thomson • com

changing the way the world learns[SM]

To get extra value from this book for no additional cost, go to:

http://www.thomson.com/wadsworth.html

thomson.com is the World Wide Web site for Wadsworth/ITP and is your direct source to dozens of on-line resources. *thomson.com* helps you find out about supplements, experiment with demonstration software, search for a job, and send e-mail to many of our authors. You can even preview new publications and exciting new technologies.

thomson.com: *It's where you'll find us in the future.*

Moral Philosophy

THEORIES AND ISSUES

Second Edition

EMMETT BARCALOW
Western New England College

Wadsworth Publishing Company
I(T)P® *An International Thomson Publishing Company*

Belmont, CA ■ Albany, NY ■ Bonn ■ Boston ■ Cincinnati ■ Detroit ■ Johannesburg
London ■ Madrid ■ Melbourne ■ Mexico City ■ New York ■ Paris ■ Singapore
Tokyo ■ Toronto ■ Washington

Philosophy Editor: *Peter Adams*
Editorial Assistant: *Kerri Abdinoor*
Marketing Manager: *Dave Garrison*
Production: *Cecile Joyner*
Print Buyer: *Stacey Weinberger*
Permissions Editor: *Robert Kauser*

Designer: *Terri Wright Design*
Copy Editor: *Margaret C. Tropp*
Cover: *Dare Porter*
Compositor: *Bookends Typesetting*
Printer: *Maple-Vail Press*

Printed in the United States of America
2 3 4 5 6 7 8 9 10

For more information, contact Wadsworth Publishing Company, 10 Davis Drive, Belmont, CA
94002, or electronically at http://www.thomson.com/wadsworth.html

International Thomson Publishing Europe
Berkshire House 168-173
High Holborn
London WC1V 7AA England

International Thomson Editores
Campos Eliseos 385, Piso 7
Col. Polanco
11560 México D.F. México

Thomas Nelson Australia
102 Dodds Street
South Melbourne, 3205
Victoria, Australia

International Thomson Publishing Asia
221 Henderson Road
#05-10 Henderson Building
Singapore 0315

Nelson Canada
1120 Birchmount Road
Scarborough, Ontario
Canada M1K 5G4

International Thomson Publishing Japan
Hirakawacho Kyowa Building, 3F
2-2-1 Hirakawacho
Chiyoda-ku, Tokyo 102, Japan

International Thomson Publishing GmbH
Königswinterer Strasse 418
53227 Bonn, Germany

International Thomson Publishing Southern Africa
Building 18, Constantia Park
240 Old Pretoria Road
Halfway House, 1685 South Africa

Library of Congress Cataloging-in-Publication Data
Barcalow, Emmett.
    Moral philosophy : theories and issues / Emmett Barcalow.—2nd ed.
        p. cm.
    Includes bibliographical references and index.
    ISBN 0-534-52645-4
    1. Ethics. 2. Social problems.   I. Title.
BJ1012.B369 1998
170—dc21
                                                97-28869

*This book is printed on
acid-free recycled paper*

Contents

Preface

WHY BRING ANOTHER ETHICS TEXT INTO THE WORLD?

It's only a slight exaggeration to say that the world is awash with introductory ethics textbooks. There is an almost endless variety of anthologies in both moral theory and applied ethics as well as a growing number of single-authored or joint-authored books introducing students to moral theory. A few books even try to strike a roughly equal balance between moral theories and moral issues. I believe that in an introductory course in moral philosophy, moral theories and moral issues deserve equal time and attention, and none of the books satisfied me (or my students).

Anthologies that focus on moral issues have two problems. First, they merely give a brief nod toward philosophical theories about morality, as though getting acquainted with moral theory is a wearisome duty: If it must be gone through, this is best done as quickly as possible before getting to the really interesting stuff—discussions about concrete moral issues. Second, almost all anthologies are made up of essays that were not written expressly for students. No matter what anthology I've used, most of my students complain that the essays are too long and involved, so that they find them incomprehensible. That usually forces me to spend a lot of time explaining what they have read rather than discussing the concrete moral issues.

Most textbooks that focus on introducing students to moral theory have slightly different problems. First, they don't pay enough attention to applying the theories they discuss to concrete moral issues. That usually means that I have to supplement the book with an anthology on moral issues, which has at least two strikes against it: It adds to the students' costs for the course, and I'm still stuck with essays that my students cannot understand. Second, most of the textbooks I've seen don't cover enough ground in moral theory and don't go into sufficient depth.

A few books are out now that try to blend moral theory and moral issues in about equal proportions. That seems to me to be the right solution if the author writes the chapters on each moral issue rather than relying on excerpts and articles in an anthology format. It is more likely that a single author writing with today's college students in mind will produce something comprehensible to that intended audience than if he or she selects articles and essays written for a different audience. Then class time can be spent on well-informed (we hope) class discussions of moral issues rather than on explanation of the assigned essays. Although a few books now take that approach, none of them has appealed to me, for various reasons. In some cases, the writing is at fault; in other cases, the coverage of either theories or issues leaves something to be desired. After reviewing and using many texts over the years, I decided to write my own.

A ROAD MAP AND AN EXPLANATION

As you can see if you peruse the table of contents, I have covered a lot of ground in moral theory. I begin with basics of moral reasoning and argument and establish some preliminary touchstones for further development, including the important statement that moral claims require justification and reasons. I then proceed to discussions of impartiality and universality. I next tackle the connections between religion and morality and the Divine Command theory because I think that is the starting point for most students when they think about morality and moral issues. In this discussion, I try to show some of the problems with relying on a theological base for resolving moral issues and answering moral questions. It seems logical to me to then proceed to versions of Moral Nonobjectivism (Nihilism, Subjectivism, Relativism, and Egoism), because it is easy to conclude that if there is no theological foundation for morality, all moral codes and moral beliefs are more or less arbitrary. In those chapters I do not claim to refute such skeptical theories about morality; rather, I present reasons for doubting that we are justified in accepting them. All too many students seem to assume that some version of moral skepticism, such as the strongest form of Protagorean Relativism, is self-evidently true and needs no justification. I have tried to counter that notion. Some form of Moral Nonobjectivism may be true, but because of powerful objections, we are justified in accepting some version of Moral Nonobjectivism only if there are very good justifying reasons supporting it. Whether there are such reasons must be carefully investigated, not simply assumed.

After the discussion of Egoism, which focuses on the pursuit of self-interest, I have included a chapter on a topic that is often not covered in introductory ethics books: conceptions of the good life. I emphasize that morality is not hostile or indifferent to self-interest. In fact, in some traditions people consider the study of ethics important primarily as a guide to living well; moral philosophy is seen as providing insight into how best to pursue self-interest and find happiness and satisfaction. From discussion of the good life it seems natural to proceed to a discussion of the good person, and I introduce students to virtue and vice ethics, a topic that has seen renewed interest in the past decade or two.

It is pretty standard to cover Utilitarianism and Kantian moral theory, as well as social contract theory. However, to provide breadth, I have also included chapters on Natural Law theory, moral duties and rights (focusing especially on the United Nations Universal Declaration of Human Rights), feminist moral theory and liberty. These chapters round out what I hope is a fairly complete trip through the thicket of moral theories for students. Throughout, my aim has been to ensure both breadth and depth of coverage, so each chapter is designed to be a complete and comprehensive introduction to the topic at hand. I have tried to ensure that the writing is well organized, lively, and understandable to today's students. I have also applied the theories to concrete moral problems and issues within each chapter so that moral theory will not appear to students to be divorced from real life. This anticipates the second section of the book, the moral issues.

PHILOSOPHY SHOULD NOT BE A SPECTATOR SPORT

For the second section of the book I have selected those moral issues that seem most interesting to today's students. Each chapter introduces students to the major issues and to the core of the debates or disagreements. I have attempted to be fair in presenting alternative views and arguments; however I have tried hard not to do all the thinking for students. My goal is to have them do some of the thinking for themselves. I designed the chapters to facilitate class discussions and provide students with enough background to stimulate them to further thought but not so much detailed argumentation that everything that can be said has been said. In some cases, I provide them more with information and alternative viewpoints than with detailed arguments. My aim is to encourage students to make up their own minds about the issues and participate in the debates rather than to treat philosophy as a spectator sport.

Many students think that having an opinion on a moral issue is the end of the story, even if people have different opinions. It's as though they are saying, "That's what I think about that. You can think what you want and I'll think what I want." I try to get them to see that having an opinion on a question or issue is the beginning of the story rather than the end of it. The important question is not so much "What do you think?" but "What justification is there for thinking that? Is what you think reasonable or unreasonable, justified or unjustified?" This corresponds with my view of philosophy. The major tasks of philosophy, whether moral philosophy or some other branch, include both the creative enterprise and the critical enterprise. The creative enterprise formulates answers to philosophical questions or solutions to philosophical problems; the critical enterprise evaluates the truth and reasonability of alternative answers or solutions by carefully investigating the justifying reasons for and against each answer or solution. I encourage students to take both enterprises seriously.

WHY SHOULD YOU USE THIS BOOK?

I believe that this book offers the right blend of moral theories and issues with the right breadth, depth, and comprehensiveness of coverage. I also believe (or at least hope) that it is written well enough to be both interesting and comprehensible to today's college students. While focusing on moral theory and concrete moral issues, I also introduce students to the thoughts on morality of some major philosophers of the past as well as the thoughts of many philosophers, past and present, on important moral issues of the day. Thus, although the book is not intended as a historical introduction, it provides students with much information about the history of moral philosophy. The analytical table of contents provides an overview of what is going on in the book, so that you can decide whether it covers what you want covered. Each chapter ends with exercises designed to encourage students to apply what they have learned in the chapter to lifelike situations and with a list of suggested readings for further research. Most of the exercises are appropriate for motivating class discussions as well. Also at the end of the book are an index and glossary. In addition, I have provided, at the end of the book, a series of case studies in several issue areas designed to stimulate class discussion. Finally, I have prepared an instructor's manual that includes chapter summaries, as well as multiple-choice questions and sample essay questions for each chapter.

WHAT'S NEW IN THIS EDITION?

Chapter 1 contains a new discussion of the distinction between descriptive and evaluative language used to talk about moral justification, as well as a new emphasis on dividing moral theories into two families: Moral Objectivism and Moral Nonobjectivism. Chapter 2, on the Divine Command theory, has been entirely rewritten. In Chapter 3, I have reshaped the discussion of Nihilism, Relativism, and Subjectivism around Moral Nonobjectivism and added material to better explain the nature of and objections to these theories.

Chapter 4 introduces the concept of "commonsense morality" as a touchstone for moral evaluation. The material on Psychological Egoism has been completely rewritten to make it more understandable. Chapter 5 includes a new section on happiness and the meaning of life. Chapter 6, on virtue and vice, has also been completely revised, adding more examples, connecting the issues to Moral Objectivism and Nonobjectivism, and amplifying the discussion of Aristotle's views. Chapter 8 has been revised to increase clarity and coherence. The discussion of Rawls in Chapter 10 and of moral duties in Chapter 11 has been expanded. A new Chapter 13 discusses liberty, with emphasis on the nature and value of autonomy, Mill's discussion of the harm principle, and Feinberg's analysis of the harm and offense principles, paternalism, and legal moralism. The chapter on morality and interpersonal violence (formerly Chapter 22) has been eliminated.

Material on pornography and censorship has been added to the chapter on morality and sex, and the discussion of seduction has been eliminated. In the chapter on abortion, I have strengthened the discussion of personhood and added a discussion of Judith Jarvis Thomson's views. The chapter on capital punishment, now Crime and Punishment, has been broadened to include new material on crime and on other forms of punishment besides execution. In the chapter on economic inequality, poverty, and equal opportunity, I have added material on the flat tax versus graduated income tax. The chapter on racism and affirmative action includes new material on racial disadvantages, new arguments and data on affirmative action, and a new section on multiculturalism and diversity. The chapter on the environment includes expanded coverage of environmental threats, new material on sustainable development, increased coverage of life-centered versus human-centered ethics, and a new discussion of environmental justice. Finally, a new series of case studies for classroom discussion has been added as a separate feature at the end of the book.

ACKNOWLEDGMENTS

I first want to thank reviewers whose comments were so helpful during revision of the manuscript: Jean Badgley, Brookdale Community College; Ronald R. Cox, San Antonio College; Erick R. Egertson, Midland Lutheran College; Roger W. Gilman, Northeastern Illinois University; Peter Horn, Capital University; Robert Kane, University of Texas, Austin; John Modschiedler, College of DuPage; Wayne P. Pomerleau, Gonzaga University; and Bambi Robinson, Southeast Missouri State University. Of course, I remain responsible for (and blameworthy for) any errors or inadequacies that remain in the text.

CHAPTER 1

Morality and Moral Reasoning

Imagine a world without morality. It would be a world where no one had any moral beliefs about what's morally right and wrong, good and bad. Consequently, it would be a world where no one had a conscience, where no one ever felt guilt or remorse for what they did or didn't do. There would be no moral restraints or constraints on people's behavior. It would also be a world in which there was no conception of vice and virtue; kindness, honesty, and compassion would not be considered morally better than cruelty, dishonesty, and malevolence. No distinction would be made between justice and injustice. No one would believe that anyone has any moral rights or duties: no one would ever claim or believe that people have a moral right to life or a right to freedom of expression or that we have a moral duty to refrain from harming others.

Beyond that, in a world without morality nothing would really *be* morally right or wrong, good or bad. In a world without morality genocide would not *be* immoral; kindness would not *be* morally better than cruelty; slavery would not *be* unjust; no one would have a moral right to a fair trial when accused of a crime; no one would have a moral duty to minimize the risks of serious harm they impose on people against their will. Moral beliefs would not influence the laws. If rape is not immoral and not believed to be immoral, then it is probable that no laws prohibiting it will be established.

A world or universe in which there was no life, not even of the one-celled variety, might plausibly be considered a world without morality.[1] Certainly nothing would be believed to be morally right or wrong because there would be nothing capable of having beliefs of any kind. Rocks don't have beliefs.[2] But probably nothing would *be* morally right or wrong, either, because there would

---

[1]Of course, if the universe contained spiritual beings that were not biologically "alive"—for example, angels—things might be different. I'll ignore such complications here.

[2]If someone asks how I know that rocks don't have beliefs, all I can say is that there are absolutely no reasons for thinking that they do and fairly good reasons for thinking that they don't. They don't have anything even approximating a brain and central nervous system, which is probably necessary for having mental states such as beliefs.

be nothing and no one to whom moral requirements could be addressed or to whom they would apply. There would be no moral agents capable of altering their behavior to conform to moral requirements. What moral requirements could be directed at a rock?

A universe in which there is life but no moral agents may also be plausibly viewed as a universe without morality. Consider a jungle with creatures such as snakes, rodents, antelope, and lions. Snakes may eat rodents. The death of these creatures may be slow and agonizing. Rodents may be swallowed alive and suffocated inside the snake's body or slowly killed by its digestive juices. Lions may chase down and tear apart an antelope before devouring it. Could we plausibly say that such behavior is wrong because it causes such great suffering? Does the antelope have a right to life that the lion violates? Does the lion have any moral duties toward the antelope? It wouldn't make much sense to talk about moral requirements applying to snakes and lions because they are not moral agents; they cannot alter their behavior to conform to moral requirements. In order for there to be morality in the universe, there must be something to which or to whom moral requirements can apply. There must be moral agents. We might say, then, that morality comes into existence in a universe when, but only when, moral agents arrive on the scene.

In order to be a moral agent, someone or something must be capable of altering its behavior to conform to moral requirements (requirements to do or not do certain things in certain circumstances). This capability, in turn, requires the ability to understand and form beliefs about moral requirements, beliefs that will or can guide behavior. But that ability requires a high level of mental sophistication, probably involving connections among a whole system of beliefs, emotions, attitudes, and feelings as well as reasoning ability.

Consider a cat playing with a mouse before killing it. The mouse may suffer terribly during the cat's "game." The cat may not need to eat the mouse in order to survive. Is it morally wrong for a cat to play such games with a mouse? It's difficult to imagine how we could answer yes to this question. A cat cannot decide whether or not to play with a mouse before killing it. Its behavior is instinctive, not under its control, not the product of deliberation. It cannot be taught that playing cruel games with mice before killing them is wrong. Therefore, it's hard to see how it could *be* wrong. On the other hand, if it were a human being playing with a mouse before killing it in the same way that a cat does, it would make sense to say that it would be wrong. A normal human being can decide whether or not to act that way toward a mouse; her behavior is under her control; she can be taught that such behavior is wrong. A cat is not a moral agent, but a human being is.

Can a world with moral agents—beings *capable* of understanding moral requirements and of altering their behavior to conform to them—be a world *without* morality? It seems unlikely. It seems highly probable that almost all moral agents will at least form moral beliefs, so it is very likely that a world that includes moral agents will include a variety of moral beliefs. For example, it is likely that human beings naturally make moral judgments and therefore have moral beliefs. We have moral views about big issues such as war and peace

(Would it be morally acceptable for a foreign dictator to invade the United States? Was it morally acceptable for the United States to drop atomic bombs on Japan?) as well as smaller issues. We have moral views about capital punishment, abortion, government spending on social programs, and environmental regulations. We have moral views about selling drugs, cheating on income tax returns and examinations, driving while intoxicated, spouse and child beating, sexual harassment, and so on.

If a universe includes moral beliefs, then it is a world that includes morality. But we may wonder whether a world that includes morality contains *only* moral beliefs. In addition to its being the case that some people *believe*, for example, that slavery is immoral, is it also the case that slavery *is* immoral? One way of expressing this question employs the concepts of truth and fact. Some beliefs are true, others false. For example, the belief that Earth is spherical is true; the belief that it's shaped like a cube is false. Many people would say that the belief that Earth is spherical is true because it's a fact that Earth is spherical, whereas the belief that Earth is shaped like a cube is false because it's not a fact that Earth is shaped like a cube. Some claims are facts, and some aren't. This way of talking—employing the language of beliefs, truth, and fact—raises a host of perplexities that require careful attention. We can't give it that attention here, but we will in a later chapter. At this point I would simply like to raise the following question without answering it: If a universe contains morality, does it include moral facts as well as moral beliefs, or does it only include moral beliefs?

A universe that contains morality must include moral agents. Moral agents are beings capable of having moral beliefs. But how do moral beliefs differ from nonmoral beliefs? For example, how does the belief that rape is immoral differ from the belief that rape is illegal in the United States? How does the belief that it's wrong to lie differ from the belief that many people do lie? Here we need to introduce the distinction between evaluative and nonevaluative beliefs, because moral beliefs are a kind of evaluative belief.

EVALUATION

We can do many things with language. Consider the following nine sentences:

1. John is 6'1" and weighs 185 pounds.
2. How old is John?
3. John, stop making that noise!
4. John, please pass the salt.
5. John is depressed because he scored lower on the SAT than he hoped to.
6. John, if you don't raise your grades, you're grounded for a month.
7. John, watch out for the bee's nest.
8. The noise John is making is loud and shrill.
9. The noise John is making is awful.

The first sentence describes John. When we describe something, we provide details about its characteristics and relationships. The second sentence asks a question. The third issues a command. The fourth is a request rather than a command. The fifth explains why something is the case. The sixth issues a threat. The seventh issues a warning. The eighth sentence describes again. It describes the noise John was making rather than describing John. The ninth, however, evaluates the noise that John was making rather than describing it.

Here we will focus on evaluation, one of the many things we do using language. Suppose that a new pizza parlor has opened in town. Because you have eaten there, someone asks you how the pizza is. You might say it's excellent, good, mediocre, or terrible. You would then be evaluating the pizza. Suppose that you say it's terrible. This evaluation implies that you have in mind certain standards that pizzas should meet and that the pizza at the new pizza parlor fails to meet those standards even to a minimal degree. On the other hand, if you say it's excellent, that statement implies that it meets to a very high degree the standards you think pizza should meet. The standards you're applying in evaluating the pizza might include such factors as the size of the pizza, the amount of cheese and other toppings, the amount and flavor of the sauce, the crispness and thickness of the crust, and the degree of doneness (neither undercooked nor burned).

You evaluate as good, bad, or indifferent all sorts of things: food, movies, music, television programs, books, computer programs, colleges or universities, even people. Evaluation is central in our lives because we use our evaluations as the basis for selection when we face choices. If you have a negative evaluation of a television program, you're not likely to watch it even if you have the opportunity. You'll choose a television program you think is good (or that you like) over a program you think is bad (or that you dislike). Similarly with music. If you think that the music of a certain band is awful, you're not going to buy tapes or CDs by that band. Then, too, if someone doesn't meet the standards you apply to people with whom you wish to be friends, you won't want that person as a friend. You would be evaluating the person from the perspective of friendship and concluding that he or she does not meet those standards.

Not only do you do evaluating of your own, but often you or things you produce are the object of evaluation. Papers you have written for classes are evaluated by your teachers, receiving grades from A to F. The standards that are applied to papers generally include considerations of content (accuracy of claims made, depth of thought, sophistication of ideas), as well as clarity, organization, and adherence to the rules of grammar, punctuation, and spelling. If you're trying out for the basketball team, a part in a play, or the school band or symphony, you're evaluated by others who must decide whether to select you. Your characteristics, abilities, or achievements are compared to the appropriate standards. If you meet the standards, you will be selected; if you fail to meet them, you won't be. In the world of work you have been or will be evaluated in the context of hiring, promotion, and salary decisions.

Evaluation, then, is a basic human activity, and it presupposes standards. There will be different standards for different kinds of evaluation. Standards appropriate for evaluating racing cars, tractor-trailer trucks, and passenger cars or for evaluating basketball players, rock-and-roll guitarists, and baby-sitters are not the same.

MORAL EVALUATION

One kind of evaluation is moral evaluation. As we have seen, in moral evaluation we can evaluate from a moral point of view people's behavior or actions, their character traits, and their social institutions. Following are some examples of moral evaluations:

> John should not have hit Jean.
>
> John's hitting Jean was wrong.
>
> Men shouldn't hit women.
>
> It's wrong (immoral) for a man to hit a woman.
>
> It was cowardly of John to hit Jean.
>
> Cowardice is contemptible (or is a vice).
>
> John is contemptible (or is an SOB).
>
> Laws permitting men to hit women are wrong (or are unjust).

Often the same vocabulary is employed in moral evaluation as in nonmoral evaluation. "Men *should not* hit women" is an example of moral evaluation, whereas "Men *should not* wear sneakers to a formal affair" is an example of non-moral evaluation. Nevertheless, it is useful to scout out some of the vocabulary central to moral evaluation. The basic concepts employed in moral evaluation include the following:

right/wrong	ought/ought not
good/bad	just/unjust
should/should not	fair/unfair

In addition, moral evaluation may employ such general concepts as praise-worthy/blameworthy, as well as more specific and descriptive concepts such as mean, arrogant, cowardly, irresponsible, offensive, and rude.

However, we will focus most intensely on what I take to be the three most basic concepts of moral evaluation, at least when it comes to evaluation of actions or behavior. We can say that an individual action or kind of action is

> morally unacceptable (immoral),
>
> morally acceptable, or
>
> morally required.

Moral evaluation, like other forms of evaluation, presupposes standards—in this case, moral standards. (We will have a lot to say about moral standards later.) To say that behavior is *morally unacceptable* or *immoral* means that it fails to meet the standards appropriate to moral evaluation. It is therefore (morally) wrong and morally prohibited or forbidden. To say that behavior is *morally acceptable* means that it does meet the standards appropriate to moral evaluation. Therefore, it is not wrong and morally prohibited or forbidden. Finally, to say that behavior is *morally required* means that *not* doing it fails to meet the standards appropriate to moral evaluation. Therefore it is (morally) wrong to *not* do it; *not* doing it is morally prohibited or forbidden. Following are some concrete examples of these three basic concepts of moral evaluation:

> Pushing a blind person into the path of an oncoming bus is morally unacceptable (immoral).
>
> Listening to rock-and-roll music is morally acceptable.
>
> Contributing some money to charity when one is rich is morally required.

We will return to these three basic concepts of moral evaluation later.

Moral evaluation probably cannot be clearly distinguished from nonmoral evaluation (evaluations that are not from a moral point of view, such as evaluations of food, books, basketball players, and baby-sitters) by appeal only to vocabulary. Something else probably is needed. One way to help distinguish between moral and nonmoral evaluation is to focus on the concept of a *moral issue*. We might say that an instance of evaluation is moral evaluation if it arises within the context of a moral issue rather than a nonmoral issue. We then must distinguish between moral and nonmoral issues.

WHAT MAKES AN ISSUE A MORAL ISSUE?

Suppose someone says that you shouldn't wear sneakers with a tuxedo or ball gown at a formal affair. Is this statement a moral evaluation? Probably not. If you went on to ask whether it's *morally* wrong or immoral, the speaker would probably say no. However, if someone says that you shouldn't torture young children to death, that statement certainly is a moral evaluation. These two statements use the same vocabulary, so why is the second but not the first an instance of moral evaluation?

We might say that in the first case there is no moral issue. Whether to wear sneakers with formal clothing generally does not create a moral issue. In the second case, however, whether to torture young children to death does raise a moral issue. But why is the second but not the first a moral issue? What makes the second but not the first a moral issue?

Let's test out your own understanding. Here is a list of choices someone might face. For each set of alternatives, decide whether it does or does not create a moral issue, and explain your reasoning.

1. Whether to wear a blue shirt to school
2. Whether to sell heroin
3. Whether to go to the movies tonight or tomorrow night
4. Whether to drive while intoxicated

5. Whether to put your right sock on before your left sock

6. Whether to have a second cup of coffee before class

7. Whether to sexually abuse children

8. Whether to starve a dog to death

If you're like me, you said that numbers 2, 4, 7, and 8 raise moral issues, whereas 1, 3, 5, and 6 do not. How might we explain the difference? Here's a hypothesis for your consideration: Moral issues arise most fundamentally when the choices people face will affect the well-being of others by either increasing or decreasing it, causing either harm or benefit. Whether we wear a blue shirt or have a second cup of coffee does not affect the well-being of others; in each case, neither alternative will harm or benefit anyone. Therefore, they are not moral issues. On the other hand, whether or not to sell drugs or sexually abuse children do represent choices that affect the well-being of others; therefore, they are moral issues. The well-being involved can be physical or psychological. Forms of physical harm include death, injury, disease, disability, and physical pain. Behavior can also cause psychological harm (1) by creating or intensifying such painful psychological states as loneliness, fear, depression, hopelessness, despair, unhappiness, anxiety, and sadness and (2) by eroding such positive psychological states as self-confidence, self-esteem, self-respect, happiness, and feelings of self-worth.

Although moral issues arise most often when a person faces choices that will affect the well-being of others, many people maintain that moral issues also arise in cases where only the agent's well-being is affected. For example, a person stranded alone on an island may have to decide between committing suicide and continuing to struggle for existence. Another person who has a special talent or ability—for example, artistic or mathematical—may have to choose between spending her time and effort cultivating that talent in order to actualize her potential or spending her time amusing herself. Many people consider these to be moral issues as well. Of course, we might insist that these are moral issues only because, if we look carefully enough, we will see that the choices involved will affect the well-being of others, not merely the agent's own well-being. However, other people claim that even if only the agent's well-being is affected, it constitutes a moral issue. On this slightly broader view of what makes something a moral issue, if an agent's behavior will affect anyone's well-being, whether the agent's own or someone else's, it creates a moral issue.

Isn't it true, however, that *any* behavior can be evaluated as morally unacceptable, morally acceptable, or morally required? These three concepts are exhaustive, in the sense that at least and at most one applies to any form of behavior. For example, wearing a blue shirt to school is either morally unacceptable, morally acceptable, or morally required. Would it follow that whether to wear a blue shirt to school is a moral issue? The answer is no. If we face a choice situation in which all of the alternatives that we seriously consider are morally acceptable, there is no moral issue involved. We do not face a moral issue unless at least one of the alternatives we are considering is either morally unacceptable or morally required.

For example, suppose that you're trying to decide whether to wear a blue, green, brown, black, or red shirt to school. If all five alternatives are morally acceptable, then you are probably not dealing with a moral issue. It would be a moral issue if and only if at least one of the alternatives you are considering is either morally unacceptable or morally required, and those concepts would be appropriately applied if and only if what alternative you select will affect someone's (or something's) well-being. If someone would be deeply offended by your wearing a black shirt to school today, perhaps because members of a white supremacist group have all agreed to wear black shirts to school today, then whether to wear a blue or a black shirt might be a moral issue.

As we will see, the hypothesis that a moral (as opposed to a nonmoral) issue arises if and only if considerations of harm and benefit or of increases and decreases in well-being come into play has interesting consequences. It suggests that reasons for and against moral evaluations are connected to considerations of harm and benefit.

STANDARDS OF MORAL EVALUATION

Evaluation presupposes standards of evaluation. When we evaluate something, we are making judgments about the extent to which it satisfies or meets the appropriate standards of evaluation. Consider the evaluation of baby-sitters. Someone is a good baby-sitter if he is reliable (in the sense that if he agrees to baby-sit at a certain day and time, he shows up rather than being late or forgetting), responsible (he is attentive to the needs of the children under his care and does not do things that would dangerously distract him such as invite friends over to party), levelheaded (he knows what to do in an emergency and will do it), and good with children (he can get along with them well enough that they are not alienated from him). Moral evaluation, then, presupposes moral standards. If I evaluate an individual concrete action or a kind of behavior as right or wrong, a person as good or bad, a character trait as a virtue or a vice, I am applying moral standards.

Let's look first at moral evaluation of individual concrete actions. Suppose that John goaded a relatively immature, insecure 16-year-old boy, Paul, into playing "chicken" with an oncoming train. At the very last minute Paul leaped aside and suffered no more serious injuries than a twisted ankle; however, if he had remained on the tracks another second or two he would have been killed. We can evaluate from a moral point of view John's action of goading Paul into playing "chicken" with a train, judging it to be either morally acceptable or immoral. But in order to morally evaluate John's action as either morally acceptable or immoral, we must apply or appeal to moral standards. What are moral standards like?

We will call the standards applied in moral evaluation moral *principles*. Moral principles can take many different grammatical forms and can be expressed employing many different concepts, as shown in the following examples:

It is *wrong* (immoral or morally unacceptable) to try to persuade someone to play chicken with a train.

People *should not* (or *ought not to*) try to persuade others to play chicken with a train.

People *have a moral duty* to refrain from persuading people to play chicken with a train.

Thou shall not try to persuade others to play chicken with a train.

Moral principles constitute moral evaluations of a *kind* of behavior. They are moral generalizations, unlike the moral evaluation of an individual concrete action. John's trying to persuade Paul to play chicken with a train is an individual concrete action; trying to persuade someone to play chicken with a train is a kind of action.

If you think that John's action of trying to persuade Paul to play chicken with an oncoming train was wrong, your position is probably based on a more general position that it's wrong to try to persuade people to play chicken with trains. In that case, you are appealing to the moral standard or principle that this kind of behavior is wrong.[3] But then, the moral evaluation of the *kind* of action of trying to persuade people to play chicken with trains itself presupposes standards or principles. These standards or principles will be even more general. If you think that it's wrong for people to try to persuade others to play chicken with a train, then it may be because you think that in general, it's wrong to try to persuade people to do things that are unreasonably dangerous—another moral standard or principle.

Justifying Moral Claims and Beliefs

Suppose that someone claims that it's immoral for people to own pets such as dogs and cats. A proper response to this claim would be the question or challenge "Why?" which is a challenge to provide reasons that support the moral evaluation—in other words, a request for justification. Surely we would wonder what reason there could be for thinking that it's immoral to own pets. If the person who claims or believes that it's immoral to own pets replies that *there are no reasons* for thinking that it's immoral to own pets, most of us would be puzzled. How could it be immoral if there are no reasons for thinking that it's immoral? This example suggests that moral evaluations require reasons.

Similarly, suppose that three people disagree about whether it is morally acceptable for sexually active couples to use contraceptives. Brown claims that

---

[3]Of course, if you only think that it's wrong to try to persuade *Paul* to play chicken with the train but that it wouldn't be wrong to try to persuade others to play chicken with a train, then you must be applying some other moral principle.

it's immoral for them to use contraceptives; Green maintains that use of contraceptives is morally acceptable but not morally required; Black says that use of contraceptives is morally required if couples do not want to conceive children. Each is asked why she believes as she does; that is, each is asked for the reasons that support her moral evaluation of contraception. Imagine that Brown replies, "There's no reason to think that the use of contraceptives is immoral; it just is." Such a reply would be puzzling. One might be tempted to respond, "But if it's immoral, then there must be some reason why it's immoral or some reason to think that it's immoral." Surely moral evaluations require reasons.

Finally, suppose that you face a moral question about which you have not yet made up your mind. You wonder whether it is morally acceptable to genetically alter corn in order to make it more resistant to disease and able to thrive in more arid environments. How would you go about making up your mind? If you approach the question in a reasonable way, you probably will try to come up with reasons for thinking that it is immoral and reasons for thinking that it is not immoral and then weigh the conflicting sets of reasons to determine which set of reasons is more compelling. Reasons are crucial for moral evaluations.

Justification is the process of providing or weighing reasons. But when a question of justification arises, one of the first things that must be determined is where the burden of justification lies. We are most familiar with this concept in the context of the criminal justice system. When someone is accused of a crime, he must be judged either guilty or not guilty. There is no third alternative. In a trial, the defense provides reasons for thinking that the accused is not guilty, while the prosecution presents reasons for thinking that the accused is guilty. Where does the burden of proof or justification lie? Should we decide that a verdict of "not guilty" will be given if and only if the defense has "proved" that the accused is not guilty—that is, if and only if the reasons for thinking the accused is not guilty are far stronger than the reasons for thinking that he is guilty? Or instead should we decide that a verdict of "guilty" will be given if and only if the prosecution has proved that the accused is guilty?

As far as I know, in all criminal justice systems the burden of justification lies with the prosecution. People accused of crimes don't have to prove that they are innocent; the prosecution has to prove that they are guilty. The operative maxim is that a person is innocent until proved guilty. One reason for this maxim is that it is much more difficult to prove that something is not the case than it is to prove that it is the case. Suppose we wonder whether the Abominable Snowmen of the Himalayas exist. If they exist, then we could readily prove that they exist by finding one. But how could we prove that they do not exist? Just because we have looked and not found one doesn't prove that they don't exist. We may not have looked in the right places. Thus, we might say that it would be more reasonable to suspend judgment about their existence. On the other hand, if many expeditions have failed to turn up any evidence that they exist, we might consider that good reason to conclude that they do not exist. (We might say that if they existed, at least one of the expeditions would have found evidence of their existence.) Similarly, suppose that you have been accused of cheating on an examination. Should it be up to you to prove that you're innocent, or should it be up to your accuser to prove that you are guilty? If you are innocent, how could you prove that you did not cheat? On the other hand, if you did cheat, your accuser should be able to present evidence. Perhaps he saw you cheat or discovered that your answers are identical to your neighbor's or found notes up your sleeve. I think we would all agree that it should not be up to you to prove that you're innocent but rather up to your accuser to prove that you're guilty.

The principle that moral evaluations require reasons presents us with a situation a bit like that of a criminal trial. The main difference is that rather than having only two alternatives—guilty or not guilty—moral evaluation presents us with three alternatives: immoral (not morally acceptable), morally acceptable, and morally required. For example, suppose that Arif claims that it is immoral for adults to drink wine with meals, Bea claims that it's morally acceptable for adults to drink wine with meals but not morally required, and Cara claims that it's morally required that adults drink wine with meals (it's immoral to *not* drink wine with meals). If moral evaluations require reasons or justification, then we may legitimately ask each of them what reasons they have for their evaluations. Suppose that you're the judge in this case and none of the three can provide much justification for their moral evaluations. Nevertheless, you must make a judgment and issue one of three verdicts: immoral, morally acceptable but not morally required, or morally required. (I hope it's obvious that what's morally required is also morally acceptable, but not vice versa.)

Which of the three alternatives most closely approximates the verdict of guilty, and which most closely approximates the verdict of innocent? I advance the following hypothesis for your consideration: "Morally acceptable but not required" most closely approximates "innocent" because it entails that, regarding the behavior in question, it is *not* wrong to do it and *not* wrong to not do it. On the other hand, both "immoral" and "morally required" closely approximate the verdict of "guilty." "Immoral" entails it's wrong to do it; "morally required" entails it's wrong to not do it. Thus, "morally acceptable (but not morally required)" is in certain ways like a negative proposition that something is *not* the case (*not* wrong to do; *not* wrong to not do), whereas "immoral" and "morally required" are like positive propositions that something *is* the case (immoral—*is* wrong to do; morally required—*is* wrong to not do). And as we saw, the maxim that one is innocent until proved guilty makes sense in part because it is much easier to prove that something is the case than it is to prove that something is not the case.

The suggestion here is that the maxim "innocent until proved guilty" can apply to behavior as well as to people accused of crimes. If we say that behavior is to be considered innocent until proved guilty, we mean that behavior is to be considered morally acceptable—neither immoral nor morally required—until and unless it can be proved either immoral or morally required. For example, drinking wine with meals is to be considered innocent (it's morally acceptable to drink it and morally acceptable to not drink it) until and unless it has been proved guilty (either immoral or morally required). In that case, it's not up to Bea to prove that drinking wine with meals is OK (morally acceptable though not morally required). Rather, it's up to Arif and Cara to try to prove their cases. If Arif can't prove that it's immoral, then we shouldn't consider it immoral. If Cara can't prove that it's morally required, then we shouldn't consider it morally required. Therefore, there's only one alternative left; we should consider it morally acceptable though not required.

When we say that moral evaluations require reasons, if we accept the hypothesis that I have suggested about considering behavior innocent until proved guilty, then we will say that the burden of justification lies with those who claim that a form of behavior is either immoral or morally required, not on those who say that a form of behavior is morally acceptable (but not required).

MORAL AGREEMENT AND DISAGREEMENT: WHO AM I TO SAY WHAT'S RIGHT AND WRONG?

When it comes to some issues, almost everyone today agrees in their moral evaluations. For example, almost everyone today agrees that rape, stealing, murdering one's own parents or children, genocide, and slavery are immoral. However, there are also many issues about which people disagree: abortion, physician-assisted suicide, capital punishment, sex outside marriage. When philosophers are faced with moral disagreement, they wish to examine carefully the justifications for the differing views in order to determine which of the competing views is most reasonable. After all, moral evaluations require justification.

Sometimes when people face moral disagreement, they throw up their hands and ask the rhetorical question "Who am I (or who are you) to say what's right and wrong?" This question is an unfortunate one. It seems to imply that only people with a certain moral expertise have a right to make or express moral evaluations and that the speaker lacks the required expertise. But do we require some special moral expertise to have a right to make and express moral evaluations? What kind of expertise is required?

What is an appropriate answer to the question "Who am I to say what's right and wrong?" The question seems to betray a lamentable lack of confidence in one's own moral judgment; the implied answer is "I'm nobody." The implication is that one's views have no value or credibility. But why should we have such little confidence in our own moral views? If we have never thought carefully and critically about our moral views, if we have unthinkingly accepted whatever we have been taught, then perhaps this lack of confidence would be justified. But if we have critically examined our moral views, if our moral views are the result of careful and well-informed deliberation, then perhaps confidence is called for.

Sometimes we find it difficult to make up our minds on an issue even after careful and well-informed deliberation. For example, someone may find it difficult to decide whether physician-assisted suicide is right or wrong, even after thinking about it, because she finds that the reasons for it and against it are nearly equal. Suppose she concludes that the reasons favoring it are slightly better than the reasons against it and consequently comes to believe that it's morally acceptable. However, given how nearly equal the reasons are, her judgment may be quite tentative. She may admit to herself, "I think it's morally acceptable, but I may be wrong." In this case lack of confidence in her moral views may be justified, and she might ask in exasperation, "Who am I to say whether it's right or wrong?"

But not all moral issues are so closely balanced. Other times, after careful deliberation one finds that all or almost all the reasons go in one direction. For example, suppose that after careful deliberation someone finds that there are no good reasons supporting the view that it's morally acceptable for men to rape women, whereas there are abundant good reasons supporting the view that it's immoral. She concludes that rape is immoral. But now suppose she asks, "But who am I to say that rape is immoral?" Such lack of confidence in her moral views seems unjustified. The question itself seems inappropriate. Rather than ask "Who am I to say what's right and wrong?" we ought instead to focus on reasons. A better question might be "Which view has the best reasons favoring it?"

MORAL ARGUMENTS

Rather than ask the rhetorical question "Who I am to say what's right and wrong?" when faced with moral disagreement, philosophers prefer to ask "Which of the conflicting moral evaluations has the strongest reasons on its side?" Or "Which of the conflicting moral evaluations is most justified?"

Justifying reasons for moral evaluations takes the form of moral arguments. An argument is a set of statements, one of which is the conclusion and the others, the premises. The conclusion is the statement to be "proved" or argued for; the premises are the reasons that support the conclusion. Here's an example of an argument in a nonmoral context:

1. All fish have gills.

2. No whales have gills.

   _____

3. Therefore, whales are not fish.

Statements 1 and 2 are the premises of the argument; statement 3 is the conclusion. Statements 1 and 2 constitute good reasons supporting the claim that whales are not fish. Conversely, they constitute good reasons *against* the claim that whales are fish. Given the truth of statements 1 and 2, it is reasonable to believe that whales are not fish and unreasonable to believe that whales are fish.

The following are examples of moral arguments:

A. 1. Tina's friend is depressed.

   2. We should try to cheer up our friends who are depressed.

      _____

   3. Therefore, Tina should try to cheer up her friend.

B. 1. Joe intentionally filed a false income tax return.

   2. Intentionally filing a false income tax return is lying.

   3. It's wrong to lie.

4. Therefore, it was wrong for Joe to intentionally file a false income tax return.

C. 1. Capital punishment will reduce the murder rate.

2. Whatever will reduce the murder rate is morally acceptable.
_____

3. Therefore, capital punishment is morally acceptable. ·

D. 1. Driving while intoxicated recklessly endangers the lives of innocent people.

2. It's wrong to recklessly endanger the lives of innocent people.
_____

3. Therefore, it's wrong to drive while intoxicated.

E. 1. Suicide is self-murder.

2. Murder is immoral.
_____

3. Therefore, suicide is immoral.

Moral justification or reasoning appeals to three different kinds of considerations: what the facts are (nonevaluative claims and beliefs), what moral principles apply, and what the words mean. For example, the claims that Tina's friend is depressed, that Joe intentionally filed a false income tax return, that capital punishment will reduce the murder rate, and that driving while intoxicated recklessly endangers the lives of innocent people are nonevaluative beliefs about what the facts are. On the other hand, the claims that we should try to cheer up our friends who are depressed, that it's wrong to lie, that whatever will reduce the murder rate is morally acceptable, that it's wrong to recklessly endanger the lives of innocent people, and that murder is immoral are moral principles. Finally, moral argument requires an understanding of the words or concepts employed. For example, in argument B we may need to clarify the concept of *intentionally* doing something in order to determine whether Joe "intentionally" filed a false income tax return. Additionally, we may need to clarify the concept of *lying* in order to determine whether intentionally filing a false income tax return constitutes lying. Similarly, in argument D we may need to clarify the concept of *recklessly endangering* people's lives in order to determine whether driving while intoxicated does or doesn't "recklessly endanger" people's lives. Finally, in argument E we may need to clarify the concept of *murder* in order to determine whether suicide constitutes self-murder. Therefore, moral reasoning requires appeal to all three considerations.

Consider the argument about intentionally submitting a false tax return. If we merely say that it constitutes lying, someone might respond "So what?" We have to explicitly include the principle that lying is wrong. On the other hand, if we merely say that lying is wrong, one may wonder what that has to do with intentionally submitting a false tax return. We have to explicitly include the claim that it constitutes lying. Thus, moral argument requires appeal to both moral principles and beliefs about what the facts are.

In what follows we will ignore the third kind of consideration in moral argument—what the words mean—and will concentrate on (1) nonevaluative claims and beliefs about the facts and (2) moral principles. We will assume that disputants have reached agreement about the meaning of their words. For example, if the issue involves sexual harassment or rape, we will assume that there is agreement about what constitutes sexual harassment or rape. Of course, such agreement is not always the case. Often people talk past each other because they mean different things even though they are using the same words. Thus, clarification of the meaning of words is often vital in moral argument.

We can construct a tree diagram that reveals the structure of reasoning about moral evaluations. At the top is the moral evaluation to be justified. The two branches give the two kinds of reasons that jointly provide support.

MORAL EVALUATION

NONEVALUATIVE BELIEFS ABOUT THE FACTS   *MORAL PRINCIPLES*

For example, we can diagram the argument for Tina's trying to cheer up her friend as follows:

MORAL EVALUATION
Tina should try to cheer up her friend.

NONEVALUATIVE BELIEFS ABOUT THE FACTS   *MORAL PRINCIPLES*
Tina's friend is depressed.   We should try to cheer up our friends who are depressed.

Good reasons for moral principles have the same logical structure. Being justified in accepting a moral principle requires good reasons, and good reasons are a combination of nonevaluative beliefs about the facts and other moral principles. Thus, for example:

MORAL PRINCIPLE
Capital punishment is morally acceptable.

NONEVALUATIVE BELIEFS ABOUT THE FACTS   *MORAL PRINCIPLES*
Capital punishment will reduce the murder rate.   Whatever will reduce the murder rate is morally acceptable.

Nonevaluative Beliefs about the Facts Must Be Reasonable

Beliefs about the facts are good justifying reasons for moral evaluations only if they're reasonable. The topic of reasonable belief is a complicated one. As a rough approximation, let us say that an individual S's belief that some statement P is true is a reasonable belief if and only if

1. P is self-consistent (it is not self-contradictory).[4]

2. P is logically consistent with other beliefs of S.

3. S has some evidence that P is true.

4. S does not have strong evidence that P is false.

For example, suppose that one argued as follows:

1. Dancing to heavy metal music inevitably leads to sexual orgies.

2. Sexual orgies are immoral.

3. Whatever inevitably leads to immoral behavior is itself immoral.

4. Therefore, dancing to heavy metal music is immoral.

Surely the belief that dancing to heavy metal music inevitably leads to sexual orgies is unreasonable because there is no evidence that it is true and abundant evidence that it is false. (Every time people dance to heavy metal music without its leading to a sexual orgy, conclusive evidence is provided that it does not inevitably lead to sexual orgies.) An unreasonable belief cannot be a good justifying reason for a moral evaluation. Therefore, the argument for the claim that it is immoral to dance to heavy metal music is defective.

Moral Principles Must Be Reasonable

Similarly, the moral principles appealed to must be reasonable. Consider the following argument:

1. Tina's best friend is depressed.

2. We should try to drive our depressed friends to commit suicide.

3. Therefore, Tina should try to drive her best friend to commit suicide.

If we think that the moral principle appealed to in premise 2 is unreasonable, then we will consider the argument defective. Generally, people consider the fact that something causes harm to other people a reason *against* it rather than for it. Therefore, most people would consider the principle expressed in premise 2 unreasonable. The point is that a moral principle is a good justifying reason for a moral evaluation only if the principle is reasonable.

Reasons for and against Moral Claims

Let's pause for a moment over the last argument. Earlier we said that a moral issue arises when considerations of increases and decreases in well-being (harm

---

[4]An example of a self-contradiction would be "There are and there are not trout in this stream now."

and benefit) are at issue. And just now I said that, all other things equal, people generally consider the fact that something causes harm to be a reason for thinking that it's wrong rather than right. This point deserves emphasis.

First, if moral issues arise when considerations of harm and benefit arise, then the nonevaluative beliefs and claims about the facts—one of the two kinds of moral reasons—should ultimately be facts about harm and benefit. The non-evaluative facts most relevant in the moral evaluation of actions (or character traits) are facts about their effects on someone's or something's well-being, and we should expect most moral arguments to appeal to considerations of harm and benefit somewhere along the line.

Second, if nonevaluative beliefs and claims about the facts are about harm and benefit to someone or something, then we must decide between the following two pairs of claims about reasons:

A. The fact that something caused or will cause harm to someone or something is a reason for thinking that it's morally *wrong*.

A'. The fact that something caused or will cause harm to someone or something is a reason for thinking that it's morally *right*.

B. The fact that something benefited or will benefit someone or something is a reason for thinking that it's morally *wrong*.

B'. The fact that something benefited or will benefit someone or something is a reason for thinking that it's morally *right*.

For example, suppose someone argues that rape is wrong because it harms the victim. Obviously, this person is treating the fact that rape causes harm as a reason for thinking that it's wrong rather than a reason for thinking that it's right. On the other hand, imagine someone disputing the issue saying, "I know that rape harms the victim; that's why I think it's morally acceptable." This person is treating the fact that rape harms the victim as a reason for thinking that it's right rather than a reason for thinking that it's wrong.

Could someone accept A' and B as principles of reason governing moral evaluation? Some of us would say that given the meaning of *moral* in "morally right" and "morally wrong" someone could not possibly adopt A' and B for *moral* evaluation. We might say that A' and B are necessarily false and that A and B' are necessarily true. (We will return to the concepts of necessary truth later.) Of course, there are probably others who would deny that A' and B are necessarily false and A and B' necessarily true. They might maintain that someone could adopt A' and B without logically contradicting themselves and that the choice between A and A' and B and B' is open, even if we in our moral tradition would consider A' and B perverse.

Conflicting Moral Arguments

So far I have oversimplified moral argument and evaluation. Sometimes we face situations in which several good arguments lead to contradictory conclusions.

Suppose that members of a terrorist group have hijacked an airplane and intend to execute everyone who is a French citizen. One of the flight attendants knows that there is a French family on board the aircraft, but she lies to the terrorists and insists that the family is Swiss, saving their lives. On the one hand, we can construct the following argument:

1. Telling the terrorists that the family was Swiss was a lie.

2. It's wrong to lie.

   _____

3. Therefore, it was wrong to tell the terrorists that the family was Swiss.

However, we can also construct a different argument.

1. Telling the terrorists that the family was Swiss saved the lives of several innocent people.

2. It's right to save the lives of innocent people if you can.

   _____

3. Therefore, it was right to tell the terrorists that the family was Swiss.

Individual reasons for moral conclusions are rarely conclusive. Often moral reasoning is like identifying and weighing symptoms in medical diagnosis. For example, having a fever and red spots on the body may suggest that a patient has disease W. However, a blood test may suggest instead that she has disease X. Further tests, such as x-rays and additional blood tests, may suggest that she has disease Y. Finally, an exploratory operation may suggest that she has disease Z. Different symptoms and test results may lead to different conclusions. Similarly, in moral evaluation several considerations and principles may lead to contradictory conclusions, and we must decide which principles have priority. Should the principle that forbids lying take priority over the principle requiring one to save innocent lives, or should it be vice versa? Here the degree of harm and benefit from following different principles may come into play in deciding on the priority of various principles. We may judge that saving lives takes priority over telling the truth in this situation because saving lives produces far more important benefits and fewer harms than would telling the truth.

According to an influential tradition in philosophy, a person's moral evaluation is reasonable or justified if and only if she has good reasons for it; that is, she has good arguments supporting it. It is important to point out that the fact that you cannot persuade others to accept your moral evaluation does not show that your moral evaluation is unreasonable or unjustified. Similarly, the fact that you cannot persuade others to alter their moral evaluations does not show that their moral evaluations are reasonable or justified. For example, if you believe that rape is immoral but Jones believes that it isn't immoral, the fact that you cannot persuade him to change his mind does not show that your moral evaluation of rape is unreasonable nor that his moral evaluation of rape is reasonable. Whether a moral evaluation is reasonable depends solely on the arguments for and against it.

Justification Chains and Basic Moral Principles

As we have seen, a moral principle is a good justifying reason for a moral evaluation only if it is itself justified or reasonable. So far we have assumed that a moral principle is justified or reasonable only if there are good justifying reasons supporting it. For example:

1. Lying harms people.

2. Harming people is wrong. (P_B)

3. Therefore, lying is wrong. (P_A)

Moral principle P_A in the conclusion 3 is justified by appeal to the belief about the facts in premise 1 and a deeper or broader moral principle P_B in premise 2. In the tree diagram the argument looks like this:

MORAL PRINCIPLE
Lying is wrong. (P_A)

NONEVALUATIVE BELIEFS ABOUT THE FACTS
1. Lying harms people.

MORAL PRINCIPLES
2. Harming people is
wrong. (P_B)

Thus, a moral principle is justified in part by appeal to an underlying or more general moral principle.

This reasoning suggests a chain of justification in which one principle, say P_A, is justified because it is supported by a deeper or more fundamental principle P_B, which in turn is justified because it is supported by a still deeper or more fundamental principle P_C, and so on. Alternatively, we might visualize the chain structure of justification in the following way:

MORAL PRINCIPLE
(Level 1)

NONEVALUATIVE BELIEFS ABOUT THE FACTS
(Level 2)

MORAL PRINCIPLES
(Level 2)

NONEVALUATIVE BELIEFS ABOUT THE FACTS
(Level 3)

MORAL PRINCIPLES
(Level 3)

NONEVALUATIVE BELIEFS ABOUT THE FACTS
(Level 4)

MORAL PRINCIPLES
(Level 4)

Moral principles on level 2 are justified by appeal to moral principles on level 3, which in turn are justified by appeal to moral principles on level 4, and so on. Principles at each lower level are more general or more basic than those at higher levels.

Given this model, we seem to be faced with three alternatives. Either there are an infinite number of levels and moral principles, so that the chain of justification is infinite; or the chain is somehow circular, so that eventually moral principles at a deeper level are justified by appeal to principles at a less deep level; or there are some fundamental or basic moral principles that establish a kind of foundation.

A basic moral principle is fairly general; an example might be the well-known Golden Rule: "Treat other people as you would have them treat you." Such a fundamental or basic moral principle would be both the starting point in moral reasoning and the end point in moral justification. On the one hand, that is, we might begin with a general principle and try to determine what behavior it requires. Basic principles would generate the nonbasic moral principles that guide our behavior, such as "Don't steal" and "Help others when their need is great and the cost to you would be small." On the other hand, we might begin with the behavior being evaluated and descend to deeper and deeper principles in justification. Thus, if we appeal to moral principle P_A to justify a moral evaluation and we are challenged (by ourselves or others) to justify P_A, we will appeal to a more general principle P_B. If we are challenged to justify P_B, we will appeal to a more general principle P_C. The end point of such chains will be one or more basic or fundamental moral principles beyond which we cannot go.

Many people believe that this alternative is the most plausible: that moral argument or justification ultimately depends on basic moral principles that serve as the foundation for the moral code of individuals or groups of individuals. One possibility is that all people accept (or should accept) only one basic principle—in which case it is natural to ask what that principle is. On the other hand, there may be many possible basic principles. In that case, it may be that everyone accepts (or should accept) the same set of principles, but it is also possible that different people accept different, and perhaps incompatible, basic moral principles.

In succeeding chapters we will see various possible responses to this set of puzzles. For example, some people maintain that there are many possible, incompatible, basic moral principles and that they are nothing but arbitrary assumptions, so that none is more correct or reasonable than any other. We will examine such views in Chapter 3. Others maintain that there is one and only one correct basic moral principle; however, people disagree as to what that principle is. In subsequent chapters we will examine some of the most influential theories about what that one basic moral principle is. In Chapter 2 we'll examine the Divine Command theory, according to which the one principle is "Obey God's Law." In Chapter 4 we'll examine Moral Egoism, according to which the one principle is "Do whatever is in your own best interest." In Chapter 7 we'll examine Utilitarianism, according to one version of which the one principle is "Maximize total well-being." In Chapter 8 we'll examine Kantian moral theory, according to which the one principle is "Act only on the maxim that you can consistently will to be a universal law." Finally, in Chapter 10 we'll examine social contract theory, according to one version of which the one principle is something like "Conform to rules that everyone would agree to abide by if they were in the Original Position." (The meaning of these terms and principles will become clearer in later chapters.)

IMPARTIALITY AND THE MORAL POINT OF VIEW

Moral issues arise most commonly when people's interests and well-being conflict. For example, if the issue is murder or theft, it's pretty obvious that the interests of the murderer and his victim and of the thief and his victim conflict. Most philosophers maintain that, almost by definition, morality involves judging or evaluating from an impartial point of view. A moral (as opposed to a nonmoral) point of view or perspective presupposes impartiality rather than partiality or bias.

We can be partial or biased against our own interests as opposed to the interests of others, or partial to or biased against the interests of one group as opposed to the interests of another group. An example of the former would be someone who always sacrifices the interests of other people in order to further her own interests. She may steal from others, lie to them, exploit them, assault and even kill them. She acts as though the interests of other people don't count. She is partial to or biased toward her own interests. Of course, the opposite is also possible. Someone may always put the interests of others before her own interests and engage in constant self-sacrifice because she has no self-esteem and considers her own interests to be valueless. She is biased *against* her own interests.

Examples of bias toward or against some group abound. The most obvious example in this century is the Nazi extermination of Jews. Nazis were biased against Jews (and toward "Aryans") and treated them as though their interests did not count. Other examples include the Turkish massacre of Armenians during World War I, "ethnic cleansing" in the war in Bosnia (Serbs killing and assaulting non-Serbs, Croats killing and assaulting non-Croats), black slavery in the United States (there were no white slaves), and the treatment of native Americans by European settlers in the eighteenth and nineteenth centuries (killing them and stealing their land). Nazis didn't exterminate other "Aryans"; Turks didn't massacre other Turks; whites didn't enslave other whites; European settlers didn't follow a systematic policy of killing other Europeans and stealing their land.

Many people maintain that when judging behavior from a moral point of view, one must strive to be impartial rather than partial, treating each individual's and group's interests as equal. One must judge (and act) like a referee at a basketball game or the judge in a criminal trial. One must not favor one's own interests over the interests of others or the interests of one's own religion, class, race, ethnic group, or nation over the interests of other religions, classes, races, ethnic groups, or nations.

However, strict impartiality may not always be called for. Suppose that two children, Ned and Sam, both need braces. Ned is Helen's son, but Sam is unrelated to her. Surely Helen would not be violating the moral requirement of impartiality if she were to pay for Ned's rather than Sam's braces. In at least some situations, parents should favor the interests of their own children over the interests of others. Similarly, suppose that two people, Jan and Jean, are depressed and need someone to listen to them and offer comfort. Jan is Anne's friend, but Jean is a stranger. Surely Anne would not be violating the moral requirement of impartiality if she were to listen to and comfort Jan rather than Jean. It is at least sometimes appropriate to be partial and to favor the interests of our relatives and friends over the interests of strangers and casual acquaintances. The problem is to specify the circumstances in which morality requires us to adopt an impartial point of view, counting everyone's interests and well-being equally, and the circumstances in which morality permits or even requires us to be partial.

Marilyn Friedman suggests that

> the abstract ideal of impartiality should not be the primary reference point around which to orient methods for eliminating bias from moral thinking. Instead, our reference points should be particular forms of *partiality*, that is, nameable biases whose distorting effects on moral thinking we recognize and whose manifestations in moral attitudes and behavior can be specifically identified.[5]

Examples of named biases would be racism and sexism. Examples of nameable biases "whose distorting effects on moral thinking we recognize" include biases based on religion, ethnic background, caste, economic class, and sexual orientation. Following Friedman, we might say that the requirement of impartiality in moral deliberation and action is that we minimize such named and nameable biases.

The requirement of impartiality can play an important role in moral argument. We can rationally criticize our own or another's moral views by showing that we would not have the view in question if we were judging from the kind of impartial perspective required by morality. Similarly, we can rationally criticize our own or another's actions by showing that we would not act that way if our actions were guided by the impartial perspective required by morality. If a moral belief or claim would not be accepted if we were judging from the impartial perspective required by morality, then it is not justified or reasonable from a moral point of view.

UNIVERSALITY

Another requirement of morality accepted by almost all philosophers is universality: Moral standards or principles, in order to be considered *moral* (as opposed to nonmoral) standards or principles, must be considered universal. Moral principles apply to *everyone*. If "Stealing is wrong" is accepted as an authoritative (or true) moral principle, then it is wrong for anyone to steal. If stealing is wrong, then it's not only wrong for you to steal from me, it's also wrong for me to steal from you.

---

[5]Marilyn Friedman, *What Are Friends For? Feminist Perspectives on Personal Relationships and Moral Theory* (Ithaca, NY: Cornell University Press, 1993), p. 31.

The requirement of universality also means that moral reasons are universal. If one judges that some act is morally wrong (right) because it has features A, B, and C, then the requirement of universality entails that all similar acts that have features A, B, and C are morally wrong (right). For example, suppose that Tang judges that it's morally acceptable for Tina to have the abortion she wants because her pregnancy is the result of rape and she is less than four months pregnant. The requirement of universality entails that he must (on pain of logical contradiction) judge that it would be morally acceptable for anyone else who is pregnant because of rape and is less than four months pregnant to have an abortion if she wants one. What is a good moral reason for Tina to have an abortion is a good moral reason for anyone to have an abortion. Similarly, if Hassan judges that it was morally wrong of Joe to physically attack him because of his religious beliefs, then the requirement of universality entails that he must (on pain of logical contradiction) judge that it would be morally wrong for him to attack Joe for his religious beliefs or for anyone to physically attack someone because of his or her religious beliefs.

Just as the requirement of impartiality is important in moral argument, so, too, is the requirement of universality. If someone would be unwilling to have everyone act on a principle she appeals to in moral argument, then she is not treating the principle as universal, and the principle cannot be considered an acceptable *moral* principle.

UNIVERSAL VERSUS ABSOLUTE PRINCIPLES

That moral principles must be considered universal doesn't entail that they must be considered absolute. A *universal* principle applies to everyone; an *absolute* principle doesn't permit exceptions. To say that the principle "Stealing is wrong" is universal means that it applies to everyone; to say that it is absolute means that there are no circumstances in which stealing would not be wrong. If the moral prohibition on stealing were absolute, then whether a person steals a blind man's seeing-eye dog for personal gain or steals an atomic bomb from a terrorist to prevent him from blowing up New York City wouldn't matter. Because it is theft, it is wrong. But few people would find it plausible to consider many moral principles absolute, especially if they're fairly general, such as "Don't steal" or "Don't break promises." As we saw in the case of the flight attendant's lying to the terrorists to save the French family, moral principles that seem equally acceptable can yield contradictory conclusions in some circumstances. Therefore, we might maintain that although the moral principle "Lying is wrong" is universal, it is not absolute because there can be situations in which lying would not be wrong.

A moral system that includes more than one absolute moral principle raises the likelihood that these principles will come into conflict with each other. If two absolute principles come into conflict with each other, there is no way to resolve the conflict without conceding that at least one of the principles is not absolute. If there is an absolute moral principle prohibiting lying under any circumstances and another absolute moral principle requiring people to do whatever is necessary to save the lives of innocent people, and if we can only save the life of an innocent person by lying, what must we do? Most people find it implausible to maintain that moral principles are absolute.

QUALIFIED VERSUS UNQUALIFIED MORAL PRINCIPLES

Unqualified moral principles, such as "It's wrong to steal," "It's wrong to kill," and "It's wrong to lie," are not good candidates for the status of absolute principles because we can easily imagine situations in which it would be right rather than wrong to violate them. Surely it would be right for me to steal my neighbor's shotgun if I know that he intends to use it to murder his family. Surely it would be right for a Secret Service agent to kill a man who is about to assassinate the President if that is the only way to prevent the assassination. And surely it would be right for an airline flight attendant to lie to terrorists in order to save the lives of innocent passengers. Generally, unqualified moral principles should be considered as nonabsolute guidelines that we should strive to follow but that may be legitimately overridden by more important moral concerns.

Moral principles, however, can be qualified. A moral principle could specify that under certain circumstances C a form of behavior is wrong (or right). For example, rather than the unqualified "Stealing is wrong" we could have the qualified principles "Stealing from someone for gain when you have other ways of acquiring money is wrong" and "Stealing from someone in order to prevent the death of many innocent people is not wrong." Such qualified principles, if carefully formulated, may plausibly be considered absolute.

Obviously, unqualified principles have their use even if they are not absolute. Imagine how many qualified principles regarding stealing we could generate. We could probably generate dozens if we thought about it. If all principles had to be suitably qualified, we'd have to formulate and remember hundreds, perhaps thousands or tens of thousands, of moral principles. It's much more efficient to formulate and remember a few basic, unqualified moral principles, even if they are accepted as nonabsolute and must be balanced against potentially competing moral principles.

WHAT KIND OF PERSON SHALL I BE?
HOW SHALL I LIVE?

Decisions about what kind of person to be and how to live our lives also present important moral issues. We may be selfish or unselfish, kind or cruel, compassionate or callous, violent or nonviolent. We may focus our lives on acquiring wealth and power or on developing and nurturing close, caring relationships with other people. We may seek happiness in being party animals or in acquiring knowledge and understanding, in drink and drugs or in athletic or artistic achievement. We will explore moral issues involving what kind of person to be and how to live in Chapters 5 and 6.

MORAL OBJECTIVISM AND MORAL NONOBJECTIVISM

Finally, let's return to our earlier discussion of a universe that includes morality. There I said that we might ask whether a world that includes morality contains moral facts as well as moral beliefs. For our purposes right now, we will narrow that issue to the question of whether a world that includes morality contains true as opposed to false moral standards or principles as well as moral beliefs, since all moral beliefs presuppose some moral standards or principles.

Some thinkers maintain that no moral principles are objectively true or false and that none are objectively better justified than any others. It follows that no moral beliefs and claims of any kind are objectively true or false or objectively better justified than any others. The concept of objectivity is a slippery one. We will look at it more carefully later, but for now let's just say that a claim or belief is objectively true (false) if its truth (falsity) is independent of anything that anyone believes, thinks, or feels. In contrast with objective truth is relative truth. Some claims or beliefs may be true only relative to a specific individual, group of individuals, or other frame of reference.

For example, consider the following two statements:

Steak tastes better than lobster.

Steak tastes better than lobster to Jean.

The first statement is not objectively true. Steak tastes better than lobster to some people but not to all people. It is not true independent of what anyone believes, thinks, or feels. On the other hand, the second statement may be objectively true. If Jean likes the taste of steak more than she likes the taste of lobster, then steak tastes better than lobster to her. Similarly, consider the statement "*David Copperfield* is a boring book." It is not an objectively true statement because although some people may find the book boring, not everyone does. On the other hand, "Joe found *David Copperfield* boring," if true, is objectively true. It's true regardless of what others may think or feel about the book.

Moral Nonobjectivism[6] is a family of theories that maintain that no moral claim, belief, or principle is either objectively true or objectively false (or objectively better justified than another). Moral Objectivism,[7] in contrast, is a family of theories that maintain that at least some moral claims, beliefs, and principles are objectively true and others are objectively false. The following chart identifies some of the members of these two families of moral theories that we will be examining in future chapters:

MORAL NONOBJECTIVISM	MORAL OBJECTIVISM
Moral Nihilism	Divine Command Theory
Moral Subjectivism	Moral Egoism

---

[6]Some philosophers call it Moral Noncognitivism or Moral Nonrealism.

[7]Some philosophers call it Moral Cognitivism or Moral Realism.

Moral Relativism   Utilitarianism

Kantian Moral Theory

Social Contract Theory

Natural Law Theory

First, however, we turn to what is probably the most widely accepted moral theory in the world, the Divine Command theory.

EXERCISES

In constructing moral arguments for the following exercises, be sure to appeal both to nonevaluative beliefs about what the facts are and to moral principles. Wherever necessary, clarify the concepts that you employ in the argument. You may use either the

Premises

Conclusion

form or the tree diagrams.

1. Jean is a 15-year-old high school student who is three months pregnant. Her boyfriend broke up with her when she informed him of her pregnancy. She wants to finish high school and go on to college, and she fears that continuing the pregnancy will make it much more difficult for her to do so, even if she were to give up the baby at birth for adoption. She doesn't want her father to know that she is pregnant because he has a very bad temper and she's afraid of what he'll do to her or to her ex-boyfriend. She also doesn't want other people to know that she is pregnant because she believes that many people will form a negative opinion of her and consider her a "slut." She has told her mother. They have talked it over, and they both agree that having an abortion is the best alternative. Would it be immoral for Jean to have an abortion? Why or why not? Construct a moral argument or arguments to defend your view. Then try to construct a moral argument or arguments to defend the opposite view. Which arguments are stronger? Why?

2. Burton murdered a store clerk during a robbery when he was 19. He was caught and convicted and has been sentenced to die in the electric chair. Reporters recently revealed that Burton had been severely abused as a child. Some psychologists maintain that such abuse interferes with the development of conscience and increases the likelihood of sociopathic behavior, especially violence. Should Burton's sentence be carried out? Why or why not? Construct an argument or arguments to defend your position.

3. Sheila has three children, ages two, four, and six. Her husband, Jeff, left her for another woman and did not contest Sheila's request for custody of their children. Although he was ordered to pay $300 a month in child support as part of the divorce decree, he rarely pays. Even if he does pay, Sheila and her children cannot live on $300 a month. Her rent alone for a modest two-bedroom apartment is $500 a month, not including utilities such as heat and electricity. Sheila has little education and has not worked in over six years. The only jobs available for which she would be qualified pay $5 to $6 per hour and do not provide

health insurance. If she works, she will need to have her two younger children in day care, which will cost a minimum of $150 a week. She will need to pay another $50 a week for after-school care for her oldest child, who is in first grade. Health insurance would cost at least $300 a month. Calculating the expenses, Sheila concludes that she can't afford to work. If she goes on welfare, she will receive about $500 a month in cash benefits, $150 a month in food stamps, a clothing and heat allowance, and Medicare that pays for her and her children's health care. Although she would like subsidized housing, the long waiting list means a wait of at least three years. Sheila reluctantly applies for welfare benefits. Is she doing anything wrong in applying for welfare? Should she be given welfare benefits? Why or why not? Construct an argument or arguments to defend your view.

4. Several male high school students talk a 17-year-old girl they know to be mildly retarded into having sexual relations with them. (We'll call her Joan.) Because they are not using force or coercion, and because they consider her to have freely consented, they believe that they are doing nothing wrong. They argue as follows:

   A. Joan is 17 and freely consented to have sex with us.
   B. There's nothing wrong with having sex with a 17-year-old girl who has freely consented to it.

   _____

   C. Therefore, there's nothing wrong with our having sex with Joan.

   Do you agree? Why or why not? Construct an argument to defend your view. What criticisms, if any, do you have of the boys' argument?

5. Write a paragraph explaining the difference between universal moral principles and absolute moral principles.

6. Timothy maintains that abortion is immoral unless it is necessary to save the life of the mother. When he learns that Frieda, a girl he despises, has had an abortion although her life was not threatened, he strongly condemns her action as immoral. However, when he learns that Gloria, a girl he likes very much, has had an abortion in similar circumstances, he maintains that she has not done anything immoral. Are there any defects in Timothy's moral evaluations? Discuss your answer from the point of view of universality and impartiality.

7. Consider the following two alternative moral principles:

   A. Capital punishment is immoral.
   B. Capital punishment is morally acceptable.

   With which do you agree? Construct an argument defending the principle that you accept. After constructing an argument, try to construct a new argument (level B) defending the moral principles to which you appealed in defending your view on capital punishment. After constructing that argument (level B), try constructing yet another argument (level C) defending the moral principles that you appealed to on level B. Do you think that the chain of argument can go on without end? If not, where did you find yourself stopping? Discuss the moral principles with which your chain of justification ended.

CHAPTER 2

Morality and Religion

In Sophocles's *Antigone,* the heroine, Antigone, deliberately disobeys the commands of the king, Creon, who ordered her not to bury her brother after he was killed in an attempt to topple Creon from power. Creon is enraged at the deliberate disobedience, but Antigone is unmoved. As far as Creon is concerned, his commands are law because he is king. It was wrong of Antigone to disobey his laws. Antigone responds,

> For me it was not Zeus who made that order.
> Nor did that Justice who lives with the gods below
>   mark out such laws to hold among mankind.
> Nor did I think your orders were so strong
>   that you, a mortal man, could over-run
>   the gods' unwritten and unfailing laws.
> Not now, nor yesterday's, they always live,
>   and no one knows their origin in time.[1]

Antigone maintains that over and above human law is divine law, the laws that are promulgated by and enforced by the gods, chief among them their ruler, Zeus. The divine laws of the gods are the appropriate standard of right and wrong. They serve as the basis for evaluating one's own conduct, the conduct of others, and the laws and institutions of one's society. They are laws that all people should follow, even if following them requires disobeying the human laws of one's society. Divine laws take precedence over human laws.

Most of us are probably familiar with similar views that pervade the major religious traditions of the Western world: Judaism, Christianity, and Islam. According to these religious traditions, there is one and only one correct or true moral code: God's Law. God's Law—a system of commandments or moral requirements—is binding on all people. It is the correct standard of right and wrong, good and bad. Its divine laws take precedence over all human laws, although God's Law may include a requirement to obey the laws of one's society

---

[1]Sophocles, *Antigone,* in *The Complete Greek Tragedies: Sophocles I,* ed. David Grene and Richard Lattimore (Chicago: University of Chicago Press, 1954), ll. 450–457. (The play was originally produced around 440 B.C.E.)

provided that those human laws are just and are consistent with the rest of God's Law. For example, we can easily imagine someone arguing in the following way:

1. God forbids suicide.

2. Whatever God forbids is immoral.

3. Therefore, suicide is immoral.

Most people who are members of one of the world's organized religions assume that their religious tradition provides them with knowledge of God's Law.

For example, the Judeo-Christian tradition provides its adherents with the Ten Commandments from the Hebrew Bible (the Old Testament). Among those commandments are the following:

Honor your father and your mother . . .

You shall not murder.

Neither shall you commit adultery.

Neither shall you steal.

Neither shall you bear false witness against your neighbor.

- Deuteronomy 5:16-20[2]

The Hebrew Bible also includes many stories that are intended to teach moral lessons. One example is the story of Adam and Eve, who were cast from paradise for disobeying God's command not to eat the fruit of the tree of knowledge; this story teaches that obedience, especially obedience to God, is an important virtue. Poems, too, have moral messages, as in Psalm 10:

In arrogance the wicked persecute the poor
. . . Their mouths are filled with cursing and deceit and oppression;
. . . They sit in ambush in the villages
in hiding places they murder the innocent.

Christians turn to the pronouncements and stories of Jesus in the New Testament for insight into God's Law. For example:

In everything do to others as you would have them do to you; for this is the law and the prophets.

- Matthew 7:12

[O]ne of [the Pharisees] asked him [Jesus] a question to test him. "Teacher, which commandment in the Law is the greatest?" He said to him, "You shall love the Lord your God with all your heart, and with all your soul, and with all your mind." That is the greatest and first commandment. And a second is like

---

[2]All translations are from *Holy Bible: The New Revised Standard Version* (New York: Oxford University Press, 1989).

it: "You shall love your neighbor as yourself."

- Matthew 22:36-40

Muslims turn to the Koran and the traditions of Islam for moral guidance. The Koran condemns some forms of behavior and praises others. For example:

> But you [the wicked] show no kindness to the orphan, nor do you vie with each other in feeding the poor. Greedily you lay your hands on the inheritance of the weak, and you love riches with all your heart.[3]

Similarly, consider the following passages from the Koran:

> Give to the near of kin their due, and also to the destitute and to the wayfarers.
> Be neither miserly nor prodigal. . . .
> You shall not commit adultery. . . .
> You shall not kill any man that Allah has forbidden you to kill, except for a just cause.
> Keep your promises. . . .
> Do not walk proudly on the earth.[4]

THE DIVINE COMMAND THEORY OF MORALITY

According to the Divine Command theory of morality, the true standard of moral right and wrong is God's Law. The Divine Command theory is a member of the family of moral theories labeled Moral Objectivism in the previous chapter, because it maintains that moral evaluations are either objectively true or objectively false. For example, according to the Divine Command theory, "Suicide is immoral" is objectively true if God's Law includes a prohibition against suicide. Conversely, "Suicide is immoral" is objectively false if God's Law includes a permission or requirement to commit suicide (although perhaps only under certain circumstances).[5]

MORAL EVALUATION
Suicide is immoral.

NONEVALUATIVE BELIEF
God's Law includes a prohibition
on suicide.

MORAL PRINCIPLE
Whatever God's Law
prohibits is immoral.

---

[3]*The Koran,* "The Dawn," trans N. J. Dawood (Harmondsworth, England: Penguin, 1956), p. 25.

[4]Ibid., "The Night Journey," pp. 235-236.

[5]Although one might be tempted to say that "Suicide is immoral" is objectively false merely if God's Law does *not* include a prohibition against committing suicide, that would be hasty. For example, if (1) God's Law includes a requirement to obey the laws of one's society provided that they are not unjust, (2) the laws of one's society prohibit suicide, and (3) the laws prohibiting suicide are not unjust, then it would *not* be the case that "Suicide is immoral" is objectively false, even though God's Law does not include an explicit prohibition against committing suicide.

The fundamental moral principle to which Divine Command theorists appeal is "Whatever God's Law prohibits is immoral." Divine Command theorists clearly consider this fundamental moral principle to be true. Some may make the stronger claim that it is necessarily true because *immoral* means nothing more than "prohibited by God's Law." On this view, "Whatever God's Law prohibits is immoral" is like "All raisins are grapes" or "All bachelors are unmarried"—true by definition.

TWO VERSIONS OF THE DIVINE COMMAND THEORY
Morality Is Logically Independent of God's Will

The Divine Command theory has at least two different versions. According to one version, God—having perfect and unlimited knowledge and wisdom and being perfectly good—has perfect and unlimited knowledge of right and wrong. Given such unlimited knowledge and perfect goodness, God necessarily prohibits only what is morally wrong and permits and requires only what is morally right. God's perfect nature ensures that God's Law can never be mistaken about moral right and wrong. In terms of motivation, human beings who want to do right rather than wrong have good reason to conform to God's Law because God's knowledge of right and wrong far surpasses their own. (They may also have an incentive to conform to God's Law if they believe that failing to conform will bring punishment while conforming will bring reward—if not during life, then after death.)

According to this first version of a Divine Command theory of morality, God's commands do not *make* things right or wrong. Rather, God prohibits some behaviors, such as torture and rape, *because* they are immoral; permits other behaviors, such as drinking wine with dinner, *because* they are not immoral; and requires other behaviors, such as treating one's parents with respect, *because* not to do them is immoral. According to this view, moral right and wrong are logically independent of God's will and God's commands. To put the point provocatively, even if God did not exist, the same things would be immoral (and not be immoral).

On this first version, human beings can acquire moral knowledge in one of two ways. The first is through divine revelation. God may reveal moral truths in sacred scriptures, such as the Bible or the Koran, or may reveal them directly to an individual in a personal revelation. Some people maintain that conscience is the voice of God within each individual revealing moral truths. The second possible way of acquiring moral knowledge, in this version of the Divine Command theory, is for human beings to use their own cognitive capacities to discover moral truths. We will construe human cognitive capacities broadly to include reason, perception, and emotions or feelings. This second possibility means that human beings can know what's morally right and wrong without it's being revealed to them by God. Whatever is morally right and wrong will still be incorporated into God's Law, but human beings can come to know at least some parts of God's Law without having to rely on divine revelation.

Morality Is Logically Dependent on God's Will

According to the second version of the Divine Command theory, God's commands *make* things morally right and wrong. On this view, if rape is immoral, it is only because God forbids it. If God did not forbid it, it would not be immoral. Consequently, we cannot say that God forbids rape *because* it is immoral. In fact, on this version of the Divine Command theory, it seems that if we ask why God forbids rather than permits rape, we can only say that there is no reason—he simply forbids it. One way of defending this version of the Divine Command theory is to maintain that *immoral* means nothing more than "forbidden by God." On this view, if God did not exist, *nothing* would be immoral, morally permitted, or morally required.

As for moral knowledge, on this version of the Divine Command theory, the only way for human beings to acquire moral knowledge is to have it revealed to them by God. There can be no source of moral knowledge independent of God's revelation.

MORAL MOTIVATION

One problem for moral theory is to identify plausible sources of moral motivation. Suppose that we agree that there are moral truths, such as "It's wrong to steal." Such moral principles are supposed to be "normative"—that is, guides to action. If they are true, people are supposed to conform their behavior to them. If someone believes that "It's wrong to steal" is true, then that belief is supposed to make a difference in how they behave. It is supposed to provide them with a very powerful reason for not stealing, a reason that will serve as a disincentive to steal. But what reason can people have to conform their behavior to a moral principle even if they concede that it's a true moral principle? Someone could simply say, "Yes, it's true that it's immoral to steal, but so what? I intend to steal anyway. I don't care about moral right and wrong."

Either version of the Divine Command theory can provide motivation for conforming one's behavior to true moral claims. First, if one believes that God will severely punish those who fail to conform to the demands of morality (God's Law) and will significantly reward those who do, perhaps by sending sinners to hell and nonsinners to heaven, then one has what many consider the best possible kind of reason for conforming to true moral claims: self-interest. It's in one's long-term self-interest to conform and against one's long-term self-interest to fail to conform. Second, if one believes that God created all of life on Earth, including human life, and if one believes that God loves and cares about humans and has provided an abundance of good things for their well-being, then one might believe that gratitude is appropriate. In turn, one may believe that an appropriate way of expressing such gratitude is by conforming to God's Law. Thus, the Divine Command theory does seem able to resolve the problem of providing motivation for conforming one's behavior to moral truths.

MORAL LAWS

According to the Divine Command theory, there is one and only one correct moral code, and it applies to all individuals and all societies. This position may strike some people as rather rigid. How can there be just one moral code when there are so many individuals and societies whose circumstances and conditions can vary widely? But as we saw in the previous chapter, although God's commands (laws) may be expressed as unqualified principles, such as "Don't steal" or "Stealing is wrong," they also could be expressed as qualified principles having the form: "Don't steal under circumstances C_1" and "Don't steal under circumstances C_2." The moral rules embodied in God's Law may require one behavior under one set of circumstances and another behavior under different circumstances. This qualification was recognized by Saint Augustine:

> I also did not know that true inward justice which judges not by custom but by the most righteous law of almighty God. By this law the moral customs of different regions and periods were adapted to their places and times, while the [moral] law itself remains unaltered everywhere and always. It is not one thing at one place or time, another thing at another.

Augustine continues:

> An act allowed or commanded in one corner is forbidden and subject to punishment if done in an adjacent corner. Does that mean that justice is "liable to variation and change"? No. The times which it rules over are not identical.[6]

For example, in a situation of abundance with more than enough food for everyone, God's justice may place no limits on how much food people may hoard or acquire. If my putting away a hundred bushels of apples will not prevent you from getting as many apples as you want, then it would not be unjust for me to take a hundred bushels of apples. In a situation of scarcity, however, God's justice may place limits on how many apples I may take for myself. If ten bushels of apples would satisfy my needs, and if my taking a hundred bushels would deprive others of apples, then God's justice might limit me to ten bushels of apples. To take more under circumstances of scarcity would be unjust.

The point is that God's Law need not be insensitive to differences in circumstances. A law may apply under one set of circumstances but not under entirely different circumstances.

PROBLEMS FOR THE DIVINE COMMAND THEORY

A number of problems face the Divine Command theory that, in the eyes of many people, reduce its plausibility.

---

[6]Saint Augustine, *Confessions,* trans. Henry Chadwick (New York: Oxford University Press, 1991), pp. 44–45.

Not Everyone Believes That God Exists

Central to the Divine Command theory, of course, is the assumption that God exists. If we doubt or reject that assumption, then the theory is undermined. We can appeal to God's Law as the standard of moral right and wrong only if we believe that God exists. Therefore, atheists (those who believe that God doesn't exist) and agnostics (those who suspend judgment about whether God exists) cannot accept the Divine Command theory, and they do not appeal to God's Law to resolve their moral perplexities and problems.

The fact that not everyone believes that God exists also poses problems for theists (those who believe that God exists). A theist might think, "I don't care what others believe; I believe that God exists and I shall obey God's Law, the only correct moral code." However, in addition to seeking moral guidance for their own behavior, people often engage in public discussion of moral issues. They try to convert others, to justify their behavior to others, and to defend or justify the moral evaluations they make. In such public discussion, people often hope to be persuasive. However, an appeal to God's Law will not persuade people unless they accept the fundamental assumption that God exists.

For example, suppose Smith believes that employing "artificial" methods of birth control, such as intrauterine devices and birth control pills, is immoral and therefore should be legally banned. Jones disagrees. Imagine the following exchange.

> Smith: Using artificial methods of birth control is immoral. People should not be legally permitted to buy or sell things that are immoral. Therefore, people should not be legally permitted to buy or sell artificial methods of birth control.

> Jones: What reason is there for thinking that using artificial methods of birth control is immoral?

> Smith: It's against God's Law. God has forbidden people to use artificial methods of birth control.

> Jones: I don't believe that there is a God, and if there's no God, there's no law of God forbidding the use of artificial methods of birth control. You'll have to give me a better reason to convince me.

Obviously, an appeal to God's Law to justify moral evaluations will be unpersuasive if the other disputant doesn't believe that God exists.

How Do We Know What God's Law Is?

Even among theists, appeal to God's Law to resolve moral perplexity or to defend moral evaluations can present problems, for theists may disagree about what God's Law is. Theists may agree that God forbids rape, murder, theft, and dishonesty, but does God forbid divorce, sex between unmarried adults, suicide if a person is suffering from a very painful, incurable illness, artificial methods of birth control, abortion in the early stages of pregnancy, or homosexuality? Does God permit the government to execute killers, soldiers to fight in wars, parents to hit their children, husbands to beat their wives, or people to tell racist and sexist jokes? Does God require us to ensure that everyone who needs medical care gets it, that everyone has equal opportunity, and that no one is homeless and hungry?

If God's Law is the correct standard of moral right and wrong, how do we determine what God forbids, permits, and requires? We can appeal to what our religion considers the revealed word of God; for example, a Christian can consult the Bible or a Muslim can consult the Koran. However, such sacred writings do not provide explicit guidance on every moral issue that a person may face. For example, the Bible says nothing about the issues of affirmative action, environmental pollution, or so-called passive euthanasia (refraining from aggressive medical treatment in order to keep patients alive). Then, too, sacred writings require interpretation, and people's interpretations may differ. How do we know which interpretation is correct? For example, in the sermon on the mount, Jesus says, "You have heard that it was said, 'An eye for an eye, and a tooth for a tooth.' But I say to you, Do not resist an evil doer. But if anyone strikes you on the right cheek, turn the other also" (Matthew 5:38–39). Should we interpret this passage as condemning capital punishment? Similarly, Jesus encountered a man who asked what he should do to ensure that he went to heaven. "Jesus said to him, 'If you wish to be perfect, go, sell your possessions, and give the money to the poor, and you will have treasure in heaven.'" The man, who was rich, wasn't pleased to hear this, but "Jesus said to his disciples, 'Truly I tell you, it will be hard for a rich man to enter the kingdom of Heaven'" (Matthew 19:21–24). Should we interpret this passage as requiring people to give away their wealth to the poor in order to ensure that they don't die rich? Can we guarantee that our interpretation of sacred writings is correct?

Saint Augustine acknowledges the problem of interpreting texts (scriptures) that are taken to be the word of God. He asks of God, "May your scriptures [for Augustine, the Bible] be my pure delight, so that I am not deceived in them and do not lead others astray in interpreting them." He continues, "It is not for nothing that by your will so many pages of scripture are opaque and obscure." He then prays, "O Lord, bring me to perfection . . . and reveal to me the meaning of these pages."[7] Augustine concedes that many biblical passages are difficult to understand because they are ambiguous or obscure. Often one needs aid in deciphering what is written there. Augustine suggests that it is difficult for people to rely on their own cognitive capacities in seeking to understand biblical passages; that is why he asks God to reveal their meaning to him. The point is that it is not easy to be sure that we truly understand or are correctly interpreting passages in scriptures that we take to be revealing God's Law or that we are using to guide our behavior.

Then, too, some theists maintain that not everything in sacred writings is truly the word of God. For example, both the Bible and the Koran were written down by human beings, even if according to tradition they were inspired by

---

[7]Ibid., p. 222.

God. Some theists believe that such sacred writings include the human voices of their authors as well as the voice of God. They may point to inconsistencies in sacred writings, passages that at least appear to contradict other passages, and maintain that such inconsistencies make it highly probable that human voices are intermingled with God's voice. The problem, then, is to determine what is the genuine voice of God and what are merely the voices of human beings.

For example, the New Testament appears to forbid divorce.

> Some Pharisees came to him and to test him [Jesus] they asked, "Is it lawful for a man to divorce his wife for any cause?" He answered, "Have you not read that the one who made them at the beginning made them male and female?"; and said, "For this reason a man shall leave his father and mother and be joined to his wife, and the two shall become one flesh. So they are no longer two, but one flesh. What God has joined together, let no one separate."
>
> *— Matthew 19:3-6*

How can we tell whether this passage is an accurate report of the words of Jesus and whether it truly reveals God's Law? Passages in sacred writings may truly reveal God's Law, but there is at least the possibility that instead they embody the moral convictions of the human beings who wrote them down.

If we do not rely on sacred writings that are considered revelations of God's Law, we may consult our conscience, hoping that God will speak to us in an audible and intelligible voice. What we hear may be God's voice, but it also may be our own voice, reflecting our moral traditions and upbringing. How can we determine whether it is God's voice? And even if it is God's voice, what we hear may require interpretation, just as sacred writings do. How can we determine whether our interpretation is correct?

People disagree about what God's Law forbids, permits, and requires. Such disagreements arise not only between different religions but even within the same religion or denomination. For example, not all Roman Catholics, let alone all Christians, agree about such issues as suicide, abortion, birth control, divorce, and sexual behavior. Therefore, theists face the problem of determining what God's Law is, and it's difficult to see how to justify the claim that we *know* what God's Law forbids, permits, and requires.

If God's Commands Make Things Right and Wrong, Is Morality Arbitrary?

Suppose that everyone agrees that God forbids adultery. According to the second version of the Divine Command theory, it follows that adultery is immoral. However, what if someone now asked how God's commands can *make* things right and wrong and *why* God forbids adultery. Could God's commands make rape, torture, and human sacrifice morally acceptable or make honesty, promise-keeping, and charity immoral? If God did not forbid rape, would rape be morally acceptable? The problem is that according to the second version of the Divine Command theory, if God required human sacrifice, then it would be wrong not to practice human sacrifice and if God permitted human beings to torture and kill each other for amusement, it would be morally acceptable to kill and torture for amusement. According to this theory, if God requires or permits something, it's right, regardless of what's required or permitted; if God prohibits something, it's wrong, regardless of what's prohibited.

Such an approach is troubling because it seems to rely on the principle that might makes right. God's commands alone determine moral right and wrong, regardless of what is commanded or what the reasons for the command may be. Doesn't that make the foundation of morality nothing but arbitrary power? Because God has the power to enforce His/Her will, God's commands are law. Then, too, we cannot say that God prohibits rape or torture *because* they're wrong and requires honesty and promise-keeping *because* they're right, since there is no right and wrong independent of God's commands. Rather, according to the second version of the Divine Command theory, rape is wrong only because God forbids it and honesty is right only because God requires it. Rape wouldn't be wrong if God didn't forbid it, and honesty wouldn't be right if God didn't require it.

Contrary to this version of the Divine Command theory, many theists maintain that God commands things because they are right or wrong. For example, consider the Spanish Roman Catholic philosopher Francisco Suarez (1548–1617). Suarez refers to the moral law as "natural law," and he maintains that the Natural Law is God's Law. According to Suarez, "Even in God, an intellectual act of judgment logically precedes an act of His will, a judgment indicating that lying is wicked, that to keep one's promises is wholly right and necessary [and so forth] (sic); therefore, . . . there will be a true natural [moral] law, even with respect to God Himself."[8] He goes on to say that "this divine volition, in the form of a prohibition or in that of an [affirmative] (sic) command, is not the whole reason for the good or evil involved in the observance or transgression of the natural [moral] law; on the contrary, it necessarily presupposes the existence of a certain righteousness or turpitude in these actions."[9] Therefore, "certain evils are prohibited, because they are evil" and "the natural law prohibits those things that are bad in themselves."[10] Suarez is emphatic that

> the natural law differs from other laws in this very respect, namely, that the latter *render* [my emphasis] evil what they prohibit, while they render . . . righteous what they prescribe; whereas the natural law *assumes* [my emphasis] the existence in a given act or object, of the rectitude which it prescribes, or the depravity which it prohibits. Accordingly, it is usual to say that this law forbids a thing because that thing is evil, or prescribes a thing because it is good.[11]

---

[8]Francisco Suarez, "On Law and God the Lawgiver," in *Moral Philosophy from Montaigne to Kant,* vol. 1, ed. J. B. Schneewind (Cambridge, England: Cambridge University Press, 1990), p. 77.

[9]Ibid.

[10]Ibid., p. 78.

[11]Ibid., p. 80.

Many theists such as Suarez deny that God's commands make things right and wrong, which presents an additional problem for the Divine Command theory. We may well suspect that in many cases, rather than relying on knowledge of God's commands to determine what's right and wrong, we rely on our convictions of right and wrong to determine what God does and doesn't command; that rather than a theist's moral convictions being dependent on her beliefs about God's commands, her beliefs about God's commands are dependent on her moral convictions. For example, does God permit people to smoke marijuana? It's likely that the answer depends on whether we think that smoking marijuana is morally wrong. If we think that it's wrong, we will maintain that God forbids it; if we think that it's not wrong, we will maintain that God doesn't forbid it. The point is that in many cases, rather than first discovering what God commands in order to discover what's morally right and wrong, as would have to be the case if the second version of the Divine Command theory were true, people rely on their beliefs about moral right and wrong in order to reach conclusions about what God commands.

These points are not new. As long ago as the fourth century B.C.E. in Athens, Greece, the philosopher Socrates clearly articulated the problem. In Plato's dialogue *Euthyphro,* Socrates asks Euthyphro, "Is the pious loved by the gods because it is pious, or is it pious because it is loved by the gods?"[12] His point was that if something is "pious" or right simply *because* it's loved by the gods, then it would be senseless to say that the gods love something *because* it's right. Yet many people in Socrates's time wished to claim that the gods often do love things because they're right (and hate things because they're wrong).

A contemporary philosopher, Robert M. Adams, has suggested a revision of the Divine Command theory to overcome some of these objections. He claims that something is right if and only if a *loving* God permits or requires it and something is wrong if and only if a *loving* God forbids it.[13] A loving God, Adams implies, would never permit rape, require human sacrifice, or prohibit honesty; therefore, the possibility of God's commanding such things is eliminated because God is loving. If a nonloving God (or Satan) were to permit rape or require human sacrifice, it would not automatically be right, contrary to what the unmodified Divine Command theory says. According to the modified Divine Command theory, only the commands of a loving God make moral law.

However, this modification still seems to presuppose prior knowledge of what's right and wrong. Suppose that someone claims that God has provided her with a new revelation. She maintains that God (who is loving) has revealed to her that He/She now commands that men will be the slaves of women and that women will perform human (male) sacrifice every Sunday. I am certain that almost all of us would immediately deny that God has commanded any such thing. Why? Because we believe that a loving God would not command enslave-

---

[12]Plato, "Euthyphro," in *Five Dialogues,* trans. G. M. A. Grube (Indianapolis, IN: Hackett, 1981), p. 14.

[13]Robert M. Adams, "A Modified Divine Command Theory of Ethical Wrongness," in Robert M. Adams, *The Virtue of Faith* (New York: Oxford University Press, 1987).

ment and human sacrifice. But why would we feel so certain that a loving God would not command enslavement and human sacrifice? Surely because we believe that they are immoral. Again, we have to rely on our moral convictions about right and wrong to decide what a loving God would command, rather than rely on what a loving God has commanded to determine what is right and wrong.

CONCLUSION

Theists who reject the second version of the Divine Command theory maintain that God requires certain things *because* they're right and forbids certain things *because* they're wrong. God doesn't arbitrarily select some things to forbid and other things to require; rather, God has reasons for His/Her commands. Theists who reject the second version of the Divine Command theory believe that moral right and wrong do not depend on God's will in the sense that God's commands make things right and wrong; because God is all-knowing and infallible, God *knows* rather than makes moral law. They maintain that actions such as rape and torture would be wrong even if God commanded us to do such things. In their view, we should obey God's commands not because they make moral right and wrong but because God, who is perfectly good, only commands us to do what is morally right and to refrain from doing what is morally wrong. God's Law is still the one and only correct moral code, even though God's will doesn't make things right and wrong.

People frequently appeal to their religious traditions and teachings in order to settle questions of moral right and wrong because they believe that their religion has knowledge of God's Law. Critics of this approach maintain that it constitutes an invalid appeal to authority. In their view, appealing to our religion as the final arbiter on moral questions is no more legitimate than appealing to our parents or to government officials. Such critics say that even if we should appeal to God's Law, there is no guarantee that our religion is correct about God's Law. Given that different religions and denominations within religions disagree on many issues, it's clear that some religious authorities are mistaken.

Some people point out that if God knows rather than makes the one correct moral code, it may be possible for human beings to come to know the moral law without having to appeal to religious authority or even to divine revelation. Perhaps individuals can employ their own reason or feelings and emotions to discover what's morally right and wrong. Or perhaps they can (and must) use their own reason to decide whether sacred writings or passages in sacred writings really are the word of God, and if they are, to come to a correct interpretation of them. The point is that some people maintain that even if God's Law is the one correct moral code, we may still have to think for ourselves and be our own moral authority. According to some people, whether theists, atheists, or agnostics, we must ultimately rely on our own reason and feelings in order to settle questions of moral right and wrong.

SKEPTICISM ABOUT MORAL LAW

Some agnostics and atheists suspect that if (or since) there is no God, then there is no moral law and nothing is morally prohibited or required. For example, consider the words of the French existentialist philosopher Jean-Paul Sartre (1905–1980).

> The existentialist . . . finds it extremely embarrassing that God does not exist, for there disappears with Him all possibility of finding values in an intelligible heaven. . . . Dostoievsky once wrote "If God did not exist, everything would be permitted"; and that, for existentialism, is the starting point. Everything is indeed permitted if God does not exist.[14]

That would be correct if moral right and wrong can only be created by God's commands, because if there is no God to issue commands, there is no moral right or wrong. However, if moral right and wrong are not created by God's commands, then even if God doesn't exist, some things may be morally right and others morally wrong.

Nevertheless, some people still think that moral rules cannot be binding on and authoritative for individuals if there is no God. They think that if morality is not created by God, it must be created by human beings, and if it is created by human beings, it has no binding authority on people. In their view, if one individual or society creates a moral rule, those individuals or societies who are not its creators cannot be obliged to conform to it. They may choose to accept it, but they may equally well choose to reject it. For example, suppose that a rule that people may not have sexual relations with their siblings (brothers and sisters) is created by human beings. We might maintain that because the rule is a human rather than a divine creation, no one is obligated to accept it and conform to it, and it does not apply to those who choose not to accept it. We will examine these skeptical views in subsequent chapters, beginning in the next chapter with a discussion of Moral Nihilism, Moral Relativism, and Subjectivism.

EXERCISES

1. If God doesn't exist, is nothing morally forbidden or required? Defend your answer.

2. Many people in the United States are homeless, although no one knows exactly how many. Santiago maintains that God requires society to ensure that no one is homeless. Trevelyan disagrees. How might Santiago and Trevelyan defend their views? Assuming that you are a theist, how would you decide which of them is correct?

3. If God exists, do you think that He/She requires monogamy (having only one spouse at a time)? Defend your answer.

---

[14]Jean-Paul Sartre, "Existentialism Is a Humanism," in *Existentialism,* ed. Robert C. Solomon (New York: Modern Library, 1974), pp. 201–202.

4. Suppose that God requires monogamy. First, try to provide reasons for requiring monogamy. Second, try to think of situations in which polygamy (having more than one spouse at a time) would be more reasonable than monogamy and try to provide a justification for permitting polygamy. Do you think that God's prohibiting polygamy would be sufficient to show that polygamy is immoral? Defend your answer.

5. The claim that we *should* obey God's Law because God will reward those who obey and punish those who disobey constitutes an appeal to self-interest. Try to construct an argument that does not depend on self-interest to defend the claim that we have a moral obligation to obey God's commands, whatever those commands might be.

6. Do you think that individuals should appeal to their religious traditions as the ultimate authority on moral matters in order to settle issues of moral right and wrong? Defend your answer.

7. Write down your responses to the claim that we should think for ourselves on moral matters and rely on our own reason and feelings.

SUGGESTED READINGS

Robert M. Adams. *The Virtue of Faith.* New York: Oxford University Press, 1987.

Saint Augustine. *Confessions.* Translated by Henry Chadwick. New York: Oxford University Press, 1991.

J. B. Schneewind, ed. *Moral Philosophy from Montaigne to Kant,* Vols. 1 and 2. Cambridge, England: Cambridge University Press, 1990.

CHAPTER 3

Nihilism, Relativism, and Subjectivism

MORAL OBJECTIVISM AND MORAL NONOBJECTIVISM

Moral Nihilism, Moral Subjectivism, and Moral Relativism are all forms of Moral Nonobjectivism (sometimes call Noncognitivism). According to Nonobjectivism, no moral claim or belief is objectively true or false—that is, true (or false) independent of what anyone thinks or believes. On the other hand, according to Moral Objectivism, some moral claims and beliefs are objectively true and others are objectively false—that is, true (or false) independent of what anyone thinks or believes.

Moral objectivists might defend their position by appealing to the requirement of consistency. A minimal requirement of rationality is consistency; that is, our beliefs should at least not contradict each other. A contradiction involves both affirming and denying the same thing. For example, the statements "Dogs are mammals" and "Dogs are not mammals" contradict each other. So, too, do the following pairs of statements:

A1. John is ten years old.

A2. John is not ten years old.

B1. Tom is allergic to shrimp.

B2. Tom is not allergic to shrimp.

When statements contradict each other, they cannot possibly both be true. One must be true and the other false. John cannot possibly be ten years old and not ten years old. Tom cannot possibly be allergic to shrimp and not allergic to shrimp.

When we say that two statements that contradict each cannot both be true—that one must be true and the other false—we are not saying that we *know* which one is true and which one is false. Consider the following pair of statements:

C1. The Democratic candidate will win the presidential election in 2012.

    C2. The Democratic candidate will not win the presidential election in 2012.

Statements C1 and C2 cannot both be true. I know that one must be true and the other false. However, I don't know which one is true and which one is false.

    A moral objectivist might apply this principle to moral claims. Consider the following pairs of statements:

    D1. Slavery is immoral.

    D2. Slavery is not immoral.

    E1. Rape is immoral.

    E2. Rape is not immoral.

A moral objectivist might maintain that when two moral statements contradict each other, they cannot both be true. One must be true and the other false. In some cases, especially when the issue is complex or controversial, we may not know which is true and which is false, but that does not change the fact that they cannot *both* be true.

    Many moral objectivists reject Moral Nonobjectivism because all members of this family of moral theories violate the principle that when statements contradict each other, they cannot both be true. In their view, the requirement of consistency justifies the claim that there is a presumption in favor of (some version of) Moral Objectivism. This presumption means that it is more reasonable to accept Moral Objectivism unless there are very strong reasons or arguments supporting Moral Nonobjectivism. Therefore, we should not accept Moral Nonobjectivism unless there are good arguments that "prove" it. We will examine each of the three members of the family of nonobjectivist theories—Nihilism, Subjectivism, and Relativism—and the arguments supporting them to see whether there are good reasons for accepting any of them.

    The Divine Command theory of morality is only one of various possible versions of Moral Objectivism, some more modest than others. The most extreme version of Moral Objectivism claims that there is one and only one correct moral code or system of moral principles and that it supplies the single correct answer to every moral question. The correct moral code must be a *system,* rather than just a set, of moral principles because if it is to provide the single correct answer to all moral questions, it must establish a hierarchy that governs situations in which principles conflict. For example, a principle requiring us to preserve human life may be more important than a principle requiring us to respect people's property; similarly, a principle forbidding us to cause psychological harm to others may be more important than a principle requiring us to tell the truth.

    Two possible misconceptions about Moral Objectivism, even the most extreme version, can make it seem less plausible than it may be. First, the moral principles making up the system or moral code need not be expressed in unqualified form, such as "Stealing is wrong." Rather, they can be expressed in a qualified form, such as "In circumstance C, stealing is wrong." Thus, a moral objectivist could deny that an unqualified principle such as "Stealing is wrong" is part of the one correct system of moral principles. Instead, she could claim that a variety of principles regarding theft are part of the system; in some circumstances theft may be immoral, but in other circumstances it may not be immoral. The correct moral code may thus include principles of the form "In circumstance C_1, it is wrong to steal" and "In circumstance C_2, it is not wrong to steal." For example, it may be wrong to steal if there are other things we could do to survive but not wrong to steal if it is necessary to save innocent human lives. (The system may also include principles that require compensation to the victim of theft, even if it was not wrong to steal under the given circumstances.)

I want to emphasize the importance of distinguishing between qualified and unqualified moral principles. Someone might reject Moral Objectivism because he thinks that Objectivism commits us to the view that certain forms of behavior are wrong in all circumstances. For example, someone might think that because Moral Objectivism maintains that some moral principles are objectively true, it commits us to saying that an unqualified moral principle such as

Killing is wrong

is objectively true. But a moral objectivist could say that this principle is not objectively true because it is unqualified and entails claims that are false. For example, in its unqualified form it entails that it is wrong for me to kill the mosquito that is about to drill for blood on my arm—a dubious claim.

We can immediately see one way to qualify the principle that would make it less implausible.

Killing people is wrong.

Does Moral Objectivism commit us to the claim that this newly qualified moral principle is objectively true? Not necessarily. If we think that it is not wrong for a police officer to kill an attacker in self-defense when it is the only way to save her own life, or to kill someone about to kill an innocent victim when that is the only way to save innocent life, then we can say again that before it can be accepted as objectively true it must be qualified further. The qualification may be vague in order to apply to a variety of circumstances—for example,

Killing people without a morally good reason is wrong.

Alternatively, we could specify a variety of more precisely qualified principles and maintain that they are all objectively true—for example,

Killing people in self-defense as a last resort is not wrong.

Killing someone who is about to kill innocent people is not wrong if that is the only way to save them.

Killing innocent people for financial gain is wrong.

Killing people for pleasure is wrong.

The point to emphasize is that a moral objectivist need not maintain that all, only, or any unqualified moral principles are objectively true.

The second point is that the moral objectivist may insist that the one correct moral code provides the correct answer to *every* moral question, but only if the question is properly expressed. For example, a moral objectivist may deny that we can answer such questions as "Is theft immoral?" or "Is polygamy immoral?", insisting instead that we can only answer a question such as "Is theft (polygamy) under circumstances C_1 immoral?" We must specify the relevant circumstances. We might ask such questions as "Is polygamy immoral in a society in which the number of men and women is equal?" "Is polygamy immoral in a society in which there are far fewer men (women) than women (men)?" "Is polygamy immoral in a society where almost everyone believes that it is (is not) immoral?" If we ask, "Is polygamy (theft) *always* immoral?", a moral objectivist may insist that the correct answer is "No."

A moral objectivist could say that polygamy is not immoral in situations (or societies) where the number of men and women is very unequal or in situations where almost everyone in a society believes that it is not immoral. On the other hand, she might insist that rape, torturing people for amusement, and killing members of despised minorities are always wrong. In her view, these are correct moral principles that apply to all individuals and societies, whether or not they accept and live by them. Thus, if people from society A condemn people from society B as immoral because they practice polygamy, a moral objectivist may insist that A is mistaken in its belief that people in B are behaving immorally. Similarly, a moral objectivist may insist that if an individual believes that rape is not immoral, he is mistaken; or that if a society believes that it is not immoral to kill members of despised minorities, it is mistaken.

A moral objectivist could say that some contrary forms of behavior are equally morally acceptable. For example, a moral objectivist could claim that under certain circumstances polygamy and monogamy are equally morally acceptable and that it is as morally acceptable for a society to forbid as to permit polygamy. Thus, Moral Objectivism should not be confused with Moral Absolutism. Moral objectivists need not claim that all or even most of the principles making up the correct moral code are absolute, unqualified, or unconditional.

MORAL NIHILISM

Some people reject Moral Objectivism, whether the principles are qualified or unqualified, conditional or unconditional. Moral nihilists reject Moral Objectivism because they maintain that nothing is right or wrong since there is no correct or incorrect moral code or system of moral principles. They claim that all moral evaluations are more or less meaningless or senseless. Therefore, they neither accept (believe) nor make any moral evaluations of their own behavior or the behavior of anyone else. They do not have a moral code that they live by because they reject the very idea of a *moral* code. Consider the following imaginary dialogue between Pablo and Mike, a moral nihilist.

Pablo: You shouldn't be selling drugs. It's immoral.

Mike: Immoral? Don't be naive.

Pablo: I mean it. It's wrong. And so is using that garbage.

Mike: If it feels good, do it. It feels good. And I get rich selling it.

Pablo: That doesn't matter. It's wrong.

Mike: You've been brainwashed. This morality talk is for suckers. Nothing is really right or wrong; anything goes.

Pablo: What do you mean?

Mike: Because you live in the United States, the laws of Russia don't apply to you. I say that moral laws don't apply to people any more than the laws of Russia apply to people who don't live in Russia. Moral rules are just rules that people invented; they're not authoritative or binding. I reject all moral rules as I reject the laws of Russia; they just don't apply to me. I don't obey them, and I don't make moral evaluations. As far as I'm concerned, nothing is really morally right or wrong, morally good or bad, morally forbidden, permitted, or required.

According to Moral Nihilism, nothing is morally right or wrong, good or bad, required or prohibited. (The word *nihilism* comes from the Latin word *nihil*, which means "nothing.") Something can be morally permitted, required, or forbidden only if there are genuine moral rules. But moral nihilists maintain that moral rules are in a sense mere fictions.

Some moral nihilists claim that moral sentences cannot be either true or false because they make evaluations rather than statements and only statement-making sentences—those that describe rather than evaluate (or prescribe)—can be true or false. According to this view, "This is a 1600-pound car" describes the car and therefore makes a statement that is either true or false, whereas the sentence "This is a good family car" evaluates rather than describes the car and therefore does not make a statement that is either true or false.

However, critics of Nihilism point out that sentences can be used to do several things simultaneously. For example, the sentence "You are obese" can be used both to describe and to insult.[1] British philosopher Philippa Foot points out that the concept "rude" is both descriptive and evaluative, so that one who says "It was rude of you to insult the host" both describes and evaluates the behavior.[2] Similarly, one could plausibly claim that "This is a good family car" both evaluates and describes the car. It describes the car if "This is a good family car" means something like "This car satisfies the standards appropriate for evaluating family cars." The standard appropriate for evaluating family cars may be somewhat vague, but surely some minimal requirements are clear. Obviously a

---

[1]One is "obese" if one's weight is more than 20% above the norm for one's height.

[2]Philippa Foot, "Moral Arguments," in Philippa Foot, *Virtues and Vices* (Berkeley: University of California Press, 1978). (The paper first appeared in the journal *Mind* in 1958.)

two-seater sports car is not a good family car because a family car must be roomy enough for a group of adults and children. Similarly, in a family car safety is a more important feature than speed. A good family car need not have a top speed of 180 mph or be able to accelerate from 0 to 60 mph in five seconds, but it must be reasonably safe.

Could we not say that a moral sentence such as "Slavery is immoral" both evaluates and describes? One way of defending the assertion that it *describes* slavery is to claim that the sentence attributes the property of being immoral to the institution of slavery just as the sentence "This is a 1600-pound car" attributes the property of weighing 1600 pounds to the car. We might go on to say that a social institution has the property of being immoral if it fails to satisfy the moral standards appropriate for evaluating social institutions. Of course, this claim leaves us with the problem of specifying (and defending) those moral standards. The point is that we need not agree with moral nihilists who claim that moral sentences are neither true nor false because they are not used to describe and hence to make statements.

Another possible defense of Moral Nihilism is to claim that moral sentences don't make statements, and therefore are neither true nor false, because they are meaningless. The string of words "The to be green weeps" is neither true nor false and makes no statement because it is meaningless. A nihilist such as the British philosopher A. J. Ayer can claim that moral sentences are meaningless and therefore are neither true nor false.[3] According to Ayer and others sympathetic to a school of philosophy called Logical Positivism, a sentence is meaningful if and only if it can be *verified* by appeal to perception and observation. Because sentences making moral evaluations cannot be verified by appeal to observation and perception, they are meaningless. However, critics of Nihilism have pointed out that if moral sentences such as "Slavery is immoral" are meaningless, they are not meaningless in the way that "The to be green weeps" is meaningless. And critics of Logical Positivism have denied that a sentence is meaningful if and only if it can be verified by appeal to observation and perception.

If moral sentences can be used to make statements as well as to evaluate, then Moral Nihilism violates the principle that when statements are inconsistent with each other, one must be true and the other false. According to Nihilism, neither member of the pair "Slavery is immoral" and "Slavery is not immoral" is true, and neither is false.

Finally, moral nihilists cannot have moral beliefs or make moral claims. For example, a moral nihilist who is being tortured to death for the amusement of a sadistic fiend cannot believe or claim that what the fiend is doing is wrong because the nihilist is committed to the view that nothing anyone does is wrong (or right). Similarly, a nihilist cannot have the belief that it would be wrong to start a nuclear war or to exterminate whole societies of people because one disagrees with their religion. Opponents of Nihilism find these implications and claims of Nihilism implausible, and so they reject Nihilism.

---

[3]A. J. Ayer, *Language, Truth, and Logic,* 2d ed. (New York: Dover, 1946).

MORAL RELATIVISM

For centuries, people have pointed out that different societies or cultures at least appear to have vastly different moral codes. For example, the French philosopher Montaigne (1533–1592) pointed out:

> There is nothing in which the world is so varied as in customs and laws. A given thing is abominable here, which brings commendation elsewhere: as in Lacedaemon [in ancient Greece] cleverness in stealing. Marriages between close relatives are capital offenses among us, elsewhere they are in honor.
>
> > There are nations, it is said,
> > Where mothers sons, and fathers daughters wed;
> > And thus affection grows, doubled by love.
> > > *- Ovid*
>
> The murder of infants, the murder of fathers, sharing of wives, traffic in robberies, license for all sorts of sensual pleasures, nothing in short is so extreme that it is not accepted by the usage of some nation.[4]

According to the moral codes of some societies, incest, infanticide, and wife sharing are immoral; however, according to the moral codes of other societies, they are not immoral. Different societies or cultures disagree about the moral acceptability of slavery, capital punishment, abortion, euthanasia, wife beating, suicide, sex outside marriage, sexual equality, homosexuality, and so on. And it's difficult to maintain that they are merely applying the same principles under different circumstances.

Acquaintance with the wide diversity of moral beliefs across societies may lead us to deny that there really is only one correct moral code that applies to and binds all societies. This view is called Moral Relativism. Moral Relativism is actually a family of theories rather than a single theory. Some versions of the theory are more moderate than others.

Protagorean Relativism

According to one of the earliest moral relativists, the ancient Greek philosopher Protagoras (485–415 B.C.E.), "I hold that whatever practices seem right and laudable to any particular state are so, for that state, so long as it holds by them."[5] Plato had Socrates sum up Protagoras's views in this way:

> And again in social matters, the theory will say that, so far as good and bad customs or rights and wrongs . . . are concerned, whatever any state makes up

---

[4]Michel de Montaigne, "Apology for Raymond Sebond, in *Moral Philosophy from Montaigne to Kant,* vol. 1, ed. J. B. Schneewind (Cambridge, England: Cambridge University Press, 1990), p. 44.

[5]Plato, "Theaetetus," in *Collected Dialogues of Plato,* ed. Edith Hamilton and Huntington Cairns (Princeton, NJ: Princeton University Press, 1961), p. 873 (167c). Whether Plato has accurately expressed the views of Protagoras is an open question, but the views that he attributes to Protagoras, whether or not Protagoras held them, have been influential.

its mind to enact as lawful for itself, really is lawful for it, and in this field no individual or state is wiser than another.[6]

Similarly, the sociologist William Graham Sumner (1840–1910) wrote, "In the folkways [customs, traditions, and moral beliefs], whatever is, is right."[7] He continued, "'Immoral' never means anything but contrary to the mores of the time and place. [T]here is no permanent or universal standard by which right and truth in regard to these matters can be established and different folkways compared and criticized."[8] More recently, anthropologist Ruth Benedict (1887–1948) wrote, "Morality differs in every society, and is a convenient term for socially approved habits." She continued, "The concept of the good . . . is that which society has approved."[9]

We'll call this most extreme form of Moral Relativism "Protagorean Relativism" after Protagoras. According to Protagorean relativists, each society or culture has its own moral code, and whatever a society's moral code says is right and wrong *is* right and wrong for that society. The moral codes of all societies are equal; no society's moral code is more correct or reasonable than any other society's moral code. Each society's moral code is immune from rational criticism. For example, if polygamy is immoral according to the moral code of society A, then it is immoral in society A. On the other hand, if polygamy is not immoral according to the moral code of society B, then it is not immoral in society B. Furthermore, it makes no sense to ask whether polygamy is "really" immoral or to ask which society's moral belief about polygamy is correct. They are both correct for their respective societies. There is no higher court of appeals on moral matters than a society's own moral code. There are no universal moral standards or principles that apply to all societies; there are only local standards and principles.

To take a concrete example, so-called "tribal law" among Palestinians in the West Bank of the Jordan River and the Gaza Strip considers some actions morally permissible that most people in the West consider immoral. Not only may a rapist be killed by relatives of the victim, but the victim may be killed by relatives for bringing shame to the family. Recently a 3-year-old girl in a town on the West Bank was raped by a 25-year-old man seeking revenge against her father because of a quarrel over money. Tribal law would encourage the little girl's relatives to kill her rapist, but also to kill her. Palestinian leader Yasser Arafat, wanting to prevent recourse to tribal law that many Palestinians no longer subscribe to, quickly brought the rapist to trial. He was sentenced to life in prison at hard labor.[10] If Moral Relativism is correct, then "tribal law" according to which it is morally

---

[6]Ibid., p. 877 (172a).

[7]William Graham Sumner, "Folkways," in *Ethical Relativity*, ed. John Ladd (Belmont, CA: Wadsworth, 1973), p. 31.

[8]Ibid., pp. 37–38.

[9]Ruth Benedict, "A Defense of Ethical Relativism," in *Ethical Theory*, ed. Louis Pojman (Belmont, CA: Wadsworth, 1989), p. 23.

[10]"Palestinian Court Dispenses Justice," *The Boston Sunday Globe*, October 20, 1996, p. A6.

permissible to kill a 3-year-old rape victim for causing her family shame is no less correct, true, or reasonable than is a moral code that prohibits such behavior.

Similarly, suppose that someone from the United States was visiting Nazi Germany in the 1930s and saw Nazi thugs drag an old Jewish man from his home and brutally beat him to death in the street. The visitor might say that this act was viciously immoral. But suppose that the Nazi thugs say that in Nazi Germany, beating innocent Jews to death is not considered immoral. A moral relativist would be committed to saying that the Nazis' belief that it is not immoral to beat innocent Jews to death is no less correct, true, or reasonable than the American's belief that it is immoral to beat to death innocent Jews.

Protagorean relativists would probably go on to say that an individual's moral beliefs are correct if and only if they are consistent with the moral beliefs of the individual's society. Thus, suppose that individual X is a member of society A (according to whose moral code polygamy is immoral) and individual Y is a member of society B (according to whose moral code polygamy is morally acceptable). If X believes that polygamy is immoral, he is correct, but if Y believes that it's immoral he is mistaken. On the other hand, if X believes that polygamy is immoral and Y believes that it is not immoral, they are both correct even though they have contradictory beliefs. Whatever a society's moral beliefs are, they're correct for the members of that society.

Most people find these claims implausible when they consider certain moral issues. Suppose that a society's moral code permits slavery, torture during interrogation of people accused of crimes, infanticide, the killing of rape victims, and wife beating. If Protagorean Moral Relativism is true, then those things *are* morally acceptable in this society and no one can legitimately say that this society's moral code is incorrect. These things may be immoral according to our moral code, but our moral code is no better than (more correct or more reasonable than) this society's moral code, according to Protagorean relativists. Furthermore, if any individual members of this society believe that these things are immoral, they are mistaken.

Why should we agree with Protagorean relativists that our society's moral code is no better or worse, no more correct or reasonable, than any other society's moral code? What *reason* is there to think that the Protagorean relativist's claims are true?

Reasons for Accepting Protagorean Relativism

God May Not Exist   Some people believe that only God's Law could furnish a standard for judging the moral codes of different societies. However, if God doesn't exist, then God's Law doesn't exist, and no such standard exists. Those who doubt that God exists may conclude that whatever a society's moral code says is right is right for that society. However, if the most extreme version of Divine Command theory of morality is false and there is a secular basis for morality, then even if God doesn't exist, it does not follow that all moral codes are equally correct or reasonable. Even if God doesn't exist, that would not prove that Protagorean Moral Relativism is true.

There Are No Moral Principles That All Societies Accept   Protagorean moral relativists often point to the wide diversity of moral beliefs as proof that whatever a society's moral code says is right is right for that society. They often argue somewhat as follows:

There are no moral principles that all societies accept.

Therefore, there are no moral principles that are correct for all societies.

For example, even as fundamental a moral principle as the prohibition against killing innocent people is not accepted by all societies. Consider the Hindu custom of suttee, the burning to death of widows on the funeral pyres of their husbands. In nineteenth-century India a Hindu reformer, Rammohan Roy, came to oppose suttee because in 1811 he "had witnessed the suttee of his sister-in-law, whom relatives kept on the pyre even though she was screaming and struggling to escape. He knew that in Calcutta alone there were over 1,500 such immolations between 1815 and 1818."[11] If some societies can consider a practice such as suttee or the killing of rape victims morally acceptable, then surely, we might conclude, there are no moral principles that all societies accept.

However, even if it is true that there are no moral principles that all societies accept, it does not follow that the moral principles of all societies are equally correct or reasonable. For example, the fact that societies disagree about the moral acceptability of suttee does not prove that all moral principles about suttee are equally correct or reasonable, and the fact that suttee is morally acceptable according to Hindu society's moral code does not prove that suttee is morally acceptable for that society. It proves that suttee is *believed to be* morally acceptable by that society, but the fact that something is believed to be true, correct, or reasonable by a society does not prove that it really is true, correct, or reasonable. Because only five planets are visible to the naked eye, ancient societies believed that there are five planets in our solar system. Having the use of telescopes, we now believe that there are at least nine planets. The fact that different societies have disagreed about the number of planets in our solar system does not show that the belief that there are five planets is as correct or reasonable as the belief that there are at least nine planets. Similarly, societies have disagreed about whether there is one God, many gods, or no God. That doesn't prove that all answers to the question "How many gods are there?" are equally correct or reasonable. Thus, the argument is invalid. The conclusion that the moral codes of all societies are equally correct or reasonable does not follow from the premise that there are no moral principles that all societies accept.

Furthermore, the premise of the argument is itself questionable. Instances of moral disagreement can be dramatic. Consider disagreements over suttee, slavery, human sacrifice, and infanticide, for example. Not all moral disagreement, however, shows that the societies accept different *moral principles.* Disagreement over a particular moral issue could arise even when the societies

---

[11]Denise Carmody and John Carmody, *Eastern Ways to the Center* (Belmont, CA: Wadsworth, 1983), p. 43.

accept the same moral principles, if they are applying them in radically different circumstances or if they have very different beliefs about the facts. Suppose that a society, S, practices human sacrifice. We believe that human sacrifice is immoral. Does this show that our society and S accept very different moral principles? Not necessarily. The explanation may be that members of S have different beliefs about the facts. Suppose that members of S believe that the gods sustain the universe, but that their power to do so will wane and vanish (destroying the universe) unless it is periodically renewed by human sacrifice. The people of S believe that they face a choice between the destruction of the universe and human sacrifice, and they choose the latter to avert the former. They may accept many of the same moral principles that we do—for example, principles forbidding indiscriminate killing and placing a high value on human life. If our beliefs were the same as theirs, we too would probably maintain that human sacrifice is morally required because we have a duty to prevent the destruction of the universe.

Similarly, suppose that the moral code of one society, G, requires children to kill their parents when they reach a certain age, say 65, while the moral code of another society, H, forbids children to kill their parents. Would this show that the two societies accept radically different moral principles—one society requiring children to honor and care for their parents, and the other society rejecting this principle? No. Suppose that members of G believe that they will spend eternity in the condition they were in when they died. If they are blind and crippled at the time of death, they will spend eternity blind and crippled. If they are strong and healthy, they will spend eternity strong and healthy. Suppose further that members of the tribe know or believe that the probability of remaining strong and healthy after age 65 declines precipitously. In their view, someone who lives beyond age 65 faces a great risk of spending eternity in a deteriorated state. Therefore, children kill their aged parents in order to ensure that they will not spend eternity in a poor state—blind, deaf, crippled, or otherwise weakened by age. Given their beliefs, the best way of following the moral principle requiring children to honor and care for their parents is to kill them by age 65. Therefore, the moral disagreement is not necessarily due to one society's rejecting a moral principle that the other society accepts.

Not only may moral disagreement be due to disagreement about the facts rather than due to societies' accepting radically different moral principles, but sometimes it's due to applying the same or similar moral principles in radically different circumstances. Suppose that there are two societies, A and B. A is an affluent, technologically advanced society with extensive, accurate information about reproduction and reliable methods of birth control. Population growth has been controlled, and overpopulation is not a problem. B, on the other hand, is technologically backward and poised on the edge of subsistence, barely able to support its current population. People in B lack accurate information about reproduction and have no reliable methods of birth control. If unchecked, population growth will outstrip available resources, leading to widespread starvation, malnutrition, and disease. People in A believe that infanticide is immoral; people in B believe that infanticide is a morally acceptable method of population control. Does this moral disagreement prove that these two societies have no moral principles in common? No. We could find that people in both A and B place a high value on human life, love children, condemn unjustified killing and the deliberate infliction of suffering on other people, and place a high value on the survival of the community and its members. However, because their circumstances differ, people in society B must choose between infanticide and widespread starvation.

The claim that there are no moral principles that all societies accept is a breathtakingly sweeping claim. How could anyone know it to be true? To confirm it, we would have to look at every moral principle that has ever been accepted by any society and examine the moral codes of all human societies in order to determine what principles they accept and reject. Finding many moral principles that some societies accept and others reject would not prove that there is not even *one* moral principle that all societies accept. For example, are there societies with moral codes that permit parents to kill their children for amusement, friends to steal from friends, or people to break agreements and promises they have made for any and every reason? To prove that there is not even one moral principle that all societies accept would be a colossal undertaking. In fact, no one has proved any such thing.

No One Can Prove Who's Correct in a Moral Dispute   Protagorean relativists might argue as follows: No one can prove which society is correct in a moral dispute. If no one can prove who is correct in a dispute, then no one is correct or incorrect. Therefore, no society's moral principles are correct or incorrect.

There are two problems with this defense. First, it is not obviously true that no one can prove who's correct in a moral dispute. As we saw in the first chapter, moral evaluations require reasons. If the nonmoral beliefs that justify some of a society's moral principles are incorrect or unreasonable, then we may say that the moral principles based on them are unreasonable or incorrect. Therefore, if we can show that those nonmoral beliefs are false or unreasonable, we have shown that the moral principles they justify may be incorrect or mistaken. For example, if human sacrifice is not required to prevent the destruction of the universe and if people will not spend eternity in the condition they are in when they die, then moral principles permitting human sacrifice and requiring children to kill their parents by age 65 may be considered incorrect. If we can show that the beliefs on which they are based are unreasonable, then we have shown that the moral principles based on them may be incorrect or unreasonable.

Second, even if we cannot prove who's correct in a moral dispute, it does not follow that all moral principles are equally correct or reasonable. Many people are convinced that no one can prove whether God exists. Nevertheless, it does not follow that there is no correct answer to the question "Does God exist?" or that all answers are equally reasonable. Similarly, human beings may never be able to prove whether there is intelligent life beyond our solar system. Nevertheless, that would not show that there is no correct answer to the question "Is there intelligent life beyond our solar system?" There's only one correct answer to the questions "Does God exist?" and "Is there intelligent life outside our solar system?" whether or not we can come to *know* what the correct answer is or prove which is the correct answer. Therefore, the fact that we cannot prove who is correct in a dispute does not show that all answers to the question at issue are equally good.

The Virtue of Tolerance   Some people accept Protagorean Relativism because they think that people should not judge other societies on the basis of their own moral code and they think that Protagorean Relativism requires that kind of toleration. This reasoning is mistaken for two reasons. First, even if a theory entails that behavior we approve of is morally required, it does not follow that the theory is correct. Second, Protagorean Relativism does not require toleration of other societies. According to Protagorean Relativism, whatever a society's moral code says is right is right for that society. If a society's moral code requires its members to forcibly convert other societies to its beliefs and moral code and to exterminate those who refuse to be converted, its moral code is no worse than the moral code of a society that requires toleration. If Moral Relativism is correct, there is no true moral principle requiring toleration that applies to all people in all times at all places. A moral code that requires toleration is no more reasonable or correct than one that doesn't.

Finally, we might insist that tolerance is not always good and praiseworthy. Is it a virtue to be tolerant of a society's moral code if it permits slavery, racial or sexual discrimination, suttee, the killing of rape victims, or mass extermination of despised minorities? Should we refrain from judging and condemning them in the name of toleration? Many people maintain that there are limits to what should be tolerated; in their view, toleration of evil is no virtue.

People Should Conform to the Moral Code of Their Society   Some people accept Protagorean Relativism because they think that people should conform to the moral code of their society and because they believe that Protagorean Relativism entails that people have such a duty. However, Protagorean Relativism does not entail any such duty. If there are no universally correct moral principles, then there can be no correct universal moral principle requiring people to conform to the moral code, or even to the laws, of their society. That is, the question "Should people obey the moral code or the laws of their society?" does not have a single correct answer, according to Protagorean Relativism. Even if our society has a moral rule requiring that we obey its moral code and laws, it doesn't follow that we should obey because that would presuppose the very question at issue: "Should people obey the moral code or laws of their society?" A Protagorean Relativist *cannot* claim that people should conform to the moral code or laws of their society.

Criticisms of Protagorean Relativism

According to many opponents of Protagorean Relativism, not only are there no good reasons to believe that it is true, but there are good reasons for thinking that it is false.

Relativism Violates Logical Laws   Some people claim that Protagorean Relativism violates the principle of logic that contradictory statements cannot both be true. For example, if society A believes "Slavery is immoral" and society B believes "Slavery is not immoral," according to Protagorean Relativism they both have true beliefs, even though the two statements contradict each other. Moral Objectivists claim that these two statements cannot both be true; one must be true and the other false.

Does Believing Make It So?   Ordinarily, we distinguish between a society's believing that something is true and its really being true. It makes little sense to maintain that whatever a society believes to be true *is* true. A society may believe that witches exist, but believing doesn't make it so. It is possible for entire societies to have false beliefs. Protagorean Relativism collapses the distinction between someone's believing that something is true and its really being true, at least for moral matters, by claiming that whatever a society believes is right really *is* right. However, we might maintain that this claim makes no more sense for moral matters than it does for nonmoral matters, such as beliefs about witches. Just as believing that something is true doesn't make it true, believing that something is right doesn't make it right.

A Society's Moral Code Is the Moral Code of the Majority   According to Protagorean Relativism, whatever a society believes to be right is right for that society. However, there is often disagreement *within* societies. For example, not all Americans agree about the morality of sex outside marriage, birth control, abortion, suicide, euthanasia, affirmative action, or capital punishment. Therefore, when we talk about the moral code or moral beliefs of a society, we can only mean the moral code or moral beliefs of the *majority* in a society. To say that a society believes that infanticide is immoral, then, means that a majority of its members believe that infanticide is immoral. But if the moral beliefs of individual members of a society are correct if and only if they conform to the majority's beliefs, then the majority *makes* moral truth and is always right.

That claim has consequences that many of us find difficult to accept. For example, if a majority of Americans in the 1940s and 1950s believed that racial segregation was morally acceptable, then according to Protagorean Relativism, it *was* morally acceptable. Furthermore, civil rights leaders such as Martin Luther King, Jr., who fought segregation because they thought it was immoral, were mistaken. Similarly, if a majority of people in early nineteenth century U.S. society believed that slavery was morally acceptable, then it *was* morally acceptable, and the abolitionists who condemned it as immoral were mistaken and had incorrect moral beliefs. Protagorean Relativism implies that we can discover moral truth simply by taking an opinion survey.

However, many of us deny that the majority is always correct in moral matters, and the minority always mistaken. Many of us deny that a majority's believing something is right *makes* it right. Many of us believe that at least some things are right and others wrong independent of what the majority of people in a society believe. For example, many of us insist that racial and sexual discrimination, slavery, wife beating, rape, suttee, and extermination of despised minorities are wrong even if the majority in a society believes they are not wrong. What counts is not the number of people who believe that something is right or wrong, but rather the weight of the arguments. In order to be justified, moral principles require reasons, and not all reasons are equally good. As we have seen, moral principles can be based on false and unreasonable beliefs. It is more likely that the moral principles justified by the best reasons or arguments are correct than that the moral principles believed by the most people are correct.

The Problem of Subgroups According to Protagorean Relativism, whether an individual's moral beliefs and claims are true depends on the moral beliefs of the majority in that person's society. However, people belong to many subgroups. For example, an individual may be a citizen of the United States, of California, and of San Francisco; a member of a certain religion; and an employee of a certain company in a certain industry. Each subgroup may have its own moral code. For example, the moral code of the majority of people in the United States may not be identical to the moral code of the majority of people in California or San Francisco. The moral codes of various industries or professions—the police, the military, the medical professions, law, teaching, architecture, accounting—may differ in important ways, as may the moral codes of individual companies.

Suppose that Smith belongs to a Los Angeles street gang. A majority of people in the United States and in Los Angeles believes that selling drugs is immoral, but a majority of people in street gangs believes that it isn't immoral. Which society's moral code constitutes the standard of moral correctness for him? U.S. society? Los Angeles society? Street gang society? Similarly, suppose that a majority of people in the world believes that exterminating despised minorities is immoral but that the majority of people in nation S believes that exterminating despised minorities is morally acceptable. Is a nation's moral code the ultimate standard of right and wrong, or is the world's moral code the ultimate standard of right and wrong? Protagorean Relativism gives no guidance on identifying which of the many groups to which people belong constitutes the appropriate standard of right and wrong.

Other Versions of Moral Relativism

Moral principles can be unqualified, as in "Stealing is (always) wrong," or qualified, as in "In circumstances C, stealing is wrong." According to a modest form of Moral Relativism that should not be confused with the extreme views of Protagorean Moral Relativism, most if not all plausible moral principles are qualified rather than unqualified—that is, they apply in some circumstances but not in others. For example, such a moral relativist might say that polygamy is immoral in some circumstances but not in others or that brother-sister marriages are immoral in some circumstances but not in others. This kind of Moral Relativism actually is compatible with what I have called Moral Objectivism because it may maintain that there are objectively correct and incorrect conditional moral principles. That is, such a moral relativist may insist that it is correct that in circumstance C_1 polygamy is immoral but that in circumstances C_2 polygamy is not immoral.

Another modest version of Moral Relativism might claim that societies may be equally justified or reasonable even though they have contradictory moral beliefs about certain forms of behavior. For example, such a moral relativist might say that society A's belief that brother-sister marriages are morally acceptable is as reasonable or correct as society B's belief that brother-sister marriages are immoral. But such a moral relativist may insist that such Relativism applies only to some forms of behavior. It may apply to marriage conventions but not to issues such as slavery, suttee, and so on. In a sense, such a relativist claims that Protagorean Moral Relativism applies to some forms of behavior but not to others.

However, it may be that such local rather than global Protagorean Moral Relativism should be considered in the following way. It is as (objectively) morally acceptable for a society to forbid as to permit brother-sister marriages because each alternative is equally (objectively) morally acceptable, just as wearing a red shirt is as (objectively) morally acceptable as is wearing a blue shirt. In this case, such Moral Relativism is compatible with what I have called Moral Objectivism.

All Systems of Moral Principles Are Arbitrary

Perhaps the most compelling argument for the claim that no moral principle can be incorrect begins with the premise that all systems of moral principles are based on one or more fundamental principles that are nothing but arbitrary assumptions. For example, a system of principles that includes a prohibition against exterminating despised minorities may be based on the fundamental principles that all people are equal in most respects relevant to how they should be treated and therefore that they should be treated equally regardless of racial, ethnic, sexual, religious, or political differences. If a society rejects these fundamental principles, it is unlikely to believe that it is immoral to exterminate or enslave despised minorities. And if such fundamental principles are merely arbitrary assumptions, a society may accept or reject them without being vulnerable to the charge of having made a mistake.

Are fundamental moral principles according to which all people should be treated equally regardless of such differences as race, nationality, sex, religion, and social class nothing but arbitrary assumptions, so that it would be as reasonable for a society to reject as to accept them? We could argue that the denial of such assumptions would be based on false and unreasonable beliefs about the inherent superiority of members of some groups—for example, the belief that men are inherently superior to women, Christians inherently superior to non-Christians, or Caucasians inherently superior to non-Caucasians. Even fundamental moral principles are based on or influenced by nonmoral beliefs about what the facts are. Therefore, we could maintain that it is unreasonable for a society to reject the fundamental moral principle that all people should be treated equally because their rejection is based on a false and unreasonable belief about the superiority of members of one group and the inferiority of members of other groups.

If a society would be mistaken if it rejected the fundamental moral principle that all people should be treated equally regardless of differences of race, nationality, sex, religion, and social class, then we could maintain that moral principles permitting such things as rape, the extermination or enslavement of despised minorities, and suttee are incorrect because they are inconsistent with fundamental moral principles that all societies *should* accept. Then, too, we could say that any moral principles, fundamental or nonfundamental, that are based on false or unreasonable beliefs are incorrect. It would follow that at least *some* moral principles are correct and others incorrect independent of what the majority of people in a society happen to believe. As I am using the term, that would be a version of Moral Objectivism.

Can a Relativist Have Any Moral Beliefs?

Suppose that Jean says that she is a moral relativist but that she also has moral beliefs of her own. For example, she says that like virtually everyone in her society, she believes that slavery is wrong, that oppressing women is wrong, and that child abuse is wrong. She discovers that another society, Bruteland, has the opposite moral beliefs. They believe that it is not wrong to enslave people, oppress women, or abuse children. Her Moral Relativism commits her to the following position:

> I believe that it is wrong to enslave people, oppress women, or abuse children, but my moral beliefs are no more true, correct, or reasonable than those of Brutelanders who believe that it is not wrong to enslave people, oppress women, or abuse children.

In what sense, then, can it be said that Jean has moral beliefs? Believing something means believing that it is true. "I believe that P (is true) but my belief (that it is true) is no more true or correct than someone else's belief that it is not true" seems unintelligible and contradictory. Yet that contradiction seems to be what Relativism commits one to if one is going to both have moral beliefs and accept Relativism.

Relativism and Moral Inquiry

Suppose that Jean has not yet made up her mind on a moral issue. For example, she wonders whether it is wrong for a therapist to date an ex-patient or whether it is wrong for a husband whose wife is in a persistent vegetative state with no hope of recovery to begin an intimate relationship with another woman. How can she resolve her moral perplexity and answer the moral questions she has asked? If Moral Relativism is correct, all she can or needs to do is consult a public opinion poll to find out what a majority of people in her society believe about these issues. If a majority of people in her society believe that it is wrong for a therapist to date an ex-patient, then it is wrong; if a majority of people believe that it isn't wrong, then it isn't. If a majority of people have no opinion on the issue, then presumably it is neither right nor wrong. It will become right or wrong when a majority of people have finally made up their minds.

But is consulting a public opinion poll really the best way to answer moral questions? Wouldn't it be better to carefully examine the reasons for and against therapists' dating ex-patients? A positive answer suggests that Moral Relativism is mistaken, because the procedure of weighing reasons implies that some moral claims are more reasonable than others.

MORAL SUBJECTIVISM

Relativists claim that whatever a society believes to be right and wrong is right and wrong for that society. There is no nonrelative or objective moral truth; the highest court of appeals on moral matters is a society's own moral code. Moral Subjectivists, on the other hand, claim that whatever an individual believes to be right and wrong is right and wrong for that individual. Like relativists, subjectivists deny that any moral statements or beliefs are objectively true or false. If two individuals disagree about a moral issue, neither can be mistaken; they're both correct in some sense. According to subjectivists, the highest court of appeals on moral matters is an individual's own moral code. Thus, if Black believes that it is immoral to kill rape victims for bringing shame to their families and Green believes that it is not immoral, neither has a false belief. It is true for Black that it is immoral, but it is not true for Green, and there is no other kind of true than "true for" some individual. If we ask "Who is really right? Which of them really has a true belief?" the answer is that both have true beliefs.

The Massacre of Black Kettle and His People: A Case Study

In 1864, a U.S. Army officer, Colonel John Chivington, ordered his troops to attack a peaceful Cheyenne village, despite the fact that the American Indians, under the chieftainship of Black Kettle, had been guaranteed safety by the local military commanders in what is now Colorado. According to Dee Brown,

> Captain Silas Soule, Lieutenant Joseph Cramer, and Lieutenant James Connor protested that an attack on Black Kettle's peaceful camp would violate the pledge of safety given the Indians . . . , "that it would be murder in every sense of the word," and any officer participating would dishonor the uniform of the Army. Chivington became violently angry at them and brought his fist close to Lieutenant Cramer's face. "Damn any man who sympathizes with Indians!" he cried. "I have come to kill Indians, and believe it is right and honorable to use any means under God's heaven to kill Indians."[12]

---

[12]Dee Brown, *Bury My Heart at Wounded Knee* (New York: Washington Square Press, 1981), p. 85. (Originally published in 1970.)

The camp held 600 Cheyenne Indians, two-thirds of them women and children. Without warning, the soldiers under Chivington's command attacked the sleeping, unguarded village at dawn. The Indians were massacred. Robert Brent, a soldier who reluctantly participated in the attack, offered the following eyewitness account.

> I saw five squaws [female Indians] under a bank for shelter. When the troops came up to them they ran out and showed their persons to let the soldiers know they were squaws and begged for mercy, but the soldiers shot them all. . . . There seemed to be indiscriminate slaughter of men, women, and children. There were some thirty or forty squaws collected in a hole for protection; they sent out a little girl about six years old with a white flag on a stick; she had not proceeded but a few steps when she was shot and killed. All the squaws in the hole were afterwards killed. . . . The squaws offered no resistance. Every one I saw dead was scalped. I saw one squaw cut open with an unborn child, as I thought, lying by her side. . . . I saw the body of White Antelope with his privates cut off, and I heard one soldier say he was going to make a tobacco pouch out of them. I saw one squaw whose privates had been cut out. . . . I saw a little girl about five years of age who had been hid in the sand; two soldiers discovered her, drew their pistols and shot her. . . . I saw quite a number of infants in arms killed with their mothers.[13]

A total of 28 men and 105 women and children were killed.

Clearly, some of Colonel Chivington's soldiers believed both before and after the massacre that killing the Indians was wrong. However, just as clearly, Chivington himself and many of his soldiers believed that what they did was morally permissible, perhaps even a moral duty, rather than morally forbidden. In addition, some of the soldiers seemed to believe that mutilating their victims was morally acceptable.

If Moral Subjectivism is true, then Colonel Chivington's moral judgments and principles were no less correct than were the moral judgments and principles of Soule, Cramer, and Connor, regardless of what moral principles were accepted in their society. (Was their society the United States? Western society? the U.S. Army?) Similarly, if someone believes that it is morally acceptable to set a building afire in order to collect the insurance on it or to rape women in order to obtain sexual gratification and to humiliate and dominate them, then those principles are no less correct than principles prohibiting arson and rape.

Reasons Supporting Moral Subjectivism

Moral Beliefs Are Based on Feelings   One common argument for Moral Subjectivism is as follows:

Moral beliefs are based only on feelings.

Feelings are subjective and are neither true nor false.

Therefore, moral beliefs are subjective and are neither true nor false.

---

[13]Ibid., p. 88.

This argument has several problems. First, if being "based on" means being caused by, it is not obvious that the first premise is true. Many moral beliefs are learned from the moral teachings of family, friends, religious groups, and teachers; they may not be caused by or associated with any feelings. If you were taught at an early age that stealing is wrong, how is that belief based on feelings?

Although feelings often do play a role in moral evaluation, they are not alone. Often experience, reason, and imagination also play a crucial role in the generation of moral beliefs. Let us return to an earlier example. A visitor from the United States sees Nazi thugs drag an old Jewish man from his home and beat him to death in the street. The Nazis believe that they are not doing anything wrong. The visitor from the United States believes that they are. It may be that the Nazis believe and act as they do in part because they hate Jews and lack sympathy and compassion for the old man they are beating to death. But we should ask why they hate Jews and why they lack sympathy and compassion. Feelings do not stand alone. They have causes rooted in perception, imagination, belief, reasoning, and so on. These Nazis may hate Jews because they have been brainwashed into believing that Jews are destroying their society. They may have no compassion or sympathy for their victim because they lack the imagination necessary to imagine his suffering as well as because of their beliefs about Jews. Similarly, the visitor from the United States may believe as he does because he does not hate Jews and because he does have sympathy and compassion for the man being beaten to death. But his feelings also do not stand alone. They have causes.

The second premise is also problematic. Feelings are neither true nor false, but it does not follow that they cannot be assessed or evaluated as reasonable or unreasonable. Consider fear. If someone feels intense fear at the sight of a mouse, the fear is unreasonable given that mice pose no threat. Similarly, we often maintain that hatred of people because of their religion or race is irrational. Hating Jews, Arabs, African-Americans, or Asians is almost universally regarded as irrational (as well as deplorable). If a moral belief is based on hatred, for example, it does not follow that it is then immune from rational criticism.

Finally, the cause of a belief has little to do with whether it is true. Thus, even if the premises of the argument were true, the conclusion would not follow. Suppose that a doting mother believes that her son did not commit a heinous crime of which he has been accused only because she loves him. Her belief in his innocence is based solely on her feelings. Would it follow that her belief is neither true nor false? Of course not. Whether her belief is true depends on whether he committed the crime. The same logic applies if the belief based on feelings is a moral belief.

People Disagree about Moral Issues We saw this argument with respect to Moral Relativism. Many people think that it can also be applied to defend Moral Subjectivism. The same criticisms apply that we developed previously. Although people disagree about some moral issues, it may be that there are some moral beliefs that all people agree on. Even if there aren't, the mere fact that people disagree does not prove that conflicting moral beliefs can both be right.

No One Can Prove Who Is Correct in a Moral Dispute   We also saw this argument with respect to Moral Relativism. Its plausibility depends on how stringently we construe "proof." It may be that we can provide strong arguments for a moral claim and against its negation. For example, those who believe that it is wrong to commit genocide may be able to construct strong arguments to support their claim, whereas those who believe that it is not wrong to commit genocide may not be able to construct strong arguments to support their claim or to construct arguments to rebut or refute the arguments of their opponents. In that case, there is a kind of "proof" that genocide is wrong.

Second, that we cannot prove that something is true does not show that it is not true. Similarly, that we cannot prove that something is false does not show that it is not false.

Criticisms of Moral Subjectivism

Like Nihilism and Relativism, Subjectivism violates the principle that statements that contradict each other cannot both be true—one must be true and the other false. For example, a subjectivist is committed to the view that both of the following statements can be true if two different people believe them.

Killing people for pleasure is wrong.

Killing people for pleasure is not wrong.

In the eyes of objectivists, this sort of contradiction makes Subjectivism implausible.

Can a Subjectivist Have Any Moral Beliefs?   Suppose that Jean says that she is a moral subjectivist but that she also has moral beliefs of her own. For example, she says that she believes that killing people for amusement is wrong. However, Tony believes that it is not wrong. Jean's subjectivism commits her to the following position:

I believe that it is wrong to kill people for amusement, but my moral belief that it is wrong is no more true, correct, or reasonable than someone else's belief that it is not wrong.

In what sense can it be said that Jean has moral beliefs? Believing something means believing that it is true. "I believe that P (is true) but my belief (that it is true) is no more true or correct than someone else's belief that it is not true" seems unintelligible and contradictory.

Moral Inquiry and Moral Improvement   Suppose that Jean has not yet made up her mind on a moral issue. For example, she wonders whether it is wrong for her to cheat on her chemistry final exam. How can she resolve her moral perplexity and answer the moral question she has asked? If Moral

Subjectivism is correct, it doesn't matter what she believes or how she comes to believe it. Whatever she comes to believe will be correct, whether or not she follows any rational procedure of moral deliberation or moral inquiry. A moral decision based on tossing a coin would be as correct as one based on carefully considering arguments. Objectivists find this position implausible.

In addition, if Moral Subjectivism is correct, it makes no sense to talk of moral progress or of improving one's system of moral beliefs. When we know that our beliefs may be false as well as true, we can try to improve our set of beliefs by deleting false ones and adding true ones. We can try to correct our mistakes and add new knowledge—in other words, to learn. But learning and improvement make no sense when it comes to morality if Subjectivism is true, because we cannot possibly make mistakes and can never have a reason for changing our minds. If I believe that it is morally acceptable to rape women, according to Moral Subjectivism my belief is true solely because it's mine. If it is guaranteed to be true, why should I ever consider changing my mind and coming to believe that it's wrong to rape women? The belief that raping women is wrong is no improvement over the belief that raping women is not wrong.

Believing That Something Is True Does Not Make It True Objectivists say that believing that something is true doesn't make it true. Subjectivism, they maintain, collapses the important distinction between something's being *believed* to be true and its really *being* true.

WHERE DO WE GO FROM HERE?

If the various versions of Nonobjectivism—Nihilism, Relativism, and Subjectivism—are mistaken and some version of Moral Objectivism is correct, several questions remain. Objectivist theories agree that some moral claims are true and others false, but how do we distinguish between those that are true and those that are false? Objectivist theories need to provide a test that will enable us to distinguish between moral claims that are true and moral claims that are false. This test (or tests) may help us in moral deliberation when we are trying to answer moral questions for ourselves, as well as provide moral arguments and justification when we are engaged in defending our views in conversation or debate. The objectivist theories that we will be examining in future chapters differ on the tests that they propose. They all agree that moral truths exist, but they disagree on the tests we can use to discover them.

EXERCISES

1. Construct an argument to persuade someone that Moral Nihilism is true.
2. Construct an argument to persuade someone that Moral Nihilism is false.
3. Construct an argument to persuade someone that Protagorean Relativism is true.

4. Construct an argument to persuade someone that Protagorean Relativism is false.

5. Construct an argument to persuade someone that Moral Subjectivism is true.

6. Construct an argument to persuade someone that Moral Subjectivism is false.

7. Do you think that there are *any* moral principles, whether qualified or unqualified, that are correct for all societies? Defend your answer.

8. Should societies show unlimited toleration for the behavior and moral principles of other societies? Is it wrong for a society to judge other societies according to its own moral code? Are "yes" answers to these questions consistent with either Protagorean Moral Relativism or Moral Subjectivism? Defend your answers.

SUGGESTED READINGS

David Copp and David Zimmerman, eds. *Morality, Reason, and Truth*. Totowa, NJ: Rowman and Allanheld, 1984.

William Frankena. *Ethics*. 2d ed. Englewood Cliffs, NJ: Prentice-Hall, 1973. (See especially Chapter 6.)

Gilbert Harman. *The Nature of Morality*. New York: Oxford University Press, 1977. (See especially Chapters 1–4, 8, and 9.)

John Ladd, ed. *Ethical Relativism*. Belmont, CA: Wadsworth, 1973.

Ellen F. Paul, Fred Miller, and Jeffrey Paul. *Cultural Pluralism and Moral Knowledge*. Cambridge, England: Cambridge University Press, 1994.

Louis Pojman. *Ethics: Discovering Right and Wrong*. Belmont, CA: Wadsworth, 1990. (See especially Chapter 2.)

Walter Sinnott-Armstrong and Mark Timmons. *Moral Knowledge? New Readings in Moral Epistemology*. Oxford: Oxford University Press, 1996.

David Wong. *Ethical Relativity*. Berkeley: University of California Press, 1984.

CHAPTER 4

Psychological Egoism and Moral Egoism

COMMONSENSE MORALITY

According to what we might call "commonsense" morality, harming others to benefit ourselves or some group with whom we identify is generally wrong, and helping others when the need is great and the cost of help small is generally right. Examples of harmful behavior that commonsense morality considers wrong are theft, rape, enslavement, murder, treason, terrorism, and genocide. The fact that you or a group to which you belong would benefit from such behaviors makes no difference; they would still be wrong according to commonsense morality. Similarly, commonsense morality says that we should help others when the need is great and the cost to us is small, even if we would not benefit from it and even if we would suffer a net loss. If someone is drowning and you could save her by throwing her a rope, commonsense morality says that you should throw her the rope even if you gain nothing you value by saving her and even if you would be a net loser by it (perhaps you get your clothes muddy and wind up with a dry-cleaning bill). Commonsense morality does not demand that you jump into the water to save the drowning person if you're not a good swimmer or if there would be significant danger to you, but according to commonsense morality it would be wrong for you to do *nothing*—to merely walk away and let the person drown.

According to commonsense morality, then, sometimes we should do things even if we will not benefit from doing them or even if doing them would impose a net cost on us. Similarly, commonsense morality says that we should refrain from doing some things even if we would benefit from doing them. Commonsense morality says that sometimes we should sacrifice our own self-interest in order to further or protect the interests of others.

Is commonsense morality correct? Some people claim that commonsense morality is wrong. They claim that we do not have a moral duty to sacrifice our own self-interest in order to benefit or protect others. We have no duty to refrain from harming others if it would be in our self-interest to harm them, and we have no duty to help others if it would not be in our self-interest to help them. On this view, it's not wrong to harm people to benefit ourselves, and it's not wrong to fail to help others when we don't benefit from helping them. This claim, called Moral Egoism, conflicts with commonsense morality. Is Moral Egoism correct, or is commonsense morality correct?

What reasons are there for thinking that Moral Egoism is correct and commonsense morality incorrect? One reason appeals to the principle that *ought* implies *can*. According to this principle, it makes sense to say that morally you *ought* to (should) do something (have a moral duty to do it) only if you *can* do it. Alternatively, we might express this principle as claiming that if you cannot refrain from doing something, then it would make no sense to say that it is wrong to do it. For example, suppose someone says that morally we ought to (we have a moral duty to) breathe underwater for at least ten minutes a day. That claim would be absurd because it is physically impossible for us to breathe underwater. We cannot possibly have a moral duty to do something that is physically impossible for us. Similarly, suppose someone says that it's morally wrong for us to age and grow old (while still living). That claim would be absurd because it is physically impossible for us to refrain from aging and growing old while still remaining alive. It cannot be morally wrong to do what we cannot help doing. On the other hand, if you *can* eat without putting your elbows on the table, then it would not be wholly senseless to claim that you have a moral duty to refrain from eating with your elbows on the table or that it is morally wrong for you to eat with your elbows on the table. Similarly, if you could not possibly refrain from scratching when you itch, then it would make no sense to say that morally you should not scratch when you itch. On the other hand, if it is physically possible for you to refrain from scratching when you itch, then it would not be wholly senseless to say that it is morally wrong for you to scratch when you itch. (Of course, that it would not be wholly senseless to say that it is morally wrong to eat with your elbows on the table or scratch when you itch does not show that either claim is true or reasonable. If we accept the principle that actions are innocent until proved guilty, we would want to know what reasons there are for thinking that it is morally wrong to eat with one's elbows on the table or scratch when one itches. If there are no good reasons for thinking that it's morally wrong to do these things, then we ought to conclude that it is not morally wrong to do them.)

The principle that *ought* implies *can* has interesting implications for commonsense morality. If people *cannot* sacrifice their own self-interest in order to refrain from harming others or to help others (because of our psychological makeup), then "*ought* implies *can*" entails that commonsense morality is mistaken. If we *cannot* help others if we don't benefit by it, then it makes no sense to say that we ought to help others or that it's morally wrong not to help others. If we *cannot* refrain from harming others when we would benefit by it, then it makes no sense to say that we ought to refrain from harming others or that it is morally wrong to harm them. But why should we think that people *cannot* sometimes sacrifice their own self-interest in order to benefit others or to refrain from harming them?

A theory called Psychological Egoism, if true, may entail that people *cannot* ever sacrifice their own self-interest in order to benefit others or to refrain from harming them. If Psychological Egoism is true and entails that people *cannot* sacrifice self-interest, then commonsense morality is mistaken and Moral Egoism is correct. Before we examine Moral Egoism, then, let's investigate Psychological Egoism.

PSYCHOLOGICAL EGOISM

Psychological Egoism is a descriptive theory about human nature and behavior, whereas Moral Egoism is a theory about moral right and wrong. Sometimes Psychological Egoism is expressed as the theory that

Everyone always behaves selfishly.

The term *selfishly* is used purely descriptively rather than evaluatively, because Psychological Egoism is a theory about human psychology, not a theory about moral right and wrong. It's a theory about how people *do* behave, not about how they should or should not behave. According to this theory, we always behave selfishly because that's human nature; it's how we're "built." But what does it mean to call an action "selfish"?

According to Webster's Dictionary, *selfish* means

1: concerned excessively or exclusively with oneself; seeking or concentrating on one's own advantage, pleasure, or well-being without regard for others
2: arising from concern with one's own welfare or advantage in disregard of others[1]

The dictionary definition of *selfish* emphasizes sacrificing the interests of others in order to advance one's own interests. If everyone always behaved selfishly according to this definition (because that's the way we're made and we cannot help behaving selfishly), then commonsense morality would violate the principle that *ought* implies *can*. In that case, commonsense morality would be mistaken; it would require us to do things we can't possibly do and to refrain from doing things we can't help doing.

But given this definition of *selfish,* is Psychological Egoism true? Surely not. Is someone behaving "selfishly" if she

1. goes to the doctor for an annual physical examination?
2. contributes $500 to the Sierra Club?
3. works every Saturday as an unpaid volunteer at the local hospital?
4. works overtime in order to get promoted?
5. embezzles money from her employer?

---

[1]*Merriam-Webster's Collegiate Dictionary,* 10th ed. (Springfield, MA: Merriam-Webster, 1994).

6. burns down a factory she owns in order to collect the insurance money?

7. refuses to share her lunch with a friend who forgot to bring hers, even though she brought more food than she can eat and will throw half of it away?

Given the definition of *selfish,* it is obvious that items 1–4 are not selfish acts because they do not involve sacrificing someone else's interests in order to protect or further one's own interests in the way that items 5–7 do. Given that many people perform actions such as those in items 1–4, it is obviously *not* the case that everyone *always* behaves selfishly. Of course, it may be true that everyone *sometimes* behaves selfishly, but that claim is not Psychological Egoism.

Perhaps a better formulation of Psychological Egoism would be

Everyone's actions are always ultimately based on self-interest.

Suppose that you volunteer to work in the local hospital every other Saturday. According to this formulation of Psychological Egoism, your action is ultimately based on self-interest. What does that mean?

Ordinarily, when people act they act for a reason. Reasons may vary widely. Consider three people who do unpaid volunteer work at the local hospital every other Saturday. Green volunteers because he is a politician who is looking for votes; he believes that by volunteering his time at the hospital he will impress voters with his altruism and gain votes. Brown is a businesswoman who wants to get more business; she hopes to impress potential clients with her good character by volunteering at the hospital. Finally, Black feels compassion and sympathy for the sick; she wants to help reduce suffering and make a constructive contribution to her community. She knows that the local hospital is financially strapped and understaffed and that patient care will suffer unless unpaid volunteers fill in some of the gaps. She wants to help, and she believes that she can help by volunteering her time every other Saturday.

An individual's action is based on self-interest if the reason or motive for the action is to increase his own well-being (to benefit himself) or to prevent a reduction in well-being (to prevent harm to himself). On the surface, doing unpaid volunteer work at a hospital looks like it's *not* based on self-interest because it seems to benefit others rather than the agent. But if we look below the surface at the agent's actual reasons or motivation, we can see that Green's and Brown's actions are ultimately based on self-interest. They are volunteering their time because they believe that they will benefit from doing so. Their intention is to benefit themselves through benefiting others. If they didn't benefit from volunteering (have their well-being increased), they would not volunteer. We might diagram the structure of their motivation or reasons as follows:

I want to → I will benefit → I volunteer. → I benefit and others
benefit myself. by volunteering. benefit.

The main goal of the action is to benefit the agent himself, not to benefit others. It may be that as a result others will benefit, but that benefit is not part of the motivation. Benefiting others is a means to an end (benefiting the agent himself), rather than an end in itself. In both cases, the action only appears to be altruistic; ultimately it benefits, and it is intended to benefit, the agent. These seemingly altruistic actions are ultimately based on self-interest.

However, what of Black? Is her action also ultimately based on self-interest? Even if we say that it is, surely it's obvious that the structure of her motivation or reasons is quite different from that of Green and Brown. We might diagram the structure of her motivation or reasons as follows:

I want to → I will benefit them → I volunteer. → Others benefit
benefit others. by volunteering. and I benefit.

Black's main concern is to benefit others rather than to benefit herself. Of course, she may benefit from her action because she gets satisfaction or happiness from helping other people. But her intention is to benefit others rather than herself, even though as a result of her action she also benefits. Her action may *not* be based on self-interest in the sense of being undertaken in order to benefit herself.

The claim that everyone's actions are always ultimately based on self-interest entails that every time we look below the surface of someone's action, we will discover that it was motivated by the desire to further that person's own self-interest, as in the cases of Green and Brown. What reason is there to think that this rather sweeping generalization about *every* action of *every* person is true? Do Psychological Egoists have proof of this claim? What would such proof look like? It is by no means obvious that there is or even could be proof of this theory. And if it is possible for people to have the structure of motivation I have attributed to Black (what reason could there be for thinking it's impossible?), then Psychological Egoism is probably false.

But even if Psychological Egoism in this form is true, would it follow that commonsense morality violates the principle that *ought* implies *can*? If Psychological Egoism is true, given human nature is it physically impossible for people to benefit others or to refrain from harming others? No. If it's in your self-interest to benefit others—for example, because you benefit financially or get satisfaction from it—then you can. Similarly, if it's not in your self-interest to harm others, then you can refrain from harming them. It seems obvious that human nature does not prevent people from ever helping others or from avoiding harming others. However, what of cases where self-interest and commonsense morality diverge? Commonsense morality says that people should refrain from harming others even when it is in their self-interest. Psychological Egoism then poses the following questions: If it's not in your self-interest to benefit others, then given human nature (our psychological makeup), is it physically possible for you to benefit them anyway? Similarly, if it's in your self-interest to harm others, then given human nature, is it physically possible for you to refrain from harming them anyway?

Psychological egoists seem to think of human nature (our human psychology) as both universal and fixed or unalterable. However, opponents of Psychological Egoism might object that human nature, especially our psychological nature, is both remarkably variable and alterable. Consider the psychological makeup of an Adolf Hitler and a Mother Teresa; surely there are vast and fundamental differences. Moreover, a person's psychological nature can change. At the extreme, it may be possible to alter the genetic makeup of the whole human species through genetic engineering. On a less dramatic and sweeping level, an individual's psychological makeup can be altered by conditioning, social circumstances, learning, and experiences. Human beings in one society or set of social circumstances may, on average, have one kind of psychological makeup while human beings in another society or set of social circumstances have, on average, a very different kind of psychological makeup. Some critics of Psychological Egoism might say that human beings in a competitive capitalist economic system may tend to have a narrowly self-interested psychological makeup of the sort described by Psychological Egoism only because they have been socialized to have such a psychological makeup. Change their social circumstances (the economic and political institutions within which they function), and you would change their psychological makeup and thus their human "nature." According to these critics, human nature, especially our psychological nature, is not fixed and unalterable.

To examine one final possible response to Psychological Egoism, let's return to our example of the three hospital volunteers who volunteer for different reasons. If Black got no satisfaction from helping others, is it likely that she would do unpaid volunteer work at the hospital without some other self-interested reason such as the ones that Green and Brown have? It may be unlikely, but is it physically impossible, given human nature? According to the German philosopher Immanuel Kant (1724–1804), human beings have a sense of duty. We can come to believe that we have a moral duty to do certain things even if they are not in our self-interest and a moral duty to refrain from doing other things even if they are in our self-interest. Besides having beliefs about moral duties, we can also develop the desire to conform our behavior to those moral duties. (This aspect of human nature is connected to the concept of *conscience.* Having a conscience seems to imply, among other things, believing that one has certain moral duties and having the desire to live by those duties.) For example, you could come to believe that, independent of your self-interest, you have a moral duty not to steal from others and a moral duty to help others sometimes, especially when the need is great and the cost or risk is low. Surely it is plausible to claim that if you *believe* that you have a moral duty not to steal even if it is in your self-interest and you have the *desire* to do your duty, then you *can* refrain from stealing even when it would be in your self-interest.

Thus, there seems to be no good reason to think that commonsense morality violates the requirement of *ought* implies *can.* The theory of Psychological Egoism cannot be used to defend the claim that commonsense morality is mistaken because it requires human beings to do things that, given human nature, they physically cannot do (because of psychological laws of human behavior). Human beings can do what commonsense morality requires of them. The question, then, is whether the claims of commonsense morality are correct. Moral Egoists maintain that they are not.

MORAL EGOISM

Psychological Egoism is a theory about human nature; Moral Egoism is a theory about morality. According to Moral Egoism—in contrast to commonsense morality—it's always morally acceptable to do what one believes to be in one's own self-interest. People have no moral duties to one another. Moral egoists claim that morality never requires people to sacrifice their own self-interest to help others or to avoid harming others; rather, morality permits people to do whatever is in their own self-interest. This view may be summarized as follows:

> It's a jungle out there, a dog-eat-dog world. Nice guys finish last. The strong prey on the weak, and the weak go under. You can't afford to reach out a helping hand to the other guy, because he'll either bite it off or drag you under with him. The world doesn't owe you anything, and you don't owe the world anything. The only rule is, Look out for number one!

For example, take a used-car salesperson who cheats his customers, disguising serious defects in the cars he sells. If he's a moral egoist, he'll claim that anything that helps him sell cars is in his self-interest and is therefore morally acceptable because it's never wrong to do what's in our own self-interest. Similarly, if committing arson is in our self-interest, it is morally acceptable to commit arson.

In many situations it is not wrong to pursue our self-interest. Eating properly and exercising regularly are in our self-interest, yet it's certainly not wrong to eat properly and exercise regularly. However, the case is less clear when our self-interest is in conflict with the interests of others. For example, although it may be in the self-interest of the owner of the antiquated apartment building to torch it and collect the insurance, it is not in the interests of the tenants, the fire department, or the insurance company that the building be torched. When people's interests conflict, is it always morally acceptable for people to do what's in their self-interest, regardless of any effect on the interests and well-being of others? Moral Egoism entails that theft, rape, torture, assault, and murder are morally acceptable if the agent believes that they are in his or her self-interest. Surely that is a startling claim.

Critics of Moral Egoism insist that people have moral duties to one another, such as duties to help and to avoid harming each other. What reason is there for thinking that people don't have such moral duties—that morality permits one to simply look out for number one? One reason that moral egoists have given is Psychological Egoism. However, we have seen that this theory does not provide a good defense of Moral Egoism. Another line of argument claims that ultimately everyone benefits if people pursue their own self-interest.

Moral Egoism and the Common Good

Adam Smith (1723–1790), the intellectual godfather of capitalism, maintained that the common good is best promoted when people focus on their own private good. When people pursue their own self-interest, he claimed, an unintended consequence is that everyone is better off.

For example, if Joe concentrates on making Sam rather than himself happy, the result may be that neither will be happy. In neglecting his own happiness, Joe may fail to be happy. And despite his best efforts to make Sam happy, he may not succeed. He may be mistaken about what will make Sam happy, or if his goals are correct, his means may be ineffective. According to Smith, each individual is most likely to achieve happiness for himself if he concentrates on making himself rather than other people happy. Therefore, the best way of maximizing happiness is for each person to concentrate on making himself happy and to leave his neighbor's happiness to his neighbor, who after all can be expected to know best what will make him happy and how to achieve it.

This defense of Moral Egoism has several problems. First, its justification appeals to principles that at least appear to be in conflict with Moral Egoism; that is, the justification proceeds in terms of what is good for *others* rather than what is good for oneself. But if Moral Egoism is correct, the good of others should not count when we are considering what we should or should not do. When you're considering what to do, you should think about what's good for you, not what's good for others.

Second, the argument seems to be based on a false dichotomy: Either you focus exclusively on your own self-interest when deciding what to do, or you focus exclusively on the interests of others. It suggests that you can do either what's in your self-interest (what benefits you) or what's in the interest of others (what benefits them), but not both. But surely we can often do both. We can do things that make both us and others happy, things that benefit us and benefit others. Often we don't have to choose between them.

Third, the argument misleadingly suggests that we must choose between always pursuing our own self-interest and never pursuing our self-interest. Both are extremes. In fact, we could choose to pursue self-interest 80 to 90 percent of the time and promote or protect the interests of others 10 to 20 percent of the time. We can do sometimes one, sometimes the other, and sometimes both simultaneously.

Finally, the argument ignores the very different ways in which people can make themselves happy. Some ways of making oneself happy are harmless. If I go out birdwatching or go to a movie, I'm not making myself happy *at the expense of others.* I'm not harming anyone. But other ways of making oneself happy are toxic to others. Suppose that a man derives happiness from raping children. Should he do what makes him happy and ignore its effect on the children he rapes? Would that be the best way to maximize everyone's well-being or promote the common good? Commonsense morality says no. We should not make ourselves happy in ways that impose serious harm, or the risk of serious harm, on others. Pursuing our own self-interest while ignoring its effects on others is not likely to maximize happiness and make everyone better off.

Moral Egoism and Universality

As we saw in the first chapter, moral principles are often said to be universal. They apply to everyone. Given universality, if it is morally acceptable for you to do what is in your self-interest regardless of its effect on others, then it is morally acceptable for others to do what is in their self-interest regardless of its effect on you. If Moral Egoism is correct, then a person who tortures and kills you or someone you love has done nothing wrong so long as it was in that person's self-interest. Someone who cannot accept that implication of Moral Egoism cannot consistently accept Moral Egoism.

Moral Egoism and Social Harmony

Many people maintain that a purely self-interested point of view is inconsistent with a moral point of view because if we evaluate and act solely on the basis of our own self-interest, we are not evaluating or behaving on the basis of moral considerations at all. To evaluate and act on the basis of moral as opposed to nonmoral considerations, we must give serious thought to the interests of others. Indeed, many people say that the basic function of a moral code is to resolve conflicts between people so that they can live together in harmony. The Greek philosopher Aristotle (384–322 B.C.E.) argued that human beings are social animals; that is, they live together in groups, not alone as isolated, self-sufficient hermits. Since Aristotle's time, many thinkers have claimed that a moral code has the function of enabling people to live together.

If everyone does whatever is in his or her self-interest regardless of how it affects the interests and well-being of others, people cannot live together peacefully in groups. By its very nature, then, morality sometimes requires people to sacrifice their own self-interest in order to benefit and protect others. For example, if everyone always stole, lied, broke promises, assaulted, and killed people when it was in their self-interest, no group could survive. Thus, many people claim that morality requires that people sometimes follow the common good rather than their own private good.

For example, Samuel Pufendorf (1632–1688) wrote, "In the natural [moral] law it is asserted that something must be done because the same is gathered by right reason as necessary for sociability between men."[2] The natural law "is so adapted to the rational and social nature of man, that an honorable and peaceful society cannot exist for mankind without it."[3] Pufendorf pointed out,

> Man is indeed an animal most bent upon self-preservation, helpless in himself, unable to save himself without the aid of his fellows, highly adapted to promote mutual interests; but on the other hand no less malicious, insolent, and easily provoked, also as able as he is prone to inflict injury upon another. Whence it follows that, in order to be safe, he must be sociable, that is, must be united with men like himself, and so conduct himself toward them that they may have no good cause to injure him, but rather may be ready to maintain and promote his interests. The laws, then, of this sociability, or those which teach how a man should conduct himself, to become a good member of human society, are called natural laws.[4]

---

[2]Samuel Pufendorf, "On the Duty of Man and Citizen," in *Moral Philosophy from Montaigne to Kant*, vol. 1., ed. J. B. Schneewind (Cambridge, England: Cambridge University Press, 1990), p. 158.

[3]Ibid., p. 161.

[4]Ibid., p. 163.

Thus, Pufendorf claimed,

> Among the absolute duties, i.e., of anybody to anybody, the first place belongs
> to this one: let no man injure another. For this is the broadest of all duties. . . . .
> Again, it is likewise the most necessary duty, because without it the social life
> could in no way exist. For with the man who confers no benefit upon me . . . I
> can still live in peace provided he injure me in no way. . . . But with the man
> who injures me, I cannot by any means live peaceably.[5]

Further, the next most basic duty is

> that every man promote the advantage of another, so far as he conveniently
> can. For since nature has established a kind of kinship among men, it could
> not have been enough to have refrained from injuring . . . others; but we must
> also bestow such attentions upon others . . . that thus mutual benevolence
> may be fostered among men.[6]

Many philosophers have insisted that morality requires people to do what is
for the common good rather than what is in their own self-interest when the
common good and their own private good are in conflict. Thus, for example,
Richard Cumberland (1631–1718) wrote that "the common good is the supreme
law."[7] Moral Egoism directly contradicts this view. If Moral Egoism is true, it's
morally acceptable for people to completely ignore the interests and well-being
of others. Critics of Moral Egoism maintain that life in a society of moral egoists
would be, in the memorable words of the philosopher Thomas Hobbes
(1588–1679), "solitary, poor, nasty, brutish, and short."[8]

Short-Term versus Long-Term Self-Interest

Moral egoists may distinguish between a person's short-term self-interest and a
person's long-term self-interest. What may be in a person's immediate or short-
term self-interest may not be in his or her long-term self-interest. For example, it
may be in a person's short-term self-interest to steal from her roommate because
she will get money she wants and not be caught. However, if success at this theft
encourages her to further thefts, she may eventually be caught and punished,
which would not be in her self-interest. The short-term benefit of stealing has to
be weighed against its potential long-term effects. Similarly, it may be in our
short-term self-interest to smoke a cigarette because it makes us feel good; however, the long-term effects of continuing to smoke may include various serious
health problems that would not be in our self-interest.

---

[5]Ibid., p. 165.

[6]Ibid., p. 167.

[7]Richard Cumberland, "A Treatise of the Laws of Nature," in *Moral Philosophy from Montaigne to Kant*, vol. 1, ed. Schneewind, p. 144.

[8]Thomas Hobbes, *Leviathan* (New York: Collier, 1962), chap. 13, p. 100. (Originally published in 1651.)

Moral egoists may insist that it is morally acceptable for people to do whatever they believe is in their long-term self-interest, but not necessarily what they believe is in their short-term self-interest; that is, long-term self-interest takes priority over short-term self-interest. They may then claim that if we do what we believe is in our long-term self-interest rather than what we believe is in our short-term self-interest, we will not behave as critics assume that moral egoists will behave. Moral egoists who pursue their long-term self-interest will not ignore the interests and well-being of others, because they will recognize that it is not in their long-term self-interest to do so. Such moral egoists will often sacrifice their short-term self-interest in order to benefit and protect others because they believe that doing so is in their long-term self-interest. Thus, they might claim that life in a society of moral egoists who pursue their long-term rather than their short-term self-interest would not be "solitary, poor, nasty, brutish, and short."

British philosopher and theologian Joseph Butler (1692–1752) made this point in the following way:

> Neither does there appear any reason to wish that self-love were weaker in the generality of the world, than it is. . . . Men daily, hourly sacrifice the greatest known interest, to fancy, inquisitiveness, love or hatred, any vagrant inclination. The thing to be lamented is, not that men have so great regard to their own good or interest in the present world, for they have not enough; but that they have so little to the good of others. . . .

> Upon the whole, if the generality of mankind were to cultivate within themselves the principle of self-love; . . . and if self-love were so strong and prevalent, as that they would uniformly pursue this as their supposed chief temporal good, without being diverted from it by any particular passion; it would manifestly prevent numberless follies and vices.[9]

Butler maintained that long-term self-interest is rarely if ever in conflict with the common good. People are happier in the long run if they care about others, refrain from harming others, and benefit others.

Critics might point to two problems with this view. First, why must long-term self-interest take priority over short-term self-interest? That assumption is crucial for maintaining that although it is not morally acceptable to pursue our short-term self-interest regardless of its effect on the interests and well-being of others, it is morally acceptable to pursue our long-term self-interest. Second, what if a person believes that it is in his long-term self-interest to ignore the interests and well-being of others? Might he be mistaken? And even if he is mistaken, Moral Egoism entails that it would be morally acceptable for him to ignore everyone else's interests and well-being in pursuing his own long-term self-interest. Critics of Moral Egoism find that position unacceptable.

---

[9]Joseph Butler, "Fifteen Sermons," in *British Moralists: 1650–1800*, vol. 1, ed. D. D. Raphael (Indianapolis, IN: Hackett, 1991), pp. 335–336. (Originally published in 1726.)

EXERCISES

1. Are people always ultimately motivated by self-interest, even when their actions appear altruistic? Defend your answer and provide examples.

2. Is it impossible for people ever to sacrifice their self-interest in order to protect or benefit others? Defend your answer.

3. White owns a chemical company. To increase his profits, he's decreasing his costs by disposing of toxic chemical wastes in a residential area. The toxic waste is contaminating the water supply of about 30 percent of the local residents. White's country has no laws forbidding his action.
   a. Develop an argument to persuade people that White isn't doing anything wrong because he's simply doing what's in his self-interest.
   b. Develop an argument to persuade people that White is doing something wrong, even if it is in his self-interest.
   c. Do you think that White's action is immoral? Defend your answer.

4. Jill is in her car when she sees two children fall through the ice. No one else is around to help them. She knows that if she doesn't come to their aid, they will almost certainly drown. She could call for help on her car phone and throw the children a rope in order to keep them above water until help arrives. Alternatively, she could do nothing and simply drive on to keep her appointment. She reflects that it is not in her self-interest to do anything to save the children because she does not know them or care about them, would get no benefit from saving them, and would not have any loss of well-being—for example, from guilt—if she did nothing. Would it be morally acceptable for her to drive on and do nothing to help the children? Defend your answer. What would a moral egoist say about this case?

5. Jones believes that it is in her self-interest to exaggerate her charitable deductions on her income tax return. Is it therefore morally acceptable for her to exaggerate them? Defend your answer.

6. Tom believes that it is in his self-interest to cheat on his economics examination in order to pass it. Is it therefore morally acceptable for him to cheat on the exam? Defend your answer.

7. Should our long-term self-interest always take priority over our short-term self-interest? Defend your answer.

8. Is it always in our long-term self-interest to refrain from exaggerating charitable contributions on income tax returns and to refrain from cheating on examinations? Defend your answer.

SUGGESTED READINGS

Joseph Butler. "Fifteen Sermons." In *British Moralists, 1650–1800,* vol. 1, edited by D. D. Raphael. Indianapolis, IN: Hackett, 1991.

Joel Feinberg. "Psychological Egoism." In *Reason and Responsibility,* 5th ed., edited by Joel Feinberg. Belmont, CA: Wadsworth, 1981.

CHAPTER 5

Self-Interest: The Good Life

Vain is the word of a philosopher which does not heal any suffering of man.

Epicurus

In the last chapter we saw that according to many people, morality sometimes requires people to sacrifice their self-interest, especially their short-run self-interest, in order to benefit and protect others. They think that the unrestrained pursuit of self-interest is harmful to society and to its members and therefore that it is contrary to the demands of morality. However, it does not follow that they think that morality requires the opposite extreme—unlimited altruism and sacrifice of self-interest. It is only the *unrestrained* pursuit of self-interest that they condemn. Most people, on reflection, would probably agree that morality does not prohibit people from being happy.

In fact, many philosophers believe that a moral code should not only provide guidance on how to treat other people but should also provide guidance on how to achieve happiness. Most people are sufficiently self-interested to pursue happiness and to aim at living what we could call the "good life"; however, many of them seem unable to achieve happiness. According to Henry David Thoreau (1817–1862), "The mass of men lead lives of quiet desperation."[1] If it is true that few people achieve happiness although so many seek it, one explanation may be that many people simply don't know what will make them happy. Perhaps people are ignorant of or mistaken about the central ingredients of the good life and happiness; perhaps they mistakenly pursue things that they think will make them happy but that will not. Many philosophers have thought it important to

---

[1]Henry David Thoreau, *Walden* (New York: Harper & Row, 1965), p. 7. (Originally published in 1854.)

provide people with a blueprint for happiness because they have thought that many people are mistaken about what will make them happy.

If we pay careful attention to popular television programs and movies and to commercials and advertisements, we might conclude that the central ingredients of the good life—the keys to happiness—are such things as wealth, power, prestige, fame, material possessions, and physical pleasure. The mass media suggest to many people that the more of these things we have, the happier we will be. However, do these things bring happiness? Are they the central ingredients of the good life?

ARISTOTLE

The ancient Greek philosopher Aristotle (384–322 B.C.E.) acknowledged that all people seek happiness, which they identify with "living well and faring well."[2] However, different people have different conceptions of happiness, and even the same people may have different conceptions of happiness at different times. According to Aristotle, most people (wrongly, as he thought) identify happiness with "things like pleasure, wealth, or honour," and "often the same man identifies it with different things, with health when he is ill, with wealth when he is poor."[3] However, Aristotle believed that a genuine source of happiness must provide permanent happiness and must be very resistant to being changed into its opposite, unhappiness. For example, he rejected honor as the key ingredient in happiness because "it is thought to depend on those who bestow honour rather than on him who receives it, but the good we divine to be something of one's own and not easily taken from one."[4]

Aristotle stressed that he was seeking to uncover the good, or the key ingredients of happiness, for *human beings.* Different species of animals have different goods, or sources of happiness, that are appropriate to members of the species. For example, what would be good for a cow would not be good for a hawk or a shark; similarly, what would make a cow happy would not make a hawk or a shark happy. Therefore, what would be good for a human being and what would make a human being happy would not necessarily be good for or make happy a member of some other species, such as a cow or a hawk. The way of life of a cow is not appropriate for a human being, and vice versa.

Aristotle believed that we must understand the unique nature of human beings in order to uncover the appropriate good for a human being. Only if we know how human beings differ from cows and hawks and turtles can we know what goods are appropriate for human beings.

The ancient Greeks believed that the best explanation for the difference between living and nonliving things is soul. Stones aren't alive, but trees and

---

[2] Aristotle, *Nicomachean Ethics,* in *The Complete Works of Aristotle,* ed. Jonathan Barnes (Princeton, NJ: Princeton University Press, 1984), p. 1730 (Book I, Section 4, line 1095a 19).

[3] Ibid., p. 1731 (1095a 20–25).

[4] Ibid., p. 1731 (1095b 24–26).

cows are. Why? According to the ancient Greeks, it must be because something is added to the physical matter making up trees and cows, giving them the activities associated with life: nutrition, growth, reproduction, and so on. That something is soul. According to many ancient peoples, all living things have souls, which are responsible for their being alive.

Aristotle recognized that although trees, cows, and human beings are similar in that they are all alive, they are also different; they have capabilities for different levels of activity. This observation led Aristotle to theorize that there are different "grades" of soul. Some grades of soul have higher capabilities than others. The most primitive kind of soul is the nutritive soul that is responsible for nutrition, growth, and reproduction. Plants have a nutritive soul. A higher grade of soul is the sensitive soul, which incorporates all the functions of the nutritive soul but also gives the organism the capacity to perceive its environment, to feel pain, and to move about. Animals such as cows, deer, dogs, and cats have a sensitive soul. Finally, there is the highest grade of soul, the rational soul. The rational soul includes all the functions of both the nutritive and sensitive souls, but it also gives an organism the capacity of reason. Only human beings have a rational soul, which enables them to think, understand, and know.

According to Aristotle, the function of an organism is activity that is directed by the highest capacities of its soul. Therefore, the function of a tree is to nourish itself, grow, and reproduce. The function of a dog is to use its senses to perceive the world and to move about in the world directed by its senses and desires. The rational souls of human beings enable them to nourish themselves, grow, and reproduce, like all living things. They also enable them to use their senses to perceive the world and to feel, as well as to move about. In addition, however, their rational souls enable them to reason. Theoretical reason enables human beings to discover truths about the world; practical reason enables them to set goals for their activity, to discover effective means for attaining their goals, and to govern their appetites and desires. Because having a rational soul rather than merely a nutritive or sensitive soul makes human beings unique and provides them with their highest capacities, the function of human beings is not simply to eat and drink, to reproduce, or to feel and perceive, but is tied to their possession of a rational soul. Therefore, the greatest good for a human being, unlike the greatest good for a dog or a cat, is tied to the use of reason.

According to Aristotle, then, the key to the good for human beings is "an activity of soul in accordance with, or not without, rational principle."[5] Aristotle believed that reason is definitive of or essential to the identity of human beings. He defined human beings as the rational animals. He maintained that "for man, therefore, the life according to intellect is best and pleasantest, since intellect more than anything else *is* man. This life therefore is also happiest."[6]

Aristotle believed that contemplative activities (thinking, learning, striving to understand and know) rather than pleasures and other external things are the

---

[5]Ibid., p. 1735 (1098a 8).

[6]Ibid., p. 1862 (Book X, Section 7, lines 1178a 6–8).

central source of happiness for human beings, in part because they are enduring and within a person's power. So-called "externals" cannot be the greatest good, in part because they are not sufficiently durable and permanent. Wealth, power, fame, and pleasure can be here today and gone tomorrow; knowledge and understanding cannot be taken away so easily. Similarly, pursuing pleasure, wealth, fame, and power can have unhappy consequences. We can become jaded with these things and discover that they do not bring the happiness and contentment that we expect from them. It is by now a cliché that wealth, power, and fame do not guarantee happiness. How many people have attained their heart's desire of wealth, fame, or power only to feel it turn to dust and ashes in their hands? Pursuit or attainment of these things can also bring unpleasant side effects. The pleasure of drink can lead to a hangover; the pleasure of sex can lead to diseases such as AIDS; wealth and power can bring with them a host of false friends and real enemies. On the other hand, Aristotle believed that acquiring knowledge and understanding and using our minds do bring happiness and contentment without unpleasant side effects. Finally, he believed that using one's mind is under a person's own control and not dependent on others the way that wealth, fame, and pleasure are. Other people can easily take away our wealth, power, fame, and pleasure, but they cannot take away our knowledge, wisdom, and rationality.

According to Aristotle, then, the highest good for a human being is a life of contemplation, a life in which a person uses reason. However, Aristotle did not deny that external goods contribute to happiness. For example, he conceded that "there are some things the lack of which takes the lustre from blessedness, as good birth, satisfactory children, beauty; for the man who is very ugly in appearance or ill-born or solitary and childless is hardly happy."[7] Similarly, he acknowledged that good health contributes to happiness and ill health detracts from it; he stressed that friends and loved ones are an important source of happiness, and the lack of them an important source of unhappiness. Human beings are social animals; they need each other in order to survive and flourish.

Aristotle emphasized happiness over a lifetime. Momentary, fleeting happiness is hardly an ideal to pursue; the aim is long-run rather than short-run happiness. Therefore, when Aristotle said that a life of contemplation is the best life for a human being, he did not mean that contemplation alone is sufficient for human happiness. Rather, his point was that a human being cannot live a fully human life without the activities of contemplation and that these activities should play a central role in a human being's life. Whatever other goods human beings pursue should be consistent with and not opposed to reason. Finally, other goods, such as wealth, power, attractiveness, friends, and prestige or fame, should be put into perspective. Although they are goods, they are not the highest good. They should not come to dominate a person's life, nor should they be pursued in a way that interferes with the highest activities of the rational soul.

---

[7]Ibid., p. 1737 (1099a 32–1099b 4).

HEDONISM

Aristotle denied that pleasure is the highest good for a human being. Hedonists disagree. According to Hedonism, what makes life worth living—the secret of happiness—is pleasure. Hedonists claim that only pleasure is intrinsically good and only pain is intrinsically bad; all other good things are good only because they increase pleasure (or decrease pain) and all other bad things are bad only because they increase pain (or decrease pleasure). Hedonists claim that we achieve happiness and the good life by maximizing pleasures and minimizing pains.

Hedonism should not be confused with Egoism or selfishness. A hedonist doesn't claim that the only pleasure that's valuable or the only pain that's bad is his or her own; rather, pleasure is valuable and pain bad, no matter whose it is. However, a hedonist would say that pursuing self-interest requires us to maximize our own pleasures and minimize our own pains. But how should a hedonist live in order to maximize pleasures and minimize pains?

EPICUREANISM

The Greek philosopher Epicurus (341-270 B.C.E.), founder of Epicureanism, is perhaps one of the most famous hedonists. Epicurus was a materialist who believed that everything that exists is composed of physical matter, the smallest bit of matter being the atom. Thus, according to Epicurus, the soul, like the body, is physical and composed of atoms, albeit a much finer variety of atoms than the body is composed of. At death, when the soul detaches from the body, we cease to exist; all consciousness permanently ceases, including sensing, perceiving, thinking, and remembering. Therefore, according to Epicurus, happiness must be achieved while we are alive. As a hedonist, Epicurus taught that we achieve happiness by maximizing pleasures and minimizing pains.

Epicurus distinguished between physical and mental pleasures and pains. Physical pleasures and pains come from the senses; they arise from sight, hearing, taste, touch, and smell. Pleasure from smelling a flower, tasting pepperoni pizza, seeing a sunset, and engaging in sex are all physical pleasures, pleasures derived from using our senses. Pain from stepping on a tack, touching a hot pot, and smelling a skunk are examples of physical pains. On the other hand, mental pleasures and pains come from using our minds. Mental pleasures could come from playing chess, reading poetry, acquiring knowledge and understanding, and scoring high on a computer game. Mental pains could include fearing some future calamity, having an unsatisfied desire, and feeling depressed, frustrated, or lonely.

Pleasures and pains can be mixed, both physical and mental. Consider the pleasure derived from attending the theater or listening to music. They appeal to the senses and to the mind. Thus, pleasures and pains may be purely physical, purely mental, or a combination of both physical and mental. As we will see, Epicurus maintained that in the long run mental pleasures are superior to physical pleasures, and he advocated a way of life that bears many resemblances to Aristotle's life of contemplation.

Banishing Fear of the Gods and Fear of Death

Epicurus believed that two sources of mental pain were particularly acute: fear of the gods and fear of death. People fear the gods because they believe that the gods will bring them evils such as poverty and illness or deny them goods such as wealth and friends. Then, too, people fear death, and the anticipation of the nothingness of death spoils their happiness. They especially fear being punished for their misdeeds in the afterlife and spending eternity in pain. In Epicurus's view, banishing these twin fears would do much to increase peace of mind, which brings happiness.

Epicurus taught that there's no reason to fear the gods. He didn't deny that the gods exist; rather, he insisted that the gods don't care about Earth and its human inhabitants. Living a blessed life, the gods are indifferent to what happens on Earth. Thus, they don't reward or punish people for their deeds, they don't answer prayers, and they don't intervene in earthly events. The gods don't act to benefit human beings or to harm them; therefore, there's no reason for human beings to fear them.

Epicurus insisted that people shouldn't fear death because when a person dies, he or she ceases to exist. The gods neither reward nor punish people after death; there's no mental or physical pain or pleasure after death. There's nothing, in fact, after death, just as there was nothing before birth. In Epicurus's view, we should feel no more unhappy about the nothingness after death than about the nothingness before birth.

> Become accustomed to the belief that death is nothing to us. For all good and evil consists in sensation, but death is deprivation of sensation. And therefore a right understanding that death is nothing to us makes the mortality of life enjoyable, not because it adds to it an infinite span of time, but because it takes away the craving for immortality. For there is nothing terrible in life for the man who has truly comprehended that there is nothing terrible in not living. . . . So death, the most terrifying of ills, is nothing to us, since so long as we exist, death is not with us; but when death comes, then we do not exist.[8]

Simplicity and Moderation

Once people stop fearing death and the gods, they can get on with the business of finding happiness here on Earth while they're alive by maximizing pleasures and minimizing pains. Epicurus taught that maximizing pleasure and minimizing pain does not mean dedicating our lives to the more obvious physical pleasures such as those afforded by food, drink, and sex. Rather, Epicurus taught that the good life is a life of moderation devoted to health and peace of mind, for he

---

[8]Epicurus, "Letter to Menoeceus," in *Stoic and Epicurean Philosophers,* ed. Whitney J. Oates (New York: Random House, 1940), pp. 30–31.

assumed that tranquillity and serenity were the greatest pleasures available. According to Epicurus, we should "refer all choice and avoidance to the health of the body and the soul's freedom from disturbance, since this is the aim of the life of blessedness."[9]

The principle of maximizing pleasure and minimizing pain does not mean that one should satisfy every desire for immediate pleasure. Some pleasures lead to future pain and some pains lead to future pleasures. For example, the pleasure of drunkenness leads to the pain of a hangover and can lead to poor health; the pleasure of unprotected sexual intercourse can lead to venereal diseases and AIDS; the pain of having a tooth filled leads to the pleasure of having healthy teeth that do not give pain. Epicurus, influenced by Aristotle's reminder that the goal is not happiness for the moment but happiness over the course of a person's whole life, taught that the goal of life should be to maximize pleasures and minimize pains not for the present moment but rather over the course of a lifetime. That goal requires people to focus on long-run rather than on short-run pleasures and pains, which will often require denying themselves immediate pleasures that will lead to future pains and accepting immediate pains if they will lead to future pleasure or a lessening of future pain. Thus, according to Epicurus,

> since pleasure is the first good and natural to us, for this very reason we do not choose every pleasure, but sometimes we pass over many pleasures, when greater discomfort accrues to us as a result of them. . . . Every pleasure then because of its natural kinship to us is good, yet not every pleasure is to be chosen: even as every pain also is an evil, yet not all are always of a nature to be avoided.[10]

Similarly, Epicurus insisted, "No pleasure is a bad thing in itself: but the means which produce some pleasures bring with them disturbances many times greater than the pleasures."[11]

Epicurus believed that the best way of life for a human being is a life focused on maintaining health and tranquillity. Over the course of a lifetime, maximum pleasure and minimum pain come from a life of moderation; overindulgence in the pleasure of the senses has painful consequences. Similarly, according to Epicurus, mental pleasures often should be preferred to physical pleasures because the mental pleasures don't have painful consequences and they banish the superstitions and fears that bring mental turmoil.

> When, therefore, we maintain that pleasure is the end [goal], we do not mean the pleasures of profligates and those that consist in sensuality, . . . but freedom from pain in the body and trouble in the mind. For it is not continuous drinkings and revellings, nor the satisfaction of lusts, nor the enjoyment of . . . luxuries of the wealthy table, which produces a pleasant life, but sober reasoning,

---

[9]Ibid., pp. 31–32.

[10]Ibid., p. 32.

[11]Epicurus, *Principal Doctrines,* Fragment VIII, in *Stoic and Epicurean Philosophers,* p. 35.

searching out the motives for all choices and avoidance, and banishing mere opinions, to which are due the greatest disturbance of the spirit.[12]

Epicurus also emphasized simplicity and moderation in life because according to him, desire for physical pleasure quickly becomes insatiable if not controlled and moderated, leading to frustration and pain. As he put it, "The wealth demanded by nature is both limited and easily procured; that demanded by idle imaginings stretches on to infinity."[13] We want a million dollars; once we have it, we want two million dollars, then four million. Epicurus thought that the wise person would focus on acquiring physical necessities—food, drink, shelter, and clothing—rather than on acquiring luxuries. Equally important, Epicurus insisted that satisfying our basic needs does not require nearly as much work as does acquiring luxuries and the grosser forms of physical pleasure. In his view, the more we want, the more work we must do in order to satisfy those wants (or to get the money to afford what we want). According to Epicurus, work is a source of pain, not pleasure. Therefore, the more wants or desires we have, the more we must work, making us slaves of our desires and setting us on a treadmill of work. The fewer wants or desires we have, the less work is required to satisfy them and the more leisure we have for pleasant activities. Thus, Epicurus said,

> The flesh perceives the limits of pleasure as unlimited and unlimited time is required to supply it. But the mind, having attained a reasoned understanding of the ultimate good of the flesh and its limits and having dissipated the fears of the time to come, supplies us with a complete life. . . .[14]

Nothing is sufficient for him to whom what is sufficient seems little.[15]

Relations with Other People

Again like Aristotle, Epicurus stressed that other people are an important source of pleasure. He did not mean the pleasures of exploitation and oppression; rather, he meant the pleasures of friendship. As he said, "Of all the things which wisdom acquires to produce the blessedness of the complete life, far the greatest is friendship."[16] Loving and being loved are fundamental sources of pleasure; being alone and friendless is a fundamental source of pain. To have friends, you must of course be a friend; you must care about others and treat them with respect if they are to be friends. To maximize pleasures and minimize pains, then, you must have friends, other people who love and are loved in return.

Epicurus also believed that rational self-interest would lead us to refrain from harming others. Trying to maximize pleasures and minimize pains does not mean riding roughshod over other people. Even if we derive pleasure from harm-

[12]Ibid., p. 32

[13]Ibid., Fragment XV, p. 36.

[14]Ibid., Fragment XX, p. 36.

[15]Epicurus, *Fragments,* Fragment LXVIII, in *Stoic and Epicurean Philosophers,* p. 44.

[16]Epicurus, *Principal Doctrines,* Fragment XXVIII, in *Stoic and Epicurean Philosophers,* p. 37.

ing others, we should not satisfy the desire to injure others, because if we harm others, we risk being harmed in return. Consider these pronouncements of Epicurus.

> The most unalloyed source of protection from men . . . is in fact the immunity which results from a quiet life and the retirement from the world.
>
> The just man is most free from trouble, the unjust man most full of trouble.
>
> Those who live most pleasantly with others have greatest immunity from others.
>
> Let nothing be done in your life, which will cause you fear if it becomes known to your neighbor.
>
> The greatest fruit of justice is serenity.
>
> A man who causes fear cannot be free from fear.[17]

According to Epicurus, harming others cannot be in our self-interest. People create societies and governments by mutual agreement or compact. If we are unjust and harm others, we may be punished for it, and the pain of punishment would probably outweigh the pleasures gained from the injustice. But even if we are not immediately punished, our peace of mind and sense of security will be forever shattered because there's always the possibility of being caught and punished; there is never a guarantee that we will escape detection and punishment. The pain of fear and insecurity will almost surely outweigh the pleasure derived from the injustice.

> It is not possible for one who acts in secret contravention of the terms of the compact not to harm or be harmed, to be confident that he will escape detection, even if at present he escapes a thousand times. For up to the time of death it cannot be certain he will indeed escape.[18]

Therefore, a rational, self-interested person will harm no one.

STOICISM

Moral Goodness Is Necessary and Sufficient for Happiness

Epicureanism's strongest competitor in the ancient world was Stoicism, which originated in Athens around 300 B.C.E. and has influenced Western thought for more than 2,000 years. Stoics heaped scorn on the Epicurean claim that pleasure is the only thing intrinsically good and pain the only thing intrinsically bad. They derided the Epicurean recipe for happiness—maximizing pleasure and minimizing pain—insisting that such a philosophy is more appropriate for cattle than for human beings. For example, the Roman writer Cicero (106–43 B.C.E.), identifying

---

[17]Ibid., pp. 38–51.

[18]Ibid., p. 38.

pleasure primarily with physical pleasure, said that "bodily [physical] pleasure is not sufficiently worthy of the superiority of man and it should be scorned and rejected."[19] Stoics claimed that moral goodness is sufficient for a happy life and that concern about pleasure and pain are incompatible with it. Again we can cite Cicero, who wrote that "pleasures . . . , the most alluring of mistresses, twist the hearts of most men away from virtue [moral goodness]."[20]

According to Cicero, "in order to live a happy life the only thing we need is moral goodness."[21] Moral goodness would not be sufficient for happiness if there were other forms of good and evil. Good things contribute to happiness, and evil or bad things to unhappiness. If other things besides moral goodness or virtue were good, then moral goodness would probably not be necessary for happiness, because we could get happiness from other good things. Similarly, if there were other evil or bad things besides moral vice or moral evil, then moral goodness might not be sufficient for happiness, because if we had enough bad things in our lives, we would probably be unhappy even if we were morally good.

Most of us assume that things such as wealth, power, health, family, and friends are good things, and their absence evils. Aristotle certainly held this view. Although he denied that these things constitute a human being's highest good, he conceded that they are good and that they contribute to happiness. Paradoxically, Stoics denied that such things are good at all. Although they admitted that such things as wealth, power, and health are to be preferred to their opposites, they denied that they deserve to be called "good." Cicero defended this position by claiming first that we shouldn't call something "good" that we can't ourselves control and that isn't durable. He then pointed out that such things as wealth, power, honor, and health are neither under our control nor durable. Events over which we have no control have a profound impact on whether we will be wealthy or poor, powerful or powerless, healthy or unhealthy. Similarly, they are not durable because we may be wealthy today and poor tomorrow, healthy today and ill tomorrow. Therefore, since these things are neither under our control nor durable, they are not good. What is not good is neither necessary nor sufficient for anyone's happiness.

Tranquillity Is the Key to Happiness

Like Epicureans, Stoics claimed that peace of mind and tranquillity are central to happiness. Cicero referred to tranquillity and the absence of distress as the "supreme object of our desires and aspirations."[22] It's not pleasure, excitement, or thrills that bring happiness, but rather, tranquillity, serenity, internal harmony, and peace of mind.

---

[19]Cicero, *On Duties,* ed. M. Griffin and E. Atkins (Cambridge, England: Cambridge University Press, 1991), p. 41.

[20]Ibid., p. 76.

[21]Cicero, "Discussions at Tusculum, V," in *On the Good Life,* trans. Michael Grant (Harmondsworth, England: Penguin, 1971), p. 52.

[22]Ibid., p. 75.

According to Stoicism, tranquillity or peace of mind does not come from the things that most people value and pursue: wealth, power, fame, physical pleasure, attractiveness, health, and so on. Why not? Because such externals are not completely under our control. No matter how hard we try, we cannot do anything to guarantee that we will become or remain wealthy, powerful, famous, healthy, or attractive. If our happiness depends on things over which we have little control, we are bound to be unhappy. For example, suppose that your happiness depends on your being rich. If you won't be happy unless you're rich, and there's nothing that you can do that will guarantee that you will become rich, then your happiness is jeopardized. Even if you become rich, there's nothing that you can do to guarantee that you'll remain rich, which will breed fear and insecurity, the opposite of tranquillity and peace of mind.

Stoics claimed that as long as we consider "good" what's neither in our control nor durable, we will lack tranquillity. As Cicero expressed it,

> Nothing that there is the slightest possibility of eventually losing can be regarded as an ingredient of the happy life. . . . For once a man starts fearing that one of these supposedly "good" possessions is going to vanish, it is out of the question for him to be happy any longer. For the happy man, as I see him, has to be safe, secure, unconquerable, impregnable: a man whose fears are not only just insignificant but non-existent.[23]

Many people erroneously assume that possessions, reputation, power, youth, good looks, and so on are necessary for happiness. However, according to Cicero, none of these is truly good.

> As for the other so-called "good" things, it is erroneous to describe or regard them as good, since it is perfectly possible to possess them in abundance and still be miserable all the same! Imagine a man who is favoured with excellent health, great physical strength and extremely good looks. . . . Then throw in wealth, distinction, great offices of state, power, and glory. But suppose also that the person thus endowed is at the same time unjust, intemperate, cowardly, slow-witted or downright stupid. You will surely have to admit that he is an unhappy man.[24]

According to Stoicism, tranquillity and peace of mind are the keys to happiness, and they come not from pursuing such externals as wealth and fame but from limiting, controlling, and moderating our desires.

Moderation of Desire

Like Epicureans, Stoics saw desire as insatiable, addictively demanding. The more we satisfy a desire, the more insistent is the demand for continued satisfaction. Suppose that we desire power. If we have power over ten people, we want power over twenty-five; if we have power over twenty-five, we want power over

---

[23]Ibid., p. 74

[24]Ibid., p. 76

fifty. Because desire is insatiable and addictively demanding, people spend ever more time and energy satisfying their uncontrolled and uncontrollable desires, while satisfaction becomes ever more elusive. The danger is that desires will control our lives rather than be controlled. Like many Greeks, such as Plato and Aristotle, Stoics believed that reason should be in control of desire. Reason will control desire primarily by moderating desire. Cicero, for example, wrote,

> We concluded that violent commotions and upheavals of the soul, when it is agitated and troubled by some irrational impulse or other, are altogether incompatible with happiness.

> Or when you see a man driven to a mad frenzy by lust, so that he plunges himself insatiably into every sort of sensuality, and still, the deeper the draughts he takes from every source, the more furious and rabid his thirst becomes: there, obviously, is another thoroughly unhappy man.

> Now, the exact opposites to these unhappy people are the happy ones who are alarmed by no fears, anguished by no distresses, disturbed by no cravings. . . . When there is not the smallest breeze to ruffle the waves of the sea one speaks of it as calm: and in the same way you are entitled to describe the condition of the soul as peaceful when no agitation disturbs its tranquility.[25]

Cicero concluded,

> The wise man is free from all those disturbances of the soul which I describe as passion; his heart is full of tranquil calm forever. And anyone who is self-controlled, unwavering, fearless, undistressed, the victim of no cravings or desires, must inevitably be happy.[26]

Above all, Stoicism preached the importance of self-control; desire should be carefully controlled by reason.

Stoic Resignation

Stoics believed that the universe is governed by divine law, by reason and intelligence, and that everything that occurs is part of a series of events that was preplanned in the far distant past. Because the universe is governed by reason and intelligence, everything that occurs is good, even if it doesn't appear good to us because we're not familiar with the plan. Therefore, a wise person will be content with whatever occurs, recognizing that it is inevitable and part of the master plan of the universe. To feel regret, anger, disappointment, discontent, or frustration about the course of events is unreasonable and virtually guarantees unhappiness. We will be happier and have more peace of mind if we simply accept what occurs. A Stoic will face the world with a sense of calm resignation and acceptance and will therefore be happy, come what may.

As the Stoic Marcus Aurelius (A.D. 121–180) put it,

---

[25]Ibid., pp. 60–61.
[26]Ibid., p. 78.

You must consider the doing and perfecting of what the universal Nature decrees in the same light as your health, and welcome all that happens, even if it seems harsh, because it leads to the health of the universe, the welfare and well-being of Zeus. For he would not have allotted this to anyone if it were not beneficial to the Whole. No sort of nature brings anything to pass which does not contribute to that which it governs. You must therefore welcome with love what happens to you, for two reasons: first, because it happens to you, is prescribed for you . . . , a fate spun for you from above by the most venerable of causes; second, because whatever comes to an individual is a cause of the well-being and the welfare . . . of that which governs the Whole.[27]

Stoics use an arresting image. They compare human beings to a dog tied behind a moving cart. The dog has no control over the cart; it must follow where the cart leads. The dog can either resist and be discontented with where the cart leads it, thus being forever unhappy, or it can make up its mind to follow along without resistance and be resigned to the inevitable, being contented with whatever path and speed the cart takes. That is, it can desire to go someplace other than where the cart will take it, or it can desire to be in harmony with the cart and desire to go wherever the cart takes it. If the dog takes the latter position, it need never be frustrated or unhappy.

According to Stoicism, human beings are like dogs tied to carts in that the course of their lives is predetermined. Like the dog, human beings are carried along by the course of events over which they have no control. People can resist the inevitable course of events and desire what they don't have, or they can resign themselves to accepting without resentment, despair, or discontent whatever fate has in store for them. They'll be happier if they follow the latter course.

LOVE AND FEAR OF GOD

Many religious people believe that the morally good life is the good life and the key to happiness because of God's existence and relation to human beings. Many adherents of Western religions such as Judaism, Christianity, and Islam maintain that a human being's essence is her nonphysical soul and that after death, when the soul detaches from the body, God punishes those who have been bad by committing their souls to hell, the place of eternal torment and suffering, and rewards those who have been good by lifting their souls to heaven, the place of eternal and perfect bliss. Therefore, if happiness over the course of our whole existence is the goal, we cannot concentrate merely on happiness in earthly life. How we spend eternity after the death of the body is the most crucial determinant of happiness over the course of our entire existence.

This view did not originate with Western religions; its roots go back in time at least to the world of ancient Egypt and probably beyond. It was a common belief in the ancient world. For example, in Plato's (427–347 B.C.E.) early dialogue *Gorgias,* Socrates, the main speaker, is urging Callicles, a rather cynical young

---

[27]Marcus Aurelius, *The Meditations,* trans. G. M. A. Grube (Indianapolis, IN: Hackett, 1983), p. 40.

man, that it's far more important to care for one's soul than one's body, wealth, or power. Callicles is contemptuous and insists that Socrates's views are silly; it's not in our self-interest to deny ourselves anything. Socrates disagrees.

> Now there was a law concerning human beings . . . that the gods even now continue to observe, that when a man who has lived a just and pious life comes to his end, he goes to the Isles of the Blessed, to make his abode in complete happiness, beyond the reach of evils, but when one who has lived in an unjust and godless way dies, he goes to the prison of payment and retribution, the one they call Tartarus.[28]

According to Socrates, in Tartarus the souls of the dead are judged by the sons of Zeus: Minos, Rhadamanthus, and Ajacus. Every evil deed has left its mark on a person's soul and is plainly visible to the judges; we cannot conceal our wickedness from these judges, even if we were able to conceal it from other human beings while alive. The judges impose punishment; the amount and duration of suffering are proportional to our degree of wickedness.

Socrates tells Callicles,

> So I disregard the things held in honor by the majority of people, and, by practicing truth I really try . . . to be and to live as a very good man, and when I die, to die like that [with a healthy rather than corrupt soul]. And I call on all other people as well . . . to this way of life, this contest, that I hold to be worth all the other contests in this life. And I take you to task, because you won't be able to come to protect yourself when you appear at the trial and judgment I was talking about just now.[29]

It is self-interest that requires us to protect our souls from corruption and wickedness.

Finally, some religious people emphasize the happiness in this life that comes from opening ourselves up to God, loving God and being loved in return. They claim that having a personal relationship with God provides the most satisfaction and happiness that life has to offer. Forming and maintaining such a relationship with God, a loving God, requires that we lead, or at least try to lead, a morally good life. As the Stoics do, they might claim the moral goodness is both necessary and sufficient for happiness because it enables one to get into the right relationship with God, which is the greatest source of happiness imaginable. All other things—wealth, power, glory, fame, possessions, sex—pale in comparison to the rewards of loving and being loved by God.

For example, St. Thomas Aquinas (1225-1274), one of the most influential Roman Catholic philosophers and theologians, maintained, "It is impossible for any created good to constitute man's happiness. For happiness is the perfect good. . . . Now the object of the will, i.e., of man's appetite, is the universal good. . . . This is to be found . . . in God alone. . . . Therefore, God alone consti-

---

[28]Plato, *Gorgias,* trans. Donald Zeyl (Indianapolis, IN: Hackett, 1987), p. 107.
[29]Ibid., pp. 111-112.

tutes man's happiness."[30] Aquinas said that "man's happiness consists in the knowledge of God."[31] Another Roman Catholic philosopher and theologian, John Buridan (1300–1358), maintained that knowledge of God is not alone sufficient for human happiness, for "a man clearly seeing God without delight and without the love of God would [not] be called happy." He pointed out that "many authoritative texts of Holy Scripture seem clearly to say that human happiness consists in the vision of God, and many others, in the love of God. This is because it is not merely in this or in that, but in both conjointly and together."[32] Then, too, the Jewish philosopher Benedict de Spinoza (1632–1677) taught that "the man whose main love and chief delight is the intellectual knowledge of the most perfect being, God, is necessarily most perfect, and shares most fully in supreme blessedness. Our highest good and blessedness, then, is summed up in this— knowledge and love of God."[33]

HAPPINESS AND THE MEANING OF LIFE

Human Life as Furthering God's Purposes

Some people can be happy only if they think that human life in general has a purpose or meaning that gives it a special significance. Usually such purpose or meaning is derived from religious beliefs. According to the major religions of the Western world, God created the human species (whether by means of a special act of instant divine creation, as in the biblical story of Adam and Eve, or by means of evolutionary processes) as part of a master plan for the universe. According to this view, human life has special significance, a significance radically different from that of any other form of life, because human beings are the crowning glory of creation. In fact, according to this tradition, the universe was created for human beings, and human beings are the most important forms of life in God's eyes.

We human beings are said to be unlike other living organisms in that we each have an immortal soul that contains our "essence" and that makes us the individual person we are. When other creatures die, they simply cease to exist, returning to the nothingness from which they came. However, human existence does not cease with death. When our bodies die, our souls are released and continue to exist; therefore, since you are identical to your soul, you will continue to exist after your body dies. In fact, you will exist forever, because your soul is immortal. The traditional religious view in the West is that you will continue to

---

[30]Thomas Aquinas, *Summa Theologica,* first part of the second part, Question II, in *Philosophy in the Middle Ages,* 2d ed., ed. Arthur Hyman and James Walsh (Indianapolis, IN: Hackett, 1983), p. 558.

[31]Ibid., p. 559.

[32]John Buridan, "Questions on the Ten Books of the Nicomachean Ethics of Aristotle," in *Philosophy in the Middle Ages,* p. 772 (Book X).

[33]Benedict de Spinoza, "A Treatise on Religion and Politics," in *Moral Philosophy from Montaigne to Kant,* vol. 1, ed. J. B. Schneewind (Cambridge, England: Cambridge University Press, 1990), p. 241.

exist in heaven if you have lived a good life or in hell if you have lived a bad life. You will also be ultimately reunited with all your loved ones who have died. Because our physical life on Earth is temporary but our existence after death is eternal, physical earthly life is far less important than our nonphysical existence after death. However, physical earthly life is not insignificant or purposeless; rather, it is important as a kind of testing ground. The kind of life we lead here on Earth will determine how we spend eternity—whether rewarded in heaven or punished in hell.

According to this view, God created human beings for His/Her own purposes, many of which we cannot understand, but a primary purpose is connected to our working toward our own salvation of eternal existence in heaven. God wants as many human souls as possible to join Him/Her in heaven, but only if they have proved worthy of heaven.

Thus, human life in general—the entire species *Homo sapiens*—is objectively important, significant, and meaningful. It is important that human beings exist because it is important to God and God's purposes that human beings exist. Similarly, the lives of individual human beings are meaningful, significant, and important because we are members of an important species and because our existence will not cease with death. Each individual life is also important because each of us is placed here on Earth to further God's purposes, even if we are partly or wholly ignorant of what those purposes are.

Human Life as a Cosmic Accident

However, many thinkers have rejected this view. They claim that the universe was not created or designed by God. Either it has always existed in some form or other or it was created billions of years ago in an event whose cause we cannot possibly understand. The history of the universe since then—including the birth of suns and galaxies, the origin of life on Earth, and the origin of human beings—has not proceeded according to any plan and serves no purpose; it is purely the result of the chance operation of natural forces. If an asteroid or comet had not stuck the Earth 65 billion years ago, driving the dinosaurs into extinction, human beings would almost certainly not have arrived on the scene. The catastrophe was not planned; it was a cosmic accident. Similarly, another cosmic accident millions of years from now may exterminate the entire human race just as the dinosaurs were exterminated, unless we manage to exterminate ourselves before then through our own stupidity. But even without such a cosmic accident, we know for certain that in a few billion years the sun will die, leaving our entire solar system devoid of life, extinguishing the entire human race (which may in any case have evolved into creatures that hardly resemble contemporary human beings). We may imagine that by then our technology will have enabled us to colonize far distant stars, thus preserving the human race, but that scenario is in the realm of science fiction rather than science. Human life, whether of the individual or the species, has no purpose, significance, or meaning. Our species came into existence by chance, without anyone or anything planning it, and it will probably go out of existence in the same way. The universe didn't cheer when our species came onto the stage, and it will not cry when it leaves it forever.

From the cosmic perspective of time and space, human life to these thinkers appears utterly insignificant. The physical universe as we know it has existed for ten to twelve billion years. Earth has existed for about five billion years. However, modern human beings, members of the species *Homo sapiens,* have existed for only a few tens of thousands of years. All of human existence so far has taken place during the blink of an eye. Since human beings did not exist throughout almost all of time, how could they be considered important or significant from a cosmic point of view? The universe got along fine without human life for almost all of time.

What of the future? Will human beings continue to exist for eternity? The dinosaurs existed for tens if not hundreds of millions of years, but even they were cast into the nothingness of extinction. Can human beings duplicate the feat of the dinosaurs and continue in existence for tens of millions of years into the future? Who knows? But even if we can, the time will inevitably come when *Homo sapiens,* as the dinosaurs, will be cast into the nothingness of extinction and the universe will continue without us, perhaps for many billions of years.

Then, too, these thinkers point out that Earth is like a minuscule grain of sand floating in the vast immensity of space. Our sun is simply an average star in a galaxy that has tens of billions of stars. Within our own galaxy we are a dot. But our galaxy is but one of tens of billions of galaxies visible to us, so our entire galaxy is like a small dot in the immensity of space. Thus, from a cosmic perspective, the planet we call home is but a tiny dot within a tiny dot. How could our species be significant or important from a cosmic point of view? According to these thinkers, the ideas that human beings play an important role in the universe and are the apple of God's eye are preposterous. All of human life occupies a tiny point in nearly infinite space and time.

This view also denies that human beings have souls. According to this view, we are purely physical organisms. Just like any other form of life, when we die we cease to exist. We return to the nothingness from which we came, a nothingness that will be eternal. All consciousness permanently ceases. Of course, this view of death entails that we will not be reunited with our loved ones who have died. They are gone forever, just as we will be gone forever when we die. Therefore, individual human lives cannot have a significance or meaning that depends on earthly life's being a test or preparation for eternal existence with God or on furthering God's purposes or plans. Neither the human species nor any individual human being has significance or meaningfulness in that sense.

Happiness or Despair?

Many people think that our happiness depends on the first view's being true rather than the second (or at least on our believing that the first view is true rather than the second). They think that as long as we view the existence of our species as important and significant, our individual lives as important, meaningful, and significant, and our existence as extending beyond death, then we will be happy even in the face of inevitable suffering and death in our physical existence on Earth. On the other hand, if we accept the second view, happiness inevitably will be replaced by despair and unhappiness. Life will be meaningless and not worth living.

We will not examine these two views to determine which one is correct. Each individual must decide for herself. Instead we will address the question of whether someone who takes the second view must inevitably be unhappy and filled with despair. Interestingly, as we saw, Epicurus claimed that we would be happier if we believed the second story rather than something like the first. He probably exaggerated the fear of hell and underestimated the hope for heaven of those who accept the first view. It seems that few people are comforted by Epicurus's reassurance that when we're dead we return to eternal nothingness and simply cease to exist.

Can We Be Happy if We Believe Human Life Is a Cosmic Accident? Will we inevitably be unhappy if we believe that the species *Homo sapiens* is the product of a cosmic accident and was not created to further God's plans and purposes? It is not entirely clear precisely why that belief should make us unhappy. Our species may have no importance or significance from the point of view of the universe (if we can intelligibly speak of such a point of view), but that doesn't mean that our species cannot or should not have importance and significance to *us*. So what if the universe didn't cheer (or nothing in the universe did cheer) when our species came on the scene and will not weep when it departs? What should count is our own point of view (since, after all, it's *our* point of view), not anyone or anything else's. Similarly, why should we care if human life in general does not further the plans or purposes of someone or something else? You can still be happy that human life came on the cosmic stage because if it hadn't, you would not exist.

Can We Be Happy if Our Individual Lives Do Not Further God's Purposes and Plans?   Similarly, suppose that you believe that your life on Earth does not fit into some cosmic plan or blueprint, does not contribute to the furthering of God's plans and purposes. Your life has no significance or meaning to God or the universe. You came into existence only because of the union of your parents; you were not born in order to play a role in a play written by anyone—not God, not the universe, not your parents.

Again, precisely why should such a belief make you unhappy? Although it may make your individual life meaningless or insignificant from a cosmic point of view, why should that bother you? What should count is your point of view, not God's or the universe's. And from your own point of view, *your* individual human life may be very important, significant, and meaningful indeed. After all, it is your life, the only life you will have. Surely it matters to you, and should matter to you, whether it goes well or badly. Why should you adopt the attitude that your life can be significant or meaningful *to you* only if it is significant or meaningful to someone or something beyond or outside of the human race?

Can We Be Happy if We Believe That We Cease to Exist at Death?
Finally, suppose that you believe that your existence ends at death—that you return to eternal nothingness because all consciousness permanently ceases. Does that make your life meaningless or insignificant (which in turn would make you unhappy) from *your* point of view? Not necessarily.

Furthering your own purposes and plans can make you feel that your life is meaningful and significant, in turn leading to happiness rather than despair and unhappiness. Most of us need to have purposes and plans beyond that of merely staying alive, meeting our basic needs for food, clothing, and shelter. Many of us need to have plans and purposes that include making a contribution, however small, to other human beings or human institutions. We may do work that contributes to creating world peace, ending hunger, or protecting our environment. We may contribute by participating in the activities or the governing of our church, labor union, civic organization, or club. We may feel that the work we do on the job is meaningful and significant to us and others. Whether we are doctors, lawyers, computer programmers, financial analysts, teachers, writers, auto mechanics, or garbage collectors, we can see our activities as contributing something of value. Such contributions make our lives meaningful and significant to ourselves as well as to other human beings. Engaging in activities that *we* find meaningful and significant helps make our lives meaningful and significant to *us*.

Then, too, engaging in activities that we enjoy or that give us satisfaction, even if they do not contribute anything of value to others, can make us feel that our lives are significant and meaningful and can give us happiness rather than despair. Someone may get satisfaction and a sense of personal significance from running, playing the piano, taking a walk in the woods, listening to music, painting, carpentry, cultivating flowers, reading, or quilting.

Of course, our relations with others, as Aristotle and the Epicureans saw, play a central role in our feeling that life is meaningful or meaningless. Friendship and love may be the most important ingredients of a meaningful life. The life of an isolated hermit or an Ebeneezer Scrooge (prior to his conversion by the spirits of Christmas past, present, and future) would fail to satisfy or provide meaning for most people. Few people would freely choose a life without love and friendship. The love of and for relatives—grandparents, parents, siblings, aunts and uncles, children, grandchildren—can be the greatest source of joy and meaning. Similarly, romantic or sexual love—for example, between husband and wife—can make an otherwise dark existence bright. Sex with someone we love can bring deep happiness and satisfaction and can contribute to making us feel that life is meaningful.

On the other hand, the absence of the things we have mentioned could easily make one feel that one's life is meaningless and insignificant, leading to despair rather than happiness. A life lived without friendship or love, that contributes nothing of even the slightest value to anyone, that is without intrinsically satisfying activities would indeed be a meaningless and insignificant life, a life not worth living. But the fact that a life will someday end does not show that it is not meaningful and significant to the person whose life it is, as well as to others. Imagine someone who his whole life will never leave his room, will never have a visitor or interact in any way with other people, and will simply watch television every second that he is awake. Would that person have a meaningful life? Now suppose that this person will never die but live this way forever. Would immortality make his life more meaningful or significant?

What makes a human life meaningful or significant from a human point of view—which is the only point of view we can take and the only point of view we should consider—is not its length but rather the common things of ordinary daily existence. Therefore, even if one adopts the second view—that human existence is the product of a cosmic accident and that inevitably the human species will die out and all individual human lives will end—that view should not lead one to despair. Our lives can be meaningful from the only point of view that counts—our own.

CONCLUSION

What way of life is most likely to make a human being happy? What are the necessary or sufficient ingredients of the good life? There's plenty of disagreement about the proper answer to these questions, so each individual has to make up his or her own mind. Many philosophers are convinced that answering these questions is the most important task that a person faces. However, even if we agree that determining or deciding how we should live is a crucial question, we might object that each of the views we've examined assumes that there is a one-size-fits-all conception of happiness—one blueprint for happiness and the good life that fits every human being. Many people today would vehemently deny such a view. They insist that different things make different people happy. Wealth, power, possessions, or sex may be the key to happiness for one person, even if they're not the key to happiness for someone else. They are confident that everyone is and must be his or her own expert on happiness and the good life and that people are unlikely to make mistakes about what will make them happy.

EXERCISES

1. Can people make mistakes about what will make them happy? Defend your answer.
2. Describe what you consider to be the good life for you—the kind of life that you think is most likely to make you happy. Defend your claim that the kind of life you have described will make you happy.
3. If there is no one-size-fits-all conception of happiness and the good life, does it follow that no way of life is any better or worse than any other?
4. Do you agree with Aristotle that because human beings alone have the capacity to reason, the good for human beings must include contemplative activities and that other pursuits should not be inconsistent with reason? Defend your answer.

5. Callicles tried to persuade Socrates that the best life is one in which a person gratifies every appetite and desire and accumulates wealth, prestige, and power. Do you agree with him? Why or why not?

6. Is it always in our self-interest to avoid harming others, as Epicurus maintains? Suppose that an Epicurean believes that he is so clever that the risk of getting caught and punished is very small and that the pleasure to be derived from harming others is very great. Do the potential benefits outweigh the potential costs? Defend your answer.

7. According to Epicurus, the pleasures of tranquillity and peace of mind are greater than physical pleasures such as sex or excitement. Do you agree? Why or why not?

8. Do you agree that moderating and controlling our desires rather than seeking to satisfy every desire as it arises is a key to happiness? Defend your answer.

9. Do you think that a human being's greatest happiness comes from knowledge of and love of God? Defend your answer.

SUGGESTED READINGS

Marcus Aurelius. *The Meditations.* Translated by G. M. A. Grube. Indianapolis, IN: Hackett, 1983.

Cicero. *On Duties.* Edited by M. Griffin and E. Atkins. Cambridge, England: Cambridge University Press, 1991.

Cicero. *On the Good Life.* Translated by Michael Grant. Harmondsworth, England: Penguin, 1971.

Terence Irwin. *Classical Thought.* New York: Oxford University Press, 1989. (See especially Chapters 8 and 9 on Epicureanism and Stoicism.)

E. D. Klemke, ed. *The Meaning of Life.* New York: Oxford University Press, 1981.

A. A. Long and D. N. Sedley. *The Hellenistic Philosophers.* Vol. 1, *Translations of the Principle Sources, with Philosophical Commentary.* Cambridge, England: Cambridge University Press, 1987.

Wallace Matson. *A New History of Philosophy.* Vol. 1. New York: Harcourt Brace Jovanovich, 1987. (See especially Chapters 21 and 22 on Epicureanism and Stoicism.)

Whitney J. Oates, ed. *The Stoic and Epicurean Philosophers.* New York: Random House/Modern Library, 1940.

Plato. *Gorgias.* Translated by Donald Zeyl. Indianapolis, IN: Hackett, 1987.

CHAPTER 6

The Good Person: Virtue and Vice

CHARACTER AND BEHAVIOR

Why do people engage in moral thinking and deliberation? Surely it is because they have questions they want answered. What moral rules or principles should I accept and try to live by? What are my duties toward others? What is the right thing to do under the circumstances that I now face? What kind of person should I be? The last question, you will notice, is a bit different from the other three. The first three questions deal with how one should behave or act, either generally or in specific circumstances; the fourth question deals with how one should *be*. Of course, the kind of person one is will have a great effect on how one behaves. However, the issue of the kind of person one should be goes beyond behavior.

As we mentioned earlier, we can evaluate from a moral point of view both actions and persons, both conduct and character. On the one hand, we can claim that Tom's action of stealing John's bicycle was wrong. We could also say that a whole class of actions is wrong by saying that it's wrong to steal people's bicycles. On the other hand, we can claim that Tom's stealing of John's bicycle is something that a good person would not do, so that we have reason to conclude that Tom is not a good person.

Suppose that Johnny Jones, a student at Thomas Jefferson Elementary School, picks on children who are smaller and weaker than he is. We observe him as he extorts money from a small boy, threatening to beat the boy up unless he hands over his lunch money. After the boy hands over his lunch money, Johnny Jones beats him up and forces him to kiss his shoe. We would evaluate Johnny's actions as morally wrong. But in addition, we would evaluate Johnny *himself* from a moral point of view. We would call him a bully. The term *bully* is both descriptive and evaluative. It is descriptive because we can correctly call someone a bully only if he tends to coerce, intimidate, and assault others, usually those who are weaker than he is. But it is also usually an evaluative concept as well. *Bully* is rarely a term of approval and admiration. On the contrary, if we call someone a bully, we are usually criticizing and condemning him. According to what we have been calling commonsense morality, being a bully is bad and someone who is a bully is a bad person, at least when it comes to the treatment of people who are weaker than they are.

Being a bully is what we can call a character trait. A character trait is, in part, a tendency to behave in certain ways under certain circumstances. Someone who is a bully tends to pick on people if they are weaker than he is but not if they are stronger. Now, the trait of being a bully often is accompanied by other traits. For example, in addition to saying that Johnny Jones is a bully, we might also say that he is mean and a coward. If he is mean, he tends to do things intentionally to cause others to suffer. If he is a coward, he would not take the risk of picking on or standing up to people who are likely to be as strong as or stronger than he is. Being a bully, being mean, and being a coward may constitute a kind of package of character traits. We may then talk about Johnny Jones's *character*—the kind of person that Johnny Jones is. To describe an individual's character, the kind of person she is, we list that person's character traits. Thus, an individual's character is a cluster, or perhaps a system, of character traits.

As we will see, a character trait is not only a tendency to behave in certain ways. Traits are more complicated and include tendencies to feel, desire, and believe in certain ways. But it's important to keep in mind that part of what we may call our commonsense view of people includes the assumption that character plays a causal role in behavior. People who have the character trait of being a bully generally behave in bullying ways, and we assume that their trait of being a bully causes them to behave that way; people who have courage generally behave courageously, and we assume that their trait of courage causes them to behave courageously. Similarly, people with the trait of selfishness generally behave selfishly, and we assume that their trait of selfishness causes them to behave selfishly.

The concept of character raises a number of important questions. One type of question involves our own character: What kind of person shall I (or do I want to) be? For example, should I be a bully (like Johnny Jones)? Another type of question involves the character of other people: What kind of people should I (or do I want to) hang out with (or date or marry)? For example, do I want to hang out with people who are boastful and arrogant? Do I want to marry someone who is selfish? Being a parent raises other questions: What kind of person do I want my child to be or become? For example, do I want my child to be mean, cowardly, and dishonest? In answering such questions, we need to get clear on which traits are good and which are bad. A traditional term for good traits is *virtue* and for bad traits is *vice*. Part of our task as moral beings is to try to develop virtues within us and to avoid or extinguish vices. Put another way, one of our tasks as moral beings is to behave virtuously and refrain from behaving viciously. But which traits are virtues, and which are vices?

EXAMPLES OF VIRTUE AND VICE
FROM HISTORY AND LITERATURE

Both history and literature are filled with heroes (people of good character) and villains (people of bad character). In his books about Rome, the historian Livy

(59 B.C.E.–17 C.E.) retold traditional legends about many of the heroes of early Rome—among them, Horatius. Rome was threatened with invasion by an army of Etruscans. According to Livy, "the most vulnerable point was the wooden bridge [over the Tiber River], and the Etruscans would have crossed it and forced an entry into the city, had it not been for the courage of one man, Horatius Cocles."[1] Horatius was one of the guards at the bridge when the Etruscans attacked. His comrades panicked and began to flee. Horatius tried to encourage them to take a stand, but when that failed he told them that they had to destroy the bridge to prevent the Etruscans from crossing it to attack Rome. Because the Roman soldiers feared that the Etruscans would be upon them before they succeeded in destroying the bridge, Horatius told them that he would stand alone at the far end to delay the Etruscan advance until the bridge was destroyed. Two Roman soldiers, feeling ashamed of themselves, went with Horatius to confront the enemy. The three men fought to hold off the Etruscan forces while their comrades set about demolishing the bridge. After several minutes of fierce fighting and when the bridge was nearly demolished, Horatius commanded his two comrades to save themselves while he fought alone until demolition was complete. They retreated, and Horatius battled the entire Etruscan army single-handed on the remains of the bridge. The bridge finally collapsed, and Horatius dove into the water to try to swim to his comrades on the other bank of the Tiber, dodging the missiles that the frustrated Etruscans hurled at him. He made it safely to shore and was celebrated as a hero who saved Rome at the risk of his own life.

Horatius was celebrated in Roman history both for his skill as a fighter and for the important and admirable character traits of courage and patriotism shown by his actions. In the face of danger, he mastered the fear that sent his comrades running in panic; rather than run away, he stood his ground to fight, even though it seemed almost certain to lead to his death. The motivation for his heroism was patriotism or public-spiritedness rather than self-interest; his goal was to save his city from invasion even at the cost of his life. Clearly Livy admired Horatius for these character traits and for the behavior that manifested these traits. In his book, Livy was holding Horatius up as a model for others to admire and, more important, to emulate. In his view, behavior that is courageous and patriotic is morally good. Livy clearly considered courage and patriotism to be virtues that we should admire and cultivate.

Another hero in Livy was Cincinnatus. Once again Rome was threatened by enemies who had trapped a Roman army and were besieging it. At times of great peril, the Roman constitution permitted appointment of a temporary dictator with power that would last for six months. At the time, the great aristocrat Cincinnatus was living in retirement on his small three-acre farm outside Rome. The Senate decided to invest him with the dictatorship in order to save Rome. The representatives of the Senate found Cincinnatus doing farmwork and begged him to assume the dictatorship, which included absolute command over

---

[1]Livy, *The Early History of Rome,* trans. Aubrey De Selincourt (Harmondsworth, England: Penguin, 1960), p. 115.

all of Rome's armies. (The fact that Cincinnatus, a wealthy aristocrat, was doing the same kind of hard manual labor as common people showed his simplicity. He was not so arrogant and puffed up that he considered manual labor to be beneath his dignity.) Reluctantly, Cincinnatus agreed. He immediately traveled to Rome, where many of the common people feared what he would do with his absolute power if he succeeded in defeating the enemy armies. Cincinnatus succeeded in a lightning campaign that lasted only a few days. Immediately after his victory, Cincinnatus resigned the dictatorship and returned to his farm, having ruled only fifteen days of the six months he could have ruled.[2]

Cincinnatus was celebrated in Roman history not only for his courage and military prowess but for his patriotism, his humility, and his lack of greed for power and wealth. Cincinnatus could have lived in splendor, but he lived as a working farmer. He could have made himself even richer by taking a big share of the booty seized from the defeated enemy, but instead he gave all of it to his men. Similarly, he could have held onto his dictatoral power for the full six months and used it to accumulate more power and influence. Instead, he resigned and gave up his power and authority. He was more concerned about the well-being of Rome than about his own well-being. Livy held up Cincinnatus, like Horatius, as a model of good character. In Livy's view, a moderate or limited desire for wealth and power is a virtue, while an unlimited desire for wealth and power is a vice.

We don't have to limit ourselves to Rome, nor to wartime, to find examples of heroism in history. For example, we can turn to the civil rights movement in the United States in the 1960s. One heroine of that era is Anne Moody.

Anne Moody was a young African-American student at Tougaloo College in Jackson, Mississippi, in the early 1960s when she participated in a peaceful demonstration to end the legally enforced racial segregation of store lunch counters in Jackson. She and a few of her friends sat down at the lunch counter that was reserved for whites in a Woolworth's department store and refused to move when ordered by the waitresses to sit at the lunch counter designated for blacks. After being heckled and verbally harassed by many white employees and patrons, Anne Moody and her friends were physically assaulted.

> We bowed our heads and all hell broke loose. A man rushed forward, threw Memphis [one of her friends at the lunch counter] from his seat, and slapped my face. Then another man who worked in the store threw me against an adjoining counter. Down on my knees on the floor, I saw Memphis lying near the lunch counter with blood running out of the corners of his mouth. As he tried to protect his face, the man who'd thrown him down kept kicking him against the head.[3]

Anne and another friend, a white Tougaloo student named Joan Trumpauer, were physically dragged from the counter. Anne was pulled across the floor by her hair for about 30 feet before her attacker released her. Instead of leaving,

---

[2]Ibid., pp. 212–216.

[3]Anne Moody, *Coming of Age in Mississippi* (New York: Dell, 1968), pp. 265–266.

however, Anne Moody and her friend returned to sit at the lunch counter, knowing that the hostile crowd might harm or even kill them.

> The mob started smearing us with ketchup, mustard, sugar, pies, and everything on the counter. Soon Joan and I were joined by John Salter, but the moment he sat down he was hit on the jaw with what appeared to be brass knuckles. Blood gushed from his face and someone threw salt into the open wound. [4]

The demonstrators sat at the counter for about three hours, bravely accepting the physical and verbal abuse of the mob while numerous police officers outside the store did nothing to protect them. Finally, the manager closed the store and the demonstrators left, as the white mob outside hurled various objects at them, kept back only by a line of police. Anne Moody and people like her in the civil rights movement of the 1950s and 1960s nonviolently resisted racial segregation and the violation of the basic human rights of African-Americans, putting their lives on the line to work for justice.

Recent history also furnishes us with examples of some of the greatest villains the world has ever seen. Surely the most notorious man in history (so far) is Adolf Hitler. Hitler was a fanatical racist who orchestrated genocide. He was cruel, unscrupulous, dishonest, selfish, and manipulative. He unleashed the Holocaust that led to the systematic extermination of at least six million Jews. He started World War II, which led to almost unimaginable misery and death for tens of millions of soldiers and civilians caught up in a global war. Given his character and the consequences of the behavior that flowed from his character, he certainly deserves the epithet "moral monster."

We can also turn to literature to see myriad examples of virtue and vice. Consider Ebeneezer Scrooge in Dickens's *A Christmas Carol*. Prior to his conversion by the spirits of Christmas past, present, and future, Scrooge is a cold, unfeeling, selfish miser who has no friends. He is no moral monster on the scale of Hitler, but he is a less than admirable person. For example, when two businessmen ask him for a donation for a Christmas charity, Scrooge's reply is almost ferocious.

> "At this festive season of the year, Mr. Scrooge," said the gentleman, taking up a pen, "it is more than usually desirable that we should make some slight provision for the poor and destitute, who suffer greatly at the present time. Many thousands are in want of common necessaries; hundreds of thousands are in want of common comforts, sir."
>
> "Are there no prisons?" asked Scrooge.
>
> "Plenty of prisons," said the gentleman, laying down the pen again.
>
> "And the Union workhouses?"[5] demanded Scrooge. "Are they still in operation?"

---

[4]Ibid., p. 266.

[5]In Victorian Britain, more and more of the poor who depended on aid from the government were forced into workhouses, where conditions were abominable.

"They are. Still," returned the gentleman, "I wish I could say they were not."

"The Treadmill and the Poor Law are in full vigour, then?" said Scrooge.

"Both very busy, sir."

"Oh! I was afraid, from what you said at first, that something had occurred to stop them in their useful course," said Scrooge. "I'm very glad to hear it."

"Under the impression that they scarcely furnish Christian cheer of mind or body to the multitude," returned the gentleman, "a few of us are endeavouring to raise a fund to buy the Poor some meat and drink, and means of warmth. We choose this time because it is a time, of all others, when Want is keenly felt, and Abundance rejoices. What shall I put you down for?"

"Nothing!" Scrooge replied.

"You wish to be anonymous?"

"I wish to be left alone," said Scrooge. "Since you ask me what I wish, gentlemen, that is my answer. I don't make merry myself at Christmas, and I can't afford to make idle people merry. I help to support the establishments I have mentioned: they cost enough: and those who are badly off must go there."

"Many can't go there; and many would rather die."

"If they would rather die," said Scrooge, "they had better do it, and decrease the surplus population. Besides—excuse me—I don't know that."

"But you might know it," observed the gentleman.

"It's not my business," Scrooge returned. "It's enough for a man to understand his own business, and not to interfere with other people's. Mine occupies me constantly. Good afternoon, gentlemen!"[6]

Dickens holds up pre-conversion Scrooge as a model of bad character. He is selfish and greedy, and he lacks compassion and sympathy.

The great British novelist Jane Austen presents her readers with a number of interesting characters in her marvelous comic novel *Pride and Prejudice.* Elizabeth Bennet is witty, independent, and strong. The wealthy Mr. Darcy, unfortunately, is disagreeably proud and arrogant when he first makes his appearance, managing to alienate Elizabeth. However, Darcy's pride is as nothing compared to the arrogant pomposity of his aunt, Lady Catherine deBourgh. She puts down everything and everyone she sees as inferior to herself and what she owns. However, as Jane Austen shows, Lady Catherine deBourgh's pretensions are empty. She is an ignorant woman without manners, intellect, or talent. Elizabeth's mother is vain and foolish, a chronic whiner and complainer. Her father is irresponsible. Her cousin, the Reverend Mr. Collins, is an obsequious, scatterbrained, insincere flatterer who shamelessly promotes his patroness, Lady

---

[6]Charles Dickens, *A Christmas Carol* (New York: Bantam Books, 1966), pp. 10-11. (Originally published in 1843.)

Catherine deBourgh. For example, when Elizabeth's father asks him whether Lady Catherine's daughter, who is sickly and ill-tempered, has been presented at the king's court, Collins replies,

> "Her indifferent state of health unhappily prevents her being in town; and by that means, as I told Lady Catherine myself one day, has deprived the British court of its brightest ornament. Her Ladyship seemed pleased with the idea, and you may imagine that I am happy on every occasion to offer those little delicate compliments which are always acceptable to ladies. I have more than once observed to Lady Catherine, that her charming daughter seemed born to be a duchess, and that the most elevated rank, instead of giving her consequence, would be adorned by her. —These are the kind of little things which please Her Ladyship, and it is a sort of attention which I conceive myself peculiarly bound to pay."
>
> "You judge very properly," said Mr. Bennet, "and it is happy for you that you possess the talent of flattering with delicacy. May I ask whether these pleasing attentions proceed from the impulse of the moment, or are the result of previous study?"
>
> "They chiefly arise from what is passing at the time, and though I sometimes amuse myself with suggesting and arranging such little elegant compliments as may be adapted to ordinary occasions, I always wish to give them as unstudied an air as possible."[7]

Finally, there is Mr. Wickham, an unscrupulous, lying, selfish fortune hunter who fails to repay debts and who carelessly harms other people.

Austen, like Dickens, presents her readers with characters, some to admire, some to deplore. Both Austen and Dickens had serious purposes in mind. They were engaged, in part, in moral education, presenting their readers with models of conduct and character, some to avoid, some to emulate.

SKEPTICISM ABOUT MORAL VIRTUE AND VICE

When we call a trait a virtue or a vice, we do not always necessarily mean that it is a *moral* virtue or vice. Specialists in Greek often claim that in ancient Greek writings on ethics, such as those of Aristotle, the term *arete,* which some translate as "virtue," is more accurately translated as "excellence." A trait may be "excellent," or a virtue, only in a certain context or for a specific purpose. For example, for the purposes of gaining and retaining political power, Machiavelli argued that honesty, fairness, scrupulousness, and generosity are not virtues. Rather, traits such as ruthlessness and dishonesty help one gain and retain power and, therefore, are virtues for those purposes. A trait is a virtue for purpose X if possession of the trait helps its possessor do or gain X. Conversely, a trait is a vice for

---

[7]Jane Austen, *Pride and Prejudice* (London: Oxford University Press, 1965), pp. 67–68. (Originally published in 1813.)

purposes of X if possession of the trait hinders its possessor from doing or gaining X.

Thus, fearlessness is a virtue of a warrior; it helps its possessor win battles. Sympathy and compassion may be virtues of a therapist because they help the therapist succeed in helping clients with their problems. Ferocity may be a virtue of a street brawler because it helps him win fights. Dishonesty may be a virtue of a propagandist because it helps her persuade people.

Our concern here is with *moral* virtues and vices. A moral virtue is a trait that is good or admirable from a moral point of view; a moral vice is a trait that is bad from a moral point of view. Moral virtues are traits that, from a moral point of view, all people should have; moral vices are traits that, from a moral point of view, no people should have. If a trait is a moral virtue, then there are good moral reasons why people who don't have the trait should try to acquire it, and those who do have the trait should try to retain and cultivate it and, most important, act on it. Conversely, if a trait is a moral vice, then there are good moral reasons why people who have it should try to extinguish it and resist acting on it, and those who don't have it should try to avoid acquiring it.

As we have seen, there are two families of moral theories, Moral Objectivism and Moral Nonobjectivism. Moral Nonobjectivism includes Nihilism, Subjectivism, and Relativism. How do these theories view the concepts of moral virtue and vice?

Moral Nihilism: No character trait is morally good or bad, a moral virtue or a moral vice.

Moral Subjectivism: Whatever an individual believes to be a morally good (or bad) character trait is morally good (or bad) for that individual. No trait is objectively a moral virtue or a moral vice; it is only a moral virtue (vice) according to some individual. An individual's belief that a trait is a moral virtue (vice) is no more true, correct, or reasonable than another individual's belief that it is not a moral virtue (vice).

Moral Relativism: Whatever a society believes to be a morally good (or bad) character trait is morally good (or bad) for that society. No trait is objectively a moral virtue or a moral vice; it is only a moral virtue (vice) according to some society. A society's belief that a trait is a moral virtue (vice) is no more true, correct, or reasonable than another society's belief that it is not a moral virtue (vice).

Moral Objectivism: Some character traits truly are moral virtues, and others truly are moral vices.

Thus, according to Moral Nihilism, traits such as selfishness, cruelty, intolerance, and dishonesty are neither morally good nor morally bad, neither moral virtues nor moral vices. On the other hand, according to Moral Subjectivism, if someone believes that the traits of selfishness, greed, cruelty, dishonesty, and ingratitude are all moral virtues, then his view is no less true, correct, or reasonable than the views of someone who believes that these traits are moral vices. Finally, according to Moral Relativism, if a society believes that the traits of intolerance, cruelty, and mercilessness are all moral virtues, then their view is no less true, correct, or reasonable than the views of another society that believes that these traits are moral vices.

In contrast, according to Moral Objectivism, some character traits truly are moral virtues while others truly are moral vices. On this view, if kindness is a moral virtue, then those who believe that kindness is a moral virtue have a true moral belief, whereas those who believe that it is not a moral virtue have a false moral belief. Similarly, if kindness is a moral virtue, then people should behave kindly and should be, or try to be, kind.

We will not examine the case for the various nonobjectivist views about moral virtue and vice. What we said in Chapter 3 about Moral Nonobjectivism (Nihilism, Subjectivism, and Relativism) applies equally to claims about moral virtue and vice. Instead, we will examine some common objectivist views about moral virtue and vice.

COMMONSENSE MORALITY: MORAL VIRTUES AND VICES

Commonsense morality is objectivist about moral virtue and vice. According to the morality that most people accept and try to live by, some character traits really are moral virtues and others really are moral vices. Consider the character traits included in the following list.

CHARACTER TRAITS

Arrogance	Fanaticism	Integrity	Patriotism
Boastfulness	Generosity	Intolerance	Politeness
Callousness	Gratitude	Irascibility	Prejudice
Chastity	Greed	Jealousy	Pride
Compassion	Honesty	Justice	Prudence
Conscientiousness	Humility	Kindness	Reliability
Courage	Ignorance	Laziness	Responsibility
Cowardice	Immodesty	Loyalty	Rudeness
Cruelty	Impatience	Manipulativeness	Self-control
Dishonesty	Imprudence	Meanness	Self-deception
Disloyalty	Independence	Mercilessness	Self-indulgence
Envy	Industriousness	Modesty	Self-reliance
Faithfulness	Ingratitude	Openmindedness	Self-respect
Faithlessness	Insincerity	Patience	Self-sufficiency

Selfishness	Strength	Tolerance	Unscrupulousness
Servility	Tactfulness	Trustworthiness	Unselfishness
Shamelessness	Tactlessness	Unreliability	Weakness
Sincerity			

I suspect that most people would agree with the following division into moral virtues and vices.

MORAL VIRTUES

Compassion	Integrity	Patriotism	Sincerity
Courage	Justice	Politeness	Strength
Faithfulness	Kindness	Prudence	Tactfulness
Generosity	Loyalty	Reliability	Tolerance
Gratitude	Mercifulness	Responsibility	Trustworthiness
Honesty	Modesty	Self-control	Unselfishness
Humility	Openmindedness	Self-reliance	
Independence	Patience	Self-respect	

MORAL VICES

Arrogance	Greed	Jealousy	Shamelessness
Callousness	Ignorance	Laziness	Tactlessness
Cowardice	Impatience	Manipulativeness	Unreliability
Cruelty	Imprudence	Mercilessness	Unscrupulousness
Dishonesty	Ingratitude	Prejudice	Untrustworthiness
Disloyalty	Insincerity	Promiscuity	Weakness
Envy	Intolerance	Rudeness	
Faithlessness	Irascibility	Selfishness	
Fanaticism	Irresponsibility	Servility	

Of course, not everyone would agree with this division of traits. For example, in the movie *Wall Street,* the character played by Michael Douglas preaches that "greed is good." He justifies this claim by appealing to the supposedly good effects of greed under capitalism. Similarly, the Nazis in Germany preached that cruelty and mercilessness are good because they show strength and determination, whereas compassion, kindness, and mercy are bad because they show weakness. But it is clear that people who take such positions recognize that their views are in opposition to traditional commonsense morality and turn it on its head.

It is one thing to construct a list of moral virtues and vices; it is another to provide principles that explain why one trait is a moral virtue and another a moral vice and that enable one to determine whether a trait should be considered a virtue or a vice. Our concern is with principles providing guidance on whether and why a trait is a virtue or a vice.

THEORIES OF MORAL VIRTUE AND VICE

Philosophers have suggested several competing theories of moral virtue and vice. One set of theories focuses on the consequences of a particular character trait—specifically, its relation to benefit and harm.

1. A character trait is a moral virtue if and only if it is beneficial to its possessor. A trait is a moral vice if and only if it is harmful to its possessor.
2. A character trait is a moral virtue if and only if it is beneficial to others. A trait is a moral vice if and only if it is harmful to others.
3. A character trait is a moral virtue if and only if it is beneficial to its possessor and to others. A trait is a moral vice if and only if it is harmful to its possessor and to others.

Another theory of moral virtue and vice focuses on moral rules or principles.

4. A character trait is a moral virtue if and only if the behavior definitive of the trait is required by a correct moral rule or principle. A trait is a moral vice if and only if the behavior definitive of the trait is prohibited by a correct moral rule or principle.

We will focus first on those theories that emphasize consequences: benefit and harm. One of the earliest and most influential of these theories is that of the Greek philosopher Aristotle (384–322 B.C.E.).

ARISTOTLE ON VIRTUE AND VICE

One question of concern to Aristotle is, What character traits are good for a human being to have? He is concerned not only with traits that are good from a moral point of view but also with traits that are good from a nonmoral point of view. In fact, his inquiry proceeds largely from a self-interested point of view. He theorizes primarily about traits that contribute to the well-being of their possessor. In his view, a virtue (many translators prefer the term *excellence*) is a character trait that is beneficial to its possessor. A virtue helps its possessor achieve happiness or a state of well-being; it helps its possessor "flourish."

Because Aristotle's concerns go well beyond the relatively narrow issue of *moral* virtues and vices (in fact, it is not clear that Aristotle recognized a distinction between the moral and the nonmoral), his work does not fit entirely comfortably with the prevailing focus of much modern moral philosophy. Moral philosophy in the West has been greatly influenced by Christianity, which emphasizes that the moral point of view is not a purely self-interested point of view and often is in conflict with self-interest. However, in the past twenty or thirty years some philosophers have returned to Aristotelian themes.

Happiness, Well-Being, Flourishing

Aristotle begins with the assumption that all people want to be happy, to maximize their own well-being, and to "flourish." To flourish is, at least in part, to live a life that enables you to meet your needs and satisfy at least some of your desires. Most important, however, flourishing involves actualizing your potential and making some use of your talents and abilities.

Aristotle knew that sometimes people seek happiness but fail to find it; that people want to live lives that maximize their well-being but instead sometimes live lives that keep their well-being at unacceptably low levels; that people want to flourish but sometimes fail to. He believed that we can acquire knowledge about the conditions under which human beings are most likely to be happy, have maximum well-being, or flourish. (From now on, I will use only the term *flourish* for economy. But please keep in mind that the term *flourish* is connected to happiness and well-being.) In his view, if we can discover what conditions enable human beings to flourish, then we can use that knowledge to guide us in our decisions about how to live so that we will flourish. He also believed that having certain character traits makes it more likely that one will flourish, whereas having other character traits makes it less likely that one will flourish. Traits that contribute to their possessor's flourishing are virtues; traits that detract from their possessor's flourishing are vices.

Knowing which traits are virtues and which are vices is important. Assuming that I have some control over my character, if I take steps to acquire virtues I don't have, nourish the virtues I do have, avoid acquiring vices I don't have, and extinguish vices I do have, I will have a better life. I will maximize my chances of flourishing, at least when it comes to those things within myself over which I have some control. (Aristotle concedes that conditions and events in the world over which I may have little or no control also affect whether I will flourish.) Knowledge of the conditions under which we are most likely to flourish and of the character traits that are most and least likely to promote flourishing can provide us with at least the outline of a blueprint or recipe for living well.

Aristotle thought that we can discover such a blueprint or recipe that would apply to all human beings. Today most people are suspicious of the idea of a one-size-fits-all blueprint or recipe for living. After all, it's obvious that different things make different people happy. People have vastly different likes and dislikes, preferences, desires, and interests. Reading philosophy may make me happy but another person very unhappy. Some people love playing golf; others loathe it; some love watching sports on television, others hate it; some crave the excitement of risky activities, others would do anything to avoid them. At a further extreme, some people may want to live their lives in an alcoholic stupor or drug-induced haze while others consider such a life an abomination. Therefore, many people are convinced that the conditions conducive to flourishing differ for different people and that the quest for a general account of what will enable every human being to flourish is doomed because there are no such conditions.

The One Way of Life Suitable for Human Beings

Aristotle was impressed by the fact that individual organisms are members of species. In general, the conditions that enable one member of a species to flourish enable each member of that species to flourish, and vice versa. If one member of a species of cactus cannot flourish in an environment that is cold and wet, then no member of the species can flourish there. Conversely, if one member of that species of cactus can flourish in an environment that is hot and dry, then every member can. Thus, the conditions that enable a single cactus plant to flourish apply to all members of the same species. Similar generalizations apply to other species. We can make generalizations about the conditions under which a rose bush, fungus, mosquito, shark, deer, penguin, or dog will survive and flourish. Those conditions apply to each member of the species. Whales and swordfish must live in water; they cannot live on land. Lions and cows must live on land; they cannot live in the water. Whales, unlike swordfish, must periodically come to the surface and breathe air. Lions, unlike cows, must hunt and eat meat; they cannot live on plants.

Aristotle was aware of the fact that all human beings are members of the same species. Therefore, what applies to cactus, whales, and lions should also apply to human beings. The conditions required for one human being to survive and flourish should also be required for all other human beings to survive and flourish. Recall from the previous chapter Aristotle's concepts of nutritive (plant), sensitive (animal), and rational (human) souls, and that each level includes all the capacities of the levels below it. Aristotle's theory of human nature—that only human beings have rational souls—shaped his views about what is required for humans to flourish.

Aristotle assumed that any creature with a rational soul requires certain conditions to survive and flourish. Under those conditions, such a creature has a high probability of surviving and flourishing; without those conditions, such a creature has a very low probability, perhaps no chance, of surviving and flourishing. Since each human being is a creature (a living physical organism) with a rational soul, these conditions apply to each human being. At the level of basic life processes, it is obvious that every human being requires food, clean air, clean water, clothing, and shelter to survive. Survival is necessary although not sufficient for flourishing. Equally obviously, since human beings are capable of perception, sensation, and self-initiated and self-directed movement, we need to be as free as possible of unpleasant and debilitating sensations such as pain, to have minimal interference with our perceiving the world, and to have at least some minimal opportunity to engage in self-initiated and self-directed movement. The probability that a human being will flourish is clearly reduced if she is in constant intense pain, has lost one or more of her senses,[8] or has little opportunity for self-initiated and self-directed movement (because of imprisonment or paralysis). Optimizing these conditions contributes to human flourishing.

Aristotle also emphasized that human beings are social animals. We are more likely to flourish if we live in groups than if we try to live entirely alone. We are better able to satisfy our basic needs for food, shelter, clothing, and so on by cooperating with others than we are if we try to satisfy them entirely by our own unaided efforts. With cooperation, a farmer who grows food can depend on others to provide the tools he uses, the clothing he wears, the house he lives in, the book he reads, or the television he watches during his leisure time, the dishes and pots he uses for cooking and eating, and the soap he uses to wash his dishes and clothes. If he tries to furnish everything he needs entirely by his own unaided efforts, his life will be radically impoverished, like that of someone cast naked on an uninhabited desert island or planet with no human-created resources.

In addition to needing other people to help us satisfy our basic physical needs, all human beings also seem to need other people to satisfy certain psychological needs. How many of us believe that someone marooned for a long time, perhaps forever, on an island or planet that has no other people on it could be happy and flourish? Surely she would soon crave contact with others. Human beings need what we can vaguely call "affiliation" with others. We need to love and be loved, to have friends and acquaintances whom we care about and respect and who in turn care about and respect us. We need to engage in a variety of activities with other people, whether work or play. Indeed, one of the most severe forms of punishment is "solitary confinement." People who undergo long periods of solitary confinement have difficulty remaining sane. Surely that shows that we need other people in order to flourish. Similarly, how many of us believe that Ebeneezer Scrooge prior to his conversion—when he had no friends or loved ones, when he was isolated from others, spending all of his time outside work alone—was really happy, was really flourishing? Probably not many.

So far, nothing I've said is likely to be controversial. In order for a human being, any human being, to flourish, she needs life's basic physical necessities, room and opportunity to exercise her functions of perception and self-movement, freedom from pain, and relationships with other people. More controversially, Aristotle claimed that the highest kind of life of which human beings are capable is one of contemplation—one that makes maximum use of the human capacity for reason or rationality. A life of contemplation would be what is sometimes called the life of the mind, spending as much of one's time as possible studying and learning. Aristotle believed that human beings, having a rational

---

[8]People who have lost one or more of their senses, such as someone who is blind or deaf, obviously can live deeply satisfying and constructive lives despite their loss. However, I assume that everyone would agree that if someone has lost one or more of her five senses, she has lost something that is valuable.

soul, have an innate desire or need to acquire knowledge and understanding. Living a life devoted to contemplation, one would presumably spend a minimal amount of time playing games or sports, watching television, partying, or having sex. But Aristotle, who did not believe that all human beings are equal, did not believe that all human beings are capable of a life of contemplation. Such a way of life, he thought, although superior to all others, is suitable only for the intellectually superior. Others must be content with lives that are less satisfying, even if they do not know that their lives are less satisfying.

Most people today reject Aristotle's view that a life devoted to contemplation is the best way of life for a human being. However, in the spirit of Aristotle we might make more modest claims that are more plausible. Given that we have rational souls, Aristotle believed that reason should play some role in our lives. We should not live like cows who lack a rational soul. One way to moderate Aristotle's extreme view that the best life for a human being is devoted almost exclusively to contemplation is to say instead that a life appropriate for a human being should at least *include* the activity of contemplation—studying in order to learn and understand. Without study, we are mired in ignorance and error. Thus, flourishing requires some attention to contemplation, some level of education, some form of lifelong learning.

Also, because we have rational souls, not merely nutritive or sensitive souls, we should behave in a way that is not contrary to reason. Aristotle says that the best way of life for a human being involves "an activity of soul in accordance with, or not without, rational principle."[9] Unfortunately, it is not exactly clear how to distinguish with any precision between forms of behavior that are contrary to reason (without rational principle) and those that are not. However, the quoted phrase does emphasize one element of Aristotle's thought that Aristotle himself sometimes emphasized and sometimes ignored or contradicted: Flourishing requires activity. One cannot flourish if one is completely immobilized—for example, chained to a wall or locked in a closet. We need to be physically active as well as intellectually active in order to flourish.

Although this characterization does not provide anything like a detailed recipe for a life that will enable a human being to flourish, it does provide an outline of some of the basic ingredients. But as we have noted previously, Aristotle also emphasized that certain character traits contribute to their possessor's flourishing, whereas other traits do not. Those character traits are the virtues and vices.

Traits That Promote Their Possessor's Flourishing

Aristotle identifies several character traits as virtues: courage, temperance, liberality (generosity), proper pride, good temper, ready wit, modesty, and justice. Aristotle does not claim that these are the only virtues, only that they are some

---

[9]Aristotle, *Nicomachean Ethics,* in *The Complete Works of Aristotle,* vol. 2, ed. Jonathan Barnes (Princeton, NJ: Princeton University Press, 1984), p. 1735 (1098a 7–8).

of the virtues. In any case, they are virtues because they contribute to their possessor's flourishing.[10] To understand this relationship, we must examine more closely Aristotle's ideas about the nature of virtues and vices.

According to Aristotle, a virtue or vice is not only a relatively stable and permanent tendency (or disposition) to act in certain ways under certain circumstances, it is also a tendency to have certain feelings and desires in certain circumstances. Let's look at courage. Courage involves how one responds to threatening and dangerous situations. It is fairly natural to feel fear in such situations, and when we feel fear we are often tempted to run away or back down. For example, in Stephen Crane's *The Red Badge of Courage,* a young soldier feels intense fear in his first battle during the Civil War and rather than standing to fight, he runs away. Afterwards, he feels ashamed and guilty because he considers his behavior a disgraceful act of cowardice. We might say that his cowardice first manifested itself in what he felt: He felt too much fear. It was so intense that it overpowered him and made him run away. A more courageous person would not have felt such intense, debilitating fear. Second, his cowardice manifested itself in his actions. Because his feelings of fear were so intense, he ran away rather than standing his ground and fighting with his fellow soldiers. Courage, then, involves both what we feel and how we act. A courageous person does not feel more fear than the circumstances warrant, and does not act inappropriately because of his fear. It is inappropriate for a soldier to run away from battle when not ordered to retreat.

Similarly, Aristotle claimed that having a virtue involves having certain attitudes and desires. A person who truly has the trait of courage wants to behave courageously and "delights" in courageous actions. Someone who feels fear that is inappropriately intense (such as terror at the sight of a mouse) who nevertheless stands his ground, but who hates every second of it, does not really have courage.

Similar things may be said about the virtue of temperance. A temperate person does not overindulge in physical pleasures; for example, she generally does not overeat or drink to excess. But temperance involves more than behavior. A temperate person's desires for physical pleasure are moderate. If you resist the temptation to overindulge in physical pleasures, but resent it because the desire and temptation are so strong, then you are not really temperate. Thus, Aristotle said,

> the man who abstains from bodily pleasures *and delights in this very fact* is temperate, while the man who is annoyed at it is self-indulgent, and he who stands his ground against things that are terrible *and delights in this* or at least is not pained is brave, while the man who is pained is a coward [my emphasis]. For moral excellence is concerned with pleasures and pains.[11]

---

[10]One possible criticism of Aristotle is that the traits he identifies as virtues help their possessors flourish *in fourth century B.C.E. Athenian society.*

[11]Ibid., p. 1744 (1104b 5–10).

We tend to think that virtues and vices come in pairs. For example, courage is paired with cowardice, temperance with self-indulgence, honesty with dishonesty, and so on. However, Aristotle maintained that when thinking of traits as virtues and vices, we must think of triples. Every virtue is a mean between two vices.

Virtue as a Mean between Two Extremes

Suppose that while walking in the woods John encounters a large Kodiak bear. Feeling no fear although he is wholly unarmed, he walks up to it and offers to shake its hand. The bear declines, whereupon John punches it in the nose. John is never heard from again. Did John display courage? Aristotle would say that of course he did not. John was foolhardy. He should have felt fear when he saw the Kodiak bear because fear is entirely appropriate in such circumstances, whereas a total lack of fear is inappropriate. And acting on that fear by carefully retreating is also appropriate.

Aristotle emphasized that one can feel more fear than the circumstances warrant but one can also feel less fear than the circumstances warrant. Being courageous does not mean that one feels no fear, but that one feels the amount of fear that is warranted under the circumstances. It is not courageous to feel abject terror at the sight of a mouse, because the threat posed by a mouse does not justify intense fear or terror. But it is also not courageous to feel no fear when suddenly encountering a highly dangerous animal such as a bear or lion, because fear under such circumstances is appropriate. The capacity to feel fear has survival value.

Courage is a virtue because it helps its possessor survive and flourish. It is a mean between foolhardiness, a tendency to feel too little fear, and cowardice, a tendency to feel too much fear. Someone who is foolhardy—who feels less fear than is appropriate—will probably shorten his life by recklessly engaging in dangerous activities. On the other hand, someone who is cowardly—who feels more fear than is appropriate—will probably live a life of frustration. He will probably fail to satisfy many of his desires and to achieve many of his goals because he will often retreat out of fear. He may fail to have dates because he won't ask someone out for fear of rejection. He may fail to get promotions because he won't take risks on the job for fear of failure. He may sit by silently while injustice is done because he is afraid to speak out and face disapproval or retaliation.

To distinguish courage from cowardice, on the one hand, and foolhardiness, on the other, requires judgment. Courage is a mean between the two vices, but it is not a mean that we can locate by some mechanical procedure. It is sometimes difficult to decide what is the courageous thing to do. Suppose that someone challenges you to a fistfight. Is it courageous to accept and fight and cowardly to decline, or vice versa? If an employee knows that her employer has engaged in illegal conduct, is it courageous or foolhardy to blow the whistle? If you see someone cheating on an examination, is it courageous or cowardly to turn him in to the instructor? Even if we know in the abstract which traits are

virtues and which are vices, we still face the task in concrete situations of deciding what virtue is called for and what the particular virtue called for requires in
that set of circumstances.

Temperance is also a mean between two extremes, according to Aristotle.
We can want too much physical pleasure, but we can also want too little physical pleasure. The person who wants too much physical pleasure and therefore
overindulges lacks self-control. He will probably eat and drink too much, eat and
drink things that taste good but are unhealthy, become promiscuous or engage
in unsafe sex, and become addicted to alcohol, cigarettes, or drugs. His behavior
will adversely affect his health and will probably shorten his life. On the other
hand, a person who denies himself all physical pleasures will deny himself often
harmless experiences and activities that would make his life more pleasant and
rich. Imagine someone who never allowed himself to have sex, good-tasting food
and drink, a hot bath or sauna, and other harmless physical pleasures. Aristotle
finds nothing admirable in such behavior because there is no good reason to
deny oneself all physical pleasures. The virtue of temperance involves a mean
between overindulgence and underindulgence in physical pleasures. When physical pleasures become unhealthy or addictive, they should not be pursued. But if
they are not unhealthy, addictive, or otherwise harmful, they may be pursued.
Again, it takes judgment to know where the mean between overindulgence and
underindulgence lies.

Aristotle generalizes this insight, noting that with respect to most things that
may be good for us,

> it is the nature of such things to be destroyed by defect and excess, as in the
> case of strength and health . . . ; both excessive and defective [deficient] exer-
> cise destroys the strength, and similarly drink or food which is above or below
> a certain amount destroys the health, while that which is proportionate both
> produces and increases and preserves it.[12]

Both too much and too little exercise, as well as too much or too little food, can
be harmful rather than beneficial. Balance is required. But Aristotle emphasizes
that the proper mean will not be the same for everyone. Too little food for a 300-
pound football player might well be too much food for someone who is 175
pounds and sedentary. Each person has to find the mean that is appropriate for
her situation and circumstances; there is no one-size-fits-all recipe for identifying
the proper mean.

Another trait that Aristotle identifies as a virtue is proper pride. One can
think too well of oneself, which will probably lead to arrogance and boastful-
ness, but one can also think too little of oneself, which will probably lead to servility and obsequiousness. If we are to flourish, we must think well enough of
ourselves that we consider ourselves and our projects to have worth or value.
Without self-respect or self-esteem, we will probably permit others to walk all
over us and will sabotage ourselves. On the other hand, we must not think so

---

[12]Ibid., p. 1744 (1104a 11–17).

well of ourselves that we get delusions of perfection or infallibility. Thinking too well of ourselves makes us act superior to others. Such behavior may make us look ridiculous to others if we have no grounds for considering ourselves superior, or it may antagonize others, who will find ways of putting us in our place. Proper pride is a mean between having too lofty a view of ourselves and having too low a view of ourselves.

Good temper is also a mean between extremes. We may be too quick to anger, making us irascible. Being irascible is not likely to make us lots of friends, and Aristotle emphasizes how important friends are to flourishing. But we may also be too slow to anger, to have what we might call righteous indignation. A person who never feels and acts upon anger, indignation, or outrage is not likely to stand up for herself or others. She will tend to let others walk all over her and is unlikely to protest at the mistreatment of others.

Another aspect of good temper involves one's expression of anger. A person of good temper will feel the degree or intensity of anger appropriate to the circumstances and will express her anger appropriately. She will not become enraged at a small slight or only mildly irritated at a significant provocation. She also will not act out her anger by swearing, shouting, insulting people, throwing objects, and so on. She will deal appropriately with her anger—for example, by saying she is angry and walking away until she has calmed down. Too much anger can lead to self-destructive or destructive behavior that alienates or harms others. Too little anger can lead to self-abasement.

Aristotle also considers liberality or generosity a virtue. It helps one flourish (in Athenian society) because it enhances one's reputation and standing within the community. It brings respect. Others admire and respect those who are generous with their money while deploring those who are selfish. If one gives too little to others, one will be considered miserly. However, if one gives too much, one will go broke. Therefore, in order to flourish, we need to ensure that we neither give too much nor give too little.

Justice and Moral Virtue

According to Aristotle, virtues are beneficial to their possessor because they help their possessor flourish; vices are harmful to their possessor because they interfere with their possessor's flourishing. Aristotle also emphasized that many virtues (we should hesitate to say all, even if Aristotle would) represent a mean between two extremes, where the extremes—an excess or a deficiency of something—are the vices. Each trait that is a virtue or vice is a tendency or disposition to behave and feel in certain characteristic ways under certain characteristic circumstances. Thus, if we know what traits are beneficial and help their possessor flourish, we know what traits are virtues.

But modern moral philosophy is based on the assumption that the moral point of view is not a purely self-interested point of view. According to most modern philosophers, the moral point of view is impartial (although most agree that there are limits to the impartiality demanded by morality.) A person is not judging character traits from a moral point of view if he only considers their effect on his own well-being. Traits that benefit only their possessor may be valuable and morally acceptable, but how our behavior affects others is surely relevant from a moral point of view. Therefore, many people would maintain that a trait can be a *moral* virtue only if it benefits others. Of course, it need not be harmful to its possessor. A trait can be beneficial both to its possessor and to others.

Consistent with this view, Aristotle maintained that justice is also a virtue and admitted that unlike the other traits he identified as virtues, justice is beneficial fundamentally to others. The trait of justice involves treating people who are equal in the same way and giving people what they are due or what they deserve. One is unjust if one treats equals unequally or unequals equally and if one does not give people what they deserve. (Justice also does not seem to fit well with Aristotle's contention that virtues are a mean between two extremes.) If you steal from people, you are behaving unjustly because you are not giving people what they deserve. If you discriminate against people on the basis of irrelevant characteristics—for example, by refusing to hire a black applicant simply because she is black—you are behaving unjustly. Obviously, if someone has the character trait of being just, it benefits others because the just person will not oppress or exploit others or otherwise unjustifiably harm them.

Justice benefits others. Does it also benefit its possessor, or does it harm its possessor? Does justice contribute to or detract from the just person's flourishing? We are all familiar with the cynical slogans "Nice guys finish last" and "No good deed goes unpunished." Sometimes it seems that injustice pays better than justice, that vice pays better than virtue. Those who rise to the top in business and politics often seem to be ruthless and unscrupulous.

However, even if it is true that wealth, power, and fame come more readily to the unjust than to the just (which is debatable), Aristotle did not think that wealth, power, and fame are the only or even the most important ingredients of flourishing or well-being. Honor or good reputation is also important—the respect or even admiration of others. Someone who is unjust is less likely to earn the respect of others. Love and friendship are also important ingredients of flourishing. Just people are more likely than the unjust to have love and friendship. Also, because human beings are social animals, we depend on others; we cannot flourish outside a society or community. Injustice injures the community, whereas justice strengthens it. If most people behaved unjustly to each other, they could not live together in peace and harmony, and they could not maintain a community. Those who injure their community ultimately injure themselves. Therefore, we should conclude that the trait of justice benefits its possessor as well as others.

What has been said of justice can probably be said of other traits that commonsense morality identifies as moral virtues. Even though Aristotle did not discuss such traits as honesty, kindness, loyalty, and politeness, it is not too hard to see that they usually benefit others but also that they usually benefit their possessors. On the other hand, moral vices are those traits that usually cause their possessor to harm others. Dishonestly, cruelty, disloyalty, and rudeness usually bring harm to others; however, they often also bring harm to the person who behaves in those ways.

The Mean, Again

Can one be too kind as well as not kind enough? Too honest as well as not honest enough? It is fruitful to look at many of the traits that commonsense morality identifies as virtues, even those traits that Aristotle did not discuss, in terms of a mean between two extremes. Take honesty—a tendency or disposition to say to others what one believes to be true. Obviously, one defect is lying—saying to others what one believes to be false with the intention of misleading them. If someone asks you for directions and you intentionally give them the wrong directions, you're not being honest and you are harming them. However, does honesty demand that you tell everyone what you think even if they have not asked for your views? If you hate someone's hairstyle or clothes, and you know that she is insecure and lacks self-esteem, should you tell her unasked in order to ensure that you are honest? Suppose she asks you what you think of her new hairstyle, and you think it makes her look ugly. Should you say "I think it makes you look ugly"? Here we might say that behavior characteristic of one virtue conflicts with behavior characteristic of other virtues. It would not be kind to say "I think it makes you look ugly," even though it might be honest. It would be kinder to use softer language—for example, to say "I liked your hair better in the old style."

In some cases, should we actually lie? Suppose that in Nazi Germany, Martin is hiding a Jewish family in the attic of the apartment building he owns. If they are found, they will be sent to a concentration camp and murdered. Martin will probably be sent to prison for aiding them. One day a Gestapo officer asks Martin if there are any Jews hiding in his building. He cannot avoid answering the question. Martin is an honest person. Should he tell the truth and say "yes," or may he lie and say "no"? Surely almost all of us would say that if Martin tells the truth to the Gestapo officer, he is being much too honest. He should lie. Telling the truth under these circumstances would be cruel and disloyal to the Jewish family. It would contribute to the injustice of organized murder. We might say that Martin does not *owe* it to the Gestapo officer to be truthful. Now one dishonest act, which is the only appropriate behavior in the circumstances, would not make Martin a dishonest man. In order to have the trait of honesty, it is not necessary that one *always* say what one believes to be the truth.

Thus, in terms of truth-telling, honesty as a virtue should be seen as a mean between two vices: too much truth-telling and too little truth-telling. Locating the appropriate mean requires judgment. The same may be said of many other virtues and vices.

Virtues and Vices as Guides to Action

For Aristotle, knowledge of which traits are virtues and which are vices provides guidance. First, it provides us with guidance on what kind of person to be. We should try to cultivate and nurture within ourselves the virtues and extinguish the vices. It also provides us with guidance on how to act. In any situation, we should try to act as a virtuous person would act. Knowing about the virtues, we will know what virtue is called for in any given situation. If we know what virtue is called for, we should try to behave the way someone with that virtue would behave. For example, if I'm in a burning building, I will know that courage is called for and I should try to behave the way a courageous person would behave. On the other hand, I know that loyalty is called for in friendship. Therefore, I should try to behave toward friends the way a loyal person would behave. Knowing about loyalty, I know that a loyal person would not betray the confidences of a friend behind his back. Such behavior would be disloyalty. Therefore, because I should not act disloyally, I should not betray a friend's confidences.

HOBBES AND HUME

The English philosopher Thomas Hobbes (1588–1679) maintained that virtues are those characteristics that enable people to live together in peace and harmony. He claimed that virtues such as gratitude, modesty, equity, and mercy "come to be praised, as the means of peaceable, sociable, and comfortable living."[13] For most virtues there are corresponding vices. For example, justice, the characteristic of keeping our agreements, is a virtue and its opposite a vice; pride is a vice and its opposite, humility, is a virtue. However, the basis of Hobbes's theory is self-interest. Characteristics that are virtues promote social harmony, but in the long run it is in an individual's self-interest to have such characteristics. Virtues are beneficial both to others and to their possessors, and they are beneficial to their possessors because they are beneficial to others. Virtues enable an individual to live well and be happy in society; vices prevent a person from living well and being happy in society.

The Scottish philosopher David Hume (1711–1776) also claimed that at least some traits are considered virtues because they're beneficial to their possessor and other traits are considered vices because they're harmful to their possessor.

> It seems evident, that where a quality or habit [character trait] is subjected to our examination, if it appear in any respect prejudicial to the person possessed of it, or such as incapacitates him for business and action, it is instantly blamed, and ranked among his faults and imperfections. Indolence, negligence, want of order and method, obstinacy, fickleness, rashness, credulity; these qualities were never esteemed by any one indifferent to a character, much, less, extolled as accomplishments or virtues.[14]

---

[13]Thomas Hobbes, *Leviathan* (New York: Collier, 1962), chap. 15, p. 124.

[14]David Hume, *An Enquiry Concerning the Principles of Morals* (LaSalle, IL: Open Court, 1960), p. 68 (Section VI, Part I). (Originally published in 1777.)

Among virtues he listed discretion, caution, frugality, good sense, honesty, fidelity, enterprise, industry, prudence, temperance, sobriety, patience, constancy, perseverance, forethought, considerateness, cheerfulness, and philosophical tranquillity.

However, Hume noted that people approve of and consider to be virtues those traits that are beneficial to their possessor even when it's other people who have the traits. In such circumstances the trait may not be beneficial to the person who judges it to be a virtue. Thus, if Jones considers perseverance (the tendency to persist in undertakings despite setbacks) to be a virtue, then if Smith has the trait, Jones will consider Smith's perseverance to be a virtue, even though Jones doesn't benefit from Smith's perseverance. In fact, Jones may benefit from no one's perseverance but his own. If Jones considers perseverance to be a virtue, it's a virtue regardless of whose perseverance it is; therefore, his reason for considering perseverance a virtue is not simply that perseverance is in his self-interest. If self-interest were the only reason for considering a trait to be a virtue, Jones would consider his own perseverance to be a virtue but would not consider perseverance in general to be a virtue. As Hume declared, "Now as these advantages are enjoyed by the person possessed of the character, it can never be self-love which renders the prospect of them agreeable to us, the spectators, and prompts our esteem and approbation."[15]

Like Hobbes, Hume also noted that many traits are considered virtues because they are beneficial to others and promote social harmony. "Whatever conduct promotes the good of the community is loved, praised, and esteemed by the community."[16] Similarly,

> As the mutual shocks, in *society*, and the opposition of interest and self-love
> have constrained mankind to establish the laws of *justice,* in order to preserve
> the advantages of mutual assistance and protection: in like manner, the eternal
> contrarieties, in *company,* of men's pride and self-conceit, have introduced the
> rules of Good Manners or Politeness, in order to facilitate the intercourse of
> minds, and an undisturbed commerce and conversation.[17]

Hume maintained that all human beings have at least some benevolence toward their fellows. Without that sympathy, the view that some traits, whoever has them, are virtues and other traits, whoever has them, are vices could not get off the ground.

> Let us suppose a person originally framed so as to have no manner of concern
> for his fellow-creatures, but to regard the happiness and misery of all sensible
> beings with greater indifference than even two contiguous shades of the same
> colour. . . . Such a person, being absolutely unconcerned, either for the public
> good of a community or the private utility of others, would look on every
> quality [character trait] however pernicious, or however beneficial, to society,
> or to its possessor, with . . . indifference.[18]

---

[15]Ibid., p. 69.

[16]Ibid., p. 79.

[17]Ibid., p. 98 (Section VIII).

[18]Ibid., p. 70.

Given that we do distinguish between virtues and vices, "There seems here a necessity for confessing that the happiness and misery of others are not spectacles entirely indifferent to us."[19]

> It cannot be disputed, that there is some benevolence, however small, infused into our bosom; some spark of friendship for human kind; some particle of the dove kneaded into our frame, along with the elements of the wolf and the serpent. Let these generous sentiments be supposed ever so weak; . . . they must still direct the determinations of our mind, and where everything is equal, produce a cool preference of what is useful and serviceable to mankind, above what is pernicious and dangerous.[20]

According to Hume, everyone naturally has some benevolent feelings toward other human beings; no one is completely indifferent to the happiness or suffering of others. This gives everyone a reason for approving of and considering to be virtues those traits that are beneficial to their possessor or to others, and for disapproving of and considering to be vices those traits that are harmful to their possessor or to others. Hume thought that conceptions of virtue and vice are not based on self-interest but rather on the universal characteristics of benevolence and sympathy. Whether everyone naturally has (and retains) such characteristics of sympathy and benevolence is an open question.

VIRTUES AS DISPOSITIONS TO OBEY MORAL RULES

As we have seen, theories about virtue and vice can be divided into two families. One family of theories focuses on the helpfulness or harmfulness of traits, either to their possessor or to others. This family includes theories that claim that moral virtues are those traits that enable their possessor to flourish, whereas moral vices are those that reduce their possessor's likelihood of flourishing. It also includes those theories in which moral virtues (vices) are traits that are beneficial (harmful) primarily to others.

Theories in the second family claim instead that virtues are dispositions to obey (true) moral rules, whereas virtues are dispositions to disobey (true) moral rules. For these theories, moral rules, laws, or principles come first and are more fundamental than the concepts of virtue and vice. In order to know which traits are moral virtues and vices, we first must know what is morally permitted, prohibited, and required—a prior knowledge that is not required by theories that emphasize harm and benefit either to their possessor or to others.[21] However, the differences between these two families of theories should not be exaggerated. It may be that there will be substantial agreement among different theories about which traits are virtues and which are vices, even if they appeal to different principles to justify their claims.

---

[19]Ibid., p. 79.

[20]Ibid., p. 111 (Section IX).

[21]Perhaps this claim needs to be qualified. The first family of theories presupposes at least some moral principles—for example, that what contributes to flourishing is good and what detracts from flourishing is bad.

As an example of the second family of theories, we will look at contemporary American philosopher Bernard Gert. Gert maintains that moral virtues are tendencies to avoid unjustified violations of correct moral rules, whereas vices are tendencies to unjustifiably violate correct moral rules. In his view, virtues and vices cannot be identified independent of or prior to the identification of the correct moral rules: that is, virtues and vices presuppose moral principles, laws, and rules. He also distinguishes between moral virtues and personal virtues. Personal virtues—traits primarily or exclusively beneficial to their possessor— are not *moral* virtues at all. Moral virtues are those traits that are exclusively or primarily beneficial to others.[22]

Consider cruelty, the tendency to deliberately or negligently cause other people pain and suffering. Following Gert, we might say that it's a moral vice because it is a tendency to violate a correct moral rule that prohibits people from deliberately or negligently causing other people pain and suffering. Kindness, on the other hand, is a moral virtue because it is a tendency to conform to a correct moral rule that requires us to avoid causing others to suffer and enjoins us to relieve suffering where we can. Similarly, correct moral rules require us to be merciful, loyal, and honest while prohibiting us from being merciless, disloyal, and dishonest, so the former traits are moral virtues and the latter are moral vices. On this view, to determine what traits are moral virtues and what traits are moral vices, we must first determine what the correct moral rules, laws, and principles are.

CHARACTER AND FREEDOM

Aristotle believed that, to some extent, our character is up to us. He believed that people can change and shape their own character. If we want to be good, we can take effective steps to cultivate the virtues and extinguish the vices. He claimed that "moral excellence comes about as the result of habit,"[23] rather than being innate or inborn. He emphasized that human beings have natures that are to some extent malleable; people have the inborn capacity to acquire a variety of traits. People can be unselfish as well as selfish, courageous as well as cowardly, temperate as well as self-indulgent, good-tempered as well as irascible, kind as well as cruel. Such character traits are acquired rather than innate.

However, aren't our early environment, training, and conditioning (over which we have no control) decisive in shaping our character? Aren't our character traits acquired very early in life and thereafter quite stable? Aristotle thought not. He believed that we can, in a sense, decondition and recondition ourselves. The potential for acquiring other traits remains after we have been conditioned early in life. Thus, according to Aristotle, "we become just by doing just acts, temperate by doing temperate acts, brave by doing brave acts."[24]

---

[22]Bernard Gert, *Morality* (New York: Oxford University Press, 1988), pp. 182–196.

[23]Aristotle, *Nicomachean Ethics*, in *Complete Works*, ed. Barnes, p. 1742.

[24]Ibid., p. 1743.

It is from the same causes and by the same means that every excellence is both produced and destroyed, and similarly every art; for it is from playing the lyre that both good and bad lyre players are produced. And the corresponding statement is true of builders and of all the rest; men will be good or bad builders as a result of building well or badly. For if this were not so, there would have been no need of a teacher, but all men would have been born good or bad at their craft. This, then, is the case with the excellences also; by doing the acts that we do in our transactions with other men we become just or unjust, and by doing the acts that we do in the presence of danger, and being habituated to feel fear or confidence, we become brave or cowardly. The same is true of appetites and feelings of anger; some men become temperate and good tempered, others self-indulgent and irascible, by behaving in one way or the other in the appropriate circumstances. . . . It makes no small difference, then, whether we form habits of one kind or of another in our very youth; it makes a very great difference, or rather *all* the difference.[25]

If Aristotle is correct, we deceive ourselves if we think that our character is not at all up to us; it is simply an excuse for lack of effort. If we discover that we are cowardly, or disloyal, or selfish, we can take steps to perform courageous, loyal, and unselfish actions. If Aristotle is correct, by repeatedly practicing such actions we can eventually extinguish the unwanted trait and acquire the wanted trait.

EXERCISES

1. Consider the list of character traits on pages 106–107. What kind of person do you think your parents would like you to be? (Alternatively, what kind of character do you think your parents would like you to have?) Why do you think they would like you to be that way?

2. What kind of person do *you* want to be? (Alternatively, what kind of character do you want to have?) Which of the traits listed (and perhaps others not listed) do you want to have, and which do you not want to have? Why?

3. When or if you have children, what kind of people do you want them to be? (Alternatively, what kind of character do you want them to have?) Why?

4. Construct a list of the people you most admire and the people you least admire. What are some of the traits characteristic of the people you most admire? What are some of the traits characteristic of the people you least admire? Why do you admire or deplore these traits?

5. What character traits do you value most in a friend? What character traits do you most deplore in a friend? Why?

6. If you could change one of your traits, either by adding or subtracting, what trait would it be? Why?

7. Of the character traits listed on pages 106–107, which do you consider to be moral virtues, and which do you consider to be moral vices? Defend your view.

---

[25]Ibid.

8. Should education in public schools try to influence character by praising virtues and criticizing vices? Defend your answer.

9. Should the society in general and government in particular be concerned about the moral character of its citizens? Defend your answer.

10. What, if anything, is admirable or deplorable about Horatius, Cincinnatus, Ebeneezer Scrooge, Mr. Collins, and Anne Moody in the stories that began the chapter? Defend your answers.

11. Is lack of self-respect a vice? Why/why not? How does the behavior of someone who has self-respect differ from the behavior of someone who lacks self-respect?

12. Would it be courageous or foolhardy to "blow the whistle" on one's employer for illegal activity, given that it could lead to one's firing? Defend your answer.

13. John sees Tom cheating on his chemistry final examination. He wonders whether he should report Tom to the professor. What, if any, virtues would be manifested by his reporting Tom? What, if any, vices would be manifested by his reporting Tom? Should John report Tom? Defend your answer.

14. What difference, if any, would it make in question 13 if (a) Tom was John's best friend? (b) Tom was John's enemy? (c) John and Tom had signed an honor code pledging that they would not cheat and would report anyone they saw cheating?

15. Is the tendency to gossip a vice? Why/why not?

16. Do you think that a person's character is formed early in life and is unalterable, or do you think that people can make changes in their character by extinguishing certain character traits and replacing them with others? For example, if you are not entirely the kind of person that you would like to be, would it be possible for you to become more like your ideal person? If yes, how? Defend your answer.

SUGGESTED READINGS

St. Thomas Aquinas. *Introduction to St. Thomas Aquinas.* Edited by Anton Pegis. New York: Modern Library, 1948.

Aristotle. *Nicomachean Ethics.* In *The Complete Works of Aristotle,* vol. 2, edited by Jonathan Barnes. Princeton, NJ: Princeton University Press, 1984.

John Cooper. *Reason and Human Good in Aristotle.* Cambridge, MA: Harvard University Press, 1975.

Philippa Foot. "Virtues and Vices." In *Virtues and Vices.* Berkeley: University of California Press, 1978.

David Hume. *An Enquiry Concerning the Principles of Morals.* LaSalle, IL: Open Court, 1960.

Amelie Oksenberg Rorty, ed. *Essays on Aristotle's Ethics.* Berkeley: University of California Press, 1980.

James Wallace. *Virtues and Vices.* Ithaca, NY: Cornell University Press, 1978.

CHAPTER 7

Utilitarianism

Paul: I'm in favor of capital punishment. I think it's morally acceptable to kill criminals convicted of premeditated murder.

Peter: Why? What justifies taking human life?

Paul: First, by putting murderers to death, you guarantee that they'll never murder again. Second, capital punishment deters people from becoming murderers, thus reducing the murder rate. People won't be so casual about committing murder if they know that they will face the ultimate punishment—death. As you can see, capital punishment saves the lives of countless innocent people who are potential murder victims. Therefore, more lives are saved by the death penalty than are lost. That's why I think that capital punishment is morally acceptable.

The proponent of capital punishment in this brief dialogue is appealing to the *consequences* of capital punishment to justify his claim that it's morally acceptable. In his view, the good consequences of killing murderers outweigh the bad consequences; therefore, the death penalty is morally acceptable.

According to an approach to moral decision making called Consequentialism, right and wrong are purely a function of the consequences of actions or behavior. According to consequentialists, no action is intrinsically right or wrong; it's only the consequences of the action that make it right or wrong. Act Consequentialism recognizes only one correct standard or test of right and wrong for individual actions: If the good consequences outweigh the bad consequences, it's right; if the bad consequences outweigh the good consequences, it's wrong. According to most consequentialists, relevant consequences are any increases or decreases in the pleasure, happiness, or well-being of people. (Some consequentialists claim that increases or decreases in the well-being of nonhuman animals who are sentient are also relevant, but for the sake of simplicity, let's limit consideration to people.) An increase in pleasure, happiness, or well-being (or a decrease in pain or unhappiness) is a good consequence; a decrease in pleasure, happiness, or well-being (or increase in pain or unhappiness) is a bad consequence.

Suppose that you didn't finish a term paper by the instructor's deadline because you began researching and writing it too late. In order to avoid being penalized for handing it in late, you are considering lying to her, telling her that a close relative's illness has delayed your completing the paper. Would it be wrong to lie to your instructor? Act consequentialists maintain that whether it would be wring for you to lie in this situation depends entirely on what the consequences will be, because no actions are intrinsically right or wrong. If the good consequences of lying will outweigh the bad consequences, lying is the right thing to do; if the bad consequences of lying will outweigh the good consequences, lying is the wrong thing to do. The most widely known and accepted version of Act Consequentialism is Act Utilitarianism.

ACT UTILITARINISM

Moral egoists can be act consequentialists, claiming that an action is right if and only if the good consequences outweigh the bad consequences. However, moral egoists will be concerned ultimately only with their own pleasure, happiness, or well-being. Therefore, when they claim that an action is right if and only if its good consequences outweigh its bad consequences, they mean if and only if its good consequences *for them* outweigh its bad consequences *for them.* If it will produce more happiness than unhappiness *for them,* then it is right.

Act utilitarians are not egoists. They deny that the only consequences that matter in determining the rightness and wrongness of actions are the increases and decreases of happiness for the agent. They agree that a moral point of view is impartial and does not permit people to ignore the happiness and well-being of others. Therefore, Act Utilitarianism requires people to consider the happiness of others when deciding what is morally right and wrong.

Jeremy Bentham

British philosopher Jeremy Bentham (1748–1832) is generally considered to be one of the earliest utilitarians. Bentham was a hedonist who believed that individual happiness is based upon pleasure and pain: Increased pleasure and decreased pain bring happiness; decreased pleasure and increased pain bring unhappiness. He used the word *utility* to refer to the tendency of something to increase or decrease happiness.

> By utility is meant that property in any object, whereby it tends to produce benefit, advantage, pleasure, good, or happiness (all this in the present case comes to the same thing) or (what comes again to the same thing) to prevent the happening of mischief, pain, evil, or unhappiness.[1]

In his view, what is most in an individual's self-interest is to have pleasure (happiness) rather than pain (unhappiness).

---

[1]Jeremy Bentham, "An Introduction to the Principles of Morals and Legislation," in *The Utilitarians* (New York: Doubleday, 1961), p. 18. (Originally published in 1789.)

Bentham agreed that morality often requires people to pursue the common good rather than their own private good, especially when the two are in conflict. However, the idea of the common good is rather vague, and Bentham tried to make it more precise. He began by noting,

> The community is a fictitious body, composed of the individual persons who are considered as constituting . . . its *members*. The interest of the community then is, what? the sum of the interests of the several members who compose it.[2]

According to Bentham, "A thing is said to promote the interest, or to be *for* the interest, of an individual, when it tends to add to the sum total of his pleasures: or, what comes to the same thing, to diminish the sum total of his pains."[3] As it is for an individual's private good that his or her total happiness be increased and total pain be decreased, so it is for the common good that the total happiness of the community be increased and the total unhappiness be decreased. The total happiness of the community is nothing but the sum of the individual happiness of its members, as the total unhappiness of the community is the sum total of individual unhappiness of its members.

Bentham believed that the correct standard of right and wrong is the principle of utility. As he put it, "An action . . . may be said to be conformable to the principle of utility [meaning with respect to the community at large] . . . when the tendency it has to augment the happiness of the community is greater than any it has to diminish it."[4] Bentham continued,

> Of an action that is conformable to the principle of utility one may always say either that it is one that ought to be done, or at least that it is not one that ought not to be done. One may say also, that it is right it should be done; at least that it is not wrong it should be done.[5]

According to the principle of utility as expressed by Bentham, then, it is wrong for people to do what will reduce the total happiness of the community.

Let's apply this theory to a concrete issue. Suppose that Martinez must choose between (1) mowing his own lawn, (2) paying someone to mow his lawn, and (3) leaving his lawn unmowed. Martinez hates to mow his own lawn. He likes paying someone else to mow it even less than he likes mowing it himself. Because he doesn't care what his lawn looks like, leaving his lawn unmowed makes him happiest. However, if his lawn remains unmowed, his neighbors will be very unhappy; if his lawn is mowed, they will be very happy. Finally, if Martinez pays someone to mow his lawn, that person will be happy.

Imagine that we have calculated the probable effect of each alternative on the happiness and unhappiness of all concerned, using "happiness units" (+ for happiness, – for unhappiness). The results appear in the following table.

---

[2]Ibid.

[3]Ibid.

[4]Ibid.

[5]Ibid., p. 19

	(1) M. MOWS	(2) M. PAYS MOWER	(3) LAWN UNMOWED
Martinez	-100 h. units	-110 h. units	+100 h. units
Neighbors	+500 h. units	+500 h. units	-500 h. units
Mower	0 h. units	+50 h. units	0 h. units
Total	+400 h. units	+440 h. units	-400 h. units

Alternative 3, leaving his lawn unmowed, would provide the most happiness for Martinez and would therefore be in his self-interest. However, according to Bentham's principle of utility, it would be wrong for Martinez to choose alternative 3 because it would diminish the total happiness of the community.

Bentham's principle of utility seems to entail that alternatives 1 and 2 are morally acceptable, or not wrong, because both increase the total happiness of the community and neither diminishes the total happiness of the community. Whether this conclusion is what Bentham had in mind may be an open question; however, there is no doubt that utilitarians after Bentham proposed a more stringent utilitarian standard of right and wrong. Alternative 2 would produce more total happiness than would alternative 1. In that case, can they both be equally right?

Mill, Act Utilitarianism, and the Greatest Happiness Principle

John Stuart Mill (1806–1873), a disciple of Bentham, explained the utilitarian theory as follows:

> The creed which accepts as the foundation of morals, Utility, or the Greatest Happiness Principle, holds that actions are right in proportion as they tend to promote happiness, wrong as they tend to promote the reverse of happiness. By happiness is intended pleasure and the absence of pain; by unhappiness, pain and the privation of pleasure.[6]

The principle of utility, or the Greatest Happiness Principle, as formulated by Mill maintains that rightness and wrongness are matters of degree. An act is right "in proportion as" it tends to promote happiness. Therefore, the more happiness it will produce, the more right it is; the more unhappiness it will produce, the more wrong it is.

Mill is quite explicit that "that standard is not the agent's own happiness, but the greatest amount of happiness altogether."[7]

> The happiness which forms the utilitarian standard of what is right in conduct is not the agent's own happiness, but that of all concerned. As between his

---

[6]John Stuart Mill, "Utilitarianism," in *Essential Works of John Stuart Mill,* ed. Max Lerner (New York: Bantam, 1961), p. 194.

[7]Ibid., pp. 198–199.

own happiness and that of others, utilitarianism requires him to be as strictly impartial as a disinterested and benevolent spectator.[8]

Most people since Mill have interpreted his Greatest Happiness version of Act Utilitarianism as requiring people to do whatever will produce the most total happiness in any given situation. For example, Henry Sidgwick (1838–1900) wrote,

> By Utilitarianism is here meant the ethical theory, that the conduct which, under any given circumstances, is objectively right, is that which will produce the greatest amount of happiness on the whole; that is, taking into account all whose happiness is affected by the conduct.[9]

According to contemporary American moral philosopher William Frankena,

> Act-utilitarians hold that in general . . . , one is to tell what is right and obligatory by . . . trying to see which of the actions open to him will or is likely to produce the greatest balance of good over evil [happiness and unhappiness according to Bentham, Mill, and Sidgwick] in the universe.[10]

Similarly, the contemporary American moral philosopher Richard Brandt describes Act Utilitarianism as maintaining that "an act is morally right if and only if the total welfare-expectation [expected happiness] for everyone affected by it is at least as great as from any alternative action open to the agent."[11] Since Mill, Act Utilitarianism has been interpreted as requiring people in a given circumstance to do whatever act will maximize total happiness.

If we apply the Greatest Happiness Principle to Martinez's case, it would be right for him to pay someone to mow his lawn (alternative 2) and wrong for him to mow his own lawn (alternative 1) because alternative 2 would produce the most total happiness, despite the fact that he would get even more unhappiness from paying someone to mow his lawn than he would get by mowing it himself. According to the Greatest Happiness Principle, it is wrong for someone to do action X if an available alternative action would produce even more total happiness than would be produced by doing X. (Because people must rely on estimates of the most likely consequences of various courses of action, we may think of the Greatest Happiness Principle as requiring people to do what will *probably* produce the greatest amount of total happiness.)

Let's look at another application of the Greatest Happiness Principle. Suppose that Jones owns a truck-cleaning firm and discovers that nontoxic solvents for cleaning trucks are roughly three times as expensive as toxic solvents. The runoff from Jones's operation ultimately finds its way into the wells of nearly 100 families to the south of him. Scientific studies suggest that long-term

---

[8]Ibid., p. 204.

[9]Henry Sidgwick, *The Methods of Ethics,* 7th ed. (Indianapolis, IN: Hackett, 1981), p. 411. (The first edition was published in 1874, the seventh and last in 1907.)

[10]William Frankena, *Ethics,* 2d ed. (Englewood Cliffs, NJ: Prentice-Hall, 1973), p. 35.

[11]Richard Brandt, *A Theory of the Right and the Good* (New York: Oxford University Press, 1979), p. 271.

exposure to the toxic solvents will probably damage an individual's immune system and may cause neurological problems. Because he will have more profits if he uses the toxic solvents and because he does not live in the area of water contamination, Jones will be happier if he uses the toxic solvents. However, because they may be injured by long-term exposure to the toxic solvents, the people whose wells will be contaminated by the runoff will be made unhappy if Jones uses the toxic solvents.

Let's assume that Jones would gain 100 units of well-being by using the toxic solvents and would lose 200 units of well-being by using the more expensive nontoxic solvents. On the other hand, using the toxic solvents would decrease the well-being of each of the 100 neighboring families by 20 units, for a total of 2,000 units, while using the nontoxic solvents would increase their well-being by 5 units, for a total of 500 units. These assumptions result in the following table.

	USE CHEAPER TOXIC SOLVENTS	USE MORE EXPENSIVE NONTOXIC SOLVENTS
Jones	+ 100	–200
Neighbors	–2,000	+500
Total	–1,900	+300

Someone applying the Greatest Happiness Principle would conclude that it would be wrong for Jones to use the toxic solvents; the right thing to do is to use the more expensive nontoxic solvents.

OBJECTIONS TO THE GREATEST HAPPINESS PRINCIPLE

Many people have criticized the Greatest Happiness version of Act Utilitarianism. Let's look at some of the reasons.

The Greatest Happiness Principle Requires Too Much

According to the Greatest Happiness version of Act Utilitarianism, even though Martinez would prefer to mow his own lawn rather than pay someone to do it, it would be wrong for him to mow his own lawn because paying someone to mow it would produce even more total happiness. Critics of the Greatest Happiness version of Act Utilitarianism believe that such examples show that it requires too much of people. According to that principle, it is wrong for people *not* to do whatever will produce the most total happiness. Richard Brandt, for example, points out that the Greatest Happiness Principle "makes extreme and oppressive demands on the individual, so much so that it can hardly be taken seriously. . . . A moral code is oppressive if it leaves no area of freedom, to do what one wants to do to achieve one's goals, and simply enjoy oneself."[12]

Suppose that you are considering going to a movie with your friends. Instead of going to the movies, you could tutor illiterate adults or work as a volunteer in a hospital, each of which would almost certainly produce more total happiness than would be produced by your going to the movies. Therefore, according to the Greatest Happiness Principle, it would be wrong for you to go to the movies because you would not be doing the alternative action that would produce the most total well-being.

Of course, what was said of going to the movies applies to almost anything we do. If we watch television, exercise, listen to music, read a book, go to a party, walk in the park, or play sports, for example, there are alternative courses of action that would have produced more total happiness; therefore, it would be wrong to do these things. Similarly, if we give $100 to charity we could have given $150 and produced more total happiness; therefore, it would be wrong to give only $100. According to the Greatest Happiness Principle, these actions would be immoral because we could always be doing something else that would produce more total happiness. Critics of the Greatest Happiness Principle such as Brandt find this consequence of the theory highly implausible; it would not allow a person any rest.

Bentham's Alternative to the Greatest Happiness Principle

If we reject the Greatest Happiness version of Act Utilitarianism, an act utilitarian can still fall back on the formulation that Bentham gave at the beginning of his *Principles of Morals and Legislation.* We might call this formulation a negative version of Act Utilitarianism. Recall that according to Bentham, "An action may be said to be conformable to the principle of utility . . . when the tendency it has to augment the happiness of the community is greater than any it has to diminish it."[13] Rather than claim that an action is *right* if and only if it would produce more total happiness than would any alternative action available to the agent, Bentham's formulation seems to suggest that an action is *wrong* if and only if (1) it would reduce total happiness and (2) alternatives are available that would either not reduce total happiness or would reduce total happiness less. The right thing to do is to increase the total happiness of the community, if it is possible to do so, but not necessarily to maximize it. If several alternative courses of action are available to an agent, all of which will increase total happiness, each is morally acceptable. Applying this negative version of Act Utilitarianism, it is morally acceptable for you to go to the movies even though there are other courses of action available that would produce even more total

---

[12]Ibid., pp. 276–277.
[13]Bentham, "Principles of Morals and Legislation," p. 18.

happiness, because your going to the movies (1) doesn't diminish total happiness and (2) does increase total happiness (by increasing your happiness).

On the other hand, suppose that you are considering cheating an old woman of her life's savings. If you do, your happiness will increase, but her happiness and the happiness of others (for example, her relatives and friends) will diminish. It is very probable that other people's loss of happiness will be greater than your increase in happiness; therefore, it is highly probable that by stealing her life savings you will diminish total happiness. You have an alternative course of action available that will not diminish total happiness: not stealing her life savings. Therefore, according to the negative version of Act Utilitarianism, it would be wrong to cheat her of her life savings.

Many people, on reflection, find the negative version of Act Utilitarianism more plausible than the Greatest Happiness version because it doesn't require so much of people. Rather than requiring everyone to maximize total happiness, the negative version of Act Utilitarianism forbids everyone to reduce or diminish total happiness. That would probably require people not to harm one another, at least when total happiness would be reduced by it. Does it also require people to sometimes help one another?

Suppose that an elderly woman asks you for directions because she is lost. You could stop for a few moments and give her directions, or you could walk on, ignoring her request. Let's suppose that the probable consequences are represented in the following table.

	GIVE DIRECTIONS	IGNORE REQUEST
You	–5 h. units	+5 h. units
Woman	+20 h. units	–20 h. units
Total	+15 h. units	–15 h. units

If you ignore the woman's request and simply walk away, her worry and confusion will increase, she will feel more insecure and dejected, and so on. Therefore, ignoring her request will actually reduce her happiness, not merely fail to increase it. In that case, the negative version of Act Utilitarianism requires you to give the woman directions because not to do so would reduce total happiness. Thus, the negative version of Act Utilitarianism at least sometimes requires people to aid and benefit others.

However, critics of Act Utilitarianism see other problems with the theory, whether the Greatest Happiness version or the negative version.

Act Utilitarianism Ignores the Distribution of Happiness

One problem is that both versions of Act Utilitarianism focus exclusively on total happiness and ignore the distribution of happiness. Suppose that you face a choice; you must do either act A or act B. Let's assume that acts A and B will make you equally happy but that if you do A, you will make three people slightly unhappy and, if you do B, you will make one person extremely unhappy. The total decrease in happiness for each alternative is the same.

	A	B
Person 1	–10 h. units	–30 h. units
Person 2	–10 h. units	0 h. units
Person 3	–10 h. units	0 h. units
Total	–30 h. units	–30 h. units

According to Act Utilitarianism, alternatives A and B are equally acceptable because all that counts is total happiness. (We would get the same results if we focused on average rather than total happiness.) However, many critics of Act Utilitarianism deny that A and B are equally acceptable. They claim that it's worse to impose great losses on one person if we could instead impose slight losses on several people.

Similarly, suppose that you face a choice between acts C and D. If you do C, you'll produce a moderate increase in happiness for three people; if you do D, you'll produce a large increase in happiness for one person. As before, the total increase in well-being is the same.

	C	D
Person 1	+10 h. units	+30 h.units
Person 2	+10 h. units	0 h. units
Person 3	+10 h. units	0 h. units
Total	+30 h. units	+30 h.units

Again, according to Act Utilitarianism, alternatives C and D are equally acceptable. However, critics claim that it's better to produce a moderate increase in well-being for several people than to produce a large increase in well-being for only one person.

Proponents of Act Utilitarianism claim that their critics are mistaken. First, they claim that when the total happiness that would be produced by two or more alternative actions is equal, the actions are equally right and neither is better than the other. They claim that their opponents don't have adequate justification for their claim that how happiness is distributed matters. Second, they insist that their critics oversimplify reality. Proponents of Act Utilitarianism claim that it is very difficult to come up with realistic, reasonably probable examples of a choice situation in which (1) one action would produce a moderate loss (or increase) of happiness for several people, (2) the alternative would produce a large loss (or increase) of happiness for one person, and (3) the total change in happiness resulting from each alternative would be the same. On closer inspection, they insist, we will almost always find that the total change in happiness is unlikely to be the same for each alternative.

For example, suppose that you face a choice of giving $1,000 each to three people or $3,000 to one person. A critic of Act Utilitarianism might use the following table to show that here is exactly the kind of example that proponents of the principle claim to be unrealistic or implausible. We'll initially assign one unit of increased happiness for each dollar.

	A	B
Person 1	+1,000 h. units	+3,000 h. units
Person 2	+1,000 h. units	0 h. units
Person 3	+1,000 h. units	0 h. units
Total	+3,000 h. units	+3,000 h. units

According to Act Utilitarianism, alternatives A and B are equally right. However, critics maintain that it is morally better to give $1,000 each to three people than to give $3,000 to one person.

A proponent of Act Utilitarianism would deny the claim that it is better to give $1,000 to each of three people than to give $3,000 to one person. Moreover, even in this case, the total happiness in each situation may not be equal. A more careful analysis might reveal that each person does not receive the same one unit of happiness for each dollar. For example, suppose that person 1 is destitute but persons 2 and 3 are affluent. Person 1 would get more happiness from each dollar received than would person 2 or 3. Thus, although person 1 would get one unit of happiness for each dollar, persons 2 and 3 might get only half a unit of happiness because a dollar means less to them. (Economists have a technical term for this difference: the declining marginal utility of money. Simply put, the more money we have, the less value we place on an additional dollar; the less money we have, the more value we place on an additional dollar.) Under this scenario, the alternatives would no longer be equal.

	A	B
Person 1	+1,000 h. units	+3,000 h. units
Person 2	+500 h. units	0 h. units
Person 3	+500 h. units	0 h. units
Total	+2,000 h. units	+3,000 h. units

In this case, more total happiness is likely to result from giving $3,000 to person 1 (alternative B) than giving $1,000 to each of them (alternative A).

Proponents of Act Utilitarianism claim that, given significant differences in the distribution of well-being, it's quite unlikely that situations will arise in which several alternative actions would produce the same change in total well-being. Whether or not the distribution objection is fatal to Act Utilitarianism remains an open question.

Act Utilitarianism Ignores Duties and Justice

Some critics of Act Utilitarianism object to its fundamental assumption that the rightness or wrongness of an individual action is determined solely by its future consequences. They think that it unjustifiably ignores past behavior that might create obligations and duties. For example, suppose that although John has promised to take you to the doctor this afternoon, he decides instead to work at a soup kitchen for the homeless because he believes that more total well-being will be produced by working at the soup kitchen than by keeping his promise and taking you to the doctor. According to Act Utilitarianism, only the consequences—namely, the effect on total happiness—determine whether what he did was right or wrong. The fact that in one situation he broke a promise and in the other situation he kept a promise is irrelevant.

Many critics maintain that Act Utilitarianism is mistaken in believing that it provides the single correct ultimate test of right and wrong for individual actions. Critics might concede that Act Utilitarianism provides a useful standard of right and wrong for individual actions *if* there are no other moral considerations that tug in other directions. For example, focusing on the effect on total happiness of a truck-cleaning firm's using toxic as opposed to nontoxic solvents may strike many people as plausible because there are no other moral considerations that lead to a conclusion different from an act utilitarian's. However, critics of Act Utilitarianism think that other considerations are relevant and that when they tug in a different direction, it is not obvious that the act utilitarian standard should always have the final word.

Individual Actions versus Kinds of Actions

Suppose that Sabrina is considering killing her uncle. He is the most hated man in town because he's such a miser. Although he wants to go on living, he is old and sickly, suffering from painful maladies and depression; she's convinced that he'd be better off dead. She has a drug that will make it appear that he died of a heart attack, so there's virtually no chance of her being caught. His fortune will be left to her, and she will use the money for various charitable purposes that will increase total well-being. Everyone in the town will be happy when they learn of her uncle's death; no one will mourn him. Therefore, Sabrina reasons that killing him will produce more total happiness than not killing him.

According to the Greatest Happiness version of Act Utilitarianism, it would be wrong for Sabrina *not* to kill her uncle; according to the negative version of Act Utilitarianism, it would not be wrong for her to kill him because killing him would not reduce total happiness. Critics of Act Utilitarianism balk at these conclusions. They say that even if more total well-being would result from killing him than from letting him live, it would nonetheless be wrong to kill him. Some critics of Act Utilitarianism who are nevertheless sympathetic to Utilitarianism claim that Act Utilitarianism errs by focusing on individual actions rather than on kinds of action. They advocate a version of Utilitarianism called Rule Utilitarianism.

RULE UTILITARIANISM

In *Utilitarianism* John Stuart Mill's words suggest that he himself was working toward distinguishing between Act and Rule Utilitarianism.

> In the case of abstinences . . . —of things which people forbear to do from moral considerations, though the consequences in the particular case might be beneficial—it would be unworthy of an intelligent agent not to be consciously aware that the action is of a class which, if practised generally, would be generally injurious, and that this is the ground of the obligation to abstain from it.[14]

To the objection that there is often insufficient time to calculate the increases and decreases in total happiness for each alternative individual action available to an agent, Mill replied that much knowledge has been acquired about the "tendencies of actions." He suggested that "the beliefs which have thus come down [about the tendencies of actions] are the rules of morality for the multitude, and for the philosopher until he has succeeded in finding better."[15] Mill conceded that this application of rules undercuts the need to test each individual action against the ultimate standard of the Greatest Happiness. His position was that ordinarily we should follow moral rules or principles, appealing to the ultimate principle of utility for individual actions only when the "secondary" principles conflict.

Mill seems to suggest that most commonsense moral reasoning involves the application of moral rules and principles. Consider the case of Sabrina and her uncle. In trying to decide whether it would be morally acceptable for Sabrina to kill her uncle, most people would unhesitatingly reason along the following lines:

Killing Sabrina's uncle would be murder.

Murder is wrong.

Therefore, it would be wrong for Sabrina to kill her uncle.

Most people would not even consider calculating the increases and decreases in total happiness that would result from Sabrina's killing her uncle. They're convinced that murder is wrong and that killing her uncle would be murder.

---

[14]Mill, "Utilitarianism," chap. 2, p. 206.
[15]Ibid., pp. 210.

Similarly, most people rely upon rules or principles to guide their own conduct as well as to judge the conduct of others—rules such as "Stealing is wrong," "Don't lie," "Don't cheat," and "People should help those in need." Few people rely solely or predominantly upon a single rule for evaluating conduct—for example, a rule requiring people to maximize total well-being or to refrain from reducing total happiness. Rule utilitarians recognize the importance of moral rules and principles, but they go on to ask how we can reasonably decide which rules are correct and which are incorrect, or which should be followed and which shouldn't. Thus, we could follow a rule that permits lying or one that forbids lying. Which rule should we follow, and why?

Act utilitarians apply the utilitarian test to individual actions; rule utilitarians apply the utilitarian test to kinds of actions, or rules. According to Rule Utilitarianism, we should follow a correct moral rule. A moral rule is correct if people's conforming to it would result in more total happiness than if people did not conform to it.

Whereas an act utilitarian would approach the case of Sabrina's uncle by asking whether more total happiness would result from killing him or not killing him, a rule utilitarian would approach it by asking which rule is correct: (1) "Kill rich relatives" or (2) "Don't kill rich relatives." Rule Utilitarianism requires us to follow correct rather than incorrect moral rules, and it furnishes a test for the correctness of moral rules: A rule is a correct moral rule if and only if more total happiness will likely result if everyone conforms rather than doesn't conform to it. To apply Rule Utilitarianism, then, we must determine whether more total happiness will result if people conform to rule 1 or rule 2. If, as seems almost certain, more total happiness will result if people conform to rule 2, then rule 2 is a correct moral rule. Rule 1 is an incorrect moral rule, and it would be wrong for Sabrina to kill her uncle.

What about telling a lie? A rule utilitarian would probably claim that a rule forbidding lying is correct and a rule permitting lying is incorrect because more total well-being will likely result if everyone conforms to a rule forbidding rather than permitting lying. Therefore, it is wrong to lie.

However, it's easy to imagine circumstances in which almost everyone would agree that lying would be the right thing to do. Suppose that a Gestapo officer knocked on the door of a couple who were hiding Jews in Nazi Germany and asked them if they knew the whereabouts of any Jews. If they told the truth, the Jews they were hiding would almost certainly be killed and they themselves would be severely punished. Almost everyone would agree that the couple should lie and claim that they don't know the whereabouts of any Jews. Therefore, we have to be careful in applying Rule Utilitarianism.

Perhaps we must formulate the moral rules derived from Rule Utilitarianism more guardedly, not as categorical rules such as "Don't lie" but rather as conditional rules such as "Don't lie in circumstance C." Alternatively, we could consider moral rules as what W. D. Ross (1877–1971) would call *prima facie* rules.[16]

---

[16]Actually, Ross talked of prima facie duties rather than rules, but the point is the same.

A prima facie rule directs one to do or refrain from doing something, but it recognizes that its directive may be overridden by another equally important or more important moral rule directing one to an opposite course of action. Prima facie rules are "all things being equal" rules. For example, one might express a prima facie rule prohibiting lying as follows: "So long as no other equally or more important moral rules require you to lie, don't lie." If the rule prohibiting lying is considered prima facie, we are not committed to the claim that we should never lie. What the correct prima facie moral rules are would be determined by appeal to Rule Utilitarianism, and the relative importance of conflicting rules might be determined in the same way. In the case of the Gestapo, the prima facie rule prohibiting lying conflicts with the prima facie rule requiring saving lives. We could maintain that putting the rule requiring people to save lives over the rule prohibiting people from lying would produce more total happiness.

An Objection to Rule Utilitarianism

Critics of Rule Utilitarianism find that in at least some cases, applying it yields conclusions that are inconsistent with their moral convictions. They reject Rule Utilitarianism rather than their moral convictions. For example, suppose that in a society one out of 10,000 babies is born with green skin. Because they detest green-skinned infants and consider them to be "unnatural," the society kills all green-skinned infants. Let us suppose that, because of people's intense revulsion, total happiness in society would be reduced if green-skinned infants were allowed to live and that total happiness is increased by killing them. If members of the society follow the rule "Kill green-skinned infants" rather than the rule "Let green-skinned infants live," total well-being is enhanced. Therefore, according to Rule Utilitarianism, "Kill green-skinned infants" is a correct moral rule. Critics of Rule Utilitarianism disagree. According to their moral convictions, it is wrong to kill green-skinned infants even if killing them does increase total happiness.

Rule utilitarians might respond by maintaining either that the moral convictions of their critics are wrong and without foundation, or that such examples are unrealistic and implausible. They might insist that an example such as the society's killing of green-skinned infants is far-fetched and based on a very superficial sketch that leaves out too much detail. If such a society really existed, closer inspection might show that total happiness really isn't increased by killing green-skinned infants. Whether this defense is adequate is an open question.

Act versus Rule Utilitarianism

Utilitarians who favor Rule over Act Utilitarianism emphasize that Rule Utilitarianism maintains the connection between morality and well-being or happiness and the dependence of right and wrong on consequences, but without the objectionable implications of Act Utilitarianism. For one thing, Rule Utilitarianism does not seem to be as open as the Greatest Happiness Principle to the objection that it requires too much. Rule utilitarians might maintain that there would be more total well-being if everyone followed the rule "Get some rest and relaxation" than if everyone followed its opposite, "Don't ever rest or relax." Unlike the Greatest Happiness version of Act Utilitarianism, Rule Utilitarianism does not seem to forbid going to the movies, listening to music, and so on because it does not require people to always do what will produce the most total happiness. Similarly, problems with the distribution of happiness are less likely to arise with Rule Utilitarianism; even if in some concrete circumstance two alternative actions would produce the same total amount of happiness but a vastly different distribution of it, the question is what rule is correct in this circumstance.

Finally, whereas Act Utilitarianism focuses exclusively on the future consequences of an action, ignoring past behavior that may have resulted in duties and obligations, Rule Utilitarianism does not. Whereas an act utilitarian would determine whether you should keep a particular promise solely by comparing the effect on future total happiness of keeping it or breaking it, a rule utilitarian would have to look at the future effects on total happiness of the *practice* of keeping or breaking promises. If the practice of keeping promises would produce more total happiness than the practice of breaking them, then a rule requiring you to keep promises is correct. And in that case, you should keep this particular promise because you should follow correct moral rules. Therefore, the fact that you made a promise is relevant under Rule Utilitarianism in a way that it isn't under Act Utilitarianism.

Does Rule Utilitarianism Reduce to Act Utilitarianism?

One serious challenge to Rule Utilitarianism is the claim that it reduces to Act Utilitarianism and therefore is identical to it, so it is not really a different theory at all. According to rule utilitarians, people should abide by whatever rules would produce the most total happiness if followed by everyone. However, wouldn't the rule "Do whatever will produce the most total happiness" be the one rule that would, if followed by everyone, produce the most total happiness? If so, then Rule Utilitarianism reduces to the Greatest Happiness version of Act Utilitarianism because that rule *is* the Greatest Happiness Principle.

A proponent of Rule Utilitarianism may be able to disarm this criticism by denying that the most total happiness would be produced by everyone's following such a rule. For one thing, people are often unreliable estimators of the probable future effect on total happiness of individual courses of action. Often they are ignorant of or overlook relevant facts, and they are prone to self-deception, especially when their own interests are at stake. For example, we might insist that Sabrina cannot know whether killing her uncle will result in more total happiness in the future, and because she stands to gain from killing him she is particularly prone to deceive herself into believing that total happiness will increase. Therefore, a proponent of Rule Utilitarianism could deny that total happiness will be maximized if people follow a rule requiring them to maximize total happiness. Rather, people should follow rules such as "Don't kill relatives for their money," "Don't steal," and so on. In that case, the claim that Rule Utilitarianism reduces to Act Utilitarianism would be blocked.

PROBLEMS FOR ALL VERSIONS OF UTILITARIANISM

To apply either Act or Rule Utilitarianism with any precision, we must be able to measure and compare increases and decreases in people's happiness. However, many critics of Utilitarianism point out that we have no reliable way of making such measurements and comparisons. In our examples I assigned numbers to increases and decreases in happiness, but the numbers assigned were arbitrary. Perhaps we can justifiably say that someone's happiness increased and someone else's happiness decreased as a result of a particular course of action, but we cannot measure degrees of change in happiness. Yet we must do so to apply Act Utilitarianism and Rule Utilitarianism with any precision.

A proponent of Utilitarianism could concede that changes in happiness cannot be measured with any precision yet insist that precise measurements are often unnecessary; comparative judgments can be made with some reliability in a large percentage of cases. Take the case of Jones and his cleaning solvents. A utilitarian might insist that even if we can't make precise measurements, the judgment that there would be more total happiness if Jones used nontoxic cleaning solvents is reliable and accurate. Similarly, a proponent of Rule Utilitarianism might insist that the judgment that more total well-being would be produced if people were to follow a rule prohibiting stealing than if they were to follow a rule permitting stealing is reliable and accurate, even if we can't make precise measurements.

EXERCISES

1. Tom is considering cheating on his chemistry final examination because he hasn't studied and is fairly certain that he'll fail it if he doesn't cheat. Apply Act Utilitarianism to determine whether it would be wrong for Tom to cheat.

2. Tina wants the latest CD from her favorite group but she doesn't have enough money to purchase it. She is considering stealing it from the record store. Apply Act Utilitarianism to determine whether it would be right or wrong for her to steal it.

3. Dave has been drinking heavily at a party and is drunk. One of his friends is urging him to leave his car there and accept a ride back to the dormitory. Apply Act Utilitarianism to determine whether it would be right or wrong for Dave to drive his car home while he's drunk.

4. Sandra works at an amusement park for the summer at the admission counter. Her best friend has asked her to let her in for free. Apply Act Utilitarianism to determine whether it would be right for Sandra to comply with her friend's request.

5. Do the results of applying Act Utilitarianism in cases 1 through 4 accord with your commonsense moral convictions? If yes, does that show that Act

Utilitarianism is a completely adequate moral theory? Why or why not? If the results of applying Act Utilitarianism in these cases does not accord with your commonsense moral convictions, explain the conflict.

6. Apply Rule Utilitarianism to the case of Jones who has a truck-cleaning firm and faces a choice of using toxic or nontoxic cleaning solvents. Would it be morally acceptable for him to use the toxic solvents? Explain and defend your answer.

7. Sally is considering buying a paper to submit as her own work in philosophy class. Apply Rule Utilitarianism to determine whether it would be right to do so. Explain and defend your answer.

8. Sherman is producing and marketing a pill that he claims cures cancer. He knows that it has no effect on cancer, but he also knows that desperate cancer patients will buy the pill. Apply Rule Utilitarianism to determine whether Sherman is doing anything wrong. Explain and defend your answer.

9. Apply Rule Utilitarianism to the issues of suicide, abortion, and capital punishment.

SUGGESTED READINGS

Jeremy Bentham. "An Introduction to the Principles of Morals and Legislation." In *The Utilitarians.* New York: Doubleday, 1961.

Fred Feldman. *Introductory Ethics.* Englewood Cliffs, NJ: Prentice-Hall, 1978. (See Chapters 2-5.)

John Stuart Mill. "Utilitarianism." In *The Utilitarians.* New York: Doubleday, 1961.

Anthony Quinton. *Utilitarian Ethics.* New York: St. Martin's Press, 1973.

CHAPTER 8

Kantian Moral Theory

Do not impose on others what you yourself do not desire.

Confucius (551–479 B.C.E.), *The Analects*

Always treat others as you would like them to treat you.

Jesus, the Sermon on the Mount (Matthew 7:12)

The quotations from Confucius and Jesus and the comic strip "Calvin and Hobbes" illustrate an approach to moral decision making and moral argument that differs from Utilitarianism, which emphasizes the consequences of actions. In contemporary Western philosophy, this approach is most closely associated not with the names of Confucius, Jesus, or Calvin and Hobbes but with the German philosopher Immanuel Kant (1724–1804).

Suppose that John steals Janine's car and wrecks it while joyriding. Janine confronts him.

Janine: It was despicable of you to steal my car and wreck it.

John: Chill out. It's no big deal. There's nothing wrong with stealing people's cars.

Janine: What do you mean, there's nothing wrong with stealing people's cars?

John: You heard me.

Janine: Oh, I suppose if someone stole your car you wouldn't think he had done anything wrong.

John: He who steals my wheels dies.

Janine: Why? You think it would be wrong for someone to steal your car?

John: Absolutely.

Janine: But you just said there's nothing wrong with stealing people's cars. If there's nothing wrong with stealing people's cars, how can it be wrong for someone to steal your car?

This pattern of moral reasoning does not appeal to the consequences of stealing cars. Rather, it appeals to considerations of logical consistency: Rational agents should avoid self-contradiction. Just as it is irrational for someone to maintain that tigers both are and are not mammals, it is irrational for someone to say there's nothing wrong with stealing people's cars but it would be wrong for someone to steal my car.

KANT AND THE GOOD WILL

Kant began his *Foundations of the Metaphysics of Morals* with the words "Nothing in the world—indeed nothing even beyond the world—can possibly be conceived which could be called good without qualification except a GOOD WILL."[1] Goods such as wealth, power, and fame; talents such as strength, agility, intelligence, skill, and endurance; character traits such as courage, industriousness, and perseverance are all good, but they are not good without qualification

---

[1]Immanuel Kant, *Foundations of the Metaphysics of Morals,* 2d ed., trans. Lewis White Beck (New York: Library of Liberal Arts, 1990), p. 9. (Originally published in 1785.)

because they can be put to evil purposes. Wealth can be used to destroy people; strength and intelligence can be used for murder; courage can be used for robbery. All such goods can be used for evil ends unless a person has a good will. Therefore, only a good *will* can be good without qualification.

To understand the concept of will, we begin by asking how we can explain human actions. Suppose that Pablo carries an umbrella to work. How can we explain why he brought the umbrella rather than leaving it home? Part of the explanation might be that Pablo believed there was a high probability of its raining that day, believed that if it rained he would get wet, and believed that if he used an umbrella he could stay dry even in the rain. But these beliefs are not enough to explain why he brought the umbrella. After all, if he desired to get wet rather than stay dry, he would still have no reason to bring an umbrella. A crucial part of the explanation has been omitted: his desires. We can complete our explanation of Pablo's action by adding that he desired to stay dry rather than get wet. Now we have a plausible explanation of his action.

But there's still one ingredient missing, according to Kant. We have to decide whether to act on a desire. After all, sometimes we decide to resist a desire rather than satisfy it. Consider an alcoholic who has a desire for a drink, a recovering drug addict who has a desire to smoke crack, someone trying to quit smoking who has a desire for a cigarette, and a dieter who has a desire for a piece of chocolate cake. In each case, the individual must decide whether to satisfy the desire or resist it. In cases like these, we usually think (and so does the person involved) that one ought to resist the desire and not act to satisfy it.

In such cases we often talk of "will power." We say that the individual who successfully resists the temptation of desire has will power, whereas the person who succumbs and acts to satisfy the desire lacks will power. This concept suggests the following model of human action: The agent starts with a cluster of beliefs and desires that are motives to action; they are like forces that get the body into action. The agent, however, must (or at least should) evaluate the desires to determine whether they should or should not be satisfied. The role of evaluator is played by the agent's reason. When reason is functioning as evaluator, it is also governor, because it is the last thing that determines the will, which in turn determines action. In any event, before a desire can be acted on, there must be an act of willing to attempt to satisfy the desire. The agent must choose or decide to act on the desire or, alternatively, to not act on the desire. Only then does the body act. Thus, we might imagine human action schematically in the following way:

Beliefs + desires ➔ evaluation by reason ➔ act of will to satisfy desire (decision) ➔ action to satisfy desire.

Beliefs + desires ➔ evaluation by reason ➔ act of will to *not* satisfy desire (decision) ➔ refrain from action to satisfy desire.

When reason is not functioning as evaluator, the model becomes

Beliefs + desires ➔ act of will to satisfy desire ➔ action to satisfy desire.

Kant recognized that desires often conflict. Sometimes acting to satisfy one desire will guarantee that we cannot satisfy another desire. In such cases, we must decide which desire to satisfy. If we are rational, we will let our reason decide between conflicting desires. No action will be undertaken until our will has been activated. Until that time, we are still deliberating and trying to decide which desire to act to satisfy. Deliberation ends only when the will is activated, which then causes us to do the action we have decided on. So our will is master of our actions. According to Kant, if we are rational, our will will not be the slave of our desires, merely doing their bidding. Our will instead will cooperate with our reason and be master of our desires.

If the one thing that is good without qualification is a good will, what makes a will good and what makes it bad?

Kant was a supporter of what we have called commonsense morality. He thought that the moral views common to most people are pretty much correct. Therefore, he would take it as obviously true that a person with a good will would not commit major moral offenses such as murder, robbery, rape, kidnapping, oppression, or exploitation of others. A person with a good will would not behave unjustly, cheating or deceiving others, behaving disloyally to friends, betraying people. Similarly, a person with a good will would not commit minor moral offenses, such as maliciously gossiping about people or behaving rudely or insensitively to others, offending or insulting people. But having a good will is not defined only in terms of how one would *not* behave. It must also be defined in terms of how one would behave. A person with a good will would behave beneficently toward others, helping those in need in a variety of ways by donating time, energy, money, and attention to others.

Kant took these things for granted. But he recognized that a person might have a good will and not be able to actually do any of the things a good person would do or refrain from doing the things a good person would not do. Similarly, someone without a good will might do all the things that a good person would do and refrain from doing all the things that a good person would not do. Thus, one's behavior is not an infallible sign of whether one has a good will. For example, someone may contribute to charity only because it's in his self-interest. Perhaps he's a politician who believes that he will gain votes by (publicly) contributing a thousand dollars to a soup kitchen that feeds the poor. Kant does not think that his contributing money to charity shows that he has a good will. Similarly, someone may be very attentive to her sick uncle, visiting him often, helping him clean his house and cook his meals, reading to him in the evening, and so on. Would that show that she has a good will? No. What if she's being so attentive only because she hopes that he will leave her lots of money when he dies? She's motivated purely by self-interest. Then her behavior would not show that she has a good will.

What of the performance of actions that normally would be considered to show that someone lacks a good will? Suppose that Martin in Nazi Germany betrays a Jewish family to the Gestapo? Wouldn't that show that he lacks a good will? Not necessarily. What if the betrayal to the Gestapo was completely unintentional? Suppose that Martin is seen carrying food up to his attic, making a rabid Nazi neighbor suspicious so that he calls the Gestapo to investigate. Martin's carrying food up to his attic for the Jewish family caused them to be found by the Gestapo, but he did not intend his action to have that outcome. It was an accident. His betrayal of the Jewish family to the Gestapo, because unintentional, does not show that he lacks a good will. Similarly, someone might act in a way that is deeply offensive or insulting to someone else. Would that show that he lacks a good will? No—not if he did not intend to be offensive or insulting.

Thus, Kant points out that we cannot tell whether someone has a good will by looking only at what he does or does not do, or only at the effects or consequences of his actions. One's intentions are the key to whether one has a good will. It is what one wants or tries to accomplish—what one wills—that counts. A person has a good will if she tries to do what is right and tries to avoid doing what is wrong. But the trying must be a genuine trying, a summoning of all one's capacities to work hard toward doing what's right and to refrain from doing what's wrong.

Kant says that the concept of duty contains the concept of a good will, but it probably would be more accurate to say that the concept of a good will entails the concept of duty. One has a good will if one tries to do one's duty. But Kant emphasized that for a will to be truly good, it must try to do its duty from a purely moral motive rather than from a self-interested motive. That purely moral motive is the desire to do one's duty out of respect for the moral law.

Suppose that Juan refrains from cheating his customers. Because he has a duty to refrain from cheating his customers, his actions are in conformity with his duty. But if he refrains from cheating his customers not because he knows that it is his duty and he desires to act dutifully, but rather because it is in his self-interest to refrain from cheating his customers, then he is not acting from the motive of duty. In that case, his actions do not reflect a good will. Juan's refraining from cheating his customers shows that he has a good will only if he refrains from cheating them because he knows that he has a duty not to cheat them and he desires to act dutifully. A person with a good will respects the moral law and tries to act dutifully because he desires to act in ways that conform to what his duties are.

A person with a good will tries to act in a way that satisfies her moral duties; put another way, she tries to ensure that her behavior conforms to the moral laws. That one's acts are in fact consistent with the moral laws does not show that one has a good will. As Kant put it, a good will not only tries to act "in accordance with" duty but acts "from" duty. In summary,

> the first proposition of morality is that to have genuine moral worth, an action must be done from duty. The second proposition is: An action done from duty does not have its moral worth in the purpose which is to be achieved through it but in the maxim whereby it is determined.[2]

---

[2]Ibid., pp. 15–16.

ACTIONS AND MAXIMS

Kant believed that people act as they do for a reason (whether or not they are immediately conscious of the reason or engage in deliberating before acting). For example, suppose that Brown, Gray, and Green each contribute $1,000 to charity. According to Kant, each has a reason for his or her action. Let's assume that we know each person's reason. Brown approves of the goals of the charity and wants to help it accomplish its goals. Gray knows that the names of large contributors will be publicized; he wants to impress his business associates and customers, which he thinks will improve his business. Green, who is running for office, also knows that the names of large contributors will be publicized; she wants voters to think she's generous because she thinks that perception will help her win the election. Reasons for action, then, at the simplest level, include the individual's beliefs and desires.

Kant believed that when people act for a reason, they're following a *maxim*—a kind of personal rule of action. Of course, people do not always consciously formulate maxims and then deliberately follow them. Rather, people often act as though they formulate and follow maxims. However, Kant seemed to assume that we can discover what maxim we were following, even if we did not consciously formulate and follow it. Thus, given Brown's, Gray's, and Green's reasons for contributing to charity, we might express the maxims they were following as M1 (Brown's maxim), M2 (Gray's maxim), and M3 (Green's maxim).

M1. I will contribute to charity when I approve of the charity's goals and I want to help it achieve its purposes.

M2. I will contribute to charity when I think that doing so will help improve my business and I want to improve my business.

M3. I will contribute to charity when I think that doing so will help me win an election and I want to win the election.

A maxim takes the form "I will do action X in circumstance C for purpose P." It is a personal principle of action, a kind of prescription of how a person will act in certain circumstances to achieve what he or she wants. Thus, a maxim must specify (1) what I will do, (2) the concrete circumstances in which I will do it, and (3) why I will do it.

For example, suppose that a social worker faces the following situation. The agency where she works is funded by the state. In order to save money, the state has instituted a screening system. All children who are referred to the agency for counseling must be given a questionnaire designed to quantify the severity of their problems or symptoms. Children who score 80 or above will receive treatment; children who score below 80 will not receive treatment. The social worker and her colleagues believe, first, that the questionnaire's results are not entirely reliable and, second, that almost all children who score in the 70s on the questionnaire need services. Consequently, they are considering falsifying the results of the questionnaire so that children who actually score only in the 70s will have a score of 80 entered in their records. Their intention is to deceive the state authorities so that treatment for these children will be authorized.

What *maxim* would the social worker and her colleagues be following? We must be careful not to identify a maxim that is overly general, such as

I will deceive people.

It must be qualified to include the circumstances and the motivation. Will the social worker deceive everyone under all circumstances? No. A more accurate statement of the maxim she would be following is:

I will deceive state authorities by falsifying the scores of children on a questionnaire designed to quantify the severity of their psychological symptoms/problems when I believe that the test is probably unreliable and when falsification is necessary in order to get children the help that, in my best professional judgment, they need.

The action contemplated is an act of deception, but we must expand the description of the act to include (1) the circumstances (the deception is limited to deception of state authorities about the results of a questionnaire that may not be reliable and may deprive children of services that they need) and (2) the motive (the deception is intended not to benefit the social worker but to benefit others). So a maxim must be properly qualified.

Of course, self-deception is possible. Ascertaining the maxim one is actually following (or would follow) requires a great deal of self-reflection. Some people may not be able to engage in such deep reflection because they are not fully aware of their own motives. Others may rationalize and convince themselves that they are following one maxim (believing that the motive is not self-interest and the circumstances are appropriate) when in fact they are following a different maxim (the motive really is self-interest or the circumstances are not appropriate). However, people who are conscientious will try to be honest with themselves about the maxims they are (or would be) really following.

According to Kant, an action done from duty has moral worth based only on the maxim that the agent was following, which specifies the action, the circumstances, and the motive. But surely an action cannot have moral worth if the agent is following a bad maxim, such as "I will kill people whenever it is advantageous to me." Presumably an action has moral worth if and only if the maxim being followed is a morally acceptable maxim. But what makes a maxim morally acceptable or morally unacceptable?

Before turning to this question, however, let us reflect a bit more on Brown's, Gray's, and Green's maxims and behavior. Did Brown, Gray, or Green do anything *wrong* in contributing to charity? If they were following morally unacceptable maxims, then they were doing something wrong, but if they were following morally acceptable maxims, they were not doing anything wrong. Whether they did anything wrong, then, depends on whether their maxims are morally acceptable. Undoubtedly Kant would agree that none of these people did anything wrong in contributing money to charity, so he would surely agree that the maxims they followed are morally acceptable. However, he would say that Gray's and Green's actions lacked moral worth because the maxims they were following were purely self-interested. (Lacking moral worth, their actions do not merit praise; but it does not follow that because they lack moral worth, they merit condemnation instead.) So once again, we face the task of distinguishing between morally acceptable and morally unacceptable maxims.

Thus, whether we are talking about the moral worth of actions or the rightness and wrongness of actions, we need to distinguish between morally acceptable and morally unacceptable maxims. We require a test of maxims that will enable us to distinguish between those that are and those that are not morally acceptable to act on.

Kant did not think that we need to invent a totally new test to determine the rightness and wrongness of maxims. He believed that there is a test that most ordinary people apply and that has been endorsed by most of the world's major religions, including Christianity. This test is the so-called Golden Rule: Treat people the way you want to be treated. However, he did think that the Golden Rule needs to be made more precise in order to be applied correctly. He called his reformulation of the Golden Rule the Categorical Imperative. It's an imperative because it takes the form of a rule. It's categorical because it applies in all circumstances, regardless of an agent's desires, and because it binds all rational agents.

THE CATEGORICAL IMPERATIVE: UNIVERSAL LAW FORMULATION

Kant's first formulation of the Categorical Imperative was "I ought never to act in such a way that I could not also will that my maxim should be a universal law."[3] Because the Categorical Imperative is commanded by a person's own reason, it applies not just to that person but to all creatures with reason—that is, to all rational creatures. And because an essential feature of the moral law is universality—that is, that it applies to everyone—it follows that universality is the essence of the Categorical Imperative. Therefore, it cannot be expressed merely in terms of "I." Thus, more formally, Kant presented the following universal law formulation of the Categorical Imperative:

> Act only according to that maxim by which you can at the same time will that it should become a universal law.[4]

According to Kant, all people in all times in all places are morally forbidden to act on maxims that they can't consistently will to be universal laws. But what does this formulation mean?

---

[3]Ibid., p. 18.
[4]Ibid., p. 38.

Maxims and Universal Laws

According to Kant, an action is morally acceptable if and only if the maxim the individual is following is morally acceptable. Kant maintained that a maxim is morally acceptable if and only if one could consistently will that it become a *universal law*. According to Kant, people are morally forbidden to act on maxims that they cannot consistently will to be universal laws. To determine whether we can consistently will a maxim to be a universal law, we must transform the maxim from a personal policy expressed in terms of "I" into a universal policy that applies to everyone.

Recall Brown's maxim (M1), Gray's maxim (M2), and Green's maxim (M3):

M1.   I will contribute to charity when I approve of the charity's goals and I want to help it achieve its purposes.

M2.   I will contribute to charity when I think that doing so will help improve my business and I want to improve my business.

M3.   I will contribute to charity when I think that doing so will help me win an election and I want to win the election.

To determine whether their maxims are morally acceptable, we must transform M1, M2, and M3 into universal laws and determine whether Brown, Gray, and Green can consistently will that the maxims they're acting on become universal laws. A maxim only applies to the individual whose maxim it is; a universal law applies to everyone. Thus, M1 becomes UL1, M2 becomes UL2, and M3 becomes UL3.

UL1.   Everyone will contribute to charity when they approve of the charity's goals and they want to help it achieve its purposes.

UL2.   Everyone will contribute to charity when they think that doing so will help improve their business and they want to improve their business.

UL3.   Everyone will contribute to charity when they think that doing so will help them win an election and they want to win the election.

If Brown can't consistently will that the maxim she's following, M1, become the universal law UL1, then M1 is an immoral maxim, and the action she performs in following that maxim is immoral. The same applies to Gray and his maxim (M2) and to Green and her maxim (M3). What might prevent Brown (or Gray or Green) from being able to consistently will that M1 (M2, M3) become the universal law UL1 (UL2, UL3)?

Inconsistencies in Willing That a Maxim Become a Universal Law

Kant's test of maxims involves looking for contradiction. Contradiction or inconsistency is always a relationship between two things. "I am sleepy" contradicts "I am not sleepy." "2 + 2 = 4" is inconsistent with "2 + 2 = 5." According to Kant, a maxim is unacceptable (it fails the test) if willing it to be a universal law generates contradiction. In order to generate contradiction, just as "I am sleepy" must be juxtaposed with "I am not sleepy," so the universal law must be juxtaposed with something else. What might that something else be?

To answer this question, let's analyze one of Kant's own examples. Kant asks us to imagine a prosperous man who "sees others (whom he could help) . . . struggle with great hardships." He asks himself whether it is morally acceptable for him to *not* help them. His maxim might be expressed as

> M4. When I am prosperous, I will refrain from helping others if I won't benefit from helping.

The question for Kant would then be whether he can will that maxim to be a universal law of nature without contradicting himself. The universal law would be

> UL4. When people are prosperous, they will refrain from helping others if they won't benefit from helping.

Kant claims that the man cannot possibly will UL4 without contradicting himself.

> It is . . . impossible to will that such a principle should hold everywhere as a law of nature. For a will which resolved this would conflict with itself, since instances can often arise in which he would need the love and sympathy of others, and in which he would have robbed himself, by such a law of nature springing from his own will, of all hope of the aid he desires.[5]

The key to this passage is that willing the universal law conflicts with *desires* the man has. According to Kant, the man desires or will desire help, but by willing UL4 he virtually guarantees that this desire will be frustrated: He will not get help if or when he needs it. Thus, one potential source of contradiction is for a universal law to conflict with our desires in the sense of making it virtually certain that the desires will be frustrated. Thus, one test of whether our willing a universal law generates contradiction is to juxtapose the law with our desires. If the law would virtually guarantee that our desires would be frustrated, then there is a contradiction in our willing: We are willing that our desires be satisfied at the same time that we are willing something that will virtually guarantee that our desires will *not* be satisfied.

But how does Kant know that the man in his example desires help? First, Kant emphasizes that human beings are both rational and "dependent." Rational beings who are dependent inevitably need help. (Kant would give angels as an example of independent rational beings.) Humans, because they are dependent as well as rational, are vulnerable to a variety of harms; therefore, they need others to refrain from harming them. Additionally, they always need the help of others at various stages and points in their lives. Kant implies that rational beings

---

[5]Ibid., p. 40.

desire or want what they need. (It would be irrational not to want what we need.) Therefore, since the man in his example is a dependent rational being, he will inevitably need help even if he does not need help at this moment; he knows he will need help; and he desires what he needs. Kant would probably maintain that the man necessarily desires the help he will inevitably need because he is rational. (If he does not desire the help he will inevitably need, he is not rational.) Therefore, it is necessarily the case that the man desires help, even if he does not desire help at this precise moment.

Let's look at another example. Suppose that I'm considering having an affair and deceiving my wife. My maxim would be

> M5.   I will have an affair and deceive my wife when I want to have sex with someone else.

I may act on that maxim only if I can will that it be a universal law of nature without contradicting myself. The universal law would be

> UL5.   Everyone will have an affair and deceive his/her spouse when he/she wants to have sex with someone else.

In order to determine whether I can will UL5 without contradicting myself, I need to determine whether it conflicts with any *desires* I have. Suppose that I don't want my wife to have an affair with someone else nor to deceive me. Then I am contradicting myself. If UL5 became a law of nature, my desire that my wife not have an affair or deceive me would almost certainly be frustrated: She would probably have an affair and deceive me. Therefore, it would be wrong for me to act on this maxim.

Let's return for a moment now to Brown, Gray, and Green who contributed money to charity for a variety of reasons, some of them purely self-interested. If they have no desires that would almost certainly be frustrated if their maxims became the universal laws UL1, UL2, and UL3, respectively, then they are not contradicting themselves and their maxims pass the test. They would be doing nothing wrong by acting on their maxims (even if their actions would not be praiseworthy because they are purely self-interested). There is no reason to think that Brown and Gray *must* have some desires that would be frustrated if UL1 and UL2 became universal laws of nature. Therefore, it seems reasonable to assume that their maxims pass the test.

However, one problem with this test is that it appears to be subjective. It depends on one's desires. Suppose that John, like me, is considering cheating on his spouse and deceiving her about it. However, unlike me, he does not care whether she has an affair and deceives him; he has no desire that she remain faithful and honest. In that case, he can will that maxim M5 be the universal law UL5 without contradicting himself (it is not in conflict with any of his desires), although I cannot will that it be a universal law without contradicting myself. Therefore, it would be morally acceptable for him to cheat on his wife, although it would not be morally acceptable for me to cheat on my wife. Kant certainly did not intend his test to be subjective.

Is there a solution? Perhaps. Kant claims that all rational beings necessarily pursue or desire happiness.

> There is one end, however, which we may presuppose as actual in all rational beings . . . , so far as they are dependent beings. There is one purpose which they not only *can* have but which we can presuppose that they all *do* have by a necessity of nature. This purpose is happiness. It belongs to [a rational being's] essence.[6]

Someone whose goal in life is to be as unhappy as possible would not be rational. Necessarily, rational beings want to be happy rather than unhappy.

If there are no limits or requirements regarding what can constitute happiness for rational dependent beings, then Kant's claim, even if true, cannot provide a solution to our problem. However, if there are limits or requirements, it may be able to provide a solution. Kant would probably agree that happiness for rational dependent beings, all other things being equal, requires continued existence, health, some degree of liberty, and enough resources to meet one's basic needs. Imagine someone's claiming that death, illness, or poverty would make him happy as an end in itself (rather than as a means to some other valued end) while admitting that he has no good reason for wanting to be dead, ill, unfree, or poor. Such a claim would be irrational. Similarly, if dependent rational beings care about other people (and probably almost all care about some other people), then their happiness will require that those they care about be happy. Thus, Kant would probably agree that the happiness of rational beings also requires that the lives, health, liberty, and access to basic resources of those they care about be preserved.

If there are some desires that all rational dependent beings necessarily have and others that necessarily no rational dependent being has, then the test of the Categorical Imperative is not wholly subjective. For example, consider the prosperous man in Kant's example who is considering not helping others in need. We suggested that he necessarily has a desire that he receive help when he needs it. Such a desire is inherent in all human beings, all of whom are dependent rational beings. Thus, Kant could say that no human being lacks the desire to be helped. Therefore, no rational dependent being could will UL4 without contradicting herself.

Can we say the same thing about UL5—that no rational dependent being can will it without contradicting herself? If we cannot, then there seems to be an element of subjectivity in applying the Categorical Imperative: The test of noncontradiction that requires juxtaposing a law with an agent's desires will have different results for people with different desires. In the case of UL5, I cannot will it without contradicting myself while it appears as though John can will it without contradicting himself. In that case, it would be wrong for me but not for him. But are appearances deceiving? Perhaps there are desires that all dependent rational beings necessarily have or desires they necessarily do not have that are in conflict with UL5. Unfortunately for Kant and the Categorical Imperative,

---

[6]Ibid., p. 32.

it is not obvious that there are desires that John, as a rational dependent being, must have or must not have that would conflict with UL5. It is not obvious that John *must* desire that his wife be faithful to him and honest. Therefore, it is not obvious that John will necessarily be made unhappy if his wife is unfaithful and deceptive. Willing UL5 may not conflict with the happiness that Kant claims all rational dependent beings necessarily seek.

If this reasoning is correct, then there is an element of subjectivity in applying the Categorical Imperative. Given agents with different desires, some actions may be wrong for some people but not for others. However, if Kant is correct that there are some desires that all rational dependent beings necessarily have and others that they necessarily do not have, then some actions are wrong for every human being—namely, those actions whose maxims, if transformed into a universal law, would conflict with desires that all rational dependent beings necessarily have.

Here's an example for you to analyze for yourself. Albertson cheats his customers when he thinks he can get away with it in order to increase his profits, acting on the following maxim:

M6.   I will cheat my customers when I think I can get away with it and it will increase my profits.

His action is morally acceptable only if he can will that M6 become the universal law UL6 without contradicting himself.

UL6.   Everyone will cheat their customers when they think they can get away with it and it will increase their profits.

Is UL6 in conflict with desires that *you* have? (If the answer is yes, then it would be wrong for you to act on M6; if the answer is no, then it might not be wrong for you to act on M6.) Is UL6 in conflict with desires that Albertson, as a dependent rational being, *must* have?

Kant considered one more possible source of inconsistency: We could will something to be a universal law that couldn't possibly be a universal law. To take Kant's own example, suppose that Abdul borrows money by making a promise to repay that he does not intend to keep. The maxim he's following is

M7.   I will make a promise to repay a loan that I don't intend to keep when I need money.

M7 is morally acceptable only if Abdul can consistently will that it become the universal law.

UL7.   Everyone will make promises to repay loans that they don't intend to keep when they need money.

According to Kant, UL7 could not possibly be a universal law because if everyone followed it, soon no one would be able to follow it because the practice of lending money on the basis of a promise to repay would soon be extinguished. UL7 is self-destroying. It would not take long for people who lend money to realize that people were following UL7, and when they did, they simply would stop lending money on the basis of a promise to repay. Once promises were no longer accepted, the practice of lending money would cease. Therefore, it would be impossible for everyone to make false promises to repay a loan with no intention to repay.

There are, then, two primary ways that inconsistency can arise in willing that a maxim become a universal law. First, in some cases, if a maxim became a universal law, it would jeopardize our own survival and happiness. Because as dependent rational creatures we will that our survival and happiness *not* be jeopardized, we would be willing contradictory things. Second, we may will something to be a universal law that couldn't possibly be a universal law.

We can use the Categorical Imperative to rationally criticize our own or others' behavior. Consider the acts of genocide committed by Serbs in Bosnia, primarily against Muslims, and by Hutus in Central Africa, primarily against Tutsis. Imagine that Sara is having a discussion with a Serb or Hutu who has participated in these acts of genocide. Challenging him, Sara asks what maxim he was following. He replies that he was following

> M8.   I will participate in killing members of groups that my people despise or fear in order to exterminate them.

Sara, applying the Categorical Imperative, asks him whether he can consistently will that M8 become a universal law.

> UL8.   Everyone will participate in killing members of groups that their people despise or fear in order to exterminate them.

Sara points out that UL8 will probably lead to acts of genocide against his own people in order to exterminate them. Surely he wills that acts of genocide against his own people, which could lead to his own murder or the murder of many people he cares about, *not* occur. Thus, he contradicts himself. He wills a universal law that will probably ensure that acts of genocide against his people will occur, at the same time that he wills that acts of genocide against his people *not* occur.

Similarly, suppose that a terrorist is considering planting a bomb on a civilian airplane carrying hundreds of passengers. If he desires to behave morally, he will ask himself whether such an act is morally acceptable. Applying the Categorical Imperative, he can ask himself what maxim he would be following. The maxim would be something like

> M9.   I will kill innocent people when I believe it will advance a cause that I think is worthy and important.

He must then ask himself whether he can consistently will that it become a universal law.

> UL9.   Everyone will kill innocent people when they believe that it will advance a cause that they think is worthy and important.

Given UL9, it is very probable that he or someone he cares about will become the victim of a terrorist. Thus, if he wills that he and those he cares about *not* be killed by a terrorist, he contradicts himself in also willing UL9. In that case, M9 is not a morally acceptable maxim, and it would be wrong to plant the bomb on the airplane.

Duties Derived from the Categorical Imperative

Kant derived a variety of duties from the Categorical Imperative. For example, he argued that everyone has a duty to help those in need, using the following reasoning:

> A . . . man, for whom things are going well, sees that others (whom he could help) have to struggle with great hardships, and he asks, "What concern of mine is it? Let each one be as happy as heaven wills, or as he can make himself; I will not take anything from him or even envy him; but to his welfare or his assistance in time of need I have no desire to contribute." If such a way of thinking were a universal law of nature, certainly the human race could exist. . . . It is nevertheless impossible to will that such a principle should hold everywhere as a law of nature. For a will which resolved this would conflict with itself, since instances can often arise in which he would need the love and sympathy of others, and in which he would have robbed himself, by such a law of nature springing from his own will, of all hope of the aid he desires.[7]

Thus, Kant argued that no one can consistently will that the maxim

   M10.   I will refrain from helping others in need when I won't benefit.

become the universal law

   UL10.   Everyone will refrain from helping others in need without personal benefit.

Everyone has required the help of others in the past and will need the help of others in the future. Because we're dependent and rational, we want the help of others when we're in need, and thus we will that we be helped when we're in need. However, if we will that M10 become the universal law UL10, we'll guarantee that we won't get help when we're in need. Therefore, no one can consistently will that M10 become the universal law UL10 because we would will both that we get help when we need it and that we not get help when we need it. Everyone, therefore, has a *duty* to help others who are in need.

In a later work, Kant again maintained that

> to be beneficent, that is, to promote according to one's means . . . the happiness of others in need, without hoping for something in return, is every man's duty.

> For every man who finds himself in need wishes to be helped by other men. But if he lets his maxim of being unwilling to assist others in turn when they are in need become public, that is, makes this a universal permissive law, then

---

[7]Ibid., p. 40.

everyone would likewise deny him assistance when he himself is in need. . . . Hence the maxim of self-interest would conflict with itself if it were made a universal law, that is, it is contrary to duty.[8]

Kant also claimed that gratitude or "honoring a person because of a benefit he has rendered us"[9] is a duty, and it is a duty generally to respect other rational agents.

THE CATEGORICAL IMPERATIVE: RESPECT FOR PERSONS FORMULATION

Kant provided a second formulation of the Categorical Imperative that he claimed is equivalent to the first. Whereas the first formulation is expressed in terms of universal law, the second formulation requires that we treat all people with respect.

> Act so that you treat humanity, whether in your own person or in that of another, always as an end and never as a means only.[10]

In *The Metaphysics of Morals,* Kant elaborated.

> Man regarded as a *person* . . . is exalted above any price; for as a person . . . he is not to be valued merely as a means to the ends of others . . . , but as an end in himself, that is, he possesses a *dignity* (an absolute inner worth) by which he exacts *respect* for himself from all other rational beings in the world. He can measure himself with any other being of his kind and value himself on a footing of equality with them.[11]

Trees, insects, snakes, and squirrels are living beings but they're not persons (or people). Human beings, although only one species among many, are thought to be special. What makes them special? What makes them people? To Kant it is rationality; in his view, it is reason that makes persons especially valuable. However, contemporary thinkers generally focus on at least three major features that define what we might call "personhood": (1) People are conscious; they're aware of their environment and can perceive the world around them. (2) People are self-aware; they're aware of themselves as separate beings persisting through time with a past, present, and future. (3) People have a developed capacity or ability to reason; they can think, solve problems, communicate, and so on.[12]

Because trees, insects, snakes, and squirrels don't have all of these characteristics, they're not people. However, that doesn't mean that only human beings are people. If there is intelligent life elsewhere in the universe, alien beings who

---

[8]Immanuel Kant, "The Doctrine of Virtue," in *The Metaphysics of Morals,* trans. Mary Gregor (New York: Cambridge University Press, 1991), p. 247. (Originally published in 1797.)

[9]Ibid., p. 248.

[10]Kant, *Foundations of the Metaphysics of Morals,* p. 46.

[11]Kant, *Metaphysics of Morals,* p. 230.

[12]Compare this definition with those discussed in Chapter 15 on abortion.

satisfy these criteria, they would be people even though they're not human beings. Consider the creature E. T. from the movie of the same name. Although viewers knew that E. T. was not human, they certainly thought of E. T. as a person. Similarly, it may be possible for nonbiological organisms to have these characteristics; if so, they would also be people. Consider the robot R2D2 from the *Star Wars* movies or the android Data from the television series *Star Trek: The Next Generation.* If such nonbiological organisms existed, they would be people and not mere things.

Kant insisted that people are supremely valuable and that they should not be treated as we might treat things that are not people, such as television sets or cows. Kant also seems to presuppose that all people have *equal* moral worth or value. In his view, it's morally permissible to use mere things purely as means to our ends. For example, it's morally permissible for you to use your television set as you please (as long as you don't use it to harm people). If you would derive satisfaction from smashing it to pieces, it's morally acceptable for you to do so. Similarly, many people believe that it's morally acceptable to raise cows in order to eat them. But it is not morally acceptable to use *people* purely for our own purposes, because people have inherent and equal moral worth.

Let us say that if we use another person *purely* for our own purposes, we are merely using the person. We do and must use people all the time for our own purposes, but it does not follow that we *merely* use them. For example, suppose you hire a tutor in calculus. You're using the tutor for you own ends, but you are not *merely* using that person. Here, it would be helpful to distinguish between hiring a tutor in calculus, on the one hand, and enslaving or raping people, on the other. In the second and third cases you are *merely* using people, but not in the first case.

How does the tutor-tutee relationship differ from the slave-master or the rapist-victim relationship? First, the tutor-tutee relationship, unlike the slave-master and the rapist-victim relationship, is purely voluntary. We *merely* use another person when we enter into the relationship against the person's will. Second, there's mutual and roughly equal benefit in the tutor-tutee relationship, but not in the slave-master or rapist-victim relationship. You benefit by receiving instruction, and the tutor benefits by receiving payment. The same cannot be said of the slave-master and rapist-victim relationship. Finally, we may presume that in the tutor-tutee relationship there is mutual respect and consideration of one another's interests and well-being, manifested in such behaviors as politeness, honesty, and openness. Each refrains from insulting, manipulating, exploiting, degrading, humiliating, or otherwise harming the other. Again, the same cannot be said of the slave-master or rapist-victim relationship. Rape and enslavement can serve as paradigm examples of *merely* using people.

According to Kant, because people are special, because they have great (and equal) value or worth, they should be treated with respect, which means that they should never be treated *merely* as a means. We treat others with respect when (1) we ensure that our interactions with them are purely voluntary, (2) we ensure that our interactions with them are mutually beneficial or are just and fair, and (3) we ensure that we take account of their needs, desires, and interests.

Kant emphasized that we must treat other people with respect simply because they're people, but he also emphasized that we should treat ourselves with respect because we, too, are people. He thought that we have duties to others, but also duties to ourselves. For example, he maintained that every person has a duty of self-perfection.

> This duty can . . . consist only in *cultivating* one's *capacities* . . . the highest of which is *understanding*. . . . Man has a duty to raise himself from the crude state of his nature, from his animality . . . , more and more toward humanity . . . ; he has a duty to diminish his ignorance by instruction and to correct his errors.[13]

As for our duties to others, Kant insisted that when we are acting toward others from the duty of beneficence, we must never undermine their self-respect or humiliate them, for that would violate the requirement that we treat people with respect.

> We shall acknowledge that we are under obligation to help a poor man; but since the favor we do implies that his well-being depends on our generosity, and this humbles him, it is our duty to behave as if our help is either merely what is due him or but a slight service of love, and to spare him humiliation and maintain his respect for himself.[14]

EXERCISES

1. Torvaldson's neighbor has fallen from the roof she was repairing and is lying unconscious on the ground. Torvaldson saw the accident. Because he's late for a basketball game for which he has tickets, Torvaldson does not wish to come to his neighbor's aid or call for assistance; he intends to ignore his neighbor's plight and go about his business. Apply (a) the universal law formulation and (b) the respect for persons formulation of Kant's Categorical Imperative to determine whether it would be morally acceptable for Torvaldson to ignore his neighbor's plight.

2. Tom normally charges $2.50 per hour for baby-sitting. His neighbor, who is poor, asked Tom to baby-sit her young daughter while she took her son to the hospital for an emergency appendectomy. She was gone for ten hours and owes him $25.00. Tom has decided that he will not charge her because she is poor and it was an emergency situation. Apply (a) the universal law formulation and (b) the respect for persons formulation of the Categorical Imperative to determine whether it would be morally acceptable for Tom to refrain from charging his neighbor for his baby-sitting services.

3. According to a story in the *New York Times*, two executives of a food company were charged with knowingly selling eggs tainted with salmonella, which causes food poisoning, and with falsifying lab reports to hide the fact that the

---

[13]Kant, *Metaphysics of Morals*, p. 191.
[14]Ibid., p. 243.

eggs were tainted.[15] For our purposes, assume that the charges were true. Apply (a) the universal law formulation and (b) the respect for persons formulation of the Categorical Imperative to determine whether their actions were morally acceptable.

4. Brad has a date with Sara. He hopes to encourage her to drink enough to get drunk so that he can either seduce her or have her pass out so that he can have sex with her while she's unconscious. Apply (a) the universal law formulation and (b) the respect for persons formulation of the Categorical Imperative to determine whether it would be morally acceptable for Brad to do what he intends.

5. Phil has gone to Boston to view the St. Patrick's Day Parade. For the first time, a gay-pride group of homosexual and lesbian Irish-Americans has been permitted to march. As they pass him on the parade route, Phil shouts out insults, makes threatening gestures and remarks, and finally throws a rock at the group. Apply (a) the universal law formulation and (b) the respect for persons formulation of the Categorical Imperative to determine whether Phil's actions are morally acceptable.

6. Brenda hasn't studied for her philosophy test, so she cheats by copying from another student's exam in order to pass it. Apply (a) the universal law formulation and (b) the respect for persons formulation of the Categorical Imperative in order to determine whether her action is morally acceptable.

7. Explain the difference between Rule Utilitarianism and the universal law formulation of the Categorical Imperative.

8. Apply both formulations of the Categorical Imperative to the issues of abortion, capital punishment, euthanasia, and suicide.

9. Pedro claims that the principle "Treat others as you want them to treat you" is dangerous. He says that a masochist who enjoys having pain inflicted on him would then inflict pain on others in following this principle. He claims that a masochist could consistently will as a universal law a principle permitting people to inflict pain on others. Consuela disagrees. She says that a masochist could not consistently will that such a principle be a universal law and that "Treat others as you want them to treat you" does not have that consequence. With whom do you agree, and why?

10. Suppose that two duties derived from the Categorical Imperative conflict. For example, suppose that we have a duty to protect human life and a duty not to lie. However, suppose that we can save an innocent life only by lying. Would this pose a problem for Kant's theory? Can you think of any way of resolving it?

SUGGESTED READINGS

Fred Feldman. *Introductory Ethics.* Englewood Cliffs, NJ: Prentice-Hall, 1978. (See especially Chapters 7 and 8.)

Immanuel Kant. *Foundations of the Metaphysics of Morals.* 2d ed. Translated by Lewis White Beck. New York: Library of Liberal Arts, 1990. (Originally published in 1785.)

---

[15]*New York Times,* March 18, 1992.

Immanuel Kant. *The Metaphysics of Morals.* Translated by Mary Gregor. New York: Cambridge University Press, 1991. (Originally published in 1797.)

Onora Nell. *Acting on Principle.* New York: Columbia University Press, 1975.

Roger J. Sullivan. *Immanuel Kant's Moral Theory.* New York: Cambridge University Press, 1989.

_____. *An Introduction to Kant's Ethics.* Cambridge, England: Cambridge University Press, 1994.

Robert Paul Wolff. *The Autonomy of Reason: A Commentary on Kant's Groundwork of the Metaphysics of Morals.* New York: Harper Torch, 1973.

CHAPTER 9

Natural Law Theory

If a human being were to eat worms he would be considered demented by most people, who would be disgusted by the thought. Yet birds eat worms and no one considers them demented; no one after childhood appears to be disgusted by the thought of birds' eating worms. Why is that? The reason is that eating worms is considered "natural" for birds but not for human beings. It is part of a bird's nature but not part of a human being's nature. Similarly, adult rabbits often eat their own feces. If an adult human being eats his own feces, it is usually considered a sign of mental illness; however, if a rabbit does it, it is not considered a sign of mental illness. Again, the reason for the different judgments despite the similarity of circumstances is that it is considered "natural" for rabbits to eat their feces but not for human beings to eat their feces. It is part of a rabbit's nature.

NATURE AND PHYSICAL LAWS

In a manner of speaking, nature has established certain physical laws. For example, it is a physical law of nature that pure water freezes at 32 degrees Fahrenheit at sea level. It is also a physical law of nature that when water freezes (turns to a solid), it expands. According to an influential tradition in Western thought, physical laws of nature describe how things do and must behave under certain conditions. If it is a law of nature that water freezes at 32 degrees Fahrenheit, then *all* water freezes at that temperature. Further, if it is a law of nature that water freezes at 32 degrees Fahrenheit, then a collection of pure water at sea level whose temperature drops to 32 degrees Fahrenheit or lower *must* freeze. Conversely, if its temperature remains above 32 degrees Fahrenheit, it *cannot* freeze. Similarly, if a collection of water freezes—for example, the water in your car's radiator—then it *must* expand. In a sense, the physical laws of nature establish guidelines on how things must, can, and cannot behave. Because of the physical laws of nature, frozen water must expand; it cannot contract. It must turn into a solid; it cannot remain a liquid or turn into a gas.

The physical laws of nature are the same everywhere. Pure water freezes at 32 degrees Fahrenheit at sea level (at a certain pressure) whether the water is in the United States or China, on Earth or on Mars. Similarly, water expands when it freezes whether it is in our solar system or in another solar system. Physical laws of nature are discovered rather than created or established by human beings. It is nature rather than human beings that "decreed" that water shall freeze at 32 degrees Fahrenheit and expand when it freezes. The physical laws of nature are what they are and operate as they operate independent of human beliefs, desires, and feelings. Before human beings even came into existence, water froze at 32 degrees Fahrenheit. Regardless of how you feel or what you desire, if the water in your car's radiator freezes, it will expand, probably cracking the radiator.

In addition to such physical laws of nature as the laws that water freezes at 32 degrees Fahrenheit and expands when it freezes, physical laws of nature pertaining to biological organisms specify what is "natural" for members of certain species. The physical "law" that birds eat worms is a law of that kind. According to this view, each kind of thing has its own inherent "nature." A thing's inherent nature is a system of capacities and ways of behaving that are "natural" for or characteristic of members of its species. For example, it is part of a cat's nature that it tends to stalk and kill birds and mice; it is part of a dog's nature that it tends to chase cats; it is part of a cow's nature that it grazes on grass; it is part of a lion's nature that it catches, kills, and eats other animals. Each kind of thing or species has its own characteristic way of life and way of behaving that is part of its inherent nature. In turn, an organism's inherent nature provides norms or standards of what is good for things of that kind. Some conditions, ways of life, or forms of behavior enable members of a species to survive and flourish; others do not. It is good for a shark but not for a cat to live in water; it is good for a lion but not for a cow to eat meat.

According to the Natural Law tradition in moral theory, there are moral laws of nature that are analogous to physical laws of nature. Theological versions of Natural Law theory are substantially identical to the Divine Command theory of morality. According to the theological versions, the moral laws of nature are simply the laws or commands of God. However, there are secular versions of Natural Law theory. Because we have already discussed the Divine Command theory of morality, in this chapter we will concentrate on secular versions of Natural Law moral theory.

MORAL LAWS OF NATURE

General Moral Laws

Natural Law theorists maintain that there are moral laws of nature that are analogous to physical laws of nature. For example, St. Thomas Aquinas claimed that certain general moral principles or rules constitute moral laws of nature, "decreed" by nature just as physical laws are. Among them are rules requiring people to return things that have been entrusted to them by others and to honor their parents, as well as rules forbidding people to kill the innocent, commit adultery, or steal.[1] These moral laws are analogous to such physical laws as the laws that water freezes at 32 degrees Fahrenheit and that it expands when it freezes. The moral and physical laws of nature are similar in that they are the same everywhere, they are established by nature rather than by human beings, and they operate or apply independent of what people believe, desire, or feel. However, whereas things in the physical world do and must behave in accordance with the physical laws of nature, they do not necessarily behave in accordance with the moral laws of nature. If it is a physical law of nature that water freezes at 32 degrees Fahrenheit, then no collection of water can possibly violate that law. However, if it is a moral law of nature that people should or must not steal, people can and do violate the law. Similarly, whereas the physical laws of nature apply to everything in the physical world, moral laws of nature only apply to rational creatures who are capable of understanding and following the moral laws of nature. Thus, the moral laws of nature do not apply to such animals as lions, tigers, sharks, and snakes because they are not rational creatures; the moral laws do apply to human beings because they are rational.

According to Aquinas, the moral laws of nature are self-evident. Human beings can discover what the moral laws of nature are, just as they can discover the laws of logic, by using their reason. Reason informs us, for example, that things equal to the same thing are equal to each other (for example, if $A = C$ and $B = C$, then $A = B$) and that every whole is greater than any of its parts.[2] These laws of logic are self-evident in the sense that one knows that they are true as soon as one understands them. According to Aquinas, the first principle of the moral law of nature is that "good is to be done and pursued, and evil is to be avoided."[3] He maintained that this principle is self-evident in the same way that the principle that things equal to the same thing are equal to each other is self-evident, and that nature has "bestowed" this and other practical principles on us.[4]

> All other precepts of the natural law are based upon this, so that whatever the practical reason naturally apprehends as man's good (or evil) belongs to the precepts of natural law as something to be done or avoided. . . .

> All those things to which man has a natural inclination are naturally apprehended by reason as being good and, consequently, as objects of pursuit, and their contraries as evil and objects of avoidance.[5]

For Aquinas, such general moral principles as the prohibition on adultery were self-evident moral principles that are "bestowed" on human beings by nature. To violate one of the moral laws of nature is to do what is contrary to reason.

---

[1]St. Thomas Aquinas, *On Law, Morality, and Politics,* ed. William Baumgarth and Richard Regan (Indianapolis, IN: Hackett, 1988), p. 85 (Summa Theologiae I–II, Question 100, Article 1).

[2]Ibid., pp. 46–47 (Summa Theologiae I–II, Question 94, Article 2).

[3]Ibid., p. 47.

[4]Ibid., p. 2 (Summa Theologiae, I, Question 79, Article 12).

[5]Ibid., p. 47 (Summa Theologiae I–II, Question 94, Article 2).

Moral Laws Derived from
a Creature's Inherent Nature

According to most Natural Law theorists, moral laws of nature that apply to human beings are rooted in human nature. As we saw, some physical laws of nature are rooted in a creature's inherent "nature"—that is, in the way of life and tendencies to behave characteristic of members of the creature's species. A certain way of life is appropriate for a cow because of the nature of cows: to graze all day eating vegetation. The way of life appropriate for a cow is different from the way of life appropriate for a lion because the nature of lions differs from the nature of cows. The way of life of a lion is to stalk other animals in order to kill and eat them. A lion could not flourish or survive if it tried to live a life appropriate for a cow, just as a cow could not flourish or survive if it tried to live a life appropriate for a lion. The way of life appropriate for a creature is determined by its nature.

Aquinas pointed out that

> under the divine lawgiver, various creatures have various natural inclinations, so that what is, as it were, a law for one is against the law for another; thus I might say that fierceness is, in a way, the law of a dog but against the law of a sheep or another meek animal. And so the law of man, which, by the divine ordinance, is allotted to him according to his proper condition, is that he should act in accordance with reason.[6]

According to Natural Law theorists, human nature determines what way of life is appropriate for a human being, just as a lion's and a sheep's inherent natures determine what way of life is appropriate for them. Human nature determines the correct moral laws of nature that human beings should follow.

Aquinas was following Aristotle. Aristotle emphasized that each kind of thing has its own nature and that this nature sets down the conditions of its surviving and flourishing, the way of life appropriate to its species. Although there is no single, unique way of life appropriate for all creatures, there is only one way of life appropriate for members of the same species, a way of life "required" by the inherent nature of members of the species. It is good or right for a creature to live according to the way of life natural for members of its species because only in that way can it survive and flourish. Thus, a creature's inherent nature establishes what is good and bad, right and wrong for it. For example, because of their inherent nature, ants and bees live together in large groups with a division of labor and a kind of hierarchy that enables them to cooperate and flourish. On the other hand, because of their inherent nature, bears live largely isolated lives. A bear could not live as ants and bees do, just as ants and bees could not live as bears do. If a creature's way of life or behavior is not consistent with its inherent nature as a member of a certain species, it will not survive and flourish.

Aristotle believed that the key to the way of life appropriate for members of a species is whatever makes members of that species different from members of

---

[6]Ibid., p. 28 (Question 91, Article 6).

other species. Therefore, what differentiates birds from fish rather than what they have in common is the key to the way of life appropriate for each of them. Aristotle maintained that rationality separates human beings from other species. It follows, then, that the way of life appropriate for a human being will be closely connected to her capacity for reasoning. He claimed that a contemplative life—a life dedicated to acquiring knowledge and understanding—is one key to human flourishing.

In the Aristotelian view, it is natural for an organism to live in accordance with the way of life that is characteristic of members of its species and unnatural to live in any other way. Furthermore, what is natural is right and what is unnatural is wrong. Thus, it is natural and right for a bee to live in a close community with other bees and unnatural and wrong for it to live in isolation, just as it is natural and right for a bear to live in relative isolation and unnatural and wrong for it to live in a close community with other bears. What is natural for a human being, therefore, is right for a human being and what is unnatural is wrong. Just as a bee's and a bear's inherent natures provide rules for correct living for them, so, too, a human being's inherent nature provides correct rules of living for human beings.

Aquinas accepted Aristotle's claims that reason makes human beings unique among the animals. He maintained, "Every will at variance with reason . . . is always evil"[7] and "the rule and measure of human acts is reason."[8] Every creature should live and act in accordance with its inherent nature. The "natural inclinations" of a creature, which are determined by its inherent nature as a member of a certain species, determine the laws of behavior appropriate to creatures of its kind. According to Aquinas, "all those things to which man has a natural inclination are naturally apprehended by reason as good and, consequently, as objects of pursuit, and their contraries as evil and objects of avoidance."[9]

According to Aquinas, because human beings naturally seek to preserve themselves, the law of nature dictates that human beings act so as to preserve themselves. Therefore, suicide is immoral. Similarly,

> there is in man an inclination to good according to the nature of his reason, which nature is proper to him; thus man has a natural inclination to know the truth about God and to live in society, and in this respect, whatever pertains to this inclination belongs to the natural law, for instance, to shun ignorance, to avoid offending those among whom one has to live, and other such things regarding the above inclination.[10]

Further, Aquinas maintained that "all sins are against nature" and that

> each thing is inclined naturally to an operation that is suitable to it according to its form; thus fire is inclined to give heat. Wherefore, since the rational soul

---

[7]Ibid., p. 7 (Question 19, Article 5).

[8]Ibid., p. 12 (Question 90, Article 1).

[9]Ibid., p. 47.

[10]Ibid, p. 48.

is the proper form of man, there is in every man a natural inclination to act according to reason, and this is to act according to virtue.[11]

According to Aquinas, acting according to reason is acting according to nature for human beings. Whatever is contrary to reason is unnatural and therefore immoral. For example, on this basis Aquinas condemns homosexuality; "certain special sins are said to be against nature; thus, contrary to heterosexual intercourse, which is natural to all animals, is male homosexual union, which has received the special name of the unnatural vice."[12] Other moral laws of nature, as we have seen, require returning goods entrusted to us and honoring our parents and prohibit killing the innocent, committing adultery, and stealing. According to Aquinas, stealing, committing adultery, and not honoring our parents are contrary to reason and therefore are unnatural. Being unnatural, they are wrong.

PROBLEMS FOR NATURAL LAW THEORY

Self-Evidence

According to Natural Law theory, any kind of behavior that is "contrary to reason" is forbidden. Behavior is "contrary to reason" if it violates a self-evident moral principle that reason has discovered or established. For example, Aquinas thought that adultery and homosexuality are contrary to reason because they violate self-evident moral rules that reason has either discovered or established.

However, many philosophers maintain that a sentence is self-evidently true only if its negation is self-contradictory and *cannot* possibly be true. For example, the sentence "Earth is either spherical or not spherical" is self-evidently true because its negation, the sentence "It is not the case that Earth is either spherical or not spherical," is equivalent to the self-contradictory sentence "Earth is both spherical and not spherical." It is logically impossible for Earth to be both spherical and not spherical. Someone who understands the sentences knows without having to appeal to evidence that "Earth either is or is not spherical" is true and that "Earth is both spherical and not spherical" is false.

Are there self-evident moral laws? According to many philosophers, proposed moral laws that prohibit killing innocent people, theft, adultery, and homosexual acts are not self-evidently true because their negations are not logical contradictions. The negation of "Theft is prohibited" is "Theft is permitted (not prohibited)." "Theft is permitted" is not a logical contradiction.

It seems that either we must give up the claim that such moral principles are self-evidently true or we must provide a different and plausible theory of self-evidence. The challenge is for Natural Law theorists to come up with a theory of self-evidence that will enable them to establish that proposed moral laws are self-evidently true.

---

[11]Ibid., p. 49 (Article 3).

[12]Ibid., p. 50.

Human Nature

Natural Law theorists argue as follows:

> Behavior/action X is not in accordance with a human being's inherent nature.
>
> It is contrary to reason for a human being to act in a way that is not in accordance with a human being's inherent nature.
>
> Whatever is contrary to reason is immoral.
> _____
>
> Therefore, behavior/action X is immoral.

However, many critics of Natural Law theory doubt that human nature can provide moral guidance, and they doubt that whatever is "natural" or in conformity with an organism's inherent nature must be morally right and good.

The concept of the inherent nature of an organism is complicated. On the one hand, it can include purely biological features that all members of a species have. For example, it is part of the inherent nature of whales that they have lungs rather than gills; it is part of the inherent nature of sharks that they have gills rather than lungs. Consequently, whales must breathe in air and cannot breathe in water, whereas sharks must breathe in water and cannot breathe in air. Similarly, it is part of a chicken's inherent nature that it lays eggs; it is part of a cow's nature that it bears live calves. It is part of a termite's inherent nature that its digestive system can derive nourishment from eating wood; it is part of a crocodile's nature that its digestive system cannot derive nourishment from eating wood. In this sense of an organism's inherent nature, an organism either physically cannot do certain things (lay eggs, breathe in water, digest wood) because of its inherent nature or it cannot survive and flourish if it acts contrary to its inherent nature.

Human nature, too, includes certain biological features. For example, all human beings have lungs rather than gills; therefore, they breathe in air and cannot breathe in water. Similarly, because of the nature of their digestive systems, human beings cannot digest and gain nourishment from wood or stones. Therefore, a human being who attempted to breathe in water or eat wood would not be acting in accordance with his inherent nature as a human being.

However, the biological features of the species *homo sapiens* do not establish the most common moral laws that Natural Law theorists claim to derive from human nature. Adultery, polygamy, homosexuality, theft, physical assault, cruelty, rape, and killing the innocent are not contrary to the biological nature of human beings the way that breathing in water and eating wood are; they obviously do not have the same effects on a person as eating wood or breathing in water. Therefore, they are not "unnatural" in the sense of being contrary to the biological nature of human beings. If Natural Law theorists wish to maintain that such behavior is contrary to reason and immoral for human beings because it is not in accordance with human nature, they must appeal to some other conception of what it is to act or not act, to live or not live, in accordance with human nature.

An organism's inherent nature as a member of a certain species often establishes characteristic patterns of behavior common to all or almost all members of the species. For example, spiders spin webs, sparrows build nests, bees construct hives, cats hunt mice and birds, hyenas hunt in packs, and polar bears hunt alone. It would be unnatural, in the sense of unusual or uncharacteristic, for a spider not to spin a web, for a sparrow to spin a web, for a hyena to hunt alone, or for a polar bear to hunt in a pack of polar bears. Similarly, it would be contrary to a lamb's nature to attack a lion, just as it would be contrary to a lion's nature to run from a lamb. In a sense, an organism's inherent nature as a member of a certain species establishes laws of behavior for it that are physical laws of nature.

Critics of Natural Law theory, however, doubt that the inherent nature of *Homo sapiens* establishes laws of behavior for human beings in the same way that the nature of cats, lions, and polar bears establishes laws of behavior for them. Human nature is surprisingly diverse. For example, are human beings naturally as fearless and aggressive as lions, or are they naturally as timid and pacific as rabbits and lambs? Human nature has room for both kinds of personality. Human beings also don't seem to have the relatively simple inherent or "instinctive" behavior patterns of animals lower on the evolutionary tree. Cats "instinctively" chase mice and birds; therefore, such behavior is natural for them. It is not easy to identify such "instinctive" behavior patterns in human beings because so much of human behavior is shaped by the environment—that is, by deliberate and nondeliberate conditioning, training, and education.

If behaviors such as polygamy, adultery, homosexuality, physical assault, cruelty, rape, and killing the innocent are not contrary to the inherent nature of human beings, then we cannot appeal to the inherent nature of human beings in order to show that such behaviors are wrong. The challenge facing Natural Law theorists, then, is to provide a plausible account of the inherent nature of human beings so that they can show that the kinds of behavior they condemn are contrary to that inherent nature and therefore immoral.

Is What Is Natural Right and What Is Unnatural Wrong?

Natural Law theorists assume that it is morally right and good for an organism to act in accordance with its inherent nature. Only on the basis of that assumption can the inherent nature of human beings provide moral laws of conduct for them. However, critics doubt that all behavior that is in accordance with an organism's inherent nature is morally good and all behavior not in accordance with its inherent nature is morally bad. For example, biologist Stephen Jay Gould writes of a group of wasps named Ichneumonidae comprising hundreds of thousands of different species. These wasps reproduce by laying their eggs inside the living body of another insect, most commonly a caterpillar. The wasp stings the caterpillar and then injects its eggs into it. As Gould writes, "Usually the host is not otherwise inconvenienced for the moment, at least until the eggs hatch and the ichneumon larvae begin their grim work of interior excavation."[13] Then, the larvae slowly eat the helpless caterpillar from the inside out. "The ichneumon larva eats fat bodies and digestive organs first, keeping the caterpillar alive by preserving intact the essential heart and central nervous system. Finally, the larva completes its work and kills its victim, leaving behind the caterpillar's empty shell."[14] Such behavior is in accordance with the inherent nature of Ichneumonidae wasps. However, one may doubt that such natural behavior is morally praiseworthy.

It may be that human beings, or at least male human beings, are naturally aggressive and prone to violence. After all, war and fighting seem to be such universal pastimes of men in all ages that one might conclude that the inherent nature of male human beings includes a strong tendency to behave violently. If that is so, should men act in accordance with their inherent nature or should they try to resist their inherent natural tendencies? Similarly, many people believe that the image of childhood as a time of innocence and purity is sentimental nonsense. In their view, children are inherently cruel and are brought to extinguish or control their inherent cruelty only through education and socialization. Consider the tendency of children to mercilessly taunt or bully those who are weaker than or different from themselves. We might maintain that the purpose of moral education is not to encourage people to give their inherent natures free rein but rather to tame their inherent natures.

Similarly, suppose that human beings are inherently selfish or primarily self-interested and that altruism is not in accordance with the inherent nature of human beings. If this were true, would it follow that altruism is immoral and contrary to reason because it is not in accordance with the inherent nature of human beings? Many people would deny that altruism is wrong even if it is not in accordance with the inherent nature of human beings. They would say, "So much the worse for the inherent nature of human beings." In their view, moral education often needs to go against rather than with the inherent nature of human beings. They deny that actions in accordance with the inherent nature of human beings are always right and good for human beings and that actions not in accordance with the inherent nature of human beings are always wrong and bad for human beings.

EXERCISES

1. Is theft contrary to reason? Defend your answer.
2. Is it self-evident that adultery is immoral? Defend your answer.

---

[13]Stephen Jay Gould, "Nonmoral Nature," in Stephen Jay Gould, *Hen's Teeth and Horse's Toes* (New York: W. W. Norton, 1983), p. 34.

[14]Ibid., p. 35.

3. Is theft a kind of action that is not in accordance with the inherent nature of human beings? Defend your answer.

4. Tommy is a third grader. Because he is overweight and wears glasses, most of his classmates make fun of him. Try to apply Natural Law theory to determine whether it is morally acceptable for his classmates to make fun of Tommy.

5. The Omega Corporation has trimmed its staff by 12 percent in order to increase its profits. Some of the employees who were dismissed had worked for the company for more than 15 years. Try to apply Natural Law theory to determine whether it was morally acceptable for the Omega Corporation to dismiss these people.

SUGGESTED READINGS

St. Thomas Aquinas. *On Law, Morality, and Politics.* Edited by William Baumgarth and Richard Regan. Indianapolis, IN: Hackett, 1988.

Stephen Buckle. "Natural Law." In *A Companion to Ethics.* Edited by Peter Singer. Cambridge, MA: Blackwell, 1991.

Robert P. George, ed. *Natural Law Theory.* Oxford: Oxford University Press, 1992.

Morality as Social Contract

Advocates of the Divine Command and Natural Law theories believe that morality is independent of human decision, belief, and desire. Other people, however, think that societies *construct* their moral codes rather than *discover* them. In their view, a system of moral rules is a social creation, just as a system of legal rules is a social creation. They point to the obvious facts that no individual creates his own moral code (individuals are in a sense born into a moral code and are taught its rules and principles) and that different societies have different moral codes.

According to these theorists, a moral code comes into existence or is created when a group of individuals reach agreement on laws of conduct to regulate their interactions and agree to conform to these laws. Traditionally the agreement has been called a social contract and the theories have been called social contract theories. According to the most extreme version of social contract theory, represented by the British philosopher Thomas Hobbes (1588-1679), all moral laws and duties are created by the social contract. The only moral prohibitions, requirements, and duties binding on an individual are those established by the social contract to which he or she has agreed.

HOBBES

The State of Nature

Hobbes claimed that society, government, law, and morality are human creations. According to Hobbes, individual human beings came into existence before society; prior to their creation of society, they lived in a "state of nature." In the state of nature, individual human beings do not live together in any organized way; there is not even the smallest tribe or village. The state of nature is a state of anarchy, a ceaseless war of all against all, because no one has the power to create and enforce laws that would enable individuals to live together harmoniously and to cooperate for mutual advantage. The strong prey upon the weak; the strong prevail and the weak perish. The ceaseless competition and struggle for security and survival ensures that individual life is "solitary, poor, nasty, brutish, and short."[1]

Hobbes believed that moral laws do not exist in the state of nature: Nothing is immoral; nothing is prohibited; nothing is required.

> The desires, and other passions of man, are in themselves no sin. No more are the actions, that proceed from these passions, till they know a law that forbids them; which till laws be made they cannot know; nor can any law be made, till they have agreed upon the person that shall make it. . . .

> To this war of every man, against every man, this also is consequent; that nothing can be unjust. The notions of right and wrong, justice and injustice have there no place. Where there is no common power, there is no law: where no law, no injustice. Force, and fraud, are in war the two cardinal virtues. . . . It is consequent also to the same condition, that these is no propriety [property], no dominion, no *mine* and *thine* distinct; but only that to be every man's, that he can get: and for so long, as he can keep it.[2]

According to Hobbes, laws of conduct come into existence when and only when some individual or group of individuals with legitimate authority creates them. We cannot violate moral laws if they don't exist; therefore, in the state of nature nothing is immoral.

The Right and Laws of Nature

Hobbes claimed that in the state of nature there is a Right of Nature and a Law of Nature. The Right of Nature is a right that everyone has to do whatever is necessary for his or her own self-preservation.

> The Right of Nature . . . is the liberty each man hath, to use his own power, as he will himself, for the preservation of his own nature; that is to say, of his life; and consequently, of doing anything, which in his own judgment, and reason, he shall conceive to be the aptest means thereunto.[3]

According to the Right of Nature, nothing is prohibited that we believe to be in our own self-interest.

Hobbes's view of the Law of Nature should not be confused with the views of Natural Law theorists that we examined in the previous chapter. What Hobbes called the Law of Nature is not a system of moral rules unconditionally prohibiting and requiring certain forms of behavior. Rather, Hobbes's Law of Nature describes the natural or inherent drives of all human beings. The most fundamental drive is self-preservation. In Hobbes's view, it is a Law of nature that all human beings strive to preserve themselves. The Law of Nature is akin to a physical law such as Newton's law of universal gravitation. Hobbes believed

---

[1]Thomas Hobbes, *Leviathan*, ed. Michael Oakeshott (New York: Collier, 1962), chap. 13, p. 100. (Originally published in 1651.)

[2]Ibid., p. 101.

[3]Ibid., chap. 14, p. 103.

that every individual has an innate or natural drive toward self-preservation. Therefore, every individual naturally (innately) is driven to do what he thinks is necessary for self-preservation and to refrain from doing what he thinks will jeopardize his continued existence. Human beings obey (and must obey) the Law of Nature, which dictates self-preservation, just as physical objects obey (and must obey) the law of universal gravitation.

We need to distinguish between the Law of Nature and laws of nature. Laws of nature identify effective means for the goal of self-preservation that all human beings naturally have. They are conditional principles that might be most accurately expressed as "If you want to survive, then you should do/should not do X." Thus, according to Hobbes,

> A LAW OF NATURE . . . is a precept or general rule, found out by reason, by which a man is forbidden to do that, which is destructive of his life, or taketh away the means of preserving the same: and to omit that, by which he thinketh it may best be preserved.[4]

Laws of nature specify forms of behavior most conducive to self-preservation. The first and most fundamental of these laws directs us to escape the state of nature—the state of war of all against all—and to seek peace. Because the state of nature is so insecure and dangerous, we best assure our self-preservation by leaving it. Individuals can only escape the state of nature by creating society and government, which in turn will create and enforce laws of conduct that will enable them to live together harmoniously and to cooperate for mutual benefit. Once society and government are created, other laws of nature or principles of self-preservation come into play.

The Creation of Society

Individuals leave the state of nature by voluntarily renouncing the Right of Nature to do whatever they believe to be in their self-interest and by agreeing to obey an authority (sovereign) they establish. The sovereign (an individual or group of individuals) creates and enforces laws of conduct, including moral laws, that enable them to live together peacefully and harmoniously. According to Hobbes, the additional laws of nature that are derived from the fundamental axiom of self-preservation become applicable once the state of nature has been replaced by society. These laws of nature are "a means of the conservation of men in multitudes."[5] They are rules of rational prudence rather than moral laws, strictly speaking, and they are discovered rather than created. For example, there's a law that requires people to be just—that is, to adhere to agreements that they've made; to express gratitude for benefits conferred; to strive to accommodate themselves to others—that is, to avoid retaining "those things which to himself are superfluous and to others necessary";[6] to not by word or deed

---

[4]Ibid., p. 103.
[5]Ibid., chap. 15, p. 122.
[6]Ibid., p. 118.

"declare hatred, or contempt of another";[7] to avoid undue arrogance and pride; and to not treat others as inferior to themselves. Hobbes claimed that the laws of nature regarding our relations with other people may ultimately be derived from one fundamental principle: "Do not that to another, which thou wouldest not have done to thyself."[8] Self-preservation also dictates laws of nature regarding people's treatment of themselves: "There be other things tending to the destruction of individual men; such as drunkenness, and all other parts of intemperance; which may therefore also be reckoned amongst those things which the law of nature hath forbidden."[9] Hobbes summarized, "These dictates of reason, men used to call by the name of laws, but improperly; for they are but conclusions, or theorems concerning what conduceth to the conservation and defence of themselves."[10]

In leaving the state of nature, an individual agrees to (or promises to) live by the laws of nature and the rules of conduct that the sovereign establishes. Hobbes suggests two reasons for individuals to conform to the laws of conduct established by the sovereign. First, they have a moral duty to conform because they have agreed to do so. Second, not to do so would be irrational, which for Hobbes meant against their own self-interest. Failure to conform to the rules of conduct (legal and moral) established and enforced by the sovereign is contrary to an individual's self-interest because it is likely to bring severe punishment.

Agreement Creates Duties

Hobbes claimed that individuals in society have a moral duty to conform to the laws of nature because they have agreed to (or promised to) live by them. However, many people would maintain that they have made no such agreement or promise.

Hobbes argued that an agreement or promise can be expressed in either words or deeds.

> Signs of contract, are either *express,* or by *inference.* Express, are words spoken with understanding of what they signify: . . . as *I give, I grant.* . . . Signs by inference, are sometimes the consequence of words; sometimes the consequence of silence; sometimes the consequence of actions; sometimes the consequence of forbearing an action: and generally a sign by inference, of any contract, is whatsoever sufficiently argues the will of the contractor.[11]

According to Hobbes, then, people can make agreements and promises without actually saying "I agree" or "I promise." For example, the driver of a bank robber's getaway car may not have said, "I agree to drive the getaway car." However, if he did not refuse when his cohorts assigned him the responsibility of driving the

---

[7]Ibid., p. 119.

[8]Ibid., pp. 113–122.

[9]Ibid., p. 122.

[10]Ibid., p. 124.

[11]Ibid., chap. 14, p. 106.

getaway car and if he drives them to the bank and waits outside while they are robbing it, his silence and his actions show that he has agreed to drive the getaway car.

Another social contract theorist, John Locke, distinguished between explicit and implicit agreements. Locke focused on a problem with the social contract theory that Hobbes said little about. The story of the origin of society might explain how and why the original parties to the social contract are obligated to obey the law, but how can it explain why later generations are obligated? Can people who weren't parties to the original contract really be said to have *agreed* to its terms? Can someone born into an already existing society be said to have agreed to conform to its laws of conduct? According to Locke, we must distinguish between explicit and implicit agreement: Members of a society who weren't parties to the original social contract have implicitly or tacitly agreed to its terms, even if they haven't explicitly agreed to them. Implicit agreement is a function of one's behavior rather than of one's speech. Thus, Locke wrote:

> No body doubts but an *express Consent,* of any Man, entering into any Society, makes him a perfect Member of that Society, a Subject of that Government.
> The difficulty is, what ought to be look'd upon as a *tacit Consent,* and how far it binds, i.e. how far anyone shall be looked on to have consented, and thereby submitted to any Government, where he has made no Expressions of it at all.
> And to this I say, that every Man, that hath any Possession, or Enjoyment, of any part of the Dominions of any Government, doth thereby give his *tacit Consent,* and is . . . obliged to Obedience to the Laws of that Government.[12]

According to Locke, people who enjoy the benefits of a society and who on reaching maturity choose to remain in that society have, by their deeds if not their words, agreed to obey its laws. They are therefore as obligated to obey the laws as anyone who has expressly agreed. Agreement to abide by the social contract of our society is almost always implicit for those of us born into an already functioning society.

Whether tacit consent is really consent remains problematic. Hobbes stressed that words and deeds are signs of agreement or consent only because they are indicators of a person's will. That suggests that people can consent to or agree to something only if they intend to consent to or agree to it. Hobbes's point is that acts and omissions as well as words can be *signs* of such an intention. However, if there are such acts and omissions *without* the intention, then the sign that there is consent or agreement is misleading. For example, the fact that the driver of the getaway car actually drove it and waited while his companions robbed the bank clearly indicates that he intended to drive the getaway car. On the other hand, we may intend to *not* live by the laws of conduct established by the sovereign and yet still remain in the society as outlaws because we have nowhere else to go or because we are too lazy to move. In that case, con-

---

[12]John Locke, *Two Treatises of Government,* ed. Peter Laslett (New York: NAL, 1965), p. 392 (Second Treatise, Chapter VIII, Section 119). (Originally published in 1690.)

tinuing to live in the society does not show that we intend to live by the laws of conduct established by the sovereign, including the laws of nature; if we do not intend to live by them, then we have not consented or agreed to live by them.

Another problem with the claim that we have a duty to live by the laws of society because we have agreed to do so is the threat of circularity. On the one hand, Hobbes suggested that all moral obligations are *created* by an agreement or promise. On the other hand, the moral obligation to keep agreements or promises must be prior to any agreement.

Hobbes argued as follows:

You have agreed to do X.

Therefore, you have a moral duty to do X.

However, as we saw in Chapter 1 on moral reasoning, the premises of a moral argument must include both nonevaluative beliefs about the facts and moral principles. The only premise in the preceding argument is a nonevaluative belief. The conclusion does not follow from that premise alone; the argument is incomplete. To reach the desired conclusion, Hobbes must add as a premise the moral principle that people have a moral duty to do what they have agreed to do.

You have agreed to do X.

People have a moral duty to do what they have agreed to do.

Therefore, you have a moral duty to do X.

What if someone challenges Hobbes's second premise—the claim that people have a duty to do what they have agreed to do? What justification can Hobbes provide for this moral principle? According to Hobbes, the *only* source of moral duties is agreement. Therefore, according to Hobbes's theory, you have a moral duty to keep your agreements if and only if you have agreed to keep your agreements. Thus, Hobbes would have to argue as follows for the claim that you have a moral duty to keep your agreement (here I will use a tree diagram):

MORAL PRINCIPLE
You have a moral duty to keep your agreements.

NONEVALUATIVE BELIEFS
ABOUT THE FACTS
You agreed to keep your agreements.

MORAL PRINCIPLES
You have a moral
duty to keep your
agreements.

The argument is clearly circular. Hobbes must assume the very principle at issue in order to justify his conclusion. If Hobbes wants to claim that people have a moral duty to keep their agreements, he cannot base that moral duty, as he has based all others, on agreement. He must find some other foundation for this duty. However, his theory provides no other foundation.

Self-Interest and the Laws of Nature

Hobbes's second reason for conforming to the laws of nature or the laws of conduct established by the sovereign is that *not* to conform is irrational—contrary to our long-term self-interest. For Hobbes, reasons of self-interest are the best reasons we can have for doing or not doing something. According to Hobbes, actions that benefit the individual are most reasonable for that individual. We might conclude that, for Hobbes, by definition actions in our self-interest are reasonable and actions contrary to our self-interest are unreasonable. He insisted that living by the laws of nature in society is reasonable (in our self-interest) and that failing to do so is unreasonable (contrary to our self-interest).

Hobbes believed that it's unreasonable for an individual to do what *may* be self-destructive—for example, play Russian roulette. In his view, to violate the laws of nature when living in society is self-destructive and hence unreasonable in exactly the same way that playing Russian roulette is. A person who fails to conform faces the possibility of discovery; if discovered, the potential losses are enormous. Others may refuse to continue to cooperate for mutual benefit with the violator; the violator may be cast out of society or severely punished. If the violator counts on not being caught, she is still behaving irrationally because if she does escape detection, it is only because others have accidentally failed to detect her violations.

> When a man doth a thing, which notwithstanding any thing can be foreseen, and reckoned on, tendeth to his own destruction, howsoever some accident which he could not expect, arriving may turn it to his benefit; yet such events do not make it reasonably or wisely done. . . . He . . . that breaketh his covenant . . . cannot be received into any society, that unite themselves for peace and defence, but by the error of them that receive him . . . ; which errors a man cannot reasonably reckon upon as the means of his security.[13]

However, it is not obvious that "unreasonable" means nothing more than "contrary to our self-interest," even if we have in mind our long-term self-interest. Therefore, critics may question whether whatever is contrary to our self-interest or long-run self-interest is unreasonable. Then, too, critics may wonder how we can derive the claim that failing to live by the laws of nature is immoral (or that we have a moral duty to live by them) from the claim that failing to live by them is unreasonable, even if Hobbes can justify his claim that whatever is contrary to self-interest is unreasonable.

PROBLEMS FOR THE FOLLOWERS OF HOBBES

According to Hobbes, the state of nature may not have actually existed; it may be a purely hypothetical state. However, he believed that actual social contracts exist and that people have agreed to live by them. Individuals have a moral duty to live by the laws of nature and the laws of conduct established by the sover-

---

[13]Hobbes, *Leviathan*, chap. 15, p. 115.

eign primarily because they have agreed to do so. However, social contract theorists have to rely on the idea of implicit agreement or consent. Critics might claim that implicit agreement is nothing but a convenient fiction. They might insist that the only genuine agreement is one where the individual intends to agree. If implicit agreement is nothing but a fiction, then the social contract itself is a fiction.

Critics of social contract theories also ask how we can know the content of the actual social contract. How do we know what people have actually agreed to when the agreement or social contract, if it exists, is unwritten and agreement is implicit rather than explicit? What is the content of the social contract of our society? Does it permit suicide, euthanasia, abortion, or the death penalty? Does it include a clause requiring individuals to contribute to relieve poverty? Does it include a clause permitting unlimited economic inequality or a clause permitting involuntary redistribution of economic resources to reduce economic inequality?

For the most part, social contract theorists must *infer* the content of the agreement. They might try to determine what duties, rights, prohibitions, requirements, and so on would be most conducive to social harmony and would maximize the probability that individuals in a society will live satisfactory lives, and then conclude that the actual agreement includes these provisions. Thus, for example, we might think that killing, assault, theft, and rape reduce social harmony and then conclude that the social contract of our society includes prohibitions against killing, assault, theft, and rape. Unfortunately, the fact that some laws of conduct would be conducive to social harmony and would maximize the probability of individuals' living satisfactory lives does not prove that the social contract actually includes those prohibitions. Discovering the clauses of an actual but unwritten contract that people in society have supposedly agreed to is indeed a daunting task.

Of course, it may be that at any instant of time the binding clauses of a society's social contract are all, and only, the duties and laws accepted or agreed to at that time by the majority of people in that society. If a majority opinion has not yet formed about an issue such as suicide, euthanasia, or abortion, the social contract is silent on the issue.

Is a Society's Social Contract Immune from Rational Criticism?

If a society's morality is created by its members' agreeing to a social contract, and if there is no other basis for morality, it seems to follow that a society's social contract is immune from rational criticism. Whatever the majority in a society accepts as right is right. As we've seen, however, many philosophers balk at this kind of Relativism.

Gilbert Harman, a contemporary American philosopher, suggests that even if a social contract theory of morality is correct, it doesn't follow that the actual social contract is immune from rational criticism. Clauses of the contract may contradict one another, and some may be based on irrational beliefs.

To say that morality derives from rules that are socially enforced [and created] is not to say that whatever is customary is right. Slavery, for example, can be wrong, according to a social custom theory, even if it is customary and there is no social pressure against it. For, even where slavery itself is customary, it can conflict with other customs that are socially enforced; this conflict may not be recognized by the members of society because of ignorance of fact, stupidity, and self-deception. According to the social custom theory, if slavery is wrong in the society, it is wrong because of the rules that are socially enforced with respect to people who are not slaves. These rules may really apply to everyone and not just to non-slaves, even though members of the society do not recognize this because they falsely believe that there is an important relevant difference between slaves and other people.[14]

Similarly, suppose that the social contract of a society requires that women be subordinate to men or prohibits homosexuality.

It may be that the socially enforced rules for relations between men are the rules with reference to which the treatment of women is wrong in the society. . . . For it may be that the treatment of women is based on false assumptions about differences between men and women. Similarly, social restrictions on homosexual behavior may derive from false beliefs about homosexuality.[15]

Thus, a social contract theory of morality does not entail that a society's moral code is immune from rational criticism.

Is There No Moral Law in the State of Nature?

According to Hobbes, these are no moral duties or laws in the state of nature prior to their creation by agreement. Many philosophers, such as Locke, have found that position difficult to accept. One corollary of the Hobbesian view is that there are no mutual moral duties, requirements, or prohibitions between societies. Different societies are in a state of nature relative to each other unless they have reached an agreement and created a social contract to govern their interactions. Thus, suppose that societies A and B have no agreement with each other about how their members will treat each other. Individuals X and Y are from society A and individual Z is from society B. Society A's social contract forbids members of the society from killing each other but includes no prohibition on killing members of other societies. According to Hobbesian social contract theory, X has a moral duty not to kill Y but doesn't have a moral duty not to kill Z. Consequently, X would do nothing wrong were he to kill Z. Many philosophers find this consequence of Hobbesian social contract theory implausible.

Gilbert Harman provides just such an example. As a contemporary social contract theorist, he claims that "the judgment that it is wrong of someone to do

---

[14]Gilbert Harman, *The Nature of Morality* (New York: Oxford University Press, 1977), pp. 94–95.
[15]Ibid., p. 97.

something makes sense only in relation to an agreement or understanding."[16] Harman asks us to imagine the following scenario:

> Intelligent beings from outer space land on Earth, beings without the slightest concern for human life and happiness. That a certain course of action on their part might injure one of us means nothing to them: that fact by itself gives them no reason to avoid the action. In such a case it would be odd to say that nevertheless the being ought to avoid injuring us or that it would be wrong for them to attack us.[17]

Because there is no agreement or social contract between earthlings and the space aliens, they are in a state of nature relative to each other, and according to both Hobbes and Harman, nothing is prohibited in such a state of nature. Suppose that the space aliens found human beings tasty and proceeded to round up thousands of them to send to their home planet as a delicacy. According to Hobbes and Harman, the aliens would not be doing anything morally wrong in eating human beings because they would not be violating any agreement or social contract that they had made with human beings. The aliens presumably have a social contract that governs their relations with each other, but they have no social contract with earthlings; therefore, there are no moral laws governing their treatment of earthlings. Many philosophers find such a consequence of social contract theory unacceptable and therefore consider social contract theory implausible.

FROM ACTUAL TO HYPOTHETICAL SOCIAL CONTRACTS

Some philosophers sympathetic to the social contract approach have abandoned the claim that there is an actual social contract and appeal instead to a hypothetical social contract. The most important contributor to hypothetical social contract theory is the contemporary U.S. philosopher John Rawls.

The Original Position

Rawls has proposed an influential modification of the social contract theory for political philosophy that may be generalized and applied to morality. According to Rawls, the correct standards of justice are those that rational, self-interested individuals in a certain hypothetical state analogous to the state of nature (the Original Position) would accept if given the choice.[18] (Notice, it is *would* accept, not *do* accept.) Extending this theory, we might say that the moral duties and laws that are binding on an individual are those that she would agree to accept in the Original Position.

---

[16]Gilbert Harman, "Moral Relativism Defended," in *Relativism: Cognitive and Moral,* ed. Michael Krausz and Jack Meiland (Notre Dame, IN: University of Notre Dame Press, 1982), pp. 189–190.

[17]Ibid., p. 191.

[18]John Rawls, *A Theory of Justice* (Cambridge, MA: Harvard University Press, 1971).

As Rawls conceives it, the Original Position is analogous to Hobbes's state of nature in that it's a situation prior to the creation of society. There is no government, law, or morality in the imaginary Original Position. The people there must create society, with all its institutions and rules, and construct a moral code that will govern their interactions once they leave the Original Position and enter society. Their purpose in creating society is the same as for Hobbes and Locke: They want to gain the benefits of social cooperation and avoid the defects of a state of nature. However, for Rawls the Original Position is a purely hypothetical situation that we enter through imagination only; it is not a historical reality.

People in the Original Position call a kind of constitutional convention to construct, among other things, a moral code to regulate their interactions once they have left the Original Position (state of nature) and entered society. Whatever moral duties and laws the members of the constitutional convention unanimously agree to adopt will be binding on them in society. Of course, the agreement is not an actual agreement because the Original Position and its inhabitants are imaginary. It's a hypothetical agreement. What counts is the duties and laws that rational, self-interested individuals *would* agree to adopt *if* they were in the Original Position. Although the Original Position is imaginary, we can ask ourselves what we would agree to if we were part of its constitutional convention. According to the hypothetical social contract theory, an individual is bound by whatever duties and laws he *would* agree to *if* he were a member of the constitutional convention in the Original Position.

The Veil of Ignorance

Imagine that three of us—you, John, and I—have to divide a cake among us. I suggest that I get the whole thing and that you and John get none of it. You and John are not likely to agree willingly to that proposal. If I'm stronger than both of you together I may be able to force you to accept this division, but neither of you is likely to consider it a fair division. Similarly, if you suggest that you get the whole thing, neither John nor I will agree to that division. We need a principle for the division of the cake that all three of us can willingly accept. If we can't come up with a solution that we all agree is fair and can accept, we're liable to resort to violence to resolve our problem.

Suppose that I make another suggestion: The tallest person gets half the cake, and the other two each get a quarter of the cake. If you are the tallest you might happily go along with this suggestion, but if you're not you would probably veto it. In fact, I am likely to suggest such a principle of division only if I know that I am the tallest. John might suggest an alternative: The oldest gets half the cake, and the others each get a quarter of it. If I'm the oldest, I might happily agree to this alternative, but if I'm not the oldest I will probably veto it. Again, John will likely make this proposal only if he knows that he is the oldest.

Rawls and other social contract theorists stress the importance of agreement. Acceptable moral rules are those that everyone can agree to and that can be publicly justified. Without agreement and public justification, the only alternative seems to be force. In the case of the cake, we are assuming that agreement must be unanimous, that we each have a veto. If one of us doesn't agree, he or she will make a very unpleasant fuss. So what principle of division might we be able to agree on? The problem with each of the principles proposed so far is that it is designed to favor the individual who suggested it. We are not likely to reach agreement if we each try to foist on the others a principle that will benefit us more than the others. How can we avoid trying to design a principle of division that will favor ourselves?

Consider the following four alternative ways of distributing the cake:

A	B	C	D
X gets 1/2.	X gets 1/4.	X gets 1/4.	X gets 1/3.
Y gets 1/4.	Y gets 1/2.	Y gets 1/4.	Y gets 1/3.
Z gets 1/4.	Z gets 1/4.	Z gets 1/2.	Z gets 1/3.

Suppose that the three of us must choose among A, B, C, and D. Which would you vote for? If you know which of the three you are—X, Y, or Z—you will probably vote for the alternative in which you get half the cake. If you know that you are X, you will probably vote for A; if I know that I am Y, I'm likely to vote for B. Thus, if we each know who we are, we are likely to find it difficult to reach agreement.

But suppose that none of us knows whether we are X, Y, or Z. In that case, which alternative are we likely to vote for? Rawls thinks that we would each vote for D. If we agree to any of the others, we have a 2/3 probability of getting only 1/4 of the cake. However, if we agree to D, we are guaranteed to get 1/3 of the cake, which is bigger. Rawls argues that making the decision when we are deprived of information that would enable us to tailor things to our own advantage will make the decision fairer and more likely unanimous. Thus, he imposes one key limitation on the members of the constitutional convention deciding on the social contract: They have no personal information about themselves.

Decisions about principles in Rawls's theory are made behind a Veil of Ignorance. Individuals do not know whether they will turn out to be old or young, strong or weak, knowledgeable or ignorant, intelligent or unintelligent, able-bodied or disabled, male or female, black or white, rich or poor, Christian or non-Christian, and so on, when they enter society. Lacking such personal information about themselves, they cannot deliberately tailor the principles they choose to benefit people like themselves. For example, if they do not know what their own race or sex will be, they cannot try to garner privileges for males at the expense of females, or for whites at the expense of blacks. The Veil of Ignorance is designed to ensure that agreement and choice occur from an *impartial* perspective, which most philosophers believe to be constitutive of morality. As Rawls says, "Moral judgments are, or should be impartial. . . . An impartial moral judgment . . . is one rendered in accordance with the principles which would be chosen in the original position."[19] It is easier to be impartial if one lacks the personal information that tends to bias judgment and decision.

For example, suppose that the members of the constitutional convention consider two possible principles:

1. Men may beat women to "keep them in their places."
2. Men may not beat women to "keep them in their places."

No one in the Original Position behind the Veil of Ignorance would agree to adopt principle 1 because they would not know whether they will be male or female when they emerge from behind the Veil of Ignorance. Because they are rational and self-interested, they do not want to risk being beaten. Because they do not know whether they will be men or women, everyone in the Original Position would agree to and insist on adopting principle 2.

Rawls believes that all rational, self-interested individuals in the Original Position behind the Veil of Ignorance would agree on two principles of justice to regulate the distribution of freedoms and economic resources in society.

(I) Each person is to have an equal right to the most extensive basic liberty compatible with a similar liberty for others.[20]

(II) Social and economic inequalities are to be arranged so that they are both (a) to the greatest benefit of the least advantaged and (b) attached to offices and positions open to all under conditions of fair equality of opportunity.[21]

With respect to the first of Rawls's principles, imagine that the issue is how much freedom people should have and that the following alternatives have been proposed regarding freedom of speech:

A	B	C	D
X has freedom of speech.	X does not have freedom of speech.	X does not have freedom of speech.	X has freedom of speech.
Y does not have freedom of speech.	Y has freedom of speech.	Y does not have freedom of speech.	Y has freedom of speech.
Z does not have freedom of speech.	Z does not have freedom of speech.	Z has freedom of speech.	Z has freedom of speech.

If I know that I am X, I may be tempted to push for alternative A because that alternative would most favor my interests. I would be at an advantage if I have freedom of speech while Y and Z do not. However, if I don't know whether I am X, Y, or Z, I am unlikely to vote for alternative A, B, or C because with each one

---

[19]Ibid., p. 190.
[20]Ibid., p. 60.
[21]Ibid., p. 83.

there is a 2/3 probability that I will wind up not having freedom of speech. If I don't know whether I am X, Y, or Z, the only safe course for me is alternative D where there is equal freedom of speech for all.

Similarly, I may be tempted to propose that only Republicans, or only whites, or only people who agree with the government have freedom of speech, largely because I am a Republican, or white, or agree with the government. However, if I don't know whether I'm a Republican or Democrat, white or non-white, in agreement or disagreement with the government, I am unlikely to support such principles. Instead, I will probably support equal free speech for everyone. According to Rawls, if we were in the Original Position behind the Veil of Ignorance, trying to reach agreement on the principles (social contract) that will govern society, we would only agree to a system of extensive equal basic liberties. These basic liberties include freedom of thought, religion, expression, association, movement, choice of occupation, and so on.

The second principle focuses on the economic resources of a society. Consider the following alternative principles regarding the distribution of annual income:

A	B	C	D
X: $150,000	X: $ 25,000	X: $ 5,000	X: $60,000
Y: $ 25,000	Y: $ 5,000	Y: $150,000	Y: $60,000
Z: $ 5,000	Z: $150,000	Z: $ 25,000	Z: $60,000

If I know that I'm X, I will probably insist on alternative A because I know I'll do best in that situation, having an annual income of $150,000. I'll certainly fight tooth and nail against alternative C because in that situation I'll only have an annual income of $5,000, which would probably leave me homeless. However, if you know that you are Z, you will fight with equal ferocity against A because under A you would have the $5,000 annual income. You would vote for B. It is unlikely that X, Y, and Z, knowing who they are, could reach agreement about either A, B, or C.

Suppose now that we are behind the Veil of Ignorance. We do not know whether we are X, Y, or Z. Which of the four alternatives would you vote for under those conditions? Rawls claims that you would vote for D. With A, B, and C you have a 1/3 probability of striking it rich, but you also have a 1/3 probability of catastrophe—homelessness with an annual income of only $5,000. With each of these you also have a 1/3 probability of having a very modest income, $25,000. However, with alternative D you are guaranteed an annual income of $60,000 regardless of whether you are X, Y, or Z. Thus, Rawls claims that if we don't know who we are, we will agree to an equal share for each. If you don't know whether you have characteristics that will likely bring you a big income (high intelligence, good education, skills in demand, wealthy parents, good health, ambition, self-confidence) or characteristics that will likely bring you a low income (low intelligence, inferior education, few skills, poor parents, poor health, lack of ambition, low self-esteem), then according to Rawls you will play it safe and press for an equal distribution of economic resources.

We could apply Rawls's theory of justice to moral issues by maintaining that the (or a) correct system of moral principles binding on all individuals is one that all rational, self-interested people would agree to adopt if they were in the Original Position behind the Veil of Ignorance. If we think of the agreement as a social contract, then according to Rawls's theory it is not a social contract that we have *actually* agreed to that counts; rather, it's the social contract that we *would* agree to *if* we were in the Original Position behind the Veil of Ignorance.

Rawls connects his hypothetical social contract theory to Kant's Respect for Persons formulation of the Categorical Imperative. According to that formulation, we are forbidden to treat people merely as things or merely as means to our ends. As Kant puts it, people must be treated as "ends in themselves." According to Rawls, "On the contract interpretation treating men [people] as ends in themselves implies at the very least treating them in accordance with the principles to which they would consent in an original position of equality."[22] To treat people with respect is to treat them according to the system of principles that all self-interested, rational people would accept if they were in the Original Position behind the Veil of Ignorance.

Rawls derives other moral principles from the Original Position. For example, he identifies what he calls natural duties.

> The following are examples of natural duties: the duty of helping another
> when he is in need or jeopardy, provided that one can do so without excessive
> risk or loss to oneself; the duty not to harm or injure another; and the duty not
> to cause unnecessary suffering.[23]

They are "natural" duties in that they apply to everyone and are not based on promises, agreements, or any other actions. They are binding on people simply because all rational, self-interested individuals would accept them as duties binding on everyone if they were in the Original Position behind the Veil of Ignorance. Rawls is not suggesting that he has discovered new duties that no one was aware of before. Based on commonsense morality, most people would acknowledge a similar set of duties. But Rawls provides a theoretical justification for such duties.

Problems for Hypothetical Contracts

Suppose that if I were in the Original Position behind the Veil of Ignorance I would agree to adopt a rule prohibiting the strong from exploiting and oppressing the weak. According to the extension of Rawls's theory, it follows that I have an actual duty to refrain from exploiting and oppressing the weak. A moral law prohibiting the exploitation and oppression of the weak is binding on me because of what I would agree to if I were in the Original Position. But why

---

[22]Ibid., p. 180.
[23]Ibid., p. 114.

should what I have not really agreed to bind me? Why should agreements I would make if I were in certain circumstances bind me when I haven't really been in those circumstances and haven't really made such agreements? This question is difficult to answer, and it lies at the heart of the hypothetical social contract theory.

If I am actually strong and would benefit from exploiting and oppressing the weak, why should I consider the principles I would agree to if I were in the Original Position relevant when I'm not in the Original Position? Perhaps the only answer is that judging from the perspective of the Original Position guarantees impartiality, and impartiality is constitutive of the moral point of view. Therefore, if we wish to make a *moral* judgment about our behavior and wish to be guided by *moral* principles, we should try to determine what moral principles we would agree to *if* we were in Rawls's Original Position. Of course, that may be a big "if."

EXERCISES

1. Have you agreed to conform to your society's moral code? If yes, does that impose a moral duty on you to conform to it? Explain and defend your answer.

2. Assuming that each society has an actual social contract, does the actual social contract of your society permit (a) abortion, (b) euthanasia, (c) suicide, (d) capital punishment, (e) sex between unmarried people, (f) adultery (g) discrimination on the basis of sexual orientation, or (h) affirmative action? Defend your answer.

3. We saw that for a Hobbesian social contract theorist, there are no binding moral principles regulating the behavior of people from different societies with different social contracts. For example, according to Gilbert Harman, visitors from another planet would not be acting immorally if they enslaved everyone on Earth because they have no agreement with us that they would be violating. How might a hypothetical social contract theorist handle this issue?

4. Suppose that a society's social contract permits its members to have more than one spouse at a time. Is it then morally acceptable for members of this society to have multiple spouses? Defend your answer.

5. Would all rational, self-interested individuals agree to accept a moral principle prohibiting polygamy if they were in the Original Position behind the Veil of Ignorance? Defend your answer.

6. Consider the following list of possible moral principles.
   A. It's morally acceptable for a man to lie in order to seduce a woman.
   B. It's immoral for a man to lie in order to seduce a woman.
   C. It's morally acceptable for a man to encourage a woman to get drunk in order to have sex with her.
   D. It's immoral for a man to encourage a woman to get drunk in order to have sex with her.
   E. It's morally acceptable to cheat on an income tax return.
   F. It's immoral to cheat on an income tax return.
   G. It's morally acceptable to pad a business expense account.
   H. It's immoral to pad a business expense account.

If you were in Rawls's Original Position behind the Veil of Ignorance, which of these rules would you agree to accept as binding moral rules for your society? Explain and defend your answer.

7. Suppose that Jones concedes that if he were in the Original Position he would reject principles A, C, E, and G and agree to the adoption of B, D, F, and H. However, he says that since he is not and never has been in the Original Position, the fact that he would reject some principles and agree to the adoption of others if he were in the Original Position is irrelevant to what would be morally acceptable and unacceptable behavior for him. How would you respond?

SUGGESTED READINGS

David Gauthier. *Morals by Agreement.* New York: Oxford University Press, 1986.

Gilbert Harman. "Moral Relativism Defended." In *Relativism: Cognitive and Moral.* Edited by Michael Krausz and Jack Meiland. Notre Dame, IN: University of Notre Dame Press, 1982.

————. *The Nature of Morality.* New York: Oxford University Press, 1977. Chapter 8.

Thomas Hobbes. *Leviathan.* Edited by Michael Oakeshott. New York: Collier, 1962. (Originally published in 1651.)

John Rawls. *A Theory of Justice.* Cambridge, MA: Harvard University Press, 1971.

C H A P T E R   11

Moral Duties and Moral Rights

After leaving the store where he had made some purchases, Naguib discovered that the clerk had accidentally given him twenty dollars too much in change. He wondered whether he should return the money. He framed his question using the concept of duty: "Do I have a duty to return the money?"

Sentences that make moral evaluations or ask moral questions often include the related concepts of duty, obligation, and responsibility. Someone involved in a discussion with Naguib might say, "You have (or do not have) a duty to return the money," "You have an obligation to return the money," or "You have a responsibility to return the money." Although philosophers make important distinctions between these concepts (for example, obligations arise only as a result of our voluntary actions, whereas duties can arise independent of our voluntary actions), we will treat them as roughly synonymous here and focus on the concept of duty.

MORAL AND LEGAL DUTIES

In *All God's Children,* Fox Butterfield claims that there has been a "culture of violence" in parts of the South in the United States. This culture, he says, derives in part from a traditional code of honor that puts a remarkably high value on an individual's reputation and that requires or expects a man to fight or kill in order to defend his honor if he is challenged or insulted. Any behavior that a man interprets as indicating a lack of respect toward him may impel him to resort to violence, such as a duel. In this culture, men believe that in order to attain and maintain the status of "gentleman," they have a duty to protect their and their family's honor from any slight. In their view, only the shedding of blood can restore their honor after it has been sullied by insult or disrespect. If a man permits someone to act disrespectfully toward him or his family without demanding a public apology or bloody retaliation, he shows that he is a coward and no gentleman.

For example, in a speech in the United States Senate in 1856, U.S. Senator from Massachusetts Charles Sumner, a passionately committed abolitionist (abolitionists advocated an end to slavery), criticized and ridiculed the state of South Carolina and its pro-slavery state senator Andrew Butler. Butler's cousin, U.S. Representative from South Carolina Preston Brooks, felt that the honor of his family and of his state had been sullied by Sumner's disrespectful remarks. If Brooks had considered Sumner a gentleman, he would have challenged him to a duel. However, Butler considered Sumner his social inferior, and in South Carolina a gentleman would never honor a social inferior with a duel. Instead, a gentleman would simply whip, beat, or kill a social inferior who had shown disrespect.

> Under the code of honor, Butler was obliged to flog Sumner, but "this Butler was unable to do," Brooks reasoned, because Sumner was thirty pounds heavier and in more robust health [than Butler]. "Under the circumstances," Brooks concluded, "I felt it to be my duty to relieve Butler and avenge the insult to my State."[1]

Butler approached Sumner at his desk in the Senate chamber.

> "I have read your speech twice over carefully," Brooks began. "It is a libel on South Carolina, and Mr. Butler, who is a relative of mine." Sumner tried to rise from his desk, but his long legs were tucked under it and it was bolted to the floor. Before the senator could move, Brooks gave Sumner "a slight blow" with the smaller end of his cane. When Sumner tried to cover his head with his arms, Brooks felt "compelled to strike him harder than he intended," raining down blow after blow.

> Blood was now streaming from Sumner's head. Finally, with a huge effort, he ripped the desk from the floor and staggered down the aisle semiconscious.[2]

Sumner took three years to fully recover from the beating. Brooks became a hero in the South. Although the House of Representatives moved to expel him, the vote failed because every congressman from the South voted against it except one. To demonstrate how popular he had become, Brooks voluntarily resigned his seat and ran for reelection in his South Carolina district. He was reelected in a landslide. To those who shared the code of honor of the "gentleman," Brooks had simply done his duty. As Butterfield sums it up, "To Northerners, Brooks's attack had been brutal and lawless, a criminal act. To Southerners, Brooks had been a gentleman, justifiably defending a relative and his state."[3]

A duty can be either a legal duty, a moral duty, or both. If the laws of the South actually required a "gentleman" to avenge insults to his or his family's honor by violence, on pain of judicial punishment for failure to act, then it would be a legal duty. If there are no such laws, then it is not a legal duty. However, if

---

[1]Fox Butterfield, *All God's Children: The Bosket Family and the American Tradition of Violence* (New York: Avon Books, 1995), pp. 16–17.

[2]Ibid., p. 17.

[3]Ibid., p. 18.

the moral code of a community requires such behavior, and if the members of the community would experience and express moral disapproval if he failed to behave in that way, then it is (believed to be) a moral duty in that community. Moral duties, unlike legal duties, are imposed by a moral code rather than by laws.

Something may be a moral duty but not a legal duty. For example, people may have a moral duty to not lie but not have a legal duty because there are no laws against lying. Similarly, something may be a legal duty but not a moral duty. For example, some people claim that we have no moral duty to obey unjust laws. They would probably claim that even though people in the Northern states prior to the Civil War had a legal duty to hand over runaway slaves to the authorities, they did not have a moral duty to do so. Finally, some duties may be both legal and moral duties. Because there are laws in the United States requiring people to submit tax returns and pay income tax, people in the United States have a legal duty to file a tax return and pay their taxes. But most people would also claim that people have a moral duty to obey the law by filing a tax return and paying their taxes. So paying taxes is both a moral and a legal duty.

Legal duties are purely local rather than universal. People in one society may have legal duties that people in other societies do not have. For example, a citizen of one country may have a legal duty to salute the flag of her nation every time it is publicly displayed, whereas a citizen of another country may not have that legal duty. Where it is a legal duty, it is a legal duty only because a government has created it by passing laws requiring that behavior.

Sometimes we want to say that people in a certain society have a legal duty that they should not have, or that they do not have a legal duty that they should have. For example, consider the law in Nazi Germany requiring people to inform on Jews to the Gestapo, who would then send them to a concentration camp where they would almost certainly be murdered. Given the law requiring such behavior, people in Nazi Germany had a legal duty to inform on Jews to the Gestapo. However, most people would agree that they should not have had such a legal duty. Similarly, in Nazi Germany laws protecting people from physical assault did not apply to Jews. Thus, people did not have a legal duty to refrain from physically assaulting Jews. Nonetheless, people should have had the legal duty to refrain from physically assaulting Jews.

It may have been that in the South in the mid-nineteenth century, people did not have a legal duty to refrain from using violence to avenge insults to their honor. If there were no laws against it, then people did not have a legal duty to refrain from employing violence to uphold their honor. But some people claim that even though there was no *legal* duty to refrain from acts of violence, there was and is a *moral* duty to refrain from violence. Certainly, Northerners who considered Brooks's act criminal believed that he had a moral duty to refrain from violence. But apparently many, if not most, Southerners believed not only that Brooks did not have a moral duty to refrain from violence but also that he had a moral duty to resort to violence.

If we wonder whether someone *really* has a legal duty, we can consult the laws of the community. But suppose we wonder whether someone *really* has a moral duty. As we saw in an earlier chapter, we often distinguish between an individual's or group's *believing* that something is right (or wrong) and its *really* being right (or wrong). Similarly, we can distinguish between an individual's or group's *believing* that something is a moral duty and its *really* being a moral duty. If Southerners believe that men have a moral duty to avenge perceived insults and disrespect, does it follow that men (or Southern men) really do have this moral duty? What if others—for example, Northerners—believe that all people have a moral duty to refrain from violence in their personal lives?

We might say that we have a moral duty to do something if there are strong moral arguments in favor of the claim that it would be immoral for us not to do it. A good moral argument requires, first, that the nonevaluative beliefs underlying or justifying the claim be true or reasonable. It also requires that all relevant information or facts be carefully considered. Next, it requires that the moral principles appealed to in justifying the moral claim be reasonable. Finally, it requires that the premises either guarantee the truth of the moral conclusion or make the conclusion highly probable.

In the case of the code of honor, in order to decide whether men (or Southern men) really have a moral duty to use violence to preserve their honor, we need to look at the arguments that can be constructed to defend the claim and the arguments that can be constructed to challenge it. We need to examine carefully the effect of the code of honor on the society and the individuals within it, the moral principles that may be appealed to in defending it or in challenging it, and so on. If there are good moral arguments against the claim that men have this moral duty, and weak or few moral arguments in favor of the claim that men have this moral duty, then we would be justified in claiming that men do not *really* have a moral duty to use violence to avenge slights to their honor.

Special and General Moral Duties

Some moral duties everyone has. Other moral duties only some people have because of their roles or voluntary actions. For example, we may say that everyone has a moral duty to minimize the pain and suffering they cause others. We also may say that everyone has a duty to help others when the need is great and the cost or risk to themselves small. Because everyone has them, we can call them general duties.

Special moral duties are those that not everyone has. Often special moral duties are attached to certain roles or relationships. For example, firefighters have a moral duty to attempt dangerous rescues of people from burning buildings. People who are not firefighters do not have that duty. This duty attaches to the role of firefighter. Many occupations or professions have special duties that people who do not fill these roles do not have. A Catholic priest has a duty to hear confessions; people outside that role do not. A parent has a duty to nurture and support his/her children; people unrelated to a child do not necessarily have those duties. A person has a duty to listen compassionately and sympathetically to his/her spouse; a stranger or casual acquaintance has no such duty.

Positive and Negative Duties

We can have a duty to do something, and we can have a duty to *not* do something. A duty to do something is a positive duty; a duty to not do something is a negative duty. A duty to file an income tax return is a positive duty. A duty to not behave cruelly toward animals is a negative duty. In practice, the distinction may blur. The duty to treat people with respect is a combination of positive and negative. It is a duty to treat people with respect and to *not* treat them with disrespect.

Violating Moral Duties

We can violate moral duties by doing things we have a moral duty to not do or by not doing things we have a moral duty to do. For example, suppose that because of taking an oath, Tom, a cadet at a military school, has a moral duty to inform authorities of violations of the honor code, including instances of hazing and sexual harassment. If he sees instances of hazing and harassment but does not inform the authorities, he has violated a moral duty by his inaction. Similarly, if Tom has a moral duty to not cheat on an examination but cheats anyway, then he has violated a moral duty by his action.

Philosophers point out that certain feelings and attitudes are warranted when we know that we have failed to do our moral duty. Such feelings include guilt, remorse, and regret. Although we sometimes hear in popular culture that guilt is bad, philosophers think that sometimes we should feel guilty. If we have violated a moral duty, guilt is called for. To not feel guilty is to show an insensitivity and indifference to moral duty. Similarly, remorse and regret are called for. We should feel sorry for what we have done or not done and should wish that the past could be altered. Guilt, remorse, and regret may lead us to attempt to compensate victims of our dereliction of duty, which is usually appropriate, and to try to do better in the future.

WHAT MORAL DUTIES DO WE HAVE?

Do we have a negative moral duty to refrain from

talking when our mouths are full of food?

interrupting people in conversation?

saying negative things about people behind their backs?

resorting to violence to avenge perceived insults?

behaving cruelly toward people?

exploiting people who are vulnerable and weak?

competing with friends for a job?

Do we have a positive moral duty to

bathe, brush our teeth, and change our clothes regularly?

turn in a friend who has broken the law?

help push out someone's car stuck in the snow?

contribute to charity?

obey the laws of our community?

According to commonsense morality, some of these things are moral duties, but others are not. Refraining from talking when our mouths are full, refraining from interrupting others in conversation, and regularly bathing, brushing our teeth, and changing our clothes are generally not seen as *moral* duties. (They may be duties of etiquette, but not of morality.) Although talking with our mouths full, interrupting others, and ignoring personal hygiene may cause mild *offense* to others, they probably do not *harm* others. According to commonsense morality, we have a moral duty to refrain from doing something only if it would cause harm or serious offense, and we have a moral duty to do something only if *not* doing it would cause harm or serious offense. (See the material on the Offense Principle in Chapter 13.)

On this view, we have a moral duty to refrain from saying negative things behind people's backs if that behavior is harmful, not just mildly offensive. Of course, it is not hard to see why commonsense morality says that we have a moral duty to refrain from violence, cruelty, and exploitation. They cause harm. But what about refraining from competing with a friend for a job? Clearly, there is no such moral duty according to commonsense morality. Yet if I get the job and my friend doesn't, it probably harms him. (Commonsense morality does not *forbid* you to withdraw from the competition; it simply does not *require* you to withdraw.) Commonsense morality holds that as long as the competition is fair, morality does not require you to withdraw because the sacrifice required is too great. Furthermore, it holds that fair competition is a legitimate way to make social decisions about employment.

However, we have to beware of moral absolutism. We need to recognize that in some situations, a person may have a moral duty to refrain from competing with a friend for a job. Suppose that Sue and Sheila are friends. Sue already has a good job that pays well and that she likes. A job is advertised that pays 5 percent more. Sue considers applying for it, knowing that she has a good chance of getting it. Her friend Sheila has been jobless for more than a year and is in dire straits as a result. She has been searching frantically for a job. Her savings are exhausted, her debts have mounted, her car is threatened with repossession, and she may be evicted soon if she cannot pay her rent. As a result of her financial woes and prolonged joblessness, she has been extremely depressed. Sheila excitedly tells Sue that she has seen the job advertised and is applying for it. She believes that she has a good chance of getting it. Sue realizes that if she applies, it will reduce the probability that Sheila will be offered the job.

Commonsense morality holds that certain moral duties arise as the result of friendship. We have a moral duty to at least sometimes put the needs of our friends before our own needs, desires, or wants. Sue doesn't *need* the job; Sheila does. Sue owes Sheila concern, loyalty, and compassion because she is a friend, not a stranger. Applying for the job would not manifest concern, loyalty, or compassion. If Sue got the job, Sheila would justifiably feel betrayed. We can imagine Sheila's confronting Sue and asking, "How could you? You knew how desperate I was for that job. You have a good job. I thought you were my friend." It is not far-fetched to claim that in this set of circumstances, Sue has a moral duty to refrain from applying for the job that her friend is applying for.

Do people have a moral duty to turn in a friend who has broken the law? In such an unqualified form, the claim cannot be accepted. It depends on the law, for one thing. If the law is unjust, commonsense morality denies that we have such a duty. For example, suppose that in Nazi Germany Hans's friend Herman discovers that, contrary to German law, Hans is hiding a Jewish family from the Gestapo. Commonsense morality denies that Herman has a moral duty to turn in his friend to the Gestapo.

What if the law is not unjust? Surely the magnitude of the offense matters. Breaking a law that forbids one to park in a no parking zone is a lot different from breaking a law that forbids murder. Suppose that Hank notices that his friend Dennis's car is parked illegally in a no parking zone and immediately goes in search of a police officer to inform so that Dennis's car can be ticketed. Did Hank have a moral duty to do that? Commonsense morality says no. The harm caused by Dennis's having parked or continuing to park in a no parking zone is probably small. There is a reasonable probability that a police officer will discover Dennis's car and ticket it without Hank's help. If Dennis manages to get back and move his car before a police officer sees it, the impact will be negligible. Weighed against these considerations are the considerations that arise from the fact that Dennis is Hank's friend. Hank owes Dennis some loyalty and some effort to protect his interests. (Imagine if Hank did bring a police officer to ticket Dennis's car and Dennis found out. We can imagine Dennis's reaction. "You did what? Are you crazy? I thought you were my friend. Well, we're no longer friends.")

But the duties of friendship cannot cancel all other moral duties. Hank's duties of friendship to Dennis would not justify his beating up a police officer to prevent her from ticketing his friend Dennis's car. They would not override Hank's moral duty to refrain from violence. Similarly, if the law that Dennis broke was the law against murder, the duties of friendship would not justify Hank's helping Dennis escape detection. In fact, if he knows that Dennis has committed a murder, commonsense morality says that he has a moral duty to inform the police. (He also has a legal duty to inform the police.)

What of positive moral duties? Do people have a moral duty to help someone whose car is stuck in the snow (at least when they are physically able to)? Again, commonsense morality says it depends on the circumstances. We don't have an unqualified moral duty to help all people whose cars may be stuck in the snow. (Of course, generally it is a good, nice, or generous thing to do, but not a moral duty. I say "generally" because it is not a good thing, for example, to help extricate from the snow a bank robber being chased by the police, enabling him to escape.) In deciding whether we have a moral duty to help someone, we need to examine the seriousness of the need. The more serious the need—that is, the greater the harm caused by failure to help—the more likely it is that we have a moral duty to help. It is more likely that we have a moral duty to rescue a drowning child than that we have a moral duty to help someone extricate his car from the snow.

Then, too, the more we are capable of helping, the more likely it is that we have a moral duty to help. If I'm in poor health, old, or small and weak, I'm less able to help someone dig or push his car from the snow than is someone who is big, strong, young, and healthy. Also, the amount of sacrifice counts—how much my interests will be set back by helping. The greater the cost or risk to me, the less likely it is that I have a moral duty to help; the less the cost or risk to me, the greater is the probability that I have a moral duty to help. I could injure myself trying to push or dig someone from the snow. But if saving a child from drowning only requires me to throw her a rope, which might get my hands and clothes dirty and delay me five minutes on my way to the grocery store, those costs hardly represent a big setback to my interests. Weighing my sacrifice against the seriousness of harm if I don't help, commonsense morality would surely conclude that I have a moral duty to throw the rope to save the child's life.

Trying to determine what moral duties we have and what our moral duty is in a given situation requires *judgment.* We have to weigh circumstances. Sometimes, when duties conflict, we have to decide what duty takes priority. For example, you may have a moral duty to keep promises and a moral duty to help people. Suppose that you have promised to pick up your friend to go to the movies. On the way, on a lonely stretch of road, you come across a bicyclist who has been struck by a hit-and-run driver. You stop to help, see that she is bleeding profusely from a major wound on her leg, and realize that if you don't get her to a hospital she might die. If you take her to the hospital, you will wind up breaking your promise to your friend because you won't be able to pick her up to go to the movies. Should you violate your duty to keep your promises or your duty to help those in dire need?

In using our judgment to determine what our moral duties are, we may appeal to some of the moral theories we have examined.

UTILITARIAN CONCEPTIONS OF DUTY

According to utilitarians, moral duties are derived from the fundamental principle of utility. According to the Greatest Happiness version of Act Utilitarianism, a person has a moral duty to do whatever will maximize total happiness. If lying will maximize total happiness in a given situation, then we have a duty to lie in that situation. If in another situation telling the truth will maximize total happiness, then we have a duty to tell the truth in that situation. According to the negative version of Act Utilitarianism, a person has a moral duty to refrain from behaving in a way that will reduce total happiness. If in a given situation lying will reduce total happiness, then a person has a duty to not lie. On the other hand, if telling the truth will reduce total happiness, then a person has a duty to not tell the truth.

According to Rule Utilitarianism, we have a general moral duty to act in conformity with principles or rules that, if generally followed, would maximize total happiness. If more total happiness would be produced by people generally telling the truth than by people generally lying, then we have a duty to tell the truth. Alternatively, in terms of conditional rules, if more happiness would be produced by people generally telling the truth in circumstances C, then people have a duty to tell the truth in circumstances C. On the other hand, if more total happiness would be produced by people generally lying in circumstances C, then people have a duty to lie in circumstances C.

For utilitarians, there is one fundamental moral duty linked to considerations of total happiness. From that fundamental duty, we derive more specific duties regarding specific behavior. To derive specific duties, we employ experience to discover what effect on total happiness certain forms of behavior will have (Act Utilitarianism) or what effect on total happiness following certain rules will have (Rule Utilitarianism).

KANTIAN CONCEPTIONS OF DUTY

According to Kant, a person with a good will acts in conformity with the demands of duty because she wants to do her duty out of respect for the moral law. Duty "subdue[s] the vice-breeding inclinations."[4] Kant emphasized that "the principle of duty is derived from pure reason."[5] Moral duties are not imposed by external authority; they are imposed by an agent's own reason. An agent's reason recognizes or establishes certain principles of conduct and demands that the will conform to those principles, subduing and controlling the feelings and passions (inclinations) that lead us astray.

> Man feels in himself a powerful counterpoise against all commands of duty
> which reason presents to him as so deserving of respect. This counterpoise is
> his needs and inclinations, the complete satisfaction of which he sums up
> under the name of happiness. Now reason issues inexorable commands.[6]

Thus, Kant maintained that "the constraint that the concept of duty contains can only be *self-constraint*."[7] The most fundamental moral duty presumably is the duty to conform our behavior to the Categorical Imperative—that is, to act only on maxims that we can consistently will to be universal laws and to treat all people with respect. Other, more specific duties are derived from the Categorical

---

[4]Immanuel Kant, *The Metaphysics of Morals,* trans. Mary Gregor (New York: Cambridge University Press, 1991), p. 181.

[5]Ibid., p. 183.

[6]Immanuel Kant, *Foundations of the Metaphysics of Morals,* 2d ed., trans. Lewis White Beck (New York: Macmillan, 1990), p. 21.

[7]Kant, *The Metaphysics of Morals,* p. 186.

Imperative. For example, Kant spoke of a duty to preserve our life,[8] a duty to be kind where we can,[9] a duty to keep promises,[10] and so on.

In *The Metaphysics of Morals* Kant identified two general moral duties that are of basic importance. The first is a duty to ourselves, a duty to cultivate

> one's *capacities* (or natural disposition), the highest of which is *understanding*. . . . At the same time this duty includes the cultivation of one's *will* (moral cast of mind), so as to satisfy all the requirements of duty. [H]e has a duty to diminish his ignorance by instruction and to correct his errors. . . . Man has a duty to carry the cultivation of his *will* up to the purest virtuous disposition, in which the *law* becomes also the incentive to his actions that conform with duty and he obeys the law from duty.[11]

Reason imposes on us a duty to make ourselves as perfect as possible, a duty that has both positive and negative aspects. Because Kant considered the capacity for reason that which gives human beings their inherent worth, we have a duty to cultivate our reason and understanding. Cultivating our reason requires us to acquire knowledge, to exercise our mental capabilities by thinking and reasoning, and to cultivate our talents, whatever they may be. Failure to cultivate our mental capacities means living like a beast rather than like a human being. The basic duty of self-perfection imposes more specific duties—for example, duties to avoid drunkenness and gluttony,[12] which cloud or incapacitate our reason. Rational agents have a duty to respect within themselves that which gives them inherent worth; therefore, they have a duty to behave in ways that will maintain their self-esteem and avoid servility, which is degrading.[13] They must also cultivate their will both to behave as required by duty and to respect the moral law.

The second general duty that reason imposes is a duty to promote the happiness of others.[14] That duty has both positive and negative aspects. It includes the connected duties of benevolence and beneficence. To be benevolent is to love and respect others; it involves our feelings and attitudes. To be beneficent is to do good for others, to act with the intention of benefiting them. Kant emphasized that the duty of benevolence must be effective in leading to beneficence.

> The duty of love for one's neighbor can . . . also be expressed as the duty to make others' *ends* my own (provided only that these are not immoral). The duty of respect for my neighbor is contained in the maxim not to degrade any other man to a mere means to my own ends.[15]

---

[8]Kant, *Foundations of the Metaphysics of Morals,* p. 13.

[9]Ibid., p. 14.

[10]Ibid., p. 39.

[11]Kant, *The Metaphysics of Morals,* pp. 191–192.

[12]Ibid., p. 222.

[13]Ibid., pp. 230–231.

[14]Ibid., pp. 192–193.

[15]Ibid., p. 244.

More specific duties are derived from this general duty to others, including a duty of gratitude[16] and a duty of sympathetic joy and sadness (joy from another's pleasure, sadness from another's suffering)—that is, "a duty to sympathize actively in [others'] fate; and to this end an indirect duty to cultivate the compassionate natural feelings in us, and to make use of them."[17]

Kant seemed to imply that the duties he identified are absolute and categorical, and he tended to ignore the possibility of a conflict between duties. The British philosopher W. D. Ross (1877–1971), profoundly influenced by Kant, presented an extension of Kant's theory.

CONCEPTION OF PRIMA FACIE DUTIES

W. D. Ross maintained that people have several different kinds of moral duties. Some are duties to others that are based on previous acts of their own; some are duties to others that are independent of any of their past actions; and some are duties to themselves.

1. Duties to others based on our previous acts
   a. Duty of fidelity (duty to keep promises and abide by agreements)
   b. Duty of reparation (duty to compensate people for injuries and harm that we have caused)
   c. Duty of gratitude (duty to repay people with thanks for benefits that they have conferred on us)
2. Duties to others not based on our previous acts
   a. Duty of beneficence (duty to help others in need)
   b. Duty of nonmaleficence (duty to not unjustifiably harm others)
   c. Duty of justice (duty to conform to the demands of justice)
3. Duties to ourselves
   a. Duty of self-improvement (duty to improve ourselves physically, intellectually, and morally to reach our fullest potential)[18]

We have a duty of fidelity, reparation, or gratitude toward someone only if we have acted in the requisite way toward that person (made a promise, caused injury, or accepted a benefit). We have the duties of beneficence, nonmaleficence, and justice to all people, regardless of our past actions.

Ross listed what we might call basic duties; various more specific duties may be derived from them. For example, from the duties based on our previous actions, we can derive a duty of parents to provide financial support to their children under age eighteen. Having acted to bring children into the world, parents have a duty to provide for their needs. Thus, fathers who refuse to provide financial support to their children after desertion or divorce are violating a moral duty they have because of their past acts. From the duty of nonmaleficence, we can

---

[16]Ibid., p. 248.

[17]Ibid., pp. 250–251.

[18]W. D. Ross, *The Right and the Good* (Indianapolis, IN: Hackett, 1988), pp. 21–22. (Originally published in 1930.)

derive duties to not unjustifiably kill, maim, assault, rape, steal from, threaten, discriminate against, restrain, coerce, deceive, subjugate, manipulate, or oppress others. From the duty of beneficence we can derive duties to call for help when someone's life or health is jeopardized, to provide directions when asked by people who are lost, and so on.

According to Ross, these are *prima facie* duties. A prima facie duty is a form of behavior (such as keeping a promise) that is morally required *if* there are no other important moral considerations pulling in opposite directions. A prima facie duty is not an absolute duty that does not admit exceptions. For example, to say that someone has a prima facie duty to tell the truth is to say that telling the truth is generally morally required, although not necessarily in all circumstances. Prima facie duties must be distinguished from what we have an actual duty to do in a given situation, all things considered. We may have a prima facie duty to tell the truth, and yet telling the truth may not be our actual duty in a given situation, all things considered.

We determine what our actual duty is in a given situation by examining all the prima facie duties that apply in that situation. For example, suppose that John's wife has returned from the hairstylist with a new hairstyle and hair color. She asks him, "Do you like it?" John doesn't like it; he thinks it looks hideous. However, he knows that if he tells her the truth, her feelings will be hurt. Moreover, because she is insecure about her appearance, his telling the truth will cause her a fair amount of psychological suffering. Unfortunately for him, he cannot evade the question; he must answer either "yes" or "no." Let us suppose that John has (and knows that he has) a prima facie duty to tell the truth rather than lie and a prima facie duty to avoid hurting his wife's feelings and causing her psychological suffering. In this case, there is a conflict between his prima facie duties; in satisfying one duty he must violate the other. Only one of these conflicting prima facie duties can be his duty, all things considered. He has to decide which of his prima facie duties has priority and is his actual duty (all things considered) in this situation.

How do we decide in a given situation which of our prima facie duties is our actual duty, all things considered? According to Ross, "When I am in a situation ... in which more than one of these *prima facie* duties is incumbent on me, what I have to do is to study the situation as fully as I can until I form the considered opinion (it is never more) that in the circumstances one of them is more incumbent than any other."[19] We must decide after careful reflection and deliberation which of the prima facie duties has prority as being more important. Although Ross does not for the most part try to establish a priority ranking for the prima facie duties, he does maintain that the prima facie duty of nonmaleficence takes priority over the prima facie duty of beneficence. After all, Ross claimed, "We should not in general consider it justifiable to kill one person in order to keep another alive, or to steal from one in order to give alms to another."[20]

---

[19]Ibid., p. 19.

[20]Ibid., p. 22.

Ross maintained that what prima facie duties we have is self-evident.

> That an act is ... *prima facie* right, is self evident; not in the sense that it is evident from the beginning of our lives, or as soon as we attend to the proposition for the first time, but in the sense that when we have reached sufficient mental maturity and have given sufficient attention to the proposition it is evident without any need of proof, or of evidence beyond itself. It is self-evident just as a mathematical axiom, or the validity of a form of inference, is evident.[21]

When a person is sufficiently mature, then if she carefully reflects on such claims as "People have a duty to keep their promises" or "People have a duty to refrain from harming others," she will recognize that the claims are true. Our reason is as capable of recognizing the truth of these self-evident moral truths as it is capable of recognizing the truth of such self-evident mathematical truths as "Things equal to the same thing are equal to each other" and such self-evident logical truths as "Something cannot simultaneously have and not have a certain property." We don't need proof or evidence for the truth of these claims.

Critics of Ross deny that what prima facie duties we have is self-evident. In their view, a statement is self-evident only if its denial is a contradiction. For example, it is self-evident that all dogs are dogs because its denial, "Some dogs are not dogs," is a logical contradiction. Similarly, because raisins are nothing but dried grapes, to deny that all raisins are grapes is to affirm that some dried grapes are not grapes, once again a logical contradiction. In some respects, Ross is claiming that statements such as "People have a prima facie duty to not harm others" are like "All dogs are dogs" or like "All raisins are grapes." However, it is not obvious that "People do not have a prima facie duty to not harm others" is a logical contradiction. Therefore, it is not obvious that prima facie duties are self-evident.

MORAL RIGHTS

People are said to have moral rights as well as moral duties. Moral rights are not created or conferred on individuals by a legal system, but rather derive from a system of moral principles.

The content of a right can best be specified in terms of the duties it imposes. Having a right imposes on others either a positive or a negative duty. For example, if Jones has a moral right to freedom of expression, then others have a moral duty to *not* prevent him from expressing his opinions. On the other hand, if Jones has a moral right to basic medical care, then others have a duty to provide him with basic medical care. The first is a negative duty, the second a positive duty. Not all moral rights are either wholly positive or wholly negative; some rights may impose a combination of positive and negative duties. Consider the right to life. We might maintain that it imposes on others not merely the negative duty to not unjustifiably kill the right-holder but also the positive duty to save

---

[21]Ibid., p. 29.

the right-holder's life when the threat is grave and the cost of saving it is low. For example, we might maintain that if you are choking and I could save you by performing the Heimlich maneuver, I would violate your right to life were I to let you die. Such a claim presupposes that your right to life imposes on others a positive duty to save your life when the cost is small.

THE UNITED NATIONS UNIVERSAL DECLARATION OF HUMAN RIGHTS

In this section, we will concentrate on one aspect of moral rights—namely, the moral rights that are listed in the United Nations Universal Declaration of Human Rights.

In 1948 the United Nations set out to provide a list of the moral or human rights that all people have. Among these rights are (1) the right to life, (2) the right to political participation, (3) freedom rights, and (4) subsistence rights.

The Right to Life

Article 3
Everyone has the right to life....[22]

Most people consider the right to life the most basic and fundamental moral right. The right to life imposes on others at least a negative duty to *not* arbitrarily (or unjustifiably) deprive the right-holder of life. The right to life, even as a negative right, however, may not be absolute; overriding or violating the right by killing someone may be justified. For example, many people think that when it's necessary to defend themselves or others from serious physical harm (in peace or in war) or to punish someone for a very serious crime, they are justified in killing another person.

Is the right to life a purely negative right, imposing on others only negative duties toward the right-holder, or does it also impose positive duties toward the right-holder? For example, does it impose on others a duty to save the right-holder's life when they can do so without undue cost? If we did not throw a rope to a drowning man, letting him drown, would we violate his right to life? To answer that question, we must examine the justification for the right to life.

Most of us in the West do not attribute a right to life to all living things. For example, few people think that mosquitoes, flies, fish, chickens, cows, and pigs have a right to life, although they do think that human beings have a right to life. Is it the result of irrational prejudice in favor of members of their own species, or can it be justified? Kant emphasized that rational agents or persons, unlike other forms of life, have inherent worth. Human beings have inherent worth, and consequently have a right to life, because they are people with developed capac-

---

[22]United Nations, *The International Bill of Human Rights* (New York: United Nations, 1988).

ities for consciousness, self-awareness, and reason. Because they have inherent worth, people should not be destroyed without very strong justification.

However, we could maintain that because people have inherent worth, not only should we not destroy them without very good reasons, but we should take steps to preserve their lives as well. Because they have inherent worth, we should not allow people to perish when we can prevent it at relatively small cost. Such considerations support the view that the right to life imposes on others both a negative duty to not destroy people without very good reasons and a positive duty to act to save people when their lives are threatened.

The Right to Political Participation

Article 21
1. Everyone has the right to take part in the government of his country, directly or through freely chosen representatives.

• • •

3. The will of the people shall be the basis of the authority of government; this will shall be expressed in periodic and genuine elections which shall be by universal and equal suffrage and shall be held by secret vote or by equivalent free voting procedures.[23]

According to the United Nations, people have a moral right to participate in their government, which strongly suggests a right to a democratic form of government. Such a right may impose a negative duty to not subvert democracy by denying people the (legal) right to vote, preventing people from running for office, corrupting or overthrowing a legitimate and popular government, monopolizing political power, and the like. It also imposes positive duties—for example, a duty to organize and conduct genuine elections for public office. What justification is there for the claim that people have a moral right to participate in the government of their country?

In many countries, past and present, the claim that everyone has the moral right to participate in political decision making would be greeted with stunned incomprehension. For example, in early nineteenth-century Britain only a small percentage of adult males, roughly 15 percent, could vote in Parliamentary elections. No women could vote, nor could men who did not meet the fairly substantial wealth requirement for voting. Similarly, only fairly wealthy males were eligible to run for Parliament. Throughout the nineteenth century almost all members of the ruling class in Britain (wealthy male aristocrats and landowners) vehemently denied that everyone, regardless of sex and wealth, has a moral right to participate in political decision making. Similarly, consider the opposition to democracy of the rulers of the People's Republic of China in the twilight of the twentieth century. In 1989 its rulers sent tanks into Tiananmen Square in Beijing to crush a student demonstration for democracy.

We might justify the claim that everyone has a moral right to participate in political decision making by pointing out that a government's decisions affect

---

[23]Ibid.

nearly every aspect of the lives of the people who live under it. Government policy affects standards of living, individual health care and public health, education, the environment, and so on. If people have no role to play in government decision making, it is easy for the government to ignore their needs and interests and to focus on protecting and satisfying the needs of those with political power. People can best protect their own lives, needs, and interests when they participate in political decision making; exclusion can leave people helpless and vulnerable.

Then, too, not permitting people to participate in political decision making that affects their lives is inconsistent with their status as rational, autonomous agents with inherent worth. Those who exclude people from political decision making violate the Kantian requirement to treat people with respect. The person who is subject to laws that she did not have a hand in enacting is ruled as a child is ruled.

Freedom Rights

Article 1

All human beings are born free and equal in dignity and rights. . . .

Article 2

Everyone is entitled to all the rights and freedoms set forth in this Declaration, without distinction of any kind, such as race, colour, sex, language, religion, political or other opinion, national or social origin, property, birth or other status.

Article 3

Everyone has the right to life, liberty and the security of person.

Article 4

No one shall be held in slavery or servitude. . . .

• • •

Article 12

No one shall be subjected to arbitrary interference with his privacy, family, home or correspondence. . . .

Article 13

1. Everyone has the right to freedom of movement and residence within the borders of each state.

• • •

Article 17

1. Everyone has the right to own property alone as well as in association with others.
2. No one shall be arbitrarily deprived of his property.

Article 18

Everyone has the right to freedom of thought, conscience and religion; this right includes freedom to change his religion or belief, and freedom . . . in public or private, to manifest his religion or belief in teaching, practice, worship and observance.

Article 19

Everyone has the right to freedom of opinion and expression; this right includes freedom to hold opinions without interference and to seek, receive and impart information and ideas.[24]

Freedom rights are like fences with No Trespassing signs posted; primarily negative, they impose duties on others to refrain from interfering with the rightholder in certain ways. They protect a person's fundamental interest in being left alone to think and do what he wants to do. For example, Jones's right to freedom of religion, thought, and expression imposes on others a duty to not interfere with his religious beliefs and activities as well as with his efforts to express his opinions and acquire information.

The United Nations documents identify certain freedoms that are thought to be basic or especially important and that deserve the protection accorded by being declared a matter of moral right. People have a moral right to be free from enslavement, from arbitrary invasions of their privacy, from interference with their movements and choice of residence, from arbitrary deprivation of their property, and from coercion regarding their beliefs and the public expression of their beliefs. If they are not protected in these crucial matters from the interference of others, including their governments, their lives and well-being will be seriously jeopardized. These freedoms are particularly important because without them, individuals are defenseless. If their thoughts and beliefs are not inviolable, if they may not move about or take up residence as and where they see fit, if they may not publicly express their thoughts in their own defense or on their own behalf, how impoverished and dangerous their lives will be.

Human beings should have freedom rights—rights to be left alone and not interfered with—simply because they are people. People have a conception of the good life that gives meaning to their lives and shapes their behavior as they try to realize that conception. To be happy, satisfied, and autonomous, an individual requires freedom to live her life according to her own, rather than others' beliefs, desires, and conception of the good life. Enforcing conformity to the standards of others in thought and action negates a person's individuality, undermining the inherent worth of the individual human being.

However, John Stuart Mill emphasized that people should not be free from interference to do absolutely anything they want. For example, virtually no one would accept the claim that people should be free to kill, assault, rape, or steal from others. Nor would they be likely to accept that people should be free to drive while drunk or to drive through stop signs without stopping, to enter other people's houses without permission, to throw bricks from overpasses onto highways, to shoot guns into crowds of people, or to commit arson. Mill maintained, "All that makes existence valuable to anyone depends on the enforcement of restraints upon the actions of other people."[25] People should be free from inter-

---

[24]Ibid.

[25]John Stuart Mill, *On Liberty* (Indianapolis, IN: Hackett, 1978), p. 5.

ference if, but only if, they are not harming others. As long as someone is not harming others, she should be free to live her life without interference.

Mill is particularly critical of paternalism. He insists that attempting to protect people from themselves is not sufficient justification for interfering with a person's thoughts and behavior. Mill would undoubtedly be opposed to mandatory seat belt laws, motorcycle helmet laws, and laws prohibiting prostitution, homosexual behavior, or drug, tobacco, and alcohol use, for example, if their only justification is that they protect people from harming themselves. Mill would maintain that people should be free to drive without seat belts, to ride motorcycles without helmets, to buy and sell sex, and to smoke, drink, and use drugs if the only people likely to be harmed are themselves. People should be left alone to live their own lives, even if they engage in very risky behavior, so long as they are not likely to cause other people harm.

However, Mill and others have recognized that in harming ourselves we may be harming others. If someone commits suicide, he may traumatize his friends and relatives or create financial hardship for his family. In that case, he is not simply harming himself. Mill's principle according to which government may only restrict freedom in order to prevent harm to others can be used to restrict our freedom to harm ourselves. However, the ultimate aim is to prevent people from harming others *by* harming themselves. Freedom to engage in self-destructive behavior that does not harm others may not be restricted. One notorious problem for Mill's harm principle is that with enough ingenuity one can find that virtually any self-destructive behavior harms others in some way. Therefore, the harm principle may not provide as much protection for freedom as Mill imagined.

Articles 1 and 2 maintain that people have a right to be free from unjust discrimination; that is, they should not be denied any of their moral rights on the basis of such irrelevant characteristics as their sex, race, or wealth. These articles reflect a commitment to the thesis that all human beings are people with equal inherent worth. Differences of race, sex, national origin, wealth, or sexual orientation do not diminish a person's inherent worth or make him less a person. Every person has a moral right to be free from discrimination on the basis of characteristics irrelevant to her personhood.

Subsistence Rights

Subsistence rights[26] are rights to goods or services that are necessary for our survival or subsistence. According to the United Nations Declaration, a person has subsistence rights that impose on others positive duties to provide the basic necessities "indispensable for his dignity and the free development of his personality."[27] Those basic necessities include food, clothing, shelter, medical care, and education. Subsistence rights protect people from serious threats to their

---

[26]Henry Shue, *Basic Rights* (Princeton, NJ: Princeton University Press, 1980).

[27]United Nations. *Universal Declaration of Human Rights,* Article 22.

lives and well-being, just as freedom rights protect people from serious threats to their autonomy.

Article 23

1. Everyone has the right to work, to free choice of employment, to just and favorable conditions of work and to protection against unemployment.
2. Everyone, without any discrimination, has the right to equal pay for equal work.
3. Everyone who works has the right to just and favorable remuneration insuring for himself and his family an existence worthy of human dignity, and supplemented, if necessary, by other means of social protection.
4. Everyone has the right to form and to join trade unions for the protection of his interests.

• • •

Article 25

1. Everyone has the right to a standard of living adequate for the health and well-being of himself and his family, including food, clothing, housing and medical care and necessary social services, and the right to security in the event of unemployment, sickness, disability, widowhood, old age or other lack of livelihood in circumstances beyond his control.

• • •

Article 26

1. Everyone has the right to education. Education shall be free, at least in the elementary and fundamental stages....[28]

Subsistence rights may be derived from the right to life if the right to life is both positive and negative. The right to life may impose on others not only the negative duty to not unjustifiably kill the right-holder but also positive duties to provide what the right-holder needs to survive. Suppose that Tatiana has pneumonia that can be cured by antibiotics but she cannot afford the antibiotics because she is poor. If she is denied medical treatment, she will probably die. Advocates of subsistence rights maintain that her right to life is violated if she is left to die without medical care. Similarly, suppose that Alfredo cannot afford to pay for rent or food. If he is left without shelter or food, he will probably die. Again, advocates of subsistence rights maintain that his right to life is violated if he is left without the shelter and food that he needs for survival. Similarly, the right to employment imposes a duty to provide paid work to people who want to work but can't find employment.

Many advocates of subsistence rights maintain that others have a duty to provide life's necessities to people only if they cannot secure them by their own unaided efforts. We might say that people have a duty to try to support themselves if they can. If someone violates that duty, then his subsistence rights do not impose on others a duty to provide him with what he refuses to provide for himself. Then, too, we might maintain that subsistence rights are contingent on a certain level of affluence. People have a duty to provide life's necessities to

---

[28]Ibid.

others only if they have a surplus beyond what they need to survive. If I'm already at the edge of starvation, I do not have a duty to provide food to others if it means that I will starve. Moral duties don't require people to virtually commit suicide. However, if I have more than enough food to survive, the subsistence rights of others would impose on me a duty to provide them with at least some of my surplus food.

Whereas freedom rights impose duties to not interfere with the right-holder in various ways, subsistence rights impose duties to provide the right-holder with certain goods and services. Does that mean that each of us has a duty to provide Tatiana with antibiotics to cure her pneumonia, or to provide Alfredo with shelter and food? Not necessarily. The duty of providing the goods and services required for survival may be imposed on the community as a whole, rather than on each individual member of the community. Each individual may have a duty to actively support social institutions that provide necessities to people who cannot meet their needs, rather than a duty to provide people with what they need to survive.

Objections to Subsistence Rights   Some people believe that subsistence rights are not genuine moral rights. One objection to subsistence rights is that they require too much sacrifice. Freedom rights primarily require people to leave each other alone, which is easily done and doesn't require a substantial sacrifice of time, energy, or resources. Subsistence rights, on the other hand, require people to provide others with life's necessities, which entails a much greater cost and sacrifice.

Advocates of subsistence rights insist that the sacrifice is not prohibitive if a society collectively shoulders and limits the responsibility. First, the sacrifice is limited if only the basic needs of right-holders rather than all their desires and wants are candidates for satisfaction. Providing antibiotics to cure pneumonia may be required, but not liposuction or other forms of cosmetic surgery. Providing access to transportation may be required, but not providing a new sports car. Second, the sacrifice is limited if only those who cannot provide for themselves by their own unaided efforts are helped. Finally, in an advanced industrial society the sacrifice required will be money, usually taken through taxes. If the tax is fair, taking only from those able to pay and proportional to their ability to pay, no individual's sacrifice will be prohibitive.

Libertarians object that subsistence rights violate freedom rights. If you are coerced into contributing to the maintenance of other people on the grounds that they have subsistence rights, you are not being left alone to live your own life. Resources that you could use in pursuing your own conception of the good life are being taken from you. It doesn't matter that you have a surplus beyond what you need to survive; you have a right to use that money as you will, and the government does not have a right to take it. Taxation is involuntary. To tax one person in order to provide life's necessities to another person is no better than theft, libertarians insist.

Advocates of subsistence rights respond in a variety of ways. Utilitarians maintain that total well-being is the ultimate moral consideration, and many utilitarians claim that recognizing and enforcing both freedom rights and subsistence rights maximizes total well-being. A utilitarian might deny that people have the specific freedom right that libertarians appeal to—the right to be free from being taxed for the purpose of providing for the needs of others. According to utilitarians, people have only those freedom rights that maximize total well-being. Because a right to be free from taxation for the purpose of providing others with what they need does not maximize total well-being, it is no more a legitimate moral right than is a right to be free to drive while drunk or free from having to stop at stop signs.

Because Kant maintained that people have the duty of beneficence derived from the universal law formulation of the Categorical Imperative, he would presumably deny that people have a right to be free from taxation for social purposes. He might also maintain that the requirement of treating people with respect is inconsistent with leaving them to die because of unmet needs.

A social contract theorist such as John Rawls might maintain that a hypothetical social contract would include subsistence rights. Rational, self-interested individuals in the Original Position behind the Veil of Ignorance would agree to advocate and accept subsistence rights because without them, their survival might be jeopardized. They might find themselves helpless and vulnerable, dependent on government programs for survival. Without such programs, helpless and vulnerable people will probably not survive. Thus, advocates of subsistence rights can respond in several ways to the claim that recognition of subsistence rights is wrong because it violates the freedom rights of those who are not weak and vulnerable.

EXERCISES

1. Which of the following possible moral duties do you believe people have? Defend your answers.
    a. A moral duty to refrain from being rude to others.
    b. A moral duty to vote in elections.
    c. A moral duty to refrain from cheating on examinations and from committing plagiarism.
    d. A moral duty to donate blood.
    e. A moral duty to refrain from committing acts of sexual harassment.
    f. A moral duty to contribute some time or money to charity.
    g. A moral duty to refrain from drinking to intoxication.
    h. A moral duty to act to prevent friends from driving while intoxicated.
    i. A moral duty to refrain from telling racist or sexist jokes.
    j. A moral duty to object if someone tells a racist or sexist joke.
    k. A moral duty to refrain from stealing from others.

2. Do you believe that people have moral duties to themselves? If yes, what are those duties? Defend your answer.

3. Do people have a moral duty to inform authorities if they have reason to believe that child abuse is occurring? Defend your answer.

4. Dave is engaged to Priscilla. He considers his engagement a contract: He asked Priscilla to marry him, and she accepted his offer. However, he has recently realized that he no longer loves her and no longer wishes to marry her. Does he have a moral duty to keep his agreement and marry Priscilla? Defend your answer.

5. Does someone who has tested positive for the HIV (AIDS) virus have a moral duty to inform past and potential future sex partners of this fact? Defend your answer.

6. Do you believe that people have a moral right to life? If yes, does it include both a negative duty to not kill people without justification and a positive duty to act to preserve people's lives? Defend your answers.

7. Do you believe that people have a moral right to participate in political decision making? If yes, how can that right best be implemented? Defend your answers.

8. Does the ban on homosexuals in the United States military violate anyone's moral rights? Defend your answer.

9. Do laws prohibiting people from buying and selling sex and from using drugs such as cocaine and heroin unjustifiably interfere with people's freedom rights? Defend your answer.

10. Do people have a moral right to commit suicide? Defend your answer.

11. Are subsistence rights genuine moral rights? If yes, what are people's specific subsistence rights? What must a society do in order to implement subsistence rights? Defend your answers.

SUGGESTED READINGS

Immanuel Kant. *The Metaphysics of Morals.* Translated by Mary Gregor. New York: Cambridge University Press, 1991.

Loren Lomasky. *Persons, Rights, and the Moral Community.* New York: Oxford University Press, 1987.

David Lyons, ed. *Rights.* Belmont, CA: Wadsworth, 1979.

John Stuart Mill. *On Liberty.* Indianapolis, IN: Hackett, 1978.

James Nickel. *Making Sense of Human Rights.* Berkeley: University of California Press, 1987.

W. D. Ross. *The Right and the Good.* Indianapolis, IN: Hackett, 1988. (Originally published in 1930.)

Henry Shue. *Basic Rights.* Princeton, NJ: Princeton University Press, 1980.

L. W. Sumner. *The Moral Foundation of Rights.* New York: Oxford University Press, 1987.

CHAPTER 12

Feminist Moral Theory

The words *feminist* and *feminism* conjure up many different images and associations. Who or what is a feminist? First and foremost, a feminist is someone who believes that men and women are inherently equal in all respects relevant to how they should be treated. Because they believe that men and women are equals, feminists insist that they should be treated as equals. They emphasize that women *do* have the same moral status as men and therefore *should* have the same legal rights, opportunities, and social status as men. Feminists are united in their opposition to patriarchy—a system in which women are subordinate to and oppressed by men—and they seek to liberate women from what they consider a pattern of systematic male domination.[1]

Feminists believe that women have been subordinated to and oppressed by men in a variety of ways. They point out that in most societies men have more power than women. Feminists believe that men have generally used that power to impose laws, customs, and traditions that systematically favor their interests over women's interests. For example, the legal systems of many societies, both past and present, have explicitly denied women the right to hold public office, to vote, to own property in their own name, to pursue a career, or to engage in certain professions. The law may permit a husband to beat, or even kill, his wife if she is not sufficiently obedient or deferential to him, and may make it easier for a husband than a wife to get a divorce. For example, in ancient Rome in the early Republic (roughly 500–200 B.C.E.), "husbands could kill their wives . . . for adultery, but wives could not prosecute their husbands for the offense." (Fortunately, "actual executions for adultery seem to have been rare.")[2] Similarly, in Britain "before 1870, a husband became by matrimony instantly and perpetually endowed with all his wife's worldly goods and indeed could disinherit her of all of them."[3] In most societies prior to the twentieth century, women were almost wholly excluded from participation in political life. Such legal discrimi-

---

[1]This characterization assumes that men as well as women can be feminists. Some female feminists would object to this assumption. According to their definition, only females can be feminists; they would call males who otherwise satisfy the definition "profeminists."

[2]Henry Boren, *Roman Society,* 2d ed. (Lexington, MA: D. C. Heath, 1992), p. 80.

[3]L. C. B. Seaman, *Victorian England* (London: Routledge, 1973), p. 181.

nation against women may be only a memory in the West, but it still persists in many parts of the world. For example, in 1992, after being liberated from Iraqi occupation by Operation Desert Storm, Kuwait organized elections for a parliament. Women were excluded both from running for parliament and from voting in the election.

Even if restrictions on women are not explicitly written into law, both custom and tradition can forge chains on women every bit as strong as those forged by law. By custom and tradition, women may be socialized to be submissive, undemanding, and obedient while men are socialized to be aggressive, assertive, and demanding. Inculcating different character or personality traits based on an individual's sex can obviously give members of one sex certain advantages over members of the other; historically, it has facilitated men's domination of women in both public and private life. Then, too, a society's dominant tradition may teach that men are superior to women and that consequently, in the natural order of things, men are destined to command and women to obey. Even if there are no laws against it, there may be strong social taboos on women's striving for success in politics, business, and the professions, or on their engaging in certain occupations outside the home. By custom and tradition, a daughter may receive far less education than a son. Husbands may be considered the "captains" of the ship with the legitimate authority to make the final decision on all family matters, including child rearing, finances, the distribution of work inside the home, and even whether the wife may work outside the home. By custom and tradition, male violence may be considered "normal," so that it is considered acceptable for men to beat their wives and children.

Recently, feminists have vehemently condemned a practice they call female genital mutilation and supporters call female circumcision, widespread in Islamic countries in sub-Saharan Africa and in Egypt, as another example of the oppression of women. The procedure involves cutting off all or part of a girl's clitoris before she reaches puberty. The procedure has been performed on girls as young as three. Some studies estimate that 97 percent of married women in sub-Saharan Africa and Egypt between the ages of 15 and 49 have undergone the procedure. (Apparently, many men in these countries are reluctant to marry a woman who has not undergone the procedure, so that a girl's parents know that her chances of getting married are low if she does not undergo it.)

Supporters of the procedure claim that it is required by Islamic law because the Prophet Mohammed ordered it. Some supporters also emphasize its utility in controlling a woman's sexual desire and ensuring that she remains faithful to her husband. For example, Egyptian Islamic cleric Sheik Yusef Badry has said, "A woman can enjoy her sexual feelings with her husband, but if we cut off this piece, she will be able to control herself."[4]

Critics of the procedure view it as another example of patriarchy—of men controlling women.

---

[4]*The Boston Globe,* June 25, 1997, p.A2.

Besides being traumatic and potentially dangerous—especially when performed by barbers and other unqualified practitioners [which is common]—the procedure has been linked to problems in childbirth and sexual relations. . . . Many Muslim scholars . . . argue [that] the practice has no basis in doctrine, noting that in Egypt it dates to pharaonic times, centuries before the advent of Islam, and is virtually unknown in such conservative Islamic societies as Saudi Arabia and Iran.[5]

But in societies where men control all the levers of power, religious as well as secular, men can impose customs, traditions, and laws that enable them to control women in a variety of ways.

Many feminists also believe that women have been socialized to accept an intellectual tradition that has been constructed primarily by males from a male point of view. By now it is widely accepted that a whole intellectual tradition can be tainted because it is constructed from and reflects a certain limited national, religious, racial, or class perspective and bias. Such a tainted intellectual tradition can be used, consciously or unconsciously, to justify oppression, exploitation, and subordination. (The most infamous example is probably Nazi ideology.) Feminists point out that many of the most influential philosophers in the Western tradition explicitly maintained that women are inferior to men in a variety of ways.

Many feminists maintain that there is both a characteristically male and a (different) characteristically female perspective on moral issues. Additionally, they maintain that there is a characteristically male and a (different) characteristically female approach to moral decision making and problem solving. In their view, the Western intellectual tradition is tainted with a male bias because it reflects male experience and the male moral perspective while ignoring or excluding female experience and the female moral perspective.[6] Many feminists believe that because of this male-centered perspective, women's values and ways of approaching moral decision making have been ignored or denigrated and many moral issues that are important from a woman's perspective have been ignored or distorted. Such issues include men's domination of and oppression of women, male violence, rape, woman and child battering, prostitution, pornography, homosexuality, sexual harassment, divorce, child rearing, and poverty (which falls more heavily on women and children than on men). As Annette Baier points out, until recently the male-dominated mainstream of moral philosophy generally ignored the issues of "wrongs to animals and wrongful destruction of our physical environment," and in much of moral and political theory there were "only hand waves concerning our proper attitude toward our children, toward the ill, toward our relatives, friends, and lovers."[7]

---

[5]Ibid.

[6]Note the use of "the" rather than "a" male and female perspective. The assumption that there is only one male perspective and only one female perspective will be called into question later.

[7]Annette C. Baier, "What Do Women Want in a Moral Theory?" in Annette C. Baier, *Moral Prejudices: Essays in Ethics* (Cambridge, MA: Harvard University Press, 1994), p. 3.

In this chapter we will focus on whether there are indeed two different approaches to moral decision making and problem solving—one characteristically female and the other characteristically male. In later chapters we will examine some of the concrete issues that are of particular concern to women.

MALE JUSTICE VERSUS FEMALE CARE APPROACHES TO MORAL DECISION MAKING

The research of psychologist Carol Gilligan, many feminists believe, confirms the difference between characteristically male and characteristically female approaches to moral decision making. Gilligan presented male and female research subjects with various moral problems and asked them how they would resolve them. For example, she tells her subjects the story of a man whose wife is dying. The town pharmacist has medicine that can save her, but he's asking so much money for it that the husband cannot afford to buy it. The question is, Should he steal it to save his wife's life? According to Gilligan, males tend to rely on impartial universal principles and rules, such as "Don't steal" or "Save your wife's life," and so-called "abstract" considerations of justice and rights, such as the right to life and the right to own property. When rights and rules conflict, as in this case, males tend to focus next on which considerations should take priority.[8] Most important, males tend to deny feelings and emotions any positive or constructive role in moral decision making because they believe that feelings and emotions distort moral judgment. Gilligan refers to the perspective that both emphasizes rules and rights and denies feelings and emotions a role in moral decision making as the "justice" perspective.

Feminists who agree that there are different characteristically male and female approaches to moral decision making consider Utilitarianism, Kantian moral theory, and hypothetical social contract theory as characteristically male because they rely on reason and the application of rules and principles to the exclusion of feelings and emotions. These theories are central examples of a "justice" as opposed to a "care" approach. For example, in *On Liberty*, John Stuart Mill noted with disapproval, "People are accustomed to believe ... that their feelings on subjects of this nature [moral subjects] are better than reasons and render reasons unnecessary."[9] Rather than rely on their feelings in moral decision making, Mill believed that people should rely on reason and rules. Similarly, Immanuel Kant emphasized that nature has appointed reason rather than feelings and emotions to be the ruler of our wills and that an action has moral worth only if it is done from duty rather than from inclination. An action that is in conformity with duty but that is done because of feelings and emotions rather than because of respect for duty has no moral worth. For example, charity done because we

---

[8]Carol Gilligan, *In a Different Voice* (Cambridge, MA: Harvard University Press, 1982).

[9]John Stuart Mill, *On Liberty* (Indianapolis, IN: Hackett, 1978), p. 5.

believe that we have a duty to be charitable has moral worth; charity done because we feel sympathy and compassion for people has no moral worth.[10]

According to Gilligan, females approach moral problems differently. Rather than relying on the application of quasi-legal rules and laws and appealing to abstract considerations of rights, women tend to rely on feelings and emotions. The feelings and emotions that guide women's moral decision making are not those of hatred, rage, fear, suspicion, or vengefulness but rather feelings of compassion, care, love, and concern. Faced with the dilemma of the man with the sick wife, some of Gilligan's female subjects refused to choose between letting the man's wife die and stealing the medicine. Instead they tried to find a compromise solution that would meet the needs of both the husband and the pharmacist. For example, they suggested that the husband borrow the money, promise to pay the pharmacist sometime in the future, or try to persuade the pharmacist to give him the medicine by getting him to feel more sympathy and compassion for his and his wife's situation. In Gilligan's view, this kind of response showed that women tend to be more sensitive than men to the needs of others and to have more compassion and sympathy. In turn, their greater capacity for care, compassion, concern, and sympathy leads women to seek solutions that will minimize pain and suffering for all concerned. Gilligan identifies this as a "care" approach rather than a justice approach to moral decision making.

According to many feminists, a justice approach relies on "abstract" rules and principles, in that formulating or applying them requires us to abstract from the concrete circumstances to uncover the similarities among situations. To formulate or apply a rule prohibiting lying, for example, we must concentrate on the features of a situation that make it a case of lying and abstract from other features of the situation that are irrelevant to its being a case of lying. The care approach to moral decision making, many feminists maintain, resists abstraction and emphasizes attention to all of the concrete details of a situation in order to understand it in all of its individuality and specificity. Consider once again Gilligan's story of the man with the sick wife. A male justice approach to moral decision making may focus on the fact that the wife will die without the medication, that the pharmacist refuses to sell the medicine to the husband for what he can afford, and that the husband's taking it will constitute theft. A female care approach would focus on many aspects of the situation that males would neglect: how the wife will feel if her husband steals the medicine; how the husband will feel if he doesn't steal the medicine and his wife dies; how the pharmacist will feel if the man's wife dies because he refused to sell the medicine; why the pharmacist refuses to sell the medicine at a price the husband can afford; whether the husband and wife have children or other relatives and, if so, what will happen to them and how they will feel; how the pharmacist's friends and relatives will feel if the woman dies because he won't sell the drug to her husband. A female approach would also emphasize imagining alternatives that

---

[10]Immanuel Kant, *Foundations of the Metaphysics of Morals,* 2d ed., trans. Lewis White Beck (New York: Macmillan, 1990), pp. 10–14.

may have been overlooked. Could a person appeal to the pharmacist's relatives or friends to plead with him to sell the drug? Could the man borrow the money from someone? Could he reach an agreement with the pharmacist to pay the money for the medicine in installments?

Feminists who adopt a care approach point out that caring people are more sensitive to and moved by the sufferings and needs of others than are noncaring people. The perception of suffering or need naturally evokes in caring people a desire to relieve the suffering or satisfy the need. Therefore, caring people can rely on their feelings, emotions, and natural impulses rather than on rules and principles in deciding what is the right thing to do in any given situation. For example, seeing someone starving naturally evokes in caring people a desire to relieve the person's hunger, and a caring person will immediately "feel" that providing food is the right thing to do.

Obligation versus Caring

In Annette Baier's view, the primary difference between justice and care approaches is that a justice approach emphasizes the concepts of duty and obligation whereas a care approach embodies an ethic of love.

> What would be a suitable central question, principle, or concept to structure a moral theory which might accommodate those moral insights which women tend to have more readily than men, and to answer those moral questions which, it seems, worry women more than men? I hypothesized that the women's theory, expressive mainly of women's insights and concerns, would be an ethic of love, and this hypothesis seems to be Gilligan's, too. . . .
>
> Like any good theory, it will need not to ignore the partial truth of previous theories. . . .
>
> So women theorists will need to connect their ethics of love with what has been the men theorists' preoccupation, namely, obligation.
>
> The great and influential moral theorists have in the modern era taken *obligation* as the key and the problematic concept, and have asked what justifies treating a person as morally bound or obliged to do a particular thing.[11]

Whereas for justice theories the principal moral question to ask in a given situation is, "What is my (one's) moral duty?" for care theories the principal question would be "What is the loving or caring thing to do?"

Furthermore, Baier laments, in men's moral theories, "their version of the justified list of obligations does not ensure the proper care of the young and so does nothing to ensure the stability of the morality in question over several generations."[12] In applying their moral theories, men tend to focus exclusively on the "public" realm of politics and economics. Issues of war and international relations, citizenship and government, crime and punishment, economic classes, and

---

[11]Baier, p. 4.

[12]Ibid., p. 6.

the like dominate in men's theorizing. Usually left out of account are considerations of moral duties to spouses, children, parents, and other relatives, as well as friends and acquaintances. Yet individual and social well-being are usually affected far more directly by the web of small-scale interpersonal relationships within which each individual is enmeshed, such as families, than by the activities of major institutions, such as government and business enterprises.

Following Gilligan, Baier hypothesizes that the difference between men's and women's perspectives and approaches is rooted in different kinds of experience. Overwhelmingly, women have been the ones to take care of children, the ill, the disabled, and the old. Gilligan suggests that this experience of caring for the weak, helpless, and vulnerable affects women's point of view, making them more conscious of the need to care and be cared for and readier to act in a caring way.

Autonomy versus Attachment

In explaining the difference between male and female perspectives, Baier notes that infants and children, whether male or female, face two vastly different threats or challenges.

> [Gilligan] postulates two evils that any infant may become aware of, the evil of detachment or isolation from others whose love one needs, and the evil of relative powerlessness and weakness. Two dimensions of moral development are thereby set—one aimed at achieving satisfying community with others, the other aiming at autonomy or equality of power.[13]

Because of their experience as caretakers, most women may be in a better position than most men to appreciate the need for both attachment and autonomy, whereas men's experience may make them more aware of the need for autonomy and power than of the need for attachment. Male-oriented justice approaches to morality thus tend to slight issues of attachment and relationships. Men's theories generally start off by assuming isolated individuals with no relationships and attachments and then try to derive principles of justice, duty, and rights to govern their interactions with the goal of protecting those individuals. Women's theories typically start off by assuming individuals enmeshed in a web of relationships that define them and that are crucial to their well-being and then try to derive principles that protect, sustain, and nurture these relationships and the individuals enmeshed in them.

Feelings and Emotions in Moral Judgment

Another feminist moral philosopher, Virginia Held, offers a feminist perspective on the role that feelings should play in moral philosophy.

> Many feminists argue . . . that emotions have an important function in developing moral understanding itself, in helping us decide what the

---

[13]Annette C. Baier, "The Need for More Than Justice," in Annette C. Baier, *Moral Prejudices,* p. 20.

recommendations of morality themselves ought to be. Feelings, they say, should be respected by morality rather than dismissed as lacking impartiality. Yes, there are morally harmful emotions, such as prejudice, hatred, desire for revenge, blind egotism, and so forth. But to rid moral theory of harmful emotions by banishing all emotion is misguided. Such emotions as empathy, concern for others, hopefulness, and indignation in the face of cruelty—all these may be crucial in developing appropriate moral positions. An adequate moral theory should be built on appropriate feelings as well as on appropriate reasoning. And that such a view requires us to suppose we already understand what feelings are appropriate is no . . . obstacle.[14]

According to this view, feelings can and should help guide us in deciding what is the right thing to do. Which feelings? Feelings that tend to cause us to behave in ways that are beneficial rather than harmful or destructive. Fundamental to human morality is the assumption that the fact that something is harmful counts against it, not for it, in moral evaluation and the fact that something is beneficial counts for it, not against it, in moral evaluation. Feelings or emotions such as hatred, envy, jealousy, and prejudice obviously cause us to behave in harmful and destructive ways. They should not help guide us in our moral deliberations. On the other hand, feelings or emotions such as love, care, sympathy, and compassion obviously cause us to behave in ways that are beneficial. They should help guide us in our moral deliberations.

This perspective demands that we focus on an aspect of our moral lives that a justice perspective ignores. One of our tasks as moral beings is to cultivate the appropriate feelings and emotions. We should try to make ourselves more empathic, sympathetic, compassionate, loving, and caring and less indifferent, hostile, and prejudiced. We should cultivate and nurture the positive moral emotions while trying to extinguish or minimize the negative moral emotions. We are feeling as well as reasoning beings.

ARE JUSTICE AND CARE APPROACHES INCOMPATIBLE?
The Case of Killing the White Crow

Roger Rigterink uses a striking example to illustrate the difference between the justice approach and the care approach. In 1988 a hunter shot a very rare white crow in Wisconsin. Many people were upset. For example, Jo Ann Munson said, "I was angry about it when I first heard of it and I still am. I don't understand why someone feels the need to shoot a bird like that. It should have been left in the wild for all of us to enjoy."[15] Apparently the bird was well known and popular with both adults and children in the area. The hunter was unapologetic. When criticized he responded, "I'm a hunter. It's fair game. The opportunity pre-

---

[14]Virginia Held, *Feminist Morality* (Chicago: University of Chicago Press, 1993), p. 30.

[15]Roger Rigterink, "Warning: The Surgeon Moralist Has Determined That Claims of Rights Can Be Detrimental to Everyone's Interests," in *Explorations in Feminist Ethics,* ed. Eve Browning Cole and Susan Coultrap-McQuin (Bloomington: Indiana University Press, 1992), p. 38.

sented itself. People blow these things out of context . . . I had been seeing it for a long time. I wanted it for a trophy."[16] Rigterink points out that there was no law prohibiting hunters from shooting the white crow.

Rigterink asked his students whether the hunter had done anything wrong. Many students claimed that the hunter hadn't done anything wrong; he had a right to shoot the crow because there was no law against it, and it was not wrong for him to do what he had a right to do. Presumably, the hunter thought the same thing. Rigterink believes that this response illustrates a justice approach to moral decision making because it appeals to rules and rights. On the other hand, many students also said that the hunter was "thoughtless, insensitive, a jerk." If they concluded that his killing the white crow was wrong because it was insensitive and thoughtless, they were employing a care approach. Applying the care approach, they might have said that killing the white crow was wrong because a caring person would not have killed it. Even with no law prohibiting shooting the white crow, a caring person would recognize that shooting it in order to have its dead body for a trophy would cause suffering to other people who value the crow as a very special creature. Both children and adults would feel resentment, anger, sadness, and a sense of loss. Only a person who thinks primarily or exclusively of his own wants and needs would shoot the crow.

Rigterink claims that the case of the white crow demonstrates a real difference between a justice and a care approach, in part because the two approaches yield incompatible conclusions in this case. He assumes that although the hunter's killing of the white crow was wrong from a care perspective, it was not wrong from a justice perspective. But is he correct that from a justice perspective it was morally acceptable for the hunter to kill the white crow? Rigterink seems to assume that the hunter had a moral right to kill the crow simply because he had a legal right to do so. However, as we've seen, a legal right to do something doesn't entail a moral right to do it. In some societies, men have had a legal right to beat their wives and whites have had a legal right to enslave blacks, but the existence of such laws doesn't require us to concede a moral right to do those things. Therefore, the fact that the hunter had a legal right to kill the crow does not necessarily show that he had a moral right to shoot it, nor does the fact that he did nothing legally wrong show that he did nothing morally wrong.

In fact, a careful application of such justice approaches as Utilitarianism, Kantian moral theory, or social contract theory would probably yield the same conclusion as a care approach. For example, an act utilitarian would probably conclude that more total well-being would result if the white crow were not shot than if it were shot and stuffed for the benefit of one hunter. A rule utilitarian would probably conclude that more total well-being would result if people followed a rule prohibiting them from killing rather than permitting them to kill very rare and popular animals in order to stuff them for their own benefit. A Kantian applying the universal law formulation of the Categorical Imperative might maintain that the hunter could not will that a maxim permit-

---

[16]Ibid.

ting him to destroy for his own benefit things that other people enjoy and value become a universal law. Applying the respect for persons formulation of the Categorical Imperative, a Kantian might maintain that killing the rare and special white crow is incompatible with treating with respect other people who value and enjoy the crow. Similarly, a person who appeals to a hypothetical social contract in the spirit of Rawls would probably maintain that people in the Original Position behind the Veil of Ignorance, who don't know whether they're hunters or bird watchers, would probably agree to a rule prohibiting people from killing very rare and special animals for sport and trophies. Thus, the case of the white crow does not demonstrate a significant difference between a justice and a care approach, because either approach would yield the same conclusion.

The Case of the Moles and the Porcupine

Rita Manning uses a different series of examples, based on Aesop's Fables, to illustrate the difference between a care and a justice approach to moral decision making. A group of moles has spent the summer industriously digging a comfortable burrow. When winter's first icy blasts make themselves felt, a porcupine begs to be admitted into their burrow for the winter. If the moles admit the porcupine, they'll be less comfortable; the burrow will be overcrowded, and the porcupine's sharp quills will often jab them. In one scenario, the porcupine is homeless because he was lazy and didn't bother to prepare a home for the winter. In another scenario, he's homeless because his burrow was destroyed through no fault of his own. In a third scenario, it's made explicit that the porcupine will die if he's not admitted into the moles' burrow for the winter.

Manning asked her students what the moles should do, and why. She classified her students' justifications in terms of (1) virtues/vices, (2) principles, (3) reciprocity, (4) self-interest, and (5) care.

> The justifications fell into the following categories:
> Virtue: Laziness should be penalized, hard work rewarded.
> Principles:
> P1. You should alleviate suffering.
> P2. You should honor your commitments.
> P3. You should protect life.
> P4. You should honor property rights.
> P5. You should maximize utility.
> P6. You should help one another.
> Reciprocity: You should help those who will be in a position to do the same for you.
> Self-interest: People should help themselves first. My group is more important than any other group.
> Care: You should try to construct a compromise that will allow you to accommodate everyone.[17]

---

[17]Rita Manning, *Speaking from the Heart: A Feminist Perspective on Ethics* (Lanham, MD: Rowman and Littlefield, 1992), p. 44.

Manning identifies the last consideration as exemplifying the care approach. How does this last approach differ from the others? With the other approaches, we either conclude that the moles should let the porcupine spend the winter with them in their burrow or conclude that they would do nothing wrong were they to keep the porcupine out. A person adopting a care approach, however, strives to use her imagination and intelligence to find a way in which the needs and comfort of both the moles and the porcupine can be accommodated. As Manning puts it, the care perspective values "compromise and accommodation." "Those who chose [a care justification] seemed to think it obvious that compromise and accommodation were good things, at least in cases of conflict."[18] Relying on conceptions of virtue and vice or on principles to answer moral questions simply yields an answer of yes/no or right/wrong; it does not encourage us to use our creativity and imagination to expand the alternatives in order to find ways of meeting everyone's needs in a given situation. Rather than focusing simply on the two alternatives of letting the porcupine in or excluding him, a person adopting a care perspective will focus on ways of altering things to limit the moles' discomfort if the porcupine is permitted to live with them for the winter. For example, a person adopting a care perspective might suggest having the porcupine help the moles enlarge their burrow so that the burrow is not so crowded and the moles are less likely to be stuck by the porcupine's quills.

> The importance of intimacy and connection to others is assumed in this [caring] voice. We compromise and accommodate in order to preserve relationships. But this voice needn't be seen as the voice of self-sacrifice. Rather we can see it as motivated by a desire to remain connected, where being connected is seen as a good thing.[19]

A person who adopts a care approach focuses on creating, preserving, and strengthening relationships and attachments, which in turn requires accommodation and compromise. As Manning sees it, one who adopts a care approach focuses less on deciding between given alternatives than on envisioning new alternatives and possibilities that will meet everyone's needs and that will create, preserve, or strengthen relationships.

Manning's analysis deepens our understanding of how a care approach differs from a justice approach. We have a duty to do what a caring person would do, but in some cases at least, a caring person would seek a compromise solution that will guard everyone's interests and well-being. In some cases, no such compromise solution is possible—for example, the case of the white crow. The desires of the hunter and the desires of those who want the white crow preserved are simply incompatible. A caring person who cannot find a suitable compromise alternative would not kill the white crow. But a caring person would at least expend some energy trying to come up with a compromise solution.

However, it is not clear that justice and care approaches are therefore *incompatible*—that we are forced to choose between a justice and a care

---

[18]Ibid.

[19]Ibid., pp. 48–49.

approach to moral decision making. Justice approaches certainly do not forbid or discourage using our intelligence and imagination to search for compromise solutions that will accommodate everyone's needs and interests wherever possible. In fact, a careful and sensitive application of such justice approaches as Utilitarianism, Kantian moral theory, and social contract theory would probably yield conclusions that encourage compromise and accommodation. Nor do justice approaches necessarily encourage us to be inattentive to the specific details of a situation, as the criticism of "abstract" principles suggests.

THE CONCEPT OF TRUST

Annette Baier agrees that justice and care approaches should not be considered mutually exclusive. A wholly adequate moral theory cannot dispense with judgments framed in terms of duty or obligation, and justice perspectives that emphasize duty and abstract principles require supplementation by incorporating feelings of love and care. According to Baier, central to an adequate moral theory that blends both perspectives is a moral concept that has been relatively neglected: trust.

> Granted that men's theories of obligation need supplementation, . . . and that the women's . . . theories will want to cover obligation as well as love, then what concept brings them together? My tentative answer is—the concept of appropriate trust, oddly neglected in moral theory. . . .
>
> I am reasonably sure that trust does generalize some central moral features of the recognition of binding obligations and moral virtues and of loving, as well as of other important relations between persons, such as teacher-pupil, confider-confidants, worker to co-worker in the same cause, and professional to client. Indeed it is fairly obvious that love, the main moral phenomenon women want attended to, involves trust.

A moral theory focusing on trust, Baier suggests, would spell out "the conditions for appropriate trust and distrust."[20]

Trust is involved in all personal relationships—love, friendship, parenting, work. Children trust that their parents will look out for their welfare. Individuals trust their spouses and friends not to betray them, oppress them, exploit them, or otherwise misuse them. Patients trust their physicians and therapists to act in their best interests. Supervisors trust their subordinates to do the work assigned; subordinates trust that supervisors will treat them fairly. Citizens trust that the power they give government and holders of political office will not be misused. In general, we trust that people will do their duty. If we didn't have at least some trust in the people and institutions around us, cooperation would be impossible. We could not possibly live together. Failure to trust can destroy relationships.

Rarely is trust complete, however. Frequently we have doubts. We must have some trust in government, or we would not give it the enormous power over our

---

[20]Baier, "What Do Women Want in a Moral Theory?" pp. 10–12.

lives that it has; at the same time, we have enough distrust that we do not give it absolute power over us, and we try to control and tame its power by various devices such as democracy and countervailing centers of power. We trust our friends to a large extent, but not wholly. We sometimes say, "I would trust this person with my life," but that level of trust is rare. More commonly, we trust our friends with some secrets but not with others. If we detect signs that our trust has been misplaced or betrayed, we may cease to trust. We must trust many people in a variety of ways at least to some extent, or social life would be impossible. But because trust leaves us vulnerable, we must also protect ourselves from violations of trust and from trusting the wrong people or trusting too deeply.

Baier's point is that trust is so central to our lives that moral theory needs to focus attention less on what moral duties people have and more on the conditions under which trust is reasonable or justified, the proper limits of trust in a variety of situations and relationships, and the conditions under which trust is unreasonable or unjustified. For example, should one trust that one's spouse is faithful to the extent of having unprotected sex that leaves one vulnerable to AIDS and other sexually transmitted diseases? What if one fails to trust and insists on using a condom in order to protect against STDs? What effect would that lack of trust have on the relationship? But what if one trusts and winds up contracting an STD such as AIDS or syphilis?

Should one trust that the advertisement on television is telling the truth and all of the truth? Should one trust a politician running for reelection who promises to cut taxes and balance the budget? Should one continue to trust a friend who has betrayed a secret? If yes, how much? Should one trust the person who says "Trust me?" These are the kinds of question that Baier thinks needs to be addressed to develop an adequate moral theory that blends men's and women's concerns as well as justice and care perspectives.

JUSTICE, CARE, AND CHARACTER

According to Gilligan and many other feminists, the differences between the sexes in moral decision making reflect a difference between male and female character and personality. In their view, men tend to adopt a justice rather than a care approach because generally they are less comfortable than women with having, expressing, and dealing with "tender" feelings and emotions. Men are more comfortable with feelings of anger, hostility, and rage than with feelings of compassion, kindness, love, and sympathy. Then, too, males tend to value and emphasize independence, competition, and conflict in social life and are more prone than women to assert themselves and to resort to violence in order to get what they want. Men tend to be primarily self-interested, detached, and relatively indifferent to the well-being of others; they think that an individual's primary task at maturity is to separate from family and society because they value separation more than connection and isolation or solitude more than relationship. Men tend to be loners with few really close attachments. Because they conceptualize people as separate, individual atoms at best loosely connected with others, men also tend to think that the main task facing a society is to contain and limit aggression between individual members caused by conflict over and competition for resources and status. Thus, from a male perspective, the core of morality is a set of rules designed to limit aggression—rules such as "Thou shalt not kill" and "Thou shalt not steal"—as well as a network of negative moral rights to limit interference with a person's life.

According to many feminists such as Gilligan, women are more likely than men to adopt a care rather than a justice approach because they are more comfortable with "tender" feelings and emotions than men; characteristically, they are more prone to have and express feelings of kindness, compassion, love, and sympathy. Then, too, women emphasize and value interdependence and cooperation in social life and tend to be more nurturing and caring than men. From a woman's perspective, people are not and cannot be individual, isolated atoms. Women recognize that people are formed by and derive their identity from their place in a network of relationships with other people and that close attachments rather than social isolation and distancing are the core of the good life. Therefore, women find separation and nonattachment threatening rather than liberating. From a woman's perspective, the main task facing an individual at maturity is not to separate from others but to strengthen the web of relationships that to some extent create, nurture, and sustain the individual. Valuing attachment and relationship, women also tend to be more caring, compassionate, nurturing, and sympathetic, and these characteristically female traits guide their moral decision making.[21] A person who has the female temperament, personality, and character described in this paragraph is a *caring* person; a person who has the male temperament, personality, and character described in the previous paragraph is a *noncaring* person.

The distinction between a care and a justice approach may be based on a fairly fundamental difference between being a caring and a noncaring person. Some of the focus of feminist thought may be on the value of being a caring person. A caring person is more likely than a noncaring person to behave morally. Caring people are more likely than noncaring people to treat others with respect, to seek compromise solutions when people's needs conflict, and to be aware of and sensitive to the needs and interests of others. Because our capacity to care can be diminished in a variety of ways, according to Rita Manning we have a duty to enhance and protect our capacity to care.[22] Then, too, being a caring person is beneficial, according to Manning. A person who doesn't care about or for other people is like Ebeneezer Scrooge before his conversion in Charles Dickens's *A Christmas Carol.* His life was lonely, empty, and meaningless because he didn't care about anyone and no one cared about him.

---

[21]See, for example, Marilyn Friedman, "Feminism and Modern Friendship: Dislocating the Community," in Marilyn Friedman, *What Are Friends For? Feminist Perspectives on Personal Relationships and Moral Theory* (Ithaca, NY: Cornell University Press, 1993); and Rita Manning, *Speaking from the Heart.*

[22]Manning, p. 70.

Sex versus Gender

Most feminists maintain that we should refer to the two different kinds of personality/character as masculine and feminine rather than male and female. Traits associated with men (for example, aggressiveness and detachment) are identified as masculine, whereas traits associated with women (for example, compassion and concern) are identified as feminine. Many feminists maintain that although *sexual* differences (male/female) are rooted in biology, *gender* differences (masculine/feminine) are largely the product of convention and are rooted in socialization. A person is either male or female depending on biological makeup. However, a person, whether male or female, is masculine if and only if the person has a preponderance of masculine traits; a person, whether male or female, is feminine if and only if the person has a preponderance of feminine traits. Thus, it is possible for men to have a feminine personality/character and be caring people and for women to have a masculine personality/character and be noncaring people. Many feminists maintain that men tend to have more masculine than feminine traits and women tend to have more feminine than masculine traits only because of socialization.

Take people's attitudes toward weakness, for example. It is not unusual for a male to feel contempt and hostility for what he perceives as weakness, especially if the weakness is manifested by another male. Many males prize strength and despise weakness as a great vice or failing. Consider fathers who feel enraged if their son is a "crybaby." This attitude can lead fathers to behave with remarkable cruelty toward their sons. Perceiving someone as weak, helpless, and vulnerable often leads to aggression and attack, whether verbal or physical. Homophobic males tend to perceive homosexuals as weak, as "sissies," and this perception frequently leads to insults, sometimes to physical attacks, occasionally to murder. Bullies, who are more likely to be male than female, prey on the weak and vulnerable in a variety of ways. Some subcultures, such as survivalists, white supremacists, and militia movements, practically worship "strength" while deploring "weakness." In contrast, females are more likely than males to feel protective rather than hostile when they perceive weakness, helplessness, and vulnerability. Rather than contempt, many females feel sympathy, pity, and compassion. The perception of weakness is more likely to provoke in a female a desire to provide care and comfort than a desire to attack.

Why Can't a Man Be More Like a Woman?

In the hit musical *My Fair Lady*, Professor Henry Higgins asks in song, "Why can't a woman be more like a man?" Higgins obviously thought that it would be better if women were more like men. Most contemporary feminists would undoubtedly sing instead, "Why can't a man be more like a woman?" because they believe that the world would be better if men were more like women, more feminine (caring) and less masculine (noncaring). In their view, if men can be socialized to be more like women, then they should be. Many feminists also believe that the world would be better if people adopted the care rather than the justice approach to moral decision making. Assuming that men tend to adopt the justice rather than the care approach to moral decision making *because* they tend to have a masculine (noncaring) personality/character and that women tend to adopt the care approach *because* they tend to have a feminine (caring) personality/character, we can increase the probability that men will adopt the (superior) care approach by socializing men to be more like women.

EXERCISES

1. Construct a list of personality and character traits that you consider masculine and associate with males and a list of personality and character traits that you consider feminine and associate with females. Do you think that your lists correspond to conventional or traditional conceptions of masculine and feminine personality/character in our society? If yes, what does that suggest? If not, how does your conception of masculinity and femininity differ from the conventional or traditional conceptions?

2. Do men tend to be less caring than women? Defend your answer.

3. Assume for the sake of argument that men tend to be less caring than women. Which state of affairs would be preferable from a moral point of view? (a) Men become more caring and less noncaring. (b) Women become less caring and more noncaring. (c) Men remain more noncaring; women remain more caring. Defend your answer.

4. If men tend to be less caring than women, is it the result of differences in socialization or in biology, or a combination of both factors? Defend your answer.

5. Try to answer the following questions by applying a care approach to moral decision making.
    a. Is capital punishment morally acceptable?
    b. Is voluntary active euthanasia morally acceptable?
    c. Do we have a duty to preserve the earth's ability to sustain human life for the benefit of future generations?
    d. What responsibilities do individuals have toward the homeless?
    e. Should material that expresses hostility or contempt for women and that associates sex with violence be made illegal and suppressed, even for adults?

6. How, if at all, would your responses to 5a–e differ if you applied a justice approach such as Utilitarianism, Kantian moral theory, or social contract theory?

7. In the case of the white crow, a hunter killed a rare white crow that many people valued. In your view, did he do anything wrong in killing the white crow? Defend your answer. Do a care approach and a justice approach yield different conclusions in the case of the white crow? Defend your answer.

SUGGESTED READINGS

Annette C. Baier. *Moral Prejudices: Essays in Ethics.* Cambridge, MA: Harvard University Press, 1994.

Claudia Card, ed. *Feminist Ethics.* Lawrence: University Press of Kansas, 1991.

Eve Browning Cole and Susan Coultrap-McQuin, eds. *Explorations in Feminist Ethics.* Bloomington: Indiana University Press, 1992.

Elizabeth Frazer, Jennifer Hornsby, and Sabina Lovibond, eds. *Ethics: A Feminist Reader.* Oxford, England: Blackwell, 1992.

Marilyn Friedman. "Feminism and Modern Friendship: Dislocating the Community." In Marilyn Friedman. *What Are Friends For? Feminist Perspectives on Personal Relationships and Moral Theory.* Ithaca, NY: Cornell University Press, 1993.

Carol Gilligan. *In a Different Voice.* Cambridge, MA: Harvard University Press, 1982.

Jean Grimshaw. *Philosophy and Feminist Thinking.* Minneapolis: University of Minnesota Press, 1986.

Virginia Held. *Feminist Morality.* Chicago: University of Chicago Press, 1993.

Rita Manning. *Speaking from the Heart: A Feminist Perspective on Ethics.* Lanham, MD: Rowman and Littlefield, 1992.

Nel Noddings. *Women and Evil.* Berkeley: University of California Press, 1989.

Susan Moller Okin. *Justice, Gender, and the Family.* New York: Basic Books, 1989.

Rosemarie Tong. *Feminist Thought: A Comprehensive Introduction.* Boulder, CO: Westview Press, 1989.

CHAPTER 13

Liberty

The only freedom which deserves the name is that of pursuing our own good in our own way, so long as we do not attempt to deprive others of theirs or impede their efforts to obtain it. Each is the proper guardian of his own health, whether bodily or mental and spiritual. Mankind are greater gainers by suffering each other to live as seems good to themselves than by compelling each to live as seems good to the rest.

—John Stuart Mill, *On Liberty*[1]

Freedom is a rare and delicate plant. Our minds tell us, and history confirms, that the great threat to freedom is the concentration of power. Government is necessary to preserve our freedom . . . , yet by concentrating power in political hands, it is also a threat to freedom.

—Milton Friedman, *Capitalism and Freedom*[2]

People in the United States are not free to buy and sell sex or to buy, sell, or use substances such as marijuana, cocaine, LSD, and heroin. Should they be? During the Prohibition era, people in the United States were not free to buy, sell, and consume alcoholic beverages. With the repeal of Prohibition, people in the United States are now free to buy, sell, and consume alcoholic beverages—but, in most states, only if they are age 21 or older. Should all people in the United

---

[1]John Stuart Mill, *On Liberty*, ed. Elizabeth Rapaport (Indianapolis, IN: Hackett, 1978), p. 12.
[2]Milton Friedman, *Capitalism and Freedom* (Chicago: University of Chicago Press, 1960), p. 2.

States regardless of age be free to consume alcoholic beverages? Prior to the Civil War, people in the United States of European ancestry were free to buy and sell other people of African ancestry. People no longer have that freedom, and no one thinks that anyone should have that freedom.

Questions of freedom or liberty are important in moral philosophy. Governments, through laws, prohibit some forms of behavior, such as committing murder or rape, stealing, embezzling, kidnapping, extortion, libel, speeding, and driving while intoxicated, and require other forms of behavior, such as stopping at stop signs and red lights, obeying a police officer's commands, and paying taxes. One is permitted to do whatever is not prohibited by law. Similarly, one is permitted not to do whatever is not required by the law. Laws regulate some forms of behavior but not others. Where law does not regulate, an individual has discretion and may choose for herself how to behave.

A person is *free* to do something if nothing prevents her from doing it. Similarly, a person is *free* to *not* do something if nothing compels or coerces her to do it. You are not free to run a one-minute mile, fly in the air unassisted, or breathe underwater because the laws of nature prevent you from doing these things. Similarly, a person who is paralyzed is not free to take a walk in the rain. Besides laws of nature and one's physical limitations, human-made laws can prevent or compel. When it is laws that prevent or compel, we will speak of *liberty*. An important moral question is how much liberty people *should* have.

Governments must decide what to permit and what to require. Often the decision is based on the moral views of those who control the government. Laws prohibit slavery, murder, rape, stealing, and assault because those who control the government believe that such behavior is immoral. If laws do not prohibit a form of behavior, such as drinking alcoholic beverages, it is usually because the authorities believe that the behavior is not morally objectionable. The question then becomes, What forms of behavior *should* the government require, permit, and forbid?

We face a variety of controversial issues in the United States and the world.

Should physicians be free to help their patients commit suicide?

Should women be free to have abortions?

Should people from other countries be free to come to live in the United States?

Should people be free to criticize their government?

Should people be free to publicly burn the flag of their country?

Should people be free to buy, sell, and use such substances as marijuana, heroin, and cocaine?

Should people be free to buy and sell sex?

Should people be free to produce and see material that is sexually explicit?

Should people be free to own every variety of weapon, such as semiautomatic rifles and hand grenades?

Should people be free to discipline their children any way they wish?

Should people be free to stage dogfights?

Should companies be free to pollute the environment if it is profitable for them?

Should wealthy people be free to contribute as much money as they want to political candidates?

Should husbands be free to beat their wives?

Should people be free to have as many spouses as they want?

Should people of the same sex be free to marry each other?

Should homosexuals be free to serve in the military?

Should people be free to sunbathe in the nude at public beaches?

Should people be free to see nude dancing at bars?

Should an employer be free to refuse to hire women?

Should an employer be free to make having sex with him a condition of employment?

Should a restaurant owner to free to refuse to serve African-Americans?

Should an African-American be free to eat at a public restaurant?

As you can see, the issues of liberty are complex and often deeply divisive. The main issue from a philosophical perspective is to find plausible *principles* that will enable us to answer these and other questions about liberty in a way that makes sense, is consistent, and is rationally defensible.

One extreme is to insist that liberty should be absolute: No laws should prohibit people from doing anything or require them to do anything. Few people find this alternative appealing, because most believe that social life would be impossible without laws. We all have some destructive tendencies, and some of us have almost nothing but destructive tendencies. Without laws that are vigorously enforced, life in society would be, in the words of the British philosopher Thomas Hobbes, "solitary, poor, nasty, brutish, and short."

The other extreme is to insist that people should have no liberty. The government, through its laws, should regulate every aspect of people's lives, from when they get up in the morning, what they have for breakfast, what they wear, and where they work, to what time they go to bed at night. This hypothetical extreme raises an important question: Why should people have *any* liberty?

THE VALUE OF AUTONOMY

Why should people be free from legal coercion to dress as they please, eat what they want, pursue the career of their choice, marry whom they want to, and spend their free time as their own interests dictate? One possible answer is that it would be too difficult and expensive for government to regulate people's lives so minutely, the way it regulates the lives of people in prison. That answer suggests, however, that liberty is not a value worth protecting and preserving for its own sake. However, most of us think that liberty is intrinsically valuable or inherently good for organisms such as human beings, and that deprivation of liberty is a form of punishment rather than a reward.

Liberty is valuable for human beings because we are capable of acting *autonomously;* that is, we are capable of making rational choices and decisions. Unlike cows, our behavior can be determined by our own beliefs, values, preferences, feelings, and desires. We can deliberate before acting. We can weigh reasons, gather information, consider our options, resolve conflicts within ourselves, and then act. The action is *our* action, caused by and reflecting our own character, personality, beliefs, and preferences. Only beings of a high level of intelligence are capable of acting autonomously. It is a rare gift. Of the approximately ten to twenty million different species of living creatures on Earth, *Homo sapiens* is among the very few species—perhaps the only one—capable of acting fully autonomously. The question, then, is whether beings *capable* of acting autonomously should be permitted an area in which to exercise this capacity—to *act* autonomously. One who is compelled to do what she does not want to do or who is prevented from doing what she does want to do is not acting autonomously.

We might maintain that some degree of liberty is good for beings capable of acting autonomously simply because autonomy is a rare and valuable capacity—a gift, as it were. Self-determination (another word for autonomy) is also good for a creature capable of acting autonomously because such a creature probably cannot be happy if it is never permitted to exercise its capacity for acting autonomously. Who could be happy as someone else's puppet? The fact that many slaves were willing to risk death in hopes of securing their freedom (autonomy) suggests just how valuable autonomy was to them. Furthermore, we might maintain that no one has a *right* to force a person capable of living autonomously to live according to someone else's life plan. In the world today there is a near-universal abhorrence of slavery, which is the ultimate and complete negation of autonomy or self-determination.

We also might argue that (some) liberty is good as a means to other valuable ends—for example, social peace and harmony. Joseph Raz points out that giving individuals some liberty not only protects them as individuals, but it also protects society as a whole. For example, religious conflict can tear a society apart; giving people freedom of religion protects the society from religious wars. Similarly, freedom of discussion and thought can prevent revolution and insurrection. People who feel oppressed, who find themselves with no freedom to voice their grievances, often feel compelled to resort to violence either to change their circumstance or to bring attention to their plight.[3] Some room to live one's life as one sees fit may be a kind of safety valve that prevents the buildup of discontent that can explode into violence.

Suppose we say, then, that people should have some liberty but not absolute or unlimited liberty. What liberties should people have, and what liberties should they not have? What principle or principles can we appeal to in deciding?

---

[3]Joseph Raz, *The Morality of Freedom* (New York: Oxford University Press, 1986), pp. 251-255.

JOHN STUART MILL AND THE HARM PRINCIPLE

In *On Liberty,* John Stuart Mill (1806–1873) concedes that society must interfere with people's doing what they want in order to prevent the strong from preying on the weak. "All that makes existence valuable to anyone depends on the enforcement of restraints upon the actions of other people." Some rules of conduct, therefore, must be imposed.[4] But Mill objects that such social interference often goes too far. Laws may prohibit or require things that the government has no moral right to prohibit or require. For example, consider laws once common in the South prohibiting interracial marriages. Virtually everyone today believes that people should be free to marry someone of a different race. Another example is laws prohibiting women from voting. There is now virtually universal agreement that women as well as men should be free to vote in elections.

Mill recognizes that law is not the only obstacle to freedom. The power of public opinion can be difficult to resist.

> Protection . . . against the tyranny of the magistrate is not enough; there needs
> protection also against the tyranny of the prevailing opinion and feeling,
> against the tendency of society to impose, by other means than civil penalties,
> its own ideas and practices as rules of conduct on those who dissent from
> them; to fetter the development and, if possible, prevent the formation of any
> individuality not in harmony with its ways, and compel all characters to
> fashion themselves upon the model of its own. There is a limit to the legiti-
> mate interference of collective opinion with individual independence.[5]

Mill fears that society has the tendency and ability to impose a mindless conformity on its members.

Mill's primary concern, though, is law. The question he asks is, When is it morally acceptable or legitimate for the government to use the power of law to coerce people—that is, to prohibit or require certain behavior and punish people who violate the prohibitions or requirements? Mill's answer is deceptively simple: Governments have the moral right to coerce people only when it is necessary to prevent them from harming others.

> The object of [*On Liberty*] is to assert one very simple principle, as entitled to
> govern absolutely the dealings of society with the individual in the way of
> compulsion and control, whether the means used be physical force in the
> form of legal penalties or the moral coercion of public opinion. The principle
> is that the sole end for which mankind are warranted, individually or collec-
> tively, in interfering with the liberty of action of any of their number is self-
> protection. That the only purpose for which power can be rightfully exercised
> over any member of a civilized community, against his will, is to prevent harm
> to others. His own good, either physical or moral, is not a sufficient warrant.
> He cannot rightfully be compelled to do or forbear because it will be better
> for him to do so, because it will make him happier, because, in the opinion of

---

[4]Mill, *On Liberty,* p. 5.

[5]Ibid., pp. 4–5.

others, to do so would be wise or even right. These are good reasons for remonstrating with him, or reasoning with him, or persuading him, or entreating him, but not for compelling him or visiting him with any evil in case he do otherwise. To justify that, the conduct from which it is desired to deter him must be calculated to produce evil to someone else. The only part of the conduct of anyone for which he is amenable to society is that which concerns others. In the part which merely concerns himself, his independence is, of right, absolute. Over himself, over his own body and mind, the individual is sovereign.[6]

According to Mill's Harm Principle, people should be free from social interference to do what they want to do and to not do what they don't want to do unless they are likely to harm others. (Mill remarks that this principle applies only to people who are "in the maturity of their faculties." It does not apply to children or to adults who have serious psychological or mental handicaps. The concept employed today is that of being *competent.* An individual who is not competent does not have the same right to autonomy as someone who is competent because an incompetent person cannot act autonomously or make rational decisions and choices.)

Applying Mill's Harm Principle, one can say that people should not be free to commit murder, rape, steal, or drive while intoxicated—that is, the government is morally justified in creating and enforcing laws prohibiting these forms of behavior—because such behaviors harm others or create a serious risk of causing harm to others. On the other hand, people should be free to decide for themselves whether to drink coffee, exercise, watch television, or play computer games because these actions do not harm anyone. The government should not pass laws forbidding or requiring such behavior.

Mountain climbing, motorcycle racing, and smoking cigarettes are dangerous activities. People who engage in them run a much higher than average risk of serious harm (to themselves). Would the government be morally justified in prohibiting such activities? According to Mill, not if they do not cause harm *to others.* Laws should not be designed to protect people from themselves. Such paternalism (or parentalism) is an unjustified encroachment on an individual's autonomy. We should be free to act as we see fit, even if our actions might bring harm to ourselves.

Appeal to the Harm Principle enables us to justify some legal prohibitions but not others. Can appeal to the Harm Principle justify legal requirements? Mill recognizes that both commissions and omissions can cause harm and, therefore, may be legitimate subjects of social interference.

> If anyone does an act hurtful to others, there is a *prima facie* case for punishing him by law or . . . by general disapprobation. There are also many positive acts for the benefit of others which he might rightfully be compelled to perform, such as to give evidence in a court of justice, to bear his fair share in the common defense or in any other joint work necessary for the interest of the society of which he enjoys the protection, and to perform certain acts of

---

[6]Ibid., p. 9.

individual beneficence, such as saving another creature's life or interposing to save the defenseless from ill usage. . . . A person may cause evil to others not only by his actions but by his inaction.[7]

Therefore, according to Mill, society may enact legal requirements as well as legal prohibitions. An example might be so-called "good samaritan" laws that require easy rescue. If you let someone drown when you are in a position to save her at virtually no cost or risk to yourself, you are failing to prevent easily preventable (serious) harm. Mill believes that his Harm Principle covers cases of preventing as well as causing harm.

FOUR POSSIBLE PRINCIPLES LEGITIMIZING COERCION

In his four volume work, *The Moral Limits of the Criminal Law,* contemporary American philosopher Joel Feinberg provides the most exhaustive treatment available of the Harm Principle and its main competitors. Feinberg identifies four different principles that we might employ in deciding whether it is legitimate[8] for the government to prohibit or require certain behavior.

1. **The Harm Principle.** The government is morally justified in prohibiting actions that will cause serious harm or high risk of serious harm to others and in requiring actions that prevent serious harm to others at small cost or risk to the agent.

2. **The Offense Principle.** The government is morally justified in prohibiting conduct that seriously offends others.

3. **Paternalism.** The government is morally justified in prohibiting actions that will cause serious harm or a high risk of serious harm to the agent, even if no one else would be harmed.

4. **Legal Moralism.** The government is morally justified in prohibiting immoral behavior, even if it will not harm or offend anyone.

Feinberg, in the spirit of Mill, (1) accepts the legitimacy of the Harm Principle, (2) accepts only a heavily qualified version of the Offense Principle, (3) accepts what he calls Soft Paternalism but rejects what he calls Hard Paternalism, and (4) rejects Legal Moralism.

THE HARM PRINCIPLE

Feinberg points out that Mill's Harm Principle leaves open a number of important questions that need to be resolved before the Harm Principle can be applied. For example, what precisely counts as a "harm"? How serious must harm

---

[7]Ibid., pp. 10–11.

[8]Feinberg distinguishes between the concepts of being "legitimized" and being "justified." Here I will ignore his distinction. See Joel Feinberg, *Harm to Others,* Volume 1 of *The Moral Limits of the Criminal Law* (New York: Oxford University Press, 1984), p. 6.

be before the government may prohibit it? Should all serious harm to others be prohibited? Let us examine each question in turn.

What Counts as Harm?

We would probably all agree that if I were to shoot you, stab you, poison you, electrocute you, hit you in the head with a brick, or kick you, I would harm you. Similarly, if I were to steal your car or your wallet, burn down your house, or ruin your reputation, I would cause you harm. But what if I give you a failing grade in a philosophy course, (truthfully) testify in a trial that I saw you shoot someone, or get a job that you applied for? What if I (truthfully) tell your fiancé that you were unfaithful to him and he calls off the wedding? What if I'm your upstairs neighbor and I (unintentionally) keep you awake at night by playing loud music? What if I spill coffee on your clothing, causing a stain? What if I'm your next-door neighbor and I leave my house unpainted and my lawn unmowed so that the value of your house declines? What if I have a lot of junk in my backyard that you see whenever you look out your window and it upsets you to look out on such an eyesore? What if my walking into your field of vision causes you to feel disgust, discomfort, and insecurity because I have technicolor spiked hair and wear a nose ring? What if I have been rude to you and my rudeness has temporarily raised your blood pressure? In each of these cases, have I "harmed" you? The answer, which is crucial to applying the Harm Principle, depends on how we understand the concept of harm. What counts as harm?

Feinberg's discussion suggests that we cannot define *harm* with absolute precision. Determining whether something constitutes harm requires judgment. Feinberg initially defines *harm* as any "thwarting, setting back, or defeating of an interest."[9] What is an interest? The concept of *an* interest is related to the concept of something's being *in* someone's interest. We could say that your remaining physically healthy is in your interest. Thus, you have *an* interest in physical health. That your remaining physically healthy is "in your interest" seems to mean something like "continued health is beneficial to you; it contributes to (or is a component of) your well-being." Thus, something is *an* interest of yours—for example, health—if its presence or absence will affect your well-being. In addition, something may be in your interest because you have needs or wants connected to it. Getting sufficient sleep is in your interest because you need sleep; without sufficient sleep you cannot function well. You could become ill and even die. Feinberg also appeals to the concepts of "flourishing" and "languishing."

> One's interests, taken as a miscellaneous collection, consist of all those things in which one has a stake. . . . These interests . . . are distinguishable components of a person's well-being; he flourishes or languishes as they flourish or languish. What promotes them is to his advantage or *in his interest;* what thwarts them is to his detriment or *against his interest.* . . . The test . . . of whether . . . an invasion [of one's interest] has in fact set back an interest is

---

[9] Ibid., p. 33.

whether that interest is in a worse condition than it would otherwise have been in had the invasion not occurred at all.[10]

One can flourish (or languish) physically, psychologically, or financially. Thus, if an act puts you in a worse condition physically, psychologically, or financially, you have been harmed (regardless of the intentions of the actor). A setback to one's interests is a decline in one's physical, psychological, or financial condition.

According to Feinberg, setbacks to what he calls "welfare" interests are the most serious harms.

> In this category [welfare interests] are the interests in the continuance for a foreseeable interval of one's life, and the interests in one's own physical health and vigor, the integrity and normal functioning of one's body, the absence of absorbing pain and suffering or grotesque disfigurement, minimal intellectual acuity, emotional stability, the absence of groundless anxieties and resentments, the capacity to engage normally in social intercourse and to enjoy and maintain friendships, at least minimal income and financial security, a tolerable social and physical environment, and a certain amount of freedom from interference and coercion.[11]

Most clearly, the Harm Principle justifies or legitimizes laws intended to prevent people from causing deterioration in the welfare interests of others, the most serious forms of harm.

Where and how do we draw the line between harm and some other unpleasant state such as mere offense? Again, if my walking into your field of vision has caused you to feel disgust, discomfort, and insecurity because I have technicolor spiked hair and wear a nose ring, or if my being rude to you has temporarily raised your blood pressure, have I "harmed" you? Feinberg thinks not.

> Not everything that we dislike or resent, and wish to avoid, is harmful to us. Eating a poorly cooked dish may be unpleasant, but if the food is unspoiled, the experience is not likely to be harmful. So it is with a large variety of other experiences. . . . These experiences can distress, offend, or irritate us, without harming any of our interests. They come to us, are suffered for a time, and then go, leaving us as whole and undamaged as we were before. The unhappy mental states they produce are . . . diverse. They include unpleasant sensations (evil smells, grating noises), transitory disappointments and disillusionments, wounded pride, hurt feelings, aroused anger, shocked sensibility, alarm, disgust, frustration, impatient restlessness, acute boredom, irritation, embarrassment, feelings of guilt and shame, physical pain (at a readily tolerable level), bodily discomfort, and many more. In all but the exceptional cases . . . , people do not have as ulterior focal aims, interests simply in the avoidance of these states as such.[12]

Thus, the items he lists do not count as harms.

---

[10]Ibid., p. 34.

[11]Ibid., p. 37.

[12]Ibid., p. 45.

"Harm" as Wronging

Providing a precise descriptive characterization of harm that will enable us to distinguish between harms and other unpleasant states is difficult, perhaps in part because the word *harm* is vague (like the word *bald*—at what number of hairs do we pass from not being bald to being bald?). But Feinberg emphasizes that for the purposes of the Harm Principle, the concept of harm that we use must have a normative or evaluative component as well as a more purely descriptive component. He refers to

> a kind of normative sense which the term [*harm*] must bear in any plausible formulation of the harm principle. To say that A has harmed B in this sense is to say . . . that A has wronged B, or treated him unjustly. One person *wrongs* another when his indefensible (unjustifiable and inexcusable) conduct violates the other's right, and in all but certain very special cases such conduct will also invade the other's interest and thus be harmful in the sense already explained.[13]

Thus, according to Feinberg, the sense of "harm" that is relevant in applying the Harm Principle includes the concepts of a setback of interests *and* of wronging. I "harm" you in this special sense only if I cause a *wrongful* setback to your interests that involves a violation of your rights. Thus, the Harm Principle justifies the government in employing coercion to prevent harm in the sense of a *wrongful* setback or thwarting of interests. If killing people for amusement would be morally wrong, then the Harm Principle permits the government to pass and enforce laws forbidding people from killing others for amusement. On the other hand, if I have not wronged you by getting a job you applied for in a fair competition, then it does not count as a harm for the purposes of applying the Harm Principle.

Harm and Consent

If someone cuts off my leg, then he has clearly harmed me in some sense. But has he harmed me in the sense relevant to the Harm Principle? Suppose a kidnapper has cut off my leg because my family has refused to pay the ransom demanded. The kidnapper has wronged me, and the government may pass and enforce laws forbidding kidnappers to cut off the legs of their victims. However, suppose instead that it is a surgeon who has cut off my leg because it is infected with gangrene and I have consented to the operation. In that case, the surgeon has not wronged me, and consequently has not harmed me in the sense relevant to application of the Harm Principle.

Feinberg points out that full and voluntary consent cancels wrongfulness. If someone fully and voluntarily consents to another's acting in a way that will set back or thwart his interests, then the action does not constitute harm in the sense relevant to applying the Harm Principle; therefore, the government is not

---

[13]Ibid., p. 34.

justified in preventing such consented-to setbacks or thwartings of people's interests. For example, the government would not be justified in passing and enforcing laws forbidding surgeons from performing surgery on patients who have voluntarily and fully consented to the surgery. However, the Harm Principle would justify the government in passing laws forbidding medical treatment, whether surgery or some other form of treatment, without the patient's full and voluntary consent. According to Feinberg, "a person's consent is fully voluntary only when he is a competent and unimpaired adult who has not been threatened, mislead, or lied to about relevant facts, nor manipulated by subtle forms of conditioning."[14]

Causing versus Permitting Harm

Does the Harm Principle justify prohibiting omissions (failures to act) as well as actions? Alternatively, we might rephrase the question as, Can the Harm Principle be used to justify laws *requiring* us to do certain things under certain circumstances as well as *forbidding* us to do certain things under certain circumstances? Feinberg calls people who fail to provide aid when the need is great and the cost of the aid is small "bad samaritans." For example, you would be a bad samaritan in Feinberg's sense if you let someone drown when you were in a position to save the victim at small cost to yourself by, say, throwing the person a rope. Does the Harm Principle justify the government in passing laws forbidding us to be bad samaritans and requiring us to be good (or acceptable) samaritans?[15] Ultimately, Feinberg concludes that a plausible formulation of the Harm Principle should both prohibit people from causing harm *and* require them to prevent harm, when the harm would be great and the cost of preventing the harm reasonably small. "Where minimal effort is required of a samaritan there seems to be no morally significant difference between his allowing an imperiled person to suffer severe harm and his causing that harm by direct action."[16] The two types of prohibition—against acting to cause harm and against failing to act to prevent harm—have the same purpose: harm prevention.

Should the Government Prevent All Harms?

According to Feinberg, "legal coercion should not be used to prevent minor harms, even though in theory it would be legitimate to do so."[17] Thus, the government has to decide which harms to try to prevent by means of legal coercion. One relevant consideration is the *seriousness* of the harms to be prevented. The more serious the harm, the stronger is the case for legal coercion to try to pre-

---

[14]Ibid., p. 116.

[15]The terms *good samaritan* and *bad samaritan* come from Jesus's parable of the good Samaritan who picked up an unconscious man who had been beaten senseless and wounded by robbers, after a priest and a Levite passed by without stopping to offer assistance.

[16]Feinberg, *Harm to Others,* p. 171.

[17]Ibid., p. 189.

vent it; the less serious the harm, the weaker the case is. "Little white lies" may constitute harm, but there may be good reasons for the government to refrain from using legal coercion to prevent people from telling each other "little white lies." The social cost of enforcing such laws would far outweigh any gains in terms of harm prevention. Feinberg emphasizes that the primary focus of the Harm Principle should be on people's basic welfare interests, among which he lists "interests in continued life, health, economic sufficiency, and political liberty."[18]

Another relevant consideration is the *probability* of harm. The more probable the harm, the stronger is the case for legal coercion to try to prevent it; the less probable the harm, the weaker the case is. If you drive while intoxicated, it is less than certain that you will cause harm to others, but there is a much greater probability of your causing serious harm to others if you drive while intoxicated than if you drive while sober. Therefore, there is a strong case for the government's prohibition against driving while intoxicated. On the other hand, there is a very low probability of your causing harm to others if you mow your lawn with a power mower, so the government would not be justified in prohibiting people from mowing their lawns with a power mower.

THE OFFENSE PRINCIPLE

Feinberg also endorses a restricted and qualified version of the Offense Principle: The government is morally justified in prohibiting conduct that seriously offends others.

Feinberg maintains that instances of offense, even serious offense, are less serious than instances of harm. As opposed to harms, which are setbacks or thwartings of interests, "offending conduct produces unpleasant or uncomfortable experiences—affronts to sense or sensibility, disgust, shock, shame, embarrassment, annoyance, boredom, anger, fear, or humiliation.[19] Feinberg provides some hair-raising examples of behavior that, because done in public, would probably offend most people but that would not cause them harm.

> A passenger on a bus plays loud music that most passengers detest.
>
> Someone who hasn't bathed in a month sits beside you on a bus.
>
> Someone on a bus vomits and then begins to eat his vomit.
>
> A bus passenger uses the American flag as a handkerchief, ostentatiously blowing his nose into it.
>
> Two people on a bus take off their clothes and begin to copulate in the center aisle.
>
> Someone on a bus is wearing a T-shirt that reads "Annihilate the Jews."

---

[18]Ibid., p. 188.

[19]Joel Feinberg, *Offense to Others*, Volume 2 of *The Moral Limits of the Criminal Law* (New York: Oxford University Press, 1985), p. 5.

Someone on a bus is wearing a T-shirt with a very erotic picture of a naked Jesus hanging on the cross.[20]

Feinberg's point is that some offensive conduct can be very offensive indeed.

Feinberg's question is whether the government may (a) prohibit *all* offensive behavior, (b) prohibit *no* offensive behavior, or (c) prohibit *some* offensive behavior but not all. Feinberg believes that neither (a) nor (b) is a plausible answer. Rather, he thinks that in the spirit of Mill, the government may prohibit some offensive conduct but by no means all. Where do we draw the line? Under what conditions may the government prohibit conduct that is merely offensive, and under what conditions may it not prohibit conduct that is offensive?

As with the Harm Principle, Feinberg limits the Offense Principle to instances of *wrongful* offense—offenses that people have a moral right to be protected from. According to Feinberg, offensive behavior may be wrongful if it violates the privacy or autonomy rights of the offended person because those who engage in offensive behavior "deprive the unwilling spectators of the power to determine for themselves whether or not to undergo a certain experience."[21] Having a right to privacy means having control or authority over some of the space or domain surrounding you. If people "invade your space" and impose very unpleasant (though harmless) experiences on you, they violate your rights.

Also, only *serious* offenses may be prohibited. The seriousness of offensive behavior depends on the intensity of the unpleasantness or discomfort of the experience, its duration, and how much inconvenience one would be put through in order to avoid or escape exposure to the offending conduct. The more intense the unpleasantness or discomfort of the offensive experience, the stronger is the case for prohibition; the less intense, the weaker the case is. Similarly, the longer the duration of the offensive experience, the stronger is the case for prohibition; the shorter the duration, the weaker the case is. As for the inconvenience required to avoid the offensive experience, the greater the inconvenience, the stronger is the case for prohibition; the less the inconvenience, the weaker the case is. Finally, the number of offended people is also relevant. The more people who would be offended, the stronger is the case for prohibition; the fewer people offended, the weaker the case is.

In addition, the reasonableness of the offending conduct and its social utility, if any, must be considered before the government may legitimately prohibit it, according to Feinberg. You may be offended (annoyed) by the noise of a nearby factory, but its behavior (producing whatever product it produces) is reasonable and its social utility may be high, providing a useful product, jobs, and tax dollars. In that case, the government would not be justified in forbidding the factory from operating merely because it offends you. On the other hand, you may be offended (annoyed) by the noise at 2:00 A.M. from your neighbor's out-

---

[20]Ibid., pp. 10–13. Some of these examples are merely suggested by Feinberg's.
[21]Ibid., p. 23.

door beer party or by the stench from the two tons of cow manure that he spread on his lawn to fertilize the grass. If such behavior is not reasonable and has little social utility, the government may be justified in prohibiting it. Besides its general social utility, the utility or importance of the offending conduct to those who engage in it must also be considered. As Feinberg points out, at one time the sight of interracial couples offended many people. Were the government to prohibit interracial couples from appearing together in public on the grounds that the sight offends people, the cost to the couples would be very great indeed given the importance of friendship and love in people's lives. The importance to the agents of the conduct being prohibited counts against the legitimacy of prohibiting it. On the other hand, playing loud, irritating music on a public sidewalk does not have the same importance for people's lives as their friendship and love relationships. Therefore, the government would be more justified in prohibiting that behavior.

In addition to the preceding considerations, the intentions of the agent and the relative inconvenience to which the agent would be put to reduce the offense to others must be considered. If Jones is wearing an offensive T-shirt merely because he wants to offend or intimidate others, then the government would be more justified in prohibiting such conduct than if Jones is wearing an offensive T-shirt in order to educate people or to make a political statement. An example of wearing a T-shirt merely to offend or intimidate might be wearing one that says "Rape: the Ultimate Spectator Sport"; an example of wearing a T-shirt to educate or make a statement might be wearing one that says "If you don't approve of abortion, don't have one." Similarly, if the offended party can easily avoid the offensive experience, then the government is less justified in forbidding the offensive behavior. Someone on a bus cannot easily avoid the sustained unpleasantness of loud, irritating music being played by an inconsiderate passenger; the only way to avoid it may be to get off the bus, which might be very inconvenient. On the other hand, if an art gallery is exhibiting erotic paintings that you would find offensive if you saw them, you can easily avoid the offense by simply not going to the exhibit.[22]

Feinberg offers no foolproof recipe for balancing these conflicting considerations when trying to determine whether it would be legitimate to prohibit offensive behavior. Applying the Offense Principle requires judgment. But Feinberg would insist that the presumption is in favor of liberty. We should not limit people's liberty unless there are compelling reasons to do so.

PATERNALISM: HARD AND SOFT

The principle of Paternalism states that it is morally legitimate for the government to employ coercion to protect people from themselves, even when they are competent adults. According to Paternalism, preventing people from harm-

---

[22]Ibid., pp. 7–9.

ing themselves is as legitimate as preventing them from harming or seriously offending others.

Few would argue that the government may and should pass laws to protect the *incompetent* (for example, children, the mentally handicapped, the mentally ill, and the extremely intoxicated) from harming themselves either deliberately or from their own carelessness or recklessness. But what of adults who are *competent*—that is, capable of making rational decisions? May the government pass laws designed to protect competent people from themselves?

On the one hand, people may directly and intentionally harm themselves by, for example, committing (or attempting) suicide or mutilating themselves (as by cutting off a hand). On the other hand, people may engage in behavior that creates considerable risk of harm to themselves, although they do not intend to harm themselves. Someone swimming alone at an unguarded beach has a higher probability of drowning than someone swimming with friends at a beach that has a lifeguard on duty. A cigarette smoker may not intend to cause herself to develop lung cancer and other diseases, but the probability of her developing lung cancer is many times higher if she smokes than if she does not smoke. Besides swimming alone at an unguarded beach and smoking cigarettes, risky activities—activities that create a higher than normal probability of serious harm (short-term or long-term) to those engaging in the activities, although the object of the activity is not to cause harm to themselves—include rock climbing, sky diving, auto racing, boxing, riding a motorcycle, riding a motorcycle without a helmet, riding in a car without seat beats, handling poisonous snakes during religious ceremonies, having unprotected sex, drinking to excess, and using cocaine or heroin.

Purely paternalistic laws are those designed solely to prevent people from directly harming themselves or from engaging in activities considered by the government to be too risky to themselves. (If a law is designed both to protect people from themselves and to protect people from others, it is not purely paternalistic.) Paternalistic laws are thus benevolent, motivated by a concern for the agent's own good. They are designed to protect people's interests rather than thwart them. Are purely paternalistic laws morally legitimate?

Feinberg distinguishes between Hard and Soft Paternalism.

> Hard paternalism will accept as a reason for criminal legislation that it is necessary to protect competent adults, against their will, from the harmful consequences even of their fully voluntary choices and undertakings.... It imposes its own values and judgments on people "for their own good"....

> Soft paternalism holds that the state has the right to prevent self-regarding harmful conduct ... *when but only when* that conduct is substantially nonvoluntary, or when temporary intervention is necessary to establish whether it is voluntary or not.[23]

Feinberg accepts the principle of Soft Paternalism. He believes that the government has a right, perhaps even a duty, to protect the *incompetent* from harm-

---

[23]Joel Feinberg, *Harm to Self,* Volume 3 of *The Moral Limits of the Criminal Law* (New York: Oxford University Press, 1986), p. 12.

ing themselves—for example, an adult who, in the middle of an episode of extreme psychosis, is about to drink poison. Because people who are incompetent are not capable of making rational choices, their actions are not fully voluntary; rather, they are nonvoluntary (as opposed to involuntary). But Feinberg also believes that it is morally legitimate for the government to *temporarily* stop an adult from doing something directly harmful or extremely risky to himself in order to ascertain whether the person is fully competent. If the person is not competent (either temporarily or permanently), then the government may continue to protect him from himself until he becomes competent. However, if the person is competent, then according to Feinberg, it would not be morally legitimate for the government to continue to prevent him from directly harming himself or from engaging in the extremely risky behavior.

Feinberg opposes Hard Paternalism as morally illegitimate. As he puts it, Hard Paternalism

> seems arrogant and demeaning. It says in effect that there are sharp limits
> to my right to govern myself even within the wholly self-regarding sphere, that
> others may intervene even against my protests to "correct" my choices and
> then (worst of all) justify interference on the ground (how patronizing) that
> they know my own good better than I know it myself.[24]

Hard Paternalism rides roughshod over personal autonomy. Given that people have the capacity for self-government—the capacity to make rational decisions and choices—then they should be given space to exercise that capacity without undue restriction. People have a moral right to an area of self-determination— that area in which their actions do not cause wrongful harm or serious wrongful offense to others. Put another way, Feinberg presupposes that others do *not* have a moral right to govern you in those areas of behavior that are not likely to cause wrongful harm or serious wrongful offense to others.

However, Feinberg emphasizes that an ideal or right of autonomy should not be equated with the extreme ideal of "rugged individualism," according to which being a fully autonomous individual means not needing or depending on others. Human beings are social animals. We are born into communities that shape our characters and personalities. Few of us can even survive, let alone flourish, without a dense network of other people who provide or help provide many of the things we need, both physical (auto mechanics do not make their own tools; doctors do not build their own houses or make their own medications or medical equipment; truck drivers do not make their own clothing, make the trucks they drive, or construct the roads they travel on) and emotional (friendship and love). The autonomous person is not, and should not be, an island. Rather, the ideal of autonomy, as Feinberg expresses it, is that of "being *able* to rely on oneself if or when others fail. It is indeed a virtue . . . to have inner resources—strength, courage, ingenuity, toughness, resilience."[25]

---

[24]Ibid., p. 23.

[25]Ibid., p. 42.

Regarding a right to autonomy, Feinberg says,

The kernel of the idea of autonomy is the right to make choices and decisions—what to put into my body, what contacts with my body to permit, where and how to move my body through public space, how to use my chattels and physical property, what personal information to disclose to others, what information to conceal, and more. . . . The most basic autonomy-right is the right to decide how one is to live one's life, . . . what courses of study to take, what skills and virtues to cultivate, what career to enter, whom or whether to marry, which church if any to join, whether to have children, and so on.[26]

LEGAL MORALISM

According to Legal Moralism, it is morally legitimate for the government to prohibit behavior that is (considered to be) inherently immoral, even if no one is wrongfully harmed or wrongfully seriously offended by it. For example, if a government were to prohibit dancing or private homosexual acts between consenting adults solely on the grounds that dancing and homosexual acts are immoral (whether or not anyone is harmed or seriously offended), then it would be applying Legal Moralism.

According to Feinberg, one justification for Legal Moralism appeals to the need to protect and preserve the way of life of a specific community. For example, a community of Puritans might maintain that adultery, divorce, birth control, drinking alcoholic beverages, and dancing are inherently immoral activities that must be prohibited in order to preserve the Puritan way of life. But does the majority of people in a community (or a powerful minority) have a moral right to force other members of the community to conform to rules they disagree with and have not consented to (or no longer consent to)? Surely it would be a serious violation of someone's right to autonomy if her community required her to live her life in strict accordance with the moral code of its rulers or the majority instead of living her life (within limits) according to her own moral code.

Of course, no community can survive for long if its members flout what we might call the fundamental core of any acceptable moral code—a core that must include rules prohibiting people from seriously harming or seriously offending each other and requiring people to help others when the need is great and the cost of help small. But outside the fundamental core, Feinberg argues that a community is strengthened if it leaves room for diversity instead of trying to enforce a rigid conformity. Trying to force people to live by rules they no longer accept as legitimate can lead to an explosion of violent resistance, as happened during the Reformation and Counterreformation when communities tried to enforce religious conformity in order to protect the community's way of life. Moral pluralism may be as necessary to social cohesion in the long run as is religious pluralism. Besides, communities naturally change and evolve, just as species

---

[26]Ibid., p. 54.

change and languages evolve. It is futile and probably dangerous to try to block all changes to a community's way of life.[27]

Of course, sometimes changes to a community's way of life may be an improvement rather than the reverse. What a majority in a community believes to be inherently immoral may not be. Some ways of life are oppressive and exploitative. If a community's way of life changes so that it no longer includes a commitment to enslavement of blacks, subordination of women, and strict racial segregation, then surely those changes are for the better. Protection and preservation of a way of life is rather weak justification for coercion of a community's members if the components of the way of life being protected and preserved are morally suspect.

Even if a particular change is considered anything but an improvement—for example, if one thinks that people's engaging in homosexual behavior is a sign of social decay rather than social progress—it does not follow that tolerating such behavior will lead to a significant change in the community's way of life (such as transforming it from a mostly heterosexual to a mostly homosexual community.) Disapproved forms of behavior are not necessarily "contagious." For example, a person's sexual orientation is highly resistant to change. (If you are a heterosexual, what would lead you to change into a homosexual?) If homosexual behavior is tolerated (not prohibited or punished), most people will still remain heterosexual. Even if adultery and divorce are inherently immoral, tolerating them (not legally prohibiting them) may not have a very profound effect on the community's way of life, leaving substantial parts of it intact.

FUNDAMENTAL LIBERTIES

Our discussion thus far has suggested that people should have some degree of liberty—or better, have a moral right to some liberties but not others. (People may forfeit their right to some of their liberties and legitimately be punished with imprisonment for criminal behavior.) Surely no one should have the liberty to rape women to whom they are sexually attracted, to take objects that belong to others without their permission, or to kill other people for amusement. On the other hand, surely people should have the liberty to choose their own religion or no religion, to apply to the college of their choice, and to drive on a public street. But are some liberties that people should have more important or fundamental than others? According to John Stuart Mill, there are two basic categories of fundamental liberties: (1) freedom of thought and discussion and (2) freedom of action.

Freedom of Thought and Discussion

Mill advocates as little social interference with thought and discussion as possible. First, people should not be punished for their thoughts or brainwashed

---

[27]Joel Feinberg, *Harmless Wrongdoing,* Volume 4 of *The Moral Limits of the Criminal Law* (New York: Oxford University Press, 1988), chap. 29.

into believing or not believing certain things. Second, they should have the widest possible freedom to discuss and argue with each other about their beliefs. Expression of thought should not be suppressed or prohibited, even if authorities are convinced that the ideas being expressed are both false and dangerous. Society should be very reluctant to silence people, even if they are criticizing their government, denouncing religion, or advocating unpopular causes and ways of living. According to Mill, censorship "is an assumption of infallibility,"[28] but no one and no institution is infallible. The silenced thoughts may be true, or at least part of the truth; if they are, then people are robbed of a great good—namely, truth. Even if they are false, the free discussion of ideas, some of which are false, is valuable because free discussion and inquiry provide people with a "clearer perception and livelier impression of truth produced by its collision with error."[29] Without free discussion of ideas, Mill claims, even a true idea will become "a dead dogma, not a living truth."[30] If an idea is a dead dogma rather than a living truth, although one may in some sense believe it, it does not guide one's behavior or influence how one lives.

There may be good reason for treating Mill's opposition to limitations on freedom of thought as absolute. Brainwashing invades your very mind, affecting who you are as well as what you do. And thoughts, at least when not acted on, do not pose threats of serious harm or offense to others. However, it is less clear that there is as good reason to treat his opposition to limitations on freedom of discussion as absolute. Words can hurt, and hurt severely. Consider laws against libel or against yelling "Fire!" in a crowded theater when you know there is no fire. Making accusations you know to be false can ruin a person's reputation, damaging the person emotionally and financially. Yelling "Fire!" in a crowded theater when there is no fire can cause a stampede that could kill or injure many people. Shouting "String him up!" in the middle of a frantic lynch mob can lead to murder. Mill himself recognizes these limitations.

> Even opinions lose their immunity when the circumstances in which they are expressed are such as to constitute their expression a positive instigation to some mischievous act. An opinion that corn dealers are starvers of the poor, or that private property is robbery, ought to be unmolested when simply circulated through the press, but may justly incur punishment when delivered orally to an excited mob assembled before the house of a corn dealer.[31]

Mill's Harm Principle would justify suppressing the discussion or expression of certain ideas if, but only if, there is strong evidence that discussing or expressing them would cause serious harm to other people. For example, consider conspiracy, or the planning of an illegal activity, such as a conspiracy to assassinate the president of the United States, to fix a horse race, or to rob a bank. Should we let people go through all the planning stages on the grounds that what

---

[28]Mill, *On Liberty,* p. 17.

[29]Ibid., p. 16.

[30]Ibid., p. 34.

[31]Ibid., p. 53.

they're doing is only discussing, and step in only after they have shot at (and possibly wounded or killed) the president, fixed the race, or robbed the bank? Our laws prohibit conspiracies to engage in illegal activity; people can be arrested and punished for merely planning or discussing such activities. Surely such laws are justified by Mill's Harm Principle. We should prevent serious harm when we can, not just punish people after the fact for causing harm.

Issues involving so-called "political correctness" are more troubling. Can we justify prohibiting the expression of ideas and views that are deeply offensive and painful to members of some groups? What if a psychology professor publicly declares that blacks are intellectually inferior to whites? A police commissioner in a city with a large Hispanic population publicly claims that Hispanics are like brutes who only understand force? A judge publicly states that gay men are all child molesters? A history teacher publicly maintains that the Holocaust, in which the Nazis exterminated millions of Jews, never occurred? Would society be justified in punishing these people for expressing such views by, for example, denying a pay raise to the psychology professor, firing the police commissioner, removing the judge from the beach, or denying the history teacher tenure? Does it matter whether the ideas expressed are true or false?

Freedom of Action

Mill believed that generally there should be fewer restrictions on freedom of thought and discussion than on freedom of action because physical acts can have more direct effects on people than mere thoughts or words. "No one pretends that actions should be as free as opinions."[32] However, Mill advocates giving individuals plenty of room for "experiments in living" in order to try our different "modes of life" so long as no one else is harmed by their behavior. He maintains that "the free development of individuality is one of the leading essentials of well-being."[33] Mill believes that people should be free to follow their own recipe for happiness, rather than the recipes for happiness that others have constructed, because they'll be happier that way. Leaving people free will thus maximize total happiness, the utilitarian test of rightness.

Of course, Mill does not think that people should be free to murder, rape, and steal or to behave with reckless indifference to the lives and well-being of others by, for example, driving drunk or dumping toxic chemicals into a river. But people should be left alone to follow their own life plans if no one else will be seriously harmed by it. Otherwise they will be forced into a mindless conformity that Mill deplores because it will destroy people's happiness and their capacity for autonomy.

> Many persons, no doubt, sincerely think that human beings thus cramped and dwarfed are as their Maker designed them to be.... But if it be any part of religion to believe that man was made by a good Being, it is more consistent

---

[32]Ibid., p. 53.
[33]Ibid., p. 54.

> with that faith to believe that this Being gave all human faculties that they
> might be cultivated and unfolded, not rooted out and consumed.[34]

Therefore, Mill urges a spirit of social tolerance for different ways of living.

What kind of harm to others justifies social interference? Mill maintains that conduct should be free from social interference if it is "not injuring the interests of [others], or rather [not injuring] certain interests which, either by express legal provision or by tacit understanding, ought to be considered as rights."[35]

Freedom/Liberty Rights in the United Nations Universal Declaration

The United Nations Universal Declaration of Human Rights lists several freedom or liberty rights, but it certainly does not offer an exhaustive list. For example, it does not include a right to wear the clothes you want to wear, to eat junk food, or to go to sleep and get up when you want to. Rather, the list includes only those freedoms that are of especially fundamental importance. Thus, it includes the right to freedom of movement and residence (Article 13), freedom to marry and found a family (Article 16), freedom to own property (Article 17), freedom of thought, conscience, and religion (Article 18), freedom of opinion and expression (Article 19), freedom of peaceful assembly (Article 20), freedom of choice in employment (Article 23), and freedom to join labor unions (Article 23). Why are these freedoms considered especially important or fundamental? Why, for example, is freedom of movement more important than freedom to choose the clothes you wear?

Suppose that you can't move from point A to point B without the government's permission, and you must wear a government-approved uniform every day. Having to wear a government-approved uniform prevents you from wearing your black leather pants and black silk blouse/shirt. That's a pain. But consider pass laws regulating your movement. Consider why you might want to move from point A to point B. You might want to visit a sick relative, attend a political speech or rally, go to the library to do research on the government's economic policies, go to an art gallery or to the theater, visit a historic sight, attend church or temple, or go to school. If the government has a veto power over your movements, then it has a veto power over your activities. If it doesn't give you permission to go from point A to point B, it can effectively prevent you from doing any of these things. Even if you almost always got permission each time you made a request to move from point A to point B, the passes would be colossally inconvenient. Imagine if every time you wanted to leave your neighborhood or town you had to first go to the police station to explain to them where you were going, how you were going to get there, and why you were going in order to get their written permission. It would be so time-consuming that you'd often give up your plans rather than go through the hassle. And of course, it would destroy spontaneity. You couldn't decide on the spur of the moment to go to the movies

---

[34]Ibid., p. 59.
[35]Ibid., p. 73.

or to a restaurant outside your neighborhood. Laws regulating your movements would have far profounder effects on your life than laws regulating the clothes you wear.

Many of the other freedom rights listed in the United Nations document are fundamental for roughly similar reasons. They are necessary if people are to maintain control over their own lives and over the conditions that affect their well-being. If people do not have freedom of thought, discussion, and expression, they cannot protest conditions, political or economic, that may be harming them or try to persuade people to change social institutions or laws. If they do not have freedom of religion, something central to their very identity may be jeopardized. The world's sorry history of religious persecution also suggests that freedom of religion will protect people from deadly religious persecution, reduce social upheaval, and promote social harmony.

Similarly, consider the right to freedom of choice in employment. If you did not have that freedom right, the government might assign you to a job whether or not you wanted that kind of job. Imagine if you wanted to be a forest ranger but your government required you to be an accountant, engineer, garbage collector, or hotel desk clerk. Being forced into a career path that is contrary to your own desires and inclinations or prevented from pursuing a career path of your choice could be a source of profound unhappiness. The right to free choice of employment imposes a duty on government to not coerce you into a career path you don't want to take by, for example, simply ordering you to follow a certain occupation. It also imposes a duty on government to protect you from other non-governmental sources of power that might interfere with your pursuing a career of your choice. The government has a duty to create and enforce laws forbidding the kind of discrimination that would prevent women, blacks, and members of other oppressed groups from pursuing the career path of their choice.

The Content of Freedom/Liberty Rights

We said earlier that specifying the content of a right involves specifying the duties toward the right-holder that it imposes on others. Let's take as an example the right to freedom of expression. To say that I have a right to freedom of expression entails that

1. Others (including the government) have a *duty not to* interfere with me in my efforts to express my thoughts.

2. Others (including the government) have a *duty to* protect me from others' interfering with my expressing my thoughts.

3. Others (including the government) have a *duty to* aid me if others have interfered with my expressing my thoughts.

However, the right is not absolute. If I bring a sound truck outside your window at 2:00 A.M. and proceed to give a philosophy lecture that awakens the whole neighborhood, the police should stop me rather than protect me from interference. Why? My expressing my thoughts in that way at that hour infringes your and your neighbors' freedom to get a good night's sleep (it wrongfully harms or seriously offends). It also makes you and your neighbors an involuntary audience. You may not want to listen to my lecture. Therefore, my behavior interferes with your freedom to *not* listen to me if you don't want to. Regulating how and when people express their thoughts in order to prevent infringements on the freedom of others seems perfectly justified. I should not be prohibited from giving a philosophy lecture in my classroom or my office, but if I give it at a time, in a place, and in a way that infringes the freedom of others, then if I am stopped I cannot legitimately complain that my right to freedom of expression is being violated. The infringement of my freedom right is justified.

EXERCISES

1. Answer the following questions, and defend your answers.

   Should physicians be free to help their patients commit suicide?

   Should women be free to have abortions?

   Should people be free to criticize their government?

   Should people be free to publicly burn the flag of their country?

   Should people be free to buy, sell, and use such substances as marijuana, heroin, and cocaine?

   Should people be free to buy and sell sex?

   Should people be free to gamble?

   Should people be free to produce and see material that is sexually explicit?

   Should people be free to own every variety of weapon, such as semiautomatic rifles and hand grenades?

   Should people be free to discipline their children any way they wish?

   Should people be free to stage dogfights?

   Should companies be free to pollute the environment if it is profitable for them?

   Should wealthy people be free to contribute as much money as they want to political candidates?

   Should people be free to engage in homosexual acts?

   Should husbands be free to beat their wives?

   Should people be free to have as many spouses as they want?

   Should people of the same sex be free to marry each other?

   Should homosexuals be free to serve in the military?

   Should people be free to sunbathe in the nude at public beaches?

   Should an employer be free to refuse to hire women?

   Should an employer be free to make having sex with him a condition of employment?

   Should a restaurant owner be free to refuse to serve African-Americans?

   Should an African-American be free to eat at a public restaurant?

   Should women be free to breastfeed their babies in public?

   Should people be free to ride skateboards or bicycles on public sidewalks?

   Should women be free to drink alcohol while pregnant?

Should people be free to smoke in enclosed public places?

Should people be free to smoke in the privacy of their own homes?

Should people be free to engage in sexual intercourse in public?

Should (adult) brothers and sisters be free to marry each other?

Should people be free to beg on the streets?

Should people be free to make alterations to their house without a permit?

2. Which of the following forms of behavior may the government legitimately *require* and punish people for failing to do? On what grounds? Defend your answers. (Assume that the people who are required to do these things are competent adults.)

Place infants and small children in car seats in moving autos.

Wear seat belts while in a moving automobile.

Wear a motorcycle helmet while on a moving motorcycle.

Serve in the military during wartime.

Vote in national elections.

Exercise regularly.

Buy automobile insurance.

Have one's automobile regularly inspected.

Register all one's firearms.

Remain at the scene of an accident one was involved in.

Report suspicions of child abuse.

3. It's winter, and the government fears that many of the homeless will freeze to death if they don't go to shelters. However, many of the homeless refuse to go to shelters. Would the government be justified in forcing homeless people into shelters against their will? Why or why not?

4. Kristol maintains that the government violates his right to autonomy when it requires him to pay taxes that are used to pay for goods and services for poor people. He claims that such laws illegitimately infringe his liberty. What *precise* liberty or liberties is the government infringing by requiring him to pay taxes, some of which will be spent on providing goods and services to the poor? Are the liberties infringed "fundamental" liberties? Should people have the liberty or liberties that such tax policies infringe? Precisely what liberties has the government *not* infringed in coercing Kristol into paying taxes, some of which will go to pay for goods and services for the poor? Is Kristol right in claiming that it is morally illegitimate for the government to require him to pay taxes for these purposes? Defend your answer.

5. Williams claims that in restricting the liberty of well-off people like Kristol by coercing them to pay taxes for social programs for the poor, the government is increasing the freedom of the poor. He says that a poor person who doesn't have money for food and shelter is not free to eat or sleep indoors when it's raining or cold. If someone is homeless and there are no public shelters or toilets and there are laws prohibiting people from defecating and urinating in public, then he is not even free to urinate or defecate. Williams says that if life's basic necessities are provided to people who would not be able to get them by their own unaided efforts, they become free to do many things that they were not free to do before. Do you agree with Williams? Why or why not?

6. Rodriguez is HIV-positive (the precursor of AIDS). She does not want her employer or fellow employees to know because she fears that she will be fired or ostracized. Would it be morally legitimate for the government to *require* health-care providers to inform employers when their patients are HIV-positive? Would it be morally legitimate for the government to *prohibit* health-care providers from divulging such information without the patient's consent? Defend your answer.

7. Because of overpopulation (its population already is over the billion mark), the government of the People's Republic of China permits married couples to have only one child. The government fears disaster if its population growth is not brought under control. The government employs coercion to enforce this law, denying couples the freedom or liberty to have as many children as they want. Is this interference with liberty morally justifiable? Should couples be free to have as many children as they want? Defend your answer.

8. Would it be morally legitimate for a town government to pass a law forbidding homosexual couples from holding hands or kissing in public on the grounds that such conduct is offensive to most of the town's inhabitants or on the grounds that such public conduct will corrupt the town's youth? Why or why not?

9. A group of neo-Nazi skinheads applies for a parade permit in order to hold a public outdoor celebration commemorating the birth of Adolf Hitler. The town they have selected for their celebration has a large Jewish population. They have selected this town for that reason. Would the town's government be justified in denying them the parade permit? Why or why not?

10. Thompson, who is white, does not want to serve black people in the restaurant he owns. He says that he should be free to serve or refuse to serve whomever he pleases since it is his restaurant. Douglass, a black woman who was denied service at Thompson's restaurant, maintains that the government should protect her freedom to eat in any public restaurant she wants to eat in by prohibiting Thompson from discriminating against her on the basis of race. In addition, Douglass says that Thompson relies on the government (police and courts) to help him discriminate. If a black person enters Thompson's restaurant and refuses to leave after being ordered to do so, Thompson calls the police to have the patron removed, claiming that the black person is trespassing on private property. Would it be morally acceptable for the government to require Thompson to serve blacks as well as whites? Why or why not?

11. Bigotburg is an all-white town that has passed an ordinance prohibiting non-whites from living or owning property in Bigotburg. They wish to preserve the "character and charm" of their community and its way of life. An African-American couple brings suit in state court to void the law. The inhabitants of Bigotburg say that they should be free to exclude nonwhites from their community. The African-American couple argues that they should be free to live wherever they want. With whom do you agree? Why?

12. Good Intentions University has instituted a speech code that prohibits "hate" speech on campus. According to the code, any words, written or uttered, that have a high probability of seriously offending a large percentage of members of any group on campus, and that tend to create a hostile or intimidating environment likely to interfere with learning, are prohibited. Punishments for

infringing the code vary from a mild reprimand to expulsion. The code applies to students, faculty, staff, and administration. The following cases are brought before the disciplinary board.

> An anti-Semitic student hung a swastika on the outside of his dorm room door.
>
> A male student in a coed dorm hung on the outside of his door a picture depicting a woman being gang-raped.
>
> A female student put on the outside of her dorm door a sign reading "All men are pigs."
>
> A faculty member wrote an essay for the university newspaper criticizing affirmative action and maintaining that most African-American and Hispanic students at the university are not qualified to be there.
>
> A drunken white student went to an interracial campus party and loudly proclaimed several times that he hates "niggers."
>
> An African-American student wrote an essay for the campus newspaper accusing all whites of being bigots.
>
> A faculty member was overheard telling sexist jokes to some colleagues at a faculty meeting.
>
> A faculty member frequently tells racist and sexist jokes in class.

Should each of these people be free to do or say the things described? Why or why not?

Should the university have a speech code prohibiting "hate" speech? Why or why not?

Suggested Readings

Isaiah Berlin. *Four Essays on Liberty*. New York: Oxford University Press, 1969.

Joel Feinberg. *Rights, Justice, and the Bounds of Liberty: Essays in Social Philosophy*. Princeton, NJ: Princeton University Press, 1980.

_____. *The Moral Limits of the Criminal Law*.

> Volume 1 *Harm to Others*. New York: Oxford University Press, 1984.
>
> Volume 2 *Offense to Others*. New York: Oxford University Press, 1985.
>
> Volume 3 *Harm to Self*. New York: Oxford University Press, 1986.
>
> Volume 4 *Harmless Wrongdoing*. New York: Oxford University Press, 1988.

John Stuart Mill. *On Liberty*. Indianapolis, IN: Hackett, 1978.

Joseph Raz. *The Morality of Freedom*. New York: Oxford University Press, 1986.

CHAPTER 14

Morality and Sex

There was a time in the not so distant past when talk of moral issues seemed to focus exclusively on sex, as though morality was only about sexual behavior. Many people are relieved that those days appear to be long gone. However, it would be a mistake to embrace the opposite extreme and conclude that morality has nothing to do with sex or that sex has nothing to do with morality. Morality is relevant in any situation in which people interact and there are possibilities of harm and benefit. Moral requirements and prohibitions, virtues and vices, duties and rights that apply in nonsexual matters also apply in sexual matters. For example, if honesty, kindness, and compassion are moral virtues, and if dishonesty, callousness, and brutality are moral vices, then they're moral virtues/vices in matters of sex as well as in other areas of life. If people have moral duties of beneficence and of nonmaleficence, then they have those duties within sexual relationships as well as outside them.

In this chapter we'll examine a number of moral issues relating to sex: sex without marriage, pornography, adultery, prostitution, and homosexual sex acts.

SEX WITHOUT MARRIAGE

Many people claim that sex between people who aren't married to each other is immoral. In their view, sexual relations are morally acceptable only within marriage. Most commonly, this claim is defended by appealing to God's Law. Proponents of this view usually claim that God forbids us to have sex outside what is often called the "sacrament" of marriage. Since God forbids it, it is immoral to have sexual relations with someone to whom one is not married.

Obviously, this argument will not persuade those who do not believe in God or who doubt God's existence. But it may also fail to persuade those who do believe in God. Many theists doubt that God really forbids people to have sex outside marriage. They may ask, "How do we know that God forbids it?" If people point to passages in sacred scriptures such as the Bible or the Koran, some theists may respond that these scriptural passages require interpretation. They may question the interpretation of those who claim that these passages show that God forbids sex outside marriage. They may also suggest that these passages reflect less God's words than the traditional moral beliefs of the human authors of the words.

We can understand why God would prohibit rape, murder, and stealing. Such actions cause severe harm to others. But why would God prohibit sex outside marriage, especially in an era of widely available, relatively effective contraceptives? We also need to keep in mind that the prohibition against sex outside marriage does not mention age. If sex outside marriage is immoral, then it applies to couples in their 30s, 40s, 50s, 60s, and 70s as well as to teenagers.

Let's reflect on how we might apply to this issue some of the moral theories we have examined.

An act utilitarian cannot make generalizations about sex outside marriage; she has to make moral judgments on a case-by-case basis. If more total well-being would result if an unmarried couple has sex than if they don't have sex, then according to Act Utilitarianism it is morally acceptable (actually, obligatory) for the couple to have sex.

The act utilitarian must weigh likely harms and benefits. Benefits include the physical pleasure the couple would experience, but there may be other benefits as well. If they are considering getting married, having sex before marriage would enable them to determine whether they are sexually compatible, which can help them decide whether to get married. One also might maintain that having sex before marriage reduces the probability of marrying purely for sex, thus reducing the probability of making a mistake in one's choice of marriage partner.

Potential harms include guilt one or both partners may feel if they believe that it is wrong to have sex outside marriage. Other potential problems include sexually transmitted diseases and unintended pregnancy. Also, when couples have sex, the emotional attachment often becomes stronger and deeper. If the relationship ends without leading to marriage, the pain may be more intense and lasting if they have had sexual relations than if they have not. (Of course, marriage cannot wholly protect us from unintended pregnancy or sexually transmitted diseases, and marriages are not necessarily permanent. Almost half of all marriages end in divorce.)

Whereas an act utilitarian must decide the issue on a case-by-case basis, a rule utilitarian may make generalizations. According to Rule Utilitarianism, if the general practice of unmarried couples' having sex would produce more total well-being than the practice of their refraining from having sex, then sex outside marriage is not wrong. On the other hand, if it would produce more harm than benefit, then it is wrong.

What might be some benefits of unmarried couples' having sex? They would experience an important source of pleasure and satisfaction; otherwise, they might feel frustrated and deprived. Couples would have the opportunity to determine their sexual compatibility before marriage. Their decision to marry at a certain time and their choice of marriage partner would not be driven primarily by their desire to have sex, which can lead to poor decision making and unfortunate choices. What might be some harms of unmarried couples' having sex? The practice might lead to more unintended pregnancies and sexually transmitted diseases. People might develop a more casual attitude toward sex, reducing its significance and meaning.

Now let's try to apply Kantian moral theory to this issue. First, we would ask the question, Could one, without contradiction, will a universal law permitting unmarried couples to have sex? It is hard to see how a rational agent would necessarily be contradicting herself by willing such a universal law. (Can you see how a contradiction would arise?) If there is no contradiction, then it passes the test of the universal law formulation of Kant's Categorical Imperative. Second, we would ask whether unmarried couples who have sex are treating each other and themselves with respect. It is difficult to see how they would necessarily be treating each other or themselves with disrespect by having sex with someone to whom they are not married. (Can you see disrespect?) If they are not treating each other or themselves with disrespect, then their behavior passes the test of the respect for persons formulation of Kant's Categorical Imperative.

We might also return to a point made early in the book: Behavior should be treated as innocent until proved guilty. It is not up to us to prove that sex between unmarried people is *not* immoral; rather, it is up to those who claim that it is immoral to prove that it is immoral. Can that claim be proved by appeal to any other consideration than the claim that such behavior is contrary to God's Law?

Moral Duties within Sexual Relationships

As we saw when we looked at the respect for persons formulation of Kant's Categorical Imperative, one fundamental aspect of treating people with respect centers on ensuring that all our interactions with them are completely voluntary. Obviously, this requirement is incompatible with rape. Thus, the first duty we have toward others regarding our sexual relationships is to ensure that they are completely voluntary. This duty not only prohibits the use of coercion or force, it also prohibits manipulation and deception. Sex is not completely voluntary if a woman has sex with a man only because he got her so drunk that she doesn't know what she's doing and is not capable of giving or withholding consent. (The law in most states now classifies that scenario as rape, and men can go to prison for it!) Similarly, it is not completely voluntary if a woman has sex with a man only because he lied to her. ("I love you." "I want to marry you.")

When couples have sex, it often reflects deep emotional attachment and strengthens that attachment. We call that emotional attachment love. When one person loves another, she usually becomes much more vulnerable to the person she loves. People we love can hurt us psychologically far more severely and deeply than people we don't care about. We come to need and depend on them. We trust them with our secrets, our feelings, our thoughts. If they betray us, are disloyal, or fail to meet our emotional needs, we may be devastated. Thus, we owe duties of special care to those who love us and who, presumably, we love in return. We have a duty to refrain from taking advantage of their vulnerability and trust; we should not exploit, oppress, manipulate, dominate, or betray them. We should ensure that our relationship is mutual, with roughly equal giving and receiving, caring and being cared for. Complete or excessive selfishness is not appropriate.

The Double Standard

Our society has often applied a double standard: Many people believe that it's far more acceptable for males than for females to have sex outside marriage. A young unmarried male with a lot of sexual experience is often called a "stud," a term of approval. On the other hand, a young unmarried woman with a lot of sexual experience is often called a "slut," a term of strong disapproval. Similarly, a man who has a sexual relationship with a woman half his age is not condemned nearly as severely as a woman who has a sexual relationship with a man half her age. Is there any justification for applying different standards of acceptable sexual behavior to males and females? Critics of the double standard say that there is no justification; they maintain that the same standards of sexual conduct should apply to men and to women. They insist that different standards can be justified only if there are relevant differences between men and women; however, they maintain that there are no relevant differences.

PORNOGRAPHY

Material that is sexually explicit is often considered pornographic, and all states have laws controlling the production, sale, purchase, and possession of pornographic material. Material deemed pornographic may include such things as videos or pictures of people having sex, pictures of naked people in suggestive poses, depictions of rape, written descriptions of sex acts, and so on. Some sexually explicit material is considered tasteful and erotic; some is nasty and vile to a degree going beyond the grotesque. Of course, one serious problem is to define *pornographic,* a notoriously difficult task. We will not attempt that task here.

The production of sexually explicit material that involves children and adolescents is obviously immoral because the children or adolescents participating are too young to give consent and their participation is not fully voluntary. Moreover, youngsters who are forced to participate in this kind of activity are psychologically harmed. Thus, there can be no rational defense for employing children and adolescents in the creation of sexually explicit material. But what of the act of selling, buying, or viewing sexually explicit material that employs children, so-called child pornography? If the material has already been produced, can the seller or buyer defend his conduct by maintaining that he had nothing to do with its production? Critics argue that the consumers of child pornography contribute to the exploitation of these children because the material would not be produced if there were no market for it. Consumers of child pornography thus share the responsibility for its creation. Accepting this reasoning, almost everyone favors laws criminalizing the production, sale, or purchase of child pornography. Almost everyone agrees that people should not be free to produce, sell, or consume child pornography.

However, what of sexually explicit material that employs only adults whose participation is fully voluntary? Clearly, if someone videotapes a real rape, the victim is not participating voluntarily. But what if it is a mock rape that is being videotaped, using adult actors and actresses who are participating voluntarily? Is it wrong to produce, sell, or buy such videotapes? Should there be laws prohibiting it, or should people be free to produce, sell, and consume such material so long as everyone participating does so voluntarily?

Defenders of such material may deplore the tastes to which it caters, but they maintain that it is not immoral to produce or consume such material. They also maintain that it is wrong to prohibit such material because it unjustifiably interferes with the liberty of those who wish to produce and sell it and those who wish to buy and view it. Defenders often claim that no one is harmed by it provided that it only uses adults who participate voluntarily and is only available to adults. In fact, some defenders might claim that overall it has a positive effect because it can increase sexual satisfaction for many people by providing heightened sexual stimulation and arousal. As for the violence that is often integral to the nastier forms of sexually explicit material, defenders sometimes claim that it reduces the amount of actual violence in society by providing an outlet, a vicarious experience, for the hostile and violent impulses that many people have.

Critics reject these claims. They think that many individuals and society in general are harmed by the kind of sexually explicit material that is violent, degrading, or dehumanizing. First, it can distort the view of sexuality and relationships of those who are frequent consumers of such material. For example, material that depicts women as getting sexual satisfaction from being hurt or degraded can lead men to believe that women want this kind of treatment. It can lead people to think of other people as mere sex objects to be used for their own gratification. It can coarsen, desensitize, and brutalize people, interfering with their capacity to feel love, sympathy, care, and compassion. Material that glorifies brutality and violence and that links violence with sex can precipitate violence, increasing rather than decreasing the amount of violence in our already violence-plagued society.

One question is whether we can distinguish between sexually explicit material that is harmful and sexually explicit material that is not harmful. Is there a difference between the effects of a movie showing two people "making love," where there is no hint of violence or hostility and every effort is made to make it "romantic," and the effects of a movie showing a woman being gang-raped? With respect to a movie showing a woman being gang-raped, does it matter whether the intention is to show that gang-rape is brutal and awful or to make gang-rape sexually stimulating? Can we formulate plausible principles that will enable us to distinguish between sexually explicit material that is morally acceptable and material that is not?

Should there be laws prohibiting the production, sale, purchase, or viewing of some forms of sexually explicit material? If yes, what forms should be prohibited, and what forms should not be prohibited? Why?

ADULTERY

Adultery occurs when a person who is married has sex with someone other than his or her spouse. Is adultery immoral?

Our society is a bit split in its thinking about this issue. On the one hand, the institution of marriage in our society seems to include the convention of sexual exclusivity. The expectation and understanding is that when people marry, they commit themselves to having sex only with their spouse. At the same time, adultery appears to be so widespread and, at least in some quarters, taken for granted that the expectation and understanding of sexual exclusivity is undermined. In a sense, people are and yet are not expected to be "faithful."

According to many people, God forbids adultery. After all, it is one of the Ten Commandments of the Hebrew Bible (Old Testament): "You shall not commit adultery." According to the Divine Command theory of morality, if God forbids adultery then it is immoral. However, as we have seen with other issues, relying solely on religious teachings and alleged revelations of God's Law presents problems. We will focus on nontheological reasons, if any, for thinking that adultery is immoral.

If a marital relationship is built on the explicit or implicit agreement that each partner is committed to sexual fidelity, then adultery involves violating that agreement. Almost every moral theory has a strong presumption against violating agreements or breaking promises (with the possible exception of Act Utilitarianism). Such behavior is justified only if there are strong moral reasons pulling in the other direction. Usually in cases of adultery it is only our own passion and lust, our own self-interest, that pulls against the anchor of our agreement or promise. A strong reason for condemning adultery, then, is that it constitutes violation of an explicit or implicit agreement that we have with our spouse.

Adultery also often involves deception as an adulterous spouse tries to conceal the adultery. Again, almost every moral theory has a strong presumption against deception (again with the possible exception of Act Utilitarianism). Self-interest alone does not constitute an acceptable moral reason that would justify violating the prohibition against deception. Therefore, if adultery involves deception, it is wrong.

Then, too, adultery, if found out, can cause great pain and suffering. The injured spouse will almost certainly feel betrayed, humiliated, and abased. We may take adultery on the part of our spouse as a sign that we have lost our spouse's love and affection or that we have lost our attractiveness and sex appeal, which may cause great anguish. The adulterous spouse, too, is harmed. Discovery of adultery can lead to unwanted divorce and other unpleasant complications and disruptions of our personal life. We may argue that we need only be discreet enough to avoid detection; however, there is always a significant possibility of detection in adultery and therefore a significant possibility of harm and suffering.

However, what if adultery involves neither the violation of an agreement nor deception? What if a couple freely agrees to have what is called an "open marriage," where each partner is free to have sexual relationships with other people? They are not violating any agreement of sexual exclusivity, and they have no reason to hide their other sexual relationships from each other. If there is no violation of an agreement and no deception, is adultery morally acceptable?

Many people insist that an open marriage is likely to be a short, unhappy marriage. They maintain that it is very probable that an open marriage will eventually generate such intense jealousy and insecurity on the part of one or both partners that the marriage will dissolve. Then, too, they point out that sexual exclusivity within marriage historically has had an important function regarding child rearing. The prohibition against adultery increases a husband's confidence that the children his wife bears within the marriage are truly his, which in turn increases the likelihood that he will fulfill the functions of a father, supporting his wife and children. We could argue that if adultery is sanctioned, no man can know whether his wife's children are really his, and this uncertainty may encourage men to ignore the obligations of fatherhood, which would have undesirable consequences for social well-being.

Even if it is true that open marriages make it more difficult to determine paternity, we could argue that if childbearing and child rearing are not at issue, then adultery that does not involve the violation of an agreement or deception is not immoral. With greater knowledge of and access to contraceptives and with sophisticated techniques for determining paternity based on biology and genetics, concerns about paternity are no longer acute. However, the likely consequences of an open marriage remain problematic. It may be that opponents of adultery are correct in maintaining that open marriages are likely to cause more disruption and suffering than marriages based on and committed to sexual exclusivity. The question is whether that fact alone would be sufficient to show that adultery that does not involve the violation of an agreement or deception is immoral.

PROSTITUTION

If sex without marriage is immoral, then obviously prostitution is immoral because it is a form of sex without marriage. However, some people maintain that buying and selling sex are particularly reprehensible, far worse than sex without marriage that occurs because of passion or love. Some people may condemn prostitution even if they do not believe that, in general, sex without marriage is immoral. Is prostitution immoral?

Not all societies have condemned prostitution as immoral. However, today most societies do. Those who condemn prostitution may assert that while it is morally acceptable to buy and sell objects such as cars and books and even to buy the labor power and services of people such as plumbers, auto mechanics, and athletes, buying and selling sex is different and immoral. One reason may be that they consider the most important aspect of sex to be its connection with love, affection, respect, and trust. Prostitution completely severs that connection. In prostitution, sex is degraded to the level of a mere animal function. Opponents of prostitution may also see sex as connected with passion, and most of the time, prostitution severs that connection, too. Prostitutes very rarely feel even a faint spark of passion for their customers, although they may fake passion. And of course, some opponents of prostitution will simply maintain that it is contrary to God's Law. We could also argue that prostitution breeds disease, and that in the age of AIDS the threat to public health is magnified.

Some critics of prostitution have a different perspective. They see prostitution as another way that women have been victimized. Prostitutes are generally women who have few economic alternatives to prostitution. (There are male prostitutes, but most are female.) Few women turn to prostitution because they enjoy the work and find it exciting; most are driven to it by dire necessity and desperation. In prostitution, women cater to men's desires, whims, and needs because they are driven to it, while the clients of prostitutes are generally not faced with the same kind of dire necessity and desperation. And historically, prostitutes have been treated far more harshly by the law than have their clients. Therefore, prostitution is just another way that men exploit women.

On the other hand, some people believe that just as people should be free to buy and sell their services cleaning houses, repairing cars, performing surgery, playing basketball, and modeling swimsuits, they should be free to buy and sell their services providing sex. In their view, a person's body belongs to that person. If a woman chooses to have sex with someone because of passion, it is her right. Similarly, if she chooses to have sex with someone for money, that, too, is her right. They maintain that many women and men marry for money or for power, ordinarily giving their spouses frequent sexual access to their bodies; they ask how that is different from prostitution.

As for the claim that prostitution severs the connection between sex on the one hand and love and passion on the other, defenders of prostitution might concede that claim and yet deny that it shows that prostitution is immoral. They might agree that sex is more satisfying if it is connected to mutual love and mutual passion, but argue that the absence of mutual love and passion does not make sex immoral. And they might say that if women are driven to prostitution by desperation, then the desperation should be condemned, not prostitution. If women are driven to prostitution by desperation, then that is a reason for taking steps to ensure that they have alternatives and are not desperate.

Finally, as for the claim that prostitution constitutes a threat to public health, defenders of prostitution claim that if prostitution were made legal and were regulated by the government, there would be no threat to public health. Prostitutes could be licensed and required to undergo regular medical examinations to ensure that they do not have sexually transmissible or other communicable diseases. If they were found to have such diseases, they could be treated, have their licenses revoked, and have their clients warned. Defenders of prostitution maintain that driving prostitution underground because of moral condemnation and legal prohibition is responsible for threats to public health.

HOMOSEXUALITY

Many people in the United States today have a strong aversion to homosexuality and to homosexuals. Many people condemn homosexuals and homosexual acts as immoral. Homosexuals have been discriminated against in a variety of ways, perhaps most obviously in government employment. Homosexuals have been forbidden to serve in the United States military and have been unwelcome in certain branches of the federal government such as the Defense Department, FBI, State Department, and Secret Service. Openly acknowledging that a person is a homosexual can jeopardize his or her career in many areas of employment. Then, too, homosexuals or people suspected of being homosexuals can become the targets of animosity and violence. People have been verbally harassed, abused, and assaulted solely because they are or are thought to be homosexuals.

Homosexual acts are sexual acts between members of the same sex; heterosexual acts are sexual acts between members of the opposite sex. Presumably, homosexuality is objectionable only if homosexual acts are objectionable. Is homosexual sex immoral? This question sidesteps the issue of whether people freely choose their sexual orientation. It can only be relevant to our concerns if homosexual sex acts are immoral or otherwise objectionable.

Homosexuality and God's Law

Many people condemn homosexual sex acts because they believe that such acts are forbidden by God. For example, the Roman Catholic Church teaches that "according to the objective moral order homosexual relations are acts deprived of the essential ordination they ought to have. In Sacred Scripture such acts are condemned as serious deviations and are even considered to be the lamentable effect of rejecting God. . . . Homosexual acts are disordered by their very nature and can never be approved."[1] However, as we have seen, many people find it difficult to justify the claim that God forbids something unless they have some reason independent of God's alleged commands for believing that it's immoral. Some people claim that homosexual acts are immoral because they are unnatural.

Are Homosexual Acts Unnatural?

Natural means in conformity with the physical laws of nature; *unnatural* means contrary to the physical laws of nature. Thus, it is natural for an unsupported rock to fall to the ground; it is unnatural for it to float in the air or rise (unless a

---

[1]"Vatican Declaration on Some Questions of Sexual Ethics," 1976, in *Social Ethics: Morality and Social Policy,* 3d ed., ed. Thomas Mappes and Jane Zembaty (New York: McGraw-Hill, 1987), pp. 246–247.

force is applied to it). The physical laws of nature include the laws of gravity, which govern the behavior of the rock. Similarly, it is natural for a lion to eat meat and unnatural for it to eat grass; it is natural for a cow to eat grass and unnatural for it to eat meat. In this sense of the words *natural* and *unnatural,* homosexual acts obviously are not unnatural. What is unnatural, in the sense of contrary to the physical laws of nature, *cannot* occur. An unsupported rock cannot simply float in the air or rise. A lion cannot eat grass, and a cow cannot eat meat. The fact that homosexual acts occur proves conclusively that they are not unnatural in the sense of being contrary to the physical laws of nature.

Perhaps *natural* means statistically normal, and *unnatural* means statistically abnormal. In this sense, because most human sex acts are heterosexual rather than homosexual, heterosexual sex acts are "normal" and natural, whereas homosexual sex acts are "abnormal" and unnatural. However, if we use *natural* and *unnatural* in the statistical sense, it's preposterous to think that what is unnatural is immoral. Most human beings have IQs between 90 and 110; therefore, it is abnormal for someone to have an IQ of 175. Surely it does not follow that it is immoral for someone to have an IQ of 175. Similarly, very few people are capable of producing artistic works of high quality, such as novels, poetry, paintings, and symphonies. Therefore, writing poetry or composing symphonies is unnatural in this sense. However, it would be preposterous to consider it immoral. Therefore, if homosexual acts are unnatural merely in the sense of being statistically abnormal, we have no reason for thinking that they are immoral.

Another line of argument is that because our sexual organs have the function of procreation, their only natural use is for procreation. In homosexual acts, one's sex organs are used for pleasure rather than for procreation, an unnatural misuse of them. According to this view, it's both unnatural and immoral to use something that has a function in a way that does not make use of its function.

This view has several problems. First, as Burton Leiser points out, something may have more than one function.[2] For example, a book may have the function of both informing and entertaining its reader; an automobile may have the function of both providing transportation and providing status. If something has more than one function, it is not unnatural if we use it for one of its functions but not another—for example, if we read a book for entertainment rather than for information. The mouth can be used for eating, drinking, speaking, breathing, and kissing. Does any of these constitute an unnatural misuse of the mouth? We might maintain that our sexual organs have the function of both procreation and providing pleasure and that if we are using them in homosexual acts for one of their functions, pleasure, they are not being unnaturally misused. After all, we might insist, they would not provide pleasure unless they have the function of providing pleasure.

---

[2]Burton Leiser, "Homosexuality and the 'Unnaturalness Argument,'" in *Social Ethics,* 3d ed., ed. Mappes and Zembaty.

As to the claim that it's immoral to use something contrary to its proper function, we might ask what could justify such a claim. After all, a book does not have the function of a ladder. Would it then be immoral to stand on it to reach something on a top shelf? Or consider the human foot. For the sake of argument we might concede that its "proper" function is for standing, walking, and running. Is it immoral to use our foot to kick a ball, squash a bug, or hold open a door?

Does Homosexuality Threaten the Family?

Another objection is that homosexuality threatens the family. Just how it allegedly threatens the family is rarely made clear, but perhaps the fear is that if enough human beings become homosexuals and engage exclusively in homosexual sex acts, then fewer and fewer children will be conceived and the human race will become threatened with extinction. Those who deny that homosexual sex acts are immoral maintain that the fear is unfounded. First, they could point out that our planet is already overpopulated with human beings. They might argue that if the birthrate declined because of decreased heterosexual sex acts, it would be a blessing rather than a curse. But they would also insist that the probability of a significant decline in the human birthrate to the point where human extinction is threatened because of homosexuality is vanishingly small.

But perhaps the claim that homosexuality undermines the family has a different focus. Perhaps the fear is that if more people become openly homosexual, the traditional family—male husband/father, female wife/mother, and their children—will be supplanted by other versions of the family, such as homosexual couples or extended groups of biologically unrelated people, including children. However, although some people think that this development would be a bad thing, others think that it would be a good thing if people were not, as they view it, forced into the "straightjacket" of the traditional family but instead had options to construct new forms of the family. We might argue that many people would still choose (and should be free to choose) to create traditional families but that others should be free to develop alternatives. Thus, we might concede that homosexuality would undermine the traditional family, but only in the sense of providing alternative versions of the family. We might see this outcome as good rather than bad.

EXERCISES

1. Is sex without marriage immoral? Defend your answer.

2. Suppose that Jack and Jill agree to have an open marriage. If they commit adultery, they will not be violating any agreement that they have made nor be deceiving anyone. Would it be immoral for them to commit adultery? Defend your answer.

3. Is prostitution immoral? Defend your answer.

4. Do you think that prostitution should be made legally permissible? Defend your answer.

5. Are homosexual sex acts immoral? Defend your answer.

6. Is homosexuality a vice? Defend your answer.

7. Would it be morally acceptable to exclude homosexuals from the police and from military service? Defend your answer.

SUGGESTED READINGS

Thomas Mappes and Jane Zembaty, eds. *Social Ethics: Morality and Social Policy.* 3d ed. New York: McGraw-Hill, 1987. (See Chapter 6.)

Jan Narveson, ed. *Moral Issues.* New York: Oxford University Press, 1983. (See Section VI.)

CHAPTER 15

Abortion

ROE V. *WADE*, 1973

Prior to 1973, almost all states in the United States had laws prohibiting abortion except when it was necessary to save the mother's life. However, in 1973 the Supreme Court ruled in *Roe* v. *Wade* that such laws are unconstitutional. Writing for the majority, Justice Harry Blackmun maintained that the right of privacy that many jurists claim is embedded in the United States Constitution "is broad enough to encompass a woman's decision whether or not to terminate her pregnancy."[1]

> The detriment that the State would impose upon the pregnant woman by denying this choice altogether is apparent. Specific and direct harm medically diagnosable even in early pregnancy may be involved. Maternity, or additional offspring, may force upon the woman a distressful life and future. Psychological harm may be imminent. Mental and physical health may be taxed by child care. There is also the distress, for all concerned, associated with the unwanted child, and there is the problem of bringing a child into a family already unable, psychologically and otherwise, to care for it. In other cases, as in this one, the additional difficulties and continuing stigma of unwed motherhood may be involved.[2]

Although Justice Blackmun concluded that the constitutional right of privacy gives a woman a right to decide whether to terminate a pregnancy, he did not hold that right to be absolute. Under certain circumstances the right may be justifiably overridden or violated.

> [The] Court's decisions recognizing a right of privacy also acknowledges that some state regulation in areas protected by that right is appropriate. [A] state may properly assert important interests in safeguarding health, in maintaining medical standards, and in protecting potential life. At some point in pregnancy, these respective interests become sufficiently compelling to sustain

---

[1] *Roe* v. *Wade,* in *Constitutional Law,* 10th ed., ed. Gerald Gunther (Mineola, NY: Foundation Press, 1980), p. 591.

[2] Ibid.

regulation of the factors that govern the abortion decision. The privacy right involved, therefore, cannot be said to be absolute.[3]

Opponents of abortion argued that because a fetus is a "person," abortion violates its constitutional rights. They argued that because the right to life is more important or fundamental than the right of privacy, the government should protect the fetus's right to life rather than its mother's right of privacy. Justice Blackmun denied that a fetus is a "person" as that word is used in the Constitution; "the word 'person,' as used in the 14th Amendment [to the Constitution], does not include the unborn."[4] The implicit conclusion is that because the fetus is not a person, it does not have a constitutionally protected right to life, because only persons (or people) have such a right. Therefore, the mother's constitutional right of privacy does not come into conflict with more fundamental rights of another person that would justify the state in prohibiting abortion.

Opponents of abortion also maintained that because (human) life begins at conception, "the State has a compelling interest in protecting that life from and after conception."[5] Justice Blackmun acknowledged the controversy over when life begins, but he concluded that the Court does not have to resolve that question. Although "there has always been strong support for the view that life does not begin until live birth,"[6] he recognized that some members of the community insist that it begins at conception. Nevertheless, Justice Blackmun implied that even if human life does begin at conception, the question of whether the fetus is a person is the deciding factor, and he reiterated that "the unborn have never been recognized in the law as persons in the whole sense."[7]

Roe v. *Wade* recognizes a woman's *nonabsolute* constitutional right to abortion. According to Justice Blackmun,

> the State does have an important and legitimate interest in preserving and protecting the health of the pregnant woman . . . , and . . . it has still *another* important and legitimate interest in protecting the potentiality of human life. These interests are separate and distinct. Each grows in substantiality as the woman approaches term [birth] and, at a point in pregnancy, each becomes "compelling" [justifying state intervention and regulation].[8]

The Supreme Court majority ruled that the state may not interfere with a woman's decision about whether to continue or terminate a pregnancy during the first trimester (the first three months of pregnancy). However, after that point, the state may impose regulations on abortion *provided that they are reasonably related to protecting the pregnant woman's health.* For example, the state may require that the person performing an abortion be a properly licensed

---

[3]Ibid., pp. 591–592.

[4]Ibid., p. 593.

[5]Ibid.

[6]Ibid.

[7]Ibid., p. 594.

[8]Ibid.

physician or that it be performed only in a certain type of medical facility such as a hospital or clinic. Similarly, the Court majority ruled that the state may not interfere with a woman's decision about abortion *for reasons of protecting potential human life* until the time of viability, when the fetus is capable of surviving outside its mother's womb (with or without medical aid). "If the State is interested in protecting fetal life after viability, it may go so far as to proscribe [forbid] abortion during that period, except when it is necessary to preserve the life or health of the mother."[9] However, prior to the time of viability, roughly the sixth month of pregnancy, the state may not prohibit abortion in order to protect potential human life. *Roe* v. *Wade*'s ruling is summarized in the following chart:

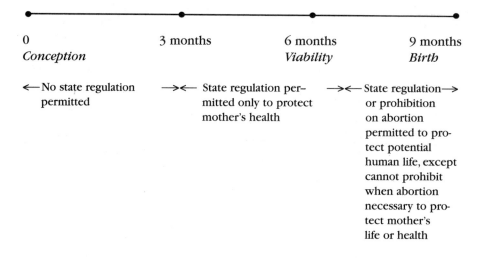

0	3 months	6 months	9 months
Conception		*Viability*	*Birth*

←No state regulation permitted   →←State regulation permitted only to protect mother's health   →←State regulation→ or prohibition on abortion permitted to protect potential human life, except cannot prohibit when abortion necessary to protect mother's life or health

CONSTITUTIONALITY AND MORALITY

The Supreme Court decides on the constitutionality of laws, including laws regulating or prohibiting abortion; it decides whether laws are consistent with or violate the United States Constitution. The Supreme Court is not a moral court; it does not decide what is morally acceptable and what is immoral. That should not be taken to imply that morality has nothing to do with law and constitutionality. After all, the moral convictions of the framers of the Constitution influenced their decisions about the Constitution; the moral convictions of legislators influence their decisions about what laws to make or not make; the moral convictions of ordinary citizens influence their decisions about whom to vote for and what laws to support or oppose. Nonetheless, the Supreme Court does not rule on the moral acceptability of laws and behavior.

---

[9]Ibid., 595.

Whether women have a constitutional right to decide whether to continue or to terminate a pregnancy based on a constitutional right of privacy is one question. Whether and under what circumstances abortion is morally acceptable is another question. We will focus on the latter question.

THE RIGHT-TO-LIFE POSITION ON ABORTION

According to what we will call the right-to-life position, from the moment of conception abortion is morally acceptable only if it is necessary to preserve the life of the mother. Most right-to-life advocates defend their position by maintaining that at conception, the fertilized egg (called a zygote until the second week, when it is implanted in the woman's uterus, an embryo from the second week until the eighth week when brain waves can be detected, and a fetus from the eighth week until birth) is a living human being with a moral right to life. Thus, for example, John Noonan insists, "If you are conceived by human parents, you are human."[10] He continues,

> The positive argument for conception as the decisive moment of humanization is that at conception the new being receives the genetic code. It is this genetic information which determines his characteristics. . . . A being with a human genetic code is [a human being].[11]

Clearly, Noonan is using "human being" in the genetic sense of being a member of the species *Homo sapiens.* Noonan maintains that from the moment of its conception, every organism that is genetically human has a moral right to life, presumably because of its potential. A genetically human zygote is a very valuable organism because it has the potential to develop into a fully functioning human being that can think, feel, love, hate, laugh, suffer, dream, and plan. A human being's zygote/embryo/fetus (from now on I will simply refer to the fetus for simplicity) is genetically human; therefore, at conception it has a moral right to life. Because the right to life is the most fundamental right, it overrides a mother's right to decide whether to terminate a pregnancy if it is not necessary to preserve her life. Only the mother's right to life can justify violating or overriding the fetus's right to life. Therefore, right-to-life advocates condemn the ruling in *Roe* v. *Wade* that until viability the state may not prohibit abortion in order to protect potential human life because they believe that it violates the fetus's moral right to life. They believe that a fetus *should* be considered a person within the meaning of the Constitution and should be granted a constitutionally protected right to life.

According to some right-to-life advocates, anything with a soul has a moral right to life. In their view, all and only human beings have souls. For them, the central question is when "ensoulment" occurs—that is, at what point a geneti-

---

[10]John T. Noonan, Jr., "An Almost Absolute Value in History," in *Social Ethics: Morality and Social Policy,* 3d ed., ed. Thomas Mappes and Jane Zembaty (New York: McGraw-Hill, 1987), p. 9.

[11]Ibid., p. 12.

cally human organism has a soul. The Roman Catholic Church teaches that ensoulment occurs at the moment of conception, and therefore at conception a zygote has a moral right to life that abortion violates. Consequently, it condemns *Roe* v. *Wade* for prohibiting the state from forbidding abortion until viability. In its view, from the moment of conception abortion is immoral unless it is necessary to preserve the life of the mother; therefore, from the moment of conception abortion should be illegal unless it is necessary to preserve the mother's life.

THE MOST LIBERAL VIEW ON ABORTION

According to the most liberal view on abortion, abortion is always morally acceptable, regardless of the stage of development of the fetus and regardless of the reason for seeking an abortion. Advocates of the most liberal view claim that women have a moral right to control their bodies, which entails that they have a right to decide whether to continue or to terminate a pregnancy. They insist that at no stage of its development does a fetus have a right to life that overrides a woman's right to control her body. They agree that a fetus is alive at conception and that it is genetically human, but they claim that only *people* have moral rights, including a right to life, and that a fetus is not a person. They maintain that the concept of a person is not based purely on biology or genetics.

Personhood

According to the liberal view, a fully functioning human being has a right to life not simply because she is genetically human but because she is a person. Trees, mosquitoes, frogs, and cows don't lack moral rights simply because of their species or genes; they lack moral rights because they're not people. What is a "person"? What criteria enable us to distinguish between persons and nonpersons? Philosopher Mary Anne Warren asks what traits or characteristics "are most central to the concept of personhood?" She says that they're (roughly) the following:

1. consciousness (of objects and events external and/or internal to the being) and in particular the capacity to feel pain;
2. reasoning (the *developed* capacity to solve new and relatively complex problems);
3. self-motivated activity . . . ;
4. the capacity to communicate . . . ;
5. the presence of self-concepts, and self-awareness.[12]

You're alive, but so is a tree. You're a person, but a tree (presumably) isn't. What are the differences between you and a tree? Unlike a tree, you're conscious,

---

[12]Mary Anne Warren, "On the Moral and Legal Status of Abortion," in *Social Ethics,* 3d ed., ed. Mappes and Zembaty, p. 16.

which at least in part involves being aware of your environment by means of perception. You see, hear, feel, smell, and taste things. Because of your perceiving things, you are aware of yourself as a separate entity different from other things. One component of perception, usually associated with the sense of touch, is the phenomenon of sensations such as pain. You have perceptual experiences called sensations that can be painful or irritating, on the one hand, or pleasurable on the other. Pains can be horrifically intense or fairly mild. Consider the difference between having a tooth drilled without anesthetic and receiving a flu shot. You also have such sensations as itches that are merely irritating. As for pleasurable sensations, those associated with sex are among the most intense. Trees cannot perceive or have sensations that are painful or pleasurable. (We can be fairly confident of this judgment because trees lack the developed brain and central nervous system that seem to be necessary for perception and sensation.) Lacking these capacities, trees cannot be considered people or "persons."

However, human beings are not the only living creatures that can perceive and have sensations. As any pet owner knows, dogs and cats can perceive and have painful or pleasurable sensations. Obviously, dogs and cats can see, hear, smell, taste, and feel. Unlike trees, they have brains and nervous systems that are very similar to those of human beings. If you kick a dog, it yelps. The best explanation of its behavior is that it felt pain at the kick. Are dogs, then, persons also? Many people maintain that they should not be considered persons (or at least not full persons) because they do not have the characteristics (to a high enough degree) of being able to reason, communicate, and have self-awareness and self-concepts.

Neither dogs nor cats are capable of constructing or even understanding scientific theories nor of performing even the simplest mathematical calculations, such as adding two and three. They cannot reason at a level of sophistication approaching that of human beings, nor communicate complex messages. Unlike dogs and cats, human beings can design and perform experiments to test scientific theories, write and interpret poetry, build jet airplanes, and create and manage gigantic business enterprises. These human activities require very sophisticated abilities to reason and communicate that dogs and cats lack. These capacities, too, are integral to the concept of a person. It is because they cannot reason or communicate at a level approaching that of human beings that we do not consider dogs and cats to be persons.

Finally, you are aware of yourself as a being having a past, present, and future. By means of memory you can remember all sorts of past experiences you have undergone. You may remember events such as birthday parties, people such as aunts and uncles, and so on. You are also aware of yourself in the present and of what you are doing. (Right now you are reading a book. You know where you are as you are reading it, and you may be aware of other things going on or of people in your immediate vicinity.) You are also aware of yourself as a being who will continue to exist into the future. By means of imagination you can project yourself into the future and imagine yourself as a spouse, parent, or professional. Because you are aware of yourself as a being having a future, you make plans and form intentions that affect your present behavior. Presumably, you are in college because of what you think a college degree will mean in the future, a future that you believe will include you. Much of what we do in the present is intended to affect the future, *our* future. It is doubtful that dogs and cats have such self-awareness—a conception of themselves as beings with a past, present, and future.

Warren's point is that only beings that meet most of these criteria to a high enough degree are persons. The question is whether a fetus meets any of these criteria of personhood.

According to the most liberal view, the mental life definitive of a person requires a certain highly sophisticated, fully functioning brain and central nervous system. In their view, the brain and central nervous system of a fetus, regardless of its stage of development, have not developed to the point where the fetus is conscious and self-aware. Therefore, regardless of its stage of development, a fetus cannot meet any of the criteria of personhood. Because it cannot meet any of the criteria of personhood, it is not a person, and consequently it has no moral rights such as a right to life.

Advocates of the most liberal view rely upon information about fetal development to defend their claim that a fetus's brain and central nervous system are not sufficiently developed to make it conscious, a necessary characteristic of personhood. The brain doesn't even come into existence until roughly the second month. They maintain that until there is a brain there cannot be a person. But the mere existence of the brain is not sufficient for consciousness; the brain has to be functioning at a certain level. Brain functioning relies very much upon connections among brain cells, but these connections develop very gradually. According to advocates of the most liberal view on abortion, there are not enough of these molecular connections essential to consciousness and brain functioning at any period of fetal development.

> In the forty weeks of gestation a human brain grows to a two-thirds-size
> likeness of the adult brain. Its anatomy at birth is remarkably complete. . . . But
> this general impression is misleading in one important respect. The formation
> of molecular connections, which take up little space but upon which the
> function of the brain depends, is far from complete.[13]

At no point in fetal development does a fetus have any of the characteristics definitive of personhood because its brain and central nervous system are not sufficiently developed. Therefore, at no stage of its development is a fetus a person with a right to life.

Warren admits that a human fetus is a *potential* person; if allowed to develop, it will develop into a person (unless it's severely damaged). But Warren insists that a potential person is not yet a person and therefore it doesn't have a right to life. In her view, only actual people, not potential people, have a right to life.

As for the right-to-life claims that every organism with a soul has a moral right to life and that ensoulment occurs at conception, advocates of the most lib-

---

[13]"Brain Development," in *The Oxford Companion to the Mind*, ed. R. L. Gregory (New York: Oxford University Press, 1987), p. 104.

eral view such as Warren could either deny that human beings have souls or insist that ensoulment occurs only at birth. Opponents of the right-to-life position would probably maintain that there is no evidence for the claim that human beings have souls or for the claim that a fetus acquires a soul at conception and that therefore such claims are not reasonable and should not be accepted.

Voluntariness

Some philosophers have pointed out that even if a fetus is a person, it does not follow that a pregnant woman has a moral duty to continue a pregnancy that she does not wish to continue. According to them, if a woman is not voluntarily pregnant, then she has no moral obligation or duty to sacrifice herself for the fetus. Judith Jarvis Thomson pursues this point by means of a thought experiment.[14] She asks us to imagine the following situation. A famous violinist is dying from kidney disease. She can be saved only if she is physically attached to you for nine months so that your kidneys can take over the functioning of her kidneys. (Being physically attached means that tubes that carry blood and other bodily fluids will connect the violinist to you. They may be long enough that you can each be in different rooms.) No one else can save her because you are the only person physically compatible with her. (Thomson asks us to ignore the implausibility of the scenario.) Suppose that you have been asked to voluntarily permit your body to be temporarily attached to the violinist for nine months, during which time your freedom will be seriously restricted because you will have to remain in the hospital. Thomson does not think that you have a moral duty to allow yourself to be attached to the violinist, even though she will die if you are not, because the sacrifice required is too great. She also does not think that the violinist has a moral right to the use of your body. (Do you agree? Why/Why not?)

Now let us change the scenario a bit. Suppose that no one has asked you whether you will voluntarily lend your body to the ailing violinist for nine months. Instead, while you are in the hospital visiting a friend you slip and fall, hitting your head so that you lose consciousness. While you are unconscious and cannot give or withhold consent, doctors attach you to the violinist. When you awaken from the temporary coma, you are told that if you are detached from the violinist, she will die. Thomson asks whether you have a moral duty to remain attached to the violinist because she will die if you do not. She answers that you do not. You did not become attached to the violinist voluntarily. (Granted you did not refuse to be attached to her, but only because you were not asked.) Thomson believes that you have no moral duty to remain attached to the violinist for nine months, or even one day. (Of course, it might be an admirable thing if you decided to remain attached to her in order to save her life, but that is different from saying that you have a duty to remain attached to her.) Thomson believes that you would be doing nothing immoral if you insisted on being detached and the violinist died.

---

[14]Judith Jarvis Thomson, "A Defense of Abortion," in *Social Ethics: Morality and Social Policy,* 3d ed., ed. Thomas Mappes and Jane Zembaty.

Thomson says that a woman's being pregnant nonvoluntarily is like your being attached to the violinist nonvoluntarily. She did not choose to become pregnant, did not take actions with the intention of and designed to make her pregnant. True, she may have voluntarily engaged in sexual intercourse, but that is not the same as acting with the intention of getting pregnant. For example, consider a couple who uses contraception during sex but experiences contraceptive failure. They took steps to prevent pregnancy. Surely pregnancy under those circumstances is involuntary. Does the involuntarily pregnant woman have a moral duty to remain "attached" to the fetus? Thomson maintains that if you don't have a moral duty to remain attached to the violinist to whom you have been nonvoluntarily attached, then the pregnant woman in this example does not have a moral duty to remain attached to the fetus and would not be doing anything wrong in having an abortion.

Moreover, not all sexual relations are voluntary. Obviously, rape is not voluntary. Incest is usually not voluntary, especially if the girl is a minor below the age of consent. A young girl below the legal age of consent is, whatever the circumstances, not competent to give her consent to sexual relations. Therefore, a girl who is pregnant and is below the age of consent cannot be considered to have engaged in sexual intercourse voluntarily and therefore cannot be considered to be pregnant voluntarily.

What if a man and a woman, both adults, voluntarily engage in sexual relations without using any form of contraception, but they do not intend pregnancy as an outcome? If the woman becomes pregnant as a result of voluntarily having sex without taking steps to prevent pregnancy, is her pregnancy voluntary? The behavior of the couple may be irresponsible and blameworthy, but it is not obvious that the pregnancy should be considered voluntary. To be fully voluntary, it seems that the behavior should have the intention of producing the outcome. But the couple in our example did not intend to conceive.

Thomson claims that if a woman becomes pregnant and the pregnancy is not voluntary or intentional, then she does not have a moral duty or obligation to remain pregnant anymore than you would have a moral duty to remain attached to the violinist if you were nonvoluntarily attached to her. Critics may claim that you do have a moral duty to remain attached to the violinist (and that a woman has a moral duty to remain pregnant), or they may claim that the situation of your being nonvoluntarily attached to the violinist is so different from a woman's being nonvoluntarily pregnant that we can conclude nothing about abortion from reflecting on Thomson's example.

Finally, what if a woman is pregnant voluntarily? Suppose that a woman intentionally becomes pregnant because she wants to have a baby and then changes her mind and wants to terminate her pregnancy? Perhaps her husband or boyfriend has left her. Perhaps she has learned that continuing the pregnancy will harm her health. Perhaps she has learned that the fetus is severely damaged. Does she have an obligation or duty to the fetus to continue the pregnancy? We could reflect on a slight variation in Thomson's example. Suppose that you have agreed voluntarily to be attached to the violinist for nine months in order to save her life. However, after two weeks in the hospital attached to the violinist you discover that it will be far more burdensome than you anticipated when you agreed to be attached to her. Therefore, you decide that you no longer wish to let the violinist use your body. Do you have a duty to remain attached to her? Does the violinist have a moral right to continued use of your body? Would it be immoral for you to change your mind and insist on being disconnected from her, knowing that she will die? We might say that if you have a moral duty to remain attached to the violinist, then the woman has a moral duty to continue with her pregnancy. But if you do not have a moral duty to remain attached, then the woman does not have a moral duty to continue with her pregnancy. Similarly, if the violinist does not have a moral right to continued use of your body, then the fetus does not have a moral right to continued use of the woman's body. Does a fetus have a moral right to the use of its mother's body in order to remain alive, even if its mother does not wish to permit the fetus to use her body to remain alive?

MODERATE POSITIONS ON ABORTION

The right-to-life view and the most liberal view on abortion are extremes. Justice Blackmun's opinion in *Roe* v. *Wade* may be thought of as suggesting a more moderate view. Whereas a right-to-life advocate maintains that abortion is immoral from the moment of conception and a supporter of the most liberal view maintains that abortion at any stage of development is morally acceptable, *Roe* v. *Wade* sets a line at viability—the point at which a fetus is capable of living outside the womb. A moderate position on abortion would be that at some stages of fetal development abortion is morally acceptable but that at others it is not. This moderate view could be defended in at least two ways. We might maintain that although a fetus is not a person at conception, it becomes a person at some point before birth. Alternatively, a moderate might maintain that although a fetus is not fully an actual person before birth (the ninth month), the closer it comes to the ninth month, the closer it comes to being transformed from a potential person into an actual person. The more its (mental) potentialities become actualized, the more valuable its life becomes and the more deserving it is of respect and protection. For example, a moderate might maintain, with *Roe* v. *Wade,* that before viability a fetus is not enough of an actual person to make abortion immoral, but that after viability a fetus is close enough to being an actual person that abortion is immoral except when necessary to preserve the mother's life or physical health.

Stage of Development

Thus, moderates claim that whether abortion is morally acceptable depends on the *stage of development* of the fetus. Although moderates agree that the line should be drawn sometime after conception and before birth, they disagree on precisely where it should be drawn. Most moderates agree that abortion in the early stages of pregnancy (within the first three months) is morally acceptable and that abortion in the late stages of pregnancy (after the sixth month) is immoral unless it is necessary to preserve the mother's life or physical health. However, within the period from the third to the sixth month, they differ on the precise point before which abortion is morally acceptable and beyond which abortion is immoral.

L. W. Sumner, for example, maintains that there are degrees or grades of personhood or moral standing. The greater an organism's developed capacities for thought, emotion, and feeling, the higher is its moral standing. The highest moral standing is full personhood, but because organisms can have none, some, or all of the characteristics associated with full personhood, and because many of these characteristics are themselves a matter of degree, there are degrees of personhood. According to Sumner, the aspect of consciousness called sentience is the most basic indicator of an organism's moral standing. "Sentience is the capacity for feeling. . . . In its most primitive form it is the ability to experience sensations of pleasure and pain, and thus the ability to enjoy and suffer."[15] In his view, an organism that is conscious or sentient, unlike one that is not sentient, is sufficiently like a full person to merit substantial protection. What gives an organism moral standing is not necessarily whether it can think, but whether it can feel and suffer.

According to Sumner, the existence of a developed forebrain is necessary for sentience. It does not appear in a human fetus until roughly the end of the first trimester (three months) and is at least minimally functional by the beginning of the third trimester. "The threshold of sentience thus appears to fall in the second trimester."[16] Because there is no sudden leap from nonsentience into sentience, no precise line can be drawn. Rather, Sumner refers to an early abortion as one that occurs sometime during the first trimester or early in the second trimester and a late abortion as one that occurs sometime in the third trimester or late in the second trimester. He then concludes, "An early abortion belongs in the same moral category as contraception. . . . A late abortion belongs in the same category as infanticide."[17] An early abortion does not violate any moral rights of a fetus because the fetus has no moral rights at that stage of development; therefore, abortion is morally acceptable. A late abortion *may* violate a fetus's moral rights because as it becomes sentient, it gains moral standing. Sumner emphasizes that the earlier an abortion is, the more morally acceptable it is.

According to Sumner, late abortions must be evaluated on a case-by-case basis. With early abortions, *any* reason a woman has justifies abortion; with late abortions, however, only very serious reasons can justify it. Sumner mentions as justifying reasons protecting the life, physical health, or mental health of the mother, as well as fetal deformity. Because a woman can choose to have an abortion early in her pregnancy, Sumner argues, "if a woman freely elects to continue a pregnancy past that stage, she will thereafter need a serious reason to end it."[18] The following diagram summarizes Sumner's position:

---

[15]L. W. Sumner, *Abortion and Moral Theory* (Princeton, NJ: Princeton University Press, 1981), p. 142.

[16]Ibid., p. 149.

[17]Ibid., p. 151.

[18]Ibid., p. 153.

```
●————————————————●————————————————●————————————————●
0                    3 months              6 months           9 months
Conception                                 Viability          Birth
←   Abortion like contraception    →←    Abortion like infanticide      →
```

Reasons for Wanting an Abortion

According to Sumner, any reason justifies an early abortion, but only very serious reasons can justify late abortions. This distinction introduces another variable: the *reasons for wanting an abortion*. Moderates may disagree on what reasons justify abortion, whether early or late. A woman might seek an abortion for many reasons. Pregnancy may be a threat to her life, her physical health, or her mental health. Pregnancy caused by rape or incest, if not terminated, may cause serious psychological damage. Pregnancy for a teenager may cause serious familial, social, or economic hardship. Pregnancy may interfere with a woman's education, career, or career plans, and may be an economic hardship. Finally, pregnancy may simply be unwanted and unplanned. It may be the result of unprotected sexual intercourse due to carelessness or ignorance, or the result of contraceptive failure. What reasons justify an abortion early or late in pregnancy?

An enormous number of answers are possible. For example, a moderate could claim that it would be morally acceptable for a woman to have an abortion at *any* stage of her pregnancy if it's necessary to preserve her life or physical health; that it would be morally acceptable only in the early stages of pregnancy if it's for financial reasons; and that it would not be morally acceptable at any stage of development if it's because one does not like the sex of the fetus. Consider the following list of reasons. In your view, which would be good reasons, and which would not be good reasons for (1) an early abortion and (2) a late abortion? (How would you defend your judgment?)

teenage pregnancy	badly damaged fetus (severe retardation)
sex selection	mother's physical health
mother's mental health	woman unmarried
family size	money
career	interferes with planned vacation
rape	incest

SHOULD ABORTION BE LEGALLY PERMITTED?

Whether and under what circumstances abortion is morally acceptable is one question; whether and under what circumstances abortion should be legally permitted is another question. For example, even if we believe that early abortions are immoral, we may believe that they should be legally permitted. After all, many people believe that not everything that is immoral should be made illegal. We may believe that women should have the legal right to decide for themselves whether to terminate a pregnancy because we place a high value on autonomy and liberty, we believe that a woman should be able to control her own body, and we believe that it is not appropriate for government to force women to remain pregnant against their wills.

Advocates of the right-to-life position may be what we will call antichoice. The antichoice position advocates making abortion illegal at any stage of development except for certain dire circumstances. Some people in the antichoice camp believe that abortion should be legally permitted only when it is necessary to preserve the life or physical health of the mother. Others believe that abortion should also be legally permitted if there are serious threats to a mother's mental health, such as those that may arise if pregnancy is due to rape or incest. Generally, people are antichoice because they believe that at conception a fetus is a full person with a moral right to life that overrides any less fundamental moral rights of its mother. In their view, the government has a duty to prevent people from violating one another's right to life. They maintain that for the government to permit women to choose abortion for any reason other than self-preservation is equivalent to permitting women to commit murder. They claim that people should not be given such choices. Therefore, the antichoice position generally opposes *Roe* v. *Wade*.

The most liberal position would presumably make abortion legally permissible at any stage of fetal development, for any reason. Because the fetus is not a person, it has no moral rights that would conflict with a woman's moral right to control her body. Furthermore, government does not have a duty to protect the life of a fetus because it has no moral standing. In their view, a woman's right to choose whether to continue or terminate a pregnancy should be absolute. However, in practice even the most liberal position may not entail that it is morally acceptable to destroy a fetus at any stage of development, even one day prior to birth. At viability a fetus is capable of surviving outside the womb. Therefore, after viability a pregnancy can be terminated without necessarily killing the fetus. An advocate of the liberal position could insist that if a woman chooses to terminate a pregnancy after viability, she may do so, but that in most circumstances every effort must be made to save the life of the fetus. If the fetus's life is saved and the mother does not want the infant, it may be put up for adoption or supported and raised by the state. Thus, an advocate of the most liberal position on abortion *could* forbid intentionally destroying a healthy, normal fetus after viability while maintaining that a woman's right to terminate a pregnancy at any stage is absolute.

The moderate position is generally that early abortions should be legally permitted for any reason. Because the fetus is not sentient, it has no moral standing that conflicts with the mother's rights. However, most moderates would probably agree that late abortions should be legally permitted only under certain very serious circumstances—for example, to preserve the life, physical health, or mental health of the mother or because of severe damage to the fetus—because sometime during the second trimester the fetus becomes sentient and gains moral standing. Because it is very personlike by this time, it has a moral right to life that only the most serious interests of the mother can justify overriding. Because of its moral standing, the state has a duty to provide it some protection.

Utilitarian Considerations

Those who believe that abortion should be legally permitted for any reason, at least in the early stages of pregnancy, also offer utilitarian reasons to support their position. In their view, the good consequences outweigh the bad consequences of such a policy. They maintain that in the long run, legalizing abortion saves the lives and health of countless women. They argue that making abortion illegal does not prevent abortion; it only drives it underground. History has shown that many women who don't want to be pregnant will find a way to terminate their pregnancies regardless of the laws. Laws against abortion were not much more effective than prohibition laws against alcoholic beverages. When abortion is illegal, it is often unsafe. If abortion is illegal, many women will be harmed by unsafe abortions, harm that can be avoided if abortion is legal. Then, too, the social costs of enforcing laws against abortion can be considerable. The sight of doctors who have performed abortions and women who have undergone abortions being sent to jail may be chilling. And the resources spent on detecting abortions, prosecuting the parties involved, and punishing those convicted may be considerable.

Public Funding of Abortion

A final issue involves the question of public funding of abortions for poor women. Abortions cost money—more money than poor women can afford. If a poor woman wants an abortion but can't afford it, should government health-care programs pay for it?

Opponents of public funding argue that abortion is immoral and that having the government pay for abortions means paying for and encouraging immoral behavior—murder. They also object to having their tax dollars used for purposes of which they strongly disapprove. Proponents of public funding argue that as long as abortion is legally permitted, it should be available to rich and poor alike. They claim that poor women rely upon government funds for their health care because they can't afford to pay for health care on their own. To deny government funds for abortions for poor women denies them an important component of health care readily available to the nonpoor. Proponents of public funding argue that to deny public funding to poor women has the same effect as making abortion legally permissible for the nonpoor but legally prohibited to the poor. That difference, they claim, is unjust.

EXERCISES

1. At what stage of development, if any, and for what reasons, if any, is abortion morally acceptable? Defend your answer.

2. Suppose that an advocate of the right-to-life position maintains that because a woman can always choose to give up an unwanted infant for adoption, abortion is morally acceptable only if it is necessary to preserve the mother's life or physical health. Do you agree? Why or why not?

3. Suppose that in the United States there is a high demand for white babies for adoption but a very low demand for nonwhite babies. What effect would that situation have on your answer to question 2? Why?

4. Do you agree with the moderate position that at least in the early stages of its development, a fetus does not have a moral right to life that could outweigh its mother's moral right to control her body because it is not sentient and therefore not sufficiently personlike? Defend your answer.

5. Should abortion be legal? If yes, under what conditions? Defend your answer.

6. Should there be public funding of abortions for poor women? Defend your answer.

7. If a poor woman has an unwanted pregnancy and cannot afford an abortion, who should have responsibility for the financial burden of supporting the child until he or she reaches maturity? Defend your answer.

8. Should minors have to have one or both parents' consent before they can legally undergo an abortion? Defend your answer.

SUGGESTED READINGS

Jane English. "Abortion and the Concept of a Person." In *Social Ethics: Morality and Social Policy,* 3d ed., edited by Thomas Mappes and Jane Zembaty. New York: McGraw-Hill, 1987.

John T. Noonan, Jr. "An Almost Absolute Value in History." In *Social Ethics: Morality and Social Policy,* 3d ed., edited by Thomas Mappes and Jane Zembaty. New York: McGraw-Hill, 1987.

L. W. Sumner. *Abortion and Moral Theory.* Princeton, NJ: Princeton University Press, 1981.

Mary Anne Warren. "On the Moral and Legal Status of Abortion." In *Social Ethics: Morality and Social Policy,* 3d ed., edited by Thomas Mappes and Jane Zembaty. New York: McGraw-Hill, 1987.

CHAPTER 16

Crime and Punishment

In February 1997 the U. S. Centers for Disease Control and Prevention released a report that revealed that the United States has the "highest rates of childhood homicide, suicide, and firearms-related deaths of any of the world's 26 richest nations. . . . The statistics show that the epidemic of violence that has hit younger and younger children in recent years is confined almost exclusively to the United States."[1] Proposed explanations include the historically low level of funding for social programs in the United States; the growing number of families in which both parents work, leaving children unsupervised; the growing number of single-parent families; the ready availability of guns, given that almost half of American households own firearms; and the social acceptability of violence in the United States.

Crime, especially violent crime, has always been a preoccupation of our society. We fear for our safety and for our property. We want the government to protect us from crime and criminals. Political careers can be made or broken on the issue of crime. We are repelled and frightened by crime, but we are also fascinated by it. Consider how many books, movies, and television programs focus on murder, rape, and robbery. More space or time in most of the news media focuses on crime than on politics or economics. Managers of newspapers and television news stations know that crime draws viewers or readers. Paradoxically, although Americans' fears about violence have been growing, the statistics show that since 1979 crime rates and the overall rate of violence in the United States have been steadily declining. And although we tend to identify crime with violence, according to Joseph Davey, "Homicide . . . accounts for .10 percent of the total serious felonies committed each year."[2]

---

[1]"U.S. Leads in Violent Child Death," *Daily Hampshire Gazette* (Northampton, MA), February 7, 1997, p. 4.

[2]Joseph Dillon Davey, *The New Social Contract: America's Journey from Welfare State to Police State* (Westport, CT: Praeger, 1995), p. 55.

CRIMINALIZING BEHAVIOR

That some actions constitute crimes and others do not is a result of human decisions. We decide (or governments decide) what is and is not a crime. Prior to the Prohibition era, producing, selling, buying, and consuming alcohol were not crimes. However, once the government passed laws prohibiting these activities, they became crimes. Then, when those laws were repealed, they stopped being crimes.

We often associate crime with violence, but not all crimes are violent. Crimes such as murder, rape, and kidnapping are violent, but embezzlement, perjury, and cheating on one's income taxes are not. Lawrence Friedman notes, "It is conventional to draw a line between property crimes, crimes against the person, morals offenses, offenses against public order, and regulatory crimes."[3] Property crimes include theft and burglary. Crimes against the person include murder, attempted murder, rape, and assault and battery. Morals offenses might include sodomy, prostitution, drug dealing, and gambling. Offenses against public order might include public drunkenness. Regulatory crimes might include fraud, insider trading, and polluting the air or water. As Friedman puts it, "All crimes are acts that society, or at least some dominant elements in society, sees as threats."[4] But criminal law also reflects a society's values and norms, its moral beliefs. Generally, acts are made crimes in a society because the society (or its dominant elements) considers the acts wrong. Not every act considered wrong is made a crime, but in general, only acts considered wrong are made crimes.

In Puritan times in New England, heresy was a crime. Heresy is proclaiming or believing doctrines that are rejected by the majority (or the powerful) in a community. Jesuits (a Roman Catholic religious order) and Quakers were heretics. They were banished for the crime of heresy. If they returned after being banished, they were hanged. Blasphemy was also a crime. One who denied the Trinity, the divinity of Jesus, the truth of the Bible, or the existence of God was guilty of blasphemy and was punished. Friedman explains, "Religion was the cornerstone of their community. It was the duty of law to uphold, encourage, and enforce true religion."[5] The laws upheld what the community considered God's Laws. Because the Puritans considered bestiality contrary to God's Law, a sin, they made it a crime punishable by death. In 1642 a 17-year-old boy was put to death for having had sex with several animals, including a cow, a sheep, and a horse. Fornication (sex between unmarried people) and adultery were also crimes. Adultery was (sometimes) punishable by death.

Besides banishment and execution, punishments included fines, being put in the stocks for public humiliation, whipping, branding, and mutilation. There were no prisons. Executions were relatively rare. Friedman writes that there

---

[3]Lawrence M. Friedman, *Crime and Punishment in American History* (New York: Basic Books, 1993), p. 7.

[4]Ibid., p. 8.

[5]Ibid., p. 33

were fifteen executions in the Massachusetts Bay colony prior to 1660: "four for murder, two for infanticide, three for sexual offenses, two for witchcraft," and four for the crime of being Quakers.[6] Then there were the infamous Salem witch trials of the 1690s during which twenty people were killed.

Friedman traces the evolution of criminal law in American history. "Law protects power and property; it safeguards wealth, and, by the same token, it perpetuates the subordinate status of the people on the bottom."[7] For example, in the South prior to the Civil War, slaves were property. The criminal law protected their masters, not them. A master could whip a slave to death, and it was not a crime. In many Southern states, it was a crime to teach a slave to read. Helping or inciting a slave to escape was a crime. Even speaking out against slavery and criticizing the institution was a crime in some Southern states. After the Civil War, the criminal law in the South still did not provide equal protection to blacks and whites. Many laws made integration a crime. Forced segregation was not a crime. Criminal acts by whites against blacks, including lynching and intimidation, frequently went unpunished. It was not a crime to deny blacks the right to vote. "And the criminal justice system was lily-white: there were no black police, prosecutors, judges, or jurors."[8]

African Americans were not the only ones not protected by the criminal law. It was not a crime in the United States to steal land from Native Americans, or even to kill them. The poor also fared ill. "Vagrancy" (which is vague enough to mean almost anything, including simply not having enough money on one's person) was a crime that was limited to the poor. Similarly, much union activity was illegal, including strikes. The law tended to side with employers rather than employees.

Gradually, whole new categories of crime evolved. Criminalization of drug use began in the 1880s. The first target was opium. Cocaine followed in the late 1890s. Some laws attempted to protect the powerless from the powerful; others merely created the appearance of protecting the powerless from the powerful. (An act may be a crime, but if the law is not enforced or the penalties are mild, the law is a charade.) Around the turn of the century it became a crime to engage in monopolistic practices or to sell adulterated products. More recently it became a crime to dump hazardous waste or pollute the air and water. Today civil rights violations are crimes, as are racially motivated "hate crimes."

PUNISHMENT

We want criminals punished, whether for violent street crime or white-collar crime. Punishment serves several purposes. Perhaps most fundamental is social protection: We want punishment to make society safer from crime. We assume that the threat of punishment will deter people from committing crimes; that is,

[6]Ibid., p. 42.

[7]Ibid., p. 81.

[8]Ibid., p. 96.

if people believe there is a high probability of being caught, convicted, and punished for committing crimes, they will be less likely to commit crimes. We also want to reform people who have already committed crimes so that they will not commit any more crimes. Punishment may create enough fear that the criminal will avoid further criminal behavior in order to avoid further punishment. Punishment may also rehabilitate, transforming a criminal's character and personality, enabling him to "see the error of his ways." Finally, if a criminal is considered a threat to society, for the protection of society he can be physically removed. He may be banished, incarcerated, or killed.

When the purpose or function of punishment is social protection, we look primarily at the future consequences of punishment in terms of its effect on crime rates. One important issue is a practical one: What form of punishment works best in terms of reducing crime rates? But punishment is not the only way to reduce crime. If we can gain knowledge about the causes of crime—what factors or conditions tend to increase or decrease crime rates—we might be able to use this knowledge to try policies of crime prevention. If substance abuse, such as alcoholism or drug use, increases the incidence of crimes such as robbery, murder, and assault, then perhaps increased availability of substance-abuse rehabilitation programs can reduce crime. If poverty increases the incidence of crime, programs to fight poverty might be effective. If inadequate or unequal educational opportunity contributes to crime, improving education might be effective. If mental-health problems, either of an individual or of an entire family—for example, physical abuse, neglect, or substance abuse—contribute to criminal behavior, then increased availability of mental-health programs might help.

Finally, punishment has at least one more purpose or function. Often we punish people not because we think it will correct their behavior but because we think that they simply deserve to be punished. Having seriously hurt society or an individual creates a kind of imbalance that must be righted by hurting in return the guilty offender who caused the hurt and created the imbalance. Criminals are said to have a "debt" to society that they must pay, and they pay it by absorbing punishment. Linked to this purpose of punishment is the desire for revenge. We want to hurt people who have hurt us, to "pay back" people in their own coin.

In the past, society did not rely on incarceration for the purposes of punishment, but rather on fines, public humiliation, physical punishment, and execution. Since around the time of the Civil War, however, imprisonment has been the punishment of choice for a wide variety of crimes, violent and nonviolent, and more money is spent on criminal incarceration each year. Between 1973 and 1991 the prison population in the United States grew from 93 per 100,000 population to 292 per 100,000.[9] In 1992 the population of U.S. jails and prisons was 1.25 million; by 1994 that number had risen to 1.5 million.[10] (Although blacks

---

[9]Ibid., p. 61.

[10]U.S. Bureau of the Census, *Statistical Abstract of the United States, 1996,* Tables 349 and 350.

comprise only about 12 percent of the U.S. population, they comprise 42 percent of inmates in jails and 47.3 percent of inmates in state prisons.)[11] Joseph Davey points out that during the 1980s, when tax cut fever struck and expenditures on federal and state social programs were slashed, expenditures on the criminal justice system skyrocketed. In 1982 the federal government spent $4.5 billion on the criminal justice system; in 1992 that figure rose to $17.4 billion. State and local governments spent $31.6 billion in 1982 and $80.3 billion in 1992.[12] Much of that money went to the prison system for construction, operating expenses, and personnel.

According to Davey, much of the rise in the prison population is due to the war on drugs. "The Justice Department estimates that in 1995 more than two-thirds of the convicts in federal prisons are inside for drug offenses."[13] Although we treat the drug problem as a criminal issue, Davey says, "most researchers in the area of drug abuse view the problem either as an emotional problem that can be alleviated only by psychological changes in the individual abuser or as a reflection of underlying social problems that can be alleviated only by social, political, and economic changes."[14] Prisons are being flooded with people convicted of such nonviolent crimes as drug selling and drug possession; prison sentences for violent offenders are being reduced to make room for them. Davey points out that the average prison sentence for violent offenders in U.S. district courts in 1985 was 135.4 months but by 1991 that figure was down to 91.2 months. At the same time the average sentence for nonviolent drug offenders (convicted of sale or possession) rose from 58.2 months to 84.5 months.[15] Ninety percent of the funds for the war on drugs is spent on law enforcement while only about 10 percent goes to education, prevention, and rehabilitation programs.

WHAT SHOULD WE DO?

If we want to reduce crime, what are the most effective means? Some argue that we should take a kind of public-health attitude toward crime and focus more on crime prevention—attacking the conditions that cause, influence, or contribute to crime, such as poverty, racism, substance abuse, psychological problems, and inadequate education. Others maintain that we should focus on punishment to deter and correct. But what form of punishment is most effective? Imprisonment? Fines? Community service? Corporal punishment (flogging)? Mutilation (such as amputation, blinding, or castration)? Execution? Of course, no form of punishment will be effective if most criminals believe they will not get caught or, if caught, will not be convicted (they'll "beat the rap"). So a system

---

[11]Ibid., Tables 349 and 351.

[12]Ibid., Table 333.

[13]Davey, *New Social Contract*, p. 128.

[14]Ibid., p. 137.

[15]Ibid., p. 142.

that relies on punishment, whatever form the punishment may take, must also consider its ability to apprehend and convict offenders.

But is effectiveness the only consideration? Many people argue that the punishment should be proportional to the crime—neither more nor less severe than the crime merits. Today we are appalled by such punishments as cutting off a person's hands for stealing a loaf of bread or hanging for cattle rustling, even if they would be effective in reducing the crime rate. (In fact, government soon learned that the severer the penalty, the less likely it was that a jury would vote to convict. Suppose that you were a member of a jury and you were convinced that the accused was guilty of stealing a loaf of bread. Would you be likely to vote for conviction if you knew it would send the thief to the gallows?) On the other hand, if a person were fined five dollars for murder, we would be appalled for the opposite reason. The penalty is far too slight for such a crime. What are the criteria of appropriateness or proportionality between a crime and its punishment?

With imprisonment, several questions arise. How long should sentences be? Should we imprison a person for life for stealing a car or cheating on income taxes? In our society, people are generally sent to prison for limited times rather than for life. But if we care about reducing crime, we want to ensure that a person will emerge from prison less likely rather than more likely to commit additional crimes. We might be tempted to try to make prison conditions so horrendous that no sane person would wish to do anything that might lead to his being returned to prison. But such prison conditions can actually make people worse than they were, failing to address or even exacerbating problems such as substance abuse, poverty, inadequate education, poor impulse control, and other psychological problems that led to crime in the first place. Prisons can actually be training schools for crime. Then, we might ask, should prison conditions be improved? Or should we rely less on prison, especially for nonviolent offenders, and more on alternative forms of punishment? Should we consider public flogging or even mutilation for some offenses?

We can also ask questions about age. Should a 10-year-old, a 15-year-old, a 20-year-old, and a 25-year-old be treated the same for the same offense? Should we execute or imprison for life 10-year-olds for murder if we execute or imprison for life 25-year-olds for murder? In our society, we do not consider 10-year-olds to be fully competent. They are not capable of fully rational decision making. They lack the maturity, experience, and knowledge required for full responsibility. Also, they are considered more amenable to rehabilitation and reform because their character and personalities are not yet fully formed. As "juveniles," they are treated differently from adults. But at what age does a juvenile become an adult, fully competent and rational? We may agree that a 10-year-old should not be treated as an adult, but what about a 12- or 13-year-old? Should we set the boundary between juvenile and adult offenders at age 14? 16? 18? 21? How do we defend the choice of boundary?

Other questions arise concerning mental and intellectual functioning. Should we treat all offenders convicted of the same crime alike even if some are mentally handicapped? Would it be just? How much of a handicap would justify differential treatment? What if a person's intelligence, as measured by IQ tests, is well below normal—say, below 90, or 80, or 70? What if an offender is diagnosed as having a severe personality disorder or psychosis? These questions and others like them need to be addressed. Some of the moral theories we have examined in the previous chapters should be helpful in answering these questions.

At this point we will turn our attention to one particular kind of punishment—capital punishment.

CAPITAL PUNISHMENT

The United States is the only nation in the developed world that still permits capital punishment. Not all U.S. states permit capital punishment, but most do, and public support for capital punishment is high. Is capital punishment morally acceptable?

One line of argument focuses on the effectiveness of the death penalty in reducing the incidence of those crimes to which it may be applied (generally premeditated murder). Supporters of capital punishment maintain that the threat of death is more of a deterrent than the threat of other, lesser forms of punishment, such as imprisonment. It also is the only form of punishment that guarantees that a murderer will not murder again. Supporters of capital punishment argue that since it is the most effective form of social protection, it is morally acceptable to rely on it. We might formalize the argument in one of two ways. First,

Capital punishment is the most effective way to reduce the murder rate.

It is morally acceptable to do whatever is most effective in reducing the murder rate.

Therefore, capital punishment is morally acceptable.

Second,

Capital punishment is an effective way to reduce the murder rate.

It is morally acceptable to do whatever is effective in reducing the murder rate.

Therefore, capital punishment is morally acceptable.

Another argument for capital punishment maintains that those who commit premeditated murder *deserve* to die. They say that death is the only punishment proportional to or appropriate for a crime that involves the killing of innocent people.

A third argument maintains that capital punishment is less costly to taxpayers than alternatives. People complain that citizens should not be taxed in order to keep murderers alive. This argument might be formalized as follows:

Capital punishment is less costly to taxpayers than alternative forms of punishment.

Whatever punishment is least costly to taxpayers is morally acceptable.

Therefore, capital punishment is morally acceptable.

A fourth argument for capital punishment focuses on the good consequences of executions for the kin of victims of violence. Relatives of victims are often filled with hate and rage for the murderer of their loved ones, and they may get relief from knowing that the murderer has been executed. We might formalize this argument as follows:

Relatives of victims of violence get psychic relief from the execution of the murderer of their loved ones.

Whatever brings psychic relief to relatives of victims of violence is morally acceptable.

Therefore, capital punishment is morally acceptable.

Finally, some people point to biblical passages, such as that in Exodus 21:23–24 requiring "life for life, eye for eye, tooth for tooth," as showing that God's Law permits the penalty of death.

OBJECTIONS TO CAPITAL PUNISHMENT

Effectiveness as Deterrence

Opponents of capital punishment argue that execution is not necessary to prevent murderers from murdering again. In their view, removing a murderer from society by imprisoning him provides sufficient social protection. If a murderer will pose a threat to society as long as he lives, then he can be imprisoned for life. The probability of a murderer killing again can be made extremely low by reforming or abolishing parole and by increasing prison security.

Further, opponents of capital punishment claim that the threat of death is no more effective a deterrent than the threat of a long prison sentence. Many studies have compared the incidence of murder in jurisdictions that have capital punishment with the incidence of murder in jurisdictions that don't have capital punishment. If capital punishment is the most effective deterrent, we would expect to find that the incidence of murder in jurisdictions *with* capital punishment would be lower than the incidence of murder in jurisdictions *without* capital punishment. However, years of social science research have failed to provide any evidence that the death penalty is a more effective deterrent than other forms of punishment. One researcher in the mid-1970s summarized the evidence on the deterrent effect of capital punishment as follows: "If there is one, it can only be minute, since not one of the many research approaches—from the simplest to the most sophisticated—was able to find it."[16] More recently, the authors of a study of murder rates between 1976 and 1987 concluded,

> We find no consistent evidence that the availability of capital punishment, the number of executions, the amount of television coverage they receive, . . . is associated significantly with rates for total and different types of felony murder. These findings are consistent with the vast majority of studies of capital punishment.[17]

Why wouldn't the threat of death be a greater deterrent than the threat of a long prison sentence? Research on deterrence suggests that the probability of being apprehended, convicted, and punished is more important in deterring crime than is the severity of the punishment. If people believe that the probability of being apprehended, convicted, and punished is low, crime rises; if people believe that the probability of being apprehended, convicted, and punished is high, crime declines.[18] No threatened punishment, however severe, will deter people who believe that there's a high probability that they can escape it. However, studies suggest that less severe forms of punishment such as imprisonment will be as effective in deterring crime as more severe forms of punishment such as death if people believe that there is a high probability of their not being able to escape punishment. Therefore, increasing the probability of detection and conviction will do more to deter crime than will increasing the severity of the punishment threatened.

The people most likely to commit violent crimes such as murder are also the least likely to be deterred by the threat of punishment, even if the punishment is death. British psychiatrist Anthony Storr claims that a certain very small minority of individuals is responsible for most of the violent crime in Western societies. A combination of genetic and environmental influences makes some people "antisocial" and predisposes them to violence; alcohol and drug use makes matters worse, suppressing ordinary inhibitions against violence. Storr believes that whereas the ordinary individual will be deterred from violence by the threat of relatively moderate punishment, antisocial people will not easily be deterred by any threatened punishment, even death. Many antisocial people have poor impulse control; many have low self-esteem; many have a sense of grievance and an excess of rage for the damage done to them by family or society—characteristics that reduce the probability that threats of severe punishment will prevent them from violent behavior. An individual who is under the influence of alcohol

---

[16]Hans Zeisel, "The Deterrent Effect of the Death Penalty: Fact and Faith," in *The Death Penalty in America,* 3d ed., ed. Hugo Adam Bedau (New York: Oxford University Press, 1982), p. 133.

[17]Ruth Peterson and William Bailey, "Felony Murder and Capital Punishment: An Examination of the Deterrence Question," *Criminology,* August 1991, p. 388.

[18]Peter Greenwood, "The Violent Offender in the Criminal Justice System," in *Violence: Patterns, Causes, Public Policy,* ed. Neil Weiner, Margaret Zahn, and Rita Sagi (Orlando, FL: Harcourt Brace Jovanovich, 1990), pp. 339–340.

or drugs is even less likely to have self-control or be able to rationally consider the probable consequences of violent behavior, regardless of the potential punishment. For such people under such conditions, the threat of death will be no more effective than any other threatened punishment.[19]

Moral Considerations

Some critics of capital punishment maintain that the effectiveness of executions as a deterrent does not settle the issue of its moral acceptability. In their view, even if it were proved conclusively that execution is a more effective deterrent than life imprisonment, that would not prove that executing murderers is morally acceptable. Suppose we discovered that slowly torturing murderers to death was a more effective deterrent than putting them to death swiftly and painlessly. Would the fact that it was a more effective deterrent justify slowly torturing murderers to death? Many people say no. They believe that there are levels to which civilized, humane people should not stoop even for social protection. They believe not only that slowly torturing murderers to death goes below that level but that even swift and painless execution of murderers goes below that level.

Many opponents of capital punishment point out that the criminal justice system is far from infallible. People can be, and have been, convicted of crimes they did not commit. Investigations can be sloppy and incompetent; prosecutors and police can conspire to deny someone a fair trial, suppressing or manufacturing evidence, bribing or intimidating witnesses; people can be represented by incompetent or ill-prepared defense attorneys; witnesses can be mistaken. Opponents of capital punishment argue that mistakes are inevitable. Even if the judge, jury, and public feel certain that a person is guilty, there's always some possibility that they're mistaken. What happens when (not if) mistakes are made? If the innocent person is in jail and the mistake is discovered, she can be released and compensated. However, if she has been executed, there is no way to rectify the mistake; death is final and irrevocable. Even if the mistake is not discovered, opponents of capital punishment maintain, it's far worse to execute an innocent person than to imprison her for life; they believe that executing an innocent person is a moral tragedy of the highest order. The only way to guarantee that innocent people will not be executed by mistake is to eliminate the death penalty. And they believe that it's more important to guarantee that we don't execute innocent people than it is to ensure that guilty people are executed or even to deter crime.

Supporters of capital punishment claim that the death penalty is the most effective way to send the message that society will not tolerate violence and therefore to reduce the level of violence in our society. However, many opponents of capital punishment claim that executing criminals brutalizes society and desensitizes people to violence. In their view, having the government resort

---

[19]Anthony Storr, *Human Destructiveness* (New York: Ballantine, 1991).

to violence sends the message that violence is a legitimate solution to problems. They argue that using violence to send the message that violence is intolerable and unacceptable is self-contradictory. Rather than reducing the violence in our society, they believe that capital punishment increases it.

In addition, opponents of capital punishment point out that the application of capital punishment in the United States has been discriminatory. Between 1930 and 1987, "more blacks than whites [were] executed, and nearly 90 percent of those who died for rape were blacks."[20] Similarly, "a study using data from Florida for 1973 to 1977 found that the race of both the defendant and the victim influenced the classification of homicides by the police and by prosecutors in a way that increased the likelihood that the death penalty would be imposed on blacks."[21] Because racism has plagued our society for generations and still has not been eradicated, racism can all too easily infect our criminal justice system. From 1930 to 1990, 4,002 people were executed in the United States.[22] More than 50 percent of them (2,122) were black, although blacks have never made up more than roughly 12 percent of the total population. At the same time, people executed are generally poor and ill educated. A middle- or upper-class white person is far less likely to be sentenced to death than a poor person— black, white, or Hispanic—even if their crimes are identical. Opponents of capital punishment claim that the death penalty is inherently discriminatory because police, prosecutors, judges, and juries cannot wholly escape the taint of racism and bias. African-Americans, Hispanics, and the poor in general will always be far more likely than anyone else to be sentenced to death. Because it is so sensitive to racism and other forms of illegitimate discrimination, capital punishment is immoral.

Supporters of capital punishment admit that discrimination is unjust, but they insist that the criminal justice system can be reformed in such a way as to minimize the effect of racism and prejudice on death sentences. They insist that the death penalty is not *inherently* discriminatory. The extent to which reforms to combat bias can or will be implemented remains to be seen.

As for the argument that executing murderers saves tax dollars that can be used for more important purposes, numerous studies have shown that executing someone actually costs far more than would imprisoning him for life. Why? To minimize the risk of executing innocent people, there is an elaborate—and very expensive—appeals process before a death sentence can be carried out. To make the death penalty cheaper than life in prison, the appeals process would have to be drastically curtailed, thereby reducing the protections against executing the innocent. Perhaps more to the point, however, opponents of the death penalty condemn any attempt to weigh dollars against lives. They say that even if execution were cheaper than life in prison, a human life is more valuable or significant than money. A criminal is still a person with inherent worth and

---

[20]Hugh D. Barlow, *Introduction to Criminology,* 5th ed. (Glenview, IL: Scott, Foresman, 1990), p. 497.

[21]John E. Conklin, *Criminology,* 4th ed. (New York: Macmillan, 1992), p. 415.

[22]*The American Almanac: 1992–1993* (Austin, TX: Reference Press, 1992), p. 200.

a right to life that cannot be forfeited, even by evil behavior, or justifiably over-ridden.

Finally, opponents of the death penalty point out that people can change. People who are a threat to society at one time may no longer be a threat at another time. A cold-blooded murderer may experience a personality and character transformation; a cruel and callous person can become kind and compassionate; violent impulses can be extinguished or people can learn to control them. Imprisonment leaves open the possibility of rehabilitation. Opponents of the death penalty believe that people should be given the chance to reform and change, an option that execution closes.

Given the considerable time that often elapses between conviction and execution, people may have already undergone substantial change by the time they face the death penalty. In a sense, they may no longer be the same persons who committed the crime or who were sentenced to death. Opponents of the death penalty disapprove of executing a murderer who may have undergone such a change of heart.

Retribution

Opponents of capital punishment may deny that death is the most appropriate punishment for even the most depraved murderer. They may believe that such a view is based on relatively "primitive" passions and emotions, including hatred, fear, and desire for revenge, rather than upon reason, humane feelings, or the principles of an enlightened conscience. They recognize that such feelings in individuals are quite natural; the more brutal, cruel, or savage the crime, the more justified people are in feeling outrage. However, opponents of capital punishment argue that public policy should not be guided by such passions, feelings, and emotions. In their view, the feelings that underlie the judgment that death is the only appropriate punishment for murder are the same that led to cruel forms of torture and execution in the past, such as burning at the stake or being devoured alive by wild animals.

It's difficult to either prove or disprove the claims that death is the only appropriate punishment for murder and that public policy should be based on "an eye for an eye." On an individual level, perhaps all we can do is appeal to considerations of logical consistency. We could ask ourselves the following question: Would I believe that death is the most appropriate penalty for murder if the person convicted of murder were the person I love most? If the answer is no, the problem is obvious. If the answer is yes, it's difficult to know what more can be said.

EXERCISES

1. What, if anything, should be done to reduce illegal drug use in the United States? Defend your answer.

2. What should be done to reduce violent crime in the United States? Defend your answer.

3. Is Friedman correct when he says that the law "protects power and property . . . safeguards wealth, and . . . perpetuates the subordinate status of the people on the bottom"? Defend your answer.

4. Construct an argument to try to persuade an opponent of capital punishment that it is morally acceptable.

5. Construct an argument to try to persuade a supporter of capital punishment that it is immoral.

6. Would applying either formulation of Kant's Categorical Imperative yield the conclusion that capital punishment is immoral? Defend your answer.

7. Apply Rawls's hypothetical social contract approach to the question of capital punishment. Would rational, self-interested people in the Original Position behind the Veil of Ignorance agree to adopt capital punishment? Defend your answer.

8. Would a good person be in favor of or opposed to capital punishment? What virtues/vices, if any, would tend to make someone support capital punishment? What virtues/vices, if any, would tend to make someone oppose capital punishment? Defend your answers.

SUGGESTED READINGS

Hugo Adam Bedau, ed. *The Death Penalty in America.* 3d ed. New York: Oxford University Press, 1982.

Joseph Dillon Davey. *The New Social Contract: America's Journey from Welfare State to Police State.* New York: Praeger, 1995.

Lawrence M. Friedman. *Crime and Punishment in American History.* New York: Basic Books, 1993.

Jonathan Glover. *Causing Death and Saving Lives.* Harmondsworth, England: Penguin, 1977. (See Chapter 18.)

Thomas Mappes and Jane Zembaty, eds. *Social Ethics: Morality and Social Policy.* 3d ed. New York: McGraw-Hill, 1987. (See Chapter 3.)

Jeffrie G. Murphy, ed. *Punishment and Rehabilitation.* 3d ed. Belmont, CA: Wadsworth, 1995.

Jan Narveson, ed. *Moral Issues.* New York: Oxford University Press, 1983. (See Section III.)

Neil Weiner, Margaret Zahn, and Rita Sagi, eds. *Violence: Patterns, Causes, Public Policy.* Orlando, FL: Harcourt Brace Jovanich, 1990.

CHAPTER 17

Suicide

Paul Bradley, 64, is suffering from bowel cancer. His doctors have informed him that he probably has less than a year to live. Paul knows that bowel cancer causes increasingly intense pain that only larger and larger doses of morphine can control. Large doses of morphine will interfere with his mental functioning and will probably cause other unpleasant side effects. Because of his disease his body weight will fall rapidly, he will grow progressively weaker, and he will become increasingly helpless. He can expect to be bedridden the last few months of his life.

Before the onset of his illness, Paul was active and healthy. Like almost everyone, he had hoped to die a dignified, swift, and painless death at a ripe old age. Unfortunately, he knows that his death will be neither dignified, swift, nor painless if his illness is allowed to take its course. He does not wish to die in that way, and he does not want his family to suffer from watching him die slowly with their last memories of him images of a disease-ravaged shadow of his former self. After several days of reflection, Paul decides that he would rather commit suicide than let his disease slowly kill him. Would it be morally acceptable for him to commit suicide?

We may believe (1) that suicide is always immoral, regardless of the circumstances, (2) that suicide is never immoral, again regardless of the circumstances, or (3) that suicide is morally acceptable in some circumstances but not in others. According to (1) it would be immoral for Paul to commit suicide; according to (2) it would be morally acceptable. Whether it would be morally acceptable for him to commit suicide according to (3) depends on the circumstances. If we accept (3), we face the task of specifying both the circumstances in which suicide is morally acceptable and the circumstances in which it is immoral.

SUICIDE IN ANCIENT GREECE AND ROME

In his dialogue *Phaedo,* Plato, speaking through Socrates, condemned suicide.

> It probably seems strange that it [suicide] should not be right for those to whom death would be an advantage to benefit themselves. . . . [However], the allegory which the mystics tell us—that we men are put in a sort of guard

post, from which one must not release oneself or run away—seems to me to
be a high doctrine with difficult implications. All the same, . . . I believe that
this much is true, that the gods are our keepers, and we men are one of their
possessions. . . . If one of your possessions were to destroy itself without
intimation from you that you wanted it to die, wouldn't you be angry with it
and punish it . . . ? So if you look at it in this way I suppose it is not unreasonable to say that we must not put an end to ourselves until God sends some
compulsion.[1]

Plato did not consider the prohibition on suicide absolute. It would be at least
morally permissible, perhaps even morally required, to commit suicide if the
gods wanted us to commit suicide and sent some sign or "compulsion." It is
wrong only if we commit suicide without the gods' permission. Plato left open
the question of whether, and if so under what circumstances, the gods ever permit or require suicide.

In his much later work, *Laws,* Plato was more equivocal about suicide.

But what of him who takes [his own life]? I mean the man whose violence
frustrates the decree of destiny by *self-slaughter* though no sentence of the
state has required this of him, no stress of cruel and inevitable calamity driven
him to the act, and he has been involved in no desperate and intolerable disgrace, the man who thus gives unrighteous sentence against himself from
mere poltroonery and unmanly cowardice.[2]

Plato clearly disapproved of such suicides, maintaining that they must be buried
alone in an isolated, desolate spot. But here Plato's disapproval is limited to a certain kind of suicide. It does not apply to suicide caused by a sentence of the state,
cruel calamity, or intolerable disgrace. Rather, it condemns suicide that reflects
"unmanly cowardice." The implication is that not all suicides are manifestations
of cowardice; those that aren't may not deserve condemnation.

Aristotle also linked suicide with the excellence or virtue of courage.

Courage is a mean with respect to things that inspire confidence or fear. . . ;
and it chooses or endures things because it is noble to do so, or because it is
base not to do so. But to die to escape from poverty or love or anything
painful is not the mark of a brave man, but rather of a coward; for it is softness
to fly from what is troublesome, and such a man endures death not because it
is noble but to fly from evil.[3]

Again, the prohibition on suicide does not appear to be absolute. Aristotle condemns suicides that are manifestations of cowardice; if suicide is done from a
"noble" motive, it is not a manifestation of cowardice. What Aristotle would consider a noble motive may be open to question.

[1]Plato, "Phaedo," in *The Collected Dialogues of Plato,* ed. Edith Hamilton and Huntington Cairns
(Princeton, NJ: Princeton University Press, 1961), pp. 44–45 (62a–c).

[2]Plato, "Laws," in *Collected Dialogues of Plato,* ed. Hamilton and Cairns, p. 1432 (IX: 873 c–d).

[3]Aristotle, "Nichomachean Ethics," in *The Complete Works of Aristotle,* vol. 2, ed. Jonathan Barnes
(Princeton, NJ: Princeton University Press, 1984), p. 1762 (1116a 10–15).

Turning to Stoicism, we find that Stoics considered suicide to be appropriate under certain circumstances. As the Roman writer Cicero put it, "When a man has a preponderance of the things in accordance with nature, it is his proper function to remain alive; when he has or foresees a preponderance of their opposites, it is his proper function to depart from life."[4] Similarly, according to Diogenes Laertius, an important source of information on Stoic doctrine, "They [the Stoics] say that the wise man will commit a well-reasoned suicide both on behalf of his country and on behalf of his friends, and if he falls victim to unduly severe pain or mutilation or incurable illness."[5] The Stoics believed that human beings should do what is "natural" and follow reason. In their view, because suicide can be reasonable, suicide can be morally acceptable. For example, if someone is about to be tortured by the enemy in order to extract information that would harm his country and the only way that he can avoid revealing the information is by committing suicide, then according to the Stoics, suicide would be reasonable. It would be motivated by principle and love of country, which justifies suicide. Similarly, if disability, injury, or disease prevents or will prevent us from living a life appropriate to a human being, then ending our life is reasonable and morally acceptable.

There were a number of famous suicides in the ancient world. Cassius and Brutus, the assassins of Julius Caesar, committed suicide when it became clear that their cause was hopeless and that they faced dishonor at the hands of Julius Caesar's successor, Augustus. Similarly, Cleopatra committed suicide rather than fall into Augustus's hands and face the humiliation of being returned to Rome as a slave rather than a queen. Her lover, Mark Antony, also committed suicide. It was not uncommon for people in the Roman world to consider suicide in order to avoid disgrace both noble and courageous rather than a manifestation of cowardice. They believed in the slogan "Death before dishonor."

SUICIDE AND RELIGION

Many people believe that suicide is always immoral because according to their religious tradition, God sets an absolute prohibition on it. Jews and Christians often appeal to the Ten Commandments, one of which is "You shall not murder." Although some Jews and Christians consider suicide to be a form of murder—namely, self-murder—and therefore prohibited by God, others disagree. Just as the book of Exodus goes on to endorse capital punishment for a variety of crimes, clearly signaling that its authors do not consider executing certain wrongdoers murder, some may doubt that suicide constitutes murder. Even if we accept the Divine Command theory of morality, discovering whether God absolutely prohibits suicide may be difficult.

---

[4]Cicero, "On Ends," in *The Hellenistic Philosophers,* vol. 1, ed. A. A. Long and D. N. Sedley (Cambridge, England: Cambridge University Press, 1987), p. 425.

[5]Diogenes Laertius, in *The Hellenistic Philosophers,* vol. 1, p. 425.

SUICIDE AND NATURAL LAW

Perhaps the most important nontheological argument against suicide relies on the Natural Law theory of morality. According to Natural Law theory, people should follow rather than go against nature. We might argue that every human being has a natural drive toward self-preservation and that suicide goes against that natural drive. Then, too, following Aristotle, we might claim that every living organism has a function and that a basic function is living. For a human being to commit suicide is wrong because it is behavior inconsistent with her natural function of living and because it is wrong to behave inconsistently with her natural function. Still others claim that suicide is wrong because it is always wrong to interfere with the normal course of nature and suicide interferes with the normal course of nature. For example, if a terminally ill patient commits suicide, she is interfering with the normal course of nature; if nature had been allowed to take its course, she would have died from her illness.

Those who believe that suicide is morally acceptable under some circumstances deny the claim of many Natural Law theorists that suicide is behavior contrary to nature. They believe that even if people have a natural drive toward self-preservation, it does not follow that behaving contrary to such a drive is immoral. The fact that people have a natural drive toward something does not entail that they are morally required to act in accordance with that drive. After all, people may have other natural drives, such as a drive to dominate people or to satisfy their sexual needs, but it does not follow that people should behave in accordance with those drives. Then, too, we could argue that the natural drive toward self-preservation is conditional—that people have a natural drive to preserve their lives *if* they consider their lives worth living.

Those who believe that suicide can be morally acceptable also dismiss the claim that it is wrong to interfere with the normal course of nature. Providing a cancer patient with morphine to control his pain interferes with the normal course of nature, as does giving someone antibiotics to cure an infection. If it is always wrong for human beings to interfere with the normal course of nature, then it is wrong to take pain relievers and medications for illness. Almost everything human beings do interferes with the normal course of nature; we clear land and farm it, dam rivers, drain swamps, build cities and roads. If it's always wrong to interfere with the normal course of nature, then almost everything we do is immoral.

SUICIDE AND THE POSSIBILITY OF ERROR

Some people think that suicide is always immoral because we can never be certain of the future. For example, they point out that medicine is not an exact science and that diagnoses may be mistaken. A patient may commit suicide because he believes that he will die soon anyway, in pain or discomfort, and there is no hope for a cure. However, doctors could be mistaken about the nature or course of a patient's illness. If a patient does not commit suicide, it is possible that he will have a remission or a miraculous cure, or that new treatments will offer new hope. Opponents of suicide may say that we should not commit suicide when our future is uncertain. In fact, our future is never certain.

Although it is possible for physicians to be mistaken about the nature and course of an illness and possible for new therapies to become suddenly available, those who believe that suicide can be morally acceptable deny that such possibilities show that suicide is always immoral. Possible does not mean probable, and they think that it is more reasonable to be guided by probability than by mere logical possibility. For example, it's logically possible that a patient will have a fatal reaction to a certain medicine her doctor has prescribed and logically possible that she'll regain her health without taking it. However, if the probability of her having such a reaction and the probability of her regaining her health without the medicine are very low, it would be more reasonable for her to take the medicine. Similarly, if it's very probable that a doctor's grim prognosis is correct, even if it is logically possible that it's mistaken, it would be more reasonable to base her decisions on probability than on mere possibility.

What reason is there to think that it's *immoral* to be guided by probability rather than by mere possibility? Suppose that a terminally ill patient acknowledges that it's possible that new therapies will unexpectedly become available that would extend his life or improve its quality. Nevertheless, suppose that he says that he doesn't want to count on that because it's much more probable that his illness will progress exactly as his doctors have predicted. Supporters of a right to commit suicide claim that it would not be immoral for him to base his decisions on probability rather than on mere possibility, even if those decisions are about whether to continue living as well as about courses of treatment.

SUICIDE AND AUTONOMY

We could maintain that mature, rational human beings have a right to freedom or autonomy and are morally permitted to live their lives according to their own values and preferences, provided that they do not impose unjustified harm on others. It may be a short step from an autonomous person's having a right to live in accordance with her values and preferences to her having a right to die in accordance with her values and preferences. We could then conclude that an autonomous person should be able to decide not only how to live her life but also whether to continue living her life, if this would not impose unjustified harm on others.

Many people think that considerations of autonomy do not generate an absolute right to commit suicide under any and all circumstances. The right to freedom or autonomy is not absolute; people do not have a moral right to do anything they want to do regardless of its effect on others. We may live or end our life in accordance with our own values and preferences *provided that* we do not impose unjustified harm on others. Committing suicide often imposes unjustified harm on others. Suppose that we have children, a spouse, parents, siblings, or other relatives and friends who love, care about, and are psychologically dependent on us. Without doubt, our committing suicide would cause them much psychological harm. We may have others who are physically and financially dependent and who would be harmed by our committing suicide. Therefore, many people argue that we have a prima facie but not an absolute moral duty to refrain from committing suicide if it would impose unjustified harm on others.

GOOD REASONS FOR COMMITTING SUICIDE

If suicide can sometimes be morally acceptable, what might be the circumstances in which suicide would be morally permitted?

Many people believe that quality of life is more important than quantity of life. They think that if (1) our quality of life has diminished to the point where on careful reflection we judge that continued life is valueless and life is no longer worth living and (2) there is virtually no chance of recovery, then it would be reasonable to end our life. Perhaps the force of this point of view can be better appreciated by first considering it in relation to decisions about taking special steps to prolong life. Suppose that Jones, 75, is crippled with severe and painful arthritis. He is also almost completely blind and partly deaf, and he has no friends or family left alive. Confined to an old age home, he is lonely and has almost no sources of pleasure and happiness left in his life. Doctors now inform him of a new treatment that will probably prolong his life 20 to 30 years, although it will not improve his condition at all. On reflection, Jones decides that 20 to 30 years of additional life have no value for him and that his life is no longer worth living. Therefore, he refuses the new life-prolonging treatment. It seems difficult to deny that it is reasonable to consider quality of life when making decisions about taking special steps to prolong life.

Similarly, we may think that it is reasonable to consider quality of life when making decisions about continuing to live our life or ending it. If our quality of life has eroded to the point where after careful reflection we judge that our life is valueless and no longer worth living, not only would it be reasonable to do nothing to prolong it, but it would be reasonable to take steps to end it. Good reasons for not taking steps to prolong our life are also good reasons for taking steps to end it. Thus, we may say that if our quality of life has been permanently eroded to a severe enough degree, that situation can outweigh some of the harm that committing suicide can cause.

Some people think that life is the supreme value and that regardless of our quality of life, life can never be valueless or no longer worth living. They think that it is illegitimate to consider quality of life when deciding whether to go on living. However, those who believe that quality of life can be a good reason for committing suicide may claim that if it is illegitimate to consider quality of life when deciding whether to continue living, it would be illegitimate to consider quality of life when deciding whether to take steps to prolong life. We must concede either that quality of life cannot be considered when deciding whether to take steps to prolong life or that there is such a big difference between not taking steps to prolong our life and taking steps to end our life that a good reason for the former cannot also be a good reason for the latter.

People sometimes commit suicide as a matter of principle. For example, during the war in Vietnam, many Buddhist monks burned themselves to death in protest against the war. People in other countries have dramatically and publicly committed suicide to draw attention to evil and injustice. Suppose that someone in Nazi Germany committed suicide to draw people's attention to and protest against the policy of exterminating Jews. Suppose further that in doing so she did not impose any unjustified harm on others. She had no dependents relying on her; her action did not jeopardize relatives or friends. Would such principled suicide be irrational? Would it be immoral or blameworthy?

Similarly, suppose that a spy is captured and is about to be interrogated. Because he will be injected with various drugs, he knows that he will divulge information that will jeopardize many of his fellow spies and that will harm his country. Would it be irrational of him to commit suicide in order to ensure that he does not divulge the information? Would it be immoral or blameworthy? Although some people believe that suicide under such circumstances would be blameworthy, others do not.

BAD REASONS FOR COMMITTING SUICIDE

Judgments that our quality of life has permanently eroded to the point where our life has become valueless and is no longer worth living can be reasonable. However, such judgments can also be unreasonable. People can believe that their diminished quality of life is permanent when in fact it is only temporary. Similarly, they can falsely and unreasonably believe that their quality of life has sunk so low that they no longer have any sources of pleasure, satisfaction, or happiness.

People can suffer from temporary depression that they believe will be permanent. For example, people who lose loved ones through death or breakup, or who suffer serious financial reverses, sometimes believe that the psychological pain they feel will never diminish. A husband whose wife has just died or a woman whose lover has just left her may believe that the crushing sense of loss and depression they feel will never go away or diminish; a businessperson who has just lost her job may believe that she will never find work again and will be permanently destitute. The belief that our quality of life will be *permanently* diminished by these catastrophic events is hardly ever reasonable. Centuries of human experience have shown that the psychological pain and the catastrophic consequences of such events almost always diminish. Similarly, we may exaggerate the degree to which our quality of life will diminish and underestimate the availability of alternative sources of pleasure, happiness, and satisfaction. For example, the woman whose lover leaves her may believe that she can't live without him and that she'll never find anyone to replace him. However, such beliefs are almost always false and unreasonable. Given time, women and men who lose their lovers recover; usually their pain diminishes and they find new loves or new sources of happiness and satisfaction.

The more harm that committing suicide would cause (to relatives, dependents, and loved ones), the more severe must be the erosion of our quality of life if it is to constitute a good reason for committing suicide. Similarly, whatever the degree of erosion, the less permanent it would be, the less it can serve as a good reason. Those who oppose suicide believe that rarely if ever will the temporary psychological pain of traumatic events such as the loss of a loved one, the loss of a job, or financial reverses constitute a good reason for committing suicide when other people would be harmed by it.

SUICIDE AND THE DUTY TO MINIMIZE HARM TO OTHERS

We have a duty to minimize the harm that we cause others, and that duty applies to suicide, even when committing suicide would be morally acceptable. There are ways of reducing the harm that suicide may cause. For example, preparing people who will be affected by our suicide rather than committing suicide without warning can reduce the harm it causes. Similarly, some ways of committing suicide can cause more harm than others.

For example, a terminally ill patient who has decided to commit suicide could reduce the pain he'll cause others by discussing his intention and preparing those who care about him. He can explain his reasoning to them and try to persuade them that committing suicide is preferable to letting nature take its course so that he dies slowly from his illness. Those who care about him may come to support his decision, preferring that he die swiftly and painlessly rather than slowly and painfully. Even if they disagree with his decision, they may at least understand his reasons and be prepared for what is to come, which will reduce the shock and surprise. Thus, we may argue that those who intend to commit suicide have a duty to those who will probably be harmed by it both to inform them and to prepare them for the event.

Similarly, method and conditions of suicide can matter. A person who finds the body of someone who has committed suicide, especially if the method used is grisly and the person discovering the body is unprepared for it, can suffer severe trauma. To reduce such trauma, we could take steps to ensure that the method used is not too grisly and that the person finding our body is prepared for it. For example, rather than slitting our wrists in a motel bathroom where we may be discovered by a hapless maid, we could take an overdose of sleeping pills in our own bedroom and ensure that our body will be discovered by someone who has been prepared for it.

If we commit suicide without trying to minimize the harm that it will cause others, we have violated our duty to minimize harm to others.

SUICIDE AND MORAL THEORY

Suicide and Utilitarianism

An act utilitarian would maintain that in any circumstance, if committing suicide would produce more total happiness than would refraining from committing suicide, then committing suicide is the right thing to do. For example, an act utilitarian might claim that by committing suicide a cancer patient would avoid pointless suffering, would relieve his family of the suffering of watching his decline, and would save money and scarce medical resources. Since he and his friends and family know that he will almost certainly die within a few months from his illness anyway, there would be an increase in total happiness from his committing suicide. Therefore, it would be the right thing to do.

Rule utilitarians would try to determine whether there would be more total happiness produced from people's following a rule such as "Commit suicide in circumstances C" than if they followed the rule "Don't commit suicide in circumstances C." Each set of rules and the circumstances in which they apply would have to be carefully examined to discover the effect on total happiness of people's following them. Rule utilitarians, like act utilitarians, would rely on experience to answer the question.

Kantian Approaches to Suicide

A Kantian approach first requires that we identify the maxim that we are following. In the case of a terminally ill patient contemplating suicide, the maxim might be

> I will commit suicide when I'm terminally ill, I have only a few months to live, I will probably have much intense pain, and I will grow ever weaker and more helpless (call these circumstances C).

According to Kant, acting on this maxim would be morally acceptable only if the individual could consistently will that it become a universal law.

> Everyone will commit suicide in circumstances C.

Kant himself believed that no rational individual could consistently will such a universal law; therefore, he believed that suicide is always immoral. However, not all people find his reasoning persuasive. Many people believe that a rational individual could consistently will such a universal law.

Kant's second formulation of the Categorical Imperative requires us to treat people with respect, including ourselves. Whether treating ourselves with respect is consistent with committing suicide is a difficult question. Some people, including Kant himself, believe that it isn't. Others believe that it can be under certain circumstances. In their view, to undergo pointless suffering and both physical and mental deterioration when terminally ill, rather than prevent it by quickly and painlessly killing ourselves, is not to treat ourselves with respect.

RIGHTS, DUTIES, AND SUICIDE PREVENTION

If someone is competent, mature, and rational, many people do not think that we have a right to *permanently* prevent her from committing suicide if she desires to end her life; permanently preventing suicide would unjustifiably interfere with an individual's right to autonomy. However, many people do think we have a right (perhaps even a duty) to prevent an individual from committing suicide, at least temporarily, if there is a question about the individual's rationality or competence. For example, if someone is not yet an adult, most people think that we have a right to prevent her from committing suicide. They think that individuals who have not yet reached maturity are not competent to decide whether their lives are worth living and should be protected from themselves until they have reached maturity.

If someone is suffering from a severe psychological disorder that is the likely cause of his desire to commit suicide, many people think that we have a right to prevent him from committing suicide in order to protect him from himself until he regains his rationality and competence, especially if there are therapies and treatments available that hold promise of relieving the psychological disorder. (We must be careful, however, not to take a suicide attempt or a desire to commit suicide as proof of a severe psychological disorder.) However, if the psychological disturbance turns out to be severe enough and if there is virtually no hope of effective therapy or treatment, we may wonder whether we have a right to permanently prevent him from committing suicide. If the person's future almost surely contains little but suffering, with almost no prospect of relief, it is not obvious that we have a right to force that individual to continue to live such a life.

Supporters of this position could justify on several grounds temporarily preventing someone from committing suicide in order to determine competence. On utilitarian grounds, such temporary prevention probably maximizes total happiness. In many cases, temporary prevention enables us to provide aid to people who need help and prevents people from acting on temporary impulses that do not reflect their true desires. It also prevents them from imposing on others unjustified harm by their committing suicide. Therefore, temporary prevention would be both a right and a duty. We might also reach the same conclusion on Kantian principles. We could maintain that we could not consistently will as a universal law a maxim that directs us to do nothing to prevent others from committing suicide, even temporarily. If such a maxim became a universal law, we might ourselves die, or someone we love might die, as a result of temporary self-destructive impulses that could have been prevented but weren't. Again, this reasoning suggests that prevention is both a right and a duty. Hypothetical social contract theory may lead to the same conclusion: Rational, self-interested people in the Original Position behind the Veil of Ignorance would agree to impose a duty to temporarily prevent suicide in order to evaluate the individual's rationality and sanity because they would recognize that they could benefit from it. If they or those they love were to suffer from a temporary self-destructive impulse, imposing a duty to intervene could save their lives.

EXERCISES

1. From a utilitarian perspective, do you think that suicide is always immoral? Defend your answer.

2. From a Kantian perspective, do you think that suicide is always immoral? Defend your answer.

3. Would a good person ever commit suicide? What virtues/vices oppose suicide? What virtues/vices support suicide?

4. Tom is a spy who has been apprehended. He has knowledge that would enable his captors to arrest an entire spy network that includes dozens of people. He is fairly certain that he will not be able to withstand the torture he can expect under interrogation and that he will reveal his knowledge to his captors. He has a cyanide capsule secreted in a false tooth. When he became a spy he took an oath promising to use the cyanide capsule to commit suicide if he was ever captured. Would it be morally acceptable for him to commit suicide? Does he have a moral duty to commit suicide? Defend your answers.

5. Paula Finn, 76, has Alzheimer's disease. Sometimes she is lucid, but at other times she is not. When she is not, she is wholly unable to care for herself. She cannot remember who she is or where she lives; she cannot recognize her family; she cannot fully control her bodily functions. She has reached the point where she is lucid about 70 percent of the time, but her condition will continue to worsen and the periods during which she is lucid will grow ever briefer. Right now Paula is lucid. She does not wish to live in a state of mental deterioration; she judges that her life is no longer worth living. Would it be irrational for her to commit suicide? Would it be immoral for her to commit suicide? Defend you answers.

6. Doug, 25, was severely injured in a motorcycle accident when he was 22. As a result of spinal injuries he is a quadriplegic, totally paralyzed from the neck down. After two years of treatment doctors told him that there is virtually no possibility of improvement; it is almost certain that he will remain a quadriplegic for the rest of his life. Six months after his doctors informed him of his prognosis, after long and careful reflection Doug decided that life as a quadriplegic is valueless and that his life is no longer worth living. He has no wife or children financially dependent on him; both of his parents are alive and in their early fifties; he has a brother and a sister, both of whom are older than he, married, and with children. He believes that the quality of his life is so diminished that it outweighs any harm to others that would be caused by his committing suicide. Would it be irrational for Doug to commit suicide? Would it be immoral for him to commit suicide? Defend your answers.

7. Nine months ago Phil, 82, lost his wife, Sara, to whom he had been married 54 years. Intensely lonely and filled with pain from his loss, he decides that life without her is not worth living. He has three grown children, all of whom live in other states. They have families of their own, and he sees them only a few times a year. No one is financially dependent on him. Would it be irrational for

him to commit suicide? Would it be immoral for him to commit suicide? Are there other possible solutions to his loneliness and grief? If you were his friend, what would you recommend? Defend your answers.

8. Would it be morally acceptable for someone to take steps to permanently prevent Phil from committing suicide? Defend your answer.

9. Paul, 19, just lost his girlfriend to another man. Believing that he cannot live without her and that life without her is not worth living, he desires to commit suicide. He has parents, siblings, and friends. Would it be irrational for him to commit suicide? Would it be immoral for him to commit suicide? Defend your answers.

10. In Shakespeare's play *Romeo and Juliet,* Romeo commits suicide when he mistakenly believes that Juliet is dead. When Juliet awakens from her deathlike state and discovers that Romeo has killed himself, she commits suicide. Were their suicides irrational? Were their suicides immoral? Defend your answers.

11. Does the fact that something is irrational entail that it is immoral? Defend your answer.

12. Paul is about to commit suicide when Jack, a casual acquaintance, comes upon the scene. Jack could try to prevent Paul from committing suicide. However, he walks away without doing anything because he tells himself that he has no duty to stop Paul, even temporarily. Do you agree with Jack? Defend your answer.

SUGGESTED READINGS

Jonathan Glover. *Causing Death and Saving Lives.* Harmondsworth, England: Penguin, 1977. (See Chapter 13.)

David Hume. "Of Suicide." In *Essays Moral, Political, and Literary,* edited by Eugene Miller. Indianapolis, IN: Liberty Classics, 1985.

Immanuel Kant. "Doctrine of Virtue," Book I, Article I, "On Killing Oneself." In *The Metaphysics of Morals,* edited by Mary Gregor. Cambridge, England: Cambridge University Press, 1991. Pp. 218–220.

Plato. "Phaedo." In *The Collected Dialogues of Plato,* edited by Edith Hamilton and Huntington Cairns. Princeton, NJ: Princeton University Press, 1961.

CHAPTER 18

Euthanasia

My dictionary defines euthanasia as "the act or practice of killing or permitting the death of hopelessly sick or injured individuals . . . in a relatively painless way for reasons of mercy."[1] An act of euthanasia may involve killing someone or it may involve refraining from trying to prevent death (permitting someone to die). However, the condition of the person undergoing euthanasia and the intentions of the person(s) performing euthanasia are crucial for distinguishing between euthanasia and other forms of killing, such as murder or self-defense. According to the dictionary definition, in order for an act to be considered an act of euthanasia, the person undergoing it must be "hopelessly sick or injured," and the motivation of the person(s) performing euthanasia must be mercy. In order to be considered an act of euthanasia, an act must be done in the interests of the person who undergoes euthanasia, and the goal must be to prevent, reduce, or end a patient's suffering, to preserve a patient's dignity, or to respect a patient's autonomy. It is not euthanasia if the person acts or refrains from acting primarily from self-interested motives.

DECISIONS ON EUTHANASIA

Issues of euthanasia can arise at the beginning of life, the end of life, or any point in between.

Impaired Newborns

Suppose that Mary Jackson gives birth to a baby with physical defects that are almost certain to cause moderate to severe mental retardation and paralysis. Ms. Jackson's physicians tell her that unless they operate as soon as possible to drain the cerebrospinal fluid that has built up in the baby's brain, the baby will very probably die within a year or two and will certainly be profoundly retarded. On the other hand, if the operation is performed without too much delay and the infant receives the best care possible, there is a 50 percent probability that the

---

[1]*Merriam-Webster's Collegiate Dictionary,* 10th ed. (Springfield, MA: Merriam-Webster, 1994).

baby will live 10 to 15 years and will be only slightly retarded. Unfortunately, regardless of what they do, the baby will be crippled or paralyzed because of irreparable spinal damage, and there is a high probability that the child will not be able to control its bladder or bowels and will suffer from chronic urinary infections.

The Jacksons recognize that even if their baby has the operation, there is a high probability that it will have a relatively short, unhappy life. If it doesn't have the operation, its quality of life may be even lower, but its life will be much shorter. Therefore, they wonder whether it would be more merciful and compassionate to refuse rather than permit the operation.

Pamela Ross has given birth to an infant with exactly the same physical disabilities and probable future as the Jacksons' infant. However, her baby also has a heart defect that, if uncorrected, will almost certainly kill the infant in a matter of days or weeks. She and her husband wonder whether it would be best to refuse permission for the operation and let their infant die quickly.

Tina Velasquez gave birth to an infant suffering from anencephaly; it was born without a complete brain. Her doctors have informed her that although her infant may live for several months, it will not be conscious in any recognizably human sense; it will not be self-aware or aware of its environment, nor will it be capable of thought, feeling, or emotion. It also has an intestinal blockage that prevents it from absorbing any nutrients; if the blockage is not corrected, the baby will starve to death over a one- to two-week period. Tina and her husband wonder whether to let the infant die by refusing to permit the operation. However, they also wonder whether it would be more merciful to give it a lethal injection in order to kill it swiftly and painlessly rather than let it die slowly from dehydration and starvation.

Irreversible Comas

In 1975 Karen Quinlan, 21, suffered severe brain damage and became comatose when she stopped breathing after mixing alcohol and barbiturates. She was placed on a respirator. After several months doctors concluded that she was in a "persistent vegetative state"—an almost always irreversible state characterized by the absence of all higher-level mental functioning, such as awareness of environment, self-awareness, thought, and emotion.

> Over the next five months, Karen's posture began to show . . . neurological
> damage. . . . Her left wrist cocked at a right angle to her hand so that it looked
> as if her fingernails were digging into her wrist; her left foot twisted inward;
> her left elbow drew into her body. These positions were held rigidly. . . .
> Karen's weight dropped [to 70–80 pounds], and because her muscles were so
> rigid that IV [intravenous] feeding couldn't be used, a naso-gastic (N-G)
> feeding tube [through the nose] was used.[2]

---

[2]Gregory Pence, *Classic Cases in Medical Ethics* (New York: McGraw-Hill, 1990), pp. 5–6.

Karen did not just lie in bed peacefully. She suffered from spasms that were like convulsions, and often her head would thrash about wildly. Because doctors told them that there was no hope of recovery, the Quinlans requested that the hospital take Karen off the respirator so that she could be permitted to die. However, the hospital refused their request and went to court to prevent the Quinlans from taking Karen off the respirator.

The case dragged on through New Jersey courts for months, but the New Jersey Supreme Court finally ruled in the Quinlans' favor. During this time, how-ever, doctors at the hospital went to great lengths to wean Karen from the res-pirator so that she would be able to breathe without it. They succeeded. When Karen was finally taken off the respirator (more than a year after her parents' ini-tial request), she did not die. In 1976 Karen was placed in a nursing home, where she lingered for another ten years without regaining consciousness until she died from pneumonia. Many people wonder whether the Quinlans should have been permitted to have Karen's respirator removed earlier to let her die. Other people wonder whether it was morally acceptable for the hospital to work to ensure that Karen could live without the respirator once it was removed.

End-of-Life Cases

Brad Felton had always been an active, healthy outdoorsman; his greatest pas-sions were hiking and climbing in the Sierra Nevada mountains of California. At age 76 he had more energy and vigor than most men half his age. Now he has had a stroke that has left him severely brain damaged. Like Karen Quinlan, he is in a persistent vegetative state with virtually no hope of recovery. Doctors have told his family that he can live another five to ten years in this condition. Although Brad rarely talked about such possibilities, his family believes that he would not want to continue to live in this condition. Brad receives nourishment and fluids through a feeding tube. If the feeding tube is disconnected, Brad will die in one to two weeks from dehydration and starvation. Doctors assure the family that he will feel no pain during this process because of the damage to his brain. The family is considering requesting that feeding be discontinued so that Brad can be permitted to die.

Frank Barker, age 52, has malignant mesothelioma, a cancer of the chest lin-ing that is untreatable and invariably fatal. He has been slowly wasting away. His weight has dropped from 180 to 125 pounds, and he is so weak that he cannot stand or walk without assistance. He is receiving large doses of morphine to con-trol the pain and discomfort, so that his mind is perpetually dulled. His medica-tions are causing bouts of constipation followed by diarrhea. Frank is now bedridden in the hospital awaiting death. Several times Frank has privately asked his physician, Dr. Nora Trent, for a lethal injection to put him out of his misery, telling her that he would prefer to die swiftly and painlessly rather than wait for his illness to kill him slowly over a period of three to six months. Dr. Trent has informed Frank's wife and children of Frank's request and they have endorsed it, assuring her that no one outside of the family would know. Dr. Trent wonders whether she should comply with the request and give Frank a lethal injection to end what he and his family consider to be his pointless suffering.

ACTIVE AND PASSIVE EUTHANASIA

Is euthanasia ever morally acceptable? To answer that question, we need to make a number of important distinctions.

Passive euthanasia occurs when someone intentionally withholds treatment or care from a patient, letting the patient die; active euthanasia occurs when someone intentionally kills a patient. For example, if the conditions for an act of euthanasia are met and a patient dies because she has been disconnected from a respirator or has had needed surgery or medication withheld, it is a case of passive rather than active euthanasia. However, if the patient dies because someone has deliberately given her a lethal injection or has shot, stabbed, drowned, smothered, or strangled her, it would be a case of active euthanasia.

Many people maintain that although passive euthanasia is sometimes morally acceptable, active euthanasia is always immoral. However, it's not easy to provide precise criteria for distinguishing between active and passive euthanasia. We may be tempted to think that we can distinguish between active and passive euthanasia simply on the basis of the difference between acting and not acting—that active euthanasia requires doing something whereas passive euthanasia simply requires not doing something. For example, consider the difference between *giving* a patient a lethal dose of morphine and *not giving* a patient an injection of antibiotics needed to cure pneumonia. However, passive euthanasia can require action as well as inaction. Discontinuing treatment in passive euthanasia can require that tubes providing medication, oxygen, or nourishment be removed or that switches on medical equipment be flipped, all of which are actions, not merely omissions.

Perhaps we could say that unlike active euthanasia, passive euthanasia involves a certain kind of inaction in that we cease to act or refrain from acting so as to prevent or delay death. We might also add a difference of intention: In active euthanasia we intend to directly cause the patient to die; in passive euthanasia we intend to refrain from taking steps to delay or prevent death. Finally, we might maintain that the direct cause of death differs in active and passive euthanasia: In passive euthanasia it is the illness or injury (that those withholding treatment or care did not directly cause) that directly causes the patient's death, but if someone gives a patient a lethal injection of morphine or smothers a patient, it is the injection or smothering that directly causes the patient's death. However, if we withhold food or fluid from a patient in passive euthanasia, it seems difficult to deny that the agent directly caused the patient's death (and intended to cause the patient's death). The starvation that caused the death is a condition that the agent directly causes, unlike the situation in which an injury or illness caused the death. To repeat, it is difficult to provide precise criteria for distinguishing between active and passive euthanasia.

EXTRAORDINARY TREATMENT
AND ORDINARY CARE

Many people claim that although it may be morally acceptable to withhold extraordinary treatment in passive euthanasia, it is never morally acceptable to withhold ordinary care. Extraordinary treatment (an unfortunate term) may include surgery and the provision of medications (oral or intravenous) and medical services such as CPR (cardiopulmonary resuscitation), kidney dialysis, blood plasma, and oxygen. Ordinary care is generally limited to things that all people need regardless of their state of health, such as food and water, or to comfort-oriented care such as bathing, massage, and pain-relief therapies. The question is whether one can be as morally justified in withholding ordinary care that is necessary for a patient's survival, such as food and water, as in withholding extraordinary treatment.

VOLUNTARY, NONVOLUNTARY,
AND INVOLUNTARY EUTHANASIA

If a fully informed, competent patient has freely requested or freely consented to undergo euthanasia, it is voluntary euthanasia. If a patient who is not competent to give or withhold consent undergoes euthanasia, it is nonvoluntary euthanasia. If a competent patient undergoes euthanasia without having freely consented, it is involuntary euthanasia. (Free consent means that the patient has not been coerced into giving consent.)

Thus, if a competent patient were given a lethal injection at his own request, it would be voluntary (active) euthanasia. It would also be voluntary euthanasia if treatment were withheld from a comatose patient who had, before becoming comatose, clearly requested or expressed a desire that treatment or care be withheld in such circumstances. Euthanasia of impaired newborn infants or of comatose patients who had never expressed a desire for or against euthanasia would be nonvoluntary euthanasia. Finally, euthanasia of a competent patient who has not requested it would be involuntary euthanasia.

There are, then, six different forms that euthanasia can take: voluntary active, voluntary passive, nonvoluntary active, nonvoluntary passive, involuntary active, involuntary passive. There is also the withholding of ordinary care and of extraordinary treatment. Our question is whether any of these forms of euthanasia can be morally acceptable.

Involuntary Euthanasia

Involuntary euthanasia, in almost all conceivable circumstances, whether active or passive, seems clearly immoral. To kill people or let them die against their will when death is (relatively easily) preventable unjustifiably violates their right to life and their right to autonomy. People don't have a right to override other people's decisions about their own lives and deaths or to substitute their judgment for another's about whether that person's life is worth living. This judgment can be easily justified by appeal to Utilitarianism, Kantian moral theory, social contract theory, or conceptions of moral rights and duties and moral virtues and vices. Involuntary euthanasia is rationally indefensible.[3]

Voluntary Passive Euthanasia

Frank Barker, the 52-year-old man slowly dying from mesothelioma, has come down with pneumonia. His doctors have told him that the pneumonia will kill him within a few days unless he is given injections of antibiotics to combat it. After discussing it with his wife, Frank refuses to consent to have the antibiotics because he wants to die sooner from pneumonia rather than later from the cancer. If he dies from pneumonia because he refused to accept medical treatment for it, it will be a case of voluntary passive euthanasia. Doctors face a choice. They can comply with Frank's request, withhold the antibiotics, and let him die from pneumonia, or they can give Frank antibiotics against his will and cure the pneumonia. What's the right thing to do?

In the United States, competent patients may not be forced to undergo medical treatment against their will; medical treatment may be provided to a competent patient only with the patient's consent. The law reflects our society's commitment to autonomy and to the fundamental importance of bodily integrity. Others may not handle our property without permission; how much more important that others be forbidden to handle our bodies, the center of our being, without permission. It also reflects our society's commitment to personal freedom. Among the most fundamental freedoms may be the freedom to choose by whom and how our bodies will be handled and the freedom to choose how energetically to resist the approach of death. The law also may reflect recognition that sometimes the most merciful and compassionate thing to do is to let someone die. It can be senseless and cruel to take energetic measures to prolong someone's life against her will if that life promises to contain little but suffering. We do not treat people with respect if we force them to continue to endure a life of suffering against their will.

There are good moral reasons for believing that voluntary passive euthanasia can be morally acceptable. Considerations of individual autonomy or freedom; appeal to virtues such as kindness, compassion, and mercy; and appeal to the requirement to treat people with respect favor the view that voluntary passive euthanasia is morally acceptable, sometimes perhaps morally obligatory. We could also justify it on utilitarian, Kantian, and hypothetical social contract grounds. Similarly, we could justify it by appeal to the fundamental moral duties of beneficence and nonmaleficence. We have a duty of nonmaleficence, a duty to minimize the harm we may cause or allow. In some situations, taking steps to

---

[3]For simplicity, I ignore situations in which medical treatment is not provided because of high cost and limited economic resources.

delay or prevent death is harmful because delayed death simply means additional suffering. We also have a duty of beneficence, a duty to help others in need. In some cases, we need to die sooner rather than later in order to end suffering, preserve dignity, or respect autonomy. Thus, the two fundamental duties of non-maleficence and beneficence appear to entail that people have a duty to comply with a competent patient's request to have treatment or care withheld.

However, suppose that Frank does not contract pneumonia; instead of refusing antibiotics he refuses food, intending to starve himself to death. Would it be morally acceptable to comply with a competent patient's request to starve himself to death? Doctors can either comply with his request and let him die from starvation, or they can forcibly keep him supplied with nourishment and fluids—either by forcing Frank to swallow food and liquid or by forcibly installing a feeding tube into his veins or stomach and restraining or sedating him to prevent him from removing them.

Although many people would probably agree that Frank's doctors should not force him to take antibiotics against his will, many people would be less certain about whether doctors should force food and fluids into Frank if he refuses to eat and drink. We could argue that the same moral considerations that justify the prohibition on forcing medical treatment on a patient against his will also justify a prohibition on forcing care such as food and water on a patient against his will. A person who takes this line could issue a challenge to those who disagree: What would justify treating the refusal to accept ordinary care differently from the refusal to accept extraordinary treatment?

Of course, we may insist that a refusal to accept care such as food and water shows conclusively that a patient is no longer competent and that there is no obligation to comply with the requests of an incompetent patient. However, it is very difficult to justify the claim that refusal to accept care such as food and water always shows that a patient is no longer competent. For example, it is by no means obvious that a patient's refusing to accept food and water in a situation like Frank Barker's is a sign of diminished competence.

Voluntary Active Euthanasia

Many people insist that although passive euthanasia can be morally acceptable, even morally obligatory, active euthanasia is always immoral. For example, suppose that rather than refusing food and water, Frank Barker asked his doctor for a lethal injection to end his life swiftly and painlessly. Many people believe that it is immoral for doctors to give patients lethal injections even if they have requested it. In their view, although it can be permissible to let someone die, it can never be permissible to kill someone.

This view appears to be based on the assumption that it's always worse to kill someone than to let someone die. However, James Rachels challenges that assumption. In his view, letting someone die is often no better from a moral point of view than killing someone. For example, suppose that a child's evil uncle comes into the bathroom with the intention of drowning her in the bathtub because he stands to inherit a million dollars. As he enters, the child slips and hits her head, loses consciousness, and slides under the water. Her uncle does nothing; he lets her drown, waiting in the bathroom for five minutes until he is certain that she is dead. According to Rachels, letting her drown is no better than drowning her.[4] Similarly, suppose that the child dies as a result of her evil uncle's starving her to death or withholding her asthma medication. Is that really better than her uncle's shooting or smothering her? Not according to Rachels. In his view, these examples show that it's not always worse to kill someone than to let someone die.

In fact, according to Rachels, letting someone die may be worse than killing him if letting him die produces far more suffering. Usually a person will die more slowly and painfully from having treatment withheld than from receiving a lethal injection that swiftly and painlessly ends his life. In Rachels's view, the moral considerations that justify passive euthanasia (autonomy and freedom; virtues such as compassion, mercy, and kindness; treating people with respect; the balance of harm and benefit; the duties of beneficence and nonmaleficence) also sometimes justify active euthanasia. On this view, giving Frank a lethal injection to end his life immediately is no more objectionable than withholding antibiotics and letting him die from pneumonia or withholding food and water and letting him starve to death. (Of course, not everyone agrees with Rachels.)

Then, too, many people believe that the moral prohibition on killing other people is not absolute. For example, most people seem to believe that it is morally acceptable to kill people in self-defense, in war, and as punishment for serious crimes. Thus, unless we take the position that it is always immoral to kill someone regardless of the circumstances, the mere fact that active euthanasia involves killing someone does not automatically show that it is immoral. We might argue that like self-defense (or perhaps capital punishment), active euthanasia can be justified as a legitimate exception to the moral prohibition on killing other people.

However, many opponents of active euthanasia fear that if we permit or legalize active voluntary euthanasia, it will inevitably lead to a kind of moral corruption. In their view, it would undermine respect for life and would act as the opening wedge for nonvoluntary and involuntary euthanasia—for example, killing people who are old, or addicted to drugs or alcohol, or retarded. However, supporters of voluntary active euthanasia maintain that such fears are exaggerated. They claim that if the intention is to minimize suffering and if the patient's desires are scrupulously respected, then the likelihood of moral corruption and decreased respect for human life is minimal.

Nonvoluntary Passive Euthanasia

Issues of nonvoluntary euthanasia arise when a patient is not competent to give or withhold consent for care or treatment, as in the case of a defective newborn infant or a comatose adult patient. In such cases, someone else must make deci-

---

[4]James Rachels, "Active and Passive Euthanasia" and "More Impertinent Distinctions and a Defense of Active Euthanasia," in *Social Ethics: Morality and Social Policy,* 3d ed., ed. Thomas Mappes and Jane Zembaty (New York: McGraw-Hill, 1987).

sions. Can it be morally acceptable for someone to make life-and-death decisions about treatment and care for another person? Is it morally acceptable for the relatives of a patient who is in a persistent vegetative state or for the parents of a defective newborn infant to decide to withhold medical treatment and let the patient die?

There is no way to avoid having others make life-and-death decisions for incompetent patients. Someone must decide between the two alternatives of providing or withholding medical treatment. However, we might claim that if we do not know what the patient wants or would want under the circumstances, we should always err on the side of caution and life—providing or maintaining rather than withdrawing or withholding treatment or care. On this view, it would be wrong for others to decide to withhold or discontinue treatment of an incompetent patient but not wrong for others to decide to provide medical treatment to an incompetent patient.

Nonetheless, many people believe that nonvoluntary passive euthanasia can be morally acceptable for much the same reasons, and under much the same conditions, as voluntary passive euthanasia. Provided that the good of the patient is the only or primary consideration, minimizing and preventing suffering for the patient or respecting the patient's dignity and autonomy can justify someone's deciding to withhold treatment or care. However, extreme caution is required in evaluating the life prospects of an incompetent patient. In order to be justified in withholding treatment or care from an incompetent patient, we must have strong evidence that there is a very high probability either that the patient's life will contain little but intense suffering or that the patient's capacity for higher-level mental functioning associated with being a person has been permanently lost. We might require that, given the patient's life prospects, virtually no reasonable person would act energetically to delay death.

That there can be such circumstances seems clear. A patient in a persistent vegetative state faces continued biological existence that does not include consciousness or self-awareness. Who would fight energetically to delay death if they were in a persistent vegetative state that could last for decades? Similarly, the life prospects for an anencephalic infant born without a complete brain are terribly grim—a short life of suffering. However, other cases are excluded. To withhold treatment or care from a newborn infant solely because it has Down's syndrome would not meet the criteria because infants with Down's syndrome do not face a life that will contain little but intense suffering. Although they face moderate to severe retardation, the degree of which cannot be predicted in very early infancy, Down's infants have many potential sources of satisfaction and can lead lives that contain little intense suffering.

Nonvoluntary Active Euthanasia

If it would be morally acceptable to withhold treatment or care from an incompetent patient, would it also be morally acceptable to kill a patient? Would the same considerations that justify withholding treatment also justify killing the patient? For example, is it worse to give a lethal injection to a patient in a persistent vegetative state than to disconnect his respirator or feeding tube? Is it worse to withhold surgery from an anencephalic infant with a bowel obstruction, letting it die from dehydration or starvation over a period of days, than to give it a lethal injection that will swiftly and painlessly kill it?

Advocates of nonvoluntary active euthanasia can appeal to the duty to minimize suffering. Letting someone die can easily produce far more suffering than would killing the person. Considerations that would justify letting someone die—such as a concern to prevent or minimize suffering, virtues such as kindness and compassion, and duties of beneficence and nonmaleficence—might also justify killing someone if killing would produce less suffering and would preserve the patient's autonomy and dignity more than would letting the person die. Of course, anyone who believes that active euthanasia is always immoral would reject this line of argument.

EXERCISES

1. Try to construct a defense for the claim that involuntary euthanasia is morally acceptable.

2. Sheila is suffering from severe postpartum depression (depression that often occurs after childbirth) when she begins to hemorrhage. To save her life doctors need to operate, but she refuses to consent to the operation because she is so depressed that she wants to die. While she is conscious, doctors cannot and will not operate; however, they have told her husband that she will become unconscious from blood loss very soon. Once she is unconscious, her husband can give consent to the operation and if he does, the doctors can operate to save her life. After she lapses into unconsciousness, her husband does give his consent and the doctors operate, saving her life. Have the doctors done anything wrong in operating on Sheila when they know that she has refused to give her consent? Defend your answer.

3. Early in the chapter we met Tina Velasquez, who gave birth to a baby that is anencephalic (born without a full brain). The infant also has a bowel obstruction that, if not surgically corrected, will cause it to die from dehydration and malnutrition over the space of a week or two. Would it be morally acceptable to withhold the surgery and let the baby die? Defend your answer. Would it be morally acceptable to give Tina Velasquez's infant a lethal injection to kill it swiftly and painlessly rather than let it die slowly? Defend your answer.

4. Frank Barker is slowly dying from mesothelioma. Because he has contracted pneumonia and refuses to accept antibiotics to cure it, he will probably die within a week. Would doctors be justified in giving him antibiotics against his will? Would doctors be justified in giving him food and fluids against his will? Defend your answers.

5. If Frank Barker asks his physician to give him a lethal injection so that he will die swiftly and painlessly, would it be morally acceptable for his physician to comply with his request? Defend your answer.

6. A 25-year-old patient has been injured in a motorcycle accident and is permanently paralyzed from the neck down. The patient refuses food and water in order to starve himself to death because he does not think that his life is

worth living in this condition. Would the hospital be justified in force-feeding the patient against his will to prevent him from starving himself to death? If he requested that a doctor give him a lethal injection to "put him out of his misery," would it be morally acceptable for a doctor to comply with his request? Defend your answers.

7. When Karen Quinlan's parents first requested that the hospital turn off her respirator, everyone knew that she would die without it. Would it have been morally acceptable for the hospital to quickly honor the Quinlan's request and disconnect Karen's respirator? Was it morally acceptable for the hospital to reject the Quinlans' request and to delay for many months before obeying the court order that the Quinlans eventually obtained? Defend your answers.

8. Was it morally acceptable for the hospital to wean Karen from the respirator to ensure that she would not die when it was disconnected? Defend your answer.

9. Would it be morally acceptable to withhold food and water from a patient who, like Karen Quinlan, is in a persistent vegetative state if the parents or spouse request it? Defend your answer.

10. Should (a) voluntary passive, (b) voluntary active, (c) nonvoluntary passive, or (d) nonvoluntary active euthanasia be legally permissible? Defend your answers. If a form of euthanasia is legally permissible, what legal safeguards would you advocate to prevent abuse? Defend your recommendations.

11. One could consider physician-assisted suicide to be a form of voluntary active euthanasia. Dr. Jack Kevorkian has assisted in several suicides and has constructed a so-called suicide machine to enable patients to kill themselves swiftly and painlessly. Can physician-assisted suicide ever be morally acceptable? If yes, under what circumstances? Defend your answers. Should physician-assisted suicide be legally permitted? If yes, what safeguards would be required to ensure that there is no abuse? Defend your answers.

SUGGESTED READINGS

Thomas Mappes and Jane Zembaty, eds. *Social Ethics: Morality and Social Policy.* 3d ed. New York: McGraw-Hill, 1987. (See Chapter 2.)

Ronald Munson. *Intervention and Reflection: Basic Issues in Medical Ethics.* 4th ed. Belmont, CA: Wadsworth, 1992. (See Chapters 2 and 3.)

Gregory Pence. *Classic Cases in Medical Ethics.* New York: McGraw-Hill, 1990. (See Chapters 1, 2, and 7.)

CHAPTER 19

Economic Inequality, Poverty, and Equal Opportunity

It seems that the world has always been divided between rich and poor. Wealth and income have rarely if ever been equally distributed among the members of a community. Economic inequality has been the norm both between nations and within nations. For example, the United States is far wealthier than Ghana; per capita income in the United States in 1990 was $21,800 while per capita income in Ghana was $380. Within the United States, there are billionaires who can satisfy their every whim and paupers who can't afford life's basic necessities, such as food, shelter, clothing, and medical care.

Consider the following table of income distribution for households in the United States.[1]

1994 INCOME	TOTAL	WHITE	BLACK	HISPANIC
Under $10,000	13.6%	11.7%	26.3%	20.5%
$10,000–14,999	9.1%	8.7%	11.5%	12.2%
$15,000–24,999	16.7%	16.4%	18.9%	20.4%
$25,000–34,999	14.2%	14.4%	12.8%	14.9%
$35,000–49,999	16.3%	16.7%	13.3%	14.4%
$50,000–74,999	16.5%	17.3%	10.8%	10.9%
$75,000 and up	13.6%	14.7%	6.3%	6.7%

As the table reveals, in 1994, 13.6 percent of households in the United States had annual incomes below $10,000: 11.7 percent of whites, 26.3 percent of blacks, and 20.5 percent of Hispanics. In 1994 the median annual household income for whites was $34,028, for blacks $21,027 and for Hispanics $23,421.[2]

---

[1]U.S. Bureau of the Census, *Statistical Abstracts of the United States, 1996,* Table 709.
[2]Ibid.

In 1994, more than 38 million people in the United States fell below the official poverty line. That represented 14.5 percent of the total population: 11.7 percent of whites, 30.6 percent of blacks, and 30.7 percent of Hispanics were below the poverty line.[3] In that year, 21.2 percent of all U.S. children were poor; however 45.3 percent of black children and 41.1 percent of Hispanic children were poor. In 1995, 4.9 percent of whites, 9.3 percent of Hispanics, and 10.4 percent of blacks were unemployed.[4]

Some people in the United States are so poor that they can barely afford life's necessities. Others are so poor that they *cannot* afford life's necessities; they're homeless, hungry, and ill. Obviously, our society tolerates a great deal of poverty.

The United States also tolerates a great deal of economic inequality. Over the past fifteen years, most of the income and wealth from economic growth in the United States has gone to the richest Americans, not to the poor or the middle class. According to a *New York Times* report, "Average household income climbed 10 percent between 1979 and 1994, but 97 percent of the gain went to the richest 20 percent."[5] In fact, the poorest 20 percent of households saw their average income fall by more than 15 percent. In 1970, the poorest 20 percent of the population received 5.4 percent of total income while the richest 20 percent received 40.9 percent. In 1994, the poorest 20 percent of the population was receiving only 4.2 percent of total income and the richest 20 percent had increased its share to 46.9 percent. For each $1 million of income, that is, the poorest 20 percent of the population gets $42,000 to share while the richest 20 percent gets $469,000. Part of the cause is the recent phenomenon of "downsizing" that affects both working class and middle class. The *New York Times* report points out, for example, "Whereas the General Motors Corporation employed 500,000 people at its peak in the 1970s, twenty years later it can make just as many cars with 315,000 workers."[6] Sears, Roebuck and Company cut 50,000 jobs between 1990 and 1996; AT&T cut 123,000 jobs. Workers with twenty or thirty years at a company have been discarded during both good times and bad. Only 35 percent of "downsized" workers have found jobs that pay as well or better than their old jobs.

Many people believe that good jobs that provide decent wages, benefits, and security are increasingly scarce. They suggest that in an economy that is more and more ruthless, people need the "safety net" provided by social welfare programs. However, in 1996 Congress passed and President Bill Clinton signed a welfare reform bill that eliminates the federal guarantee to help poor people. Federal block grants to the states have replaced the main federal welfare programs such as Aid to Families with Dependent Children (AFDC). States have

---

[3]Ibid., Table 730.
[4]Ibid., Table 616.
[5]*The New York Times, The Downsizing of America* (New York: Times Books, 1996), p. 6.
[6]Ibid., p. 17.

rushed to set time limits on benefits, establish work requirements, eliminate education benefits, and impose other regulations designed primarily to cut the cost of social programs. Critics of the legislation expect a "rush to the bottom" by states as they slash benefits so that they can cut taxes, thereby retaining businesses tempted to relocate to other states or countries and luring new businesses from other states. At the same time, so-called "corporate welfare"—federal and state tax breaks and subsidies for businesses, worth tens of billion of dollars annually—has remained remarkably resistant to reduction or elimination. Critics argue that the poor and working classes are asked to make far more sacrifices than are the rich and powerful.

IS TOO MUCH ECONOMIC INEQUALITY IMMORAL?

Egalitarians believe that economic and social inequalities should be kept to a reasonable minimum. Different egalitarians may have different conceptions of what constitutes a reasonable minimum, but all egalitarians agree that virtually all societies today have too much inequality. Economic inequality is a matter of degree. The highest-income earners in a society may receive ten times what the lowest-income earners receive, or they may receive ten million times what the lowest-income earners receive. Similarly, there can be small or colossal differences between the accumulated wealth of the richest and the poorest. Some people may have negative wealth (their debts are greater than their assets) while others have wealth counted in the billions of dollars.

The Case for Equality

According to John Rawls, there is a presumption in favor of economic equality. In his view, rational self-interested individuals in the Original Position behind the Veil of Ignorance would insist on a relatively equal distribution of the product of their social cooperation, unless some inequality would be advantageous for all. Because an individual behind the Veil of Ignorance does not know whether she will be healthy or ill, of high or low intelligence, skilled or unskilled, educated or uneducated, highly motivated or poorly motivated, she will refuse to accept principles of economic distribution that will favor one group of people over another because she may lose rather than gain from it. She will be cautious in selecting principles of economic distribution because she knows that she could be on the bottom of the economic ladder rather than on the top when she emerges from the Original Position. She will try to ensure that the worst that can happen to her is at least tolerable. Demanding an equal distribution of income and wealth, unless an unequal distribution will clearly benefit her, gives her the maximum protection from disaster if she emerges from the Original Position at the bottom of the ladder.

Thus, according to Rawls, "All social values—liberty and opportunities, income and wealth, and the bases of self-respect—are to be distributed equally unless an unequal distribution . . . is to everyone's advantage."[7] Economic inequality can have a number of bad effects. Some people may have so much that there isn't enough left over to meet even the basic needs for food, clothing, shelter, medical care, and education of many people at or near the bottom. Often, political and social power come with greater income and wealth. Great economic inequality can give some people the resources to dominate and oppress others and to gain undue influence over government and public policy, enabling them to amass and protect a variety of privileges. Great economic inequality can produce envy and an erosion of self-respect among those left behind, as well as arrogance and callousness among those who surge ahead. Therefore, Rawls maintains that rational self-interested individuals in the Original Position behind the Veil of Ignorance would accept this principle:

> Social and economic inequalities are to be arranged so that they are both
> (a) to the greatest benefit of the least advantaged and (b) attached to offices
> and positions open to all under conditions of fair equality of opportunity.[8]

"Injustice," according to Rawls, "is simply inequalities that are not to the benefit of all."[9] (Rawls makes several assumptions that lead to the conclusion that all are benefited if and only if the least advantaged are benefited.)

Rawl's presumption of equality means that economic *inequality* must be justified as benefiting everyone—most specifically, the least advantaged—if it is to be just or morally acceptable. Inequality benefits everyone if and only if it is both sufficient and necessary as an incentive for greater production. If a certain degree of inequality is required in order to get people to be more productive, and if their greater productivity increases the size of the economic pie so that everyone gets a bigger slice with the inequality than they would get without the inequality, then the equality is just and morally acceptable. However, if the inequality is more than is required to increase productivity, then it is unjust and morally unacceptable. For example, if people would be motivated to go to medical school and become good doctors only if the average income for doctors were three times the national average, then it would be just for doctors to have average incomes that were three times the national average. However, if receiving an income three times the national average is sufficient to motivate enough people to go to medical school and become good doctors, then it would be unjust for doctors to have annual incomes five times the national average. Similarly, if people could be motivated to become high corporate executives and to work at maximum efficiency if the average salary of corporate executives were five times the average salary of their workers, then it would be unjust and morally unacceptable if the average salary of high corporate executives were fifty times the average salary of their workers. Rawls implies that there is a far greater degree of economic inequality in United States society than is necessary as an incentive for production; if there is, there is too much economic inequality.

---

[7]John Rawls, *A Theory of Justice* (Cambridge, MA: Harvard University Press, 1971), p. 62.
[8]Ibid., p. 83.
[9]Ibid., p. 62.

Other egalitarians reach conclusions similar to Rawls's on other grounds. Contemporary United States philosopher Gregory Vlastos maintains that "the human worth of all persons is equal however unequal may be their merit."[10] As a corollary of this basic assumption, Vlastos claims that *"one man's well-being is as valuable as any other's."*[11] Therefore, "one man's *(prima facie)* right to well-being is equal to that of any other."[12] He then argues, "Since men have an equal right to well-being . . . , they have an equal right to the means of well-being."[13] Therefore, he concludes, people have a right to an "equal distribution [of economic resources] at the highest obtainable level."[14] According to Vlastos, because people have equal inherent worth simply because they are people, they have an equal moral right to economic resources, one of the primary means of well-being. If some people have many more economic resources than others, they have a much greater ability to achieve happiness or a satisfactory level of well-being. Too much economic inequality thus violates people's moral right to equal resources for pursuing and achieving happiness or well-being.

Australian philosopher Kai Nielson believes that an appropriate social goal is "an equality of basic condition for everyone."[15] He maintains that "everyone, as far as possible, should have equal life prospects. . . . There should, where this is possible, be an equality of access to equal resources over each person's life as a whole, though this should be qualified by people's varying needs."[16] Nielson's radical egalitarianism does not require that everyone have exactly the same amount of income and wealth. He supports Karl Marx's (1818–1883) principle, "From each according to his ability, to each according to his needs."[17] Greater need justifies greater economic resources that are required to satisfy that need. If one person is healthy and another person is ill and needs expensive medical treatment, equal economic resources will not give them equal life prospects. The person needing expensive medical treatment needs more economic resources to bring her life prospects up to the level of someone who doesn't need such medical treatment.

Nielson assumes that people should not be controlled or exploited by others. Because he believes that significant economic inequality enables the rich to control and exploit others, he believes that significant economic inequality is wrong.

---

[10]Gregory Vlastos, "Justice and Equality," in *Social Justice,* ed. Richard Brandt (Englewood Cliffs, NJ: Prentice-Hall, 1962), p. 43.

[11]Ibid., p. 51.

[12]Ibid., p. 52.

[13]Ibid., p. 59.

[14]Ibid.

[15]Kai Nielson, "Radical Egalitarianism," in *Justice: Alternative Political Perspectives,* 2d ed., ed. James Sterba (Belmont, CA: Wadsworth, 1992), p. 98.

[16]Ibid.

[17]Karl Marx, "Critique of the Gotha Program," in *The Marx-Engels Reader,* ed. Robert C. Tucker (New York: Norton, 1978), p. 531.

> Equal access to resources should be such that it stands as a barrier to there
> being the sort of differences between people that allow some to be in a
> position to control and to exploit others; such equal access to resources
> should also stand as a barrier to one adult person having power over other
> adult persons that does not rest on the revokable consent on the part of the
> persons over whom he comes to have power.[18]

Nielson maintains that egalitarians "are aiming for a society which, while remaining a society of material abundance, is a society in which there are to be no extensive differences in life prospects because some people have far greater income, power, authority, or prestige than others."[19]

Nielson believes that a radically egalitarian society will more effectively protect people's fundamental liberties and autonomy than a society that has a large degree of economic inequality. In his view, where there is great economic inequality, "power will pass into the hands of a few who will control the lives of the many and determine the fundamental design of the society."[20] Although the freedom to amass a fortune and to buy and sell at will will be restricted in a radically egalitarian society, that is a freedom that only a small minority can truly exercise. Restricting such less basic freedoms will effectively protect more basic freedoms of the majority of people, including the freedom to participate on an equal basis in political decision making and the freedom to control their own lives.

Nielson's views on equality and inequality are reminiscent of those of the European philosopher Jean Jacques Rousseau (1712-1778). According to Rousseau, freedom cannot survive without a certain degree of equality. Too much inequality destroys or undermines freedom. Equality, argues Rousseau, "must not be taken to imply that degrees of power and wealth should be absolutely the same for all, but rather that power shall stop short of violence and never be exercised except by virtue of authority and law, and, where wealth is concerned, that no citizen shall be rich enough to buy another and none so poor as to be forced to sell himself."[21] If some people are enormously wealthy, they can use their wealth to tyrannize over others, destroying freedom; if some people are terribly poor, they become so dependent on others for their very lives that they are no longer free. Both extremes are bad for society, according to Rousseau.

Some utilitarians also support equality. Contemporary British philosopher R. M. Hare provides a utilitarian argument in favor of equality: Greater economic equality almost always increases total happiness.

> Almost always, if money or goods are taken away from someone who has a lot
> of them already, and given to someone who has little, total utility [happiness or
> well-being] is increased, other things being equal. . . . Its ground is that the

---

[18]Nielson, "Radical Egalitarianism," p. 98.

[19]Ibid., p. 99.

[20]Ibid., p. 108.

[21]Jean Jacques Rousseau, *The Social Contract,* trans. Maurice Cranston (Harmondsworth, England: Penguin, 1968), p. 96.

poor man will get more utility out of what he is given than the rich from whom it is taken would have got."[22]

Arguments against Equality

Some people argue that economic equality means that everyone will be the same. In their view, if everyone has roughly equal amounts of wealth and income, all individuality will be lost. Everyone will act in the same way, dress identically, drive the same car, live in identical houses, and think the same thoughts. These opponents of economic equality maintain that human diversity is extremely valuable; the world of human beings would be terribly boring and monotonous if everyone were the same. Because economic equality would destroy human diversity, they argue, economic equality is undesirable.

Egalitarians, however, deny that people would be pretty much identical to one another if they had equal amounts of wealth and income. Suppose we know only that Juarez and Jon-Kim have the same amount of wealth ($65,000 in assets) and income ($40,000 per year). Can we confidently predict that they are pretty much alike? Egalitarians say that we cannot. Juarez may wear suits, listen to classical music, play golf, drink wine, go to the opera, and read philosophy while Jon-Kim may wear jeans, listen to rock and roll, climb mountains, jog and lift weights, drink beer, play cards, and watch televised sports. Egalitarians insist that having equal wealth and income cannot make people the same or similar in other areas, such as their religion, political beliefs, behavior, interests, tastes, and preferences. Therefore, egalitarians maintain, greater economic equality would not lead to the dreary uniformity that opponents of egalitarianism fear.

Probably the most important argument against reducing economic inequality is that achieving it requires economic redistribution and that economic redistribution violates the rights and freedoms of those from whom resources are taken. Economic redistribution occurs when economic resources (wealth or income) are taken from those who have a lot and redistributed to or given to those who have little. For example, a government may tax the nonpoor in order to give to the poor, Robin Hood style. People opposed to economic equality object that the freedom to spend their earnings as they wish or to keep all the money and resources that they have legitimately acquired is violated if they are taxed in order to reduce economic inequality—that is, to close the gap between rich and poor. They consider such taxation a form of theft. Contemporary United States philosopher Robert Nozick maintains, "Taxation of earnings from labor is on a par with forced labor."[23] Nozick appears to assume that people have a more or less absolute moral right not to be taxed in order to reduce economic inequality—a right that cannot justifiably be overridden in order to increase total

---

[22]R. M. Hare, "Justice and Equality," in *Justice and Economic Distribution*, ed. John Arthur and William Shaw (Englewood Cliffs, NJ: Prentice-Hall, 1978), pp. 124–125.

[23]Robert Nozick, *Anarchy, State, and Utopia* (New York: Basic Books, 1974), p. 169.

happiness or to respect the moral rights of other people, such as a right to equal life prospects or subsistence rights.

Egalitarians deny that people have a right not to be taxed. Some utilitarians point out, however, that redistributive policies can have negative effects on total happiness unless they are carried out with great caution. For example, Hare suggests that

> there are several empirical, practical restraints on the equality that can sensibly be imposed by governments. To mention just a few . . . the removal of incentives to effort may diminish the total stock of goods to be divided up; abrupt confiscation or even very steep progressive taxation may antagonize the victims so much that a whole class turns from a useful element in society to a hostile and dangerous one; or . . . it may merely become demoralized and either lose all enterprise and readiness to take business risks, or else just emigrate if it can.[24]

Hare emphasizes the need for empirical research to determine the probable effects on total happiness of various alternative redistribution policies.

IS POVERTY IN THE MIDST OF AFFLUENCE IMMORAL?

Is poverty in the midst of affluence immoral? It could only be immoral if poverty is subject to human control. If people can't do anything to reduce or eliminate poverty, then they cannot be blamed or morally condemned for it. It would be like asking whether gravity is immoral. Gravity is not under anyone's control; therefore, it doesn't make sense to say that gravity is immoral. However, poverty isn't like gravity; in an affluent society, poverty *is* under people's control. Poverty is a condition of having too little money to afford life's necessities; it can be cured by providing job opportunities, training, money, or life's necessities to the poor person.

Is poverty in the midst of affluence immoral if we believe that poor people are poor through their own fault? For example, we might claim that poor people are poor because they freely choose not to work hard enough to lift themselves from poverty; therefore, they're poor voluntarily rather than involuntarily. We might go on to claim that voluntary poverty is not immoral, and that all poverty is voluntary.

Even if voluntary poverty is not immoral, it is clear that not all poverty in our society is voluntary. Consider who is poor (or would be poor without assistance): children under age 18; people who are mentally or physically disabled, ill, or aged; and the working poor—people who work full- or part-time but do not earn enough to pull themselves above the poverty line, such as divorced or single mothers working low-paying jobs with no health insurance or other benefits. Their poverty is not voluntary. Even if some people are poor voluntarily, many

---

[24]Hare, "Justice and Equality," p. 125.

people are poor involuntarily. Our discussion of poverty as a moral issue will be limited to *involuntary* poverty.

Arguments for Relieving Poverty

According to both Act and Rule Utilitarianism, total happiness or well-being should be maximized, whether by acting directly to accomplish that end or by following rules that, if followed, will accomplish that end. A utilitarian could claim that total well-being is not maximized when poverty exists amidst affluence because total well-being would be greater if the rich had less and the poor had more—that is, if the basic needs of the poor were met rather than the desires of the rich for luxuries. Therefore, on utilitarian grounds we could say that poverty amidst affluence is immoral because it violates the utilitarian requirement that total well-being be maximized.

We might also appeal to Kant's Categorical Imperative. According to the universal law formulation, we should only act on a maxim that we can consistently will to be a universal law. Those who believe that poverty should be reduced or eliminated when it is possible to do so might maintain that no one can consistently will to be a universal law a maxim recommending that one ignore the suffering of the poor and refrain from relieving poverty. Kant himself took this position.

> A . . . man, for whom things are going well, sees that others (whom he could help) have to struggle with great hardships, and he asks, "What concern of mine is it? Let each one be as happy as heaven wills, or as he can make himself: I will not take anything from him or even envy him; but to his welfare or his assistance in time of need I have no desire to contribute." If such a way of thinking were a universal law of nature, certainly the human race could exist. . . . It is nevertheless impossible to will that such a principle should hold everywhere as a law of nature. For a will which resolved this would conflict with itself, since instances can often arise in which he would need the love and sympathy of others, and in which he would have robbed himself, by such a law of nature springing from his own will, of all hope of the aid he desires.[25]

A person naturally wants to have help if he needs it. If he wills as a universal law a maxim that permits him to ignore the needs of others in distress, his will is in conflict because he simultaneously wills that he be helped and yet not be helped when he is in distress and requires aid. Therefore, actions according to such a maxim are morally unacceptable. People should help those in need and relieve the sufferings of the poor.

Similarly, according to the respect for persons formulation of the Categorical Imperative, we should always treat other people with respect. We do not treat people with respect if we allow them to suffer or die or leave them unable to secure life's necessities because of poverty. A person is not being treated with respect if she is left homeless or hungry or if she is ill and left without medical

---

[25]Immanuel Kant, *Foundations of the Metaphysics of Morals,* 2d ed., trans. Lewis White Beck (New York: Macmillan, 1990), p. 40.

care. Respecting people involves caring about them and taking effective steps to promote or sustain their well-being.

We might also claim that a person's right to life is violated if he is left without life's necessities in the midst of affluence. Killing someone without sufficient justification (such as self-protection) would certainly violate his right to life; having a right to life entails that others have a duty not to kill us without sufficient justification. Some people maintain that the right to life also entails that others have a duty to save a person's life when they can do so at relatively little cost to themselves. According to this view, letting someone die when the death is preventable also violates that person's right to life. Suppose that you're choking because you've inhaled food and I could save your life by applying the Heimlich maneuver. Many people maintain that I would be violating your right to life were I to walk away and let you die. Poverty can be just as deadly as choking on food if a person does not get assistance. Thus, we might claim that leaving people in poverty when poverty is preventable and remediable violates their right to life.

We might also appeal to Rawls's hypothetical contract theory. We could maintain that rational self-interested individuals in the Original Position behind the Veil of Ignorance would not agree to accept principles that would permit the nonpoor to ignore the plight and suffering of the poor. In the Original Position a person does not know whether she will emerge rich or poor. If she agrees to accept principles that permit the nonpoor to escape from having to help the poor or that permit the poor to remain poor when it is preventable, she may be consigning herself to the sufferings of poverty.

Many people claim that people have moral rights to subsistence. According to the United Nations Universal Declaration of Human Rights, every person has a right to social security (Article 22), to work and protection against unemployment (Article 23), and "to a standard of living adequate for the health and well-being of himself and of his family, including food, clothing, housing, and medical care and necessary social services" (Article 25). If someone cannot afford life's necessities and is left without them to die, in a society affluent enough to meet those needs, that person's moral rights are being violated. The nonpoor have a duty of nonmaleficence and of beneficence—a duty to minimize harm to others and to relieve suffering caused by poverty.

Finally, those who support policies to reduce or eliminate poverty might appeal to considerations of virtue and vice and to a care approach. They may claim that a good or caring person would not ignore the sufferings of the poor. The virtues of generosity, kindness, compassion, concern, sympathy, benevolence, and beneficence would lead people to work to reduce or eliminate poverty; only the vices of selfishness, greed, and callousness would make them indifferent to the sufferings of the poor.

The Case against Reducing or Eliminating Poverty

The most fundamental arguments against reducing or eliminating poverty are identical to those against economic equality, discussed previously, because reducing or eliminating poverty requires economic redistribution. Those arguments need not be repeated here.

EQUAL OPPORTUNITY

Besides poverty and economic inequality, equal opportunity may also be a moral concern. For example, John Rawls's egalitarian principle of justice, cited previously, includes a requirement of equal opportunity.

> Social and economic inequalities are to be arranged so that they are both (a) to the greatest benefit of the least advantaged and (b) attached to offices and positions open to all under conditions of fair equality of opportunity.[26]

According to Rawls, equality of opportunity means

> that those with similar abilities and skills should have similar life chances. More specifically, assuming that there is a distribution of natural assets [innate abilities and capacities], those who are at the same level of talent and ability, and have the same willingness to use them, should have the same prospects of success regardless of their initial place in the social system, that is, irrespective of the income class into which they are born.[27]

Equal opportunity means that people with roughly the same genetic endowment have a roughly equal probability of rising to the same level in society. To the extent that people are either advantaged or disadvantaged by their environment, equal opportunity is compromised.

People can be advantaged or disadvantaged by their social environment in a variety of ways. If some people receive better nutrition and health care than most others while in the womb or in infancy, they have an advantage. If they receive better education or live in a more secure and nurturing environment than most others, they have an advantage. If they have family connections that enable them to get into desirable professional schools or career positions, they have an advantage. Conversely, if some people receive worse nutrition and health care than most others while in the womb or in infancy, they have a disadvantage. If they receive worse education or live in a less secure and nurturing environment than others, they have a disadvantage.

We might compare competition in society for income, wealth, status, education, and jobs to a huge marathon. Those who finish in the lead get the best things society has to offer; those who finish at the back get what's left over, if anything; those who don't finish may get nothing. If some people are running a rough uphill course, others are running a smooth level course, and still others are running a smooth downhill course, opportunity isn't equal—the race isn't fair.

---

[26]Rawls, *Theory of Justice,* p. 83.

[27]Ibid., p. 73.

Rawls maintains that rational self-interested people in the Original Position behind the Veil of Ignorance would insist on equal opportunity. Because they do not know what social class they are in, they will not want members of the upper classes having special advantages because they know that they may not be members of the upper classes. Similarly, they will not want members of the lower classes having special disadvantages because they may emerge as members of the lower classes. Because rational self-interested people in the Original Position would demand equal opportunity, unequal opportunity is unjust and morally unacceptable.

A Kantian would probably reach the same conclusion for similar reasons. A Kantian might maintain that rational agents could not consistently will as a universal law a maxim tolerating unequal opportunity because the willer of the maxim could be disadvantaged by it as well as advantaged. A rational agent would want her inherent intelligence, skills, talents, and abilities to determine her life prospects and position in society rather than have her place in society determine her life prospects.

A utilitarian might claim that equal opportunity will enable people to rise to the appropriate level in society so that society's human resources will be used with maximum efficiency, maximizing total well-being. With unequal opportunity, someone with the innate ability to be a nuclear physicist, engineer, brain surgeon, or conductor might be washing dishes in a diner or sweeping floors in a factory, a terrible waste of human potential.

JUSTICE, FAIRNESS, AND TAXES

In the 1996 presidential election, several Republican candidates endorsed a so-called "flat tax," maintaining that it is fairer and simpler than a graduated income tax. With a flat tax, all people pay the same percentage of their income in taxes, whether their annual income is $25,000 or $2.5 million. With a graduated income tax, on the other hand, higher income taxpayers are taxed at a higher rate.

For example, if we had a flat tax of 20 percent, then all income taxpayers would be taxed at a rate of 20 percent. Someone with a taxable income of $25,000 would pay $5,000 in taxes, leaving her with $20,000; someone with a taxable income of $2.5 million would pay $500,000 in taxes, leaving her with $2 million. Now suppose that we had a graduated income tax with three tax brackets: Income under $30,000 is taxed at a rate of 15 percent, income from $30,000 to $60,000 is taxed at a rate of 20 percent, and income over $60,000 is taxed at a rate of 30 percent. In that case, someone with a taxable income of $25,000 would pay $3,750 in taxes, whereas someone with a taxable income of $2.5 million would pay $742,500 (15% of the first $30,000 plus 20% of the next $30,000 plus 30% of the remaining $2,440,000, or $4,500 + $6,000 + $732,000 = $742,500).

Critics of the flat tax were quick to point out that moving from a graduated to a flat tax would do very little to simplify the system. Most of the complexity comes in the rules about what income is taxable and what income isn't. It is not the different tax rates that make the tax code complicated, but rather the myriad deductions and credits. When you're preparing your income tax return, it's determining that final number specifying your taxable income after all the deductions that drives you crazy. You have to determine whether contributions to retirement accounts, interest payments on a mortgage, professional expenses, losses on stocks, medical expenses, and so on are tax deductible. Once you've arrived at your taxable income, determining how much you owe is simple.

However, proponents of the flat tax maintained that it would be fairer than the graduated income tax because, unlike a graduated income tax, a flat tax treats all taxpayers *equally*. As we saw, Aristotle said that justice requires treating people who are equal in relevant respects in the same way and people who are unequal in relevant respects differently. Supporters of a flat tax seem to imply that all taxpayers are equal in the ways relevant to paying taxes and that therefore they should be treated equally by being taxed at the same rate.

Opponents of the flat tax, however, claim that not all taxpayers are equal in the ways relevant to paying taxes. They claim that someone with an annual income of $25,000 is not equal in relevant respects to someone with an annual income of $2.5 million. If both are taxed at 20 percent, the individual with an income of $25,000 pays $5,000, leaving only $20,000 on which to live. This person will find it difficult to afford life's basic necessities, let alone afford luxuries, on the money left after taxes. Paying 20 percent is a real hardship for him. On the other hand, the individual with an annual income of $2.5 million pays $500,000 but has $2 million left after taxes. Not only can he easily afford necessities, but he has ample money left over for a variety of luxuries. The 20 percent tax is no hardship for him. Thus, the two taxpayers are not equal in their *ability to pay*. Since they are not equal in all respects relevant to paying taxes, it would be unjust and unfair to treat them as if they were equal. Therefore, opponents of the flat tax claim that people with higher incomes who can afford to pay more should be taxed at a higher rate.

Interestingly, one common tax actually has the opposite structure: Those with *higher* incomes are taxed at a *lower* rate. Under the Social Security tax, income is taxed at a flat rate of 7.65 percent—but only the first $60,600 of income is taxed at all. As a result, everyone with a taxable income under $60,600 is taxed at a rate of 7.65 percent, but everyone with taxable income over $60,600 is taxed at less than 7.65 percent. Their rate is lower because no matter how much they earn, they still pay only $4,635.90 in Social Security tax. Thus, for example, someone with a taxable income of $500,000 is taxed at a rate of less than 1 percent. What is particularly galling to critics of Social Security is that for many years Congress and the president have been "borrowing" tens of billions of dollars annually from the Social Security trust funds to pay for government expenditures. (Cynics claim that it is done to hide the true size of the annual federal deficit.) Thus, Social Security taxes, which are lower for higher-income taxpayers, have been used instead of ordinary income taxes, which are higher for higher-income taxpayers. Critics consider this reverse effect very unjust.

Clearly, questions of justice and equality are central to tax policies, including the issue of a flat versus a graduated income tax.

EXERCISES

1. Review the economic data provided at the beginning of this chapter. Do you believe that there is too much economic inequality in the United States? Defend your answer. If you believe that there is too much economic inequality, what do you believe should be done to reduce it? Why?

2. Is economic redistribution to reduce economic inequality immoral? Defend your answer.

3. Is most poverty in the United States voluntary or involuntary? Defend your answer.

4. Should the United States pursue policies to reduce or eliminate poverty? Defend your answer.

5. Is economic redistribution to reduce or eliminate poverty immoral? Defend your answer.

6. If the United States sets the goal of significantly reducing or eliminating poverty, what policies are most likely to be effective? Defend your answer.

7. Try to construct an argument opposing equal opportunity.

8. What is probably required in order to ensure genuine equality of opportunity in the United States? Defend your answer.

9. Consider two people, Jim and Tom. Jim was born into a poor family. When he was in the womb, his mother suffered from malnutrition because of her poverty, and as a result Jim's brain was affected during its early development. After he was born, he continued to suffer from malnutrition and hunger. He often went without medical attention when he was ill because his family could not afford to pay for it. He has lived all his life in slums, and he went to substandard schools in the inner city that were overcrowded, dilapidated, and dangerous. During junior high school and high school he worked at least 20 hours a week in a grocery store to help his family, which took him away from his studies. He had a C average in high school, has received no encouragement to further his education, has no money for college, but has thought about college. Jim took the SAT and achieved a combined score of 900.

   Tom was born into an affluent family. He has never known hunger. He has lived in a large, comfortable, suburban house; he was sent to preschool; he attended superior suburban schools. He never had to work, and if he had trouble with a subject, his family hired private tutors. Tom had a B average in high school. Since he was ten years old he has been encouraged to attend college, and the family has the money to pay for even the most expensive private college. He plays sports, takes music lessons, and skis. Tom took an expensive SAT preparation course and achieved a combined score of 950 the first time he took it. He retook the SAT preparation course, retook the SAT, and achieved a combined score of 1020. His mother has connections among her business associates who can use their influence to help him get accepted into a good college or university.

Jim and Tom are both 18. Are they now able to compete on equal terms for admission to college? If they both go to college and are both accepted by the same college, will they be able to compete on equal terms? If their circumstances violate the requirement of equal opportunity, what can or should be done?

SUGGESTED READINGS

John Arthur and William Shaw. *Justice and Economic Distribution.* 2d ed. Englewood Cliffs, NJ: Prentice-Hall, 1991.

Robert Goodin. *Reasons for Welfare: The Political Theory of the Welfare State.* Princeton, NJ: Princeton University Press, 1988.

Immanuel Kant. *Foundations of the Metaphysics of Morals.* 2d ed. Translated by Lewis White Beck. New York: Macmillan, 1990.

Louis Pojman and Robert Westmoreland, eds. *Equality.* New York: Oxford University Press, 1997.

John Rawls. *A Theory of Justice.* Cambridge, MA: Harvard University Press, 1971.

James Sterba. *Justice: Alternative Political Perspectives.* 2d ed. Belmont, CA: Wadsworth, 1992.

CHAPTER 20

Sex Roles and Sexual Equality

In ancient Rome, women were completely subordinate to men. For example, a husband had the legal right to decide whether to keep and raise a newborn infant or to send it out to be exposed so that it would die. His wife, the infant's mother, had no legal say in the matter; it was entirely her husband's decision. Similarly, in the early years of the Roman Republic, women had no legal control over property. When they married, their property became their husband's. Women were also excluded from politics; they were ineligible for the Senate or other political offices and did not have the legal right to vote in elections.

Subordination of women was not confined to the ancient world. Shakespeare reflected the dominant attitude toward women in Elizabethan England in *The Taming of the Shrew*. Katherine was a "shrew" who needed to be "tamed" because she was ill-tempered and insufficiently submissive. Her husband, Petruchio, turned her into the perfect wife by psychological manipulation. In her final speech to two newly married women, Katherine shares her new-found wisdom about the proper relations between men and women, a wisdom that has brought her happiness.

> Thy husband is thy lord, thy life, thy keeper,
> Thy head, thy sovereign—one that cares for thee,
> And for thy maintenance commits his body
> To painful labor by both sea and land,
> To watch the night in storms, the day in cold,
> Whilst thou li'st warm at home, secure and safe;
> And craves no other tribute at thy hands
> But love, fair looks, and true obedience;
> Too little payment for so great a debt.
> Such duty as the subject owes the prince,
> Even such a woman oweth to her husband,
> And when she is froward, peevish, sullen, sour,
> And not obedient to his honest will,
> What is she but a foul contending rebel
> And graceless traitor to her loving lord?

> I am ashamed that women are so simple
> To offer war where they should kneel for peace,
> Or seek for rule, supremacy, and sway,
> When they are bound to serve, love, and obey.
>   *(V, ii, 146–164)*

In nineteenth-century Britain, according to Susan Kent, the situation was much the same.

> Under English law, wives became the property of their husbands, ceding to them their rights to own property and to earn money; apart from a limited custody over infants, mothers had no rights to their children; husbands could sue their wives for restitution of conjugal rights and could have them imprisoned if they refused sexual intercourse; they might rape their wives with impunity under the law; and they were free to indulge in extramarital sex without fear of a divorce action against them. Such a breach on the part of a married woman, however, constituted grounds for invalidation of the [marriage].[1]

In *Regina* v. *Clarence,* the British courts ruled that a man could not be convicted of raping his wife even if she refused sexual intercourse because he had a venereal disease.[2] At the same time, women were excluded from university education and from most professions.

Until well into the twentieth century, very few people believed that men and women are equal and that they have the same moral rights and moral status. Most people believed that women are inferior to men in a variety of ways—physically, intellectually, and morally—and that men should command and women obey. Many people assumed that men, much more than women, are capable of having reason control passion and feeling, which was considered a strength and a foundation of virtue. Few believed that women should have the same opportunities as men. Women were expected to be submissive to and dependent on men, to focus on being good wives and mothers, to labor inside the home for their husbands and family while men controlled the world outside the home. Families were hierarchical: The husband/father was the captain of the family ship, and the wife/mother and children were the crew.

In 1909, reports feminist Cicely Hamilton, the head of the local school board in North Surrey made the point explicit in a speech to the pupils in his district. "Addressing the girls he is reported to have used the following words—'To keep house, cook, nurse and delight in making others happy is your mission, duty, and livelihood.'"[3] According to Hamilton, women were expected and trained to be

> home-loving, charming, submissive, . . . unintelligent, . . . possessed with a
> desire to please, well-dressed, . . . self-sacrificing, . . . endowed with a talent

---

[1]Susan Kingsley Kent, *Sex and Suffrage in Britain, 1860–1914* (Princeton, NJ: Princeton University Press, 1987), p. 88.

[2]Ibid., p. 93.

[3]Cicely Hamilton, "Marriage as a Trade," in *Ethics: A Feminist Reader,* ed. Elizabeth Frazer, Jennifer Hornsby, and Sabina Lovibond (Oxford, England: Blackwell, 1992), p. 37.

for cooking, narrowly uninterested in the world outside their gates, and
capable of sinking their own identity and interests in the interests and identity
of a husband.[4]

Helplessness and fragility in women were valued far more than strength and
independence.

Since men were understood to dislike clever women, the girl who had brains,
capacity, intellect, sought to conceal, denied possession of them, so that her
future husband might enjoy, unchallenged, the pleasurable conviction of her
mental inferiority to himself.[5]

In the latter part of the twentieth century, age-old assumptions about the
proper relations between men and women began to buckle under vigorous
and sustained assault. Many people, both male and female, challenged the view
that women are inferior to men. They rejected the view that a woman's proper
place is in the home and that women should be subordinate to men. They claimed
that women should have the same opportunities for education, career and professional advancement, political participation, and personal fulfillment as men.
They rejected the idea that some work, such as housework and child rearing,
should be solely or primarily the responsibility of women while other work, such
as running the government and managing large corporations, should be the work
solely or primarily of men. They objected to "patriarchy." According to critics of
patriarchy, in a patriarchal society men have a near monopoly on political and economic power that enables them to make and interpret the laws that in turn
enable them to gain and to maintain a variety of privileges. It also enables them
to impose their values, preferences, beliefs, and perceptions on the rest of society.

People concerned about women's place in society point to a variety of ways
in which women lag behind men, thus confirming that women are still subordinate to men and that our society is still patriarchal. They note how few women
are in positions of political power. No women have been elected president or
vice president. Only two women have ever served on the Supreme Court in its
two-hundred-year history. Although women make up roughly 51 percent of the
population, very few women have been elected to the U.S. Senate or Congress
or elected a state's governor, and relatively few are judges in the higher state and
federal courts. Women don't fare much better in business and the professions.
Very few women have reached the top executive rungs of the corporate ladder
in large corporations or sit on their boards of directors. Few are influential
senior partners in large law or accounting firms. Women remain clustered in low-
pay, low-status jobs.

Many advocates for women claim that in personal relationships, too, women
remain subordinate to men. Even if a wife/mother works full-time outside the
home, she still is often expected to shoulder most of the burdens of home life,
such as cooking, food shopping, washing clothes and dishes, cleaning, and child

---

[4]Ibid., p. 38.
[5]Ibid., p. 39.

rearing. Moreover, many men still believe that the final decision on important family matters, such as major purchases, should be the husband's.

One question, of course, is whether critics are correct when they claim that our society is patriarchal and that women are still subordinate to men. That question can be answered only after careful examination that is beyond the scope of this chapter. Rather than focus on that question, we will examine two different, though related, questions. First, are men and women equal in all relevant respects so that morality requires that they be treated equally? Second, if men and women should be treated equally, what would morally acceptable relations between the sexes be like?

ARE MEN AND WOMEN EQUAL?

Plato in the *Republic* expressed views about women that were highly unusual for his society and for the ancient world in general. He divided the people in his ideal society into three classes: rulers, guardians or soldiers, and workers. Rulers make and administer the laws; guardians protect the state or city from enemies both internal and external; workers work to provide the goods and services that everyone needs. In Plato's society and time, it was almost unthinkable that women should exercise the legal and political power he assigned to the rulers, or that women should serve in the military and fight alongside men. Nevertheless, that is what Plato proposed. In his ideal society, men and women would perform the same tasks and have the same responsibilities. Women as well as men would be rulers and guardians.

Socrates, the spokesman for Plato in the *Republic,* conceded that men and women are different. However, he pointed out that not all differences are relevant for distributing the various tasks and responsibilities of social life.

> We are bravely . . . pursuing the principle that a nature which is not the same must not engage in the same pursuits, but . . . we did not examine at all what kind of difference and sameness of nature we had in mind. . . .

> We might . . . just as well, it seems, ask ourselves whether the nature of bald men and long-haired men is the same and not opposite, and then, agreeing that they are opposite, if we allow bald men to be cobblers, not allow long-haired men to be, or again if long-haired men are cobblers, not allow the others to be. . . .

> Is it ridiculous for any other reason than because we did not fully consider their same or different natures in every respect but we were only watching the kind of difference and sameness which applied to those particular pursuits? . . .

> But if they seem to differ in this particular only, that the female bears children while the male begets them, we shall say that there has been no kind of proof that a woman is different from a man as regards the duties we are talking about. . . .[6]

---

[6]Plato, *Republic,* trans. G. M. A. Grube (Indianapolis, IN: Hackett, 1974), pp. 116–117 (454b–e).

Plato advocated treating a person's sex as one might treat a person's hair color, hair length, or baldness. Such differences are irrelevant to the person's skills, intelligence, knowledge, or virtue, and consequently they are irrelevant to how a person should be treated and what tasks and responsibilities a person is fitted for. If a woman has the wisdom and virtue to be a ruler, then she should be a ruler. If she has the strength, skill, and courage to be a guardian, then she should be a guardian and fight alongside men. And Plato seemed confident that women would be found with the characteristics required of a ruler or a guardian.

Plato's attitudes toward women were highly unusual in his day, and they remained unusual until the twentieth century. For example, Aristotle wrote, "the male is by nature fitter for command than the female."[7] St. Paul enjoins in the New Testament (Ephesians, 4:22–23), "Wives, be subject to your husbands as you are to the Lord. For the husband is the head of the wife just as Christ is the head of the church." Other thinkers, too, have expressed the view that women are in some relevant ways inferior to men and that such inferiorities justify and practically demand different treatment of men and women.

Although many societies still harbor the assumption that women are inferior to and should be subordinate to men, those assumptions have been challenged in most of the modern industrialized world. For example, it used to be widely assumed that males are superior to females because males are more rational than females while females are more emotional than males. Critics of patriarchy point out that if that claim means that no female is more rational than any male and that no male is more emotional than any female, it is obviously false. Moreover, women's advocates claim that the assumption creates a false dichotomy between reason and emotion, presupposing that if a person is rational she cannot be emotional, and vice versa. Even if on average women are more emotional than men, it does not follow that they must then be less rational than men. Furthermore, the assumption that males are superior to women because they are less emotional places an unjustifiably low value on feelings and emotions. A person only mildly susceptible to such emotions as love, compassion, sympathy, and joy hardly seems a human ideal to strive for.

In 1973 sociologist Steven Goldberg wrote, in *The Inevitability of Patriarchy,* that males have a hormonal "aggression advantage." He claimed that "those individuals [with a] male anatomy . . . have hormonal systems which generate a greater capacity for 'aggression' (or a lower threshold for the release of 'aggression' . . .) than those individuals [with a] female anatomy."[8] In his view, success in industrial societies is largely a function of aggressiveness. Because males have an aggressive advantage, they will almost always triumph when women compete with men. In Goldberg's view, this aggression advantage—rather than unjust dis-

---

[7]Aristotle, "Politics," in *The Complete Works of Aristotle,* Vol. II, ed. Jonathan Barnes (Princeton, NJ: Princeton University Press, 1984), p. 1998 (1259b 3).

[8]Steven Goldberg, *The Inevitability of Patriarchy,* quoted in *Social Ethics,* 3d ed., ed. Thomas Mappes and Jane Zembaty (New York: McGraw-Hill, 1987), p. 148.

crimination and the historical oppression of women—best explains why women lag behind men. Therefore, Goldberg thought, it is imperative for women's self-esteem that a special sphere be set aside for them where they can succeed because they don't have to compete with men. Women, he argues, should be socialized to accept their limitations and to confine their interests to the special sphere where they are protected from men's aggression advantage. That sphere, not surprisingly, is the home rather than the wider world of business and government. Aggression is not necessary for success in housekeeping and child rearing, as it is for success in politics and business. Thus, because women are inferior to men in aggressiveness, they should be treated differently.

Goldberg never adequately defines his crucial term, *aggression.* What does it mean to claim that males are more aggressive than females? The dictionary defines *aggression* as

> **1:** a forceful action or procedure (as an unprovoked attack) esp. when intended to dominate or master **2:** the practice of making attacks or encroachments; . . . **3:** hostile, injurious, or destructive behavior or outlook esp. when caused by frustration[9]

These definitions suggest the use of force and violence to master or subdue. Thus, aggression might manifest itself in starting a war, beginning a barroom brawl, or battering a spouse or children. If that is what aggression means, then it is by no means clear that a high level of aggressiveness is necessary for or even compatible with success in politics and business in an industrial society, nor that high levels of aggressiveness (or a low threshold for aggression) is a good thing. A high level of aggressiveness may have been valuable in more primitive warrior cultures, but in contemporary society it seems more likely to lead to long jail terms than to the upper reaches of business and government. If Goldberg is right that men's hormones make them more aggressive than women in this sense, that claim hardly makes men superior. In fact, we could argue that it makes them inferior. Their higher levels of aggressiveness make them dangerous!

But perhaps by aggressiveness Goldberg means high levels of energy and ambition. In this sense, he is correct that aggression contributes to success outside the home, but it seems quite unlikely that men's hormones give them an "energy and ambition" advantage. Differences in male and female hormones do not seem to be good grounds for concluding that men are generally superior to women or for treating them differently.

Like Plato, many modern observers see no grounds for claiming that men are superior to women in terms of any characteristics that are relevant to how they should be treated: intellectual ability, innate potential for acquiring skills and knowledge, creativity, imagination, ambition, moral virtues and vices, and so on. Therefore, they believe that women should not be subordinate to men.

---

[9]*Merriam-Webster's Collegiate Dictionary,* 10th ed. (Springfield, MA: Merriam-Webster, 1994).

Sexual Equality in Practice

If men and women are equal, then they should be treated equally. But what does equal treatment mean in practice?

The Family and Home

Feminists insist that there is no justification for an unequal, hierarchical relationship between males and females within a relationship or family (however a family is defined). The benefits and burdens of family life should be equally shared wherever possible, with no sex having extra privileges or benefits while the other has extra burdens. For adult partners in the relationship, there should be an equal or fair division of responsibility for housework and child rearing, especially if both work outside the home. Most particularly, to identify some chores as purely or primarily women's work—such as cleaning the house, washing clothes and dishes, shopping, cooking, or caring for and playing with the children—while other tasks are identified as men's work—such as repairing the car, mowing the lawn, or fixing leaky faucets—is inconsistent with the equality of men and women.

Feminists also apply this approach to child rearing itself. In their view, children should not be treated in accordance with or socialized toward the prevailing sex-based stereotypes of men's and women's work. For example, it would be wrong to make a female child responsible for keeping her room clean while not making a male child of comparable age responsible for keeping his room clean. It would be wrong to parcel out family chores on the basis of sex—the daughters responsible for washing and drying dishes, doing laundry, cleaning the house, and making meals while the sons mow the lawn and take out the garbage.

Sons and daughters should also be given equal support and encouragement for achievement. It would be wrong to give more encouragement to sons than to daughters for success in elementary and secondary education, for going on to college, or for entering a profession such as engineering, medicine, or law. It would be wrong to spend $60,000 sending a son to an elite private college or university while spending only $20,000 sending a daughter to a less prestigious local state college solely on the grounds that a male's education is more important than a female's. It would be wrong to train a son to increase his toughness and decrease his tenderness ("Only girls cry") while training a daughter to decrease her toughness and increase her tenderness ("Don't be a tomboy"). The degree of toughness appropriate for a male should be the degree of toughness appropriate for a female; the degree of tenderness appropriate for a female should be the degree of tenderness appropriate for a male. Similarly, the same levels of dependence/independence, ambition, self-esteem, confidence, inner strength, intelligence, and competence are appropriate for both girls and boys. What is desirable or appropriate for one sex is desirable or appropriate for the other sex.

Feminists also maintain that since men and women are equal, there is no justification for a man within a family to take the role of the captain of a ship who must make the final decision on all important matters and whose final decision is law. Because men and women within a relationship are equal, decisions must be made jointly, the product of compromise and negotiation when there are differences of opinion. A man has no more right to impose his will in making the final decision when there's disagreement than a woman does. Similarly, women should not be expected to be, or be treated as, servants of their male partners. The woman should not do most of the giving and the man most of the taking; each should give and receive in equal proportion.

However, these ideals of sexual equality come into conflict with many deeply held preconceptions about the proper relations between the sexes. Many people are profoundly uncomfortable with taking sexual equality to such lengths. They believe that men should be socialized to be "masculine" and women should be socialized to be "feminine." They believe that some tasks and responsibilities—such as child rearing and caring for the home—are more suited to women because women are more nurturing and caring than men. They also believe that a man is naturally the head of the family. Disagreement thus remains in our society about how far sexual equality should go within the family and personal life.

Work

If men and women are equal, then women should not be discriminated against on the basis of their sex in employment and education. Sexual equality means equal pay for work of equal value, and equal opportunity for hiring and promotion. Women should have the same opportunities as men for entrance into and success in trades such as construction and plumbing; professions such as law, architecture, and medicine; and middle-class white-collar fields such as computer programming, accounting, and management. Sexual equality also requires a work environment free from sexual harassment.

Some women's advocates go further and maintain that because women continue to lag so far behind men, it would be appropriate to institute programs of affirmative action in order to overcome the effects of past and present discrimination against women. They believe that many men remain biased against women, considering them inferior to men. Because men monopolize the positions of greatest authority and power in our society, their bias against women (sexism) continues to handicap women who seek to achieve in the workplace. Men have most of the power when it comes to hiring and firing; their conscious or unconscious bias is a significant barrier to women's advancement. Therefore, some form of affirmative action or preferential treatment is needed to rectify the injustice.

For example, until recently most major law firms had few if any female partners. Women's advocates claimed that the reason was male bias. They maintained that the situation would not change significantly without programs of preferential treatment to force the law firms to make women partners. Similarly, ten or twenty years ago college and university faculties were overwhelmingly male. Many women's advocates maintained that women were unfairly handicapped in their quest for tenure because the decision makers were overwhelmingly men who were either consciously or unconsciously biased against women. Women's advocates claimed that unless programs of preferential treatment were instituted, women would continue to be largely frozen out of academia. Even today the percentage of full-time, tenured faculty members who are women remains far below what women's advocates believe it should be.

It goes almost without saying that affirmative action for women is controversial.

Women as Sex Objects

Many women's advocates object to society's treating women primarily as sex objects. Women's advocates believe that although they are equal, men and women are not treated with equal respect. In their view, women are systematically demeaned by a host of powerful and influential institutions. For example, advertising uses women's bodies to sell a variety of products; a huge number of advertisements on television and in magazines feature scantily clad attractive young women. MTV music videos are loaded with suggestively gyrating female bodies, and many popular songs have lyrics that express disrespect for and hostility toward women. Violence against women has become a major spectator sport on television and in movies, with the universal plot of beautiful-young-woman-pursued-by-mad-rapist/killer-who-hates-women dominating the screen.

Many women's advocates also deplore what they see as an overemphasis on youth, slenderness, and beauty that women in our society face. In their view, it is more acceptable in our society for a man to age than for a woman. A woman's value or worth is far more dependent on her appearance than a man's. Men can become distinguished as they age, but all too often women are treated as if they have been extinguished. The consequences of a man's becoming overweight, gray (or bald), and wrinkled are far less severe than the consequences of a woman's becoming overweight, gray, and wrinkled. A man can be valued more for his mind, character, and personality than for his physical appearance or his body, but far too often a woman seems to be valued primarily or exclusively for her physical appearance (the ideal being slender, unwrinkled, voluptuous beauty). For example, it's far more common for a husband to leave his aging wife for a younger woman than for a woman to leave her aging husband for a younger man.

Women's advocates maintain that many social institutions in our society both express and reflect disrespect for and hostility toward women. They believe that such disrespect and hostility should be eliminated. However, what would be required to achieve that end? Should advertisers be forbidden to employ images of scantily clad young women? Should television and movies be forbidden to portray violence against women? Should public service announcements periodically remind people that men and women should be treated equally? Some proposals obviously present problems. Some of them conflict with freedom of expression, forcing us to choose. Some people choose freedom of expression over sexual equality; others choose sexual equality over freedom of expression. Which values deserve priority is a vexing question.

EXERCISES

1. Do you believe that the oppression, suppression, and subordination of women is a relic of the past, or does it still occur? Defend your answer.

2. Are men and women equal in the respects relevant to how they should be treated? If not, in what way or ways are members of one sex superior to members of the other sex? If there are differences in personality, character, interests, and so on, between men and women, are they primarily the product of heredity or of socialization? Defend your answers.

3. Should men and women be treated equally? If not, in what ways should they be treated unequally? Defend your answers.

4. Tom believes that someone in the family has to have the final word, and he insists that that is the natural prerogative of the man of the house. Do you agree or disagree? Defend your position.

5. In 1922, Margaret Sanger wrote, "No woman can call herself free who does not own and control her own body. No woman can call herself free until she can choose consciously whether she will or will not be a mother."[10] Do sexual equality and the liberation of women require access to birth control or abortion so that women will have as much control over their bodies as men have over theirs? Defend your answer.

6. Are some tasks "women's work" and other tasks "men's work"? Defend your answer.

7. Describe in as much detail as you can what you think family life would be like if men and women treated each other as equals. Do you approve or disapprove of what that family life would be like? Why?

8. Describe how you, as a parent, would try to bring up a son and how you would try to bring up a daughter. Explain and defend your views on child rearing.

9. Do you think that our society treats women primarily as sex objects? If yes, how? Do you think that men are treated primarily as sex objects? Is there anything wrong with treating women primarily as sex objects? Defend your answer.

10. Do you think that there are influential institutions in our society that express disrespect for and hostility toward women? If yes, identify them and defend your answer.

---

[10]Margaret Sanger, "Birth Control—A Parents' Problem or a Woman's?" in *Ethics: A Feminist Reader,* ed. Frazer, Hornsby, and Lovibond, p. 55.

SUGGESTED READINGS

Elizabeth Frazer, Jennifer Hornsby, and Sabina Lovibond, eds. *Ethics: A Feminist Reader.* Oxford, England: Blackwell, 1992.

Thomas Mappes and Jane Zembaty, eds. *Social Ethics: Morality and Social Policy.* 3d ed. New York: McGraw-Hill, 1987. (See Chapter 4.)

Jan Narveson, ed. *Moral Issues.* New York: Oxford University Press, 1983. (See Section VII.)

Susan Moller Okin. *Justice, Gender, and the Family.* New York: Basic Books, 1989.

Plato. *Republic.* Translated by G. M. A. Grube. Indianapolis, IN: Hackett, 1974.

CHAPTER 21

Racism and Affirmative Action

Racism is a constellation of negative beliefs, attitudes, and feelings toward certain people based solely on their race. Racists believe that members of the target race are inherently inferior to other people. They may believe that members of the target race are less intelligent, less capable of acquiring knowledge or skills, less motivated to achieve, less capable of acquiring or exercising valued character traits such as self-discipline, and so on. Racists also have negative attitudes, feelings, and emotions—often hate or fear—toward members of the target race.

People may have racist beliefs, feelings, and attitudes and be consciously aware of them, or they may have them without being aware of it. In either case, racist beliefs, feelings, and attitudes influence behavior and lead to racist acts. Racist acts can be as dramatic as a lynching or as mundane as telling a joke that shows disrespect for members of the target race. They can include (consciously or unconsciously) refusing to associate with, hire, or promote members of the target race.

Gertrude Ezorsky distinguishes between overt and institutional racist acts.

Overt racist action . . . takes place only if a harm is inflicted or a benefit withheld either because of the perpetrator's racial bias against the victim or because of the perpetrator's obliging the race prejudice of others. . . .

Institutional racism occurs when a firm uses a practice that is race-neutral (intrinsically free of racial bias) but that nevertheless has an adverse impact on [members of the target race].[1]

A personnel manager's not hiring members of a certain race because she "doesn't feel comfortable with them" or because she does not think that members of the race "fit in with the company" would be overt racism. It would be institutional racism if a company required a high score on a standardized test that (1) is not adequately validated as reliably testing for skills or knowledge clearly related to successful job performance and that (2) members of the target race tend to do more poorly on than other people.

---

[1]Gertrude Ezorsky, *Racism and Justice* (Ithaca, NY: Cornell University Press, 1991), p. 9.

The United States has a long history of racism against African Americans. In this chapter we will examine the problem of racism against African Americans and a proposed remedy, affirmative action.[2]

RACISM IN THE UNITED STATES

African Americans were first brought to the North American continent as slaves; until the Civil War in the 1860s, most African Americans were slaves of whites. After the Civil War and Reconstruction, freed slaves and their descendants continued to be despised and oppressed by the white majority, especially in the South. However, their plight was ignored by most white people until the 1950s and 1960s.

In the 1950s and 1960s, the United States appeared to rediscover the pervasiveness of racism and its effects. Political events graphically demonstrated how far our society had to go to fulfill its promise of political equality and equal economic opportunity and focused public attention on some brutal facts of U.S. life. In some parts of the country, primarily the South, African Americans were denied the right to vote and equal protection of the laws. In most parts of the country, African Americans attended segregated public schools that were vastly inferior to the schools that white students attended. In many southern states, African Americans were denied admission to state colleges and universities. The poverty rate for African Americans was far higher than for whites: In 1959, 15.2 percent of white families but 48.1 percent of black families fell below the official poverty line. Relatively few African Americans had made it into the middle class, and fewer still had made it to the top, whether in business or politics. By almost any measure, African Americans lagged far behind their fellow citizens because they had been (and continued to be) victimized by prejudice and discrimination that affected every aspect of their lives. Society had, in a sense, conspired to oppress them solely because of their race.

In the 1950s and 1960s, positive steps were taken to improve the plight of citizens of color. A series of new laws banned discrimination in employment, housing, transportation, and public facilities such as hotels and restaurants. The Supreme Court, in *Brown* v. *Board of Education,* declared the legally segregated public schools of the South unconstitutional because they violated the Equal Protection clause of the Constitution. Although the *Brown* decision did not lead to immediate desegregation of public schools, it began a process that gradually accelerated as the federal government slowly began to enforce the Supreme Court's decision. At the same time, public and private programs were designed and at least partly implemented to bring African Americans into the mainstream of American political and economic life.

---

[2]I am not suggesting that bias and discrimination against members of other groups, such as women, Hispanics, and Native Americans, are nonexistent or unimportant. I focus on racism directed against African Americans because of its long history in the United States and its resistance to resolution.

A generation later, in the 1990s, many people appear to believe that those initiatives have succeeded—that the problems of racism, political equality, and equal opportunity have been solved, and no further positive initiatives are required. They believe that all citizens of the United States, regardless of race or national origin, now occupy a kind of level playing field that guarantees equal opportunity in the competition for wealth, power, status, and rights, with no one having special disadvantages or advantages because of their race or ethnicity. Others go further and maintain that having darker skin now confers an advantage rather than a disadvantage.

Have We Come a Long Way?

The claim that having darker skin now confers an advantage rather than a disadvantage cannot withstand serious scrutiny. In 1995, median family income was $40,884 for whites and $24,698 for blacks;[3] 11.7 percent of whites were below the poverty line, compared to 30.6 percent of blacks;[4] 13 percent of white families had an annual income below $15,000, compared to 32.2 percent of black families.[5] At the same time, 24 percent of whites had completed four or more years of college, compared to 13.2 percent of blacks and 9.3 percent of Hispanics.[6] For years, the unemployment rate among blacks has been roughly double that for whites, and the infant mortality rate has been almost three times as high.[7] By almost any measure, African Americans still lag far behind their white counterparts. Few sit on the boards of directors or are in the top ranks of management of major companies; all too many still attend inferior, segregated public schools, particularly in the major urban centers.

Why Do African Americans Still Lag Far Behind?

Why do African Americans on average continue to lag so far behind white America? Some people blame African Americans for their own situation. They maintain that although African Americans once were victimized by discrimination, unjust discrimination is now a thing of the past. According to this view, the United States is now a land of genuine equal opportunity. If people do not succeed in the economic competition, they have no one but themselves to blame. Sometimes it may be just bad luck, but bad luck has nothing to do with skin color. Often, though, it's a matter of bad attitudes and habits. African Americans who do not succeed made poor choices. Perhaps they chose to drop out of school or become pregnant. Perhaps they did not try very hard because they wallowed in self-pity or expected people to hand them things on a silver platter instead of working hard for them as other people have done. Perhaps they lacked

---

[3]U.S. Bureau of the Census, *Statistical Abstract of the United States, 1996*, Table 49.

[4]Ibid., Table 730.

[5]Ibid., Table 717.

[6]Ibid., Table 241.

[7]Ibid., Table 124.

self-discipline or ambition. Perhaps they chose to turn to crime as an easy way out rather than working at legitimate jobs. In any event, on this view, we may lament the fact that so many African Americans are behind in the race for money, status, and power, but neither American society in general nor European Americans in particular are responsible for their plight. They are responsible for their own plight, and it's up to them to pull themselves up.

However, not everyone accepts this view. On the contrary, many people believe that the best explanation of these disparities and inequalities is that the effects of past discrimination are still with us, handicapping African Americans in their efforts to compete with whites for education, training, jobs, income, and wealth, and that prejudice and unjust discrimination still exist, compounding the handicap.

That the effects of past discrimination continue to hobble African Americans seems plausible to many people. In addition to the data showing a substantial ongoing disparity between whites and blacks, the available evidence suggests that a substantial segment of white America is still prejudiced against African Americans, and it's highly probable that such prejudice results in overt discrimination, whether conscious or unconscious. Then, too, it is likely that institutional racism still exists.

A 1991 study of white attitudes by the University of Chicago's National Opinion Research Council found that "the majority of whites still believe that blacks and Hispanics prefer welfare [to working] and are lazier and more prone to violence [than whites]."[8] William Shaw found similar evidence of persistent stereotypes:

> A recent survey of Ivy League graduates, class of 1957, illustrates the prevalence of racial stereotypes and assumptions. For these men, "dumb" came to mind when they thought of blacks. Only 36 percent of the Princeton class, 47 percent of the Yale class, and 55 percent of the Harvard men agreed with the statement "Blacks are as intelligent as whites." These are graduates of three leading universities who are now in their fifties, the age of promotion into senior corporate positions.[9]

In 1992 television viewers were horrified when they were shown a videotape of white Los Angeles police officers beating a black motorist they had stopped, Rodney King. As seen in the televised videotape, King lay helpless on the ground as several white policemen continued to beat him savagely with their nightsticks. After the public outcry, four police officers were indicted and went to trial. The trial was held in a predominantly white middle-class suburb. To the surprise of almost everyone, the jury acquitted the four police officers. Many people believe that the police officers would not have beaten Rodney King so savagely if he had been white, and many believe that the jury would not have acquitted the officers if the officers had been black and King white. Many people

---

[8]*Boston Globe,* May 19, 1992.
[9]William Shaw, *Business Ethics* (Belmont, CA: Wadsworth, 1991), p. 294.

thus believe that both the beating and the jury's verdict were influenced by racism. (In 1993 two of the officers were convicted in a federal trial of violating Mr. King's civil rights.)

Evidence of bias abounds. Reports show that African Americans have a more difficult time getting mortgages than whites with comparable incomes and down payments. African Americans who enter stores are often followed by suspicious store clerks, whereas whites are not. If a black male walks down the street, women often clutch their handbags more tightly, a reflex that does not occur with white men. African Americans often have a difficult time renting apartments in primarily white neighborhoods.

Lawrence Otis Graham is an African American lawyer who graduated from Princeton University and Harvard Law School and was earning $105,000 a year in the early 1990s. He discovered that many of his white counterparts in the prestigious Manhattan law firm where he worked and hoped to become a partner were getting assignments over the weekend, whereas he got his Monday morning. On inquiring, he found out that his white male counterparts were being invited by senior partners to their Connecticut country clubs on the weekend, where a great deal of business with important clients was taking place. Graham discovered that he wasn't invited because the country clubs did not admit blacks. (Most also either did not admit or limited the membership of Jews and women.) Curious, Graham posed as a young college dropout looking for a job. Several of the county clubs that the partners belonged to had advertisements for waiters. He called and told them that he had two years' experience and two years of college. The people to whom he talked on the telephone were enthusiastic and asked him to come to the club right away to fill out an application. In almost every case, when they saw that he was black, they told him that the job he had called about a half-hour ago was no longer available.[10] The message was clear: Prejudice and discrimination are not dead.

Recent studies reinforce the claim that discrimination against African Americans still exists.

> The results of a recent research project reveal the extent of discrimination against young black men in hiring and give an insight into the connection between the discrimination and their high rate of unemployment. The Urban Institute assembled pairs of young men to serve as "testers." In each pair, one tester was black, the other white. Entry-level job openings were chosen at random from the newspaper, and a pair of testers was assigned to apply for each opening.

> The researchers made the pairs of testers as similar as possible, except with regard to race. Testers were matched in physical size and in the education and experience they claimed to have. An attempt was also made to match each pair in openness, energy level, and atitculateness. The testers were actually college students, but most of them posed as recent high school graduates and were supplied with fictional biographies that gave them similar job

---

[10]Lawrence Otis Graham, *Member of the Club* (New York: HarperCollins, 1995).

experience. They were put through mock interviews and coached to act like the person they were paired with to the greatest possible extent. The testers were then sent to apply for low-skill, entry-level jobs usually filled by young high-school graduates in manufacturing, hotels, restaurants, retail sales, and office work. The job titles ranged from general laborer to management trainee. The testers were instructed to refuse any job offered them so that the other member of the pair could have a chance at it.

The black testers posing as job seekers were carefully coached to present qualifications apparently equal to those of their white counterparts. In reality they were all, black and white, excellently qualified for the jobs they applied for. The Urban Institute researchers found that the young white men were offered jobs 45 percent more often than the young black men. This result clearly reveals that some employers were not treating male minority job seekers equally with white males of similar qualifications.[11]

PASSIVE NONDISCRIMINATION

Gertrude Ezorsky suggests that in order to eliminate the wide disparity in life prospects between whites and African Americans, social policy should aim at fully desegregating economic and social life. She maintains that programs of affirmative action are both effective and necessary for achieving this goal. However, many critics of affirmative action maintain that although its goals may be laudable, the means it employs to achieve those goals are immoral, and it is wrong to employ immoral means even for morally praiseworthy ends. They maintain that only *passive nondiscrimination* is morally acceptable.

Passive nondiscrimination involves ensuring that race-neutral criteria are used in hiring and promotion decisions and in entrance into colleges, universities, and professional schools. Many critics of affirmative action maintain that all we need to do is to establish and rigorously enforce laws prohibiting discrimination against individuals on the basis of race. If schools and employers are prohibited from discriminating against individuals on the basis of race, and if employment decisions and education admissions decisions are based solely on race-neutral qualifications, then the problem will be solved. In their view, passive nondiscrimination is an effective solution and is the only morally acceptable solution to the problem.

Other people, although they agree on the need for laws prohibiting discrimination in employment and schooling on the basis of race, maintain that passive nondiscrimination will not be effective enough in achieving the goals of racial equality and equal opportunity. First, they argue that because many African Americans have suffered from serious disadvantages all their lives—disadvantages based largely on race—it is impossible for many of them to compete on equal terms with whites for education and jobs. Although some whites are also

---

[11]Barbara Bergmann, *In Defense of Affirmative Action* (New York: Basic Books, 1996), pp. 50-51.

disadvantaged or poor, their disadvantage or poverty is not based on race, and the percentages are much smaller. Many more African Americans than whites are victims of poverty, childhood malnutrition, crime- and drug-plagued neighborhoods, substandard schools, low self-esteem, and serious family problems. Consider any successful white male, such as a doctor, lawyer, or college professor (perhaps one of your own professors). We can ask whether he would have been equally successful if he had been born with dark skin to poor parents. If we are honest, we would have to say "Probably not." Passive nondiscrimination will do nothing to erase the disadvantages that hobble many African Americans, making competition between them and middle- and upper-class whites unfair. If we rely only on passive nondiscrimination, critics argue, hobbled African Americans will remain hobbled for the foreseeable future.

Second, critics of relying only on passive nondiscrimination point out that judging credentials and qualifications is a subjective process that is affected by prejudice and bias, whether conscious or unconscious. Someone who is consciously biased and whose decision to reject an applicant for a job, promotion, or school is motivated by prejudice may nevertheless falsely maintain that he judged the rejected applicant solely on her qualifications. He may say that the applicant did not present herself well in the interview or that, in his judgment, she would not "fit" in the organization. Thus, although he may be consciously and deliberately discriminating against an applicant on the basis of the applicant's race, he can often plausibly maintain that he was not discriminating on the basis of race but instead made the decision solely based on qualifications. It is not easy to prove that discrimination on the basis of race has occurred in any given situation. Therefore, requiring only passive nondiscrimination may not be effective in eliminating discrimination.

Unconscious bias can affect our perception and judgment without our being aware of it. A person of color may not seem as bright or articulate, or might not seem to have leadership qualities, to an interviewer who is white. Written work submitted by a person of color to a white reader may not seem to the white reader as well written, perceptive, or knowledgeable as work submitted by another white person. Again, passive nondiscrimination alone may not be effective in ending discrimination because most decision makers are white. Unconscious bias may influence their judgments, so that a black applicant has to *be* twice as good as a white to *seem* even half as good in the eyes of a white decision maker.

Some people thus maintain that more than passive nondiscrimination is necessary in order to end discriminatory practices, whether conscious or unconscious, and to bring people of color into the mainstream of economic life.

AFFIRMATIVE ACTION AND PREFERENTIAL TREATMENT

Those who think that passive nondiscrimination will not solve the problem advocate *affirmative action*. Unfortunately, affirmative action is a notoriously vague concept embracing a wide variety of policies and programs. Many people tend to equate affirmative action with preferential treatment, and preferential treatment is intensely controversial. In fact, however, affirmative action programs can take many forms.

One modest form is designed to increase the number of people of color who apply for jobs or school admissions. Sometimes jobs are not advertised; applicants learn of them by word of mouth. In other cases, jobs are advertised in local media that may not be well known or popular with people of color. The result is that often people of color do not learn of job openings and therefore do not apply. In order to increase the number of applicants of color, an employer may change the way jobs are advertised. An employer may list a position with career resource centers that specialize in working with people of color or advertise in media (newspapers and magazines) that are widely circulated in communities of people of color. A company may also publicly announce that it does not tolerate discrimination as a way of encouraging people of color to apply.

Similarly, a college, in order to increase the number of applicants of color, may advertise in media popular with people of color or have special open houses or luncheons for people of color in order to show them how much the college has to offer them. A college may try to ensure that its admissions brochures include pictures of students and faculty of color in order to send the message that the college is hospitable to and values diversity. These types of affirmative action do not involve preferential treatment for people of color.

Affirmative action can also take the form of preferential treatment. With regard to hiring, promotions, and school admissions, preferential treatment generally follows one of three patterns:

1. Selecting an African American applicant over a white applicant when they are tied in terms of relevant qualifications.

2. Selecting an African American applicant over a white applicant when the African American applicant is less qualified in relevant respects than the white applicant.

3. Lowering selection standards for African American applicants.

Supporters of preferential treatment believe that it can be justified on at least two grounds. First, they maintain that virtually all African Americans have been harmed in one way or another, whether to a lesser or a greater degree, by past racial discrimination. From inferior segregated schools to inferior segregated housing, from lack of access to mortgages to lack of access to capital for business ventures, from inferior health care to inferior job prospects, African Americans have been kept from the table of American abundance. Then, too, the psychological damage of living in a racist society that brands and treats African Americans as inferior is virtually inescapable. It reduces self-esteem and self-confidence; it reduces motivation; it breeds hopelessness and despair. In the United States, someone with dark skin is handicapped; his or her road in life is uphill and rough rather than smooth and level or smooth and downhill. That is the legacy of racial discrimination. Therefore, advocates of preferential treatment maintain, African Americans deserve compensation for the harm they have suffered from the past history of bigotry. The most appropriate compensation is that, wherever possible, they be given preference over those who have not been harmed and handicapped by racism; such preferences will enable them to compete on more equal terms with people who have not been victimized and oppressed.

A second justification for preferential treatment is forward rather than backward looking. Unless more aggressive measures than passive nondiscrimination are taken, advocates maintain, African Americans will continue to lag behind white America for generations to come. In order to ensure that the future will not be like the past and present, preferential treatment is required.

Not everyone is persuaded by the backward-looking and forward-looking arguments for preferential treatment. Some people deny that most African Americans living today have suffered harm from past and present racism. Others deny that racism still holds African Americans back and that passive nondiscrimination will take generations to be effective. They think that if African Americans would work harder and stop looking for excuses for failure, they would catch up to European Americans. Finally, many people oppose preferential treatment on principle.

Does Preferential Treatment Mean Hiring the Unqualified?

Opponents of preferential treatment maintain that such programs entail hiring the unqualified for jobs, promoting the unqualified, or accepting the unqualified into colleges, universities, and professional schools. Of the three versions of preferential treatment, this objection can only apply to the second and third; in the first version, applicants are equally qualified. However, advocates of preferential treatment deny that such programs necessarily involve selecting unqualified applicants even in the second and third versions.

In the second version of preferential treatment, we may establish a qualifications threshold for being basically or fully qualified for a position or for admission. In that case, an applicant of any race must be basically or fully qualified— that is, have the relevant (objective) qualifications—in order to be considered. Of those who meet the basic qualifications, some applicants may be more qualified than others. Preferential treatment then permits hiring a less qualified applicant over a more qualified applicant; however, neither applicant is unqualified.

For example, suppose that a university requires that applicants have at least a B average in high school and a combined score of 1000 on the SAT in order to be considered for admission. Suppose that two applicants to the university have the same high school grades and test scores, but one is white and the other African American. If the university can't accept both, the first form of preferential treatment would permit using race as the tie breaker so that the African American applicant would be the one accepted. However, suppose that the white applicant has an A- high school average and a combined score of 1150 on the SAT while the African American applicant has a B+ high school average and a combined score of 1050 on the SAT. The second form of preferential treatment would permit selecting the African American over the white applicant, even though she is less qualified on the basis of high school grades and test scores. Note, however, that she is not *un*qualified because she still meets and even exceeds the basic requirements for admission to the university.

Similarly, suppose that a city is seeking to desegregate its police and fire departments. In order to be hired, an applicant must score at least 70 on a departmental civil service examination. Suppose that in fact almost no one who has scored below 90 has been hired, and suppose further that because of the segregated, inferior education to which they have been consigned, very few African Americans have scored 90 or above on the examination. If the departments were to select some African American applicants with scores in the 70s and 80s over white applicants with scores in the 90s in order to desegregate the department, they would not be hiring the unqualified.

Even the third version of preferential treatment need not entail selecting the unqualified, if by unqualified we mean not being competent to satisfactorily perform the tasks required in the job or not capable, with proper training, of becoming competent to do the job. Suppose that the police and fire departments in the last example found that very few African Americans were able to achieve scores of 70 or above on the examination. Therefore, in order to increase the representation of African Americans, it selected some African American applicants with scores in the 60s rather than white applicants with higher scores. A supporter of preferential treatment could argue that the fact that an applicant scored below 70 on the civil service examination may not prove that he or she is not competent to satisfactorily perform the tasks required of a police officer or firefighter or that he or she cannot become competent with proper training.

Does Preferential Treatment Violate the Rights of Highly Qualified Whites?

Many people believe that decision makers have a moral duty to accept, hire, or promote the most qualified applicant. Therefore, although they may have no objections to employing race in order to break ties, they do object to hiring the less qualified over the more qualified and to lowering standards.

There is a presumption in favor of hiring the most qualified applicant. One argument is utilitarian: Choosing the most qualified applicant maximizes efficiency, putting the most competent person in the job or school, thereby benefiting all of us. Second, some people maintain that the most qualified person has a *right* to the job or college admission. Partly the right derives from what can be considered legitimate expectations and the sacrifices made on the basis of those expectations. A highly qualified applicant may have made many sacrifices in order to achieve the qualifications—for example, by undergoing extensive education or training—because he expected, and was led by society to expect, that desirable positions would go to more qualified applicants. If we do not select the most qualified applicant for a job, we are violating that individual's rights, which is unjust.

Advocates of programs of preferential treatment that lead to selecting the less well qualified may respond in several ways. First, they may claim that rarely if ever have the most qualified been selected in the past, so that preferential treatment would *not* constitute a significant departure from past (and fairer) practice. For example, who we know (personal connections) is often more important than our qualifications, whether it be for appointment to the U.S. Supreme Court, admission to prestigious universities and professional schools, or selection for managerial positions in private industry. Second, they claim that decision makers have no absolutely reliable way to identify the most qualified applicant anyway. Decision makers rely on such factors as the applicant's experience, education record, test results, interviews, and letters of recommendation. However, these credentials are far from foolproof. The fact that one applicant has "better" qualifications than another, such as a higher grade point average, a higher score on an aptitude test, a degree from a more prestigious school, or a few more years of experience, does not guarantee that she is the more competent person and would do a better job. (Anyone who has been on an academic search committee knows how difficult it is to ascertain who is the "most qualified" and most likely to do the "best" job.) Much of the decision is ultimately based on personal interviews and the interviewers' evaluation of an applicant's "fit" and other personal characteristics, a notoriously subjective process that provides little protection from conscious or unconscious bias. Conscious or unconscious bias can subtly influence the decision maker's perception of the applicant and the evaluation of his or her record, undermining the supposed objectivity of the selection. For example, a male interviewer with a degree from an Ivy League college may tend to perceive male applicants with degrees from Ivy League colleges in a more favorable light than other applicants. Advocates of preferential treatment could argue that preferential treatment may actually increase efficiency by reducing the chance that less qualified white applicants will be selected over more qualified African American applicants because of conscious or unconscious bias on the part of mostly white decision makers.

Advocates of preferential treatment also point out that African Americans are not the only ones given preferential treatment. For example, veterans often benefit from programs of preferential treatment. From education grants to low-interest home mortgages, from extra bonus points on civil service examinations to free health care in Veterans Administration hospitals, veterans are given preferential treatment and privileges. Giving veterans bonus points on civil service examinations or taking steps to hire veterans as opposed to nonveterans violates the policy of hiring only the most qualified. Similarly, many colleges give preference in admission to children of alumni or to athletes who do not even come close to qualifying for admission on the basis of academic qualifications. If preferential treatment for veterans or athletes is justifiable, why not preferential treatment for African Americans? In reality, jobs, promotions, and school admissions going to the "most qualified" is more the exception than the rule; therefore, it is misleading at best to attack preferential treatment for people of color on the grounds that it departs from accepted and fairer practices.

Advocates of preferential treatment may concede that the most qualified applicant has a prima facie right to the job or school admission. However, even if we can identify the most qualified applicant, other, more important considerations may justify violating the prima facie right. Advocates of preferential treatment might argue that the most qualified applicant has a prima facie right to be selected for the job or school admission *if* everyone has an equal opportunity to become the most qualified applicant. Advocates of preferential treatment claim that African Americans are often denied the opportunity to become the most qualified applicant because of their race. Without equality of opportunity, they argue, the most qualified applicant does not necessarily have a right to be selected.

However, Gertrude Ezorsky recognizes that there is a serious problem here: If less qualified African American applicants are selected over more qualified white applicants, the white applicants are harmed. These white applicants may not be the most privileged members of our society. Suppose that in desegregating a city's police and fire departments, high-scoring white applicants are harmed by not being hired. Should they bear the total cost of compensating African Americans for past discrimination and the cost of desegregating economic and social life? They may not have benefited personally from past discrimination. Those who may have benefited most from past discrimination are escaping having to share the cost of rectifying it. The outcome seems unjust: In benefiting members of one group, we are harming members of another group.

Ezorsky advocates compensating the white victims of preferential treatment programs.[12] For example, suppose that six people are hired for the fire department, three whites and three African Americans. The whites scored 94, 92, and 91; the African Americans scored 84, 80, and 79. However, several white applicants scored higher than the African American applicants. The three highest-scoring whites had scores of 90, 87, and 86. If the department did not have a program of preferential treatment, they would have been hired instead of the three African American applicants. Because we can reliably identify those whites who have been harmed—that is, those whites who very probably would have been hired if there were no program of preferential treatment—we can and should compensate them for the harm that has been done to them. The fairest way is to use tax dollars in order to spread the burden of affirmative action. The three white applicants might receive extra unemployment compensation if they are unemployed or some other monetary compensation. In many cases, however, it is difficult to identify white victims of preferential treatment programs. A person may claim that, without affirmative action, he would have gotten a job that went instead to an African American, but it is often uncertain who actually would have gotten the job.

---

[12]Ezorsky, *Racism and Justice*, pp. 84–88.

Is Preferential Treatment Unjust Discrimination?

Many people believe that programs of preferential treatment unjustly discriminate against white males and thus constitute a kind of reverse discrimination. If a less qualified applicant is selected over a more qualified applicant solely because the more qualified applicant is white and the less qualified applicant is African American, hasn't the white applicant been unjustly discriminated against? Isn't it exactly the same as if a white applicant were selected over an African American applicant solely because of his race?

Proponents of preferential treatment deny that it constitutes reverse discrimination. First, they maintain that almost all whites have benefited from past and present racial discrimination against African Americans.

> As a group, they have been the first in line for hiring, training, promotion, and desirable job assignment, but last in line for seniority-based layoff. As whites, they have also benefited from housing discrimination in areas where jobs could be had and from the racist impact of selection based on personal connections, seniority, and qualifications. Indeed many white candidates fail to realize that their superior qualifications may be due to their having attended predominantly white schools.[13]

While people of color have been disadvantaged, whites have been unfairly advantaged, even if many of them don't realize it. If whites had had to compete on equal terms with people of color, many of them would not have risen as high as they have. Many whites owe their present level of comfort to pervasive discrimination that gave them an unfair advantage over others who had equal innate ability and potential but who were hobbled by discrimination. Proponents of preferential treatment thus argue that such programs are, in effect, returning stolen goods to their rightful owners.

Supporters of preferential treatment also maintain that the motivation and attitudes underlying these programs make them significantly different from unjust reverse discrimination. The motive underlying discrimination was racism. African Americans were discriminated against because they were despised and judged to be inferior to whites; the discrimination was pervasive, occurring in all areas and at all levels of society. It was not a question of one African American losing one good job to one white applicant; economic and educational opportunities were severely restricted everywhere but at the bottom.

If an African American is selected over a more qualified white applicant because of a program of preferential treatment, prejudice has nothing to do with it. The decision is not based on the assumption that whites are despicable or are inferior to African Americans. The purpose of selecting the African American is not to exclude a white from a social benefit solely because of his or her race, and it is not part of a pervasive pattern of exclusion based on race. It does not

---

[13]Ibid., p. 83.

consign individual whites or whites as a group to the cellar of economic life or globally deny them equal opportunity everywhere they turn. If a white applicant who is more qualified than an African American is passed over in one situation in favor of the African American, he or she will not necessarily be excluded from other opportunities.

Thomas E. Hill, Jr., argues that discrimination is generally thought unjust when it is arbitrary discrimination. Discrimination that gives preference to African Americans, however, is not arbitrary. It is based, first, on the fact that in the past not only were blacks treated differently from whites but they were treated "*as no human beings should be treated*,"[14] and second, on the claim, which some whites deny, that African Americans continue to be treated as no human beings should be treated. Justice requires that whites not be *arbitrarily* discriminated against in school admissions, hiring, and promotions. Supporters of preferential treatment for African Americans maintain that the discrimination that these programs embody is not arbitrary and not unjustified, and therefore not unjust.

Hill points out that "the values that give affirmative action its point . . . include . . . the ideals of mutual respect, trust, and fair opportunity for all."[15] He claims that what is needed is "a message to counter the deep insult inherent in racism."[16] To be believed, the message must include deeds as well as words. Inaction or passivity would send the message that our society and its (white) power structure are not very concerned about the fact that African Americans continue to lag far behind whites on almost every front. Failure to employ preferential treatment sends a message of indifference. Furthermore, it sends the message that our society is more concerned with protecting whites who have not suffered from past discrimination than it is in helping African Americans who have suffered and probably continue to suffer from racist discrimination. As Hill puts it, the message would be, "We would rather let the majority of white males enjoy the advantages of their unfair headstart than to risk compensating one of you who [might] not deserve it."[17]

On the other hand, according to Hill, if our society does employ affirmative action programs, including programs of preferential treatment, in order to help African Americans improve their economic condition, we would be sending the following message:

> We acknowledge that you have been wronged . . . by humiliating and debilitating attitudes prevalent in our country and our institutions. We deplore and denounce these attitudes and the wrongs that spring from them. We acknowledge that, so far, most of you have had your opportunities in life diminished by

---

[14]Thomas E. Hill, Jr., "The Message of Affirmative Action," in Thomas E. Hill, Jr., *Autonomy and Self-Respect* (Cambridge, England: Cambridge University Press, 1991), p. 195.

[15]Ibid., p. 205.

[16]Ibid., p. 206.

[17]Ibid., p. 208.

the effects of these attitudes, and we want no one's prospects to be diminished by injustice.[18]

The message of affirmative action to those who have been disadvantaged by racist discrimination is that of concern, care, respect, and welcome into the mainstream of American life. It is important that we send this message.

What message does affirmative action send to whites? Does it send the message that they are inferior and not worthy of respect? No. Hill thinks that we should try to send the following message to whites:

> Our policy [preferential treatment for African Americans] in no way implies the view that your opportunities are less important than others', but we estimate (roughly, as we must) that as a white male you have probably had advantages and encouragement that for a long time have been systematically, unfairly, and insultingly unavailable to most . . . minorities. . . . We appeal to you to share the historical values of fair opportunity and mutual respect that underlie this policy and hope that, even though its effects may be personally disappointing, you can see the policy as an appropriate response to the current situation.[19]

White resistance to affirmative action and preferential treatment for African Americans suggests that few whites today accept this message.

MULTICULTURALISM AND DIVERSITY

Many colleges and universities are wrestling with issues involving multiculturalism and diversity on campus. In 1995, the U.S. population was 83 percent white; some projections estimate that by 2050, that figure will fall to about 75 percent. Of the present population, 84 percent is Christian—60 percent Protestant and 24 percent Roman Catholic—2 percent are Jewish, 6 percent are identified as "other," and 8 percent list no religion. Contact with other peoples and cultures is increasing as the world economy grows ever more integrated. We must learn to understand and work with people with all kinds of backgrounds: people of Asian and African ancestry; people who speak any of a hundred languages, not just English; people who are Muslims, Hindus, and Buddhists.

Because our own country is becoming increasingly diverse, and because the world outside our country is such a diverse place, many people believe it is vital that our colleges and universities reflect that diversity. In their view, a college or university whose student, faculty, and staff populations are 90–100 percent European American is doing its students a disservice. It is not preparing them for the world in which they will live and work. Without constant exposure to diverse kinds of people, students—especially white students—may not learn how to feel comfortable and deal sensitively with people who are unlike themselves.

---

[18]Ibid., p. 209.

[19]Ibid., p. 210.

Lawrence Blum considers multiculturalism an important value that should be taught in schools.

> Multiculturalism involves an understanding, appreciation and valuing of one's own culture, and an informed respect and curiosity about the ethnic culture of others. It involves a valuing of other cultures, not in the sense of approving of all aspects of those cultures, but of attempting to see how a given culture can express value to its own members.[20]

As Blum sees it, multiculturalism also involves a desire to learn about other cultures, an openness to learning *from* other cultures, and "valuing and taking delight in cultural diversity itself."[21] It is unlikely that the value of multiculturalism can be inculcated in students unless they are in a truly multicultural environment. A campus that is almost all white is not a truly multicultural environment.

From this perspective, diversity is an important educational value. How can we ensure that a college or university has a diverse population? Many argue that true diversity can only be achieved by affirmative action programs. If they do not employ some form of affirmative action, many colleges and universities will have a population of faculty, students, and staff that is overwhelmingly white. If having a racially diverse campus is an important educational value, then affirmative action programs may be justified as a necessary means to that end.

EXERCISES

1. Could a program of preferential treatment pass the Kantian moral test of involving a maxim that one could consistently will to be a universal law? Explain and defend your answer.

2. Apply the social contract theory of morality, either the real or hypothetical version, to the issue of affirmative action and preferential treatment. Could such programs be morally acceptable from this point of view? Explain and defend your answer.

3. Jefferson City is 40 percent white and 40 percent African American, but its police force is 95 percent white. Community leaders believe that it's important to increase the number of African American police officers, believing that they are more effective than white officers in African American neighborhoods. In order to qualify for the police force, applicants must score at least 70 on the police exam. In practice, the force selects applicants with the highest scores on the exam, so almost no one has been hired who scores below 92. Of those who score 92 or above, 95 percent are white. Some community leaders claim that whites score higher because the schools they attend are so much better than those that most African Americans attend. They are proposing that the department set a goal that 50 percent of the *new* police officers it hires over the next

---

[20]Lawrence Blum, "Antiracism, Multiculturalism, and Interracial Community," in *Social Justice in a Diverse Society,* ed. Rita C. Manning and René Trujillo (Mountain View, CA: Mayfield, 1996), p. 370.
[21]Ibid., p. 374.

five years will be African Americans. To reach that goal, they recommend that African Americans be hired over whites even if they score lower on the test than some white applicants; however, they recommend maintaining the minimum score requirement of 70. Thus, an African American who scored 71 could be selected over a white applicant who scored 93. Would this program of preferential treatment be morally acceptable? Defend your answer. Would it be morally acceptable to lower the minimum passing score from 70 to 60 on the test for African Americans, but not for whites? Defend your answer.

4. Eight of 200 students (4 percent) in the entering class of Holmes School of Law are African Americans. The Dean of Admissions believes that more African American lawyers are needed; therefore, she proposes that the school have a goal of accepting at least 16 African Americans next year. In order to achieve that goal, she recommends that admission standards for African Americans and Hispanics be lowered. To be considered for admission, applicants have had to have at least a 3.2 undergraduate GPA and score at least in the 70th percentile on the LSAT; she recommends lowering the minimum to a 2.75 GPA and the 60th percentile on the LSAT for African Americans and Hispanics to increase the probability that the school can reach its goal. She emphasizes, however, that graduation standards will not be lowered. In order to ensure that underqualified students who enter this program meet the graduation requirements, she recommends a remedial program in their first and second years for those students who need it in order to help them meet the standards of the school and succeed in law school. Would this program of preferential treatment be morally acceptable? Defend your answer. Would it make a difference if it were a medical school?

5. Ted, a white male, graduated from college with a B.A. in economics, a minor in business administration, and a 3.4 GPA. He applied to the management training program at Summa Corporation. He was not hired. However, he learned that Summa has an affirmative action plan that includes a program of preferential treatment because the company has so few African Americans in management. Although Summa rejected Ted's application, the company hired an African American applicant to the management training program who has a B.A. in government and a 2.9 GPA. Ted believes that he was discriminated against because he's white and that Summa's program of preferential treatment is morally unacceptable. Do you agree with him? Defend your answer.

SUGGESTED READINGS

Barbara Bergmann. *In Defense of Affirmative Action.* New York: Basic Books, 1996.

Bernard Boxill. *Blacks and Social Justice.* Totowa, NJ: Rowman & Littlefield, 1982.

George Curry, ed. *The Affirmative Action Debate.* Reading, MA: Addison-Wesley, 1996.

Gertrude Ezorsky. *Racism and Justice.* Ithaca, NY: Cornell University Press, 1991.

Alan Goldman. *Justice and Reverse Discrimination.* Princeton, NJ: Princeton University Press, 1979.

Jan Narveson, ed. *Moral Issues.* New York: Oxford University Press, 1983. (See Section VII, Equality, and Section VIII, Justified Discrimination?)

Morality and War

The world has a long and sorry history of war. The United States was born in war, the American Revolution, and has fought numerous wars since then. Expanding European settlement precipitated a series of wars with Native Americans, including the Black Hawk War of 1832, The Seminole wars of the 1830s, and the Sioux wars of the 1870s. In 1846 the United States fought a war with Mexico in order to seize parts of what is now Texas. From 1861 to 1865 Americans fought the Civil War as the southern states attempted to secede from the Union and the northern states sought to prevent them from seceding. In 1898 the United States fought Spain; in 1917 it entered World War I; in 1941 it entered World War II. In the 1950s the United States fought in Korea; in the 1960s and 1970s it fought in Indochina (Vietnam, Laos, and Cambodia); in the 1980s it invaded Grenada and Panama. Most recently, in 1991, if fought in the Middle East in order to liberate Kuwait from Iraqi occupation.

No one knows precisely how many wars have been fought in human history, nor how many people have died as a result of war, but the numbers must be enormous. Ancient civilizations such as the Egyptians, Greeks, and Romans fought constantly. Some conflicts were major, some minor; battles on land and sea were probably annual events. Some wars practically define certain periods of history or civilizations—for example, the Trojan War, the Peloponnesian War, and the Punic Wars in ancient times, the Crusades in the Middle Ages, the Napoleonic Wars, and World Wars I and II.

Even when nations are not fighting wars, they are preparing for war, spending money to pay and equip armies and navies (and now air forces) and to buy weapons. No one knows how much money has been spent in human history waging or preparing to wage war, but again, the amount must be enormous. If we just confine ourselves to the end of the twentieth century, the numbers are breathtaking. Estimates are that from 1970 to 1990, the world spent $17 trillion on the military. By 1990, annual world military spending totaled about $1 trillion. About 5 percent of the world's GNP goes to the military—money that could be spent for other purposes.[1]

---

[1]Mostafa K. Tolba, *Saving Our Planet* (London: Chapman & Hall, 1993), pp. 210–211.

Wars have been fought for all kinds of reasons. Sometimes they're purely defensive, a reaction to some form of aggression such as an invasion. But not all wars can be purely defensive. If a nation is attacked, someone must have done the attacking. Nations may attack other nations to acquire territory or economic resources, to enhance their prestige, to settle disputes, or to protect important interests. Then, too, wars can be fought in all sorts of ways. An army can assault and massacre civilians; execute prisoners of war; besiege, starve, and bomb cities with conventional, chemical, biological, or nuclear weapons; poison water supplies; spray an enemy's land with defoliants that kill vegetation; or assassinate an enemy's leaders. Two fundamental moral issues thus arise regarding war and peace: (1) Under what conditions, if any, is it morally acceptable to resort to the organized violence of war? (2) Is everything morally acceptable in war, or are there moral limits to what is permissible in waging war?

These questions are vital not only for national leaders who must decide whether to and how to fight a war but also for ordinary citizens, especially in a democracy. Ordinary citizens have to decide whether to vote for or against political candidates and leaders in national elections that often have profound influence on their nation's military and foreign policy. They may have to decide whether to publicly support or oppose a war that their leaders have entered or threaten to enter. They may have to decide whether to support a war by volunteering to fight, consenting to conscription, remaining in the military, or working in military-related industries. If they are fighting in a war, they may have to decide whether to obey the orders of superiors who could demand that they massacre defenseless civilians, bomb cities of negligible military value in order to terrorize their inhabitants, or poison water supplies. If there are moral limits to whether and how war may be fought, they apply to ordinary citizens as well as to national leaders.

THE PRESUMPTION AGAINST WAR

Some people, fed on sanitized images of war from television and movies, view war as heroic, romantic, and exciting. Compared to flipping burgers at a fast-food restaurant, bagging groceries at the food store, or shuffling papers at an office desk, war may seem a thrilling, adventurous relief from the often boring routine of peacetime existence. However glorious, thrilling, or exciting war may seem to some people, however, for most people it brings nothing but death, destruction, injury, and suffering, often on a gargantuan scale. The sharp teeth of war tear apart huge numbers of helpless, innocent victims: children, women, the ill and injured, the aged. People die from being blown apart, crushed, burned, stabbed, and shot; they die from starvation, disease, and exposure. If they do not lose their lives, they may lose limbs, eyes, or internal organs; they may be permanently crippled, disabled, or disfigured. In addition to destroying people, war destroys property that people need to survive and creates intense emotional suffering and anguish from the loss of possessions and loved ones.

People also point out that fighting or preparing to fight wars diverts crucial economic resources from meeting the needs of people. Money spent on battle-ships, tanks, bombers, missiles, military installations, and soldiers could have been spent on education, health care, housing, child care, transportation, and other civilian-oriented goods and services.

Because war brings so much death and intense suffering, especially to the helpless and innocent, some people maintain that war is always immoral. These absolute pacifists live their principles by refusing to participate in any way in war. They will not serve in the military, and they will not work in war-related industries. Some pacifists will not do anything that they believe supports war, including serving as a civilian medic on or near the field of battle. Some even refuse to pay taxes that go to support the military.

Many pacifists appeal to religious precepts, such as the Hebrew Bible com-mandment "You shall not murder," claiming that war is nothing but organized murder. They argue that war unjustifiably and massively violates the most fun-damental moral right of innocent people, the right to life. In their view, no cause, however good, can outweigh the evil of war. Then, too, the virtues seem to be on the side of peace and the vices on the side of war. Kindness, compassion, sym-pathy, and love must lead one to deplore war; cruelty, callousness, brutality, indif-ference to suffering, greed, arrogance, and hate weigh in on the side of war.

Many people deplore war for the same reasons as pacifists but maintain that under certain circumstances war can be justified. They recognize a very strong presumption against war because it is evil, but argue that in certain extreme cir-cumstances, the presumption against war may be justifiably overridden.

THE JUST WAR TRADITION

Discriminating between circumstances under which the presumption against war may and may not be justifiably overridden requires standards or criteria. Many people appeal to criteria that have been developed in the just war tradi-tion that has been most carefully elaborated by Roman Catholic philosophers and theologians.

According to St. Thomas Aquinas, in order to be just, a war must (1) be declared by competent authority, (2) be for a just cause, and (3) be fought with the right intentions.

> In order for a war to be just, three things are necessary. First, the authority of the ruler, by whose command the war is to be waged. . . . Just as it is lawful for them to have recourse to the sword in defending the common weal against internal disturbances. . . , so too it is their business to have recourse to the sword of war in defending the common weal against external enemies.
>
> Secondly, a just cause is required, namely, that those who are attacked, should be attacked because they deserve it on account of some fault.
>
> Thirdly, it is necessary that the belligerents should have a rightful intention, so that they intend the advancement of good or the avoidance of evil. Hence Augustine says, "True religion looks upon as peaceful those wars that are

waged not for motives of aggrandizement or cruelty but with the object of securing peace, of punishing evil-doers, and of uplifting the good." For it may happen that [war] is ... rendered unlawful through a wicked intention. Hence Augustine says, "The passion for inflicting harm, the cruel thirst to vengeance, an unpacific and relentless spirit, the fever of revolt, the lust of power, and such like things, all these are rightly condemned in war."[2]

However, just cause is not the only condition on warfare in the just war tradition. The war must have a reasonable chance of success. Shedding innocent blood on behalf of an obviously lost cause is wrong. War must also be the last resort rather than a first resort. Finally, there are moral limits on how wars may be fought, even if the cause is just and there is a reasonable chance of success. We must employ just means and avoid unjust means, and the response must be proportional to the provocation. The just war tradition rejects the slogan "All's fair in love and war."

WHAT IS A JUST CAUSE?
Self-Defense and Aggression

According to the just war tradition, war is justified if it is necessary to protect innocent people from harm and to protect a nation or people from unjust aggression. Wars of aggression—wars initiated to conquer or subjugate a nation's neighbors—are illegitimate and immoral. As the National Council of Catholic Bishops expressed in their 1983 pastoral letter on war and peace, "War is permissible only to confront 'a real and certain danger,' i.e., to protect innocent life, to preserve conditions necessary for a decent human existence, and to secure basic human rights."[3]

According to the just war tradition, nations have a right to self-defense, just as individuals do. Self-defense for a nation means defending the lives, health, freedom, and property of its citizens, as well as defending its territorial integrity and political independence. We might justify the claim that nations have a right of self-defense by pointing out that in many cases a nation-state protects (and is the only entity that can and does protect) its citizens' well-being and way of life. We could maintain that such wars can be justified by appeal to utilitarian, Kantian, and social contract moral theories.

According to just war theory, resistance to military attacks and invasions constitutes just cause. However, a nation can face a variety of nonmilitary threats. For example, other nations may refuse to sell it resources it needs, such as oil or wheat, or refuse to admit its exports into their markets, jeopardizing its standard

---

[2]St. Thomas Aquinas, "Summa Theologiae," II-II, in *On Law, Morality, and Politics,* ed. William Baumgarth and Richard Regan (Indianapolis, IN: Hackett, 1988), pp. 221–222 (Question 40, Article I).

[3]National Council of Catholic Bishops, *The Challenge of Peace: God's Promise and Our Response* (Washington, DC: United States Catholic Conference, 1983), paragraph 86.

of living. In extreme cases, the lives and health of a nation's inhabitants may be jeopardized. For example, if nation X can't grow enough food to feed its population and other nations refuse to sell it the grain and meat it needs, its people may face widespread starvation and malnutrition. Whether such nonmilitary threats constitute just cause remains controversial.

Suppose that nation X faces widespread starvation because of drought. Consider three different scenarios:

1. X has money to purchase the food it needs; a neighbor, nation Y, has enough surplus food to supply X's needs and intends to sell it to other nations; X has offered to buy Y's surplus at the price that Y has been selling it; Y refuses to sell to X; X has no other likely source of food; X invades Y and seizes the food it needs.

2. X has money to purchase the food it needs; a neighbor, nation Y, has only enough food to feed its own population; X has offered to buy food from Y; Y refuses to sell food to X; X invades and seizes the food it needs.

3. X does not have any money to purchase the food it needs; a neighbor, nation Y, has a surplus of food that it intends to sell to other nations; X asks Y to either give it food or allow it to buy food on credit; Y refuses to give X food or sell it food on credit; X invades and seizes the food it needs.

Does nation X have just cause in any of these scenarios?

In all three scenarios, nation Y is innocent in that it has not caused nation X's food shortage nor has it engaged in aggression against nation X. And we might argue that nation X would violate the property rights of nation Y if it seized the food that it needs. However, in scenario 1 Nation Y refuses to sell nation X the food that it needs if it is to avoid widespread famine despite the fact that Y has a surplus that it intends to sell. Some people might argue that such behavior is not very different from aggression and that it constitutes just cause. In scenarios 2 and 3, the situation is different: In scenario 2 nation Y cannot provide nation X with food without harming its own people; in scenario 3 it is being asked to either give or sell on credit, both of which may impose financial harm on its people. If nation X does not have just cause in scenarios 2 and 3, then self-preservation alone is not sufficient for just cause.

Proving Strength and Determination

During the Vietnam War, President Nixon insisted that he would not permit the United States to appear to be a "pitiful, helpless giant." At least one reason for continuing the war, then, was to prove to the world that the United States was militarily strong and determined to use its strength to protect its vital national interests. Similarly, many people believe that President Reagan ordered the U.S. invasion of the tiny Island of Grenada in 1983 primarily to enhance the image of U.S. power and determination. Is the desire to prove a nation's military strength and determination a good enough reason to go to war?

Some people maintain that proving a nation's power and determination cannot outweigh the losses of war. Even if a war is kept limited and controlled (an increasingly difficult task), people will die and be injured. (From a moral point of view, we must include the losses of our adversaries as well as our own losses.) However, others maintain that to prove a nation's power and resolve may be worth at least some deaths because a nation's image of power and resolve is vital to its well-being. They claim that powerlessness (or the image of powerlessness) leaves a nation vulnerable to economic, political, and military threats from aggressive neighbors. In their view, an image of declining power and resolve invites attack, increasing the probability that a nation will be faced with a choice of resisting or surrendering. However, if aggressive neighbors believe that a nation is militarily powerful and willing to use that power to protect its vital national interests, they will be much less likely to threaten those national interests. Therefore, sometimes initiating "small" wars to prove a nation's power and resolve can prevent large wars, paradoxically saving lives.

Unfortunately, political leaders (and their people) are sometimes prone to exaggerate, intentionally or unintentionally, the extent to which their nation's image of power and resolve is threatened and the extent to which war will enhance that image. Similarly, political leaders sometimes tend to overestimate their ability to control and limit the level of conflict and to underestimate the losses (to themselves and others) that a war will bring. Therefore, it is often difficult to determine whether a war to enhance or protect a nation's image of power and resolve is necessary (and sufficient) to protect a nation from aggression. Often such wars of prestige simply make diplomacy easier, or enable a nation to more easily protect its standard of living and economic interests, or enable it to get its way in the international arena more frequently.

One problem, of course, is that wars of prestige to deter aggression are often fought not against the nation that threatens the aggression but against other nations. For example, if the U.S. wars against Vietnam and Grenada were wars of prestige, the message of undiminished power and resolve that U.S. leaders wanted to communicate was directed not toward those small nations but toward the Soviet Union. It's difficult to imagine how a nation can rationally defend attacking a (relatively) innocent third party in order to deter an attack from another nation. If nation X wants to show nation Y that its power and resolve remain undiminished in order to deter aggression from Y, it may be acceptable for it to attack Y, but surely it would be immoral for it to attack another nation, Z. It's even problematic whether X would be justified in attacking Y for reasons of prestige. Therefore, it is at least questionable whether projecting an image of strength and resolve constitutes just cause.

Preemption

If a nation appears to face imminent military attack, it may have a choice: wait to be attacked before responding, or attack first. Preemption is the act of attacking first in self-defense. For example, in 1967 Israel launched a preemptive military first strike against Egypt. According to Michael Walzer, for several weeks

preceding the Israeli attack Egypt had engaged in actions that almost any reasonable observer would have considered preparation for war. Egypt and the
other Arab nations had been extremely hostile to Israel since its creation in 1948
and had already fought several wars with Israel with the publicly expressed
intention of destroying and eliminating it. Believing that an Egyptian military
attack was imminent and that Israel would be more likely to survive, win, and
limit its casualties if it attacked before being attacked, Israel struck first.
Although in hindsight Walzer thinks that Egypt's leaders intended to humiliate
rather than actually attack Israel, he thinks that it was perfectly reasonable for
Israel's leaders to anticipate an attack.[4]

Walzer suggests that a first strike is justified by the right of self-defense and
morally acceptable if there is "a manifest intent to injure, a degree of active preparation that makes that intent a positive danger, and a general situation in which
waiting, or doing anything other than fighting, greatly magnifies the risk."[5] To
insist that a nation wait to be attacked before acting can, in some circumstances,
seriously jeopardize a nation's ability to protect itself. A high probability of imminent attack may therefore constitute a just cause for war. To justify attacking
first, however, there must be very strong evidence that an attack is imminent and
that waiting to be attacked would make self-defense far more costly or uncertain.

Revolution/Civil War

In the 1770s the American colonies turned to war to secure their political independence from England. In 1861 the southern states turned to war to gain their
political independence from the federal Union. From the 1950s through the early
1970s, nationalist and communist forces in Vietnam fought to overthrow the U.S.-
backed government in the South and to reunify North and South Vietnam. In the
last decade of the twentieth century, the former Yugoslavia erupted into civil war
as Bosnia-Herzegovina sought autonomy and its Serbian minority fought to seize
as much territory as possible from the majority Muslims and Croats to join to the
territory of Serbia. Is it morally acceptable to wage war to gain political independence or to seize control of the government of one's own country?

Few people find it plausible to maintain that revolution or civil war is never
justified. Governments can be unjust and oppressive and can violate fundamental moral rights of all or some of their people. They can exclude members of
some groups from political participation, or they can exploit, oppress, and even
systematically massacre people (for example, the Nazi government's policy of
exterminating Jews in Europe and the Khmer Rouge's genocidal policies in
Cambodia in the 1970s that led to the death of up to 15 percent of Cambodia's
population). According to many people, a government's systematically violating
fundamental moral rights of a large number of its members can constitute a just
cause for war, whether civil war, revolution, or international intervention. In

[4]Michael Walzer, *Just and Unjust Wars* (New York: Basic Books, 1977), pp. 82–85.
[5]Ibid., p. 81.

such cases, we are striving to protect the innocent. The more oppressive and unjust the government is, the more justified we are in resorting to violence to resist or overthrow it; the less oppressive and unjust the government is, the less justified we are in resorting to violence to resist or overthrow it.

Most people probably also accept that securing a region's or people's political independence or autonomy can be a just cause. For example, few people today condemn the leaders of the American Revolution for resorting to war to secure American independence from England. However, some people do not consider violence in order to gain political independence acceptable. Gandhi in India insisted that the campaign for Indian independence be nonviolent. Similarly, Stephen Maturin, a character in a series of stories by Patrick O'Brian, says, after a futile Irish uprising in 1798,

> With what I saw in '98, on both sides, the wicked folly and the wicked brute cruelty, I have had such a sickening of men in masses, and of causes, that I would not cross this room to reform parliament or prevent the union or to bring about the millennium. . . . Man as part of a movement or a crowd is indifferent to me. He is inhuman. And I have nothing to do with nations, or nationalism. The only feelings that I have . . . are for men as individuals; my loyalties, such as they may be, are to private persons alone.[6]

In his view, nationalistic causes dedicated to political independence are invitations to barbarism and cruelty, not moral justifications for war.

Third-Party Intervention

What of intervening in order to protect allies or friends or to protect oppressed minorities within a country? Even if a nation is not itself attacked, it may wage war to protect its allies and friends from unjust aggression or to protect the innocent from massive evil or violations of their fundamental moral rights. Many people in the United States during the Cold War were ready to attack the Soviet Union if it invaded Western Europe. The United States participated in the Korean War in the 1950s even though North Korea had invaded South Korea, not the United States. Similarly, Operation Desert Storm of 1991 ejected Saddam Hussein's Iraqi troops from Kuwaiti territory, not from United States territory. Is protecting allies, friends, or innocent people a just cause?

Such wars can sometimes be justified on the basis of self-defense. A nation's security depends at least in part on its having friends and allies in the world who are ready and willing to come to its aid. If an aggressor conquers all of a nation's friends and allies, its position may become hopeless. It will be alone in a hostile sea. However, as before, a nation must beware of intentional or unintentional exaggeration. Nations may overestimate the justice of a friend's a cause and underestimate the justice of an adversary's. They may also exaggerate a friendly nation's contribution to their security.

---

[6]Patrick O'Brian, *Master and Commander* (New York: Norton, 1970), p. 173.

Although some interventions may be based on self-defense, others may be based on humanitarian considerations. A nation may wish to protect a weak nation from a strong and aggressive one simply because the aggressive nation will oppress, exploit, enslave, or exterminate the people it conquers. A nation may wish to protect a people from its own government, not an invader, for the same reason. At least some people maintain that it would have been morally acceptable for the United States to overthrow Castro's government to "liberate" the people of Cuba. Similarly, many people maintain that it would have been morally acceptable for other nations to wage war to overthrow the genocidal Khmer Rouge government of Cambodia in the 1970s or that it was morally acceptable to wage war against the Nazi government pursuing its policy of exterminating Jews and other "undesirables" in Germany in the 1940s.

Do such humanitarian reasons constitute just cause? Many people find it difficult to rationally defend the claim that however massive the violation of basic human rights may be, other nations must stand aside and do nothing so long as their own interests are not threatened. Admittedly, a crusading mentality can be profoundly dangerous, leading to perpetual wars to right every conceivable wrong. However, the opposite mentality seems equally dangerous. Duties to minimize suffering, to resist or prevent evil, and to protect the weak and helpless do not lapse at a nation's boundaries.

OTHER CONDITIONS OF A JUST WAR

Just cause is not the only requirement of just war theory; a number of other conditions must be met. Many of these additional principles could probably be defended by appealing to Utilitarianism, Kantian moral theory, or social contract theory.

Last Resort

According to just war theory, war is justified only as a last resort, never as a first resort. Nations must first make a good faith effort to resolve issues peacefully through genuine diplomacy, negotiations, bargaining, or compromise. A resort to war can be morally acceptable only if all peaceful means of achieving a nation's (just) objectives or resolving a conflict have been exhausted.

Reasonable Chance of Success

According to just war theory, a nation (or people) is justified in resorting to war only if it has a reasonable chance of achieving its (just) objectives. To initiate violence that will kill thousands or tens of thousands of innocent people for a cause that has virtually no chance of success is immoral. For example, if violent resistance to an invader would be futile and would create far more casualties than would not resisting, it would not be morally acceptable to violently resist. (Nonviolent resistance may be a different matter.) Similarly, if a revolution has no chance of success, it would be wrong to revolt and throw lives away in what is obviously a lost cause.

Proportional Response

According to just war theory, any violent response must be proportional to the provocation. For example, if a nation is invaded, a legitimate response would be to repel the attack and perhaps to punish the aggressor to the extent required to discourage further attacks. It would not be legitimate to exterminate every citizen of the attacking nation, to enslave all of its inhabitants, or to destroy its economy. Self-defense permits only what is actually necessary to protect the lives and health of a nation's citizens, defend its territorial integrity, and preserve its political independence. The duty to minimize harm entails that a nation should cause as little harm as possible in defending itself.

JUSTICE IN WAGING WAR

General Sherman, who left a trail of devastation in Georgia and torched Atlanta during the Civil War, said that war is hell and implied that anything done to win or shorten a war is morally acceptable. Just war theory rejects this view. According to its theorists, some ways of waging war are immoral, even if one is fighting in a just cause. This understanding has been incorporated into international law, the Geneva Conventions, which prohibit some forms of warfare as too cruel to be acceptable. These international agreements, for example, prohibit mistreatment of prisoners of war and civilian populations under military control.

The distinction between combatants and noncombatants is fundamental to the moral evaluation of warfare. Combatants are regular and irregular military or paramilitary personnel (for example, members of the armed forces, guerrilla bands, and active terrorist organizations) who participate in the fighting. Noncombatants are nonparticipants and usually include children, women, the ill, the aged, ordinary farmers and industrial workers, and prisoners of war. According to just war theory, combatants pose a military threat and therefore may be attacked in a just cause; noncombatants are innocent victims who do not pose a military threat and therefore may not be attacked even in a just cause.

The distinction between combatants and noncombatants has often been ignored. Even when battles between soldiers could be clearly limited in space and time, enabling each side to clearly recognize who was a combatant and who was not, the victor sometimes killed all or most of the inhabitants of the area captured. For example, according to the Hebrew Bible, Joshua and the Israelites slaughtered all the people of Jericho, Ai, Makkedah, Hazor, and other towns after defeating their armies. The ancient Greeks and Romans, too, sometimes slaughtered all the inhabitants of towns that they conquered. Similarly, the U.S. cavalry in the nineteenth century indiscriminately slaughtered the inhabitants of Indian camps: children, women, and the aged as well as able-bodied men.

The distinction between combatants and noncombatants has become increasingly blurred as human beings have invented weapons of mass destruction and engaged in a kind of total warfare. Bombing cities has become a commonplace tactic of war, in part because things of military value are often in or near major cities: communication and transportation systems, energy sources, military installations, and factories producing war-related items such as guns, ammunition, tanks, bombs, airplanes, and ships. Even if the goal is not explicitly to kill noncombatants, it is foreseeable that large numbers of noncombatants will be killed. Nuclear, chemical, and biological weapons have made this problem even more acute. Because of their terrible destructiveness, a single weapon can literally destroy an entire city, killing and injuring millions of people, most of whom are noncombatants.

Almost everyone now agrees that it is immoral to intentionally attack defenseless noncombatants. Although such behavior still occurs in wartime, when it does occur virtually every nation condemns it. However, there is sharp disagreement about whether it is morally acceptable to attack military targets if such attacks will inevitably and foreseeably lead to numerous casualties among noncombatants. In such cases the goal is not to kill noncombatants but to destroy targets of military value; the noncombatant casualties are an unavoidable by-product, now referred to as "collateral damage."

Many people claim that a nation's interest in winning or shortening a war, or in limiting its own casualties, justifies attacking targets with important military value even if a large number of noncombatant casualties is inevitable. In their view, the right of self-defense permits a nation to harm or kill innocent people, if necessary, to limit its own injuries or to save itself. For example, if a nation can win or significantly shorten a war only by destroying an enemy's fuel supplies, it may do so even though destroying them requires destroying large parts of the cities in which refineries and storage facilities are located, killing tens of thousands of noncombatants.

However, some people believe that morality places limits on what we may do in furthering our own self-interest, whether as individuals or nations. We cannot harm innocent people just because it is in our self-interest. First, critics maintain, we must show beyond reasonable doubt that attacks that will cause noncombatant casualties are directed at targets of military value whose destruction is absolutely necessary for winning or significantly shortening a war. Second, we must make every effort to minimize noncombatant casualties in such attacks, even if it means additional risks to the attackers. Finally, if the likely cost in noncombatant injury and death is too high, we should refrain from attacking, even if it makes defeat highly probable. In their view, a nation's or individual's right of self-defense does not entail a right to inflict limitless harm on innocent people.

But are noncombatants of an enemy nation innocent? What if our own cause is just and our enemy's cause is unjust? In that case, wouldn't all citizens of the enemy's country be in some sense guilty rather than innocent? That view is difficult to justify. Not all people have influence over their government's policies, most obviously children; they cannot be held responsible for the misdeeds of their government. Some people may disapprove of or actively resist rather than support their government's policies; they, too, cannot be held responsible. Thus, many people will be innocent, even if they inhabit the country of our enemy and the enemy's cause is unjust.

Unconventional Weapons

The duty to minimize the harm that we cause to innocent people makes questionable any use of unconventional weapons, whether nuclear, chemical, or biological. High-powered unconventional weapons capable of destroying most living things within a wide radius are incapable of discriminating between combatants and noncombatants. Many people are convinced that any use of unconventional weapons would be immoral. In their view, recourse to such weapons not only indiscriminately destroys innocent noncombatants but significantly increases the likelihood of escalation to all-out nuclear war that could exterminate all of humanity.

Deterrence

Even if *using* unconventional weapons—nuclear, chemical, or biological—would be immoral, is *threatening* to use them immoral? The threat to use unconventional weapons is an essential element of a policy called deterrence: threatening to retaliate and inflict unacceptable damage on an adversary with unconventional weapons in order to discourage the adversary from attacking (whether with conventional or unconventional weapons). Rational adversaries are expected to calculate that because of such retaliation, the costs of aggression would be far greater than any conceivable benefits; therefore, they will avoid aggression that could lead to such retaliation. Thus, during the Cold War, the United States threatened to use nuclear weapons against the Soviet Union if it attacked Western Europe or the United States, whether with conventional or unconventional weapons. The threat was intended to deter such an attack, much as the threat of capital punishment is intended, in part, to deter violent crime.

Let's assume for the sake of argument that to actually use unconventional weapons in attacking the Soviet Union, even in retaliation for aggression, would be immoral because of the horrific number of innocent people who would be killed. Is it immoral to threaten to do what it would be immoral to actually do? Many people think not. From a utilitarian perspective, if the threat is effective in deterring attack, many lives are saved, making the gains far greater than the losses. And if deterrence fails and a nation is attacked anyway, it need not carry out the threat. Therefore, from a utilitarian perspective, deterrence may be morally acceptable.

EXERCISES

1. First, try to construct a defense for pacifism. Next, try to construct a defense for the rejection of pacifism.

2. Try to construct (a) a utilitarian, (b) a Kantian, and (c) a social contract defense of the requirements for a just war.

3. Was it morally acceptable for the American colonies to resort to violence in order to gain independence from England? Defend your answer.

4. Was it morally acceptable for the southern states to resort to violence in order to gain independence from the federal union? Defend your answer.

5. Was it morally acceptable for the northern states to resort to violence in order to prevent the southern states from seceding from the federal union? Defend your answer.

6. Would it have been morally acceptable for a country such as Poland, Lithuania, or Czechoslovakia to have violently rebelled against Soviet rule during the Cold War? Would it have been morally acceptable for the United States to have gone to war in order to liberate Eastern Europe from Soviet domination? Defend your answers.

7. Was it morally acceptable for the United States to go to war in order to liberate Kuwait from the Iraqis in the Persian Gulf War of 1991? Defend your answer.

8. If the Soviet Union had invaded West Germany during the Cold War, would it have been morally acceptable for the United States to destroy Moscow with a nuclear bomb in retaliation? Defend your answer.

9. Would it have been morally acceptable for the United States to have destroyed Iraq's capital, Baghdad, with either conventional or nonconventional weapons in order to force it to withdraw from Kuwait? Defend your answer.

10. The United States is the only nation in the world that has actually used nuclear weapons. U.S. leaders knew that dropping atomic bombs on Hiroshima and Nagasaki in 1945 was not necessary to win the war, but they (apparently) believed that it was the only or the best way to shorten it and save lives. Critics of the bombing insist that there were other alternatives that would have led to a swift Japanese surrender, that there were virtually no targets of military value in these cities, and that one important reason for dropping the bomb was to impress and intimidate the Soviet Union. Construct an argument defending the dropping of atomic bombs on these Japanese cities. Construct an argument condemning the bombing. What is your true opinion about the moral acceptability of the atomic bombing of Hiroshima and Nagasaki? Why?

11. Is it morally acceptable to threaten to bomb an adversary's cities with conventional or unconventional weapons in order to discourage it from aggression? Defend your answer.

12. Is it morally acceptable for members of a nationalist group seeking political independence to carry out terrorist attacks against innocent civilians—for example, by planting bombs aboard civilian aircraft or in crowded buildings and streets? Defend your answer.

SUGGESTED READINGS

St. Thomas Aquinas. *On Law, Morality, and Politics.* Edited by William Baumgarth and Richard Regan. Indianapolis, IN: Hackett, 1988.

Avner Cohen and Steven Lee, eds. *Nuclear Weapons and the Future of Humanity.* Totowa, NJ: Rowman and Allanheld, 1986.

Marshall Cohen, Thomas Nagel, and Thomas Scanlon, eds. *War and Moral Responsibility.* Princeton, NJ: Princeton University Press, 1974.

National Conference of Catholic Bishops. *The Challenge of Peace: God's Promise and Our Response.* Washington, DC: United States Catholic Conference, 1983.

Michael Walzer. *Just and Unjust Wars.* New York: Basic Books, 1977.

CHAPTER 23

Morality and the Environment

Some people maintain that we face an environmental crisis of potentially catastrophic proportions. In their view, human activities are altering Earth so dramatically that much of the planet's life, including human life, is in great danger. They insist that in order to avert these potential environmental catastrophes, human beings must significantly change their ways. Others dismiss these dire warnings as the deliberate exaggerations of "environmental extremists" who are exploiting the issue in order to advance their own economic and political agendas.

Although scientists are uncertain about the exact nature and extent of the threats to the environment posed by human activity, what they do know is not comforting. The National Academy of Sciences reports that human activities are causing significant and unusually swift changes in the earth's environment and that relatively small changes can have quite large effects. "In essence, we are conducting an uncontrolled experiment with the planet."[1]

ENVIRONMENTAL THREATS

In manufacturing products, generating energy, growing food, and transporting people and things, highly industrialized societies spew a variety of harmful substances into the air, water, and soil. Such substances adversely affect human health by causing diseases such as cancer and emphysema, neurological damage, and birth defects. In addition, some substances affect human life and health more directly by altering the environment.

The Greenhouse Effect and Global Warming

Atmospheric levels of carbon dioxide have increased significantly in the past 100 years, primarily because of the burning of fossil fuels. Carbon dioxide traps infrared rays from the sun that would otherwise be reflected out into space, rais-

---

[1]National Academy of Sciences, *One Earth, One Future* (Washington, DC: National Academy Press, 1990), p. 2.

ing the surface temperature of Earth. According to the National Academy of Sciences, without the trapped infrared sunlight, Earth's surface would be too cold to sustain life. However, human activity now threatens to increase Earth's temperature. The National Academy estimates that the average global temperature will rise 0.5–1.5 degrees Celsius (1.8–2.7 degrees Fahrenheit) in the next few decades, no matter what we do now or in the future, because of increased atmospheric carbon dioxide from *past* human activity. However, if current trends continue, it is very probable that average global temperature will rise 1.5–5 degrees Celsius (2.7–9 degrees Fahrenheit) within a few decades. This increase may seem trivial, but it isn't.

> A 3 degree C rise would create conditions that some organisms have not had to contend with in the last 100,000 years. If the temperature rises 4 degrees C, the earth would be warmer than at any time [in 40 million years]. . . . In the midst of the last glaciation when much of North America was covered by ice, the average temperature of the earth was only about 5 degrees C colder than it is now.[2]

How accurate are these predictions? Is there any solid evidence that global warming is occurring? One piece of evidence surfaced in 1996. Camille Parmesan, a research fellow at the University of California, Santa Barbara, discovered that a species of butterfly known as Edith's checkerspot, which can be found from Mexico to Canada, "is being driven north through California to escape rising temperatures." This species of butterfly is known to be particularly sensitive to small climate changes. According to Parmesan's research, "rising temperatures [are] killing off the butterfly at the southern extremes of its range, while allowing it to expand into cooler climes to the north." In addition, "where the butterflies persisted, [they have] shifted to higher elevations, where temperatures would be slightly cooler."[3] The best explanation of the change in habitat of this butterfly, according to most scientists, is that the temperature of its habitat is rising.

In order to confirm or disconfirm a scientific theory—about global warming or anything else—scientists make predictions about what they should observe if the theory is true. Observing what they should observe tends to confirm the theory (shows that the theory is probably true); failing to observe what they should observe disconfirms the theory (shows that the theory is probably not true). Scientists emphasize that even if the theory of global warming is true, they do not expect to observe that every year will be warmer than the preceding year, because weather conditions vary from year to year. However, they do expect to observe patterns over decades. In fact, some of the hottest years on record have occurred in the past decade or so. Scientists also say that if global warming is occurring, we can expect more weather extremes—severer storms and unusually cold winters followed by unusually hot summers, or the reverse. Weather patterns recently have been conforming to these predictions.

---

[2]Ibid., p. 71.

[3]"Migration of Butterfly Is Attributed to Global Warming," *Boston Globe,* August 29, 1996, p. A7.

However, we know that climate changes radically over time independent of human activity. For example, the ice ages, of which there have been several over periods of hundreds of thousands of years, were not caused by human activity. During the last ice age, which ended about 18,000 years ago, much of North America as far south as the Great Lakes was buried under a glacier of ice about a mile thick. Even if global warming is occurring, might it not be from natural causes rather than human activity? It is possible. However, given our scientific knowledge, it is highly probable that human activity is making the average global temperature warmer than it would otherwise be.

In this as in other environmental issues, certainty about the future is hard to come by. The question is what to do now in the face of predictions about the future effects of human activity when those predictions are probable but not certain. Should we continue doing what we're doing, making few or no changes, with a wait-and-see attitude? (If by 2100 the direst predictions are proved correct, then we will do something about it.) Or should we make changes now as an insurance policy against possible, though not certain, catastrophe? How probable must the predictions be in order for us to take action? How drastic should our actions be if the predictions are merely probable rather than certain? These questions apply to all of the environmental threats we will examine.

One question, then, is, How likely is it that Earth's temperature will rise as a result of human activity, and how much will it rise if it does? A second question is, Why should we care? What difference will it make to us? Scientists maintain that the probable effects are worrisome. As they heat up, the oceans will expand and take up a larger volume of space. Glaciers at the poles will partly melt, increasing the amount of water in the oceans. If the temperature rises high enough (closer to the upper limits of predictions rather than the lower limits), it will lead to flooding of coastal regions of the world, where a large percentage of the world's population resides, such as the coastal cities of Philadelphia, New York, Boston, Los Angeles, and San Francisco, leading to a massive exodus of refugees. Global warming will probably also lead to changes in precipitation. Regions that are dry may become wetter, and regions that are wet may become drier. These changes, in turn, would affect agriculture. Many scientists fear that the result will be a reduction in the world food supply. If the food supply drops, food prices will rise, increasing the cost of living for virtually everyone and increasing the incidence of malnutrition and starvation in poor countries of the world. Global warming would also cause shifts in the habitats of flora and fauna, with uncertain consequences for human well-being.

Ozone Depletion

The sun's rays include potentially destructive ultraviolet radiation. Ultraviolet radiation causes sunburn and skin cancer in human beings. Too much ultraviolet radiation reaching the surface of Earth would practically fry many living things, both plants and animals. Most of the sun's ultraviolet radiation is screened out by a chemical called ozone (O_3) that exists in the stratosphere, a band that stretches from about 9 to 22 miles above Earth's surface. Without that screen of ozone, life as we know it could not exist on Earth.

Scientists have discovered that atoms of chlorine and bromine, called halogens, destroy atoms of ozone. One chlorine atom in the stratosphere can destroy up to 100,000 atoms of ozone. One bromine atom can destroy even more atoms of ozone. Scientists have discovered that certain human-made chemicals that include halogen atoms—chlorocarbons, chlorofluorocarbons, and halon compounds—have risen to the stratosphere and seem to be destroying some of the ozone there. (Scientists have been viewing with alarm the large and growing "ozone hole" that has developed above the northern hemisphere.) These chemicals are used as industrial solvents and degreasing compounds, in refrigeration and air conditioning systems, and as fire suppressants. As a result of the thinning of the ozone layer, more ultraviolet radiation is reaching Earth's surface.

The probable effects include an increase in the incidence of skin cancer and cataracts among humans (more ultraviolet radiation entering our eyes damages them); suppression of both human and animal immune systems, leading to lowered resistance to infection and disease; reduction in crop yields, reducing the food supply (many plant varieties will be damaged by increased ultraviolet radiation); and a reduction in phyloplankton in the ocean, the small organism that lies at the base of the ocean's food chain, which would reduce the amount of fish in the ocean at every level of the food chain.

Air Pollution

The list of common air pollutants is long, including sulfur oxides, nitrogen oxides, suspended particulate matter, carbon monoxide, a variety of trace metals (for example, lead, mercury, and zinc), ground-level ozone (smog), and a veritable zoo of volatile organic materials (the Environmental Protection Agency lists 189). The primary sources are fossil fuel energy sources and industrial production.

One form of air pollution that has gotten special attention is acid precipitation. As a result primarily of sulfur and nitrogen oxides, rain, fog, and snow have far greater acidity than normal. This acidity, in turn, has increased the acidity of streams, rivers, and lakes, reducing their capacity to sustain plant and fish life. Acid precipitation damages plants, buildings, bridges, and human health. The effects of this and other forms of air pollution on human health include lung damage and disease (lung cancer, emphysema, pneumonia, bronchitis, and asthma), birth defects, cancer of vital organs, nervous system damage (especially lead and mercury), immune system suppression, and aggravation of heart disease.

The Enviromental Protection Agency is responsible for regulating air pollution in the United States. In 1996 it proposed tightening standards on suspended particulate matter and ground-level ozone (smog), which unlike stratospheric ozone is bad for living organisms. After a review of more than 300 scientific studies, the Natural Resources Defense Council concluded that "fine particles of air pollution [suspended particulate matter] from power plants, motor vehicles and other sources kill some 64,000 Americans a year."[4] The Environmental Protection Agency agreed with these conclusions and announced that it would tighten the

---

[4] "More Dying of Dirty Air Than in Cars, Study Finds," *Boston Globe,* May 9, 1996, p. A1.

standards in an attempt to reduce particulate and ozone levels in the air. As of this writing (February 1997) industry is fighting the more stringent regulations, claiming that the conclusions are based on bad science and that the cost of the new, tightened regulations would be astronomical and catastrophic.

Water Pollution

We do not have (and probably never will have) the technology to create large amounts of water. The water supply that now exists on Earth is all the water we are likely to ever have. According to recent estimates, 94 percent of it is salt water in the oceans. Thus, only 6 percent of the world's water supply is fresh water that can be used by human beings. Of that amount, 27 percent is frozen in glaciers and 72 percent is underground, leaving a mere 1 percent of the world's freshwater in the atmosphere, streams, rivers, and lakes.[5] Humans use freshwater for domestic purposes (drinking, cooking, washing), agriculture, and industry. Globally, 69 percent of freshwater is used for agriculture, 23 percent for industry, and 8 percent domestically. Contaminated water cannot be used for these purposes.

The chief sources of water pollution are untreated or inadequately treated sewage; discharge of volatile organic compounds, trace metals, and nitrogen and sulfur oxides by industry; and the runoff of fertilizers and pesticides used in agriculture. The consequences include human illness and disease, water shortages, and reductions in aquatic life. The same pollutants also affect the salt water in the oceans, leading to human illness and infection from bathing in contaminated water and eating contaminated fish, and to reductions in a variety of fish species.

Energy Consumption

Global energy consumption continues to grow as world population grows and more poor countries try to increase their standards of living. The average annual rate of growth in energy consumption has been estimated at 2.2 percent for the period 1900-1950, 5.2 percent for 1950-1970, and 2.3 percent for 1971-1990. The slowdown in energy consumption after 1970 resulted from several factors, including higher energy prices, economic slowdowns in many parts of the world, and explicit policies of energy conservation. Predicted annual growth rates after the year 2000 are 1.9 percent for developed countries, 3 percent for Russia and Eastern Europe, and 4.5 percent in the developing nations.[6]

In 1990, 32 percent of the world's commercial energy came from coal and 36 percent from oil. This dependence on fossil fuels creates two problems. First is the depletion of fossil fuels. The question is not whether we will run out of these nonrenewable energy sources, but when. Estimates are that, based on

---

[5]Mostafa K. Tolba, *Saving Our Planet* (London: Chapman & Hall, 1992), p. 46. (This book is a product of the United Nations Environmental Programme, of which Tolba is executive director.)

[6]Ibid., pp. 150-152.

known supplies, at 1990 levels of consumption the world will run out of oil around 2040, natural gas around 2060, and coal around 2200.[7] The second problem is the variety of pollutants emitted in the mining, transportation, and combustion of fossil fuels. The use of nuclear energy creates the additional problem of safe disposal of radioactive waste, which will remain radioactive for tens of thousands of years. Can we find cleaner sources of energy? Can we perfect technologies for "renewable" sources of energy such as sun, wind, and tides?

Both pollution and the depletion of natural resources are attributable largely to the developed world. Most of the world's pollution has been generated by the United States, Canada, Western Europe, and Japan, which do the lion's share of producing and consuming the world's goods. The developed world, with 22 percent of the world's population, uses 82 percent of the world's energy while the developing world, which contains the other 78 percent of humanity, uses only 18 percent of the world's energy.[8] Native Americans say that we should "step lightly on the Earth." The step of people in the developed world is far heavier than the step of people in the developing world.

Deforestation and Species Loss

Roughly 90–95 percent of the species that ever existed on Earth since life emerged about 3.5 billion years ago are now extinct, almost all from natural causes rather than from human activity. Now, however, the speed of extinction is vastly accelerating because human activity has destroyed and is destroying natural habitats at an increasing rate.

More than half the species of plants and animals currently on Earth are located in (and only in) tropical rainforests. Poor, overpopulated countries have felt compelled to overexploit their rainforests in order to meet their immediate needs. They export timber and clear the forests for agriculture and animal grazing. Additionally, global warming and ozone depletion may adversely affect the world's forests.

Some people estimate that human activity has increased the rate of species extinction as much as 10,000-fold. From a purely human point of view, such accelerated extinction is unfortunate because various species (and varieties within species) of plants and animals constitute important sources of food, energy, and medicine. They are also a fundamental and irreplaceable source of the gene pool of Earth. The National Academy of Sciences notes, "Commercial species are continuously crossbred with their wild relatives to improve yield, nutritional quality, responsiveness to different soils and climate, and resistance to pests and diseases."[9] Similarly, the World Commission on Environment and

---

[7]Ibid. It is difficult to know how seriously to take these estimates. New finds of oil, coal, and natural gas may occur that would double or triple known reserves. That we definitely will run out of these energy sources someday remains incontrovertible. The question is whether we will have developed adequate substitutes for them.

[8]Ibid., pp. 150–151.

[9]National Academy, *One Earth*, p. 128.

Development, established by the United Nations in 1983, points out, "Vast stocks of biological diversity are in danger of disappearing just as science is learning how to exploit genetic variability through the advances of genetic engineering."[10]

Besides causing species extinction, destruction of tropical rainforests affects Earth's climate. As the wood decays or is burned, it releases carbon dioxide, which accelerates the greenhouse effect. The rainforests also affect the patterns of rainfall and protect soil from erosion. Forest loss can bring drought or flooding to vast areas.

HUMAN POPULATION GROWTH

The human population has been growing at an alarming rate. Estimates are that around 6000 B.C.E. there were about 5 million human beings on the entire Earth. Then, with the agricultural revolution, human populations began to soar.

1 C.E.	250 million
1600	500 million
1800–1850	1 billion
1930	2 billion
1960	3 billion
1974	4 billion
1986	5 billion
2000	6 billion

The 1996 population is estimated at 5.7 billion. Much of the recent population growth has occurred in the developing world, whose share of world population has risen from 64 percent in 1930 to 77 percent in 1990.[11]

Since 1970, however, the rate of population growth has slowed. Population growth rates are determined by birth rates relative to death rates. From 1965 to 1970 the human population grew at an annual rate of 2.1 percent, from 1980 to 1990 the rate was 1.8 percent, and in 1995 it was about 1.6 percent. The biggest slowdown in growth has occurred in China, India, Brazil, Egypt, Indonesia, Korea, Mexico, and Thailand. Note that the human population is still growing, but at a slower rate than in the recent past.

What can we expect in the future? The most widely used population forecast is the 1992 United Nations set of projections, which includes low, medium, and high estimates. The low estimate assumes a fertility rate of 1.7 children per woman, the medium estimate a rate of 2.06 children per woman, and the high estimate a rate of 2.5 children per woman.

---

[10]World Commission on Environment and Development, *Our Common Future* (New York: Oxford University Press, 1987), p. 148.

[11]Joel E. Cohen, *How Many People Can the Earth Support?* (New York: Norton, 1995).

	2040	2100
Low	7.5 billion	6 billion
Medium	9 billion	11 billion
High	12 billion	19 billion

As you can see, the range of this forecast is very wide—from 7.5 billion to 12 billion in 2040, from 6 billion to 19 billion in 2100. Which estimate—high, medium, or low—is most likely? No one knows. In fact, estimated fertility rates for Africa, Latin America, and Asia excluding China in 1990-1991 were 6.1, 3.4, and 3.9, respectively[12]—considerably higher than the UN's "high" estimate of 2.5 children per woman. In some other countries, fertility rates have already fallen to or near the low estimate assumption of 1.7 children per woman, and these rates may continue to decline. The reality is that human population in 2040 or 2100 could actually be below the low estimates, but it also could be above the high estimates. What the future brings will depend on many factors, some of which we have control over, some of which we do not.

One thing seems clear, however. The more human beings there are on Earth, the greater will be the strain on the environment. More human beings means more energy produced and consumed, more products produced, more pollution, more transportation, and more land cleared for human purposes. Human beings have control over their fertility; the number of children a woman has can be a matter of choice and decision. The world will be better off if we choose to control our population and wind up with 6-10 billion human beings a century from now rather than make choices and decisions that will lead to a population of 15, 20, or 25 billion people.

Population is growing faster in poor countries than in rich countries. At the same time, poor countries are struggling to increase living standards. Currently, the disparity between poor and rich countries is enormous and growing greater. In 1992, average annual per capita income in the developed world (830 million people) was $22,000. In the middle-income world (2.6 billion people) it was $1,600, and in the poorest countries (2 billion people) it was $400.[13] In 1960, the richest 20 percent of the world's population had an annual income 30 times that of the poorest 20 percent; in 1991, the richest 20 percent had an annual income 59 times that of the poorest 20 percent. Part of the problem is overconsumption by the rich. Roughly 20 percent of the world's population is chronically undernourished. The world's environment probably cannot sustain 5.7 billion people living at or near the current economic level of people in the rich countries, let alone 15 or 20 billion. It may be that people in rich countries will have to consume less in order for people in poor countries to consume more. But as we saw in an earlier chapter, not everyone in rich countries is rich. Rich countries also contain poor people who want to see their standards of living

---

[12]Ibid., p. 143.

[13]Ibid., p. 53.

rise. It may be that wealthier people in wealthy countries will have to consume less to enable the poor of their own countries to consume more.

As paradoxical as it may seem, many experts believe that increasing living standards of poor people will lead to a reduction in their fertility. Recent history shows an inverse relationship between income and family size: As a society becomes more affluent, family size falls. Thus, economic development is considered one way to control population. In addition, experts call for a global campaign to promote contraception and to make it affordable and accessible. Also, empowering women and educating both men and women about the value of small families will help women gain greater control over their own fertility.

CREATING A SUSTAINABLE ECONOMY

What, if anything, can be done? What, if anything, should be done? Many environmentalists say that we now have a global economic system that is "unsustainable." In their view, because the global system of industrial capitalism creates huge amounts of waste and pollution that poison the planet and depletes scarce nonrenewable resources, it is destroying its own foundations. The system may be able to function in this way for several decades, but eventually it will cease to function. The currently unsustainable system must be transformed into a "sustainable" economy—an economic system that can continue to meet the needs of people into the foreseeable future without destroying its own foundations.

Creating a sustainable economy requires many changes. The production process must be redesigned and made more efficient so that more is produced with less—less energy consumed and fewer resources used in producing goods and services. Where possible, renewable clean sources of energy would replace the nonrenewable fossil fuels that pollute the planet. It also would mean design changes in production processes to reduce or eliminate waste, whether hazardous or nonhazardous. Where waste is generated, every effort would be made to find a way of using that waste in some other production process. Hazardous waste, if it could not be eliminated, would be stored safely.

As an example, Paul Hawken points to the 3M company, which in 1975, under the leadership of Joseph Ling,

> developed a program called Pollution Prevention Pays (3P), the first integrated, intracompany approach to designing out pollution from manufacturing processes. The plan created incentives for the technical staff to modify product manufacturing methods so as to prevent hazardous and toxic waste, and to reduce costs. By reformulating products, changing processes, redesigning equipment, and recovering waste for reuse or recycling, 3M has been able to save $537 million. During the fifteen year period, it reduced its air pollution by 120,000 tons, its wastewater by 1 billion gallons, its solid waste by 410,000 tons.[14]

---

[14]Paul Hawken, *The Ecology of Commerce* (New York: HarperCollins, 1993), pp. 60–61.

Hawken points out that companies can be more environmentally responsible if they use their ingenuity and creativity in redesigning how they produce products and the nature of the products they produce. Besides helping save the planet, it can pay handsomely.

The agricultural sector of the economy would have to reduce its reliance on human-made pesticides and fertilizers and rely more on methods of organic farming. Pesticides and fertilizers harm the environment in many ways that are now clearly recognized. Their use must be minimized. Farmers will also have to rely less on irrigation because it degrades soil in the long run and uses up so much water and energy.

Some environmentalists claim that many companies have few incentives to reduce the pollution and waste they generate as long as they don't have to pay the full cost of the environmental damage they cause. Companies that pollute are not charged for the human illnesses and damage to flora and fauna that their pollution causes. Consider oil spills and toxic waste that gets into the environment. The companies responsible generally pay only a fraction of the cost of the cleanup; the American taxpayer pays most of the bill. If companies that pollute were charged the full cost of their pollution, then they would have a great incentive to drastically change the way they do things. Hawken suggests that companies that produce toxic waste be charged for the safe storage of the waste as long as it remains toxic—a kind of rent for space at government-run toxic waste sites. In order to ensure that companies that produce the waste don't try to escape paying for it by going out of business after a few years, perhaps the first fifty years of rent would have to be paid in advance. The result would undoubtedly be that far less toxic waste would be produced. Businesses would find a way to minimize toxic waste to cut costs.

In order to create a sustainable economic system, products would themselves be redesigned so that they operate more efficiently, especially in their use of energy. For example, motor vehicles would be redesigned to be more fuel efficient and electric appliances redesigned to use less electricity. Products should also be designed to be reusable or recyclable rather than disposable.

Consumers would need to be more environmentally responsible and sensitive in their purchases. First, we would need to avoid overconsumption. We would need to refrain from buying things we don't need, especially products that use energy. We would need to stop discarding things because they are "out of style." (Do we really need to buy new cars every three or four years?) We would need to refrain from buying disposable items. Second, people would need to buy and use more environmentally friendly products and refrain from buying and using environmentally unfriendly products. We would need to buy vehicles that are fuel efficient rather than gas guzzlers. We might trade in our motorboats and snowmobiles for rowboats, canoes, snowshoes, and cross-country skis. Third, we could refrain from buying the products of companies that behave in an environmentally irresponsible way, voting with our dollars. If a company is a major polluter or produces lots of hazardous waste, if it clear-cuts tropical forests or squanders energy, we can refuse to buy what it is selling. Hawken cautions, though, "don't just avoid buying a Mitsubishi automobile because of the company's participation in the destruction of primary forests in Malaysia, Indonesia, Ecuador, Brazil, Bolivia. . . . Write and tell them why you won't. Engage in dialogue, . . . talk, organize."[15] Finally, we can employ environmental criteria in our investment decisions. We can refrain from investing in companies that do not meet our standards of environmental responsibility.

People would also need to change their habits. More reliance on mass transportation or carpooling, or on alternatives such as bicycling or walking, and less reliance on the private automobile would help preserve the environment. We need to keep our homes cooler in winter and warmer in summer and to use less hot water in cooking and bathing and less electricity in lighting. We must insulate our homes and make them more energy efficient. We must recycle and reuse products while avoiding disposable items.

Government also could help increase sustainability. It could provide more money for research and development of alternative energy sources and for mass transportation. It could pass laws regulating waste and pollution or provide incentives for conservation. It could provide funds for population control, on both a national and a global level. It could provide education to sensitize people to the necessity of being more environmentally responsible. It could provide economic assistance to poor countries to help them protect their environments and could resist the push of international economic institutions to cajole Third World countries into overexploiting their environments in order to pay back loans they received for economic development. These economic development plans often have the effect of pushing subsistence farmers off their land and replacing them with factory farms designed to grow products for the world market rather than to feed their own people.

Opposition to Sustainable Economies

If sustainable economies were cost free, there would be no resistance to implementing it. In fact, however, many industries and individual companies will have increased costs because of the expense of controlling the amount of pollution they emit or of safely disposing of hazardous wastes they generate. Owners of polluting sources of energy such as oil and coal may see the value of their investments decline if alternative sources of energy are developed. A company may lose profits or go out of business if its products are replaced by less polluting alternatives; for example, manufacturers of pesticides and fertilizers would lose business if much of the world switched to organic farming methods. Consumption patterns in the industrialized countries would have to change.

Because they believe that they face economic loss if sustainable economies are implemented, many business and political leaders have vehemently criticized as "environmental extremists" those who want to move quickly and decisively toward creating sustainable economies. They maintain that a decisive shift

---

[15]Paul Hawken, "A Declaration of Sustainability," in *People, Penguins, and Plastic Trees,* 2d ed., ed. Christine Pierce and Donald VanDeVeer (Belmont, CA: Wadsworth, 1995), p. 437.

toward sustainable economies will harm the industrialized countries by dramatically lowering their standards of living. They claim that the costs of sustainable economies for people in the highly industrialized countries are prohibitive: Jobs will be lost, salaries and wages will decline, prices and taxes will rise, and government regulation will increase.

Reasons for Shifting to Sustainable Economies

Although some industries, individual businesses, and individual people will indeed face economic losses if sustainable economies are created, it's far less clear that industrialized societies as a whole will lose out. First, and most obviously, some people will gain. If air, water, and soil pollution are reduced, the lives of some people will be saved and the health of many people will be improved. Similarly, if new technologies and new resources are developed, the owners of and workers in these new industries and companies will be economic winners even if older industries and companies are economic losers. Similarly, costs may rise and jobs may disappear in highly polluting industries, but new industries for designing and producing pollution-control equipment will spring up and become prosperous, adding jobs. Tax losses from one industry can be made up by increased tax revenues from other, newer industries.

If we apply moral theories to the question of sustainable economies, we cannot limit our gaze to its effects on just one country, such as, the United States, or one social class. The moral point of view is impartial. In order to evaluate environmental policy and sustainable economies from an impartial point of view, we must consider the interests of all people on the planet. (Whether we can limit our view to our own species is discussed later in this chapter.)

For example, if we apply Utilitarianism to questions of environmental policy, we must consider not only the gains and losses of people in the industrialized countries but also the gains and losses of people around the world. A utilitarian could thus defend creating a sustainable economy by claiming that shifting to it would increase the total happiness or well-being of the human race.

If we apply the universal law formulation of Kant's Categorical Imperative, we will ask whether a maxim such as the following could consistently be willed a universal law.

> I will use up the world's nonrenewable resources and pollute the environment when it benefits me.

If a rational agent could not will such a universal law without contradicting herself, then acting in accordance with such a maxim is immoral. A Kantian could then maintain that no rational agent could will such a maxim without contradicting herself. If we apply the respect for persons formulation of the Categorical Imperative, we must ask whether we are treating everyone with respect if we follow policies of "unsustainable" development. A Kantian might maintain that if we pollute and deplete resources, we are not treating other people with respect because some people are harmed by it when harm to them is avoidable. We are not making their ends and needs our own.

Similarly, if we apply a hypothetical social contract theory such as Rawls's to the issue of environmental policy, we must ask whether rational self-interested individuals in the Original Position behind the Veil of Ignorance would agree to environmental policies that are in conflict with sustainable development. A person applying this moral theory might maintain that people in the Original Position would only agree to policies of sustainable development because they do not know whether they will experience a net gain or a net loss from pollution and resource depletion.

We might also rely on the right to life to defend policies of sustainable development. We might claim that the right to life entails a right to a livable environment—an environment capable of sustaining people's lives and health. Because everyone has a duty to refrain from violating people's right to life and a duty to minimize the harm that they cause people, and because pollution harms people, everyone has a duty to minimize the pollution that they cause. This duty applies especially to decision makers in large institutions that have the greatest potential to create pollution, whether that pollution is in the United States, Europe, or the poor countries of Asia, South America, or Africa. Additionally, we could argue that because depleting natural resources leaves some people without the means of sustaining their lives, it violates their right to life.

PRESENT VERSUS FUTURE PEOPLE

According to many environmentalists, our industrial civilization cannot sustain itself indefinitely. Unless we change our ways, it will break down within a generation or two. But why should we care about the future? Why should we sacrifice now in order to benefit people who haven't even been born?

Suppose that some form of pollution will not affect any presently existing people. For example, suppose that highly toxic wastes could be dumped into the ocean encased in concrete that will last a hundred years. When the concrete case finally disintegrates and releases the toxic waste, no presently existing people will be harmed. Do presently existing people have moral duties only to other presently existing people, or do they also have moral duties to future people? Do only presently existing people have moral rights, or do future people also have moral rights?

We could argue that from a moral point of view, the time during which people exist is irrelevant; as long as they can be harmed or benefited by an action, their interests must be considered. Thus, for example, from a utilitarian perspective, the interests of future people are no less important than the interests of presently existing people. Similarly, we could argue that from a Kantian or hypothetical social contract perspective, the fact that the people being harmed have not yet come into existence would be irrelevant. In adopting a moral point of view, we are supposed to be impartial. Impartiality requires not only that we not be influenced by differences of race, sex, national origin, religion, and sexual orientation, but also by our location in space-time. Therefore, we could argue that presently existing people have the same moral duties toward future people as they have toward other presently existing people and that future people have the same moral rights as presently existing people.

Trudy Govier takes the position that future people do not have exactly the same moral rights and moral status as presently existing people. Presently existing people actually exist; future people are only potential—they *may* exist. The existence of people a hundred years from now may be highly probable, but it is not certain. Events could occur that will lead to human extinction—for example, an all-out war fought with chemical, biological, and nuclear weapons. "Since the probability that a . . . possible person will exist is always less than one, the interests of . . . possible people always count for something less than those of actual people."[16]

If people do exist a hundred or a thousand years in the future, however, they will have moral rights and we have moral duties to them. Counting for less than actual people doesn't mean not counting at all. Therefore, although the amount of sacrifice morally required of presently existing people to safeguard the interests of future people may not be unlimited, it is not negligible, either. Presently existing people have a moral duty to make some sacrifices in order to protect the moral rights, especially the right to life, of the people who will probably come after them. Some sacrifice is required in order to prevent our bequeathing to future people a planet that is no longer capable of sustaining human life.

Just as some pollution will affect presently existing people as well as future people, the depletion of some natural resources will affect some presently existing people. However, many of the benefits of conservation and of the substitution of renewable for nonrenewable resources will accrue primarily to future people. Again, we could argue that because future people, if they come into existence, will have a right to life, they will have a moral right to an environment capable of sustaining their lives. If we use up all or most of the natural resources they need to sustain their lives, we will have violated their right to life. Similarly, we could argue that the duty we all have to minimize the harm we cause others applies to the harm that we might cause future people. The duty to minimize harm to future people requires that we make at least some sacrifices in order to conserve the natural resources they will need to live.

ENVIRONMENTAL JUSTICE

As paradoxical as it may seem, environmental degradation provides benefits as well as burdens. Industries that pollute, deplete resources, and consume energy also make profits for their owners, generate high salaries for their managers, and provide wages for their workers—all clearly benefits. The burdens, of course, are pollution and depleted resources. Balancing the burdens and benefits of environmental degradation is complicated by the fact that these benefits and burdens are not fairly distributed. Often the people who benefit most are able to

---

[16]Trudy Govier, "What Should We Do about Future People?" in *Moral Issues,* ed. Jan Narveson (New York: Oxford University Press, 1983), p. 406.

escape shouldering the burdens while the people who bear most of the burdens receive few of the benefits.

Studies have shown that in the United States an unusually high percentage of polluting industries and hazardous waste facilities are located in communities of poor people of color—African Americans, Latinos, and Native Americans. The people who own the industries and benefit most from them do not live in the communities where they are located; the people who live in the communities where they are located generally do not benefit much from them. The reason is power. Communities that are predominantly white and middle or upper-class don't want pollutants and hazardous wastes in their communities, and they have the political influence to keep them out; communities that are predominately African American, Latino, or Native American usually don't have the same kind of political influence, and they get stuck with them.

For example, in 1970 the Harris County (Texas) Board of Supervisors forbade placement of a municipal solid waste landfill in Northwood Manor, a subdivision of the city of Houston. At the time, Northwood Manor was predominantly white. By 1979 Northwood Manor had become predominantly African American. In that year, the Board of Supervisors approved placement of the landfill there. Robert D. Bullard writes,

> Houston has a long history of locating its solid waste facilities in communities of color, especially in African American neighborhoods. From the early 1920s through the late 1970s, all five of the city-owned sanitary landfills and six of the eight municipal solid waste incinerators were located in mostly African American neighborhoods. Similarly, three of the four privately owned solid waste landfills were located in mostly African American communities during this period. African Americans, however, made up only 28 percent of the city's population.[17]

Similarly, in 1982, 30,000 cubic yards of soil was contaminated in North Carolina as a result of illegal dumping of toxic compounds known as PCBs. The site selected for burying the toxic soil was in Warren County, North Carolina, a mostly African American county. Opponents maintained that the site was not chosen because of scientific evidence showing that it was the most appropriate location. Rather, they claimed, the decision was purely political: Counties that were predominantly white were able to use their influence to keep it out of their communities.[18]

A 1983 report by the General Accounting Office of the United States government "found a strong relationship between the location of off-site hazardous waste landfills and the race and socioeconomic status of the surrounding communities."[19] For example, in EPA region IV, comprising Alabama, Florida, Georgia, Kentucky, Mississippi, North Carolina, South Carolina, and Tennessee, three of the

---

[17]Robert D. Bullard, "Environmental Justice for All," in *Unequal Protection: Environmental Justice and Communities of Color,* ed. Robert D. Bullard (San Francisco: Sierra Club Books, 1994), p. 4.

[18]Ibid., p. 5.

[19]Ibid., p. 6.

four hazardous waste landfills were located in predominantly African American communities, although African Americans made up only 20 percent of the population of region IV.

Similarly, a 1992 study by staff writers from the *National Law Journal* concluded that "there is a racial divide in the way the U.S. government cleans up toxic waste sites and punishes polluters. White communities see faster action, better results and stiffer penalties than communities where blacks, Hispanics and other minorities live."[20] In addition, Bullard claims that "African Americans and Latino Americans are more likely than whites to live in areas with reduced air quality." He quotes a report by researchers from the National Argonne Laboratory who found that "a total of 33 percent of whites, 50 percent of African Americans, and 60 percent of Hispanics live in the 136 counties in which two or more air pollutants exceed standards."[21] Bullard points to Chicago's Southeast neighborhood around Altgeld Gardens, a housing project. The neighborhood is 70-percent African American and 11-percent Latino; it is "encircled by municipal and hazardous waste landfills, toxic waste incinerators, grain elevators, sewer treatment facilities, smelters, steel mills, and a host of other polluting industries."[22]

Regina Austin and Michael Schill summarize the imbalance:

People of color throughout the United States are receiving more than their fair share of the poisonous fruits of industrial production. They live cheek by jowl with waste dumps, incinerators, landfills, smelters, factories, chemical plants, and oil refineries whose operations make them sick and kill them young. They are poisoned by the air they breathe, the water they drink, the fish they catch, the vegetables they grow, and, in the case of children, the very ground they play on.[23]

If they and Bullard are right, then our country faces a situation that is unjust. People in our country are not receiving equal protection from environmental degradation. The burdens of that degradation are being shifted to the shoulders of the least powerful and most vulnerable of our citizens, people of color—precisely those people who, from an economic point of view, benefit least from that degradation. Something needs to be done to ensure that middle- and upper-class whites, who benefit the most, shoulder their fair share of the burdens of environmental degradation. What might be some morally acceptable solutions to the problem?

One solution might be to export polluting industries and the pollution they cause to Third World countries in Latin America, Africa, and Asia. For example, chemical manufacturing plants can be moved to nations such as India so that they will pollute those nations rather than ours. An added benefit is that most poor Third World countries have far less stringent laws protecting their environ-

[20]Ibid., p. 9.

[21]Ibid., p. 12.

[22]Ibid., p. 14.

[23]Regina Austin and Michael Schill, "Black, Brown, Red, and Poisoned," in Bullard, *Unequal Protection,* p. 53.

ments, so factories can spend less on safety and pollution control. (Consider the environmental disaster in Bhopal, India, where a chemical plant leaked a highly toxic substance that killed and injured several thousand people living near it.) We could also build hazardous waste landfills and incinerators in these nations and send them our toxic wastes. (We are already exporting some toxic wastes in this way.) But the question is, Would it be just? Would it be morally acceptable? Given the moral requirement of impartiality, the answer is obvious.

LIFE-CENTERED VERSUS HUMAN-CENTERED ENVIRONMENTAL ETHICS

So far we have discussed environmental ethics as though only human well-being counts from a moral point of view. However, we should keep in mind that human beings constitute only one species out of the tens of millions that exist on Earth. Many environmentalists claim that it is arbitrary to think that only human beings have moral standing. They think that we should consider the effects of our behavior not only on other human beings but on all living creatures.

We use nonhuman living things in a variety of ways. We kill and eat many of them—for example, cows, pigs, deer, sheep, rabbits, and fish. We hunt and kill them for sport. We kill them for their fur or skin. We use them in medical experiments to test new drugs or new forms of surgery. We use them in schools, where they are dissected by students or observed and conditioned in psychology laboratories. We test cosmetics on them. We confine them in zoos, circuses, and aquariums and sometimes train them to behave in ways that are not natural to them, such as training a seal to balance a ball on its nose or a whale to leap over a net. We keep them as pets. We encourage them to fight and kill each other for our entertainment, as in rooster or dog fights. We may sacrifice them to our gods or fight and kill them for entertainment, as in bullfighting. Human beings act in ways that intentionally cause harm (suffering and death) to millions of nonhuman living creatures every day. Is our treatment of nonhuman animals morally acceptable? May we use them in any way we please, ignoring their well-being?

We also unintentionally but foreseeably cause harm to millions of nonhuman living things. Pollution harms other living things besides humans. Individual creatures or groups of creatures may be severely harmed by toxic chemicals in the air, soil, and water. When we damage or destroy an ecosystem, we make it unhabitable for a variety of creatures that will simply die because their environment can no longer support their existence. In extreme cases, we can exterminate an entire species. We came close to making the buffalo extinct. Our behavior has led to the extinction of many creatures over the past 200 years, and hundreds of species are now endangered or threatened. As environmentalists are fond of pointing out, extinction is forever. Is it morally acceptable for us to destroy entire ecosystems so that the creatures that live there cannot survive? Is it morally acceptable for us to annihilate entire species, driving them to extinction? Do we have a duty to preserve species and ecosystems for the good of nonhuman living things?

Many environmentalists claim that we have duties to nonhuman living things because they count from a moral point of view. In contrast to a human-centered ethics that assumes that only human beings have moral worth and that takes account only of human harm and benefit in moral deliberation, many environmentalists recommend a life-centered ethics that assumes that all living things have some moral worth and that takes account of the harm and benefit to all living things in moral deliberation.

Peter Singer maintains that our limiting moral worth and status to human beings is akin to whites' limiting moral worth and status to other whites (racism) and males' limiting moral worth and status to other males (sexism). Singer calls it "speciesism."[24] In his view, speciesism is as morally objectionable as other forms of arbitrary and unjust discrimination.

Paul W. Taylor has presented a theoretical defense of a life-centered ethics. He argues that all living things have what he calls "inherent worth" and should be treated with respect. According to him, human beings are superior to other creatures only from a human point of view. That supposed superiority grounds the assumption that humans have inherent worth and ought to be treated with respect. But if humans are not superior according to any objective standard, then there is no justification for treating humans considerably better than we treat nonhuman animals. That is not an invitation to treat human beings with as little respect as we treat nonhuman animals. Rather, it is an invitation to treat nonhuman animals with the same kind of respect that we treat (or should treat) human beings.

Why should we treat human beings with respect? According to Taylor, it is because human beings have intrinsic worth. We have intrinsic worth because we are alive and conscious and because we are the product of billions of years of evolution. But we cannot *prove* that we have intrinsic worth. We can only say that it is an assumption that is reasonable given a clear understanding of our nature. Similarly, according to Taylor, we cannot *prove* that nonhuman animals have intrinsic worth. But according to him it is an assumption that is reasonable given a clear understanding of the facts. Human beings are related to all other living things. We are part of a family of life. The differences between us and other living things are only a matter of degree. All other living things are as alive as we are. Many of them are conscious. Many of them have a form of intelligence akin to our own. All forms of life are interdependent in a variety of ways. All are the product of evolution that occurred over billions of years. As a result, Taylor claims, not only do all living things have inherent worth, they have equal inherent worth. Thus, an oak tree, a lizard, an insect, a fish, a cow, a dolphin, an elephant, and a human being all have equal inherent worth.

Does this mean that it is never morally acceptable for us to use or harm nonhuman living things? Is it wrong to cut down a tree to build a house? To kill a cow and eat it? To pick an apple and eat it? To wear a fur coat? To test drugs and

---

[24]Peter Singer, *Practical Ethics* (Cambridge, England: Cambridge University Press, 1979), Chapters 2 and 3.

surgical procedures on animals? To clear a plot of forested land to build a hospital, school, or museum? To hunt? To place animals in zoos and use them in circuses and rodeos? To kill insects that carry bacteria or viruses that cause human diseases? Human life would be impossible if we did not use other living things. Accepting this reality, Taylor does not advocate behavior that would lead to human extinction or mass misery. However, he does say that a commitment to the equal inherent worth of all living things requires change. "In order to share the Earth with other species, . . . we humans must impose limits on our population, our habits of consumption, and our technology."[25]

According to Taylor, all living creatures—including human beings—have a right of self-defense. Thus, "it is permissible for [human beings] to protect themselves against dangerous or harmful organisms by destroying them."[26] If a mad dog or a lion is threatening to attack you, it is morally acceptable to kill it if that is the only way to protect yourself. The right of self-defense also justifies us in killing bacteria and viruses that threaten our health, as well as other living things that may carry such bacteria and viruses, such as mosquitoes, fleas, and rats.

Taylor makes a distinction between basic and nonbasic interests.

> The interests of an organism can be of different degrees of comparative importance to it. One of its interests is of greater importance to it than another, either if the occurrence of the first makes a more substantial contribution to the realization of its good than the second, or if the occurrence of the first is a necessary condition of the preservation of its existence while the occurrence of the second is not. We might say that one interest is of greater importance than another to the extent that the nonfulfillment of the first will constitute a more serious deprivation or loss than the nonfulfillment of the second. The most important interests are those whose fulfillment is needed by an organism if it is to remain alive.[27]

When the interests of human beings and nonhuman living organisms conflict, the basic interests of human beings may prevail. However, if a nonbasic interest of human beings conflicts with a basic interest of a nonhuman living organism, then the basic interest of the nonhuman living organism should prevail.

For example, if we human beings need to kill and eat other living creatures in order to survive, then it is morally acceptable for us to do so because life is our most basic interest and we need not sacrifice our own lives or existence as a species in order to preserve the lives of other organisms. We are not morally required to commit suicide. However, our desire for entertainment is a nonbasic interest. If we are entertained by watching bullfights or by hunting and killing deer, then the basic interest of bulls and deer in continued life should prevail over our nonbasic interest in mere entertainment. Taylor gives examples of other instances where, because the interests of humans are nonbasic while the interests of the other living things are basic, a kind of action is not morally acceptable.

---

[25]Paul W. Taylor, *Respect for Nature* (Princeton, NJ: Princeton University Press, 1986), p. 258.
[26]Ibid., pp. 264–265.
[27]Ibid., p. 271.

Slaughtering elephants so the ivory of their tusks can be used to carve items of the tourist trade.

Killing rhinoceros so that their horns can be used as dagger handles.

Picking rare wildflowers . . . for one's private collection.

Capturing tropical birds, for sale as caged pets.

Trapping and killing reptiles, such as snakes, crocodiles, alligators, and turtles, for their skins and shells to be used in making expensive shoes, handbags, and other "fashion" products.

Hunting and killing rare wild mammals, such as leopards and jaguars, for the luxury fur trade.[28]

He contrasts these activities with subsistence hunting and fishing to provide food in order to stay alive.

In addition, some nonbasic interests may be so important for human well-being that even the basic interests of living organisms may be sacrificed for them if the interests can be protected in no other way. Taylor gives the following examples:

Building an art museum or library where natural habitat must be destroyed.

Constructing an airport, railroad, harbor, or highway involving the serious disturbance of a natural ecosystem.

Damming a free-flowing river for a hydroelectric power project.[29]

Although these projects are not essential for continued human existence or health, they may be so important for ensuring a meaningful, satisfying human life that we are justified in sacrificing the basic interests of other living things.

However, Taylor maintains that just as commonsense human-centered ethics assumes that we have a duty to minimize the harm we cause other humans, life-centered ethics assumes that we have a duty to minimize the harm that we cause other nonhuman living things. When basic or important human interests are in conflict with the basic interests of other living things, we should take concrete steps to ensure that we require the smallest possible sacrifice of their interests. We should harm as few living things as possible; we should minimize the destruction or disruption of ecosystems and habitats; we should take special steps and assume substantial costs to avoid causing the extinction of an organism.

EXERCISES

1. Do you believe that threats to the environment are serious? Defend your answer. (Specify particular kinds of alleged environmental threats and the basis for your evaluation of their seriousness.)

---

[28]Ibid., p. 274

[29]Ibid., p. 276.

2. How would shifting to policies of sustainable development affect the lives of individuals in the United States among (a) the rich, (b) the middle classes, and (c) the poor? How would it affect business and government? Defend your answer.

3. How would shifting to policies of sustainable development affect the lives of the poor in the undeveloped nations of South America, Africa, and Asia? Defend your answer.

4. You have been elected president of the United States. One of your first tasks is to draft a statement of principles and a detailed policy agenda for dealing with both national and international environmental problems. Construct and defend the statement.

5. Paul Kahn says that the United States should only pursue environmental policies that are beneficial to its own presently existing people. He says that people in the United States don't have any duties to people in other countries or to future people. He doesn't care if presently existing people in the United States use up all the world's resources or poison the rest of the planet beyond the boundaries of the United States. What would you say to Paul?

6. Suppose that a middle- or upper-income individual in the United States wants to help protect the earth, its ecosystems, and its living organisms. What can he or she do on an individual basis, especially in day-to-day life? Defend your answer.

7. A certain region of the country that depends on logging for its prosperity has a dilemma. Major sections of forest in that region are the last natural habitats of several varieties of insect and one bird species. If logging is permitted, the insect varieties and bird species will almost certainly become extinct. However, unemployment in the region is high. If logging is permitted, many unemployed workers in the region will be employed again; if it remains forbidden, they will remain unemployed. Should logging be permitted? Defend your answer. If logging should not be permitted, should or can the unemployed workers somehow be compensated? Defend your answer.

8. Miners in a certain region of the country are irate because the high-sulfer coal that they mine may be phased out in order to protect the environment. As a result, they will lose their jobs. Their region is already suffering from economic decay; closing the mines will make the region's problems worse. They are lobbying to get the environmental laws changed so that the high-sulfur coal that they mine can still be used. Environmentalists oppose their efforts. Whose side are you on? Why?

9. Eastern Nowhere Electric has been burning high-sulfur coal because it is cheaper than low-sulfur coal. In order to reduce by 80 percent the pollution that the company's plants emit, the Environmental Protection Agency has decreed that the company must either switch to low-sulfur coal and install moderately expensive scrubbers (pollution control equipment) or install very expensive scrubbers if it continues to use the high-sulfur coal. Either alternative will require Eastern Nowhere Electric to raise its rates for electricity by 20 percent. Many of ENE's customers oppose the Environmental Protection Agency's order because they do not want to see their electric bills rise by 20 percent. Environmentalists support it. Whose side are you on? Why?

10. Toxics-R-Us has submitted an application to the state to build a solid waste incinerator. They have chosen a site in a community that is 70-percent African American and Latino because they believe that primarily white communities have enough political influence to put up a long, hard, expensive fight over the application. Because the community has a very high unemployment rate and Toxics-R-Us promises to provide more than 100 new jobs, many of the community's political leaders have decided not to oppose the application. However, environmental activists are opposing the application, calling it a case of environmental racism and injustice. Opponents have pointed out that three of the four solid waste incinerators are in primarily minority communities in a state that has an African American and Latino population of about 20 percent. If the new incinerator is built in this community, then four of the five solid waste incinerators in the state will be located in primarily minority communities. Should something be done to prevent the building of the incinerator in this community? Why/why not? If something should be done, what precisely could be done?

11. Bug-Away is selling in Third World countries a pesticide that it manufactures in the United States. The Environmental Protection Agency has banned its use in the United States because it is considered too toxic and long-lasting. The pesticide is not prohibited by the laws of the Third World countries in which it is sold. Is there anything wrong with Bug-Away's activities? Defend your answer.

12. Is it morally acceptable to capture wild animals, such as lions, elephants, tigers, whales, dolphins, and seals, and use them in circuses and aquariums? Defend your answer.

13. A high school student has petitioned the local school board to stop the practice of dissecting dead animals in biology class. She maintains that students can learn from computer simulations everything they now learn by dissection. If you were on the school board, would you vote for or against her petition? How would you defend your decision?

14. Is it morally acceptable to eat meat? Defend your answer.

Suggested Readings

National Academy of Sciences. *One Earth, One Future.* Washington, DC: National Academy Press, 1990.

Peter Singer. *Practical Ethics.* New York: Cambridge University Press, 1979. (See Chapters 2 and 3.)

Paul W. Taylor. *Respect for Nature.* Princeton, NJ: Princeton University Press, 1986.

Mostafa K. Tolba. *Saving Our Planet.* London: Chapman & Hall, 1992.

Donald VanDeVeer and Christine Pierce, eds. *The Environmental Ethics and Policy Book.* Belmont, CA: Wadsworth, 1994.

World Commission on Environment and Development. *Our Common Future.* New York: Oxford University Press, 1987.

Case Studies in Ethics

In all cases, explain and defend your answers.

ISSUES IN INTERPERSONAL RELATIONS

1. Carl knows that Brad submitted a paper to his philosophy instructor that he (Brad) did not write. The college that he and Brad attend has strict rules prohibiting academic dishonesty, and its honor code requires students who know of cases of academic dishonesty to report them to the proper authorities. Not only is academic dishonesty punished, but so is the failure to report it. Carl considers the following alternatives: (a) Tell Brad that he will inform the proper authorities of Brad's academic dishonesty unless Brad turns himself in and then carry through with the threat if Brad refuses to confess to his academic dishonesty. (b) Inform the authorities of Brad's academic dishonesty without giving Brad the opportunity to confess. (c) Warn Brad that although he won't turn him in this time, if Brad engages in academic dishonesty again, he will inform the authorities the next time. (d) Do nothing. If you were Carl, which alternative would you act on? Which alternatives do you think are right or wrong?

2. Would your responses to number 1 be different if the college did not have an honor code that explicitly requires students to report cases of academic dishonesty to the proper authorities?

3. Gary, a highly successful architect with an annual income of about $200,000 and assets of about $2 million, is engaged in a bitter divorce struggle with his wife, Renee. He blames Renee for the breakdown of their marriage while she blames him for the breakdown. He is not contesting Renee's request for sole custody of their two teenage children. However, to minimize the amount of alimony and child support that the court will require him to pay, Gary has taken pains to conceal from Renee and her attorney as many of his assets as possible. He believes that if he does not conceal a large portion of his assets, he will be required by a court to pay so much alimony and child support that it will significantly reduce his standard of living. Is it morally acceptable for Gary to try to hide his assets from Renee and her attorney? If you were Gary's financial adviser and Gary asked you for help in concealing his assets, would you do it? Would it be morally acceptable to help Gary conceal his assets from his wife and her attorney?

4. Tamara is a 24-year-old single mother with two children ages 4 and 6. Tamara's income is not large, so she tries to live frugally. She can pay her basic expenses such as rent, food, utilities, and car payments, but she has no money for "frills" or for savings. The 6-year-old is attending the local public school while the 4-year-old is in day care, which is expensive. Tamara works for XYZ, Unlimited. XYZ gives its employees five paid sick days per year that may be used if the employee is ill, but does not give them paid time off for sickness of family members. Tamara's 4-year-old is ill today and cannot be sent to day care, so she must stay home with him. If she calls and tells her employer that she is sick, she will be paid for the day; if she calls and says that she is staying home with a sick child, she will be docked a day's pay. What should she do?

5. Adam is the plate umpire at a Little League baseball game between the Robins and the Owls. His son, Richard, plays second base for the Owls. Richard is not a talented athlete—he has the lowest batting average and highest rate of errors on the team—and he is obviously having problems of self-esteem and self-respect because of his poor performance. Richard is at bat and the count is 3 balls and 2 strikes. The next pitch, which Richard lets go by without swinging at it, looks like a strike to Adam. Should Adam declare it a strike, which will mean that Richard strikes out, or a ball, which means that Richard gets a walk? Should Adam be an umpire in a Little League game in which his son is playing?

6. Saleh has a friend, Bart, who has told her that he is so depressed that he often thinks of suicide. He does not get along well with his parents, who are always arguing. His father is always criticizing him, and nothing he does seems to please him. He is doing very poorly in school. Saleh suspects that Bart is using drugs, and she worries that he will try to commit suicide. Bart has made her promise that she will tell no one about his problems. What, if anything, should Saleh do?

7. Tom recently graduated from law school. He has been offered a high-paying position in the legal department of a major tobacco company. The tobacco company job would pay $12,000 per year more than the next highest offer he has received. Tom has reservations about accepting the job because the work would involve defending the tobacco company from lawsuits brought by people who have become ill or died as a result of smoking cigarettes and from attempts by various government agencies to regulate or discourage smoking. Tom, who does not smoke, believes that smoking causes a variety of serious health hazards. He also believes that tobacco is addictive. He comes to you for advice about what to do. What will you say to him?

8. Rose and Tom had been married for ten years when Tom was in a motorcycle accident that left him paralyzed from the neck down. He has been paralyzed for six years, and Rose has been his primary caregiver, devoting much of her time and energy to meeting his needs. Because of Tom's injury, Rose has not had sex in six years. Recently, Rose met a man she thinks is wonderful, and she feels very sexually attracted to him. He is divorced, and he has made it clear that he finds Rose very attractive. She is tempted to have an affair with him, although her religion has taught her that adultery is immoral. She feels that important needs are not being met and never will be met again by Tom. She is feeling more and more unhappy about her situation. If she were to have an affair, she would not divorce Tom, but she would never tell him of it because she believes that it would be devastating for him. She turns to you, her best friend, for advice, asking what you think she should do. What do you say to her?

9.   Brenda is a clerk in a convenience store. Over the past several weeks she has frequently seen a young mother with a 4-year-old child in the store. They are African American and obviously poor. Several times the young mother has bought milk, soda, or juice and paid for it with food stamps. The manager of the store is white, as is Brenda. Twice the manager has made racially disparaging remarks about the mother and child to Brenda after they left the store. He was also rude to them on one occasion when the mother was having trouble finding her food stamps. The mother and child have just left the store, and the manager has again used a nasty racial epithet and called them "parasites." What, if anything, should Brenda do?

10.   Agnes and Ben have been arguing. Both work full-time. Agnes complains that Ben does not do enough work around the house. She claims that she does most of the household chores such as cooking, cleaning, laundry, and shopping. She wants a more equal distribution of household chores. Ben concedes that he does not do much around the house, but he is reluctant to agree to do more of the domestic chores because he considers them "women's work." You are a good friend of both Agnes and Ben, and they have come to you to talk about their conflict. What do you say to them?

11.   Jane was caught in a speed trap. When the police officer stopped her, she told him that she was rushing to pick up her mother to take her to the hospital emergency room and begged him not to give her a ticket. Jane was lying to escape getting a speeding ticket, which would mean a $100 fine and an increase in her auto insurance premiums. Did she do anything wrong by lying to the police officer?

12.   John believes that smoking marijuana is harmless, and he strongly disagrees with laws that prohibit its use. He thinks that the government has no moral right to prohibit its use, and he believes that the government is hypocritical because it prohibits smoking marijuana but not tobacco, which is far more addictive and deadly. Would it be wrong for him to smoke marijuana?

13.   Abe has been having trouble earning the money he needs to pay his college tuition. An acquaintance has told him that he earns $2,000 a week selling cocaine part-time, and he offers to put Abe in contact with a dealer he knows. He assures Abe that the possibility of getting caught is very low. What should Abe do?

14.   Tory was having trouble earning money for her college tuition. Recently she took a job in a strip club, where she dances nude three nights a week, earning $200 per night. She does not have sex with any of the customers. Is she doing anything wrong?

15. Suppose that in number 14 Tory was earning her money by means of prostitution in a city where prostitution is legal. Would she be doing anything wrong?

ISSUES IN MEDICINE

1. Given that in a finite economy the resources available for medical care are not unlimited and that medical needs are in competition with other needs for scarce resources, people have been seriously entertaining the idea of rationing medical care. A recent study suggests that rationing is already occurring. According to the study, "doctors [are] opting to spend less and perform fewer surgeries on people over 80 than they do on people younger than 50 who have comparable illnesses and conditions." The study focused on treatment of "nine major illnesses, including heart and lung failure, multiple organ failure, and advanced lung or colon cancer. Even after accounting for the relative severity of the illnesses and for cases where elderly patients did not want aggressive care, [the] study found that over-80 patients had surgery half as often as younger patients with comparable illnesses, and about $7,000 less was spent on their care."[1] Do you think there is anything wrong with providing less care to patients over 80 than to younger patients with comparable conditions?

2. Researchers at a major university think they have discovered a technique for genetically reengineering human beings to give them an average life expectancy of 200 years with enhanced resistance to a variety of common diseases including AIDS. The technique involves reengineering the genetic code of a woman's eggs before they are fertilized. The technique has been tried successfully on mice and rats. The scientists are considering applying for permission to conduct experiments using the technique on human subjects. Should they apply for such permission? Should permission be given?

3. Joan believes that every citizen of the United States has a moral right to basic medical care. She says that the best way to ensure that this right is not violated is either to guarantee health insurance for everyone, paid for by the government if necessary, or to institute a single-payer system whereby the government directly pays for everyone's health care. She believes, furthermore, that every citizen should have access to health care of equal quality. Her friend Tina disagrees. Tina says that any such program would cost so much money that taxes would have to increase, and she is against raising taxes. Furthermore, she does not like the idea of the government's getting any more involved in health care or health insurance that it already is. She knows that many Americans do not have health insurance and do not qualify for the Medicaid program that provides medical care to the poor, but she says that life isn't completely just and we should not pretend that we can make it perfectly just. It's a shame that some

---

[1]*The Boston Sunday Globe,* September 8, 1996, p. A14. (The study was conducted by Dr. Mary Beth Hamel of Beth Israel Hospital in Boston.)

people lack health insurance, but that's life. With whom do you agree, Joan or Tina? Why?

    4. Tom, age 81, is brought into the emergency room of a hospital. He is unconscious and in full cardiac arrest. Doctors discover that he has a "Do not resuscitate" order on file with the hospital. However, his son, who brought him into the emergency room, demands that doctors provide the medical care Tom needs. He states emphatically that he does not want his father to die and he will sue the doctors and the hospital if they let him die. What should the doctors do?

    5. Legislators are considering a bill that would make physician-assisted suicide legal. The proposed law includes requirements that its sponsors hope will prevent abuse. It requires that patients have an incurable illness or condition that either is terminal within a year or so greatly diminishes the quality of the patient's life that the ordinary, reasonable person would find the condition intolerable or barely tolerable. The diagnosis must be confirmed by at least two physicians. The patient must be mentally competent to make the request, as determined by at least two mental-health professionals. The request must come from the patient in writing, countersigned by two witnesses. There must be a waiting period of at least a week after submission of the request for physician-assisted suicide, during which time the patient may change his/her mind. If you were one of the legislators, how would you vote?

    6. Frank is a patient of Dr. Gentile. Frank recently came to Dr. Gentile with symptoms that made her suspect AIDS. An AIDS test confirmed that Frank is HIV-positive. Under questioning, Frank admitted that he had had unprotected sex with a coworker with whom he was having an affair. He also acknowledged that he and his wife were having unprotected sex because his wife believed that he was faithful to her and he had had a vasectomy after their second child. Dr. Gentile asked Frank to have his wife come in for an AIDS test and told him that from now on he should be sure to use a condom when he has sex with his wife. Frank tells Dr. Gentile that he won't ask his wife to come in for an AIDS test or use a condom when they have sex because he doesn't want her to know that he is HIV-positive as a result of an affair. He tells Dr. Gentile that he has a right to privacy and confidentiality that he expects her to respect. Dr. Gentile explains to Frank that if his wife is HIV-positive, it is very important that she get medical attention as quickly as possible. She tells him that a combination of drugs is very effective if provided in the early stages of the infection. Frank still refuses to give Dr. Gentile permission to contact his wife and steadfastly refuses to tell her himself. After Frank leaves, Dr. Gentile wonders whether she should inform Frank's wife that he is HIV-positive and recommend that she come in for an AIDS test, even though she does not have Frank's permission. What should she do?

    7. Beth is a nurse at a municipal hospital. In her view and the view of the other nurses, Dr. Vincent Gaugan is incompetent. On several occasions he has given prescriptions to patients for the wrong medication or the wrong dosage. He has also given mistaken diagnoses on more than one occasion. Beth and several other nurses believe that doctors and administrators at the hospital are protecting Dr. Gaugan, because complaints to the hospital administration have not led to any disciplining of Dr. Gaugan. Beth is considering making a complaint to the state medical licensing board. The other nurses have warned her not to do it because they think the only person who would be punished would be Beth. What should Beth do?

8. Dr. Garcia has given a prescription to Mrs. Dwyer. The prescribed medication has some potential side effects that are serious but have a low probability. Mrs. Dwyer is a nervous, anxious woman. Dr. Garcia worries that if he tells Mrs. Dwyer about these possible but improbable side effects, she will not take the medication that she needs. Dr. Garcia believes he has a duty to inform Mrs. Dwyer of all the possible side effects of the medication so that her taking the medication will be fully voluntary. However, he does not think it is in her best interest to know because if it leads her to not take the medication, her health problems will get worse. He has thought of several options. (a) He could tell her everything and reassure her that the serious side effects are highly unlikely; however, he worries that she will only hear the information about seriousness and will not pay attention to the improbability because she is so anxious about her health. (b) He could ask if she wants to know anything about possible side effects and if she says no, which he thinks is likely but by no means certain, keep the information to himself. (c) He could simply say, "There are some possible side effects, but they are so unlikely that you don't need to hear about them" and hope she won't ask him about them. (d) He could simply say nothing about possible side effects and unless she asks about them on her own, which is very unlikely, not tell her anything. What should he do?

9. Currently, doctors do not perform medical experiments on prison inmates because they do not believe that the conditions for fully voluntary consent can be met in prisons. Suppose that someone began to press for a reversal of this policy on the grounds that prisoners owe a debt to society that can and should be repaid by their serving as subjects in medical experiments. The most modest suggestion is that inmates who become ill from natural causes, such as developing cancer, be given the option of participating in tests of experimental drugs and therapies in exchange for reductions in their sentences. A much more radical suggestion is that prisoners condemned to death be given deadly diseases, such as the HIV infection or tuberculosis, so that they can be treated with experimental drugs. Supporters of the latter proposal maintain that since the inmates are condemned to death anyway, their lives can be useful to society even if the diseases or the experimental therapies kill them. Do you agree or disagree with any of these recommendations?

10. Dr. Elkins is busy. Many patients are sitting in her waiting room. She has just told a patient that the diagnosis of his malady is bone cancer. The patient is shocked, frightened, and depressed. He is sitting silently in the chair with his eyes on the floor. Dr. Elkins has already explained the nature of the disease and the forms of therapy available and made a recommendation for a course of treatment that she admits has only a 20-percent probability of saving his life. She wants to move on to her next patient, but she is also sensitive to the needs of this patient. He probably needs to talk about his feelings and receive some sympathy. What alternatives are available to Dr. Elkins? What should she do?

ISSUES IN BUSINESS

1. Zed's accountant has told him that he can deduct up to 5 percent of his income for charitable contributions. If he deducts less than 5 percent, it will probably not trigger an audit and he will probably never be asked by the IRS to provide evidence of his contributions. By Zed's own calculations, he has contributed about 2 percent of his annual income to charity. He is considering inflating that figure on his income tax return to 4 percent of his annual income in order to reduce his income taxes. Would it be morally acceptable for him to do that?

2. Theodora is browsing through a tag sale sponsored by a local homeless shelter. She is quite knowledgeable about antiques. She has come across an item for sale for $10 that she knows is worth at least 100 times that amount. She wonders whether she should purchase it and pocket the profit or inform the organizers of the item's value. What should she do?

3. Would your response to number 2 be different if the tag sale were sponsored by an individual who is moving rather than by a homeless shelter?

4. You have been hired to work in the human resources department of a large company owned by a local businessman. The salary and benefits are good. You had been looking for work for almost a year and are very happy to have gotten this job. Your first day on the job, the manager comes to you and explains that the owner of the company is prejudiced against African Americans. Consequently, he would be very unhappy if any executives or middle-level managers were African Americans. He explains to you that although the law does not permit discrimination on the basis of race, one can always find some other reason for denying someone a job or promotion. He says that in order to keep his job, he has made sure that he has never been able to find any qualified African Americans for management positions within the company. He asks whether you would have a problem with this unwritten policy. How would you respond?

5. XYZ, Inc., has come up with a plan to hire and train welfare recipients for entry-level jobs. A consultant has warned them of likely problems. Many of the welfare recipients will have to receive training that focuses on such basic skills as dressing appropriately for work, coming to work every day and on time, and office etiquette, as well as basic education in reading, mathematics, speaking, and writing. Some may need substance-abuse counseling. However, the consultants have said that those welfare recipients who survive the first six months to a year will probably become loyal and competent employees. XYZ's management is divided. Some oppose the plan because it will cost the company too much and they don't consider the welfare recipients employable. They think that too few will survive the first six to twelve months to make the program a good gamble. They also complain that such a program is appropriate for a social service agency, not for a business whose goal is profit. On the other hand, supporters think it makes good business sense and is socially responsible. They maintain that although not all welfare recipients hired for the program will succeed, if the program is carefully designed and effectively implemented, enough of them will succeed to justify the investment. They also maintain that business organizations have a responsibility to society to help solve social problems. They say that helping people on welfare become employed and employable is part of a business's duty to society. With whom do you agree?

6. Titanic Enterprises has hired a phalanx of lobbyists to lobby Congress for tax breaks and other kinds of favorable treatment that critics have called "corporate welfare." Through its political action committee it has given hundreds of thousands of dollars collected from its employees, primarily at the managerial level, to political parties that use the money to finance the campaigns of members of the Senate and the House of Representatives, most of which goes to key members of committees that deal with issues important to Titanic. Critics claim that it is wrong for big companies to provide huge campaign contributions to politicians, and then lobby for tax breaks and other favorable treatment. They argue that it undermines democracy and hurts people who are less powerful and wealthy than the large corporations. Titanic maintains that it is just good business, that the company is merely exercising its rights to freedom of expression, and that there is nothing morally wrong with what it is doing because it is all perfectly legal. What do you think?

7. Titanic, Inc., has a labor problem. Its employees are talking about unionization. The management of Titanic does not want its employees to unionize. Unions give workers more power and generally enable workers to get higher wages. Therefore, Titanic has retained the services of a law firm known for its ruthlessness and effectiveness in union-busting. The law firm has a reputation for going over the line of what's legal, but rarely has it or its clients been severely punished for such behavior, and its success in keeping unions out has saved its clients millions of dollars. If there anything wrong with a company's using every means at its disposal to resist unionization?

8. A new fruit has become very popular. However, you have heard that certain groups are trying to organize a consumer boycott of the fruit because they claim that workers who harvest the crops are poorly paid, live in inhuman conditions, and are frequently poisoned by the pesticides that are sprayed on the crop. Should you buy the fruit anyway and ignore the boycott, or should you honor the boycott and refrain from buying the fruit?

9. You are in charge of produce for a supermarket chain with thirty stores. Recently a delegation of community activists came to visit you asking that your stores not stock the fruit that is being boycotted in number 8. You are wondering whether to comply with their request. You must write a memo to your superiors reporting on the meeting and making a recommendation. What is your recommendation?

10. The personnel manager of the company where you are CEO has noticed that a large percentage of the low-paid, unskilled jobs are held by African Americans and Hispanics while almost no African Americans and Hispanics are in supervisory and managerial positions. The city in which the company is located has a large African American and Hispanic population. The personnel manager has recommended implementation of an affirmative action plan to increase the number of African Americans and Hispanics in supervisory and managerial positions, even though such a plan is not required by law. Are you for or against implementing such a plan?

11. Gabe complains that as a smoker, his rights are being violated. His company has a strict rule prohibiting smoking in the building. Gabe argues that he should be free to smoke in his office. Do you agree?

12. Behemoth, Inc., is revising its policies and procedures regarding sexual harassment. One recommendation is that the new code state that a supervisor's or manager's asking a subordinate for a date constitutes sexual harassment. Do you agree?

SOCIAL/POLITICAL ISSUES

1. Jean comes from a family that is usually characterized as dysfunctional. She has been addicted to drugs since she was 15; to support her habit, she turned to prostitution when she was 17. She dropped out of school in the tenth grade, so she has little education and few marketable skills. Today she is a single mother with two young children and continues to support them and herself by prostitution. She still is addicted to drugs. However, recently she began feeling a determination to turn her life around, if not for her sake, then for her children's. She now wants to overcome her addiction to drugs and then try to get an education so that she can get a decent job to support herself and her children. She has no money to pay for a drug rehabilitation program, so she goes to the nearest publicly supported program. She is told there is a waiting list, so that she cannot be admitted for six to twelve months, and that all other drug rehabilitation programs in the city have similarly long waiting lists. Jean pleads with the intake counselor because she is afraid that her resolve to turn her life around will not survive the six to twelve months she must wait. The intake counselor says she is sorry, but a shortage of funds makes it impossible for public clinics and programs to meet the demand for services. Jean asks why not, and the counselor tells her that these programs are funded entirely by tax dollars and that taxpayers complain of high taxes and clamor for tax relief. Consequently, there simply is not enough money to meet the needs for drug rehabilitation. Politicians don't dare increase taxes to fund drug rehabilitation programs and are reluctant to take money earmarked for other purposes, such as police and fire protection, education, garbage removal, highway repair, and medical care. Jean leaves feeling hopeless and depressed. What should society do about cases such as Jean's? Does society have a duty to provide adequate services for drug rehabilitation so that people such as Jean will not be put on waiting lists? What about competing needs that are also inadequately funded? What duties do politicians have? What duties do citizens/taxpayers/voters have?

2. Raoul is a proponent of gun control. He believes that citizens in modern industrial nations should not have a constitutional right to own firearms, especially such firearms as handguns and automatic or semiautomatic weapons, because of the danger to others. He favors a ban on the ownership of such weapons and strict licensing requirements for ownership of rifles and shotguns used for hunting. He claims that part of the problem of violence in the United States is the casual attitude toward firearms and their wide availability. Gun-control opponents appeal to the Second Amendment to the United States Constitution: "A well regulated Militia, being necessary to the security of a free State, the right of the people to keep and bear Arms, shall not be infringed." Raoul maintains that people do not have a *moral* right to keep and bear firearms; therefore, he believes that the Second Amendment to the United States Constitution should be repealed. Do you agree with him?

3. Ortega is an advocate of campaign finance reform. He points out that almost all of the money for politicians' campaigns is provided by contributions from very wealthy individuals and businesses. He says that consequently the very rich have undue influence over politics while the poor and middle class have little influence; as a result, public policy in the United States favors the interests of the rich and powerful. He thinks that the way political campaigns are financed should be changed. He wants substantial public financing of all campaigns for federal office, with strict limits on the amount of private money that may be donated to candidates and parties. Critics argue that it would simply be welfare for politicians and would interfere with people's freedom. With whom do you agree?

4. The law requires males to register for the draft even though currently the United States has an all-volunteer army and there is no conscription. John does not think it's fair that men should have to register but not women. He also maintains that if conscription is ever revived, women as well as men should be conscripted into the military. Do you agree?

5. Fascistland is led by a military dictator, General Francochet, who rules undemocratically while systematically and massively violating the human rights of his people, who live in abject poverty while Francochet and his cronies live in luxury. The United States government is being pressured by many large companies to do nothing that would lead Fascistland to close its markets to American business. Defense firms are asking for permission to sell a variety of weapons to the government of Fascistland. Supporters of these policies claim that maintaining friendly ties with Fascistland benefits the United States economy and will probably lead to eventual democratization. Critics maintain that it is wrong to support and sell weapons to an undemocratic government that brutalizes its people. With whom do you agree?

ENVIRONMENTAL ISSUES

1. Jones bought a house in the suburbs on a two-acre lot. He hates to cut the grass and doesn't want to pay to have someone cut it for him. He doesn't like the trees, shrubs, plants, and flowers that grow on his property because they attract insects, need care, and shed leaves that have to be raked. He does not find any of them beautiful or aesthetically pleasing. Therefore, he has all of the trees and shrubs cut down, the plants and flowers pulled, and the whole two acres around his house covered with cement. Is there anything wrong with Jones's action?

2. Through genetic engineering, researchers have found a way to create a single-celled organism that eats oil. They are excited at the prospect of employing such organisms to clean up oil spills. Critics, however, are afraid of possible unexpected risks. They wonder if the new organism might mutate into something more harmful. They also fear that it could become uncontrollable once introduced into the world's environment and eat up the world's oil reserves. Imagine if oil tankers became infested with the organisms on their way from the Middle East to North America, critics say. Whole shiploads of oil could be destroyed. Whole oilfields might become infected. Other critics argue that creating new species of organisms is playing God and we should not try to play God.

Supporters scoff at these arguments. They maintain that the fears of catastrophe are wildly exaggerated and that the potential benefits to humans justify the risks, which are very small. They also say that creating new organisms is not like playing God. Since God gave us the ability to create such techniques and made nature in such a way that genetic engineering is physically possible, God must not mind. Also, if God exists, God created things out of nothing, whereas genetic engineering is simply rearranging already existing material.

Should scientists go on to create the organism in the laboratory? If they are successful, should they release it into the environment to clean up oil spills?

3. Through genetic engineering, researchers have found a way to create a strain of grain that is more nutritious for humans than any known grain, that grows in environments generally inhospitable to other forms of grain, and that is highly resistant to both disease and insects. Scientists estimate that cultivating the new form of grain could increase the world's food supply by about 50 percent. Critics worry about the risks. The new grain, if planted in nature, may have unexpected interactions with other living things in the ecosystem. It may kill or supplant other plants with unanticipated catastrophic results for human interests. It may be susceptible to diseases or insect predators that other strains of grain are not. If it supplants other forms of grain and then is found to have unexpected weaknesses or vulnerabilities, the food supply could shrink rather than increase. Supporters of the program maintain that the risks are greatly exaggerated. Should they go on to create the new form of grain in the laboratory? If successful, should they make the grain generally available for cultivation by farmers around the world?

4. Sheila and Dan are arguing. Dan comes from a family where hunting has been a tradition for generations. He believes there is nothing morally wrong with sport hunting, and he enjoys the activity very much. He wants to introduce their 12-year-old son, Tim, to deer hunting and plans to take him deer hunting with him this weekend. He also wants to buy Tim his own hunting rifle. Tim wants very much to have a hunting rifle and is eager to go deer hunting with his father. However, Sheila abhors hunting, believing it is immoral to kill animals for sport. She also does not like guns. Therefore, she does not want Dan to buy a rifle for Tim or take him deer hunting. With whom do you side? Why?

5. The president has proposed increasing the tax on gasoline by $1 per gallon over a five-year period to encourage conservation, which in turn would help reduce air pollution. The taxes raised would be spent on research and development of alternative forms of energy and mass transportation. Low-income people who would be hardest hit will be given a partial rebate on gasoline taxes through their income taxes. Would you be for or against this tax increase?

6. Pablo is opposed to the clear-cutting of old timber, which the government is permitting. Pablo believes that the government is permitting it because key members of House and Senate committees have received big contributions from the timber industry. To stop the clear-cutting, he and some friends have chained themselves across the road to prevent logging trucks from entering the forest and to bring the public's attention to the problem, even though their actions are illegal. Do you approve of what they are doing?

7. In order to stop a shipment of low-level nuclear waste from being moved by truck from a nuclear power plant to a temporary nuclear repository that some people claim is unsafe, Jennifer in the middle of the night damaged the vehicles that were to carry the waste. Do you approve of what she did?

Glossary

Absolute moral principle A moral principle that cannot be justifiably violated; a moral principle for which there are no exceptions.

Act Utilitarianism The positive version of the theory claims that an individual action is right if and only if it would produce more total happiness than any other action available to the agent. The negative version of the theory claims that an action is right as long as it does not reduce total happiness.

Affirmative action Programs intended to counteract unjust discrimination. *See* Preferential treatment.

Altruistic behavior Behavior motivated by concern for the well-being of others and intended to benefit others. Opposed to purely self-interested behavior.

Beneficence Altruistic behavior directed toward benefiting others or protecting them from harm.

Categorical Imperative According to Kant's moral theory, a basic principle of morality that all people should follow. The universal law formulation is "Act only on a maxim that you can consistently will to be a universal law." The respect for persons formulation is "Never treat people merely as a means to your ends."

Deterrence Threatening punishment in order to deter or discourage wrongdoing.

Divine Command theory The theory that God's commands make moral laws that are true and authoritative for all human beings.

According to this theory, an action is wrong if and only if it is forbidden by God.

Epicureanism The theory that pleasure and the absence of pain are the keys to human happiness.

Euthanasia The practice of killing someone or letting someone die for that person's own good or benefit. In active euthanasia, one kills the person. In passive euthanasia, one does not act to prevent the person's death.

Fundamental moral principle A moral principle that justifies other moral principles but is not itself justified by appeal to other, more general moral principles.

Harm Principle The principle that liberty may be limited only to prevent harm to others.

Hedonism The theory that only pleasure is good and the source of human happiness.

Legal Moralism The principle that liberty may be limited to prohibit immoral conduct even if no one is harmed or offended.

Maxim According to Kant's moral theory, a personal rule specifying how and why one will behave in certain circumstances; for example, "In circumstances C, I will do action X for purpose P."

Moral Absolutism The theory that there is only one correct moral code, many or most of whose moral principles are absolute.

Moral Egoism The theory that it is always morally acceptable for an individual to do what she believes to be in her own self-interest.

Moral Nihilism The theory that nothing is morally right or wrong, morally forbidden or required.

Moral Objectivism The theory that some moral claims are objectively true and others objectively false.

Moral Relativism The theory that moral principles can only be true relative to (or true for) some group. Moral relativists deny that there is only one correct moral code that binds all people at all times in all places.

Moral Subjectivism The theory that whatever an individual believes to be right and wrong is right and wrong for that individual.

Negative duty A duty to refrain from doing something (or to *not* do something). *Compare* Positive duty.

Negative right A negative right imposes on others a (negative) duty to refrain from behaving in certain ways toward the right-holder.

Offense Principle The principle that liberty may be limited to prevent offense to others.

Paternalism The principle that liberty may be limited to prevent people from harming themselves.

Positive duty A duty to *do* something. *Compare* Negative duty.

Positive right A positive right it imposes on others a (positive) duty to do something for the right-holder.

Preferential treatment Giving members of certain groups (usually groups that have suffered severely from unjust discrimination) preference in selection and promotion over members of groups that have not suffered from unjust discrimination.

Prima facie duty A duty required by one set of circumstances that may be overridden by duties entailed by other sets of circumstances.

Protagorean Moral Relativism The theory that whatever a society believes to be right is right for that society.

Psychological Egoism The theory that all human behavior is exclusively self-interested—that people do only what they believe is in their self-interest.

Rule Utilitarianism The theory that an action is right if and only if it is permitted or required by a correct moral rule. A moral rule is defined as correct if following it would result in more total happiness than not following it.

Stoicism The school of thought according to which moral goodness is sufficient for happiness. Stoics recommended self-control of desires and appetites as the key to happiness.

Subsistence rights (Positive) rights to goods and services necessary for one's survival.

Universal moral principle A moral principle that applies to everyone.

Index